A COURSE IN
URDU

اِبْتِدَائی اُرْدُو

MUHAMMAD ABD-AL-RAHMAN BARKER

and

HASAN JAHANGIR HAMDANI

KHWAJA MUHAMMAD SHAFI DIHLAVI

SHAFIQUR RAHMAN

VOLUME TWO

Spoken Language Services, Inc.

Library of Congress Cataloging in Publication Data

Main entry under title:

A Course in Urdu = ابتدائی اردو

    (Spoken language series)
    Reprint of the 1967 ed. published by the Institute of Islamic Studies, McGill University, Montreal.
    1. Urdu language--Conversation and phrase books.
I. Barker, Muhammad Abd-al-Rahman.
PK1975.C64 1975   491.4'39'82421   75-15183
ISBN 0-87590-341-6

Spoken Language Services, Inc.
P. O. Box 783
Ithaca, New York 14851

TABLE OF CONTENTS

UNIT TWENTY-FIVE

Shah Alami Market, a bazaar in the Old City, Lahore.

16.000. CONVERSATION

Mrs. Smith is speaking with her cook.

wonder, astonishment M1 [np]

təəjjwb

tailor M1

dərzi

although, notwithstanding, even though Conj

halāke

promise M2

vada

according to Comp Post

[ke] mwtabyq

MS: It's very strange [lit. it's a matter of great wonder] that the tailor hasn't come yet, even though he always comes according to his promise.

bəRe təəjjwb ki bat həy, ky dərzi əbhi tək nəhī aya, halāke vw həmeša əpne vade ke mwtabyq ata həy.

following, adhering, observing, bound to PA1 [A1 rare]

pabənd

C: Perhaps some necessary task has come up, otherwise he is really very punctual [lit. very bound of time].

šayəd koi zəruri kam peš a gəya ho, vərna vaqəi, vw vəqt ka bəhwt pabənd həy.

bandage F2

pəTTi

has got tied on FS [/bādhna/ "to tie, bind"; If: /ā/]

bādh rəkkhi həy

MS: Why have you got a bandage tied on [your] hand?

twm ne hath pər pəTTi kyõ bādh rəkkhi həy.

breakfast M2

našta

hearth, stove M2

culha

kept, put, placed FOS

rəkkhi hwi

kerosene [lit. earth's oil] M1

myTTi ka tel

to be scattered, strewn, spread, dispersed, dropped [I: /bəkherna/: Ig]

bykhərna

burning MOP

jəlte

charcoal, coal, coals M2

koyla

breath, life, moment M1

dəm

to extinguish, quench, put out [C1 /bwjhna/: IIc]

bwjhana

slow, gradual, soft, calm, mild; slowly, gradually A1 Adv

ahysta

at last, finally, in the end Adv

axyrkar

gardener M1

mali

to call out, cry out to [Ia]

pwkarna

poor, unfortunate, poor fellow A2 M/F2

becara

on hearing, at the moment of hearing MOS

swnte hi

running MNS

dəwRta hwa

1

C: After preparing breakfast this morning, I was washing the dishes. Suddenly my hand struck the bottle of kerosene sitting on the stove, because of which [lit. from which] all the oil [i. e. kerosene] spread out and reached the burning coals. Thus the stove caught fire all at once [lit. this way [in] a moment in the stove fire attached]. I tried hard to put out the fire, but it slowly kept spreading. At last I called to the gardener. On hearing my voice, that poor fellow came running. In this way together we both put out the fire. In this my hand got burned.

swba naŝta təyyar kərne ke bad mə̃y bərtən dho rəha tha. əcanək mera hath culhe pər rəkkhi hwi myTTi ke tel ki botəl se Təkra gəya, jys se təmam tel bykhər gəya, əwr jəlte koylõ tək pəhw̃c gəya. ys təra ek dəm culhe mẽ ag ləg gəi. mə̃y ne ag bwjhane ki bəhwt koŝyŝ ki, lekyn vw ahysta ahysta phəylti gəi. axyrkar mə̃y ne mali ko pwkara. vw becara meri avaz swnte hi dəwRta hwa aya. ys təra həm donõ ne myl kər ag bwjhai. ys mẽ mera hath jəl gəya.

just, a little A1 Adv

zəra

kitchen M2

bavərcixana

MS: I hope there wasn't much damage [lit. wasn't there much damage?]! Just come along with me. I want to see the kitchen.

zyada nwqsan to nəhĩ hwa? zəra mere sath ao! mə̃y bavərcixana dekhna cahti hũ.

basket F2

Tokri

C: No, nothing was damaged. Only two [or] three empty baskets have been burned.

ji nəhĩ, kysi ciz ko nwqsan nəhĩ pəhw̃ca. syrf do tin xali Tokriã jəl gəi həy.

burned FNP

jəli hwi

smoke M2 [np]

dhũã

wet, damp A2

gila

housefly F2

məkkhi

mosquito M1

məcchər

to cover [Id: /ə/]; cover, lid M2

Dhəkna

MS: Throw out all these burned baskets! This wall has become black because of the smoke. Clean with a [lit. any] wet cloth! Close this window! Through it [lit. from this direction] flies, mosquitoes, etc. are coming [inside]. And keep all these things covered [lit. having covered, keep!]! Finish up all these tasks quickly because arrangement[s] for a party tonight must be made also.

yy jəli hwi Tokriã bahər phẽk do! yy divar dhũẽ ki vəja se kali ho gəi həy. yse kysi gile kəpRe se saf kəro! ys khyRki ko bənd kər do! ys tərəf se məkkhiã, məcchər vəyəyra a rəhe hə̃y. əwr yn təmam cizõ ko Dhək kər rəkho! yy səb kam jəldi xətm kər lo, kyõke ŝam ko davət ka bəndobəst bhi kərna həy.

C: What [various things] should [I] cook this evening?

ŝam ko kya kya pəkana həy.

rice cooked with meat and spices M1 [np]

pwlao

meat curry cooked without much gravy M2 [np]

qorma

minced meat, hamburger M2 [np]

qima

to bring [Conjunct verb: take-come]

le ana

spicy meat patty M1

kəbab

spiced meatballs in sauce M2

kofta

household purchases, groceries, supplies M2

səwda

2

MS: pwlao and qorma. Aside from this, bring some minced meat from which [you] should make kəbab and kofta. Do [you] need any other groceries too?

pwlao əwr qorma. ys ke ylava, kwch qima bhi le ana, jys ke kəbab əwr kofte bəna lena. kya, kwch əwr səwde ki bhi zərurət həy?

potato M1

alu

onion F1 [pl. rare]

pyaz

tomato M1

TəmaTər

spices, seasoning M2

məsala

C: Yes, [I] have to bring potato[es], onion[s], tomato[es], and some seasoning too.

ji hã, alu, pyaz, TəmaTər, əwr kwch məsala bhi lana həy.

cauliflower, cabbage F2

gobhi

carrot F1

gajər

while leaving, at the time of going MOS

cəlte vəqt

had given and gone FS [Conjunct verb: give-had gone]

de gəi thi

expense, expenditure, cost, spending M1

xərc

MS: [You] should also bring cauliflower and carrot[s]. And yesterday as I was leaving [lit. going time], I gave [you] ten rupees. Where did [you] spend them?

gobhi əwr gajər bhi lana. əwr kəl cəlte vəqt mə̃y dəs rupəe de gəi thi, vw kəhã xərc kie.

bill, account M1

hysab

slip (of paper); examination paper M2

pərca

barber M1

nai

hair M1

bal

had had made and brought MS [Conjunct verb: had-made-had brought; /bənvana/ "to cause to be made, built"; DC: /bənna/: IIc]

bənva laya tha

C: [I] brought three rupees' [worth] of groceries, the account for which is written on this slip. [I] gave three rupees to the barber. Yesterday I got the girls' hair cut [lit. [having] caused the girls' to be done [I] had brought [them home]]. And the remaining four rupees are [still] with me.

tin rupəe ka səwda le aya tha, jys ka hysab ys pərce pər lykha hwa həy. tin rupəe nai ko de die. kəl bəcciõ ke bal bənva laya tha. əwr baqi car rupəe mere pas məwjud hə̃y.

while cooking, at the time of cooking MOS

pəkate vəqt

dustcloth M1

jhaRən

curtain, veil M2

pərda

to sweep, dust, brush off [If: /ə/]

jhaRna

MS: All right. Be a little careful while cooking [lit. cooking time]! Lest [lit. may it not be thus that] sometime there may be more damage. Secondly, take a dustcloth and dust the window curtains!

Thik həy. pəkate vəqt zəra yhtiat rəkkha kəro! əysa nə ho, ky kəbhi zyada nwqsan wThana pəRe. dusre, jhaRən le kər khyRki ke pərdõ ko jhaRo!

C: Very well. I'll do all these tasks right away. -- From next week, I need ten days of leave too.

bəhwt əccha. mə̃y əbhi yy səb kam kər leta hũ. -- əgle həfte se, mwjhe dəs dyn ki chwTTi bhi cahie.

MS: Why do [you] need leave?

chwTTi kyõ cahie.

mother F1

mã

father M1

bap

participating in, joining in, included in PA1

  šərik

C: I have to go to my parents [lit. mother-father]. Aside from this, my young[er] brother's marriage is [taking place]. It is necessary to take part in that also.

mwjhe əpne mā̃ bap ke pas jana həy. ys ke ylava, mere choTe bhai ki šadi həy. ws mē̃ bhi šərik hona zəruri həy.

without Comp Post

  [ke] bəγəyr

difficulty, problem, perplexity F1

  dyqqət

cook M1

  bavərci

MS: Without you, there will be a lot of difficulty in the housework. Oh well, no matter. Make arrangement for some other cook [as a substitute].

twmhare bəγəyr ghər ke kam mē̃ kafi dyqqət peš aegi. xəyr, koi bat nəhī̃. kysi dusre bavərci ka yntyzam kər dena.

C: Very well. -- Here you are [lit. please take]]! The tailor has come.

bəhwt əccha. -- lijie, dərzi a gəya həy.

early morning, dawn, early M2 [np]

  səvera

neighbour M1

  pəRəwsi [or /pəRosi/]

death; transfer M1 [np]

  yntyqal

funeral, funeral procession M2

  jənaza

T: Excuse me, Madame, I'm late [lit. to me lateness has become]. In fact, early this morning one of my neighbours died. [I] had to go to [lit. on] his funeral.

maf kərna, begəm sahəb, mwjhe der ho gəi. dərəsl aj swba səvere mere ek pəRəwsi ka yntyqal ho gəya. ws ke janaze pər jana tha.

forgiveness, pardon F2

  mafi [literary: /mwafi/]

MS: What is there to forgive about it [lit. in this what matter of forgiveness is there]? Rather this is very sad news. How old was he?

ys mē̃ mafi ki kya bat həy. bəlke yy to bəhwt əfsosnak xəbər həy. ws ki wmr kytni thi.

sixty-two A1

  basəTh

sixty-three A1

  təresəTh [or /tyrsəTh/]

T: [He] was an old man. He was about sixty-two [or] sixty-three years old. -- Now tell me, what is your pleasure [lit. order]?

buRha admi tha. ws ki wmr koi basəTh təresəTh sal thi. əb fərmaie, kya hwkm həy.

together, collected, in a mass, gathered A2 Adv

  ykhəTTa

shirt F1

  qəmis [or /qəmiz/]

loose pajama F1

  šəlvar

sport shirt: "bush-shirt" F1 [or M1]

  bwšərT [or /bwššərT/]

to sew [Ie: stem /syl/]

  sina

pants F1

  pətlun

MS: Yesterday I brought some cloth all together [i.e. various kinds of cloth purchased at one time]. Three shirts are to be made for me. Two bush-shirts and four [pairs of] pants are to be sewn for Mr. Smith, and the rest of the cloth is for the girls' šəlvars.

māy kəl kwch kəpRa ykhəTTa le ai thi. tin qəmisē̃ mere lie bənani hə̄y. do bwšərT əwr car pətlunē̃ ysmyth sahəb ke lie sini hə̄y, əwr baqi kəpRa bəcciō̃ ki šəlvarō̃ ke lie həy.

measurements F1 [or M1] [np]

  nap

T: [I] have Mr. Smith's and your measurement[s]. Please tell [me] the children's measurement[s].

ysmyth sahəb əwr ap ki nap məwjud həy. bəcciō̃ ki nap bəta dijie.

4

copybook, copy F2	kapi
imitation, copy, copying F1	nəql
length, tallness F2	ləmbai
width F2	cəwRai
inch M1	ync
to expand, enlarge, stretch out, make grow [C: /bəRhna/: IIc]	bəRhana

MS: [It] is written in this copy-book. Copy [it] from here! This measurement of the children's is from last year. I think that [you] ought to enlarge [it by] one or two inches [each] in the length and width.

ys kapi mẽ lykhi hwi həy. yəhã se nəql kər lo! bəcciõ ki yy nap pychle sal ki həy. mera xyal həy, ky ləmbai əwr cəwRai mẽ ek ek ya do do ync bəRha dena.

silken A1	rešmi

T: What is this silken cloth for?

yy rešmi kəpRa kys lie həy.

blouse M1	blawz
saRi: "sari" F2	saRi
present, gift M2	twhfa
to measure [If: /ə/]	napna

MS: This is for a blouse. Last week a friend of mine gave me a saRi as a gift. This is the blouse that goes with it. Measure this cloth! I think [it] will be enough.

yy blawz ke lie həy. pychle həfte meri ek səheli ne mwjhe ek saRi twhfe ke təwr pər di thi. yy blawz ws ke sath ka həy. ys kəpRe ko nap lo! mera xyal həy, ky kafi hoga.

complete, full, whole, entire A2	pura

T: Yes, it's sufficient [lit. complete].

ji hã, pura həy.

to be sewn [I: /sina/: Ie]	sylna

MS: By when will these clothes be sewn?

yy kəpRe kəb tək syl jaẽge.

T: [You] will get [them] after a week, God willing.

ynšaəlla[h] ek həfte ke bad myl jaẽge.

As the tailor leaves, the washerman comes in.

total, sum, whole, all M1 [np] A1	kwl
iron (for clothing) F2	ystri

MS: How many clothes are there in all? And those clothes which [I] sent yesterday for ironing [lit. for iron], have [you] brought them too?

kwl kytne kəpRe hə̃y. əwr jo kəpRe kəl ystri ke lie bhyjvae the, kya, vw bhi le ae ho?

to count [Ic: /y/]	gynna
undershirt M1	bənyan
pajama M2	pajama

W: Yes, there are thirty-three items [lit. clothes] in all. Please count them! There are eight large [i.e. adult] shirts. There are six [pairs of] pants. There are ten undershirts, and the rest are the girls' pajamas.

ji hã, kwl tẽtys kəpRe hə̃y. gyn lijie! aTh bəRi qəmisẽ hə̃y. chəy pətlunẽ hə̃y. dəs bənyan hə̃y, əwr baqi bəcciõ ke pajame hə̃y.

stocking, sock M2	moza

MS: I don't see the socks [lit. the stockings do not come to view].

moze nəzər nəhĩ ate.

5

handkerchief M1   rwmal

to be tied, bound, fastened [I: /bādhna/:   bādhna
If]

W: They're tied up in this handkerchief.   ys rwmal mē bādhe hwe hāy.

to be washed [I: /dhona/: Ie]   dhwlna

[you nonhonorific] have brought torn   phaR lae ho
MP [Conjunct verb: torn-have brought;
/phaRna/ "to tear, rip, rend"; If:
stem /phəT/ or /phəR/]

MS: These pajamas have not been washed   yy pajame əcche nəhī dhwle. dusre, yy
well. Secondly, [you] have brought   qəmis phaR lae ho.
[back] this shirt torn.

to be torn, ripped, rent [I: /phaRna/:   phəTna
If]

W: [It] is an old shirt, and [it] was torn from   pwrani qəmis həy, əwr pəhle se phəTi hwi
before.   thi.

MS: How much money do I owe you for all   yn ke kwl kytne pəyse hwe.
these [lit. All how much money of these
became]?

sixty-five   pāysəTh

included, associated in, joined in PA1   šamyl

W: Four rupees and sixty-five pəyse. One   car rupəe əwr pāysəTh pəyse. ek rupəya
rupee was left over from before. [I] have   pəhle ka baqi tha. wse bhi šamyl kər lia
included that too.   həy.

MS: Here you are [lit. take this!]. Five   yy lo! -- pāc rupəe.
rupees.

change, small coins F2   rezgari

W: I don't have change.   mere pas rezgari nəhī.

while going back, at the time of going   vapəs jate vəqt
back MOS

MS: No matter. Include [it] next time [i.e.   koi bat nəhī. əgli dəfa šamyl kər lena.
put the remaining thirty-five pəyse on   əbhi kəpRe təyyar nəhī. pəhle dusre ghərõ
next week's bill]. The clothes [for you   se kəpRe ykhəTTe kər lao! vapəs jate
to take] are not yet ready. First gather   vəqt yəhā se le jana.
and bring the clothes from the other
houses [on your route]. As you return,
take [our dirty clothes] from here.

W: Very well, Madame.   bəhwt əccha, begəm sahəb.

16.100. WORD STUDY

16.101. Section 16.000 depicts the daily activities of a typical upper-middle-class foreign household in present-day Pakistan or North India. The employment of servants for most household tasks is an old tradition in the Subcontinent, and the foreigner, whatever his own traditions, usually succumbs to being waited upon by anywhere from three to ten professional, English-speaking (or partially English-speaking) servants. As a class, these people have a long tradition of service with British families, and they have firm ideas about their respective duties and relative status. Labour-saving devices and such luxuries as super-markets are rare in the Subcontinent, and the foreign resident who wishes to avoid having a house full of servants finds himself spending much of his time learning how to shop in the bazaar, how to cook on charcoal, etc. etc. and thus wastes much of his working time. It is not uncommon for a family earning the equivalent of eight to ten thousand dollars a year to have five or six servants, and this is also true of Indian and Pakistani households as well. Even middle class families have a servant or two, and the author has even seen cases of a servant having a servant! The servant system is crumbling somewhat under the onslaught of technology and industrialisation and rising costs of living, but for the foreseeable future the servant tradition is likely to continue.

Mrs. Smith, whose household is about average for an American working in Pakistan, employs:

(1) A "bearer" (/bəyra/ M2), a sort of majordomo, whose job it is to supervise the house, make the beds, dust, serve the food, etc. It may be noted that the "bearer" is an institution in European households only; in Indo-Pakistani homes the majordomo is simply termed /nəwkər/, and the word /bəyra/ is reserved for a waiter in a restaurant, a hotel room-boy, etc.

(2) A cook (/xansamā/ M1 or /bavərci/ M1), who purchases food from the market and does the cooking, dishwashing, etc. Cooks, as well as other servants, are mostly men in foreign households. Women servants exist, of course, in the women's quarters and family areas of Indo-Pakistani homes where /pərda/ (see Sec. 16.115) is observed.

(3) A sweeper (/jəmadar/ M1, /myhtər/ M1, or /bhāgi/ M1 -- or a woman sweeper: /jəmadaryn/ F1, /myhtərani/ F2, or /bhāgən/ F1) who does the "untouchable" tasks around the house: he (or she) sweeps the floors, cleans the toilets and drains, cleans up messes left by pets, etc. These are tasks which no other servant will generally touch.

(4) A part-time gardener (/mali/ M1) who comes on certain afternoons to do the yard-work.

(5) A night-watchman (/cəwkidar/ M1) who stands guard over the Smiths' property each night.

In addition to these permanent people, the Smiths also have a washerman (/dhobi/ M1) who comes each week to collect and deliver the washing. (For drycleaning, however, Mr. Smith must take his clothing to a shop in the city.) Since most clothes are "made to measure" there is also a tailor (/dərzi/ M1) who calls occasionally. Other peddlars and merchants also frequently call at the Smiths' home.

7

16.102. /halāke/ Conj "although, notwithstanding, even though" is roughly synonymous with /əgərce/ Conj "although."

16.103. /pabənd/ PA1 "following, adhering, observing, bound to" is a Persian loan-compound: /pa/ "foot" + /bənd/ "tied, bound," /pabənd/ belongs to that class of predicate adjectives which are "possessed" by their semantic objects (see Sec. 11.306): i.e. /pabənd/ is possessed by the thing followed or adhered to: /[X ka] pabənd/ "adhering [to X], observing [X], following [X]." The possessive postposition agrees in number-gender with the grammatical subject. E.g.

    /vw admi nəmaz ka bəhwt pabənd həy./ That man is very punctual about his prayers. [Lit. ... is very observing of prayer. Here /ka/ agrees in number-gender with /admi/. Compare:]

    /vw əwrət nəmaz ki bəhwt pabənd həy./ That woman is very punctual about her prayers. [/ki/ agrees with /əwrət/.]

    /vw log vəqt ke bəhwt pabənd hə̃y./ Those people are very punctual. [Lit. bound of time. /ke/ agrees with /log/.]

16.104. /bykhərna/ Ig "to be scattered, strewn, spread out, disheveled (hair)" is the intransitive form of /bəkherna/ (or /bykherna/) "to scatter, strew, spread." The vowels of the intransitive form are irregular: one might expect */bəkhyrna/ or */bykhyrna/ instead of /bykhərna/. See Sec. 9.306.

16.105. /dəm/ M1 "life, breath, moment" occurs in a great many idioms. The student may treat /ek dəm/ Aḍv "all at once" as a unit for the present. Other common usages are given in Sec. 16.128.

16.106. /ahysta/ A1 Adv has a great many uses. Some of the commonest are illustrated in the following examples:

    /vw bəhwt ahysta cəl rəha tha./ He was going along very slowly.

    /yy bimari təmam šəhr mẽ ahysta ahysta phəylti gəi./ This illness gradually spread throughout the whole city.

    /ahysta bolo!/ Speak slowly! [Or:] Speak softly!

    /zəra rəDyo ahysta kijie!/ Please turn the radio down!

    /ws ne ahysta avaz se kəha, ky mwjhe jane do!/ He said in a soft [low] voice, "Let me go!"

16.107. /axyrkar/ Adv "at last, finally, in the end" is an Arabic-Persian compound consisting of /axyr/ M1 Adv "end; lastly, finally" + /kar/ "work" (found only in compounds in Urdu).

16.108. /becara/ A2 M/F2 consists of the Persian prefix /be/ "without" (see Sec. 11.301) + /cara/ M2 "redress, means, resource." /becara/ denotes "poor fellow, unfortunate person," and although it is found as a Type II adjective, it is commonly used as a noun. The feminine form, /becari/ F2 A2, similarly means "poor girl, poor woman." E.g.

8

/ws becari ne kəha, ky mə̄y kya kərū. / That poor [woman] said, "What shall I do?"

/vw becara ro pəRa. / That poor [fellow] burst into tears.

/ag ləgne se, ws becare ka bəhwt nwqsan hwa. / Because of [lit. from] the fire, that poor [fellow] suffered much loss.

/becare mwsafyr ka gaõ ke ləRkõ ne bəhwt tə̄g kia. / The boys of the village teased the poor traveller a lot.

16.109. /zəra/ Al Adv has two main uses: (a) alone as an adverb meaning "just, a little"; and (b) + the Type II enclitic /sa/ "like, -ish" as an adjective meaning "a little bit, a small amount of." E.g.

/zəra Thəyr jaie! / Please wait a bit!

/zəra nərs ke sath jao! / Just go with the nurse!

/vw mwjh se zəra si bat pər naraz ho gəya. / He became very angry with me over [lit. on] a very small matter. [Although /si/ agrees with /bat/ in number-gender-case and is Type II, /zəra/ is Type I and does not change.]

/cae mē̃ zəra si cini əwr Dal do! / Put a little more sugar in the tea!

16.110. Naturally any explanation of the Indo-Pakistani dishes mentioned in this Unit must remain incomplete until the student has had first-hand experience of them. All of the items introduced are very common, and no formal dinner is complete without at least some of them. Briefly, they are: (a) /pwlao/ Ml [np] is a dish known in Syrian and Armenian restaurants as "pilaff"; it consists of rice cooked with meat and spices. (b) /qorma/ M2 [np] is a type of hot curry dish cooked with /gərm məsala/ (see Sec. 16.111); it has very little excess liquid, and the meat (usually lamb or goat) is first browned in curds (/dəhi/ Ml [np]). (c) /qima/ M2 [np] denotes any minced meat, and this may be prepared in various ways. (d) /kəbab/ Ml "kabab" also comes in many forms; these include patties of ground meat, bits of roasted meat marinated in spices, the famous "shish kabab" (Urdu /six kəbab/; /six/ Fl "skewer, spit"), etc. (e) /kofta/ M2 is made of minced meat rolled into meatballs and cooked in a spicy sauce.

16.111. The term /məsala/ M2 "spices, seasoning" includes a great variety of condiments. A number of spices, however, are treated as a single unit in cooking and are called /gərm məsala/ "hot seasoning." This group includes: /kali myrc/ Fl "black pepper," /lõwg/ Fl "cloves," /darcini/ F2 [np] "cinnamon," /ylayci/ F2 "cardamon seed," /zira/ M2 "cumin seed," and sometimes a few other items. Other spices not included in /gərm məsala/ are added separately: e.g. /lal myrc/ Fl "red pepper, chili," /həri myrc/ Fl "green pepper," /həldi/ F2 [np] "turmeric," /dhənia/ M2 [np] "coriander," and of course /pyaz/ Fl "onion" and /ləhsən/ Ml [np] "garlic." It may be noted that in Indo-Pakistani cooking there is no such thing as "curry powder"; this seems to have been a foreign innovation.

16.112. /le ana/ "to bring" and /le jana/ "to take away" are two very common conjunct verbal formations: lit. "to take-come" and "to take-go," respectively. The main

9

verb, /ana/ "to come," is intransitive, and the subject of these formations is thus never marked by /ne/ in the past tenses. /lana/ "to bring" is a contraction of /le ana/ and is almost always substitutable. E.g.

> /vw ap ka səb saman le aya./ He brought all your luggage. [Never */ws ne .../!]
>
> /bavərci cabi le gəya hoga./ The cook must have taken away the key.
>
> /bazar se kwch məsala bhi le ana!/ [You] should bring some spices also from the market! [Appropriate forms of /lana/ are substitutable in all of these examples.]

16.113. Alone, /gobhi/ F2 usually denotes "cauliflower" but may mean "cabbage." More specifically, "cauliflower" is termed /phul gobhi/ (i.e. "flower-gobhi") and "cabbage" is called /bənd gobhi/ (i.e. "closed-gobhi").

16.114. "To cut the hair, give a haircut" is expressed by /bal bənana/ or /bal kaTna/. "To get a haircut" is expressed by the double causative forms of these: /bal bənvana/ and /bal kəTvana/. A complex verbal construction, /həjamət kərna/ (Arabic /həjamət/ F1 [np] "haircut, shave"), is also employed for "to cut the hair" (and occasionally for "to shave" also). Among the urban people, /šev kərna/ is commonly used for "to shave (the face)," but /DaRhi bənana/ (/DaRhi/ F2 "beard") is also common, and the latter form is commoner in rural areas.

16.115. /pərda/ M2 means not only "curtain" but also "veil." It also denotes the whole complex of customs connected with the seclusion of women from males who do not belong to the immediate family. E.g.

> /vw əwrət pərde mẽ rəhti həy./ That woman stays in "pərda." [I.e. she remains out of sight of non-family males, wears a head-to-foot veil (/bwrqa/ M2) when she goes out, etc.]
>
> /vw əwrət pərda kərti həy./ That woman practices "pərda."

16.116. /mã/ F1 "mother" and /bap/ M1 "father" are rather less honorific then /valda/ and /valyd/. /mã bap/ Mpl is also found as a loose compound meaning "parents"; */valda valyd/ is never used in this way.

16.117. /dyqqət/ F1 "difficulty, problem, perplexity, dilemma" contrasts with /təklif/ F1 "trouble, pain, hardship" and with /pərešani/ F2 "trouble, anxiety, upset, distress." E.g.

> /ajkəl cini mylne mẽ bəRi dyqqət peš ati həy, jys ki vəja se logõ ko bəhwt təklif həy./ Nowadays there is [lit. presents itself] a great problem in getting sugar, because of which people are suffering.
>
> /jəb yy dyqqət peš ai, to vw pərešan ho gəya./ When this problem arose, he became upset.

16.118. /bavərci/ M1 "cook" is synonymous with /xansamã/ M1. "Kitchen," however, is always /bavərcixana/ M2 and never */xansamãxana/.

16.119. /swba/ [literary /swbəh/] F1 "early morning" and /səvera/ M2 [np] "early morning, dawn, early" differ only in that the latter may also occasionally be used alone to mean "early" (i.e. "before the appointed time"). /pəhle/ Adv "first" or /jəldi/ F2 Adv "quickly" are usually preferable for "early" in most environments, however. In compound form, /swba səvere/ Adv or /səvere səvere/ Adv denote "early in the morning." E.g.

> /maf kijie, mə̄y zəra səvere pəhw̃c gəya hū./ Please excuse [me], I have arrived a little early. [/pəhle/ or /jəldi/ are more frequent in such contexts.]

> /davət bəhwt səvere xətm ho gəi./ The party ended very early. [/jəldi/ would be more common here.]

> /aj gaRi səvere a gəi./ Today the train came early. [/pəhle/ is perhaps a trifle more idiomatic.]

> /ap ytne səvere kyō ja rəhe hə̄y./ Why are you going so early [in the morning]? [/ytni jəldi/ or /ytne pəhle/ would both mean "so soon."]

16.120. /jənaza/ M2 denotes the bier on which the corpse is carried by his male relatives and friends to the burial ground. The word is generally used, however, for the whole Muslim funeral procession and funeral ceremony. Hindus, on the other hand, carry the corpse to a place of cremation and there set it upon a bier (/ərthi/ F2) and burn it.

16.121. /begəm sahəb/ F1 "Madame" is generally a term of address employed by persons of the lower classes for an upper class Indian or Pakistani married woman and sometimes for foreign ladies as well (although Mrs. Smith would more probably be addressed as /mem sahəb/ by her servants, tradesmen, etc.). The student should not use this term to address a lady; the honorific form is /begəm sahyba/, and this is the form which should be employed.

16.122. /ykhəTTa/ A2 Adv "together, collected, in a mass, gathered, accumulated" differs from /myl kər/ "together" (see Sec. 9.119) in that the latter refers to the subject of the verb only, whereas /ykhəTTa/ may also refer to an object, modify a noun, etc. E.g.

> /wn səb ne myl kər yy kam kia./ All of them together did this work.

> /həm səb log myl kər yy pətthər wTha səkēge./ All of us people together will be able to lift this stone.

> /səb logō ne myl kər wse nykal dia./ All the people together took it outside.

> /ys məwqe pər, təmam log ykhəTTe ho gəe./ On this occasion all of the people got together. [Here /ykhəTTe ho gəe/ is synonymous with /jəma ho gəe/.]

> /səb gaōvale ykhəTTe ho kər ləRne ke lie ae./ All of the villagers got together and came to fight.

> /ykhəTTi cizē le ao, take bar bar bazar nə jana pəRe./ Bring all the things together [in one lot], so that [you] won't have to go to the market again and again.

> /mə̄y kəl səb saman ykhəTTa le aya tha./ I had brought all of the luggage together [in one lot] yesterday.

16.123. There is almost unlimited variation in costume in India and Pakistan. Not only does the manner of dress differ from area to area but also from social class to social

11

class, and an experienced person can often identify the provenance, religion, social status, etc. of almost any passerby by his dress.

So far as Muslim women's dress is concerned, however, two general traditions can be identified: the Western /šəlvar/-/qəmis/ costume versus the Eastern /saRi/. The /qəmis/ F1 consists of a long-sleeved, collarless shirt-like garment which reaches almost to the knees. The /šəlvar/ F1 is worn under the /qəmis/; it consists of a pair of loose, baggy pajamas which are tight at the ankles. A gauzy scarf, called a /dopəTTa/ M2, is worn across the breast with the ends hanging down the back. Women may also wear a /qəmis/ over a very tight pajama which hugs the legs almost like hose (see below). The Eastern /saRi/ F2 consists of a single six-yard piece of cloth worn over a petticoat and a blouse.

The East and the West also differ in men's costumes. In the East one finds the /kwrta/-/pajama/ combination most prevalent: the /kwrta/ M2 is a thin, gauzy, long-sleeved, collarless shirt worn over an undershirt (/bənyan/ M1) and one or another style of pajama (/pajama/ M2). The latter ranges in style from the very tight, hose-like /cuRidar pajama/ or /tõg pajama/ (also worn by women, see above) to the foot and a half wide cuff of the /Dhila pajama/ (/Dhila/ A2 "loose"). In the West the /šəlvar/-/qəmis/ is worn also by men, though differing from the women's costume in colour and style. The /qəmis/ is now made to look rather like a European man's shirt, with collar, cuffs, and breast pocket, but it is worn with the ends outside the /šəlvar/. The /šəlvar/ is usually white (or some light, dull colour) and very baggy, using anywhere from four and a half to seven yards of cloth (the latter in the Northwest Frontier tribal areas and in Baluchistan).

European dress is common for men of the middle and upper classes, and during the hot season a short-sleeved sportshirt (/bwšərT/ or /bwššərT/ F1 [or M1] "bush-shirt") or a /qəmis/ are worn with a pair of pants (/pətlun/ F1, a Portuguese loanword, or /pəynT/ F1). During the cool weather the English-style suit (/suT/ M1) is worn (or at least a coat, /koT/ M1, and a necktie, /Tai/ F2). Aside from the Indo-Pakistani Christian community, however, almost NO women have adopted European styles of dress in the Subcontinent.

16.124. /pura/ A2 "complete, full, whole, entire" semantically overlaps /səb/ A1 "all, " /təmam/ A1 "complete, all, entire, " and /sara/ A2 "whole, entire. " /pura/ usually is not employed for the totality of a group of individual items; instead it indicates completeness, fullness, wholeness up to the entirety of some single entity. /kwl/ M1 A1 "total, sum, whole, all" is rather restricted in use: it denotes the totality of a countable group of individual items or entities. E. g.

> /sara šəhr təbah ho gəya. / The whole city was destroyed. [/pura/ and /təmam/ are substitutable here since the totality of a single unit is meant.]

> /sare log mər gəe. / All the people died. [/səb/ and /təmam/ are also substitutable. /pura/ cannot be used since a number of entities are included in /log/.]

> /əb yy rəqəm puri həy. / Now this amount is complete. [None of the others is quite idiomatic here.]

> /yy kam təmam ho gəya. / This work has been completed [lit. become complete]. [/pura/ can occur here, giving the sense of "becoming whole, entire"; none of the others are appropriate.]

/yn ka kwl kya həy. / What is the total of these? [None of the others can occur here.]

/vəhã kwl kytne pakystani the. / In all how many Pakistanis were there? [Lit. There total how many Pakistanis were? /səb/, /sara/, and /təmam/ may occur but are less expressive of a total number.]

/admiõ ki kwl tadad pəcas thi. / The total number of people was fifty. [Again /kwl/ is more appropriate for numerical totality than any of the others.]

/vəhã təmam admi məwjud the. / All of the people were present there. [/səb/ and /sare/ are quite appropriate here; /pure/ may also occur, providing that the totality of some unitary body of people was meant: i.e. all the members of a club, all of the members of parliament, etc.]

16.125. /rwmal/ M1 "handkerchief" consists of Persian /ru/ "face" + /mal/, the stem of the Persian verb meaning "to wipe, rub."

16.126. /phaRna/ If "to tear, rip, rend" has an irregular intransitive form: /phəTna/ "to be torn, ripped, rent." The double causative form is usually /phəRvana/, but /phəTvana/ is also occasionally found. Older dictionaries also list a causative form, /phəTana/, but this seems to be almost obsolete. See Sec. 9.306.

16.127. /rezgari/ F2 "change, small coins" does not have quite the same meaning as "change" in English: /rezgari/ does not mean "the remains of a larger amount after some sum has been taken away." For example, /rezgari/ cannot occur in the Urdu equivalent of the following context: "You gave me five dollars for this three dollar book; here is your change -- two one dollar bills." /rezgari/ means only "coins, small change." E.g.

/bazar ja kər ek rupəe ki rezgari lao! / Go to the market and bring one rupee's [worth of] change!

16.128. Some Complex Verbal Formations.

A:

/ahysta/
　　/ahysta hona/ to be, become gradual, slow, soft, mild
　　/[X ko] ahysta kərna/ to make [X] gradual, slow, soft, mild
/gila/
　　/gila hona/ to be, become wet, damp
　　/[X ko] gila kərna/ to wet, dampen [X]
/nəql/. [See also B.]
　　/[X ko] nəql kərna/ to copy [X], make a copy [of X]
/pura/
　　/pura hona/ to be, become complete, full, whole
　　/[X ko] pura kərna/ to complete, fulfill, fill [X]
/šamyl/
　　/[X mẽ] šamyl hona/ to be, become included [in X]
　　/[X ko Y mẽ] šamyl kərna/ to include [X in Y]

13

/šərik/

/[X mē] šərik hona/ to participate [in X]

/[X ko Y mē] šərik kərna/ to make [X] a partner [in Y], make [X] participate [in Y]

/xərc/. [See also F.]

/[X pər] xərc hona/ to be spent [on X]

/[X mē] xərc hona/ to be spent [in X]

/[X pər Y] xərc kərna/ to spend [Y on X]

/[X mē Y] xərc kərna/ to spend [Y in X]

/ykhəTTa/

/ykhəTTa ho jana/ to gather, collect together

/[X ko] ykhəTTa kərna/ to gather, collect [X]

B:

/nəql/. [See also A.]

/[X ki] nəql hona/ [X] to be copied, imitated

/[X ki] nəql kərna/ to imitate, ape, mimick [X]

/pabənd/

/[X ka] pabənd hona/ to adhere to, be punctual about, observe [X]. [As stated in Sec. 16.103, the presence of /ka/, /ke/, or /ki/ depends upon the number-gender of the subject.]

/[X ko Y ka] pabənd kərna/ to restrict [X to Y], to cause [X] to adhere to, observe [Y]. [In this construction X always occurs with /ko/ or its equivalent, and thus only /ka/ may occur: e.g. /ws ne ws ləRki ko nəmaz ka pabənd kia./ "He made that girl observe [her] prayer[s]. */ws ne vw ləRki nəmaz ki pabənd ki./ is not idiomatic.]

/səwda/

/[X ka] səwda hona/ [X] to be sold, a bargain to be struck [for X]

/[X ka] səwda kərna/ to strike a bargain [for X]

D:

/hysab/. [See also F.]

/[X ko Y ka] hysab dena/ to give an accounting [to X for Y]

/[X se Y ka] hysab lena/ to take an accounting [of Y from X]

/mafi/

/[X ko] mafi dena/ to forgive [X]

/[X se Y ki] mafi lena/ to obtain forgiveness [from X for Y]

/[X se] mafi māgna/ to seek forgiveness [from X]

/[X ko] mafi mylna/ [X] to be forgiven, pardoned

/nap/

/[X ko Y ki] nap dena/ to give [X] the measurement [of Y]

/[X ki] nap lena/ to take the measurement [of X]

F:

/bal/

/bal bəRhna/ hair to grow

/[X ke] bal bənana/ to cut, trim the hair [of X]

/[X ke] bal kaTna/ to cut, trim the hair [of X]

14

/dəm/

    /dəm dena/ to die, expire

    /[X pər] dəm dena/ to be infatuated [with X]

    /dəm hona/ to be simmered (as rice)

    /[X ko] dəm kərna/ to simmer [X] (as rice)

    /dəm lena/ to catch one's breath

    /[X ke samne] dəm nə marna/ to be afraid to speak [in front of X]

    /[X ka] dəm nykal dena, nykal lena/ to absorb all of [X's] energies

    /[X ka] dəm nykəlna/ [X] to become terrified; [X] to die

    /dəm toR dena/ to die, breathe one's last

/dyqqət/

    /[X ko Y mẽ, ki] dyqqət hona/ [X] to have difficulty [in the matter of Y]

    /[X ko hasyl kərne mẽ] dyqqət wThana/ to have trouble [obtaining X]

/hysab/. [See also D.]

    /[X ka] hysab ləgana/ to estimate the costs [of X]

/jənaza/

    /[X ka] jənaza wThana/ to carry the bier [of X], take part in [X's] funeral

/jhaRu/

    /[X mẽ] jhaRu dena/ to sweep [X], use a broom [in X]

/məcchər/

    /məcchər marna/ to kill mosquito[es]

/məkkhi/

    /məkkhi marna/ to kill fli[es]

/našta/

    /našta kərna/ to have breakfast, eat breakfast. [*/našta khana/ is not
        idiomatic.]

/pabəndi/

    /[X pər] pabəndi hona/ to be a restriction [on X]

    /[X pər Y ki] pabəndi ləgana/ to place a restriction [of Y on X]

    /pabəndi se/ regularly, punctually, strictly

/pərda/

    /[X se] pərda kərna/ (woman) to remain secluded [from X], practice "pərda"
        [with X]

    /pərde mẽ rəhna/ (woman) to remain in seclusion, practice "pərda"

/pəTTi/

    /[X ke] pəTTi bādhna/ to bandage [X (a person)]

    /[X pər] pəTTi bādhna/ to bandage [X (a limb)]

/təəjjwb/

    /[X ko Y pər] təəjjwb hona/ [X] to be astonished [at Y]

    /[X pər] təəjjwb kərna/ to display astonishment [at X], wonder [at X]

/vada/

    /[X ka Y se] vada hona/ [X] to have a promise [with Y]

    /[X se Y ka] vada kərna/ to promise [Y to X]

    /[X se Y ka] vada lena/ to obtain a promise [from X] [(to do) Y]

/xərc/. [See also A.]

 /[X ka] xərc wThana/ to take the expenses [of X] upon oneself, to bear the
 expenses [of X]

/yntyqal/

 /[X ka] yntyqal hona/ [X] to die

 /yntyqal kərna/ to die

/ystri/

 /[X pər] ystri kərna/ to iron [X]

16.201. Word Recognition.

(1) The following words are written with "uncommon" Arabic consonants, with final

ه = /a/, or with other special spelling conventions.

SCRIPT	PRONUNCIATION	SCRIPT	PRONUNCIATION
آهسته	ahysta	رومال	rwmal [not */rumal/]
باورچی خانه	bavərcixana	تميص	qəmis [or: تميض /qəmiz/]
	becara	قورمه	qorma
پاجامه	pajama	قيمه	qima
پرچ	pərca	كوفته	kofta
پرده	pərda	كوئله	koyla
تحفه	twhfa	مصالحه	məsala [or: مصالح ,
تعجّب	təəjjwb		or even مساله]
جنازه	jənaza	مطابق	mwtabyq
حالانكه	halāke	معافی	mafi [or: /mwafi/]
حساب	hysab	موزه	moza
دهواں	dhūā	ناشته	našta
ذرا	zəra	وعده	vada

(2) The spelling of words ending in /ūā/ is quite irregular; compare دهواں /dhūā/ M2 [np] "smoke" with كنواں /kūā/ M2 "well."

16.202. Reading Drill I: Text.

17

The following is the text of Sec. 16.000. Read it aloud several times, striving for speed and accuracy.

مسز اسمتھ۔ بڑے تعجب کی بات ہے کہ درزی ابھی تک نہیں آیا۔ حالانکہ وہ ہمیشہ اپنے وعدے کے مطابق آتا ہے۔

خانساماں۔ شاید کوئی ضروری کام پیش آگیا ہو۔ ورنہ واقعی وہ وقت کا بہت پابند ہے۔

مسز اسمتھ۔ تم نے ہاتھ پر پٹّی کیوں باندھ رکھی ہے؟

خانساماں۔ صبح ناشتہ تیّار کرنے کے بعد میں برتن دھو رہا تھا۔ اچانک میرا ہاتھ چولھے پر رکھّی ہوئی مٹّی کے تیل کی بوتل سے ٹکرا گیا، جس سے تمام تیل بکھر گیا اور جلتے کوئلوں تک پہنچ گیا۔ اس طرح ایک دم چولھے میں آگ لگ گئی۔ میں نے آگ بجھانے کی بہت کوشش کی، لیکن وہ آہستہ آہستہ پھیلتی گئی۔ آخرکار میں نے مالی کو پکارا۔ وہ بے چارہ میری آواز سنتے ہی دوڑتا ہوا آیا۔ اس طرح ہم دونوں نے مل کر آگ بجھائی۔ اس میں میرا ہاتھ جل گیا۔

مسز اسمتھ۔ زیادہ نقصان تو نہیں ہوا؟ ذرا میرے ساتھ آؤ۔ میں باورچی خانہ دیکھنا چاہتی ہوں۔

خانساماں۔ جی نہیں۔ کسی چیز کو نقصان نہیں پہنچا۔ صرف دو تین خالی ٹوکریاں جل گئی ہیں۔

مسز اسمتھ۔ یہ جلی ہوئی ٹوکریاں باہر پھینک دو۔ یہ دیوار دھوئیں کی وجہ سے کالی ہو گئی ہے۔ اسے گیلے کپڑے سے صاف کرو۔ اس کھڑکی کو بند کردو۔ اس

18

طرف سے مکھیاں مچھّر وغیرہ آ رہے ہیں ۔ اور اِن تمام چیزوں کو ڈھک کر رکھو!
یہ سب کام جلدی ختم کرو، کیونکہ شام کو دعوت کا بندوبست بھی کرنا ہے ۔

خانساماں :   شام کو کیا کیا پکانا ہے ؟

مسز اسمتھ۔   پلاؤ اور قورمہ ۔ اِس کے علاوہ کچھ قیمہ بھی لے آنا ، جس کے کباب اور
کوفتے بنا لینا ۔ کیا کچھ اور سودے کی بھی ضرورت ہے ؟

خانساماں۔   جی ہاں ۔ آلو، پیاز ، ٹماٹر اور کچھ مصالحہ بھی لانا ہے ۔

مسز اسمتھ۔   گوبھی اور گاجر بھی لانا ۔ اور چلتے وقت میں دس روپے دے گئی تھی۔وہ کہاں
خرچ کئے ؟

خانساماں۔   تین روپے کا یہ سودا لے آیا ہے۔ جس کا حساب اِس پرچے پر لکھا ہوا ہے ۔
تین روپے نائی کو دے دیے۔ کل بچیوں کے بال بنوا لایا تھا ۔ اور باقی چار
روپے میرے پاس موجود ہیں ۔

مسز اسمتھ۔   ٹھیک ہے ۔ پکاتے وقت ذرا احتیاط رکھا کرو! ایسا نہ ہو کہ کبھی زیادہ نقصان
اٹھانا پڑے ۔ دوسرے، جھاڑن سے کر کھڑکی کے پردوں کو جھاڑو!

خانساماں۔   بہت اچھا۔ میں ابھی یہ سب کام کر لیتا ہوں ..... اگلے ہفتے سے
مجھے دس دن کی چھٹی بھی چاہیے ۔

مسز اسمتھ۔   چھٹی کیوں چاہیے ؟

خانساماں۔   مجھے اپنے ماں باپ کے پاس جانا ہے ۔ اِس کے علاوہ میرے چھوٹے بھائی
کی شادی ہے ۔ اُس میں بھی شریک ہونا ضروری ہے ۔

مسز اسمتھ۔   تمہارے بغیر گھر کے کام میں کافی وقت پیش آئے گی ۔ خیر کوئی بات نہیں

19

کسی دوسرے باورچی کا انتظام کردینا۔

خانساماں۔ بہت اچھا۔ لیجئے۔ درزی آگیا ہے۔

درزی۔ معاف کرنا بیگم صاحب، مجھے دیر ہوگئی۔ دراصل آج صبح سویرے میرے ایک پڑوسی کا انتقال ہوگیا۔ اُس کے جنازے پر جانا تھا۔

مسز اسمتھ۔ اِس میں معافی کی کیا بات ہے ؟ بلکہ یہ تو بہت افسوس ناک خبر ہے۔ اُس کی عمر کتنی تھی ؟

درزی۔ بوڑھا آدمی تھا۔ اُس کی عمر کوئی باسٹھ ترسیٹھ سال تھی۔ اب فرمائیے کیا حکم ہے ؟

مسز اسمتھ۔ میں کل کچھ کپڑا اکٹھا لے آئی تھی۔ تین قمیصیں میرے لئے بنانی ہیں۔ دو بشرٹ اور چار پیٹی کوٹیں اسمتھ صاحب کے لئے سینی ہیں اور باقی کپڑا بچیوں کی شلواروں کے لئے ہے۔

درزی۔ اسمتھ صاحب اور آپ کی ناپ موجود ہے۔ بچیوں کی ناپ بتا دیجئے۔

مسز اسمتھ۔ اِس کاپی میں لکھی ہوئی ہے۔ یہاں سے نقل کرلو۔ بچیوں کی یہ ناپ پچھلے سال کی ہے۔ میرا خیال ہے کہ لمبائی اور چوڑائی میں ایک ایک یا دو دو انچ بڑھا دینا۔

درزی۔ یہ ریشمی کپڑا کس لئے ہے ؟

مسز اسمتھ۔ یہ بلاؤز کے لئے ہے۔ پچھلے ہفتے میری ایک سہیلی نے مجھے ایک ساڑھی تحفے کے طور پر دی تھی۔ یہ بلاؤز اُس کے ساتھ کا ہے۔ اِس کپڑے کو ناپ لو۔ میرا خیال ہے کہ کافی ہوگا۔

20

درزی۔ جی ہاں! پورا ہے ۔

مسزاسمتھ۔ یہ کپڑے کب تک سل جائیں گے ؟

درزی۔ انشاءاللہ ایک ہفتے بعد سل جائیں گے ۔

مسزاسمتھ۔ (دھوبی سے) کُل کتنے کپڑے ہیں ؟ اور جو کپڑے کل استری کے لئے بھجوائے تھے، کیا وہ بھی لے آئے ہو ؟

دھوبی۔ جی ہاں ۔ کُل تینتیس کپڑے ہیں ۔ گِن لیجیے ۔ آٹھ بڑی قمیصیں ہیں ۔ چھ پتلونیں ہیں ، دس بنیان ہیں اور باقی بچّیوں کے پاجامے ہیں ۔

مسزاسمتھ۔ موزے نظر نہیں آتے۔

دھوبی۔ اس رومال میں بندھے ہوئے ہیں ۔

مسزاسمتھ۔ یہ پاجامے اچھّے نہیں دُھلے ۔ دوسرے یہ قمیص پھاڑ لائے ہو۔

دھوبی۔ پُرانی قمیص ہے اور پہلے سے پھٹی ہوئی تھی ۔

مسزاسمتھ۔ اِن کے کُل کتنے پیسے ہوئے ؟

دھوبی۔ چار روپے اور پینتھ پیسے۔ ایک روپیہ پہلے کا باقی تھا۔ اُسے بھی شامل کر لیا ہے۔

مسزاسمتھ۔ یہ لو ۔ پانچ روپے ۔

دھوبی۔ میرے پاس ریزگاری نہیں ۔

مسزاسمتھ۔ کوئی بات نہیں۔ اگلی دفعہ حساب میں شامل کر لینا۔ ابھی کپڑے تیار نہیں ۔ پہلے دوسرے گھروں سے کپڑے اکٹھے کر لاؤ۔ واپس جاتے وقت یہاں سے لے جانا۔

دھوبی۔ بہت اچھا بیگم صاحب۔

21

16.203. Reading Drill II: Sentences.

Read the following sentences aloud and translate them into English.

Transportation

۱۔ سیلاب آتے ہی آمدورفت کا سلسلہ بند ہوگیا اور لوگ اپنے گھروں سے بھاگنے لگے۔

۲۔ آج ناشتہ کرتے وقت میں اپنے باورچی پر بہت ناراض ہوا کیونکہ اُس نے مجھے جلی ہوئی روٹی اور کچے انڈے دیئے دیئے تھے۔

۳۔ آج خبر آئی ہے کہ اُس بیچارے درزی کا انتقال ہوگیا۔ سیتے سیتے اُس کی طبیعت خراب ہوگئی تھی اور آخر کار اُس نے دم توڑ دیا۔

۴۔ بیٹا دوسرے شہر سے ابھی نہیں آیا تھا۔ اِس لئے اُس کے انتظار میں باپ کا جنازہ دو گھنٹے تک رکھا رہا۔

۵۔ یہ میلی ہوئی قمیص کسی غریب کو دے دینی چاہئے۔ دھوبی نے اِسے دھوتے ہوئے پھاڑ دیا۔

۶۔ میں تو یہ سمجھتا تھا کہ اُس کا انتقال ہو چکا ہے۔ لیکن جب یہ معلوم ہوا کہ وہ ابھی زندہ ہے تو مجھے بہت تعجّب ہوا۔

۷۔ میرے باپ نے ناراض ہوتے ہوئے کہا "تم نے یہ ساری رقم سینما وغیرہ پر کیوں خرچ کی ؟ یہ تمہارے اِسکول کے لئے تھی۔"

۸۔ ماسٹر نے جب لڑکوں کو اندر آتے ہوئے دیکھا تو کہا کہ تم لوگ ہمیشہ دیر سے کیوں آتے ہو ؟

۹۔ جب اسمتھ صاحب دعوت میں شلوار قمیص پہنے ہوئے آئے تو ؟ نہیں اِن کپڑوں میں دیکھ کر سب لوگوں کو تعجّب ہوا۔

۱۰۔ جب چور گھر میں داخل ہوا تو اُس نے سب لوگوں کو سوتے ہوئے پایا۔

22

۱۱- پل ٹوٹتے ہی اُس افسرنے حکومت کو اطلاع دی اور بتایا کہ اُس کے اندازے کے مطابق کوئی بیس ہزار روپے کا نقصان ہوا ہے۔

۱۲- جب میری ماں نے سامان بکھرا ہوا دیکھا تو وہ سمجھی کہ شاید کوئی چور گھس آیا ہے۔

۱۳- کسی اور باورچی کا انتظام ہوئے بغیر تمہیں چھٹی نہیں ملے گی۔ کیونکہ گھر کے کام میں بہت دِقت پیش آئے گی۔

۱۴- آگ جلاتے وقت اُس کا ہاتھ کوئلوں پر پڑ گیا۔ جس کی وجہ سے تمام ہاتھ جل گیا۔

۱۵- گوبھی، گاجر اور ٹماٹر ختم ہو گئے ہیں۔ گھر کا کام تم تم کرتے ہی بازار سے یہ سودا خرید لانا۔

16.204. Writing Drill I: Text.

Counting each speaker's part as one paragraph, write out the first ten paragraphs of Sec. 16.506 (Conversation Practice) in the Urdu script (i.e. down through /pwrani nap mẽ do do ỹc bəRha die hẽy./).

16.205. Spelling Review.

Write out the following words in the Urdu script. Check your spelling and handwriting against the correct forms of these words. Place them in Urdu alphabetical order.

(1) adaɒ		(16) Dhəkna
(2) əcanək		(17) bə̃dhna
(3) vaqəi		(18) bəhadri
(4) əlbətta		(19) pəta
(5) mwtabyq		(20) jwmerat
(6) lie		(21) ənar
(7) aspas		(22) ystemal
(8) bəɣəyr		(23) dhũã
(9) kydhər		(24) bã̃dhna
(10) myhnəti		(25) mətləb
(11) əjəb		(26) təriqa
(12) ThənDa		(27) wsul
(13) hasyl		(28) ylaj
(14) Dəraona		(29) kũã
(15) pəhw̃cna		(30) mysal

23

16. 206. Response Drill.

Answer the following questions in writing. (Answers to these questions should be based upon Secs. 16, 000 and 16, 506.)

۱۔ درزی کیوں دیرے سے آیا ؟

۲۔ مٹی کے تیل کی بوتل کہاں رکھی ہوئی تھی ؟

۳۔ آگ سے باورچی خانے میں کیا نقصان ہوا ؟

۴۔ اِسمتھ صاحب کے ہاں شام کو کون کرنے کھانے لگے تھے ؟

۵۔ مسز اِسمتھ مالی پر کیوں ناراض ہوئیں ؟

۶۔ کیا ، چلتے وقت مسز اِسمتھ باورچی کو پاکٹ روپے دے گئی تھیں ؟

۷۔ دھوبی سے مسز اِسمتھ کو کیا شکایت تھی ؟

۸۔ دوسری دفعہ درزی سب کپڑے سی کر کیوں نہیں لایا ؟

۹۔ درزی کو بچیوں کی ناپ کہاں سے ملی ؟

۱۰۔ دھوبی کل کتنے کپڑے لایا تھا ؟

16. 207. English to Urdu Sentences.

1. I saw the gardener sleeping under the tree.
2. Without going yourself, you cannot understand Pakistan.
3. How many months has it been since you went to your village?
4. We all tried together to stop the water, but it slowly kept on spreading.
5. The bill for [lit. of] these things is written on this slip.
6. According to our information, our enemy is gradually increasing his army.
7. To make [lit. cook] qorma, [you] need meat, onion[s], tomato[es], and "hot seasoning. " Some people also put [lit. pour] potato[es] in it.
8. Two weeks ago we went to our son's school, where we saw the boys playing football.
9. What is the total number of farmers in this village?
10. Yesterday while cutting [my] hair, the barber asked me, "Do you know Mr. əziz ? "

24

11. On hearing the noise, we rushed [lit. arrived fleeing fleeing] to the market. About sixty-five villagers holding [lit. taken] guns and staves, had come to complain to [/se/] the landlord.

12. Bring a wet cloth and clean this stove! Dust this room and throw these papers outside!

13. A great problem will arise in getting this silken cloth because the government has laid a restriction upon it.

14. I don't want to be associated in this mischief. Even though there will be no damage from it, still [/phyr bhi/] I don't like [it].

15. I brought this cloth all together from the market. Measure it, and from it [lit. from in it] make four shirts, two šǝlvars, and two pajamas.

16.300. ANALYSIS

16.301. The Verb: the <S + /rǝkhna/> Construction.

The <S + /rǝkhna/> formation lies on the borderline between "conjunct" and "compound" verbal constructions. Although a conjunctive participle (e. g. /kǝr ke/ "having done, " /swn kǝr/ "having heard"; see Sec. 5.308) can indeed be substituted for the stem in many instances, there are enough examples of a "compound-verb-like" nature (i. e. sentences in which /rǝkhna/ has lost its individual meaning, and a conjunct form cannot be substituted for the stem) to warrant the inclusion of this construction under the heading of compound verbal formations.

The <S + /rǝkhna/> formation denotes an action performed deliberately and with lasting effects. E. g.

/ws ki bivi ne davǝt mē saRi bādh rǝkkhi thi. / His wife had a saRi on [lit. had tie-kept] in the party. [I. e. his wife had put on a saRi and was wearing it during the party: a deliberate action with a lasting subsequent state.]

/mǣy ne ws se vada kǝr rǝkkha tha, ky mǣy šam tǝk vapǝs a jaūga. / I had made a promise to him that I would [lit. will] return by evening. [The sense is "firmly made a promise which is to be definitely kept. "]

/ws ne dǝrzi ko kwch kǝpRe sylne ke lie de rǝkkhe hǣy. / He has given the tailor some clothes to be sewn. [The clothes have been given to the tailor, who will keep them for some time.]

/wnhō ne bǝhwt dynō se gošt khana choR rǝkkha hǝy. / They have given up eating meat for a long time [lit. from many days]. [The action was deliberate, and the subsequent state still continues.]

/mǣy ne ws ki tǝsvir ǝpne kǝmre mē lǝga rǝkkhi hǝy. / I have placed [lit. attached-kept] his picture in my room.

/mã ne bǝcce ko pǝlǝg pǝr lyTa rǝkkha hǝy. / The mother has laid [lit. has laid-kept] the child on the bed.

16.302. The Verb: the Present Participle as a Substantive.

Urdu participles have, up to this point, been seen only in verbal roles. With the exception of the simple future tense, most of the tense-aspect formations of the language contain a present or past participle. It must be remembered, nevertheless, that a participle is basically a kind of "substantive" -- a word which may be employed in various contexts as an adjective or a noun. Substantive uses of both the present and past participles are many and complex, and the student will not require all of the information presented in the following two Sections. It is important, however, that the major points of the system be understood, and this material should thus be kept available for easy reference.

(1) The present participle occurs alone as a Type II noun. This usage is generally limited to such stylised formations as proverbs and to a few common verb stems. Such a "nominal participle" may be optionally followed by the past participle of /hona/ "to be, become, " which agrees with the participle in number-gender-case (compare Sec. 14.302). The present participle (+ /hwa/) denotes an actor in the act of performing the action of the

26

verb. E.g.

/mərtō ko kyō marte ho!/ Why do you kill the dying [ones]? [I.e. Why do you add to this person's troubles?]

/mərta kya nə kərta./ What wouldn't a dying [person] do? [Proverb: said of a person who is in such bad circumstances that he must adopt any course available to him, no matter how unpleasant.]

/sotō ko nə jəgana!/ Don't wake the sleeping [ones]!

/pəRhte hwe ko tōg nə kəro!/ Don't bother the reading [one]! [/pəRhte ko/ is substitutable.]

/bhagte hwō ko pəkəR lo!/ Catch the fleeing [ones]! [Note that when a participle is followed by /hwa/, only the latter has the MOP suffix /ō/; if /hwa/ does not occur, then /ō/ occurs with the participle itself, as seen in examples 1 and 3 above.]

/mərti ko kyō marte ho!/ Why do you kill the dying [woman]? [Compare example 1 above.]

(2) The present participle (+ /hwa/) is commonly employed as an adjective before a following noun. This usage indicates that the noun is engaged in the action of the participle and that this action is in process at the time of the utterance. E.g.

/jəlti hwi ag/ burning fire. [Or: /jəlti ag/.]

/cəlti hwi gaRi/ the moving car. [Or: /cəlti gaRi/.]

/dəwRta hwa admi/ the running man. [/dəwRta admi/ is possible but less common.]

/cəlti hwi həva ko kəwn rok səkta həy./ Who can stop the blowing [lit. moving] wind?

/jəlti hwi ləkRiō ko bwjha do!/ Put out [i.e. extinguish] the burning sticks!

/gyrti hwi ləRki ne mədəd ke lie pwkara./ The falling girl cried out for help.

/roti hwi ləRki ko tōg nə kəro!/ Don't tease the crying girl!

/ləRte hwe admiō ko rok dena cahie./ [You] ought to stop the fighting men.

/sote hwe mwsafyr ko nə jəgao!/ Don't wake the sleeping traveller!

(3) The present participle is also used as a predicate complement: it denotes another action performed by the subject at the same time as the action of the main verb: e.g. "Laughing, he said ...," "Falling, he cried out ...," etc. When such a participle precedes the subject and refers to it, a /,/ is usually employed, thus distinguishing this construction from the purely adjectival construction just discussed above. The participle (+ /hwa/) is likely to be in the MOS form and thus does not agree with the number-gender-case of the subject. E.g.

/cəlte hwe, mōy ne wse do rupəe de die the./ On leaving, I gave him two rupees.

/hōste hwe, vw cəla gəya./ Laughing, he went away.

When such a predicative participle follows the subject to which it refers, then four cases arise:

(a) If the participle refers to a subject not followed by /ne/, and if the participle itself has no object, and if the main verb of the sentence is a verb of motion (e.g. /ana/ "to come," /jana/ "to go," /bhagna/ "to flee," /pəhw̄cna/ "to arrive," /cəla jana/ "to go away," etc.) -- then the participle usually agrees

27

with the subject in number-gender-case. E. g.

/vw hə̃sta hwa cəla gəya./ He went away laughing. [/hə̃sta hwa/ is MNS agreeing with the number-gender of the subject. Compare:]

/vw hə̃sti hwi ai./ She came laughing.

/vw ləRka rota hwa bhag gəya./ That boy fled crying. [Compare:]

/vw ləRki cixti hwi bhag gəi./ That girl fled screaming.

/vw rota hwa mere valyd sahəb ke pas pəhw̃ca./ He came [lit. arrived] to my father weeping.

/səb əwrtẽ bolti hwi əndər a gəĩ./ All the women came inside talking.

/vw log Dərte hwe əndər a gəe./ Those people, [being] afraid, came inside.

/vw hə̃sta hwa kəmre mẽ daxyl hwa./ He entered the room laughing. [Although /hona/ "to be, become" by itself is not a verb of motion, the complex verbal formation /daxyl hona/ "to enter" does fall into this category.]

(b) If the participle refers to a subject not followed by /ne/, and if the participle itself has no object, and if the main verb of the sentence is anything OTHER than a verb of motion, then the participle tends to be in the MOP form, but it may optionally agree in number-gender-case with its subject. E. g.

/vw cəlte hwe bola./ He spoke [as he was] going along. [/cəlta hwa/ is also possible.]

/vw ləRki khate hwe boli./ That girl spoke [as she was] eating. [/khati hwi/ is also correct, though somewhat less frequent.]

/vw ləRki gyrte hwe cixi./ That girl screamed [as she was] falling. [/gyrti hwi/ is possible also.]

/vw hə̃ste hwe kəhne ləga .../ He, laughing, began to say ...

(c) If the participle refers to a subject not marked by /ne/, and if the participle has an object of its own, then it is usually in the MOS form. It may still agree with its subject in number-gender-case, however, especially if the main verb is a verb of motion. E. g.

/cor cori kərte hwe pəkRa jaega./ The thief will be caught [while he is in the act of] stealing. [/kərta hwa/ is also possible.]

/ləRki kəhani swnte hwe so jaegi./ The girl will go to sleep listening to the story. [/swnti hwi/ is also substitutable.]

/vw ys ymarət ko dekhta hwa age bəRha./ He came forward [while] looking at this building. [/age bəRhna/ "to come forward, advance" is semantically a "verb of motion." /dekhte hwe/ is also correct, of course.]

/ws ki bivi kəbab khate hwe boli./ His wife spoke [as she was] eating the kabab. [Also /khati hwi/, although less common.]

/səb əwrtẽ batẽ kərti hwi əndər a gəĩ./ All the women came inside conversing. [/a jana/ is, of course, a verb of motion; /kərte hwe/ is still possible, however.]

(d) If the participle refers to a subject marked by /ne/, then it is obligatorily in the MOS form. E. g.

/ws ləRki ne kəbab khate hwe kəha .../ That girl said [as she was] eating the kabab ...

/ws admi ne gyrte hwe avaz di./ That man cried out [lit. gave voice] [as he was] falling.

28

/ws ne hɔ̃ste hwe kəha .../ He said, laughing ...

/wnhɔ̃ ne, wse marte hwe, jəb polis ko dekha, to bhag gəe./ When they, beating him, saw the police, [they] ran away.

(4) The participle may also be a predicate complement referring to the object of the sentence. It then denotes an action performed by the object which is simultaneous with the action of the main verb: e.g. "I saw him dancing," "I found them sleeping," etc. Here again there are subtypes:

(a) If the object is not marked by /ko/ (or its equivalent), then the participle may agree with the object in number-gender-case, or it may be in the MOS form. /hwa/ is again optionally added after the participle. E.g.

/ap ag jəlti hwi paẽge./ You will find the fire burning. [/jəlti hwi/ agrees with /ag/ in number-gender; /jəlte hwe/ is also possible, and /jəlti/ or /jəlte/ are not incorrect. Forms with /hwa/ are apparently preferable for this construction.]

/mə̃y ne vw divar gyrti hwi dekhi./ I saw that wall falling. [/gyrte hwe/, /gyrti/, and /gyrte/ are also possible.]

/mə̃y ne ws məkan se dhũã nykəlta hwa dekha./ I saw smoke coming out of that house. [/nykəlte hwe/, /nykəlte/, and /nykəlta/are all possible, although the last is less preferable.]

/mə̃y ne khana pəkta hwa dekha./ I saw the food cooking. [Also /pəkte hwe/, /pəkta/, and /pəkte/.]

/polisvale ne ws ki gaRi əndər ate hwe rok li./ The policeman stopped his [i.e. some other person's] car [as it was] coming inside. [/ati hwi/ is possible, but /ate/ and /ati/ are unidiomatic -- perhaps because of the presence of a compound verb.]

(b) If the object is marked by /ko/, then the participle is likely to be in the MOS form; it may also be in the MNS form (especially in past tense sentences where the subject is marked by /ne/ and the verb is the "impersonal" MNS). E.g.

/mə̃y wse khate hwe dekhna cahta hũ./ I want to see him eating. [/khata hwa/ is also possible, though less common.]

/mə̃y wse pəhaR pər cəRhte hwe dekhũga./ I will see him climbing [lit. climbing on] the mountain. [/cəRhta hwa/ is also substitutable.]

/mə̃y ws ləRki ko pəhaR pər cəRhte hwe dekhũga./ I will see that girl climbing on the mountain. [Here /cəRhta hwa/ seems somewhat incongruous since /ləRki/ is feminine. /cəRhte hwe/ is thus the most acceptable form.]

/mə̃y ne wse dəwRte hwe dekha./ I saw him running. [/dəwRte/, /dəwRta hwa/, and /dəwRta/ are also possible, the latter two apparently "in agreement" with /dekha/.]

/həm ne ws bəcci ko rote hwe paya./ We found that girl weeping. [/rota hwa/ is possible here (though less common), in apparent agreement with /paya/.]

/mə̃y ne cəwkidar ko sote hwe paya./ I found the watchman sleeping. [/sote/, /sota hwa/, and /sota/ are also possible in that order of preference.]

/mə̃y ne bavərci ko kəbhi khana pəkate hwe nəhĩ dekha./ I never saw the cook cooking food. [/pəkate/ is possible, as are /pəkata hwa/ and /pəkata/, but the latter are less likely since the participle has an object of its own: /khana/ M2 "food, dinner."]

(5) There is one major problem in the use of the participles which is inherent in the nature of the language itself: in many cases where the participle is in the MOS form, it

may refer EITHER to the subject or to the object, and only context can clarify which is meant! As a rough rule of thumb, one may say that when the participle precedes the subject, it probably refers to the subject; when it follows the object, it probably refers to the object (although there is a possibility of ambiguity); and when the participle stands between the subject and the object, it may refer to either. This is, of course, aside from the use of the participle as an adjective, in which case it agrees with the noun it modifies. E.g.

/khate hwe, ws ne mwjhe pwkara./ While eating, he called out to me. [It is likely that he is eating, but on the basis of this utterance alone, it is also possible that I am the one who is eating.]

/ws ne khate hwe mwjhe pwkara./ He, [while] eating, called out to me. [This is ambiguous: without any context it is possible that either he or I could be eating. There is, however, a greater statistical likelihood of this referring to the subject (i.e. he), however.]

/ws ne mwjhe khate hwe pwkara./ He called out to me [as I was] eating. [This is again ambiguous, but the likelihood of the participle's referring to the object is somewhat greater.]

/polisvale ne ws ki gaRi əndər ate hwe rok li./ The policeman stopped his [i.e. some other person's] car [as it was] coming inside. [Or: The policeman stopped his car [as he -- the policeman -- was] coming inside.]

/məy ne wse dəwRte hwe dekha./ I saw him running. [Or: [As I was] running, I saw him. If /dəwRta hwa/ or /dəwRta/ are used, the participle will unambiguously refer to /wse/.]

/cəlte hwe, ws əwrət ne ws admi se pucha./ [As she was] going, that woman asked that man. [/cəlte hwe/ will almost always be taken as referring to /əwrət/.]

/ws əwrət ne cəlte hwe ws admi se pucha./ That woman, [while] going, asked that man. [Ambiguity is possible, however.]

/ws əwrət ne ws admi se cəlte hwe pucha./ That woman, [while] going, asked that man. [Again, ambiguity is possible.]

/ws əwrət ne ws cəlte hwe admi se pucha./ That woman asked that man [who was] going [along]. [Lit. that moving man. This usage is adjectival.]

(6) The present participle is repeated (e.g. /bhagte bhagte/) to signify continued or repeated action which ends or culminates in the action of the main verb. The repeated participle is usually MOS in form, but it may also agree in number-gender with the subject (whenever the subject is also the subject of the participle). When the subject of the participle is NOT the same as the subject of the sentence, then the participle will invariably be MOS in form. E.g.

/məy bolte bolte thək gəya./ I became tired from talking too much. [Lit. I became tired speaking speaking. /bolta bolta/ is possible, although less idiomatic, since the subject of /thək gəya/ and /bolta bolta/ is the same.]

/pəRhte pəRhte, ws ki nəzər kəmzor ho gəi./ From reading too much [lit. reading reading] his sight became weak. [The subject of /pəRhte pəRhte/ is understood -- he, the referent of /ws/ -- while the subject of the main verb /ho gəi/ is /nəzər/; thus, only /pəRhte pəRhte/ can occur.]

/swba hote hote, səylab ka pani yəhā tək pəhw̃c jaega./ By dawn [lit. morning becoming becoming], the water of the flood will arrive here [lit. up to here]. [As in the preceding example, the subject of the repeated participle is not the same as that of the main verb; hence only the MOS form /hote hote/ is possible.]

30

/dyn nykəlte nykəlte, həm šəhr pəhw̃c jaẽge./ As day is dawning [lit. day going out going out], we will reach the city.

/vw becara rote rote mər gəya./ That poor fellow died weeping. [Since /vw/ is the subject of both /rote rote/ and /mər gəya/ the MNS form /rota rota/ is also possible, though less frequently used.]

/mwjhe pəhw̃cte pəhw̃cte der ho gəi./ I was late getting there. [Lit. To me arriving arriving lateness became. Only the MOS form is possible here since the subject of /ho gəi/ is /der/.]

/vw ləRki bhagti bhagti ai./ That girl came running. [/bhagte bhagte/ is also substitutable.]

/axyrkar, vw dəwRte dəwRte məkan tək pəhw̃c gəya./ Finally, running [and] running he arrived at [lit. up to] the house. [/dəwRta dəwRta/ is also possible.]

/vw mərte mərte bəc gəya./ He had a narrow escape from death. [Lit. He dying dying escaped. /mərta mərta/ is also possible.]

/kysan həl cəlate cəlate thək gəya./ The farmer became tired from too much plowing [lit. plow making-go making-go]. [Again, /həl cəlata cəlata/ is possible, though less common.]

/həm hər roz cavəl khate khate tõg a gəe hə̃y./ We have become fed up with eating rice every day. [Lit. We every day rice eating eating have become straitened.]

(7) Two different but semantically related present participles are also found in the construction just described under (6). E. g.

/vw ə̃dhere mẽ gyrta pəRta həmare məkan tək pəhw̃c gəya./ Slipping and falling in the darkness, he arrived at [lit. up to] our house. [/gyrta/ "falling down" and /pəRta/ "falling, befalling" are used together to signify "tumbling about, slipping and stumbling." Since the main verb is a verb of motion (see (3a) above) and the two participles have no object of their own, the MNS form is preferable to the MOS form.]

/ys təra, vw ləRte jhəgəRte šəhr tək pəhw̃ce./ Thus, fighting [and] quarrelling they reached [lit. arrived up to] the city. [The main verb is a verb of motion, and thus /ləRte jhəgəRte/ must be taken as MNP here rather than MOS. /jhəgəRna/ "to quarrel."]

(8) The MOS present participle occurs directly before /vəqt/ M1 "time." This denotes "at the time of ..." or "while ... ing." In older Urdu this construction could have a semantic subject: an inanimate subject simply occurred before the participle + /vəqt/ (e. g. /dyn nykəlte vəqt/ "at dawn"); an animate subject possessed the participle + /vəqt/ (e. g. /badšah ke sote vəqt/ "at the time of the king's sleeping, while the king slept [sleeps]"). In present-day Urdu this construction does not seem to occur with an expressed subject of its own. It may, however, have an object. E. g.

/khana khate vəqt, batẽ kərna mwnasyb nəhĩ./ While eating [lit. food eating time] talking is not proper.

/ws ne mərte vəqt mwjhe yy bat bəta di./ He told me this thing as he was dying. [lit. dying time].

/ate vəqt, bazar se yy səwda le ana!/ When you come [lit. coming time] bring these provisions from the bazaar!

/sote vəqt, dəvai ki ek əwr xwrak pi lo!/ When you go to sleep [lit. sleeping time] take [lit. drink] one more dose of the medicine!

/mə̃y ne əpne dost ko cəlte vəqt ek twhfa peš kia./ At the time of departure [lit. going time], I gave my friend a present. [This is ambiguous without knowledge of the context: it is not clear whether I am departing or my friend is departing.]

31

(9) The MOS present participle is also found followed by the emphatic enclitic /hi/. This denotes action which has just taken place before the action of the main verb: i.e. "as soon as ..." or "the moment that ..." This construction may have a semantic subject: if the subject is an inanimate, non-rational thing, then it occurs in the nominative form; if the subject is animate and rational, then it must possess the participle (cf. (8) above). This construction may also have an object. E.g.

/bap ke mərte hi beTŏ mẽ jhəgRa š̌wru ho gəya./ As soon as the father died [lit. father's dying-emphatic], a quarrel began among the sons. [/bap/ M1 "father" is an animate, rational being; it is the semantic subject of /mərte/ and must thus possess it.]

/hwkm mylte hi vw badš̌ah ke pas gəya./ As soon as he got the command [lit. command getting-emphatic], he went to the king. [/hwkm/ M1 "command, order" is the semantic subject of /mylte/ "meeting, getting"; since it is inanimate and non-rational, however, it does not possess /mylte/.]

/mere pəhW̌cte hi, səb log meri tərəf dekhne ləge./ The moment I arrived [lit. my arriving-emphatic], everybody began looking at me.

/mere xət lykhte hi, vw a gəya./ As soon as I wrote the letter [lit. my letter writing-emphatic], he came. [The semantic subject of /lykhte/ is an animate, rational being and thus possesses it. The object is MNS.]

/mə̃y xət lykhte hi yəhã se cəla jaũga./ The moment I write the letter [lit. letter writing-emphatic], I will leave. [/mə̃y/ is the nominative subject of /cəla jaũga/; it is not grammatically connected to /xət lykhte hi/, the subject of which is unexpressed and understood.]

/pəyse lete hi, ws ne əpni jeb mẽ Dal lie./ The moment he took the money [lit. money taking-emphatic], he put [lit. poured] [it] into his pocket.

/jagte hi, ws ne cor ko dekha./ The moment he woke up [lit. waking-emphatic], he saw the thief.

16.303. The Verb: the Past Participle as a Substantive.

The past participle occurs in substantive constructions quite similar to those just described for the present participle (although there are indeed a few grammatical differences). The past participle signifies a past action resulting in a present state. Compare:

/jəlti hwi ag/ burning fire

/jəli hwi roTi/ burned bread

/mərta hwa admi/ dying man

/məra hwa admi/ dead man

/vw Topi pəhnta hwa aya./ He came [in the act of] putting on [his] cap.

/vw Topi pəhne hwe aya./ He came wearing [i.e. having put on] [his] cap.

The past participle occurs in the following substantive constructions:

(1) The past participle occurs (alone or + /hwa/) as a Type II noun. Like the present participle, such occurrences are limited to certain idiomatic constructions. E.g.

/yy ap ke kie ka nətija həy./ This is the result of your doing [lit. done].

/mə̃y ne bhule se wse yy bəta dia./ I told this to him by mistake. [/bhula/ "forgotten": /bhule se/ "through forgetfulness, by mistake."]

/ws ke kəhe pər nə cəlna cahie! / [You] should not go on his say-so!
[Lit. on his said. This usage is becoming obsolete; modern Urdu
seems to prefer /ws ke kəhne pər/.]

/yy kam mera kia hwa həy. / This work is my doing. [Lit. my done.
This usage is quite common. Another example:]

/yy khana mera khaya hwa həy. / I have eaten this [kind of] food before.
[Lit. This food is my eaten.]

/yy ymarət pətthər ki bəni hwi həy. / This building is made of stone.
[The past participle + /hwa/ functions as a kind of noun, possessed
by the substance from which the referent is made and agreeing with
the referent in number-gender. Another example:]

/yy məkan myTTi ka bəna hwa həy. / This house is made of clay. [/bəna
həy/ is also possible.]

(2) Like the present participle, the past participle (+ /hwa/) is frequently employed
as an adjective modifying a noun. E. g.

/ek məra hwa ghoRa raste mẽ pəRa tha. / A dead horse was lying in the
road.

/ws ne mwjhe ek phəTi hwi qəmis de di. / He gave me a torn shirt.

/yy meri lykhi hwi kytab həy. / This is a book I have written. [Lit.
This is my written book.]

/vw ws TuTi hwi chət se gyr pəRa. / He fell down off that broken roof.

/yy mere ghər ki syli hwi šəlvar həy. / This šəlvar was made at my
home. [Lit. This is my home's sewn šəlvar.]

/mãy ne səRək pər khəRe hwe ləRkõ se pucha. / I asked the boys standing
on the street. [Lit. I asked from the on the street standing boys.
Note that both /khəRe/ and /hwe/ are inflected as Type II MOP
adjectives.]

(3) The past participle is also employed as a predicate complement. One form of this,
the "stative" construction, has already been discussed in Sec. 14.302. Other usages are:

(a) When the past participle refers to the subject and has no object of its own, it
usually agrees with the subject in number-gender. Compare Sec. 16.302
(3a, b). E. g.

/meri qəmis syli hwi pəRi həy. / My shirt is ready. [Lit. My shirt is
sewn lying. /pəRi həy/ stands for the "stative" form /pəRi hwi həy/;
wnenever two adjoining participles would both be followed by /hwa/,
the second /hwa/ is omitted.]

/kytabẽ mez pər bãdhi hwi pəRi hãy. / The books, tied up, are lying on
the table.

/vw ləRka bəyTha hwa kam kər rəha həy. / That boy is sitting [lit. in a
state of having sat] [and] working.

/vw log bəhwt thəke hwe ae the. / Those people came [being] very tired.

/vw leTa hwa pəRh rəha tha. / He was reading [while] lying [down].

(b) If the participle has an object of its own, it is almost always in the MOS form.
Compare Sec. 16.302 (3c). E. g.

/mãy yy kytab hath mẽ lie hwe vəhã pəhw̃ca. / I arrived there holding
[lit. having taken] this book in [my] hand.

/əziz sahəb Topi pəhne hwe bazar cəle gəe. / Mr. əziz, wearing [his]
cap, went off to the market.

/nəwkər phəlõ ki Tokri wThae hwe səRək pər khəRa rəha. / The servant,
carrying [lit. having lifted] the basket of fruits, remained standing
on the street.

/qwli suTkes lie hwe mere piche dəwR rəha tha./ The coolie was running after me carrying [lit. having taken] the suitcase.

/həm ə̄dhera kie hwe dwš̌mən ka yntyzar kər rəhe the./ We, having made it dark, were waiting for the enemy.

/zəmindar sahəb sər ūca kie hwe cəle gəe./ The landlord went off with [his] head held high [lit. having made [his] head high]. [The object of the participle, /sər/ M1 "head," is MNS, and the predicate adjective /ūca/ is also thus MNS.]

(c) If the participle refers to a subject marked by /ne/, it is always in the MOS form. Compare Sec. 16.302 (3d). E.g.

/ws ne leTe hwe jəvab dia./ He answered [while] lying down [lit. in a state of having lain].

/mə̃y ne bəyThe hwe wse dur se dekha./ I, [while] sitting, saw him from afar.

/mə̃y ne pələ̄g pər bəyThe hwe khana khaya./ I ate [my] food [while] sitting on the bed.

(4) Used to refer to the object, three cases arise:

(a) If the object is not marked by /ko/ (or its equivalent), then the past participle (+ /hwa/) almost always agrees with the object in number-gender. This participle almost always follows the object. See Sec. 16.302 (4a). E.g.

/ws ne dərvaza khwla hwa choR dia./ He left the door open. [Compare:]

/ws ne khyRki khwli hwi choR di./ He left the window open.

/mə̃y ne vw əwrtē bəyThi hwi dekhī̃./ I saw those women sitting.

/mə̃y ne yy kaɣəz zəmin pər pəRa hwa paya./ I found this paper lying on the ground.

/mə̃y ne ek kwtta pələ̄g pər leTa hwa paya./ I found a dog lying on the bed.

/nəwkər ne kwtta məra paya./ The servant found the dog dead. [/məra hwa/ is, of course, also possible.]

(b) If the object is marked by /ko/, the participle may be in the MNS form (especially in past tense sentences where the subject is marked by /ne/ and the verb is the "impersonal" MNS). The participle may also be in the MOS form, especially if the object is animate and rational. See Sec. 16.302 (4b). E.g.

/ws ne dərvaze ko khwla hwa choR dia./ He left the door open. [/khwla/ is also possible. Although /khwle hwe/ and /khwle/ are also correct, the tendency for the "impersonal" MNS form to occur with an inanimate, non-rational object is greater than was seen to be the case for the present participle.]

/ws ne khyRki ko khwla hwa choR dia./ He left the window open. [Also /khwla/; again, the MOS forms /khwle hwe/ and /khwle/ are grammatically correct but are considered less idiomatic.]

/mə̃y ne ws ləRki ko bəyThe hwe dekha./ I saw that girl sitting. [The object is an animate, rational being, and hence the MOS form is more idiomatic. /bəyTha hwa/ is also possible, however.]

/mə̃y ne əwrtō̃ ko bəyThe hwe dekha./ I saw those women sitting. [/bəyThe/ or /bəyThe hwe/ are more idiomatic than /bəyTha/ or /bəyTha hwa/.]

/mə̃y ne ys kaɣəz ko zəmin pər pəRa hwa paya./ I found this paper lying on the ground. [The tendency is toward the MNS form.]

34

/DakTər ne ws buRhi əwrət ko pəlᶘg pər leTe hwe paya./ The doctor found that old woman lying on the bed. [The tendency is toward the MOS form.]

/mᶘy ne ws məkan ko gyra hwa dekha./ I saw that house [in a] fallen [state]. [The tendency is toward the MNS form. Compare:]

/mᶘy ne ws məkan ko gyrte hwe dekha./ I saw that house falling [down]. [The present participle tends to be in the MOS form in this type of sentence. See Sec. 16.302 (4b).]

/mᶘy ne ws admi ko bəyThe hwe dekha./ I saw that man sitting down [i.e. in a state of having sat down]. [The tendency is toward the MOS form since the object is animate. Compare:]

/mᶘy ne ws admi ko bəyThte hwe dekha./ I saw that man [in the act of] sitting [down]. [The tendency is for the present participle also to be in the MOS form -- whether animate or inanimate!]

(c) When the past participle itself has an object, the tendency toward the MOS form is very strong. E.g.

/mᶘy ne wse qəmis pəhne hwe dekha./ I saw him wearing a shirt.

/mᶘy ne ws əwrət ko saRi bᶘdhe hwe paya./ I found that woman wearing [lit. having tied] a saRi.

(d) As the student has seen, the past participles of certain verb stems are employed to denote a previously entered state or condition, while the present participles of these same stems are used to describe the action in progress. Common verbs of this type include: /bəyThna/ "to sit down," /khəRa hona/ "to stand, stand up," /ləgna/ "to be struck, attached, feel," /leTna/ "to lie, lie down," /pəhnna/ "to put on, wear," /pəRna/ "to fall, befall, lie," etc. Both the present and past participles of certain other verbs (e.g. /sona/ "to sleep") may denote a state and thus are identical in meaning. E.g.

/mᶘy ne wse bəyThte hwe dekha./ I saw him [in the act of] sitting [down]. [Compare:]

/mᶘy ne wse bəyThe hwe dekha./ I saw him [in the state of] sitting [lit. having sat].

/mᶘy ne wse Topi pəhnte hwe dekha./ I saw him [in the act of] putting on [his] cap. [Compare:]

/mᶘy ne wse Topi pəhne hwe dekha./ I saw him wearing [lit. having put on] [his] cap.

/mᶘy ne wse sote hwe dekha./ I saw him sleeping. [Or:]

/mᶘy ne wse soe hwe dekha./ I saw him sleeping. [Both have much the same meaning: in the state of being asleep. The act of going to sleep must be expressed differently:]

/mᶘy ne wse sone ke lie jate hwe dekha./ I saw him going [i.e. on his way] to sleep. [Or:]

/mᶘy ne wse sone ki košyš kərte hwe dekha./ I saw him trying to sleep [lit. making the attempt of sleep].

(5) The past participle is also repeated to indicate a past action resulting in a continuous or repetitive state. In a past tense sentence having a subject not marked by /ne/, the repeated participle usually agrees with the subject in number-gender; it may also be MOS in form. After a subject marked by /ne/, the repeated past participle is invariably in the MOS form, and if the participle has an object it must also be MOS. In present and future tense sentences the repeated past participle always seems to be MOS in form. See also

35

Sec. 16.302 (6). E.g.

/mə̃y bəyTha bəyTha thək gəya./ I became tired sitting [and] sitting. [/bəyThe bəyThe/ is also possible.]

/yy seb pəRa pəRa xərab ho gəya./ This apple has gone bad just lying around too long [lit. lay lay]. [Also /pəRe pəRe/.]

/ws ne leTe leTe puri kytab pəRhi./ Lying [and] lying, he read the whole book. [Only the MOS form is possible after a subject marked by /ne/.]

/mə̃y bəcce ko lie lie thək gəi hū./ I have become tired from carrying the child around [lit. child taken taken]. [The participle has an object, and hence only the MOS form is possible.]

/vw bəyThe bəyThe thək jaẽge./ They will get tired sitting [and] sitting. [Only the MOS form is possible in a present or future tense sentence.]

Certain repeated past participles can only be described as idiomatic: e.g. /dəwRa dəwRa/ and /bhaga bhaga/ both mean "running," "at a run," or "rapidly." Both carry a connotation of distractedness: running here and there, running helter skelter, against one's will, etc. E.g.

/ap ki səheli bhagi bhagi ja rəhi thi./ Your girlfriend was going along at a run. [I.e. in a hurry, rushing because of some emergency, etc.]

/vw dəwRi dəwRi həspətal pəhw̃ci./ She rushed to the hospital. [I.e. all in haste because of some emergency. Compare:]

/vw dəwRti dəwRti həspətal pəhw̃ci./ By dint of running, she arrived at the hospital. [Lit. running running. The emphasis is upon repeated, emphatic action which culminates in the action of the main verb. There is no sense of "helter skelter" or "all in a rush." Compare also:]

/vw dəwRti hwi həspətal pəhw̃ci./ Running, she arrived at the hospital. [/dəwRti hwi/ has no connotations of emergency or of repetitive action; it simply describes the way she reached the hospital. Although somewhat less idiomatic, the following is also possible:]

/vw dəwRi hwi həspətal pəhw̃ci./ Running, she reached the hospital. [This is equivalent in meaning to /dəwRti hwi/.]

(6) Two different but semantically related past participles are also employed together:

(a) A few idiomatic pairs of past participles are employed as unit nouns. Tactically, these are compounds like /mã bap/ Mp1 "parents," /chwri kāTa/ M2 "knife [and] fork." E.g.

/bimari mẽ, məriz ka səb khaya pia nykəl gəya./ Due to [lit. in] the illness, all of the patient's health and well-being [lit. eaten drunk] left [him].

/wse kysi ae gəe ka bhi xyal nəhī./ He has no thought even of visitors. [Lit. To him [there is] no thought of even any came-went. Such a usage is limited, of course, to a few idiomatic sentences; one cannot say, for example, */həmare ghər mẽ ek aya gəya həy./ "In our house is a visitor."]

(b) Similarly, certain pairs of past participles are used in loose compounds as Type II adjectives. E.g.

/vw kafi pəRha lykha admi həy./ He is quite [lit. enough] an educated man. [Lit. read wrote man.]

/yy TuTe phuTe bərtən bavərcixane mẽ kyõ rəkkhe hwe hə̃y./ Why are these broken utensils kept in the kitchen? [Lit. broken shattered utensils. /phuTna/ "to be shattered, burst, broken" is the intransitive form of /phoRna/ Ig "to shatter, burst, break."]

36

(c) The past participles of the intransitive and causative forms of the same verb
are similarly used together as unit adjectives. If the verb has no intransitive
form, then the past participle of the transitive form is used with that of the
causative instead. This sort of compound gives the meaning of "already ...
en" or "ready ... en." E.g.

/mɛ̃y yy kəpRe syle sylae laya hū. / I have brought these clothes ready-
sewn. [Lit. been-ṣewn made-sewn. /sylna/ and /sylana/ are the
intransitive and causative forms of /sina/ Ie "to sew."]

/mɛ̃y ne yy məkan bəna bənaya xərida həy. / I have purchased this house
ready-built. [Lit. been-built made-built.]

/ghər ate hi, wse pəka pəkaya khana myl jata həy. / The moment [he]
gets home, he gets ready-cooked food. [Lit. been-cooked made-
cooked.]

/cəlne ki jəldi mɛ̃, bɛ̃dha bɛ̃dhaya saman rəh gəya. / In the hurry of
leaving, the already-packed baggage was left behind. [Lit. been-
tied made-tied. /bɛ̃dhana/ is the causative form of /bɛ̃dhna/ Ie
"to tie, bind."]

/ap ne səb kia kəraya kam xərab kər dia. / You spoiled all the completed
work. [Lit. done made-done.]

/səylab ki vəja se, kəTi kəTai fəsl bhi təbah ho gəi. / Because of the
flood, the already-harvested crop was also ruined. [Lit. been-cut
made-cut. /kəTana/ is the causative form of /kaTna/ Ie "to cut."]

/ap ko swni swnai bat pər yəqin nəhĩ kərna cahie. / You ought not to rely
upon casual gossip. [Lit. heard made-heard. /swnana/ is the
causative form of /swnna/ Ic "to hear, listen."]

(7) The past participle is also found in a number of idiomatic temporal constructions.
The student must learn these individually as the need arises. E.g.

/vw do bəje cəla gəya. / He went off at two o'clock. [/bəje/ is, of course,
the MOS past participle of /bəjna/ IIc "to ring, strike, play." It is
used idiomatically for "o'clock."]

/vw rat gəe ghər pəhw̃ca. / He arrived home after midnight. [/rat gəe/
literally means "night gone"; it denotes any time from midnight
until dawn, and it is employed adverbially.]

/vw ae dyn yyhi jhəgRa kərta həy. / Every day he quarrels [on] this very
[matter]. [/ae dyn/ literally denotes "came day"; it means "every
day" or "day in, day out."]

/ap ko pakystan ae hwe kytne sal hwe hɛ̃y. / How many years has it been
since you came to Pakistan? [Lit. To you, came to Pakistan, how
many years have become? This can also be expressed in another
way:]

/ap ko pakystan mɛ̃ rəhte hwe kytne sal hwe hɛ̃y. / How many years have
you lived in Pakistan? [Lit. To you, living in Pakistan, how many
years have become?]

/mɛ̃y tin həfte hwe ap ke hã aya tha. / I had come to your place three
weeks ago. [This implies "came and left again." Compare:]

/mɛ̃y tin həfte se ap ke hã aya hwa hū. / I have come to [and have stayed
at] your place for three weeks. [A time word or phrase + /hwa/ is
used when the action is unitary and no subsequent state ensues; a
time word or phrase + /se/ "from" is employed when the action has
a subsequent state or result continuing up until the time of the
narrative. The former is often translatable as "ago" in English,
while the latter is usually rendered as "since" or "for." These words
overlap in English, however.]

37

/mə̄y ek həfta hwa kəraci gəya tha. /   I went to Karachi a week ago.   [Note that /hwa/ is nominative, rather than adverbial, and agrees with the time word in number-gender.]

/do həfte hwe, ky mə̄y wn se nəhī̃ myla. /   [It] has been two weeks since [lit. that] I did not meet him. [When the time phrase with /hwa/ precedes the main clause, it is treated like a separate verbal clause and is followed by /ky/. Another example:]

/car səw sal hwe, ky mwɣəl dyhli ae. /   Four hundred years have passed [lit. became] since [lit. that] the Mughals came to Delhi.

(8) The past participle is also used with four words meaning "without": /bəɣəyr/, /be/, /byn/, and /byna/. In modern Urdu the most frequent of these is /bəɣəyr/; the others are becoming increasingly limited to certain "frozen" idiomatic phrases. /bəɣəyr/ and /byna/ may precede or follow their participle, but the latter case is more common. /be/ and /byn/ precede their participle only. In all of these cases, the participle is obligatorily MOS in form. If the participle has a "semantic subject" of its own, then the rules given in Sec. 16.302 (8, 9) apply: an animate, rational subject always possesses the participle; an inanimate, non-rational subject is usually nominative in form (but may also rarely possess its participle). E.g.

/mə̄y yy ciz dekhe bəɣəyr nəhī̃ xəridūga. /   I will not buy this thing without seeing [it]. [Also /yy ciz bəɣəyr dekhe/, though this order is less common.]

/ws ke ae bəɣəyr, yy kam nəhī̃ ho səkta. /   Without his coming, this work cannot be [done]. [Also /bəɣəyr ws ke ae/ or /ws ke bəɣəyr ae/, but these are less common in modern Urdu. Since the referent of /ws ke/ is animate and rational it possesses the participle.]

/ap ke jae bəɣəyr, yy kam nəhī̃ hoga. /   Without your going, this work will not be [done]. [In this construction the past participle of /jana/ "to go" is the MOS form of /jaya/, previously seen in the "habitual" formation (Sec. 14.306).]

/mə̄y xət bəɣəyr lykhe nəhī̃ soūga. /   I will not sleep without writing the letter. [In modern Urdu /xət lykhe bəɣəyr/ is more idiomatic.]

/məriz ko dekhe bəɣəyr, DakTər cəla gəya. /   Without seeing the patient, the doctor went away. [Also /bəɣəyr məriz ko dekhe/ and /məriz ko bəɣəyr dekhe/, but these are less idiomatic.]

/vw be puche mere kəmre mē̃ daxyl hwa. /   He entered my room without asking. [/puche bəɣəyr/ is more appropriate in modern Urdu.]

/ws ne be soce səmjhe yy bat kəhi. /   He said this thing without thinking. [/be/ + the two semantically related past participles /soce/ "thought" and /səmjhe/ "understood" is an idiomatic "frozen" phrase denoting "thoughtlessly, without thinking. "]

/byn puche, vəhā̃ nə jana! /   Don't go there without asking! [/bəɣəyr puche/ or /puche bəɣəyr/ are more idiomatic in modern Urdu; cf. /be puche/ above, which is also correct -- though archaic -- here.]

/byn bwlae, kysi ke hā̃ nə jana cahie. /   [One] ought not to go to someone's place without being asked. [/byn bwlae/ "without being called, asked, invited" is again a "frozen" idiomatic phrase. It is common in modern Urdu.]

/vw puche byna yəhā̃ se cəla gəya. /   He went from here without asking. [This is now considered archaic; /puche bəɣəyr/ is the present form.]

/byna badšah ke hwkm die, həm ys sylsyle mē̃ qədəm nəhī̃ wTha səkte. /   Without the king giving the order, we cannot take [any] step in this connection. [Again, this usage is considered archaic: /badšah ke hwkm die bəɣəyr/ is the most likely modern form -- or without the verb entirely: /badšah ke hwkm ke bəɣəyr/ "without the order of the king. "]

16.400. SUPPLEMENTARY VOCABULARY

16.401. Supplementary Vocabulary.

The following numerals are all Type I adjectives. See Sec. 2.401.

yksəTh	sixty-one
cǎwsəTh	sixty-four

Other items are:

jhaRu F1	broom
pabəndi F2	restriction, limitation, punctuality
rešəm M1 [np]	silk

16.402. Supplementary Exercise I: Substitution.

1.	ykkys	əwr	wntalys	ka kwl kya həy.	saTh.
	thirty-six		twenty-eight		sixty-four
	thirty		thirty-one		sixty-one
	twenty-three		forty		sixty-three
	forty-eight		seventeen		sixty-five
	thirty-seven		twenty-five		sixty-two

16.403. Supplementary Exercise II: Translation.

Translate the following sentences into Urdu:

1. The girl is sweeping the room [lit. is giving the broom in the room].
2. Pakistan gets [lit. causes to ask for] silk from other countries.
3. He goes punctually [lit. with punctuality] to school every day.
4. Buy [lit. buy-bring!] another broom from the market!
5. Our government has laid [lit. attached] some restrictions upon this kind of silk.

16.500. VOCABULARY AND GRAMMAR DRILL

16.501. Substitution.

1. vw admi   <u>əpni bat</u>   ka pabənd həy.

              his principle

              his promise

              your command

              time

              prayer

2. <u>yy swnte hi</u>,   vw <u>əpne pəRəwsi</u>   ke pas cəla gəya.

   [on] saying this   the barber

   [on] seeing this   the gardener

   [on] tying the horse   the watchman

   [on] measuring the   the tailor
   cloth

   [on] cooking the   Madame
   qorma

3. vw <u>Topi pəhne hwe</u> aya.

      wearing a pajama

      carrying [lit. taken]
      a gun

      carrying [lit. picked
      up] a basket

      grasping his mother's
      hand

      wearing black socks

4. mə̄y ne wse <u>kəpRe site hwe</u> dekha.

           climbing on the tree

           brushing the curtain

           cooking pwlao

           counting the change

           eating [lit. doing]
           breakfast

5. yy <u>jəli hwi Tokri</u> phə̄k do!

    torn shirt

    broken bottle

    burning coals

    dead animal

    dried carrots

6. həm   <u>dəwRte dəwRte</u>   thək gəe.

         fighting fighting

         weeping weeping

         fleeing fleeing

laughing laughing

thinking thinking

7. <u>bal bənate vəqt,</u>   ws ne mwjhε yy bat bətai.

[at] the time of sewing the clothes

[at] the time of measuring the
silken cloth

[at] the time of ironing

[at] the time of buying groceries

[at] the time of covering the well

8. <u>səwda xəride bəɣəyr,</u>   khana nəhĩ pək səkta.

without going [to] the market

without washing the vegetables

without cleaning the stove

without cutting the onion[s]

without putting in [lit. pouring]
the seasoning

9. zəra dekhte rəho! əysa nə ho, ky yy   <u>nykəl jae!</u>

                              may spill

                              may break

                              may tear

                              may open

                              may dry [up]

10. səb logõ ne myl kər   <u>kwtte ko</u>   <u>nykalne</u>   ki košyš ki.

                                      water   catch
buffalo[1]

                                      crop   cut

                                      fire   put out

                                      bridge   make

                                      wall   break

    [1]"Water buffalo" should be marked by /ko/ since it is an animate being; the
remaining objects are inanimates and hence do not require /ko/.

11. kya, mãy   <u>baqi rəqəm</u>   bhi ys hysab mẽ šamyl kər lũ?

                  your new blouse

                  these potato[es],
cabbage[s], and tomato[es], etc.

                  the children's pants
and your shirts

                  these curtains and
carpets

                  this bush-shirt, socks
and handkerchief

12. mãy   <u>ap ke ys kam</u>   mẽ šərik nə ho səka.

his funeral

that party

my big brother's
wedding

that conversation
the prayer

13. ap ne   <u>ws ki šadi</u>   pər kytni rəqəm xərc ki.
       this saRi
       this shirt
       this gift
       these pants
       this šəlvar

14. mez pər rəkkhi hwi   <u>pətlun</u>   mwjhe de dijie!
       iron
       bandage
       basket
       copybook
       onion[s]

15. yy   <u>divar</u>   <u>pətthər</u>   ki bəni hwi həy.
    cup   glass
    chair   wood
    car   America
    saRi   Pakistan
    plate   clay

16.502. Substitution II.

1. In the following set of sentences the word "all" or "whole" in the second substitution
admits of four possible translations. Idiomatically appropriate substitutions are
indicated after each sentence by giving the numbers of the correct Urdu words in
brackets:

"1" = /səb/, "2" = /sara/, "3" = /təmam/, "4" = /kwl/, and "5" = /pura/.

məy ne	<u>ys suTkes</u>	mẽ	<u>səb saRiã</u>	<u>rəkh li hãy.</u>	[2, 3]
	this copybook		the whole account	have written	[1, 2, 3, 4, 5]
	this food		all the spices	have poured	[1, 2, 3, 5]
	this hand-kerchief		all the socks	have tied	[1, 2, 3]
	this story		all matters	have included	[1, 2, 3]
	this cupboard		all the books	have gathered	[1, 2, 3]

16.503. Transformation.

1. Change the underlined verb forms in the following sentences to the <S + /rəkhna/>
formation (e.g. /bādh lia həy/ to /bādh rəkkha həy/). Retain the same tense but
omit any other intensive auxiliary.
  a. məy ne ap ke lie khana <u>pəkaya həy.</u>
  b. wnhõ ne ap ke hwkm ke mwtabyq yy kam <u>kia həy.</u>

c. wnhõ ne yy xəbər swni thi.

d. mali ne əpne sər pər pəTTi bãdhi həy.

e. mə̃y ne kwch bərtən wn ke ystemal ke lie die hə̄y.

f. kysan ne khet mẽ khad Dali həy.

g. ws əmir admi ne bəhwt dəwlət ykhəTTi ki həy.

h. mə̃y ap ke ane tək khana pəka lūga.

i. məcchərõ ne mwjhe bəhwt tãg kia həy.

j. ws ne əpni kapi mẽ sari kytab nəql ki həy.

k. ws ne əpne sər pər rwmal bãdh lia həy.

2. The present participle as an adjective: the subject of the first sentence is repeated again in the second sentence of each set. Change the verb of the first sentence to a present participle (+ /hwa/) and make it (+ any necessary object, etc.) modify the repeated word in the second sentence. See Sec. 16.302 (2). E.g.

/səylab ka pani bəRh rəha tha. gaõvalõ ne səylab ke pani ko roka. /
  [This becomes:]

/gaõvalõ ne səylab ke bəRhte hwe pani ko roka. /

a. koyle jəl rəhe hə̄y. koylõ ko hath nə ləgao!

b. gaRi cəl rəhi thi. mə̃y ne gaRi ko pəkRa.

c. bəcce khel rəhe the. bəccõ ko pwkaro!

d. mwsafyr səRək pər ja rəha tha. mə̃y ne mwsafyr ko avaz di.

e. bəcci ro rəhi thi. bəcci ko yəhã bwlaie!

f. mali so rəha həy. mali ko jəga do!

g. yy bimariã bəRh rəhi hə̄y. yn bimariõ ko rokna cahie.

h. vw admi mər rəha həy. ws admi ko pani pylana cahie.

i. gaRi cəl rəhi thi. mə̃y ne gaRi se saman wtara.

j. ləRka dərəxt se gyr rəha tha. mə̃y ne ləRke ko pəkəR lia.

k. məwsəm bədəl rəha həy. yy məwsəm mwjhe pəsənd nəhĩ.

l. cyraɣ bwjh rəha həy. cyraɣ mẽ tel Dalo!

m. pani phəyl rəha həy. pani ko roko!

n. ləRke baɣ mẽ khel rəhe the. mə̃y ne ləRkõ ko məna kia.

o. ləRka hə̃s rəha həy. ləRke ko mere pas lao!

3. The present participle as a predicate complement referring to the subject: change the verb of the first sentence to a present participle (+ /hwa/) and insert it (+ any necessary object, etc.) after the subject to which it refers in the second sentence. See Sec. 16.302 (3). E.g.

/vw kəhani pəRh rəha tha. vw ro rəha tha./ [This becomes:]

/vw kəhani pəRhte hwe ro rəha tha./

a. məriz cix rəha tha. məriz həspətal pəhw̃ca.

b. gaõvale šor məca rəhe the. gaõvale səRək pər ja rəhe the.

c. kysan bij bo rəha tha. kysan həmari tərəf a rəha həy.

d. vw khana pəka rəha tha. ws ne mwjhe əndər bwlaya.

e. vw meri tərəf dekh rəhe the. wnhõ ne ws ke bare mẽ pucha.

43

4. The present participle as a predicate complement referring to the object: change
    the verb of the first sentence to a present participle (+ /hwa/) and insert it (+
    any necessary object, etc.) after the object to which it refers in the second sentence.
    See Sec. 16.302 (4). E.g.

    /dərzi kam kər rəha tha. mə̃y ne vəhā dərzi ko paya. / [This becomes:]
    /mə̃y ne vəha dərzi ko kam kərte hwe paya. /

    a. cor ghər mē ghws rəha tha. mə̃y ne cor ko pəkRa.
    b. əziz sahəb bol rəhe the. wnhõ ne əziz sahəb ko swna.
    c. vw so rəha tha. mə̃y wse əndər laya.
    d. bəcca ro rəha tha. mā ne bəcce ko choR dia.
    e. kysan lykh rəha tha. əfsər ne kysan ko dekha.

5. The repeated present participle: if the subject of the first sentence is the same as
    that of the second, change the verb of the first sentence to a repeated present
    participle and insert it (+ any necessary object, etc.) after the subject of the
    second sentence to which it refers. If the repeated participle is a temporal absolute
    and does not have the same subject as the main verb of the second sentence, place
    the repeated participle first in the second sentence together with its subject. See
    Sec. 16.302 (6). E.g.

    /ws ne pəyse gyne. hysab ɣələt ho gəya. / [This becomes:]
    /pəyse gynte gynte, hysab ɣələt ho gəya. /

    a. ləRka pəhaR pər cəRh rəha tha. ləRka thək gəya.
    b. swba ho rəhi həy. səylab ka pani ghəT jaega.
    c. ag phəyl gəi. ag bəhwt dur tək pəhw̃c gəi.
    d. mə̃y myhnət kərta tha. mə̃y buRha ho gəya hū.
    e. fəwj age bəRh rəhi thi. fəwj dwšmən ke qəle mē ghws gəi.

6. The present participle + /vəqt/ "at the time of . . .": change the verb of the first
    sentence to a present participle + /vəqt/ and insert it (+ any necessary object, etc.)
    at the beginning of the second sentence. See Sec. 16.302 (8). E.g.

    /dəftər bənd ho rəha həy. mə̃y məwjud hūga. / [This becomes:]
    /dəftər bənd hote vəqt, mə̃y məwjud hūga. /

    a. mə̃y a rəha tha. mwjhe xyal aya.
    b. ap pəRh rəhe hə̃y. ap ko reDyo nə swnna cahie.
    c. mə̃y dopəhr ko sota hū. mə̃y do goli khaya kərta hū.
    d. kysan fəsl bo rəha həy. kysan ko bəhwt myhnət se kam kərna pəRta həy.
    e. bivi khana kha rəhi həy. bivi ne mwjh se ws ki šykayət ki.

7. The present participle + /hi/ "as soon as . . . ," "while . . .": change the verb of
    the first sentence to a present participle + /hi/ and insert it (+ any necessary
    object, subject, etc.) at the beginning of the second sentence. See Sec. 16.302
    (9). E.g.

    /mə̃y ne ws ki fayl dekhi. mə̃y ne fəysla kia. / [This becomes:]
    /ws ki fayl dekhte hi, mə̃y ne fəysla kia. /

    a. ws ne təsvir khēci. vw məsjyd se bahər aya.

44

b. ws ne khana pəkaya. ws ne ysmyth sahəb ko bwlaya.

c. ws ne cae pi. ws pər zəhr ka əsər hwa.

d. baryš šwru hwi. həm log ghər bhag ae.

e. ws ne kaɣəz ko phaRa. wse əfsos hwa.

8.  The past participle as an adjective: change the verb of the first sentence to a past participle and insert it (+ any necessary object, etc.) as a modifying adjective before the repeated word in the second sentence of each set. See Sec. 16.303 (2). E.g.

/kytabē mez pər pəRi thī. mə̄y ne kytabō ko ykhəTTa kər lia./ [This becomes:]

/mə̄y ne mez pər pəRi hwi kytabō ko ykhəTTa kər lia./

a. ləkRiā kəT gəi hə̄y. ləkRiō ko yəhā jəma kəro!

b. kəpRe dhwl gəe hə̄y. mə̄y kəpRō ko dhobi ke hā se le aya hū.

c. botəl TuT gəi həy. botəl ko bahər phēk do!

d. bəkri mər gəi həy. vw bəkri ko yəhā se le gəya həy.

e. ws ne twhfa dia həy. ws ka twhfa əlmari mē rəkkha həy.

f. bəcce bəyThe hwe the. masTər ne bəccō se yy bat kəhi.

g. kəpRe syl gəe hə̄y. kəpRō ko ghər le ao!

h. ləkRiā sukh gəī. mə̄y ləkRiō ko jəlaūga.

i. kytab gyr gəi həy. kytab ko wThao!

j. roTi jəl gəi həy. roTi ko nəhī khana cahie.

k. ap ne pəɣɣam bheja tha. ap ka pəɣɣam mwjhe myl gəya tha.

l. khyRki khwl gəi həy. khyRki ko bənd kijie!

m. cavəl bykhər gəe. cavlō ko mwrɣi kha gəi.

n. vw admi thək gəya tha. vw admi dərəxt ke nice bəyTh gəya.

o. pətlun phəT gəi həy. dərzi pətlun si rəha həy.

9. The past participle as a predicate complement referring to the subject: change the verb to a past participle (+ /hwa/) and insert it (+ any necessary object, etc.) after the subject in the second sentence. See Sec. 16.303 (3). E.g.

/qwli ne saman wThaya. qwli mwjh se pəyse mā̄gne ləga./ [This becomes:]

/qwli saman wThae hwe mwjh se pəyse mā̄gne ləge./

a. bavərci thək gəya həy. bavərci ghər se vapəs aya.

b. Dybba khwl gəya. mwjhe yy Dybba myla.

c. saman bə̄dha hwa həy. saman ghər ke samne pəRa həy.

d. cor ne laThi li. cor ghər se bahər aya.

e. dərzi bəyTha hwa həy. dərzi si rəha tha.

10. The past participle as a predicate complement referring to the object: change the verb of the first sentence to a past participle (+ /hwa/) and insert it (+ any necessary object, etc.) after the object to which it refers in the second sentence. See Sec. 16.303 (4). E.g.

/Dybba khwl gəya. mə̄y ne Dybbe ko mez pər choR dia./ [This becomes:]

45

/mə̄y ne Dybbe ko khwla hwa mez pər choR dia./

a. cəwkidar leT gəya. ap bay mē cəwkidar ko paēge.
b. roTi sukh gəi. ws ne bavərcixane mē roTi pai.
c. cor ne pətlun pəhni. polis ne cor ko pəkRa.
d. sare phəl bykhər gəe. ws ne sare phəl zəmin pər choR die.
e. qəmisē syl gəī. mə̄y ap se qəmisē le lūga.

11. The repeated past participle: change the verb of the first sentence to a repeated past participle and insert it (+ any necessary object, etc.) after the subject of the second sentence. See Sec. 16.303 (5). E.g.

/vw dəwR rəha tha. vw ghər tək pəhw̄ca./ [This becomes:]
/vw dəwRa dəwRa ghər tək pəhw̄ca./

a. mə̄y bəyTha tha. mə̄y thək gəya hū.
b. qwli ne saman wThaya. qwli mwjhe təlaš kərta rəha.
c. məriz leTa hwa tha. məriz ne nərs ko avaz di.
d. kele pəRe hwe the. kele xərab ho gəe.
e. ws ki bivi bhag gəi. ws ki bivi polis ke pas gəi.

12. The past participle + /bəyəyr/ "without ...": change the verb of the first sentence to a MOS past participle + /bəyəyr/ and insert it (+ any necessary object, etc.) at the beginning of the second sentence. See Sec. 16.303 (8). E.g.

/ap meri šadi mē šərik nəhī hwe. ap lahəwr nəhī ja səkte./ [This becomes:]
/meri šadi mē šərik hwe bəyəyr, ap lahəwr nəhī ja səkte./

a. ap ne našta nəhī kia. ap ko nə jana cahie.
b. mə̄y ne wrdu nəhī sikhi. mə̄y pakystan nəhī jaūga.
c. nəwkər ne kəmra nəhī jhaRa. nəwkər cəla gəya həy.
d. dərzi ne kəpRa nəhī napa. dərzi pətlun kəyse siega.
e. ws ne culhe ko saf nəhī kia. vw bavərcixane mē so gəya həy.

16.504. Variation.

1. yy qəmis tə̄g syli həy, halāke dərzi ne meri nap li thi.
yəhā bəhwt məcchər əwr məkkhiā ghws ai hāy, halāke mə̄y ne khyRki ko bənd kər rəkkha həy.
ys pərde ki cəwRai kafi nəhī, halāke mə̄y ne xwd divar ko napa tha.
əziz sahəb ke bal bəRh gəe hāy, halāke wnhō ne ek həfta hwa bal bənvae the.
vw əb tək mere ghər nəhī ate, halāke mə̄y ne mafi māg li thi.
əbhi əbhi həmara pəRəwsi šykayət kərne aya, halāke mə̄y ne reDyo ko ahysta kər dia tha.

2. yn kəpRō ke kwl kytne pəyse hwe.
yn saRiō ki kwl kytni qimət həy.
saRiō, pətlunō, əwr qəmisō ki kwl qimət bətaie!
ys šəhr mē pakystaniō ki kwl tadad kytni thi.
səb hysab myla kər, kwl kytni rəqəm hwi.

46

səylab mẽ, kwl kytne məkan təbah ho gəe.

3. mwjhe yy bəyl məra hwa malum hota həy.

   həmẽ yy salən kwch jəla hwa malum hota həy.

   mwjhe yy qəmisẽ saf dhwli hwi malum nəhĩ hotĩ.

   yy rwmal mwjhe zəra sa phəTa hwa malum hota həy.

   mwjhe yy səntre kwch sukhe hwe malum hote hə̃y.

   yy ymarət pətthər ki bəni hwi malum hoti həy.

4. mera bavərci cəlte hwe mwjhe yy hysab de gəya tha.

   mera nəwkər bazar jate hwe mwjhe yy pərca de gəya tha.

   meri bivi ne ystri kərte hwe mwjhe yy bat bətai.

   pəRəwsi ne dəftər se ate hwe ap ka pəyyam mwjhe pəhw̃ca dia.

   gaõvale cor ko marte hwe polis ke pas le gəe.

   ləRke šor məcate hwe kylas se bahər nykle.

5. mə̃y ne yy kəhani bhi əpni kytab mẽ šamyl kər li həy.

   kəpRevale ne yy rešmi kəpRa hysab mẽ šamyl nəhĩ kia.

   təəjjwb ki bat həy, ky ap ne wse əpni parTi mẽ šamyl nəhĩ kia.

   xərbuza əwr tərbuz bhi phəlõ mẽ šamyl hə̃y.

   ys šadi ki vəja se, vw bhi həmare xandan mẽ šamyl ho gəya həy.

   mwjhe wmmid həy, ky ap bhi həm logõ mẽ šamyl ho jaẽge.

6. polis ki yttyla ke mwtabyq, vw bhi ys kes mẽ šərik the.

   nai ke kəhne ke mwtabyq, twm bhi ws šərarət mẽ šərik the.

   zəmindar sahəb ke kəhne ke mwtabyq, vw bhi ys kəmpni mẽ šərik ho gəe.

   meri yttyla ke mwtabyq, vw bhi ws ki šadi mẽ šərik hõge.

   ek xəbər ke mwtabyq, həzarõ admi ws ke jənaze mẽ šərik the.

   təqribən dəs sal se, mə̃y wn ke sath ys kam mẽ šərik hū.

7. mwjhe pakystan mẽ rəhte hwe dəs sal ho gəe hə̃y.

   əziz sahəb ko əmrika ae hwe pāc sal ho gəe hə̃y.

   mali ko pəwda ləgate hwe do ghənTe ho gəe hə̃y.

   dərzi ko kəpRa napte hwe bəRi der ho gəi həy.

   wnhẽ davət mẽ gəe hwe təqribən pəwn ghənTa ho gəya həy.

   mwjhe pakystani khana khae hwe bəhwt ərsa hwa.

8. yy kam mera kia hwa həy.

   yy kəbab meri bivi ke bənae hwe hə̃y.

   yy kytab meri lykhi hwi həy.

   yy pətlun ws dərzi ki si hwi həy. [1]

   yy Dyrama mera dekha hwa həy.

   yy pajama dhobi ka phaRa hwa həy.

[1]Although the FS past participle of /sina/ "to sew" should grammatically be /sii/, many people pronounce it as /si/.

9. mə̃y dəs sal hwe mwltan gəya tha.

   vw do dyn hwe yəhã ae the.

   vw saRhe tin ghənTe hwe yəhã se cəla gəya.

DakTər ne chəy məhine hwe yy məšin əmrika se mãgvai thi, lekyn əbhi tək koi
jəvab nəhĩ myla.

do məhine hwe, ky mãy yy kam xətın kər cwka hũ.

bəhwt ərsa hwa, ky mãy wn se nəhĩ myl səka.

10. baryš mē cəlte cəlte, mere səb kəpRe xərab ho gəe.

xət lykhte lykhte, səb kaɣəz xətm ho gəe.

kəpRe site site, ek dəm dərzi ki halət xərab ho gəi.

əpne dost ko pwkarte pwkarte, vw jãgəl mē bəhwt dur nykəl gəya.

dhup mē bəyThe bəyThe, mere sər mē dərd ho gəya.

axyrkar, khãste khãste, becare məriz ka yntyqal ho gəya.

16.505. Response.

1. kya, ap ne yy qəmis syli hwi xəridi thi?
2. ap ko wrdu pəRhte hwe kytne məhine ho gəe hãy.
3. kya, pakystan jae bəɣəyr, koi šəxs pakystaniõ ki zyndəgi səməjh səkta həy?
4. ap ke hã khane pər hər həfte kytna xərc hota həy.
5. kya, ap ke ghər mē koi bavərci həy?
6. ys kylas mē ləRkõ ki kwl tadad kya həy.
7. ap ko ys šəhr mē rəhte hwe kytne sal ho gəe hãy.
8. kya, ap ne kəbhi koylõ pər khana pəkaya həy?
9. ys mwlk mē əwrtē pərda kyõ nəhĩ kərtĩ.
10. gərm məsale mē kəwn kəwnsi cizē šamyl hoti hãy.
11. ap ki jeb mē ys vəqt kwl kytne pəyse hãy.
12. kya, ap vəqt ke pabənd hãy?
13. ap ko əpne mã bap se myle hwe kytne dyn hwe.
14. kya, ap swba wThte hi našta kərte hãy?
15. kya, ap kəbhi kysi pakystani davət mē gəe hãy? ap ko kəwnsa khana zyada pəsənd
    aya.

16.506. Conversation Practice.

Mrs. Smith is talking to the tailor.

MS: kya, səb kəpRe syl gəe hãy?

T: təqribən səb kəpRe syle hwe təyyar rəkkhe hãy. əlbətta saRi ke lie blawz əbhi təyyar
   nəhĩ hwa.

MS: bəcciõ ki šəlvarõ mē se, ek šəlvar kəm həy.

T: šəlvarõ ka kəpRa kwch kəm nykla. ys lie chəy šəlvarõ ki bəjae, syrf pãc bən səki hãy.

MS: mere xyal mē to kəpRa bylkwl pura tha.

T: mãy ne dwkan pər jate hi kəpRa napa tha, to malum hwa, ky kəpRa kəm həy.

MS: xəyr -- lekyn yy bat Thik nəhĩ, ky mera blawz əbhi tək təyyar nəhĩ hwa. halāke do
    həfte hwe, ky twm kəpRe le gəe the. əgərce twmhara vada syrf ek həfte ka tha! mwjhe
    blawz aj šam tək myl jana cahie, kyõke mwjhe ek səheli ke hã davət mē šərik hona həy.

48

T: mwjhe əfsos həy, ky mə̃y vade ke mwtabyq kəpRe nəhĩ la səka. dərəsl vəja yy hwi, ky dusra admi, jo mere sath dwkan pər kam kərta həy, bimar ho gəya. ys lie kafi kam pəRa hwa həy. aj bhi swba se kəpRe si rəha tha. jəb site site thək gəya, to soca, ky yy syle hwe kəpRe ap ko de aũ. ap ka blawz bhi təqribən syla hwa rəkkha həy. syrf thoRa sa kam baqi həy. mə̃y ynšaəlla[h] šam se pəhle pəhw̃ca dũga.

MS: kya, bəcciõ ke kəpRe nəi nap ke mwtabyq sie hə̃y?

T: ji hã. pwrani nap mẽ do do ync bəRha die hə̃y.

MS: bəhwt əccha. Thik həy. zəra jate vəqt bavərci ko mere pas bhej dena.

T: bəhwt əccha. xwda hafyz.

The tailor leaves, and the cook comes in. This man is a temporary replacement for the Smiths' regular cook, who is on vacation.

MS: ytni der se kəhã gəe hwe the! twmhara yntyzar kərte kərte do ghənTe ho gəe hə̃y!

C: mə̃y səwda lene ke lie bazar gəya tha. mere xyal mẽ to mə̃y ne koi xas der nəhĩ ləgai.

MS: xas der se twmhara kya mətləb həy! kya, šam tək bazar mẽ bəyThne ka xyal tha?
-- əccha, bətao, kya kya səwda lae ho.

C: pyaz, TəmaTər, gobhi, alu, gajər, əwr kwch məsala laya hũ. koyle əwr myTTi ka tel əbhi nəhĩ myla. kwl car rupəe təresəTh pəyse xərc hwe hə̃y. hysab ys pərce pər lykha hwa həy.

MS: twm həmeša səwda mə̃hga late ho. həmara bavərci yy səb cizẽ səsti lata tha.

C: begəm sahəb, vəja yy həy, ky ajkəl cizõ ki qimtẽ bəRhti ja rəhi hə̃y.

MS: yy kəyse mwmkyn həy, ky jəb se twm ae ho, qimtẽ bəRh rəhi hə̃y! ys se pəhle səb cizẽ səsti mylti thĩ. -- xəyr, jao -- əwr dopəhr ke khane ka bəndobəst kəro! pwlao əwr kofte pəkane hə̃y, əwr kwch kəbab bhi bəna lena.

C: bəhwt əccha. mə̃y əbhi yy səb kam kər leta hũ.

MS: dusre, mali do dyn se nəzər nəhĩ aya. vw kəhã həy.

C: aj swba səvere aya tha, əwr jəb ap log našta kər rəhe the, mə̃y ne wse pəwdõ mẽ pani dete hwe dekha tha.

MS: əb xyal rəkhna -- jəb vw ae, to mwjhe bətana!

C: bəhwt əccha. -- dhobi kafi der se aya hwa bəyTha həy, əwr ap ka yntyzar kər rəha həy.

Mrs. Smith goes to meet the washerman.

MS: kwl kytne kəpRe hə̃y.

W: kwl bis kəpRe hə̃y. chəy šəlvarẽ hə̃y, pãc bwšərT hə̃y, car pətlunẽ hə̃y, tin pajame əwr do bənyan hə̃y.

MS: yy pətlunẽ saf nəhĩ dhwlĩ. pychli dəfa bhi ysmyth sahəb šykayət kər rəhe the, ky bənyan əwr moze saf nəhĩ dhwle. -- əwr dekho, yn kəpRõ pər ystri bhi Thik nəhĩ hwi. əgər kəpRe saf nəhĩ dho səkte, to dhona choR do!

W: begəm sahəb, ap to naraz ho rəhi hə̃y. mwjhe to yy kəpRe bylkwl saf dhwle hwe malum hote hə̃y, lekyn əgər ap kəhti hə̃y, ky yy əcche nəhĩ dhwle, to mə̃y phyr dho laũga.

MS: yy pətlunẽ vapəs le jao, əwr saf dho kər lao!

W: bəhwt əccha.

MS: yn kəpRõ ke kwl kytne pəyse hwe.

49

W: tin rupəe basəTh pəyse. pychli dəfa ke pɔ̄ytys pəyse bhi šamyl kər lie hɔ̄y.

MS: yy lo -- əwr yy dusre kəpRe bhi gyn lo! əwr aynda kəpRe saf dho kər laya kəro, vərna pəyse nəhĩ mylēge.

W: bəhwt əccha, begəm sahəb.

16. 507. Conversation Stimulus.

Topics may include the following:

1. Buying groceries.
2. Dealing with household servants.
3. The washerman.
4. The tailor.
5. The cook.

ahysta A1 Adv	slow, gradual, soft, calm, mild; slowly, gradually
alu M1	potato
axyrkar Adv	at last, finally, in the end
bal M1	hair
bap M1	father
basəTh A1	sixty-two
bavərci M1	cook (person)
bavərcixana M2	kitchen
bādhna [If: /ə̄/]	to tie, bind, fasten
[ke] bəɣəyr Comp Post	without
bənvana [DC: /bənna/: IIc]	to cause to be made, built, done
bənyan M1	undershirt
bəRhana [C: /bəRhna/: IIc]	to expand, enlarge, stretch out, make grow, cause to advance
bə̄dhna [I: /bādhna/: If]	to be tied, bound, fastened
becara A2 M/F2	poor, unfortunate, poor fellow
blawz M1	blouse
botəl F1	bottle
bwšərT [or /bwššərT/] F1 [or M1]	sport shirt: "bush-shirt"
bwjhana [C: /bwjhna/: IIc]	to extinguish, quench, put out
bykhərna [I: /bəkherna/: Ig]	to be scattered, strewn, spread, dispersed, dropped, disheveled
cəwRai F2	width
cə̄wsəTh A1	sixty-four
culha M2	hearth, stove, fireplace
dəm M1	breath, life, moment
dərzi M1	tailor
dhū̄ā M2 [np]	smoke, vapour
dhwlna [I: /dhona/: Ie]	to be washed
dyqqət F1	difficulty, problem, perplexity, dilemma
Dhəkna [Id: /ə/] M2	to cover, conceal; cover, lid
gajər F1	carrot
gila A2	wet, damp
gobhi F2	cauliflower, cabbage
gynna [Ic: /y/]	to count, enumerate
halāke Conj	although, notwithstanding, even though
hysab M1	bill, account
jənaza M2	funeral, funeral procession, bier
jhaRən M1	dustcloth
jhaRna [If: /ə/]	to sweep, dust, brush off
jhaRu F1	broom

kapi F2	copybook, copy
kəbab M1	"kabab," spicy meat patty
kofta M2	"kofta," spiced meatballs in sauce
koyla M2	charcoal, coal, coals
kwl M1 A1 [np]	total, sum, whole, all, entire
ləmbai F2	length, tallness, height
mafi [literary: /mwafi/] F2	forgiveness, pardon
mali M1	gardener
mā F1	mother
məcchər M1	mosquito
məkkhi F2	housefly
məsala M2	spices, seasoning
moza M2	stocking, sock
[ke] mwtabyq Comp Post	according to, in accordance with
nai M1	barber
nap F1 [or M1] [np]	measurement
napna [If: /ə/]	to measure
našta M2	breakfast
nəql F1	imitation, copy, copying, mimicking
pabənd PA1 [A1 rare]	following, adhering, observing, bound to
pabəndi F2	restriction, limitation, punctuality
pajama M2	pajama[s]
pərca M2	slip (of paper); examination paper
pərda M2	curtain, veil
pəRəwsi [or /pəRosi/] M1	neighbour
pətlun F1	pants, trousers
pəTTi F2	bandage
pəysəTh A1	sixty-five
phaRna [If: stem /phəT/ or /phəR/]	to tear, rip, rend
phəTna [I: /phaRna/: If]	to be torn, ripped, rent
pura A2	complete, full, whole, entire
pwkarna [Ia]	to call out, cry out to
pwlao M1 [np]	"pwlao," rice cooked with meat and spices
pyaz F1 [pl. rare]	onion
qəmis [or /qəmiz/] F1	shirt
qima M2 [np]	minced meat, hamburger
qorma M2 [np]	"qorma," meat curry cooked without much gravy
rešəm M1 [np]	silk
rešmi A1	silken
rezgari F2	change, small coins
rwmal M1	handkerchief
saRi F2	"sari": saRi

səwda M2	household purchases, groceries, supplies
səvera M2 [np]	early morning, dawn, early
sina [Ie: stem /syl/]	to sew
sylna [I: /sina/: Ie]	to be sewn
šamyl PA1	included, associated in, joined in
šəlvar F1	"šəlvar," a type of loose pajama
šərik PA1	participating in, joining in, included in
təəjjwb M1 [np]	wonder, astonishment
təresəTh [or /tyrsəTh/] A1	sixty-three
twhfa M2	present, gift
TəmaTər M1	tomato
Tokri F2	basket
vada M2	promise
xərc M1	expense, expenditure, cost, spending
ykhəTTa A2 Adv	together, collected, in a mass, gathered
yksəTh A1	sixty-one
ync M1	inch
yntyqal M1 [np]	death; transfer
ystri F2	iron (for clothing)
zəra A1 Adv	just, a little, a bit

The Jami Masjid, Delhi, built by the Mughal Emperor Shah Jahan in 1644-58.

UNIT SEVENTEEN

17.000. CONVERSATION

Mr. Smith is chatting with Dr. Rəhim.

Islam M1 [np]	yslam
knowledge, facts, information Fpl [no sg.]	malumat

S: I'd like to obtain some facts about Islam.
məy yslam ke bare mē kwch malumat hasyl kərni cahta hū.

religious A1	məzhəbi
learned man, scholar M1	alym
Muslim religious scholar M1	məwlvi
kind, friendly, gracious M/F1 A1	myhrban
learned men, scholars Mpl [pl. /alym/]	wləma
religions Mpl [pl. /məzhəb/ M1 "religion"]	məzahyb
acquainted with, knowing PA1	vaqyf

R: This is not a difficult matter. There are many books about Islam, and if you'd like to meet a religious scholar, there is a Məwlvi [who is] my good friend. We can go to him. This Məwlvi is one of our great scholars. Aside from Islam, he is also acquainted with other religions.
yy koi mwškyl bat nəhī. yslam ke mwtəəllyq bəhwt si kytabē məwjud hɔ̄y, əwr əgər ap kysi məzhəbi alym se mylna cahte hɔ̄y, to ek məwlvi sahəb mere myhrban dost hɔ̄y. həm wn ke pas cəl səkte hɔ̄y. yy məwlvi sahəb həmare bəRe wləma mē se ek hɔ̄y. yslam ke ylava, dusre məzahyb se bhi vaqyf hɔ̄y.

good fortune F1 [np]	xwšqysməti
present, attendant, in attendance PA1	hazyr

S: What greater good fortune could there be for me, than that I pay him a visit? [Lit. For me advancing beyond this, what good fortune will there be, that I may be present in his service?]
mere lie ys se bəRh kər əwr kya xwš-qysməti hogi, ky mɔ̄y wn ki xydmət mē hazyr ho jaū.

R: Very good. This evening at five o'clock we'll go [to see] him.
bəhwt əccha. šam ko pāc bəje həm wn ke pas cəlēge.

They arrive at the religious scholar's home at the appointed time.

mention, reference M1	zykr

MS: Come in, Mr. Smith! Come in! Mr. Rəhim has [lit. had] mentioned you on the telephone. I am very glad to meet you. [Lit. Having met with you, much happiness has become.]
aie, ysmyth sahəb, təšrif laie! rəhim sahəb ne Telifun pər ap ka zykr kia tha. ap se myl kər bəRi xwši hwi.

valuable, precious A1	qimti
favour, gift, benefaction, boon F1	ynayət

S: It is kind of you to have favoured us with your valuable time.
yy ap ki myhrbani həy, ky ap ne əpna qimti vəqt həmē ynayət fərmaya.

culture F1	təhzib
civilisation M1	təməddwn

religion M1

interest, fascination F2

MS: What is there of kindness or favour in
this? It makes us happy that you take
[lit. keep] interest in our country,
culture, civilisation, and religion.

fundamental, basic A1

beliefs, tenets Mpl [pl. /əqida/ M2
"tenet, belief"]

India M1 [np]

concept, idea, conception M1

S: I want to know something about the
fundamental tenets of Islam. Especially
the concept of Islam which is [found] in
India and Pakistan; please say something
about that!

whether Conj

Iraq M1 [np]

Saudi M1 A1

Arabia, Arab M1 A1

Egypt M1 [np]

Syria M1 [np]

tenet, belief M2

worhsip, devotion F1

suitable, proper, worthy, fit, capable
A1 [/[ke] layq/ Comp Post "worthy of,
fit for, suitable for"]

star M2

sun M1

sea, ocean M1

in short Conj

administration, system, order,
arrangement M1

under, below Comp Post

MS: Islam, whether it be in Iraq or in Saudi
Arabia, in Egypt or in Syria, -- in its
basic tenets there is no difference. Our
foremost tenet is this, that God is one.
He has no partner. Aside from Him,
none other is worthy of worship. He has
created the earth, the sky, the moon,
the stars, the sun, the sea, the rivers
-- in short, [He] created everything in
the world. The entire ordering of the
world is in His hand. Therefore, under
this belief, we worship only one God,
and from Him alone do we seek assistance.

S: This belief is found in almost all of the
religions of the world.

Christian M1 A1

Jew, Jewish M1 A1

məzhəb

dylcəspi

ys mē myhrbani ya ynayət ki kəwnsi bat
həy. həmē xwši həy, ky ap həmare mwlk,
təhzib, təməddwn, əwr məzhəb se dylcəspi
rəkhte hɔ̄y.

bwnyadi

əqayd

hyndostan [common: /hyndwstan/]

təsəvvwr

mɔ̄y yslam ke bwnyadi əqayd ke bare mē
kwch janna cahta hū. xas təwr pər,
hyndostan əwr pakystan mē yslam ka jo
təsəvvwr həy, ws ke mwtəəllyq kwch
fərmaie!

xa

yraq

səudi

ərəb

mysr

šam

əqida

ybadət

layq

sytara

surəj

səməndər

yərəzke [or /yərzeke/]

nyzam

[ke] təht

yslam, xa yraq mē ho, ya səudi ərəb mē,
mysr mē ho, ya šam mē -- ys ke bwnyadi
əqayd mē koi fərq nəhī. həmara səb se
pəhla əqida yy həy, ky əllah ek həy. ws
ka koi šərik nəhī. ws ke ylava, koi dusra
ybadət ke layq nəhī. ws ne zəmin, asman,
cād, sytare, surəj, səməndər, dərya,--
yərəzke dwnya ki hər ciz pəyda ki. dwnya
ka sara nyzam wsi ke hath mē həy. cwnāce
ys əqide ke təht, həm syrf ek xwda ki
ybadət kərte hɔ̄y, əwr wsi se mədəd māgte
hɔ̄y.

yy əqida dwnya ke təqribən təmam məzahyb
mē paya jata həy.

isai [common: /ysai/]

yəhudi

56

most important A1	əhəmtərin
prophethood F1 [np]	rysalət
i.e., that is ... Conj	yani
prophets Mpl [pl. /nəbi/ M1 "prophet, apostle"]	əmbia
prophethood, apostleship F1 [np]	nəbuvvət [or /nwbuvvət/]
faith, belief M1	iman
giving, benefaction, bounty F1	əta
affair, matter, dealing M2	mwamla [less literary: /mamla/]
goodness, merit, virtue F2	əcchai
lie, falsehood M1	jhuT
truth M1 [np]	səc
discrimination, discernment, distinction F1 [np]	təmiz
heart M1	dyl
obedience, submission F1	ytaət
parents Mpl	valdəyn [literary: /valydəyn/]
love, affection F1	mwhəbbət [originally: /məhəbbət/]
tongue, language F1	zəban [also /zwban/]
goal, aim, object M1	məqsəd
explanation, statement, declaration, description M1	bəyan
favours, gifts, bounties, boons Fpl [pl. /ynayət/]	ynayat
had forgotten MS [/bhwlana/ "to (deliberately) forget"; C: /bhulna/: IIc]	bhwla bəyTha
sin M1	gwnah
to be caught, trapped, snared, entangled [IIc: /ɔ̃/]	phə̃sna
guidance, direction F1	hydayət
prophet, apostle M1	nəbi
being astray, misguidedness, error, heresy F2	gwmrahi
to save, rescue, cause to escape [C: /bəcna/: IIc]	bəcana
Muslim M1 A1	mwsəlman

MS: Yes, nearly this same sort of belief is present in the Christian and Jewish religion[s] also, and it is also found in various forms in some other religions. This is our foremost and most important tenet. After this comes the concept of Prophethood, i.e. the belief in the apostleship of all the Prophets. God created mankind. [He] gave him a brain, in order that he may think before taking a step in each matter, and that he may distinguish between virtue and vice, falsehood and truth. [He] gave [him] a heart, in order that aside from obedience

ji hã, təqribən ysi qysm ka əqida isai əwr yəhudi məzhəb mẽ bhi məwjud həy. əwr kwch dusre məzahyb mẽ bhi mwxtəlyf surtõ mẽ mylta həy. yy həmara səb se pəhla əwr əhəmtərin əqida həy. ys ke bad, rysalət ka təsəvvwr ata həy, yani təmam əmbia ki nəbuvvət pər iman rəkhna. əllah ne ynsan ko pəyda kia. take vw hər mwamle mẽ soc kər qədəm wThae, əwr əcchai əwr bwrai, jhuT əwr səc mẽ təmiz kər səke. dyl əta kia, take vw xwda ki ytaət ke ylava, valdəyn, dostõ, əwr pəRəwsiõ ki mwhəbbət rəkh səke. zəban di, take ynsan əpna məqsəd bəyan

57

to God, he may bear love for parents, friends, and neighbours. [He] gave [him] a tongue, in order that Man may express himself [lit. express his meaning]. But Man [foolishly] forgot all of these gifts and became entangled in sins. Thereupon God sent the Prophets for Man's guidance. The task of these Prophets was to show people the straight path and to save them from error. Therefore, we Muslims have faith in all of those Prophets whom God sent for people's guidance.

kər səke. lekyn ynsan yn təmam ynayat ko bhwla bəyTha, əwr gwnahõ mẽ phə̃s gəya. cwnãce əllah ne ynsan ki hydayət ke lie nəbiõ ko bheja. yn nəbiõ ka kam yy tha, ky vw logõ ko sidha rasta dykhaẽ, əwr wnhẽ gwmrahi se bəcaẽ. cwnãce həm mwsəlman wn təmam nəbiõ pər iman rəkhte hə̃y, jo əllah ne logõ ki hydayət ke lie bheje.

lord, sir, master (title of respect) Ml

həzrət

Christ Ml [np]

isa

on whom be peace! [epithet added after the names of all the Prophets except the Prophet Muhammad]

ələyhyssəlam

S: What do you people think about Christ (on whom be peace!)?

həzrət isa ələyhyssəlam ke bare mẽ, ap logõ ka kya xyal həy.

honour, dignity, respect Fl

yzzət

complete, perfected, finished Al

mwkəmməl

position, rank, status Fl

həysiət

MS: We honour him with the status of a perfect man and as a very great Prophet, but we do not consider him to be the son of God or as His partner.

həm wn ki yzzət, ek mwkəmməl ynsan əwr ek bəhwt bəRe nəbi ki həysiət şe kərte hə̃y, lekyn həm wnhẽ xwda ka beTa ya ws ka šərik nəhĩ səməjhte.

teachings Fpl [pl. /talim/]

talimat

S: What is your opinion of his teachings?

wn ki talimat ke bare mẽ ap ka kya xyal həy.

The Gospels Fl

ynjil

erring, lost, astray Al

gwmrah

last, final Al

axyri [common: /axri/]

prophet Ml

rəsul

Muhammad Ml [np]

mwhəmməd

God's peace and blessings be upon him! [epithet added only after the name of the Prophet Muhammad]

səlləllaho ələyhe və səlləm

idol, image, statue Ml

bwt

to worship (as an idol) [If: /w/]

pujna

to quarrel IIa

jhəgəRna

buried, interred PAl

dəfn

morals, ethics, manners Ml [np]

əxlaq

moral, ethical, relating to courtesy or manners Al

əxlaqi

fallen into, suffering from, involved in, embroiled in PAl

mwbtəla

MS: Christ also taught exactly what the other Prophets taught. He too was a Prophet of God, and [he] brought His message in the form of the Gospels. But after him the world again went astray. Therefore, God sent His last Prophet, Muhammad (God's peace and blessings be upon him!)

həzrət isa ələyhyssəlam ne bhi vwhi talim di, jo dusre nəbiõ ne di. ap bhi xwda ke nəbi the, əwr ws ka pəyɣam ynjil ki surət mẽ lae the. lekyn ap ke bad, dwnya phyr gwmrah ho gəi. ys lie, əllah ne əpne axyri rəsul, həzrət mwhəmməd, səlləllaho ələyhe və səlləm ko logõ ki hydayət ke lie bheja,

for the people's guidance, and [He] ended prophethood with [lit. upon] him. After him no other prophet can come. In the age in which he was born, at that time the condition of Arabia was very bad. People used to worship idols. They fought among themselves over very minor matters. They used to bury [their own baby] daughters alive -- in short, these people's morals had completely collapsed, and they were entangled in moral vices.

əwr ap pər nəbuvvət xətm ki. ap ke bad koi dusra nəbi nəhĩ a səkta. jys zəmane mẽ ap pəyda hwe, ws vəqt ərəb ki halət bəhwt xərab thi. log bwtõ ko pujte the. mamuli mamuli batõ pər apəs mẽ ləRte jhəgəRte the. ləRkiõ ko zynda dəfn kərte the -- γərəzke yn logõ ka əxlaq gyr cwka tha, əwr əxlaqi bwraiõ mẽ mwbtəla the.

S: Was it for this reason that your Prophet was born in Arabia: because the condition of Arabia was worse than that of other countries?

kya, ysi vəja se ap ke nəbi ərəb mẽ pəyda hwe -- kyõke ərəb ki halət dusre mwlkõ se zyada xərab thi?

Arabic, Arabian F2 [np] Al   ərəbi

person of the world M/F2   dwnyavala

region, area, district M2   ylaqa

MS: Yes, but that message which God sent through Muhammad (God's peace and blessings be upon him!), although it was in the Arabic language, nevertheless [lit. but] it was not only for the people of Arabia but was for all of the people of the world. Whenever God sent any Prophet, [He] did not send [him] for any special region or any special country, but His message was for the whole world.

ji hã, lekyn jo pəyγam əllah ne həzrət mwhəmməd səlləllaho ələyhe və səlləm ke zərie bheja, əgərce vw ərəbi zəban mẽ tha, lekyn syrf ərəb ke logõ ke lie nəhĩ tha, bəlke təmam dwnyavalõ ke lie tha. jəb bhi əllah ne koi nəbi bheja, to kysi xas ylaqe ya kysi xas mwlk ke lie nəhĩ bheja, bəlke ws ka pəyγam təmam dwnya ke lie tha.

S: What did your Prophet teach?

ap ke nəbi ne kya talim di.

to relate, tell, cause to hear [C: /swnna/: Ic]   swnana

nation, tribe, people, race Fl   qəwm

useless, futile, invalid, meaningless, unemployed Al   bekar

reward, prize Ml   ynam

customs Fpl [pl. /rəsm/ Fl "custom, practice"]   rwsumat

to sink, be submerged, drown [IIc: /w/]   Dubna

suddenly awoke MP   jag wThe

difficulties, troubles, problems Fpl [pl. /təklif/]   təkalif

to lose (a game, war, courage, etc.) [IIIa: /ə/]   harna

to be called; to cause to be called [C: /kəhna/: Ic; used both as a causative and as an intransitive]   kəhlana

meaning, sense, intent Mpl [no sg.]   mane [also /mani/]

The Qwran, "Koran" Ml   qwran

Tradition, a recorded saying or act of the Prophet Muhammad Fl   hədis

commentators Mpl [pl. /mwfəssyr/ Ml "commentator on the Qwran and Hədis"]   mwfəssyrin

Traditions Fpl [pl. /hədis/]   əhadis

commentaries Fpl [pl. /təfsir/ F]
"commentary on the Qwran or the Hədis"]

təfasir

MS: When our Prophet received the command of God, he related God's message to the people: "God is one. I am a Prophet sent by Him [lit. His sent Prophet], just as many other Prophets have been sent to various nations before me. The worship of idols is futile. These idols can offer nothing. Only God alone is worthy of worship. The burying of [your baby] daughters alive is a very great sin. All people are equal and are brothers to one another [lit. are brother brother among themselves]. The man who does virtuous deeds in this world, God will be pleased with him, and he will receive their [lit. its] reward in the next world. And that man who commits sins and evils here, he will receive their punishment." The people of Arabia who were sunk in the evil practices of the world, when they heard this teaching, suddenly awoke and became ashamed of their sins. At the very beginning, our Prophet had to bear [lit. pick up] many difficulties, but he did not lose courage, and he related the message of God to every person. Those people who believed [lit. brought faith], they were called "Muslims," and the name of this religion was retained as "Islam," which means submission to God. Therefore we believe in the message of God -- i.e. the Qwran -- and we follow the Traditions -- i.e. the principles related by Muhammad (God's peace and blessings be upon him!). For our convenience, the commentators have written commentaries upon the Qwran and the Hədis, from which we obtain assistance at every step of our lives.

jəb həmare nəbi ko əllah ka hwkm hwa, to ap ne logõ ko əllah ka yy pəyyam swnaya. "əllah ek həy. mãy ws ka bheja hwa nəbi hũ, jys təra mwjh se pəhle bəhwt se dusre nəbi mwxtəlyf qəwmõ ke lie bheje gəe the. bwtõ ko pujna bylkwl bekar həy. yy bwt kwch nəhĩ de səkte. syrf xwda hi ybadət ke layq həy. ləRkiõ ko zynda dəfn kərna bəhwt bəRa gwnah həy. səb log bərabər hãy, əwr apəs mẽ bhai bhai hãy. jo šəxs ys dwnya mẽ nek kam kərega, ws se əllah xwš hoga, əwr dusri dwnya mẽ ws ka ynam paega. əwr jo šəxs yəhã gwnah əwr bwraiã kərega, vw wn ki səza paega." ərəb ke logõ ne, jo ky dwnya ki bwri rwsumat mẽ Dube hwe the, jəb yy talim swni, to jag wThe, əwr əpne gwnahõ pər šərmynda hwe. šwru šwru mẽ, həmare nəbi ko bəRi təkalif wThani pəRĩ, lekyn ap ne hymmət nəhĩ hari, əwr əllah ka pəyyam hər šəxs ko swnaya. jo log iman lae, vw mwsəlman kəhlae, əwr ys məzhəb ka nam yslam rəkkha gəya, jys ke mane əllah ki ytaət həy. cwnãce həm log əllah ke pəyyam -- yani qwran -- pər iman rəkhte hãy, əwr hədis -- yani həzrət mwhəmməd səlləllaho ələyhe və səlləm ke bətae hwe wsulõ -- pər cəlte hãy. həm logõ ki asani ke lie, mwfəssyrin ne qwran əwr əhadis ki təfasir lykhi hãy, jyn se zyndəgi ke hər qədəm pər mədəd mylti həy.

S: I think that now we should ask permission [to leave], because we have taken enough of your time. God willing, we will come [lit. be present] again some time.

mera xyal həy, ky əb həmẽ yjazət dijie, kyõke həm ne ap ka kafi vəqt lia həy. ynšaəlla[h] phyr kysi vəqt hazyr hõge.

MS: You're welcome. Certainly you must come again. Please take this book with you. All of the necessary facts about Islam are in it. Moreover, it is written in very easy Urdu.

koi bat nəhĩ. ap zərur təšrif laẽ. yy kytab əpne sath le jaẽ. ys mẽ yslam ke bare mẽ təmam zəruri malumat məwjud hãy. dusre, yy bəhwt asan wrdu mẽ lykhi hwi həy.

S: Thank you very much. God willing, I will read it at the first opportunity [lit. leisure], and I will come to visit you [lit. will be present in your service] again next week. Goodbye!

bəhwt bəhwt šwkria. mãy ynšaəlla[h] yse pəhli fwrsət mẽ pəRhũga, əwr əgle həfte ap ki xydmət mẽ phyr hazyr hũga. xwda hafyz.

MS: Goodbye!

xwda hafyz.

17. 101. /malumat/ Fpl "facts, knowledge, information" has no singular, although formally it appears to be the plural of /malum/ PA1 "known. " /malumat/ is employed for a body of information: e. g. the facts about a country, a religion, etc. It contrasts thus with /yttyla/ F1 "information, " which refers to a piece of news or information about some specific event. E. g.

/jəb ap pəhw̄c jaē, to mwjhe yttyla dijie! /   When you arrive, please inform me! [/malumat/ is inappropriate here, but /xəbər/ F1 "news" can be substituted.]

/mə̃y pakystan ke bare mē kwch malumat hasyl kərni cahta hū. /   I want to get some information about Pakistan. [Both /xəbər/ and /yttyla/ are inappropriate here, unless one means "news of [events] in Pakistan. "]

/ws ki yttyla ke mwtabyq, vw vəhā̃ məwjud nəhī tha. /   According to his information, he was not present there. [Here a specific event is meant. Compare:]

/meri malumat ke mwtabyq, yy hyndostan ki səb se pwrani məsjyd həy. / According to my knowledge, this is India's oldest mosque.

17. 102. /alym/ M1 denotes "scholar, learned man (of any subject). " The Arabic plural, /wləma/ Mpl, may also be employed for scholar generally, but it more often refers to a body of Muslim religious scholars. /məwlvi/ M1, on the other hand, is used only for a Muslim religious scholar and is specifically employed for a person having a degree from a religious school or a university department of Islamic studies. This qualification is not always necessary, however, and a person may be called /məwlvi/ on the strength of his demonstrable knowledge of Islamic matters alone. Although there is no formal priesthood in Islam -- and hence no hierarchy to appoint a /məwlvi/ -- this title has indeed tended to become a profession, and now various groups, schools, mosque boards of trustees, etc. engage a person with the requisite training at a fixed salary as a /məwlvi/. His duties may include teaching at a religious school, tutoring children privately in Islamic matters, officiating at the five daily prayers, delivering the sermon at the Friday congregational prayer, holding marriage and funeral ceremonies, and delivering minor judgments in religious matters.

17. 103. /vaqyf/ PA1 "acquainted with, knowing" largely overlaps the semantic areas of /janna/ Ia "to know" and /malum/ PA1 "known. " Like /malum/, however, /vaqyf/ is not generally used for detailed knowledge of a broad general subject (e. g. a language). /vaqyf/ is also uncommon for the knowledge of a single specific fact (an area covered by /malum/). In some contexts /vaqyf/ may also denote a somewhat lesser degree of knowledge also: i. e. a difference like that found for English "acquainted with" versus "knowing. " See Sec. 3. 107. E. g.

/mə̃y ysmyth sahəb se vaqyf hū. /   I am acquainted with Mr. Smith. [This is equivalent to:]

/mə̃y ysmyth sahəb ko janta hū. /   I know Mr. Smith. [Compare:]

/mwjhe ysmyth sahəb malum həy./ I know Mr. Smith. [I.e. I would recognise Mr. Smith if I saw him; I know who he is. /malum/ is not otherwise employed for knowledge of a person.]

/mə̄y ys raste se vaqyf hū./ I am acquainted with this road. [This is generally equivalent to:]

/mə̄y ys raste ko janta hū./ I know this road. [And also to:]

/mwjhe yy rasta malum həy./ I know this road.

/mə̄y ws məzhəb ki talimat se vaqyf hū./ I am acquainted with the teachings of that religion. [The various doctrines, etc. of the religion. are considered to be individual facts with which the speaker is acquainted. One cannot say */məzhəb se vaqyf/ "acquainted with the religion" because a religion is not a set of discrete facts but rather a broad, general topic.]

/mə̄y wrdu janta hū./ I know Urdu. [Neither /vaqyf/ nor /malum/ are appropriate for knowledge of a language.]

/mwjhe yy xəbər malum həy./ I know this [piece of] news. [Neither /janna/ nor /vaqyf/ are applicable here since /xəbər/ refers to a single, specific abstract fact.]

17.104. /hazyr/ PA1 "present, in attendance" is often employed in formations which are the opposite of "honorific speech": just as honorific forms are employed when one addresses a person of equal (though formal) or higher status, so one must use special "humble" forms when referring to oneself in the presence of such a respected person. There may thus be as many as three ways to express a given concept: an honorific way, a humble way, and a neutral way. For example, /... ki xydmət mē hazyr hona/ denotes "to visit, go to, come to, be present" when referring to a respected person. /hazyr/ is also employed for "present, in attendance (as a student in class)," and the Arabic plural, /hazyrin/ Mpl, is used as a polite term for "audience, those present." E.g.

/mə̄y ap ki xydmət mē hazyr ho gəya hū./ I have come to see you. [Lit. I have become present in your service.]

/məwlvi sahəb yəhā məwjud həy./ Məwlvi Sahəb is here. [To say /... hazyr həy/ would be insulting. Used in the presence of the person, /məwjud/ is somewhat honorific: one cannot say */mə̄y ap ki xydmət mē məwjud hū./. Used outside the humble-honorific context, however, /məwjud/ is neutral.]

/həm səb log vəhā məwjud the./ We all were present there. [/hazyr/ can be substituted but would imply great respect for some person mentioned in the context.]

/mwjrym ədalət mē hazyr kia gəya./ The culprit was presented in the court. [This is equivalent to /peš kia gəya/.]

17.105. "What more ..." or "what else ..." are idiomatically expressed by /... se bəRh kər/ "having advanced from ..." E.g.

/ys se bəRh kər, əwr kya ho səkta həy./ What more can there be than this? [Lit. Having advanced from this, what else can be?]

/ap se bəRh kər, əwr kəwn dost hoga./ Who else can be more of a friend than you? [Lit. Having advanced from you, who else will be a friend?]

/valdəyn se bəRh kər, əpne bəccō ko əwr kəwn cahega./ Who will love children more than their parents. [Lit. Having advanced from the parents, who else will love one's children?]

62

/ys se bəRh kər, ap əwr kya ynam cahte hɜy./   What more reward do
you want than this?

/dwnya ka koi dusra məzhəb yslam se bəRh kər əxlaq nəhĩ sykhata./   No
other religion of the world teaches ethics more than Islam. [Lit.
Any other religion of the world does not teach ethics having advanced
from Islam.]

/ys se bəRh kər, buRhe bap ki əwr kya bədqysməti hogi, ky ws ka jəvan
beTa mər gəya./   What greater misfortune can there be for an old
father, than that his young son has died?

/ys se bəRh kər, mɜy ws ke lie əwr kwch nəhĩ kər səka./   I could do no
more for him than this.

/yy kəpRa ws se bəRh kər həy./   This cloth is better than that [cloth].
[This usage is colloquial.]

17.106. /ap se myl kər bəRi xwši hwi./   literally means "Having met with you, much
happiness has become." This is the standard way of saying "I am happy to meet you."

17.107. /ynayət/ Fl "favour, gift, benefaction, boon" is used with /kərna/ or
/fərmana/ as an honorific way of saying "to give, grant, bestow." These formations carry
the connotation of granting a favour, and they tend to be used for the granting of abstract
things rather than for material objects (although examples of the latter are also found).
/əta/ Fl "giving, benefaction, bounty" (again + /kərna/ or /fərmana/) is used to refer to
the giving of concrete objects. These two formations are, of course, "honorific language";
the corresponding "humble" form for "to give" is /peš kərna/ "to present, offer." /ynayət/
is also common as a noun (i. e. outside the complex verbal formations just mentioned), but
/əta/ is only rarely employed as a noun. E. g.

/ap myhrbani kər ke, aj thoRa sa vəqt ynayət fərmaẽ!/   Please grant me
a little time today!

/mwjhe do dyn ki chwTTi ynayət fərmaie!/   Please grant me two days'
leave!

/əllah ne ynsan ko dyl əta kia./   God gave man a heart. [/ynayət fərmana/
is also possible here.]

/məwlvi sahəb ne mwjhe dəs rupəe əta kie./   Məwlvi Sahəb gave me ten
rupees. [Compare:]

/mɜy ne məwlvi sahəb ko dəs rupəe peš kie./   I gave Məwlvi Sahəb ten
rupees.

/həm əllah ki ətaõ ka šwkr əda nəhĩ kər səkte./   We cannot thank God
[enough] for His bounties. [/ətaõ/ is quite rare; /ynayat/ Fpl
would be more common here.]

17.108. /əqida/ M2 "tenet, belief" almost always refers to a religious belief. /iman/
Ml "faith, belief" is more basic and inclusive; it refers to the totality of one's faith and
convictions. /əqida/ denotes only a single article of belief.

17.109. /ərəb/ Ml Al denotes both "Arabia" and "[an] Arab." It is also used as an
adjective before nouns denoting persons: e. g. /ek ərəb əwrət/ "an Arəb woman." It also
occurs as an adjective before words like /mwlk/ Ml "country," /dwnya/ Fl "world," etc.
/ərəbi/ Fl [np] Al, on the other hand, is employed as a noun denoting "Arabic" (i. e. the

Arabic language) and as an adjective before nouns denoting material objects: e.g. /ek ərəbi ghoRa/ "an Arabian horse."

17.110. /[ke] təht/ Comp Post "under, below, according to" is used only for abstract subordination: e.g. "under that king," "under my command," "under [i.e. according to] this law." It is never employed to denote spatial location: e.g. "under that table." This latter meaning is always expressed by /[ke] nice/ "under, underneath." E.g.

> /ws əfsər ke təht, calys admi kam kər rəhe hə̃y./ Under that officer there are forty men working.

> /ys hwkm ke təht, mwjhe lahəwr jana pəRega./ Under [i.e. according to] this command, I will have to go to Lahore.

17.111. /rysalət/ F1 [np] and /nəbuvvət/ [or /nwbuvvət/] F1 [np] both mean "porphet-hood" and are almost interchangeable in Urdu, although they have somewhat different connotations in Arabic. /rəsul/ M1 "prophet" is made from the same Arabic root /rysalət/ (r-s-l "to send" in Form IV; see Sec. 17.301), and /nəbi/ M1 "prophet, apostle" is similarly from the same root as /nəbuvvət/ (n-b-ʔ "to inform," through various phonetic changes too complex to be discussed profitably here). According to Islamic scholars, /rəsul/ is properly applicable only to those Prophets who have received a book of revelation from God. These are four: Moses, who was given the Torah (/torəyt/ F1), David, who was vouchsafed the Psalms (/zəbur/ F1), Jesus, who received the Gospel (/ynjil/ F1), and Muhammad to whom God revealed the Qwran (/qwran/ M1). /nəbi/, on the other hand, is a more inclusive term: it is applied to all of the Prophets, including the four just mentioned who received a "Book" and also those to whom Revelation came in other forms.

Islam teaches that there is a "chain of Prophecy," reaching from the first Prophet, Adam, to Muhammad. This chain includes all of the Prophets of the Old Testament, various non-Biblical Prophets mentioned in the Qwran, and many others not named in any of the Scriptures: " ... And Messengers We [i.e. God] have mentioned unto thee [i.e. Muhammad] before and Messengers We have not mentioned unto thee ..." (Qwran IV:164). Every nation has thus had its own Prophet in its own time, each of whom brought essentially the same Message: Islam -- submission to the Will of God. Each Prophet preached that God is one; that He alone is worthy of worship and obedience; that mankind shall believe in Him and in His Word and in His Prophets and in the Day of Judgment; that the way of life revealed by Him to His Prophets is to be followed; that things He has forbidden are to be avoided; that mankind is one under Him; that believers must pray, be charitable, love one another, etc. etc.

Each Prophet was thus a "Muslim" -- i.e. one who has surrendered his will to God -- and each of his followers was also a Muslim. Nevertheless, according to the Qwran, each people in turn tended to ignore His Message, to turn away from it, or even to slay their Prophet for tampering with the pagan beliefs of their ancestors. Thus it was that at last the Prophet Muhammad was endowed with the totality of the Message in its most complete form, and God allowed him to fulfill his mission successfully. He lived long enough to see that the Qwran was completely and irrevocably recorded by his followers in its original purity. He also gave the precepts of the Qwran practical shape in the example of his own life, and his sayings and doings are recorded in the Hədis. With him, the need for Prophecy is at an end, and no other Prophet will come until the end of time, when God will call forth all of His creatures to answer for their actions, good and evil, on the Day of Judgment.

17.112. /zəban/ [or /zwban/] F1 denotes the tongue (the organ) and also "language." One may thus speak of /wrdu zəban/ "the Urdu language," /ərəbi zəban/ "the Arabic language," etc.

17.113. In India and Pakistan the form /mwsəlman/ M1 Al is a more common designation for a member of the Islamic faith than the Arabic form /mwslym/. The origin of the /an/ in /mwsəlman/ is disputed. The student should avoid the terms "Muhammadan" (which implies to Muslims that the object of worship of this religion would be Muhammad) and "Moslem" (pronounced, according to the alphabet employed in this book as */mazləm/). The proper form is /mwslym/. The name of the religion is similarly /yslam/, rather than */ysləm/ or */yzləm/.

17.114. /həzrət/ M1 "lord, sir, master" is used as an epithet of respect before the names of Prophets, saints, and other esteemed persons. It is also sometimes found alone as a noun, and the Arabic plural, /həzrat/ Mpl, is employed for "gentlemen": e.g. one may open an address to an audience with /xəvatin əwr həzrat/.../ "ladies and gentlemen ..." [/xəvatin/ Fpl is the broken plural of /xatun/ F1 "lady."]

17.115. Muslims refer to Jesus Christ by the name /isa/ M1 [np] (عيسى).

Indian and Pakistani Christians call him /yəsu/ or /yysu/ M1 [np] (یسوع).

17.116. /ələyhyssəlam/ "on whom be peace!" is an Arabic epithet added by pious Muslims after the names of all the Prophets except the Prophet Muhammad, after whose name /səlləllaho ələyhe və səlləm/ "God's peace and blessings be upon him!" must be added. Even if one is not a Muslim, it is not polite to omit these marks of respect when discussing these revered personages with Muslims. The courtesy will be appreciated. See also Sec. 12.005.

17.117. According to Islam, the /ynjil/ F1 "Gospel" is the book vouchsafed by God to Jesus Christ. Moses, David, and Muhammad are the other three Prophets who were granted detailed Revelations to be retained in book form (see Sec. 17.111). The followers of these four great Prophets are termed /əhle kytab/ Mpl "People of the Book," and Islamic law permits a somewhat closer degree of relationship with them (e.g. Muslims can take a bride from amongst them, Muslims can eat meat killed by them, providing certain other restrictions are met, etc.) than with people outside the Judaeo-Christian tradition.

Muslims do not consider the present New Testament to be the original /ynjil/, however. According to Islam, the real /ynjil/ has been lost, and the books comprising the present New Testament are only a later, somewhat distorted record of what Christ taught, as

written down many years later by his followers. Muslims believe that Christ never claimed
to be more than another Prophet -- a man who had been given a revelation by God -- and
that the message he brought was the same as that already granted to Moses, David, etc.:
i.e. Islam. His followers, however, misunderstood and made him more than he was --
and more than he claimed to be. The giving of the final, complete Revelation to the Prophet
Muhammad was thus God's way of giving mankind another -- and final -- chance at the true
path.

17.118. /pujna/ If "to worship" is used only of acts of worship performed for
polytheistic deities and never for Muslim or Christian prayers.

17.119. /əxlaq/ M1 [np] "morals, ethics, manners, courtesy" is really a broken
plural of /xwlq/ F1 "civility, affability, politeness." /əxlaq/, however, is now employed
as a singular noun, and it also differs in gender from /xwlq/. The latter word is rather
uncommon in Urdu.

17.120. When referring to any respected person (particularly religious personages,
Prophets, saints, etc.), the honorific pronoun /ap/ is often found for "he." This is
especially true of references to the Prophet Muhammad. /ap/ is also employed for a
respected third person who is present: e.g. Məwlvi Sahəb may ask Dr. Rəhim about Mr.
Smith (who is present and listening): /kya, ap wrdu səməjhte hɔ̃y?/ "Does he understand
Urdu?"
    God is never spoken of or addressed as /ap/. Instead, the Deity is addressed as /tu/
"Thou" and is spoken of in the masculine third person singular. This, Muslims say, is to
preserve the concept of the oneness of God from any faintest hint of plurality (which would
otherwise appear if a plural verb were used honorifically). God's actions, however, are
often described with "honorific" formations: e.g. /ynayət fərmana/ "to give, grant,
bestow," etc.

17.121. /kəhlana/ "to be called; to cause to call" is originally the causative of
/kəhna/ Ic "to say, tell." /kəhlana/ is now employed mostly as an intransitive verb with
the special meaning "to be known as, to be called." Although /kəhlana/ is also occasionally
found in its expected causative sense, the double causative form /kəhlvana/ "to cause to
call, cause to say" is more frequent. E.g.
                /vw mwsəlman kəhlae./ They were called Muslims.
                /šəhr ka yy hyssa nəi dyhli kəhlata həy./ This part of the city is called
                New Delhi.
                /yy qəla lal pətthər ka bəna hwa həy. ys lie lal qəla kəhlata həy./
                This fort is built of red stone. Therefore it is called the Red Fort.

17.122. /mane/ [or /mani/] Mpl "meaning, sense, intent" is always treated as a
masculine plural, at least in more literate Urdu. It has no singular.

17.123. According to Muslim belief, the /qwran/ M1 "Qwran" (or "Koran") contains only the exact words of the Revelation given by God to the Prophet Muhammad. It must thus be distinguished from the Hədis (/hədis/ F1, broken plural /əhadis/ Fpl), which are the sayings of the Prophet Muhammad, reports of his actions, accounts of his practices and decisions, etc. Together, these two sources form the basis not only for Islamic theology and religious belief but also for the elaborate code of Islamic law (/šəriət/ F1), which embraces all aspects of legal and social legislation, matters of manners and morals, etc. The Hədis were recorded by many early Muslim scholars, and the work of collecting, grading, and commenting upon them has continued over the centuries and has resulted in a huge body of literature. Six great compendia of Hədis are now considered standard.

The Hədis also contain much information about the meaning and context of a great many Qwranic verses, and this, together with an author's own comments and interpretations, forms the content of a /təfsir/ F1 "commentary on the Qwran" (broken plural /təfasir/ Fpl). The term /təfsir/ is reserved for commentaries upon the Qwran (+ the Hədis) alone; a commentary on any other book is called /šəra/ [Arabic /šərḥ/] F1. A commentator on the Qwran is called a /mwfəssyr/ M1; a commentator upon another book is termed a /šaryh/ M1.

17.124. Some Complex Verbal Formations.

A:
    /əta/
        /[X ki tərəf se Y ko] əta hona/ to be given [by X to Y]
        /[X ko Y] əta kərna/ to give [Y to X]
    /bəyan/. [See also D.]
        /bəyan hona/ to be stated, explained, described
        /[X ko] bəyan kərna/ to explain, describe, state [X]
    /bekar/
        /bekar hona/ to be, become useless, unemployed
        /[X ko] bekar kərna/ to make [X] useless
    /dəfn/
        /dəfn hona/ to be buried, interred
        /[X ko] dəfn kərna/ to bury, inter [X]
    /gwmrah/
        /gwmrah hona/ to be, become lost, go astray, fall into error
        /[X ko] gwmrah kərna/ to lead [X] astray
    /hazyr/. [See also F.]
        /[X mẽ] hazyr hona/ to be present [in X]
        /[X ko Y mẽ] hazyr kərna/ to present [X in Y]. [As the police present a
           culprit in court.]
    /mwbtəla/
        /[X mẽ] mwbtəla hona/ to be, become involved [in X], embroiled [in X]
        /[X ko Y mẽ] mwbtəla kərna/ to embroil [X in Y]

/mwkəmməl/

    /mwkəmməl hona/ to be, become complete

    /[X ko] mwkəmməl kərna/ to complete, finish [X]

/ynayət/

    /[X ko Y] ynayət kərna, fərmana/ to present [Y to X]

B:

/təmiz/

    /[X ko Y əwr Z ki] təmiz hona/ [X] to [have the power of] discrimination [between Y and Z]

    /[X əwr Y ki] təmiz kərna/ to distinguish [between X and Y]

    /[X əwr Y mẽ] təmiz kərna/ to make a distinction [in X and Y]

/təsəvvwr/

    /[X ka] təsəvvwr kərna/ to conceive, imagine [X]

/ybadət/

    /[X ki] ybadət hona/ [X] to be worshipped

    /[X ki] ybadət kərna/ to worship [X]

/ytaət/

    /[X ki] ytaət hona/ [X] to be obeyed

    /[X ki] ytaət kərna/ to obey [X], submit oneself [to X], be obedient [to X]

/yzzət/. [See also D.]

    /[X ki] yzzət hona/ [X] to be honoured

    /[X ki] yzzət kərna/ to honour, show respect [to X]

    /[X ki] yzzət rəkhna/ to maintain the honour [of X]

/zykr/

    /[X ka] zykr hona/ [X] to be mentioned

    /[X ka] zykr kərna/ to mention, refer [to X]

C:

/hydayət/. [See also D.]

    /[X ko] hydayət kərna/ to give advice, guidance [to X]

D:

/bəyan/. [See also A.]

    /[X ko] bəyan dena/ to give a statement [to X]

    /[X ka] bəyan lena/ to take a statement [from X]. [E.g. as a court takes a statement of evidence.]

/həysiət/

    /[X ko Y ki] həysiət dena/ to give the status [of Y to X]

    /[X ko Y ki] həysiət mylna/ [X] to receive the status, rank [of Y]

/hydayət/. [See also C.]

    /[X ko] hydayət dena/ to give guidance [to X]. [The subject of this construction is usually God.]

    /[X ko] hydayət mylna/ [X] to receive guidance

    /[X se] hydayət pana/ to receive guidance [from X]

/nəbuvvət/

/[X ko] nəbuvvət dena/ to give [the power of] prophecy [to X]. [The subject
    of this construction is usually God.]

/[X ko] nəbuvvət mylna/ [X] to receive [the power of] prophecy

/[X se] nəbuvvət pana/ to receive [the power of] prophecy [from X (God)]

/rysalət/

/[X ko] rysalət dena/ to give [the power of] prophecy [to X]. [The subject of
    this construction is usually God.]

/[X ko] rysalət mylna/ [X] to receive [the power of] prophecy

/[X se] rysalət pana/ to receive [the power of] prophecy [from X (God)]

/ynam/

/[X ko Y ka] ynam dena/ to reward [X with/for Y]

/[X se] ynam lena/ to take, receive a reward [from X]

/[X ko Y se] ynam mylna/ [X] to receive a reward [from Y]

/[X se] ynam pana/ to receive a reward [from X]

/yzzət/. [See also B.]

/[X ko] yzzət dena/ to show respect, show honour [to X]

/[X ko Y se] yzzət mylna/ [X] to receive respect [from Y]

/zəban/

/[X ko] zəban dena/ to give [one's] word [to X]

F:

/əcchai/

/[X ke sath] əcchai kərna/ to do good [to X]

/əqida/

/[X ka Y pər] əqida hona/ [X] to believe [in Y (a tenet, etc.)]

/[X pər] əqida rəkhna/ to come to belief [in X], place [one's] belief [in X]

/bwnyad/

/[X ki] bwnyad Dalna, rəkhna/   to lay the foundation [of X]

/dyl/

/[X ko] dyl dena/ to give [one's] heart [to X], fall in love [with X]

/[X ka Y mẽ] dyl ləgna/ [X] to fall in love [with Y (an object or abstract, not
    a person)]

/[X se] dyl ləgana/ to form an attachment [for X]

/[X ka] dyl rəkhna/ to not disappoint [X], live up to [X's] expectation, not let
    [X] down

/dylcəspi/

/[X ko Y se] dylcəspi hona/ [X] to be, become interested [in Y]

/[X mẽ] dylcəspi lena/ to take an interest [in X]

/[X se] dylcəspi rəkhna/ to have an interest [in X]

/gwnah/

/[X se] gwnah hona/ [X] to have committed a sin

/gwnah kərna/ to sin, commit a sin

/hazyr/. [See also A.]

/[X ki xydmət mẽ] hazyr hona/ to visit, go [to see], be in attendance upon [X]

/[X ki xydmət mẽ] hazyr rəhna/ to remain in attendance upon [X]

/iman/

    /[X pər] iman lana/ to come to believe [in X]

    /[X pər] iman rəkhna/ to believe [in X], retain, hold a belief [in X]

/jhuT/

    /jhuT bolna/ to tell a lie. [This construction is treated both as transitive and as intransitive.]

/mwhəbbət/

    /[X ko Y se] mwhəbbət hona/ [X] to love, fall in love [with Y]

    /[X se] mwhəbbət kərna/ to love [X]

/myhrban/

    /[X pər] myhrban hona/ to show kindness [to X]

/səc/

    /səc bolna/ to tell the truth. [This construction is treated both as transitive and as intransitive.]

/vaqyf/

    /[X se] vaqyf hona/ to know, be acquainted [with X]

17.200. SCRIPT

17.201. Word Recognition.

(1) As was stated in Sec. 17.304, the plural suffix /əjat/ is usually written separately from the singular, and the final θ of the singular is retained. E.g.

SCRIPT	PRONUNCIATION	SCRIPT	PRONUNCIATION
علاقه‌جات	ylaqəjat	نسخه‌جات	nwsxəjat

(2) In some compounds, /xwš/ tends to be written separately from the second member; in others the opposite is found. The student must learn by observation which form is common for each compound. E.g.

خوش قسمتی	xwšqysməti	خوشخط	xwšxət

(3) The following words are written with "uncommon" Arabic consonants, with final θ = /a/, or with other special spelling conventions.

احادیث	əhadis	حیثیت	həysiət
إطاعت	ytaət	خواه	xa *either / or*
انبیاء	əmbia *prophets*	ذکر	zykr
إنعام	ynam *Reward*	ستاره	sytara
تحت	təht *under*	سعودی	səudi
تصوّر	təsəvvwr	صلّی الله علیه وسلّم	səlləllaho ələyhe və səlləm
تعلیمات	talimat	عالم	alym
تهذیب	təhzib *culture*	عبادت	ybadət
حاضر	hazyr	عراق	yraq
حدیث	hədis	عرب	ərəb
حضرت	həzrət	عربی	ərəbi

71

SCRIPT	PRONUNCIATION	SCRIPT	PRONUNCIATION
عزّت	yzzət	محبّت	mwhəbbət
عطا	əta *Bestowed*	محمّد	mwhəmməd
عقائد	əqayd	مذاہب	məzahyb
عقیدہ	əqida	مذہب	məzhəb
علاقہ	ylaqa	مذہبی	məzhəbi
علماء	wləma	مصر	mysr
علیہ السلام	ələyhyssəlam	معاملہ	mwamla
عنایت	ynayət	معلومات	malumat
عیسیٰ	isa	معنے	mane [orː معنی /mani/]
عیسائی	isai	مقاصد	məqasyd
غرضکہ	yərəzke	مقصد	məqsəd
قرآن	qwran	نبوّت	nəbuvvət
گمراہ	gwmrah *gone astray*	نظام	nyzam
گناہ	gwnah	یعنی	yani

17.202. Reading Drill I: Text.

The following is the text of Sec. 17.000. Read it aloud several times, striving for speed and accuracy.

استم :۔   میں اسلام کے بارے میں کچھ معلومات حاصل کرنی چاہتا ہوں ۔

رحیم :۔   یہ کوئی مشکل بات نہیں ۔ اسلام کے متعلق بہت سی کتابیں موجود ہیں ۔ اور

اگر آپ کسی مذہبی عالم سے ملنا چاہتے ہیں تو ایک مولوی صاحب میرے

مہربان دوست ہیں۔ ہم اُن کے پاس چل سکتے ہیں۔ یہ مولوی صاحب ہمارے

بڑے علماء میں سے ایک ہیں۔ اسلام کے علاوہ دوسرے مذاہب سے بھی

واقف ہیں۔

اسمتھ :۔ میرے لئے اِس سے بڑھ کر اور کیا خوش قسمتی ہوگی کہ میں اُن کی خدمت میں

حاضر ہو جاؤں۔

رحیم :۔ بہت اچھا۔ شام کو پانچ بجے اُن کے پاس چلیں گے۔

مولوی صاحب :۔ آئیے اسمتھ صاحب، تشریف لائیے! رحیم صاحب نے ٹیلیفون پر آپ کا

ذکر کیا تھا۔ آپ سے مل کر بڑی خوشی ہوئی۔

اسمتھ :۔ یہ آپ کی مہربانی ہے کہ آپ نے اپنا قیمتی وقت ہمیں عنایت فرمایا۔

مولوی صاحب :۔ اِس میں مہربانی یا عنایت کی کونسی بات ہے؟ ہمیں خوشی ہے کہ آپ ہمارے

ملک، تہذیب، تمدن اور مذہب سے دلچسپی رکھتے ہیں۔

اسمتھ :۔ میں اسلام کے بنیادی عقائد کے بارے میں کچھ جاننا چاہتا ہوں۔ خاص طور پر

ہندوستان اور پاکستان میں اسلام کا جو تصور ہے، اُس کے متعلق کچھ فرمائیے۔

مولوی صاحب :۔ اسلام خواہ عراق میں ہو یا سعودی عرب میں، مصر میں ہو یا شام میں۔ اِس کے

بنیادی عقائد میں کوئی فرق نہیں۔ ہمارا سب سے پہلا عقیدہ یہ ہے کہ اللہ ایک

ہے۔ اُس کا کوئی شریک نہیں۔ اُس کے علاوہ کوئی دوسرا عبادت کے لائق نہیں۔

اُس نے زمین، آسمان، چاند، ستارے، سورج، سمندر، دریا۔ غرضکہ دنیا کی ہر

چیز پیدا کی۔ دنیا کا سارا نظام اُسی کے ہاتھ میں ہے۔ چنانچہ اِس عقیدے کے

تحت ہم صرف ایک خدا کی عبادت کرتے ہیں اور اُسی سے مدد مانگتے ہیں۔

73

استھ :۔ یہ عقیدہ دنیا کے تقریباً تمام مذاہب میں پایا جاتا ہے۔

مولوی صاحب :۔ جی ہاں۔تقریباً اِسی قسم کا عقیدہ عیسائی اور یہودی مذہب میں بھی موجود ہے اور
کچھ دوسرے مذاہب میں بھی مختلف صورتوں میں ملتا ہے۔ یہ ہمارا سب سے پہلا اور
اہم ترین عقیدہ ہے۔ اس کے بعد رسالت کا تصور آتا ہے۔یعنی تمام انبیاء کی نبوّت
پر ایمان رکھنا۔ اللہ نے انسان کو پیدا کیا۔اُس کو دماغ عطا کیا تاکہ وہ ہر معاملے میں
سوچ کر قدم اٹھائے اور اچھائی اور برائی، جھوٹ اور سچ میں تمیز کر سکے۔ دل عطا
کیا تاکہ وہ خدا کی اطاعت کے علاوہ والدین، دوستوں اور پڑوسیوں کی محبت رکھ
سکے۔ زبان دی تاکہ انسان اپنا مقصد بیان کر سکے۔ لیکن انسان اِن تمام غنایات
کو بھلا بیٹھا اور گناہوں میں پھنس گیا۔ چنانچہ اللہ نے انسان کی ہدایت کے لئے
نبیوں کو بھیجا۔ اِن نبیوں کا کام یہ تھا کہ وہ لوگوں کو سیدھا راستہ دکھائیں اور
اُنہیں گمراہی سے بچائیں۔ چنانچہ ہم مسلمان اِن تمام نبیوں پر ایمان رکھتے ہیں
جو اللہ نے لوگوں کی ہدایت کے لئے بھیجے۔

استھ :۔ حضرت عیسیٰ علیہ السلام کے بارے میں آپ لوگوں کا کیا خیال ہے ؟

مولوی صاحب :۔ ہم اُن کی عزت ایک کامل انسان اور ایک بہت بڑے نبی کی حیثیت سے کرتے
ہیں لیکن ہم اُنہیں خدا کا بیٹا یا اُس کا شریک نہیں سمجھتے۔

استھ :۔ اُن کی تعلیمات کے بارے میں آپ کا کیا خیال ہے؟

مولوی صاحب :۔ حضرت عیسیٰ علیہ السلام نے بھی وہی تعلیم دی جو دوسرے نبیوں نے دی۔آپ
بھی خدا کے نبی تھے اور اُس کا پیغام انجیل کی صورت میں لائے تھے۔لیکن آپ
کے بعد دنیا پھر گمراہ ہوگئی۔اِس لئے اللہ نے اپنے آخری رسول حضرت

74

محمد صلی اللہ علیہ وسلم کو لوگوں کی ہدایت کے لئے بھیجا اور آپ پر نبوّت ختم کی۔ آپ کے بعد کوئی دوسرا نبی نہیں آسکتا۔ جس زمانے میں آپ پیدا ہوئے اُس وقت عرب کی حالت بہت خراب تھی۔ لوگ بتوں کو پوجتے تھے۔ معمولی باتوں پر آپس میں لڑتے جھگڑتے تھے۔ لڑکیوں کو زندہ دفن کرتے تھے۔ غرضکہ اِن لوگوں کا اخلاق گِر چکا تھا اور اخلاقی برائیوں میں مبتلا تھے۔

استمبر:۔ کیا اسی وجہ سے آپ کے نبی عرب میں پیدا ہوئے۔ کیونکہ عرب کی حالت دوسرے ملکوں سے زیادہ خراب تھی؟

مولوی صاحب:۔ جی ہاں، لیکن جو پیغام اللہ نے حضرت محمّد صلی اللہ علیہ وسلم کے ذریعے بھیجا اگرچہ وہ عربی زبان میں تھا لیکن صرف عرب کے لوگوں کے لئے نہیں تھا بلکہ تمام دنیا والوں کے لئے تھا۔جب بھی اللہ نے کوئی نبی بھیجا تو کسی خاص علاقے یا کسی خاص ملک کے لئے نہیں بھیجا بلکہ اُس کا پیغام تمام دنیا کے لئے تھا۔

استمبر:۔ آپ کے نبی نے کیا تعلیم دی؟

مولوی صاحب:۔ جب ہمارے نبی کو اللہ کا حکم ہوا تو آپ نے لوگوں کو اللہ کا یہ پیغام سنایا " اللہ ایک ہے۔ میں اُس کا بھیجا ہوا نبی ہوں۔ جس طرح مجھ سے پہلے بہت سے دوسرے نبی مختلف قوموں کے لئے بھیجے گئے تھے بتوں کو پوجنا بالکل بے کار ہے۔ یہ بت کچھ نہیں دے سکتے۔ صرف خدا ہی عبادت کے لائق ہے۔ لڑکیوں کو زندہ دفن کرنا بہت بڑا گناہ ہے۔ سب لوگ برابر ہیں اور آپس میں بھائی بھائی ہیں۔ جو شخص اِس دنیا میں نیک کام کرے گا اُس سے اللہ خوش ہوگا اور دوسری دنیا میں اِس کا انعام پائے گا اور جو شخص یہاں گناہ اور برائیاں کرے گا وہ

اُن کی سزا پانے لگا۔'' عرب کے لوگوں نے جو کہ دنیا کی بُری رسومات میں ڈوبے ہوئے تھے جب یہ تعلیم سنی تو جاگ اٹھے اور اپنے گناہوں پر شرمندہ ہوئے۔ شروع شروع میں ہمارے بنی کو بڑی تکالیف اٹھانی پڑیں لیکن آپ نے ہمت نہیں ہاری اور اللہ کا پیغام ہر شخص کو سنایا۔ جو لوگ ایمان لائے وہ مسلمان کہلائے اور اس مذہب کا نام اسلام رکھا گیا جس کے معنے اللہ کی اطاعت ہے ۔ چنانچہ ہم لوگ اللہ کے پیغام ── یعنی قرآن ── پر ایمان رکھتے ہیں اور حدیث یعنی حضرت محمؐد صلی اللہ علیہ وسلم کے بتائے ہوئے اصولوں پر چلتے ہیں ۔ ہم لوگوں کی آسانی کے لئے مفسرین نے قرآن اور احادیث کی تفاسیر لکھی ہیں جن سے زندگی کے ہر قدم پر مدد ملتی ہے ۔

استھ :۔ میرا خیال ہے کہ اب ہمیں اجازت دیجئے کیونکہ ہم نے آپ کا کافی وقت لیا ہے۔ انشاءاللہ پھر کسی وقت حاضر ہوں گے ۔

مولوی صاحب :۔ کوئی بات نہیں ۔ آپ ضرور تشریف لائیے ۔ یہ کتاب اپنے ساتھ لے جائیے۔ اس میں اسلام کے بارے میں تمام ضروری معلومات موجود ہیں۔ دوسرے یہ بہت آسان اردو میں لکھی ہوئی ہے ۔

استھ :۔ بہت بہت شکریہ ۔ میں انشاءاللہ اسے پہلی فرصت میں پڑھوں گا اور اگلے ہفتے آپ کی خدمت میں پھر حاضر ہونگا۔ خدا حافظ ۔

مولوی صاحب :۔ خدا حافظ ۔

17, 203. Reading Drill II: Sentences.

Read the following sentences aloud and translate them into English.

۱۔ ہمارے ایمان کے مطابق اللہ ایک ہے ۔ جس نے دنیا پیدا کی ۔ اُس کا کوئی شریک نہیں ۔ تمام دنیا کا نظام اُس کے ہاتھ میں ہے ۔ اُس نے لوگوں کی ہدایت کے لئے مختلف زمانوں میں مختلف نبی بھیجے ۔ جنہوں نے اُس کا پیغام پہنچایا ۔ محمد صلی اللہ علیہ وسلم اُس کے آخری نبی ہیں اور قرآن اُس کا مکمل پیغام ہے ۔

۲۔ میں اِن مولوی صاحب سے واقف تو نہیں ہوں ۔ لیکن رحیم صاحب نے اِن کا ذکر کیا تھا ۔

۳۔ میری بڑی خوش قسمتی ہوگی کہ میں آپ کی خدمت میں حاضر ہو سکوں ۔

۴۔ اگر کوئی شخص اللہ کی اطاعت نہ کرے اور گناہوں اور گمراہیوں میں مبتلا رہے تو وہ اُس کی سزا پائے گا ۔

۵۔ قرآن اور حدیث میں بہت فرق ہے ۔ قرآن اللہ کا پیغام ہے جو اُس نے ہمارے نبی کے ذریعے ہم تک بھیجا اور حدیث وہ بات ہے جو حضرت محمد صلی اللہ علیہ وسلم نے فرمائی ۔

۶۔ مصر کے ایک بادشاہ نے کہا تھا کہ میں ہوا کو روک سکتا ہوں ۔ سورج ، چاند اور ستاروں کی روشنی ختم کر سکتا ہوں اور سمندروں کو سکھا سکتا ہوں ۔ لیکن وہ بھی مر گیا اور اب کسی کو یہ بھی پتہ نہیں کہ وہ کہاں دفن ہے ۔

۷۔ کوئی ستر سال پہلے عراق میں چند ایسے پتھر پائے گئے جن پر عربی زبان میں ایک بادشاہ کی تعریف لکھی ہوئی ہے ۔

۸۔ اسلام کی تعلیم نے دنیا کے لاکھوں گمراہ آدمیوں کو سیدھا راستہ دکھایا ۔

۹۔ وہ مفسر کی حیثیت سے خواہ کتنے ہی مشہور کیوں نہ ہوں لیکن وہ زبان سکھانے کے طریقے نہیں جانتے ۔

77

۱۰۔ افسوس ہے کہ آپ اِس کام کے لائق نہیں کیونکہ آپ کی تعلیم بہت کم ہے ۔

۱۱۔ اُس مذہب میں ایک خدا کا تصوّر نہیں ہے۔وہ سمجھتے ہیں کہ دو خدا ہیں ۔ ایک روشنی اور دوسرا اندھیرا۔ روشنی اچھائی کا خدا ہے اور اندھیرا برائی کا خدا ہے ۔

۱۲۔ اسلام کے عقائد کے مطابق بتوں کو پوجنا ایک بہت بڑا گناہ ہے ۔

۱۳۔ ہمارے نبی کے بعد رسالت ختم ہوگئی اور اب کسی اور رسول کی ضرورت نہیں۔

۱۴۔ خواہ آپ اُن کی عزّت کریں یا نہ کریں لیکن میں اُنہیں ایک بہت بڑا عالم سمجھتا ہوں۔

۱۵۔ زندگی کے ہر معاملے میں آپ کو اپنے مذہب کے اصولوں پر چلنا چاہئے ۔

17. 204. Writing Drill I: Text.

Counting each speaker's part as one paragraph, write out the first nine paragraphs of Sec. 17. 505 (Conversation Practice) in the Urdu script (i. e. down through /... ky vw əllah ki ynayat ka šwkr əda kəre, əwr nek kam kəre. /).

17. 205. Spelling Review.

Write out the following words in the Urdu script and place them in correct Urdu alphabetical order.

(1) hafyz	(16) məzbut
(2) mwfid	(17) təsəvvwr
(3) təsvir	(18) mwkəmməl
(4) yntyzam	(19) mwfəssyr
(5) təšrif	(20) ynam
(6) mwsafyr	(21) vaqe
(7) təməddwn	(22) mwnasyb
(8) təəjjwb	(23) məwjud
(9) yttyla	(24) mwmkyn
(10) yhtiat	(25) xali
(11) mwjrym	(26) mwxtəlyf
(12) yšara	(27) šamyl
(13) tarif	(28) ystemal
(14) təhzib	(29) məsruf
(15) yntyqal	(30) mwxalyf

78

17.206. Arabic Forms.

Using Sec. 17.301 as a guide, identify each word given in Sec. 17.205 as to: (a) Arabic Form Number, (b) Verbal noun, active participle, or passive participle, and (c) type of verb (i.e. "sound," "initially weak," "medially weak," etc.) and probable root letters.

17.207. Response Drill.

Answer the following questions in writing.

۱۔ اسلام میں اللہ کا تصور کیا ہے ؟

۲۔ کیا آپ مذہبی معاملات سے دلچسپی رکھتے ہیں؟

۳۔ مولوی صاحب کے بیان کے مطابق حضرت محمد صلی اللہ علیہ وسلّم کے بعد کیا کوئی دوسرا نبی آ سکتا ہے ؟

۴۔ مفسّرین کا کیا کام ہوتا ہے ؟

۵۔ اِسلام میں اخلاق کی کیا حیثیت ہے ؟

۶۔ اخلاق میں کون کون سی چیزیں شامل ہیں ؟

۷۔ اگلی دنیا کی زندگی پر اِس دنیا کے اچھے کاموں اور برے کاموں کا کیا اثر پڑے گا؟

۸۔ اللہ نے انسان کو دل کیوں عطا کیا ؟

۹۔ مسلمانوں کے مطابق انجیل کس کو دی گئی تھی ؟

۱۰۔ مسلمانوں کے ایمان کے مطابق حضرت عیسیٰ علیہ السلام کی کیا حیثیت ہے ؟

17.208. English to Urdu Sentences.

1. I don't think that he is suitable for this job.
2. When she saw her mother on the bed, she [suddenly] screamed.
3. According to the tenets of Islam, Muhammad (God's peace and blessings be upon him!) is the last Prophet.
4. In our religion, breaking a promise is a sin.
5. In the time of that king, the basic teachings of Islam were spread, and many mosques were built

79

mosques were built.

6. No matter how much pain there may be, nevertheless this operation is necessary.

7. All the crops -- i.e. sərsõ, wheat, potatoes, etc. -- suffered a loss.

8. [One] ought to love [lit. keep love with] one's parents, friends, and neighbours.

9. I hope that you will take interest in our culture and civilisation.

10. In those countries they worship idols, and they have [deliberately] forgotten the teachings of their Prophet.

11. He was entrapped in this case because of my evidence, and no one can save him from punishment.

12. Our goal is the taking out of salt from sea water [lit. sea's water], in order that we may grow crops with that water.

13. According to the old religion of this nation, the sun is a god, the moon is his wife, and the stars are his children. Sitare

14. My gracious [lit. kind] friend, Məwlvi Sahəb, gave us his valuable time. He showed us his commentary [on the Qwran], which he has now completed.

15. The customs of this district are very strange, and no one [/koi bhi ... nəhĩ/] knows the language of these people.

— والدین ، دوستوں اور پڑوسیوں کو
پیار کرنا چاہیئے ،

— جس ملکوں میں بتوں پوجتے ہیں
انہوں نے ماں کے بنی کے اصولوں بھولا کئے
میں ،

17.301. Arabic Formations in Urdu.

Sections 17.301 through 17.307 are primarily for reference. The student should read these and familiarise himself with the basic principles of Arabic structure. Later he will find it useful to refer back to these Sections in order to more thoroughly understand various points of grammatical detail.

Although the elements of Urdu grammar introduced thus far are perhaps sufficient for most domestic conversation, the moment one turns to more sophisticated topics or to almost any written material, a knowledge of Persian and Arabic formations becomes of the utmost importance.

Arabic belongs to the Semitic language stock and is thus quite different in basic structure from Urdu (which, like English and the more familiar European languages, belongs to the Indo-European stock). All Arabic words are made by combining a "root" consisting only of consonants with a "pattern" composed of vowel and/or consonant prefixes, infixes and suffixes. A root usually consists of three consonants, although particles, etc. may consist of one or two only, and some four and five consonant roots are also found. The same root occurs with a great many patterns to produce all substantive and verbal forms. Substantives include nouns, adjectives, active and passive participles (which function both as nouns and as adjectives), "adverbs" (which are usually just nouns or noun-like words with special case endings), etc. Verbs include all tense-aspect-voice-mood-person forms of a "basic" form and up to fourteen "derived" forms (of which only eight are common).

Prefixes, infixes, and suffixes employed in the various patterns are limited in composition to the short vowels (ˊ /ə/, ˒ /y/, and ˒ /w/) and the consonants ا ,

ت /t/, س /s/, م /m/, ن /n/, و /v/, ی /y/, and ٴ /ʔ/.

ا , و , and ی also serve as long vowel signs: /a/, /u/, and /i/. All of these letters (except ا) may also serve as root consonants.

Some examples should make the root-pattern relationship clear:

ROOT $C^1 C^2 C^3$	PATTERN	WORD	MEANING
s l m	$yC^1C^2aC^3$	yslam	Islam
s l ḥ	"	yslaḥ	reform
s l m	$mwC^1C^2yC^3$	mwslym	Muslim
j r m	"	mwjrym	culprit
s l m	$təC^1C^2iC^3$	təslim	acceptance
f s r	"	təfsir	commentary
s l m	$mwC^1əC^2C^2əC^3$	mwsəlləm	accepted
r t b	"	mwrəttəb	compiled

81

The student will have little need for the inflected forms of the Arabic verb: as a rare

exception, one may cite ﻳَﻌﻨﻰ /yani/ "i.e., that is" -- lit. "he means," the 3rd msc.

sg. imperfect active indicative of Form I of the root ﻋﻨﻰ . A knowledge of the active

and passive participles of the nine common forms and of the verbal noun patterns for these

forms will be of considerable use, however, since Urdu contains hundreds of loanwords

constructed on these patterns. Patterns for the "sound" triconsonantal root are:

FORM NUMBER	ACTIVE PARTICIPLE PATTERN	SCRIPT	PASSIVE PARTICIPLE PATTERN	SCRIPT	VERBAL NOUN PATTERN	SCRIPT
I	CaCyC	فَاعِل [1]	məCCuC	مَفعُول	[unpredictable]	
II	mwCəCCyC[2]	مُفَعِّل	mwCəCCəC	مُفَعَّل	təCCiC [or]	تَفعِيل
					təCCyCa	تَفعِیَہ
III	mwCaCyC	مُفَاعِل	mwCaCəC	مُفَاعَل	mwCaCəCa [or]	مُفَاعَلَہ
					mwCaCəCət [or]	مُفَاعَلَت
					CyCaC	فِعَال
IV	mwCCyC	مُفعِل	mwCCəC	مُفعَل	yCCaC	إِفعَال
V	mwtəCəCCyC	مُتَفَعِّل	mwtəCəCCəC	مُتَفَعَّل	təCəCCwC	تَفَعُّل
VI	mwtəCaCyC	مُتَفَاعِل	mwtəCaCəC	مُتَفَاعَل	təCaCwC	تَفَاعُل
VII	mwnCəCyC	مُنفَعِل	mwnCəCəC	مُنفَعَل	ynCyCaC	إِنفِعَال
VIII	mwCtəCyC	مُفتَعِل	mwCtəCəC	مُفتَعَل	yCtyCaC	إِفتِعَال
X	mwstəCCyC	مُستَفعِل	mwstəCCəC	مُستَفعَل	ystyCCaC	إِستِفعَال

[1] The Arabic device of giving illustrations with a single triconsonantal root,

ﻓﻌﻞ f-'-l "to make, do," has been adopted here. ﻑ thus stands

for C^1 of any root, ﻉ for any C^2, and ﻝ for any C^3.

[2] Doubled consonants are underlined. Non-underlined sequences of CC denote
two different consonants: C^1C^2 or C^2C^3.

Form IX is not found in Urdu. Forms XI-XV are also so rare as to be unimportant. Words made from four consonant roots are sometimes seen, however: e.g. /sylsyla/ M2 "chain, sequence," /təsəlswl/ M1 "sequence, succession," made from the root s-l-s-l "to be in sequence."

Active and passive participles of all Forms except Form I differ only in the occurrence of /y/ or /ə/ after C^2.

Wherever alternate forms are found, the commonest is given first in the above table: e.g. /mwCaCəCa/ is more frequent than CyCaC.

With the exception of the təCCiC pattern, the genders of words made with these patterns are not predictable: e.g. /yslah/ F1 "reform" but /yslam/ M1 "Islam." All words of

the təCCiC pattern (except تَعْوِیذ /taviz/ M1 "amulet, charm") are feminine.

At one time these derived forms denoted causal, reflexive, reciprocal, etc. aspects of the verbal action. These distinctions have become blurred in Arabic itself, and thus the occurrence of a word in a given pattern can now be taken only as a very uncertain clue to its meaning. The eight common Forms originally signified:

I: Simple action, the primary meaning of the root

II: Emphatic, intensive, factitive; transitive of intransitive Form I verbs

III: Attempted reciprocity, attempting to perform the action reciprocally; denominative action

IV: Causative of Form I

V: Reflexive of Form II; action to or for oneself

VI: Reflexive of Form III; action performed upon one another; pretense at being what the root signifies

VII: Passive of Form I

VIII: Reflexive of Form I: action to or for oneself

X: Desiring, seeking, asking to perform the action of the root; performance of the action of Form I reflexively; considering something to have the quality expressed by the root

The symmetry of the derived patterns is complicated by various factors. Roots containing و , ی , or ء as root letters are treated somewhat differently from roots composed entirely of other consonants. These three letters are termed "weak" consonants, and "weak" verbs may be classified as follows: (a) "weak initial": v-C-C, y-C-C, or ʔ-C-C; (b) "weak medial": C-v-C, C-y-C, or C-ʔ-C; (c) "weak final": C-C-v, C-C-y, or C-C-ʔ; and (d) "doubly weak": v-y-C, v-C-y, y-C-v, ʔ-C-v, etc.

In the following tables, "AP" = "active participle," "PP" = "passive participle," and "VN" = "verbal noun." Whenever the form is regular (i.e. identical with those already given above), NO FORM HAS BEEN GIVEN BELOW. Instead, a dash marks the place of such "regular" forms, and the student should consult the preceding table of "sound" forms.

FORM NUMBER	INITIALLY WEAK (v-C-C, y-C-C)		MEDIALLY WEAK (C-v-C)		MEDIALLY WEAK (C-y-C)	
	PATTERN	SCRIPT	PATTERN	SCRIPT	PATTERN	SCRIPT
I: AP	--	--	CayC	فَاعِل	CayC	فَاعِل
I: PP	--	--	məCuC	مَفْعُول	məCiC	مَفْعِيل
I: VN	[unpredictable]		[unpredictable]		[unpredictable]	
II: AP	--	--	--	--	--	--
II: PP	--	--	--	--	--	--
II: VN	--	--	--	--	--	--
III: AP	--	--	--	--	--	--
III: PP	--	--	--	--	--	--
III: VN	--	--	CyaC[1]	فِيَعَال	--	--
IV: AP	muCyC	مُوعِل	mwCiC	مُعِيل	mwCiC	مُعِيل
IV: PP	muCəC	مُوعَل	mwCaC	مُعَال	mwCaC	مُعَال
IV: VN	iCaC	إِيعَال	yCaCa [or] / yCaCət[2]	إِفْعَالُ / إِفْعَالَت	yCaCa [or] / yCaCət[2]	إِفْعَالُ / إِفْعَالَت
V: AP	--	--	--	--	--	--
V: PP	--	--	--	--	--	--
V: VN	--	--	--	--	--	--
VI: AP	--	--	--	--	--	--
VI: PP	--	--	--	--	--	--
VI: VN	--	--	--	--	--	--
VII: AP	--	--	mwnCaC	مُنْفَال	mwnCaC	مُنْفَال
VII: PP	--	--	mwnCaC	مُنْفَال	mwnCaC	مُنْفَال

FORM NUMBER	INITIALLY WEAK (v-C-C, y-C-C)		MEDIALLY WEAK (C-v-C)		MEDIALLY WEAK (C-y-C)	
	PATTERN	SCRIPT	PATTERN	SCRIPT	PATTERN	SCRIPT
VII: VN	--	--	ynCiaC	إنْفِيَال	ynCiaC	إنْفِيَال
VIII: AP	mwttəCyC	مُتَّقِل	mwCtaC	مُقْتَال	mwCtaC	مُقْتَال
VIII: PP	mwttəCəC	مُتَّقَل	mwCtaC	مُقْتَال	mwCtaC	مُقْتَال
VIII: VN	yttyCaC	إتِّقَال	yCtiaC	إنْتِيَال	yCtiaC	إنْتِيَال
X: AP	--	--	mwstəCiC	مُسْتَقِيل	mwstəCiC	مُسْتَقِيل
X: PP	--	--	mwstəCaC	مُسْتَقَال	mwstəCaC	مُسْتَقَال
X: VN	ystiCaC	إسْتِيَال	ystyCaCət[2]	إسْتِيَال	ystyCaCət[2]	إسْتِفَاُت

[1] In Arabic, the pattern of the Form III verbal noun is CyyaC: e.g. قِيَام /qyyam/ (Urdu /qyam/ or /qəyam/) M1 "stay."

[2] Verbal nouns of Forms IV and X and the mwCaCəCa-mwCaCəCət alternate pattern of the Form III verbal noun all end in ة in Arabic. This has been replaced either by ‍ /a/ or by ت /ət/: e.g. /yrada/ M2 "wish, desire"; /yjazət/ F1 "permission." Nouns ending in /ət/ are almost always feminine in Urdu.

FORM NUMBER	FINALLY WEAK (C-C-v)		FINALLY WEAK (C-C-y)		INITIAL GLOTTAL STOP (ʔ-C-C)	
	PATTERN	SCRIPT	PATTERN	SCRIPT	PATTERN	SCRIPT
I: AP	CaCi[1]	فَاعِي	CaCi[1]	فَاعِي	--	--
I: PP	məCCu	مَفْعُو	məCCi	مَفْعِي	--	--
I: VN	[unpredictable]		[unpredictable]		[unpredictable]	
II: AP	mwCəCCi[1]	مُفَعِّي	mwCəCCi[1]	مُفَعِّي	--	--
II: PP	mwCəCCa[2]	مُفَعَّى	mwCəCCa[2]	مُفَعَّى	--	--
II: VN	təCCiət[3]	تَفْعِيَت	təCCiət[3]	تَفْعِيَت	--	--

85

FORM NUMBER	FINALLY WEAK (C-C-v)		FINALLY WEAK (C-C-y)		INITIAL GLOTTAL STOP (ʔ-C-C)	
	PATTERN	SCRIPT	PATTERN	SCRIPT	PATTERN	SCRIPT
III: AP	mwCaCi[1]	مُفَاعِي	mwCaCi[1]	مُفَاعِي	--	--
III: PP	mwCaCa[2]	مُفَاعَى	mwCaCa[2]	مُفَاعَى	--	--
III: VN	mwCaCat[3]	مُفَاعَات	mwCaCat[3]	مُفَاعَات	--	--
IV: AP	mwCCi[1]	مُفْعِي	mwCCi[1]	مُفْعِي	--	--
IV: PP	mwCCa[2]	مُفْعَى	mwCCa[2]	مُفْعَى	--	--
IV: VN	yCCa(ʔ)[4]	إِفْعَا (ءَ)	yCCa(ʔ)[4]	إِفْعَا (ءَ)	iCaC	إِيعَال
V: AP	mwtəCəCCi[1]	مُتَفَعِّي	mwtəCəCCi[1]	مُتَفَعِّي	--	--
V: PP	mwtəCəCCa[2]	مُتَفَعَّى	mwtəCəCCa[2]	مُتَفَعَّى	--	--
V: VN	təCəCCi[1]	تَفَعِّي	təCəCCi[1]	تَفَعِّي	--	--
VI: AP	mwtəCaCi[1]	مُتَفَاعِي	mwtəCaCi[1]	مُتَفَاعِي	--	--
VI: PP	mwtəCaCa[2]	مُتَفَاعَى	mwtəCaCa[2]	مُتَفَاعَى	--	--
VI: VN	təCaCi[1]	تَفَاعِي	təCaCi[1]	تَفَاعِي	--	--
VII: AP	mwnCəCi[1]	مُنْفَعِي	mwnCəCi[1]	مُنْفَعِي	--	--
VII: PP	mwnCəCa[2]	مُنْفَعَى	mwnCəCa[2]	مُنْفَعَى	--	--
VII: VN	ynCyCa(ʔ)[4]	إِنْفِعَا (ءَ)	ynCyCa(ʔ)[4]	إِنْفِعَا (ءَ)	--	--
VIII: AP	mwCtəCi[1]	مُفْتَعِي	mwCtəCi[1]	مُفْتَعِي	--	--
VIII: PP	mwCtəCa[2]	مُفْتَعَى	mwCtəCa[2]	مُفْتَعَى	--	--
VIII: VN	yCtyCa(ʔ)[4]	إِفْتِعَا (ءَ)	yCtyCa(ʔ)[4]	إِفْتِعَا (ءَ)	ityCaC	إِيتِعَال
X: AP	mwstəCCi[1]	مُسْتَفْعِي	mwstəCCi[1]	مُسْتَفْعِي	--	--
X: PP	mwstəCCa[2]	مُسْتَفْعَى	mwstəCCa[2]	مُسْتَفْعَى	--	--

FORM NUMBER	FINALLY WEAK (C-C-v) PATTERN	SCRIPT	FINALLY WEAK (C-C-y) PATTERN	SCRIPT	INITIAL GLOTTAL STOP (ʔ-C-C) PATTERN	SCRIPT
X: VN	ystyCCa(ʔ)[4]	إِسْتِقْعَا(ءِ)	ystyCCa(ʔ)[4]	إِسْتِقْفَا(ءِ)	--	--

[1]Active participles of all of the forms of the finally weak verbs and verbal nouns of Forms V and VI end in ٍ /yn/ when indefinite and in ِى /i/ when definite. Indefinite forms are rare in Urdu.

[2]Passive participles of all the forms of the finally weak verb end in ًى /ən/ (i.e. /əlyf məqsura/ + the indefinite ending ً) when indefinite, and in ِى (also written ُى) /a/ when definite. Only definite forms are found in Urdu.

[3]In Arabic these forms end in ة /t/. This has become ت /t/ in Urdu with only rare exceptions: e.g. تَرْبِيت /tərbiət/ F1 "upbringing, training," مُلاقَات /mwlaqat/ F1 "meeting, encounter, visit."

[4]These forms are written with a final ء in Arabic, but this is now generally omitted in Urdu: e.g. اسْتِعْفا (less commonly اسْتِعْفاء and even اسْتِعْفٰى in newspaper writing) /ystefa/ M1 "resignation," انْشا (also انْشاء) /ynša/ F1 "writing, composition."

Verbs having a medial or final glottal stop are infrequent and present no problem; they are not given in detail here. Similarly, although various forms of "doubly weak" roots occur, they are uncommon and complicated and will thus be omitted: e.g. إِلْتِوا /yltyva/ M1 "postponement," مُلْتَوِى /mwltəvi/ PA1 "postponed," both from the root l-v-y.

Still another problem is that of the "doubled verbs": roots whose second and third consonants are the same: e.g. q-r-r, ḥ-b-b, m-d-d, etc. Their forms are as follows:

FORM NUMBER	ACTIVE PARTICIPLE PATTERN	SCRIPT	PASSIVE PARTICIPLE PATTERN	SCRIPT	VERBAL NOUN PATTERN	SCRIPT
I	CaCC	فَاعّ	--	--	[unpredictable]	
II	--	--	--	--	--	--

87

FORM NUMBER	ACTIVE PARTICIPLE PATTERN	SCRIPT	PASSIVE PARTICIPLE PATTERN	SCRIPT	VERBAL NOUN PATTERN	SCRIPT
III	mwCaCC	مُفَاعَ	mwCaCC	مُفَاعَ	CyCaC	فِعَاع
IV	mwCyCC	مُفعَ	mwCəCC	مُفعَ	--	--
V	--	--	--	--	--	--
VI	mwtəCaCC	مُتَفَاعَ	mwtəCaCC	مُتَفَاعَ	təCaCC	تَفَاعَ
VII	mwnCəCC	مُنفعَ	mwnCəCC	مُنفعَ	--	--
VIII	mwCtəCC	مُفتعَ	mwCtəCC	مُفتعَ	--	--
X	mwstəCyCC	مُستَفعَ	mwstəCəCC	مُستَفعَ	--	--

All word-final doubled consonants are reduced to single consonants in Urdu, however, and thus the distinction between CVC and CVCC is lost in this environment: e.g. /xas/ Al "special" (Arabic خاص /xaṣṣ/), /mwqyr/ M/F1 "one admitting, confessing" (Arabic مُقرّ /mwqyrr/).

Still another complication occurs in combinations of a Form VIII pattern with a root beginning with ت /t/, ث /θ/ (Urdu /s/), د /d/, ذ /ḍ/ (Urdu /z/), ز /z/, ص /ṣ/ (Urdu /s/), ض /ḍ/ (Urdu /z/), ط /t/ (Urdu /t/), and ظ /z/ (Urdu /z/). The /t/ of the Form VIII pattern tends to partially assimilate to one of these consonants when the consonant occurs as C^1 of a root. The pattern is as follows:

ARABIC				URDU	EXAMPLE
ت	+	ت	= ت /tt/	/tt/	إتّبَاع /yttyba/ M1 following
ث	+	ت	= ت /tt/ or	--	[not found in Urdu]
			ثّ /θθ/		
و	+	ت	= دّ /dd/	/dd/	إدّعَا /yddea/ M1 claim
ذ	+	ت	= دّ /dd/ or	--	[not found in Urdu]
			ذّ /ḍḍ/		

88

ARABIC		URDU	EXAMPLE
ز + ت = زط /zd/		/zd/	إِزْدِحَام /yzdyham/ Ml crowd
س + ت = صط /ṣṭ/		/st/	إِصْطِلَاح /ystylah/ Fl term
ض + ت = ضط /ḍṭ/		/zt/	إِضْطِرَاب /yztyrab/ Ml disturbance
ط + ت = طّ /ṭṭ/		/tt/	إِطِّلَاع /yttyla/ Fl information
ظ + ت = طّ /ṭṭ/ or		--	[not found in Urdu]
ظّ /ẓẓ/			

17.302. The Gender of Arabic Nouns.

Arabic distinguishes two genders: masculine and feminine. Most feminine nouns (and any agreeing adjectives) end in ة . There are, however, a number of unmarked feminine nouns (e.g. حرب /ḥərb/ "war") and various feminine adjective patterns with no ة . In Urdu, this ة has become either ت /t/ or ه /a/. Nouns ending in ت /t/ are almost always feminine, and those ending in ه are masculine (unless they denote a female being). On the whole, Arabic gender distinctions have become obscured in Urdu, and only a few clear pairs can be cited which distinguish gender by the Arabic suffix ة : e.g. /valyd/ Ml "father" and /valda/ (Arabic /valyda/) Fl "mother," the masculine and feminine active participles of Form I of v-l-d "to give birth."

17.303. Case and Definiteness.

Every noun in Classical Arabic is marked for one of three cases (nominative, accusative, genitive) and for definiteness or indefiniteness. Of these forms, only the accusative indefinite ending (اً or ً /ən/) occurs in Urdu. This ending denotes an adverb; in Arabic most adverbs are simply nouns in the accusative case. All other case-definiteness endings are absent in Urdu. E.g. فَوْراً /fəwrən/ Adv "at once," تَقْرِيْبًا /təqribən/ Adv "almost," حَقِيْقَةً /həqiqətən/ Adv "in reality."

89

17.304. Number.

Arabic distinguishes three numbers: singular, dual, and plural. Neither the singular nor the dual present any problem since the former has no special ending, and the latter is found only in a few "frozen" constructions. Only the accusative-genitive form of the dual ending, /əyn/, occurs in Urdu. E.g. والدین /valdəyn/ Mpl "parents," جانبین /janybəyn/ Mpl "both sides, directions," طرفین /tərfəyn/ M/Fpl "both sides, parties, directions, etc. Dual formations are rare in Urdu, and the student need only be able to recognise them and to use the one or two which are common.

Plurals are of two types: (1) the "sound plural," which consists of suffixes added to the singular form, and (2) the "broken plural," made by combining the root with a prefix-infix-suffix pattern different from that of the singular.

Sound plurals employed in Urdu include:

(1) /in/ (from Arabic /inə/), the accusative-genitive form of the masculine sound plural; the nominative form, /unə/, does not normally occur in Urdu. /in/ is added to participles used as nouns and to "nouns of occupation" (see Sec. 17.305). Occurrences of /in/ are generally limited to literary or sophisticated styles. In less Arabicised styles, the same word will be found with an Urdu plural suffix. E.g.

حاضرین /hazyrin/ Mpl audience, people present. [Lit. present-plural, an active participle of Form I of the root ḥ-ḍ-r.]

مفسّرین /mwfəssyrin/ Mpl commentators. [/mwfəssyr/ Ml "commentator" is an active participle of Form II of f-s-r.]

مجرمین /mwjrymin/ Mpl culprits. [/mwjrym/ Ml "culprit" is an active participle of Form IV of j-r-m.]

(2) /at/, the Arabic feminine sound plural suffix, is very common in written Urdu and in more sophisticated styles of spoken Urdu also. It is added to Arabic loanwords of all sorts (including some to which it cannot be added in Arabic) and also to many purely Persian words. In Arabic, plurals in /at/ are feminine, but in Urdu they are usually of the same gender as their singular. There are, however, numerous cases of a singular of one gender having an /at/ plural of the other gender: e.g. /halət/ Fl "state, condition," but /halat/ Mpl "states, conditions." E.g.

سوالات /səvalat/ Mpl questions

تعلیمات /talimat/ Fpl teachings. [Note /talim/ Fl means "education."]

مکانات /məkanat/ Mpl buildings, houses

کاغذات /kaɣəzat/ Mpl papers, documents. [/kaɣəz/ Ml "paper"
is from Persian.

بیگمات /begmat/ Fpl ladies. [/begəm/ Fl "lady, madame" is from
Persian.]

دکانات /dwkanat/ Fpl shops. [The Arabic broken plural, دکاکین
/dəkakin/, is rare.]

Nouns ending in the Arabic feminine singular termination ة /ət/ (Urdu ت)
often replace /ət/ with /at/. E.g.

عنایات /ynayat/ Fpl bounties, favours. [/ynayət/ Fl "favour, gift,
bounty." Arabic عنایة .]

حرکات /hərəkat/ Fpl motions, acts. [/hərəkət/ Fl "action, motion,
act, movement"; Arabic حرکة .]

شکایات /šykayat/ Fpl complaints. [/šykayət/ Fl "complaint";
Arabic شکایة .]

Many Persian words denoting inanimate objects and ending in ہ /a/ (or even rarely
ending in ا) may have a plural in /əjat/. Although this formation is really a combination
of Persian and Arabic suffixes, many purely Arabic words and even a few Hindi items are
also found with an optional /əjat/ plural. Occurrences of /əjat/ are frequent in literary
Urdu, but there are dialect, class, style, and individual variations which govern its use.
In the author's experience, /əjat/ is more common in Pakistan than in India, and in the
former country it is frequently found in formal and governmental documents, etc., where
an Urdu plural might be used elsewhere. In writing, the final ہ of the singular is NOT
dropped, and جات is written separately after it. It may also be noted that many nouns
ending in ہ do not have an /əjat/ plural, but simply drop ہ and add ات directly,
and the student must thus make careful note of the permitted plurals of each word. E.g.

کرایہ جات /kyrayəjat/ Mpl rents, fares. [/kyraya/ M2 "rent, fare."]

91

مقدمہ جات /mwqədməjat/ Mpl lawsuits. [/mwqədma/ M2 "lawsuit."

Also مقدمات /mwqədmat/ Mpl.]

نسخہ جات /nwsxəjat/ Mpl prescriptions. [/nwsxa/ M2 "prescription, copy."]

ڈاکخانہ جات /Dakxanəjat/ Mpl postoffices. [Hindi-Persian ڈاکخانہ /Dakxana/ M2 "postoffice"; the /əjat/ plural occurs only in a term like "Department of Postoffices."]

سلسلہ جات /sylsyləjat/ Mpl chains, connections. [/sylsyla/ M2 "series, connection."]

درجہ جات /dərjat/ M2 ranks, positions. [Although the singular درجہ /dərja/ M2 "class, rank, position" ends in ہ , * درجہ جات does not occur.]

اشارات /yšarat/ Mpl signs, signals. [The singular is اشارہ /yšara/ M2 "sign, signal," but * اشارہ جات is not found.]

Various adjectives and predicate adjectives also occur with the ات /at/ plural, the resulting form being a noun. The genders of such nouns are not predictable. E.g.

باقیات /baqiat/ Fpl remnants, remains. [باقی /baqi/ A1 "remaining."]

معلومات /malumat/ Fpl facts, information, knowledge. [معلوم /malum/ PA1 "known."]

ممکنات /mwmkynat/ Mpl possibilities. [ممکن /mwmkyn/ A1 "possible."]

(3) Arabic "broken plurals" are very common in all types of written Urdu, and many are frequent in moderately sophisticated speech as well. Broken plurals are made by combining the root with a pattern different from that of the singular: e.g. حکم /hwkm/ M1 "order, command" is a singular noun (really a verbal noun of Form I) made with the root ḥ-k-m + the pattern CwCC. The broken plural of /hwkm/ is احکام /əhkam/ Mpl

92

"orders, commands," made on the pattern əCCaC. Unless they refer to rational beings
(i. e. things having a real sex gender), broken plurals are always treated as feminine singular
in Arabic grammar, whatever the gender of the singular form. In Urdu, however, these
forms are treated as plural, and they generally agree with their singular in gender. Thus,
whereas in Arabic /hwkm/ is masculine, /əhkam/ is grammatically treated as feminine
singular; in Urdu both forms are masculine, the former being grammatically singular and
the latter plural. There are, nevertheless, many cases of broken plurals of a gender
different from that of their singular: e.g. اطراف /ətraf/ Mpl "sides, directions" but
طرف /tərəf/ Fl "side, direction." Various broken plural forms are also used as
singulars in Urdu, sometimes with specialised meaning: e.g. اخبار /əxbar/ Ml
"newspaper" is really the plural of خبر /xəbər/ Fl "news."

There is no way to ascertain which plural pattern a given singular noun will follow, and
there are many examples of singulars with two or more broken plurals (e.g. حبيب /həbib/
Ml "friend," plural احباب /əhbab/ Mpl "friends, companions," or the less common
احبّاء /əhybba/ Mpl). It can be said, however, that certain singular patterns tend to
take certain broken plural patterns, and the student soon learns to make good guesses about
the likely plurals of new words. Since broken plural patterns are too numerous -- and
some too rare -- to be listed in full here, only the commonest will be given below. Most
Urdu dictionaries list broken plurals as separate entries, and the student should learn
these as needed.

(1) Broken plural pattern əCCaC: occurs with singulars of the patterns CyCC, CwCC,
CəCC, and with some singulars of the pattern CaCyC also. E.g.

        احكام /əhkam/ Mpl orders, commands. [حكم /hwkm/ Ml
"order, command."]

        اصحاب /əshab/ Mpl companions. [صاحب /sahəb/ -- Arabic
/sahyb/ -- Ml "friend, gentleman."]

(2) Broken plural pattern CwCuC: occurs with singulars of the patterns CyCC, CwCC,
CəCC, CəCəC, CəCyC, etc. E.g.

        علوم /wlum/ Mpl sciences. [علم /ylm/ Ml "knowledge,
learning, science."]

        حقوق /hwquq/ Mpl rights. [حق /həq/ -- Arabic /həqq/ --
Ml "right, truth."]

(3) Broken plural pattern CwCəCa(ʔ): occurs with singulars of the patterns CaCyC and CəCiC. E.g.

علما /wləma/ Mpl learned men. [عالم /alym/ M1 "learned man, scholar."]

امرا /wməra/ Mpl rich people. [امیر /əmir/ M1 A1 "rich man, rich."]

(4) Broken plural pattern əCCyCa: occurs with singulars of the pattern CəCiC (though less commonly than (3) above). E.g.

انبیاء /əmbia/ Mpl prophets. [نبی /nəbi/ -- Arabic /nəbiʔ/ becomes /nəbiy/ -- M1 "prophet." Note also the assimilation of /n/ to /m/ before /b/ in the plural form.]

اولیاء /əwlia/ Mpl saints. [ولی /vəli/ M1 "saint, guardian."]

(5) Broken plural pattern CyCaC: occurs with singulars of the patterns CəCC, CəCəC, CəCwC, and with Arabic adjectives of the pattern CəCiC. E.g.

جبال /jybal/ Mpl mountains, hills. [جبل /jəbəl/ M1 "mountain"; rare in Urdu.]

کرام /kyram/ A1 [pl] noble, benificent. [کریم /kərim/ A1 "benificent, kind." /kyram/ is employed only after a plural noun + the /yzafət/: e.g. /səhabəe kyram/ "the noble companions (of the Holy Prophet)."]

(6) Broken plural pattern CwCwC: occurs with singulars of the patterns CyCaC, CəCiC, CəCiCa, CwCCa, etc. E.g.

کتب /kwtwb/ Fpl books. [کتاب /kytab/ F1 "book."]

مدن /mwdwn/ Mpl cities. [مدینہ /mədina/ M2 "city"; rare in Urdu.]

نسخ /nwswx/ Mpl manuscripts, copies. [نسخہ /nwsxa/ M2 "copy, manuscript, prescription."]

(7) Broken plural pattern CwCCaC: occurs with singulars of the pattern CaCyC. E.g.

حکام /hwkkam/ Mpl rulers. [حاکم /hakym/ M1 "ruler."]

کفار /kwffar/ Mpl infidels. [کافر /kafyr/ M1 "infidel, unbeliever."]

94

(8) Broken plural pattern əCCyCa (with final ٥): occurs with singulars of patterns CəCiC, CəCaC, etc. E.g.

اودیہ /ədvia/ Fpl medicines. [دوا /dəva/ F1 "medicine," from a root d-v-y.]

امثلہ /əmsyla/ Fpl examples. [مثال /mysal/ F1 "example."]

(9) Broken plural pattern CəCayC: occurs with singulars of patterns CəCaC, CyCaC, CəCiC, CəCiCa, CəCuCa, CəCiCət, etc. E.g.

دلائل /dəlayl/ Fpl proofs. [دلیل /dəlil/ F1 "proof."]

رسائل /rəsayl/ Mpl treatises, tracts. [رسالہ /rysala/ M2 "treatise, tract, journal."]

حقائق /həqayq/ Fpl realities, truths. [حقیقت /həqiqət/ F1 "truth, reality."]

فرائض /fərayz/ Mpl duties. [فریضہ /fəriza/ M2 "duty, obligation"; many Urdu speakers use فرائض as the plural of

فرض /fərz/ M1, which is synonymous with فریضہ and somewhat more common.]

شرائط /šərayt/ Fpl conditions. [Used as the pl. of شرط /šərt/ F1 "condition," although it is originally the plural of شریطہ /šərita/, which is not used in Urdu.]

(10) Broken plural pattern CəvaCyC: occurs with singulars of patterns CaCyC and CaCyCa. E.g.

فوائد /fəvayd/ Mpl benefits, profits. [فائدہ /fayda/ M2 "benefit, profit."]

قوائد /qəvayd/ Mpl rules. [قاعدہ /qayda/ M2 "rule, statute, regulation."]

(11) Broken plural pattern CəCaCyC: occurs with singulars of the patterns CəCCəC, CəCCəCa, CəCCəCət, əCCəC, CwCiCət, etc. -- i.e. any singular pattern containing four consonants and a "short vowel" (/y/, /w/, or /ə/) as the last vowel (+ a final feminine suffix /a/ or /ət/). All of the consonants may be root letters, or they may include one of the

95

prefix consonants ت /t/, م /m/, or ا /ʔ/. E.g.

مساجد /məsajyd/ Fpl mosques. [مسجد /məsjyd/ F1 "mosque."

The four consonants are /m-s-j-d/, and the last vowel is /y/. The /m/ is part of a prefix-infix pattern (see Sec. 17.305), and the root letters are just s-j-d.]

مدارس /mədarys/ Mpl schools. [مدرسه /mədrəsa/ M2 "school."; the four consonants are /m-d-r-s/, the last vowel is /ə/, and the Arabic feminine ending /a/ (for /ət/) makes no difference. Again, the /m/ is part of a prefix-infix pattern, and the root is d-r-s.]

دفاتر /dəfatyr/ Mpl offices. [دفتر /dəftər/ M1 "office." The four consonants are /d-f-t-r/, and the final vowel is /ə/. This word has a four letter root.]

اكابر /əkabyr/ Mpl greatest ones. [اكبر /əkbər/ A1 "greatest." The four consonants are /ʔ-k-b-r/, and the root is k-b-r. ʔəCCəC is the comparative-superlative pattern for Arabic adjectives; see Sec. 17.307.]

جواهر /jəvahyr/ Mpl jewels. [جوهر /jəwhər/ M/F1 "gem, jewel." The four consonants are /j-v-h-r/ (/w/ = /v/), and the last vowel is /ə/. Again, this word is based on a four consonant root.]

(12) Broken plural pattern CəCaCiC: occurs with singulars CəCCiC, CəCCuC, etc. -- i.e. wherever the singular has four consonants and a "long vowel" (/i/, /u/, or /a/) (± a final feminine suffix /a/ or /ət/). As above, all of the consonants may be root letters, or they may include the prefix consonants ت /t/, م /m/, or ا /ʔ/. E.g.

سلاطين /səlatin/ Mpl sultans. [سلطان /swltan/ M1 "sultan." The four consonants are /s-l-t-n/, and the last vowel is /a/. This word is based on a four consonant root.]

تفاسير /təfasir/ Fpl commentaries. [تفسير /təfsir/ F1 "commentary"; the four consonants are /t-f-s-r/, and the last vowel is /i/. /təfsir/ is, of course, a verbal noun of Form II; all verbal nouns of this pattern have this broken plural form.]

مشاهير /məšahir/ Mpl famous persons, dignitaries, notables.

96

[مشہور /məšhur/ A1 "famous"; the four consonants are /m-š-h-r/,
and the last vowel is /u/. /məšhur/ is the passive participle of
Form I of the root š-h-r. The singular form cannot be used as a
noun in Urdu, and, conversely, /məšahir/ cannot be employed as an
adjective.]

قوانین /qəvanin/ Mpl laws. [قانون /qanun/ M1 "law"; the four
consonants are /q-v-n-n/, and the last vowel is /u/. This Greek
loanword into Arabic (the same source as English <u>canon</u>) is treated as
a four consonant medially weak /v/ verb.]

The preceding list is by no means exhaustive. Other patterns are, however, statistically
less common: e.g. احادیث /əhadis/ Fpl "traditions" (sg. حدیث /hədis/ F1 "tradition"),
حصص /hysəs/ Mpl "parts, shares" (sg. حصہ /hyssa/ M2 "part, share"), etc. The
student must learn these individually as the need arises.

The matter is further complicated by the fact that some singulars may have more than
one broken plural pattern. Generally these plurals will have the same meaning, but there
may be differences of connotation, and occasionally two broken plurals of a given word may
have rather different meanings. E.g.

اشراف /əšraf/ Mpl nobles. [Also شرفا /šwrəfa/ Mpl with the
same meaning. Both are plurals of شریف /šərif/ A1 "noble,
gracious."]

شیوخ /šwyux/ Mpl sheikhs, elders. [Also مشائخ /məšayx/ Mpl
with the same meaning. Both are plurals of شیخ /šəyx/ M1
"sheikh, elder."]

Many singulars occur with both a broken plural and a sound plural in /at/ (as well as
the expected Urdu plurals). E.g.

تفاصیل /təfasil/ Fpl details, explanations. [Also تفصیلات /təfsilat/
Fpl with the same meaning -- and also تفصیلوں , تفصیلیں
/təfsilē/ and /təfsilō/ -- all plurals of تفصیل /təfsil/ F1 "detail,
explanation."]

قصص /qysəs/ Mpl stories. [Also pronounced /qəsəs/ and /qəsys/.

97

Also قصّہ جات /qyssəjat/ Mpl with the same meaning -- and also

قصّے /qysse/ and قصّوں /qyssō/ -- all plurals of قصّہ /qyssa/

M2 "story."]

تحائف /təhayf/ Mpl gifts. [Also تحفہ جات /twhfəjat/ Mpl with the

same meaning -- and also تحفے /twhfe/ and تحفوں /twhfō/ -- all

plurals of تحفہ /twhfa/ M2 "gift."]

There are also many instances of "double plurals" -- a broken plural + /at/, etc.
Urdu plural suffixes are also sometimes added to broken plurals, although this usage is not
considered elegant in modern Urdu. E.g.

وجوہ /vwjuh/ Fpl reasons, causes. [Also وجوہات /vwjuhat/ Fpl

with the same meaning -- and also وجہیں /vəjhē/ and وجہوں /vəjhō/

-- all plurals of وجہ /vəjə(h)/ F1 "reason, cause."]

رسوم /rwsum/ Fpl manners, customs. [Also رسومات /rwsumat/

Fpl with the same meaning -- and also رسمیں /rəsmē/ and رسموں

/rəsmō/ -- all plurals of رسم /rəsm/ F1 "custom, ritual, manner."

/rəsm/ also means "connection," and in this meaning it has a broken

plural مراسم /mərasym/ Mpl "connections, relations" -- really

the plural of مرسوم /mərsum/, which is not used in Urdu.]

ادویہ /ədvia/ Fpl medicines. [Also ادویات /ədviat/ Fpl with

the same meaning -- and also دوائیں /dəvaē/ and دواؤں /dəvaō/

-- all plurals of دوا /dəva/ or دوائی /dəvai/ F1 [or F2]

"medicine."]

علماؤں /wləmaō/ Mpl [MOP] religious scholars. [E.g. in a

sentence like /həmare wləmaō ka xyal həy .../ "It is the opinion of

our religious scholars ..." Such a broken plural + an Urdu plural is

sometimes found but is not encouraged by modern stylists.]

17. 305. Other Arabic Patterns.

Arabic consonantal roots also combine with various other patterns to give specific meanings. Some of these are:

(1) The noun of place or time, formed on the patterns məCCəC, məCCyC, məCCəCa, or məCCyCa. E. g.

موقع /məwqa/ M2 occasion, opportunity. [Also commonly written

موقعه . From v-q-' "to fall, befall. "]

مسجد /məsjyd/ F1 mosque. [From s-j-d "to prostrate oneself. "]

مدرسہ /mədrəsa/ M2 school. [From d-r-s "to study"; Arabic

مدرسة .]

مکتب /məktəb/ M1 elementary school. [From k-t-b "to write. "]

(2) The noun of instrument, formed on the patterns myCCiC, məCCyCa, myCCaC. E. g.

مفتاح /myftah/ F1 key. [From f-t-ḥ "to open": "an instrument for

opening. "]

میزان /mizan/ F1 balance, pair of scales. [From v-z-n "to weigh. "]

(3) The emphatic noun and the noun of profession, formed on the patterns CəC̲C̲aCa and CəC̲C̲aC. E. g.

علّامہ /əllama/ M/F1 most learned scholar. [From '-l-m "to know. "]

طبّاخ /təbbax/ M1 cook. [From ṭ-b-x "to cook. "]

دلّال /dəllal/ M1 broker. [From d-l-l "to guide, direct. "]

مدّاح /məddah/ M1 one who praises much, panegyrist. [From

m-d-ḥ "to praise. "]

(4) The diminutive, formed on the pattern CwCəyC, is rare in Urdu. E. g.

حسین /hwsəyn/ M1 Hwsəyn (proper name). [From ḥ-s-n "to be

beautiful, handsome": "little handsome one. "]

(5) The comparative-superlative patterns are differentiated for gender: əCCəC is the

masculine form, and CwCCa (with a final ی) is used for the feminine. Although these

forms are adjectives in Arabic, they are used as proper names in Urdu, or in the Persian /yzafət/ formation (Sec. 18.302) in highly literary styles. E. g.

خَقِيقَتِ كُبْرٰى /həqiqəte kwbra/ the greatest reality. [The root k-b-r "to

be big, large" is used with the feminine pattern CwCCa -- feminine

because /həqiqət/ F1 "reality" is feminine. /e/ is the Persian

/yzafət/, used to connect a modifier to its preceding noun.]

مَشْرِقِ وَسْطٰى /məšryqe vwsta/ the Middle East. [The root is v-s-ṭ "to

be middle, central."]

اَكْبَر /əkbər/ M1 A1 Akbar; the greatest. [The masculine pattern

əCCəC is used with the root k-b-r "to be big, large" as a proper

name and also sometimes following the /yzafət/.]

اَعْلٰى /ala/ A1 superior. [The root '-l-y "to be high, great" + the

pattern əCCəC should = */ə'ləy/, but this is realised in Urdu as /ala/.

This word is widely employed as an adjective.]

اَكْثَر /əksər/ A1 Adv most, the majority, mostly, most often.

[The root is k-θ-r "to be many, numerous."]

(6) Although the Arabic cardinal numerals do occur in Urdu, they are of several

patterns and need not be given in detail here. The ordinal numerals, however, are all of

the pattern CaCyC except "the first," which is اَوَّل /əvvəl/ A1 in the masculine and

اُولٰى /ula/ A1 in the feminine. Only a few Arabic ordinals are found in Urdu, often

with the names of kings, etc. E. g.

مُحَمَّد ثانی /mwhəmməd sani/ Muhammad [the] Second. [/sani/ A1

"second" is from the root θ-n-y "to be two."]

مُحَمَّد خامِس /mwhəmməd xamys/ Muhammad [the] Fifth. [/xamys/ A1

"fifth" is from x-m-s "to be five."]

(7) The pattern for multiplicative numerals is the same as for the passive participle

of Form II; mwCəCCəC. E. g.

مُثَلَّث /mwsəlləs/ M1 A1 triangle, triangular, three sided. [The

root is θ-l-θ "to be three."]

مُرَبَّع /mwrəbba/ M2 A1 square, four-sided. [The root is r-b-'

100

"to be four."]

مسدّس /mwsəddəs/ M1 A2 hexagon, six-sided, a form of poetry composed in six-line stanzas. [The root is s-d-s "to be six."]

(8) Arabic fractions are of the pattern CwCC (except "one half," which is نصف /nysf/ M1 A1). E.g.

ثلث /swls/ M1 one third

خمس /xwms/ M1 one fifth

ربع /rwba/ M1 A1 one fourth

(9) Abstract nouns of quality are made with the adjective formant /i/ + /ət/. These are feminine. E.g.

انسانيت /ynsaniət/ F1 [np] humanity. [From انسانی /ynsani/ A1 "human" from انسان /ynsan/ M1 "human being, person."]

کیفیت /kəyfiət/ F1 quality. [From کیف /kəyfə/ Adv "how?"]

(10) Names of sciences, school subjects, etc. are made with /i/ + the sound plural suffix /at/. These are treated as singular, however, in Urdu. E.g.

لسانیات /lysaniat/ F1 [np] linguistics. [From لسان /lysan/ F1 "tongue, language."]

اقتصادیات /yqtysadiat/ F1 [np] economics. [From the verbal noun of Form VIII of q-ṣ-d, اقتصاد /yqtysad/, which is not used alone in Urdu.

سیاسیات /syasiat/ F1 [np] political science. [Cf. سیاست /syasət/ F1 "politics."]

17.306. Arabic Prepositions.

Some common Arabic prepositions are من /myn/ "from," علٰی /əla/ "on, upon," عن /ən/ "from, about, concerning," لِ /ly/ "to, for," ب /by/ "with, by," إلٰی /yla/ "to, towards," فی /fi/ "in," حتّٰی /hətta/ "until," مَع /ma/ "with," etc.

Most of these are found only in Arabic phrases borrowed as complete units into Urdu. E.g.

101

منتقل الیہ /mwntəqəl yləyh/ M/F1 [person] to whom [something] has been transferred. [الی /yla/ and علی /əla/ become /yləy/ and /ələy/ before the various pronominal suffixes; in Classical Arabic this would be /yləyhy/ "to him," but in Urdu (as in the modern Arabic dialects) the final short vowel is dropped.]

من جیث المجموع /myn həysylməjmu/ Adv on the whole. [Lit. from the position of the whole.]

حتّی الامکان /həttəlymkan/ Adv so far as possible. [Lit. up to the possibility.]

Only فی /fi/ "in" has any truly independent existence in Urdu. It occurs as a preposition with many nouns and denotes "per." E.g.

فی سال /fi sal/ per year

فی روز /fi roz/ per day

فی گھنٹہ /fi ghənTa/ per hour

17.307. Other Arabic Formations.

Literary Urdu abounds in borrowed Arabic constructions, but aside from those discussed above, these are either uncommon or else can be treated as individual vocabulary items without resorting to an analysis of roots and patterns. The Arabic definite article has already been treated in Sec. 10.012.

17.308. Substantive Composition: Compounds With /xwš/.

/xwš/ PA1 "happy" occurs as the first member of many compounds. These are generally antonyms of formations with /bəd/ A1 "bad" (in compounds "un-, dis-, non-"); see Sec. 9.302. Compounds of /xwš/ + a following Arabic- or Persian- derived noun are grammatically adjectives. Formations possible from the vocabulary introduced thus far include:

/əxlaq/ M1 morals, ethics	/xwšəxlaq/ A1 well-mannered, courteous
/fykr/ F1 thought, worry	/xwšfykr/ A1 well-thinking, having a healthy, positive approach
/hal/ M1 state, condition	/xwšhal/ A1 prosperous
/myzaj/ M1 nature, disposition	/xwšmyzaj/ A1 good-natured
/qysmət/ F1 fortune, destiny	/xwšqysmət/ A1 having good fortune

/təbiət/ F1 nature, disposition   /xwŝtəbiət/ A1 good-natured

/xət/ M1 letter, script   /xwŝxət/ A1 one having beautiful handwriting

As with formations made with /be/, /bəd/, and /na/, abstract nouns are made from
the above adjectives by the addition of the suffix /i/. E. g.

/xwŝəxlaqi/ F2 [np] well-manneredness, courtesy

/xwŝqysməti/ F2 [np] good fortune

17. 309. /xa/ "Whether."

/xa/ Conj occurs at the beginning of the "whether" clause. The "or" clause may be
introduced by another /xa/ or by /ya/ Conj "or." The resultative clause may begin with
/lekyn/ Conj "but, " or it may have no introductory conjunction. When followed by /kytna
hi/ or /kytna kyõ nə ho/, /xa/ may be translated as "no matter ..." E.g.

/yy ciz, xa mẽhgi ho ya səsti, mẽy zərur xəridūga./ This thing, whether
expensive or inexpensive, I will certainly purchase.

/xa ap mere sath cəlẽ, ya nə cəlẽ, ys se koi fərq nəhĩ pəRta./ Whether
you go with me or do not go, it makes no difference. [Lit. ... from
this no difference befalls.]

/xa ap jəhaz se jaẽ ya rel se, kyraya wtna hi hoga./ Whether you go by
ship or by rail, the fare will be just as much.

/xa yy kam ws ne kia, ya kysi əwr ne, mera məqsəd pura ho gəya./
Whether he did this task or somebody else, my objective has been
attained.

/xa ap kəl aẽ ya nə aẽ, lekyn yy kytab mwjhe zərur mylni cahie./
Whether you come tomorrow or not [lit. or do not come], nevertheless [lit. but] I must certainly get this book.

/xa vw mere sath kytni hi dwŝməni kərẽ, lekyn mẽy wn ke sath koi bwrai
nəhĩ kərūga./ No matter how hostile he may be to me [lit. may do
enmity with me], nevertheless [lit. but] I will do him no harm.

/xa yy kam kytna hi mwŝkyl kyõ nə ho, mẽy zərur kərūga./ No matter
how difficult this task may be, I will certainly do it.

17. 310. The Verb: Two Semantically Similar Main Verbs.

The use of two semantically similar nouns to denote intensiveness and a vague
inclusiveness of concept has been discussed in Secs. 3. 110 and 15. 301. Two present
participles, infinitives, etc. can be similarly employed, sometimes with the same
intensive-inclusive connotations and sometimes with rather divergent meanings. These
constructions are limited to certain pairs of semantically similar verbs and to the participles
(etc.) of a simplex verb followed by its causative (for a similar usage for the past participles
(see Sec. 16. 303). E. g.

/vw apəs mẽ həmeŝa ləRte jhagəRte rəhte hãy./ They are always
quarrelling [and] fighting together.

/ys qysm ke ləRkõ mẽ wThna bəyThna əccha nəhĩ./ It is not good to
remain in the company of this sort of boys. [Lit. to stand up -- sit
down. This has much the same connotation as the American expression
"to hang around with. "]

/mə̃y əwr ysmyth sahəb əksər ykhəTTe khate pite the./ Mr. Smith and
I usually used to dine together. [Lit. used to eat -- drink. The
whole concept is thus included.]

/mə̃y wn ke hã əksər ata jata rəhta hũ./ I usually visit their place. [Lit.
keep on coming -- going.]

/vw pəRhne mẽ məsruf rəhta həy, əwr kysi se mylta mylata nəhĩ./ He
remains busy in studying and doesn't meet anybody. [Lit. does not
meet -- cause to meet.]

17.311. The Verb: the < S + /wThna/ > Construction.

Another compound verb formation is the < S + /wThna/ > construction. This is rather
limited in occurrence, being found mainly with verbs denoting speaking, crying, screaming,
etc. It has connotations almost identical with those of the < S + /pəRna/ > formation (Sec.
15.309): suddenness, violence, and intensity. It occurs mostly in the past tenses but may
sometimes be found in present or future formations. Like other compound verbs, it does
not occur in negative sentences. So far as could be determined, this formation can occur
only with the following verbs of those introduced so far: /bolna/ "to speak," /cixna/ "to
scream, cry out," /jagna/ "to wake up," /jəlna/ "to burn," and /pwkarna/ "to call."

It is important to note that the < S + /wThna/ > construction is always treated as
intransitive: in the past tenses the subject of this formation is NOT marked by /ne/, even
when the main verb is otherwise transitive. E.g.

/bəcca kwtte ko dekh kər cix wTha./ The child [suddenly] screamed on
seeing the dog.

/mə̃y pəRəwsiõ ka šor swnte hi jag wTha./ The moment I heard the
neighbours' noise, I woke up.

/vw kylas mẽ əcanək bol wTha./ He suddenly spoke up in class.

/myTTi ka tel Dalte hi, ag fəwrən jəl wThi./ The moment [he] poured
the kerosene, the fire at once blazed up. [Lit. burn-arose. This
might also be considered a conjunct verb.]

/vw əksər swba səvere jag wThta həy./ He generally gets up early in
the morning. [I.e. suddenly wakes up. This also might be considered
a conjunct verb: "wake-gets up."]

/gaõvale həmẽ dekhte hi mədəd ke lie pwkar wThe./ The villagers cried
out for help the moment they saw us. [Although /pwkarna/ la "to call,
cry out to" is a transitive verb, its subject is not marked by /ne/ in
this formation.]

17.312. The Verb: the < S + /bəyThna/ > Construction.

Still another compound verb formation is the < S + /bəyThna/ > construction. Although
the distribution of this formation is also rather limited, it is more widespread and common
than the < S + /wThna/ > form just discussed above, and it can occur with a greater number
of main verb stems. The < S + /bəyThna/ > formation is found mainly in past tense forms,
although future and present forms also occur. Like the < S + /wThna/ > formation, it is
always intransitive, and in the past tenses its subject is not marked by /ne/. It cannot be
employed in negative sentences.

This construction has several rather different connotations: (a) action by error,

(b) action by force to obtain an undeserved goal, (c) completed action (equivalent to the < S + /cwkna/ > construction; Sec. 9.309). E. g.

/vw hər roz meri dwkan pər a bəyThta həy. /　He comes to my shop every day. [He forces his presence upon me.]

/dwšmən ki fəwj səməjh bəyThi thi, ky həm kəmzor hɐ̃y. /　The army of the enemy thought that we were [lit. are] weak. [They mistakenly thought that we were weak -- and they have suffered for their blunder.]

/vw ys mwamle mɛ̃ γələti kər bəyTha. /　He made a blunder in this affair.

/əgər yyhi hal rəha, to vw ek dyn ys mwlk ka badšah bən bəyThega. /　If this same state continues, one day he will become king of this country. [I. e. He will illegally and wrongfully usurp power.]

/vw meri avaz swnte hi wTh bəyTha. /　He woke right up on hearing my voice.

/mɐ̃y to puri košyš kər bəyTha, lekyn kam nəhĩ bəna. /　I made every effort, but the work didn't get done. [Completed action.]

17.313.　Casus Pendens.

When one or more unrelated or parenthetical clauses separate an element from the rest of its clause, a pronoun or demonstrative referring to that element and in apposition to it may be inserted at some later point in the sentence in order to maintain clausal (or phrasal) unity. The element thus separated is, in effect, "left hanging" with no grammatical function except that of apposition. E. g.

/yslam, xa yraq mɛ̃ ho, ya səudi ərab mɛ̃, mysr mɛ̃ ho, ya šam mɛ̃ -- ys ke bwnyadi əqayd mɛ̃ koi fərq nəhĩ. /　Islam, whether [it] be in Iraq or in Saudi Arabia, in Egypt or in Syria, -- in its basic tenets there is no difference.

In this example, /yslam/ is brought first in order to connect the sentence to the preceding context. A clause (or series of clauses) beginning with /xa/ Conj "whether" must be placed either at the beginning of the sentence or else just after some emphasised element. These clauses interfere with the usual cohesion of the possessive phrase (i. e. /yslam ke bwnyadi əqayd mɛ̃/ "in the basic tenets of Islam"). The demonstrative /ys/ "this" is thus inserted to complete the possessive phrase, and /yslam/ is left to "hang" in apposition at the beginning of the sentence.

In some cases, a whole clause may assume the character of a "casus pendens"; such clauses usually contain a relative pronoun or relative adjective, however, which has its correlative in the following clause. E. g.

/hyndostan əwr pakystan mɛ̃, yslam ka jo təsəvvwr həy, ws ke mwtəəllyq kwch fərmaie! /　That concept of Islam which is [found] in India and Pakistan; please say something about that! [The correlative of /jo/ is /ws/, which refers to the totality of the relative clause.]

/jys zəmane mɛ̃ ap pəyda hwe, ws vəqt ərab ki halət bəhwt xərab thi. /　In that age in which he was born, at that time the condition of Arabia was very bad. [/ws vəqt/ refers to the /jys zəmane mɛ̃/ clause.]

17.401. Supplementary Vocabulary.

The following numerals are all Type I adjectives. See Sec. 2.401.

chyasəTh	sixty-six
səRsəTh	sixty-seven
əRsəTh	sixty-eight
wnhəttər	sixty-nine
səttər	seventy

Other items are:

bwnyad F1	basis, foundation
*məqasyd Mpl [pl. /məqsəd/]	goals, aims, objectives
rəsm F1	custom, practice
təfsir F1	commentary [on the Qwran or Hədis]

17.402. Supplementary Exercise I: Substitution.

1. ys gaõ mẽ   cəvaly s   mwsəlman əwr   pəndra   isai rəhte hə̃y.

44

sixty-eight ar Sath	sixty-seven Sarseth	
seventy Sat	sixty-six	
forty-nine	fifty-four	
sixty-nine Unsal	sixty-four chonSat	
thirty-eight	sixty-eight	

2. kya, ap ys rəsm   ke bare mẽ kwch jante hə̃y?

this commentary

the basis of this law

the goals of education

these old customs

these commentaries

17.500. VOCABULARY AND GRAMMAR DRILL

17.501. Substitution.

1. mẽy yslam   ke bare mẽ kwch malumat hasyl kərni cahta hū.
        your religion
        your basic tenets
        these religions
        the teachings of Muhammad
        Saudi Arabia

2. ws zəmane mẽ, hyndostan   əxlaqi bwraiõ   me ınwbtəla tha.
                   Syria   religious quarrels
                   Egypt   evil customs
                   my friend   fever
                   the whole   heresy
                   country
                   man [kind]   sins

3. məwlvi sahəb qwran ke cənd hysse   swna rəhe the.
        some Traditions
        a part of his commentary
        a Tradition of Muhammad
        the command of God
        some moral stories

4. yy profesər sahəb   həmari təhzib   se dylcəspi rəkhte hẽy.
        Islam
        the civilisation of India
        the Arabic language
        our culture and customs
        the teachings of the Qwran

5. ws mwfəssyr ne yslam ke bwnyadi əqayd   bəyan kie.
        officer   the Government's goals[1]
        scholar   the meaning[s] of "faith"
        American   the principles of agriculture
        professor
        lawyer   all the events[2]
        person   the circumstances of the
                          life of Christ[3]

    [1]Use the Arabic plural, made on the pattern CəCaCyC.

    [2]The /at/ plural of /vaqea/ is /vaqəyat/ Mpl.

    [3]For "circumstances," use /halat/ Mpl.

6. ap ne əpne bəyan mẽ ys təfsir   ka zykr kyõ nəhĩ kia.
        God's bounties

107

```
                              that language
                              his virtues  haki yon
                              the last Prophet
                              his rank  hassiat
   7.  ap   yn xydmat         ka ynam paẽge.
           your labour
           your virtues
           obedience     forma badaar
           your bravery
           this kindness
   8.  ys   nyzam   ke təht,   bəhwt si yələtiā      hwi hõy.
           order                religious education   has spread
           tenet                all the idols         have been broken
           principle            a new government      has been made
           promise              this aid              has been given
           concept              Pakistan              has been made
   9.  mõy   ys ylaqe               se vaqyf nəhī hū.
           those scholars
           this commentary
           your parents
           Syria
           the civilisation of America
  10.  wnhõ ne  əpne məzhəb         ke bare mẽ kwch batẽ bətaī.
           the sun and moon
           the Prophets
           the stars
           the worship of God
           prophethood
  11.  yy qəwm  əpne rəsul ki talimat        bhwla bəyThi həy.
           its culture
           the message of the Qwran
           its ancient civilisation
           its language and culture
           the distinction between
           [lit. of] truth and falsehood
  12.  kəl mõy   məwlvi sahəb            ki xydmət mẽ hazyr ho jaũga.
           the lawyer[1]
           that scholar
           their parents
           that Jewish professor
           the village elder[1]
```

[1]Since this word is the title of a specific respected person, it should be
followed by /sahəb/.

13. aj vw   <u>buRha admi</u>   dəfn kia gəya həy.
            Christian
            Arab
            Muslim
            tailor
            farmer

14. yy <u>ylaqa</u>   <u>šam</u>   kəhlata həy.
       country   Egypt
       religion   Islam
       game   football
       city   Lahore
       food   pwlao

15. əllah ne ynsan ko   <u>zəban</u>   əta ki.
                       voice
                       honour
                       intellect
                       life
                       this virtue

17.502. Transformation.

1. Change the underlined Urdu plural nouns in the following sentences to the corresponding Arabic "broken plural" forms. The relevant consonants of the Arabic singular and the proper broken plural pattern are given at the end of each sentence. [Note: ' = the Arabic letter /ayn/; ? = the glottal stop (/həmza/); the pharyngealised consonants /ṣ, ḍ, ṭ, ẓ/, the two interdental fricatives /ḍ/ and /θ/, and the pharyngeal /ḥ/ are transcribed according to Urdu pronunciation (i.e. /s, z, t, z, z, s, h/) rather than according to Arabic pronunciation or the Arabic script. For correct spelling, see Sec. 17.201.

a.   log <u>dəftərō</u> se vapəs a rəhe həy. [/d-f-t-r/; CəCaCyC]
b.   ws vəqt log <u>məsjydō</u> mē nəmaz pəRh rəhe the. [/m-s-j-d/; CəCaCyC]
c.   əyse <u>məwqe</u> bar bar nəhī̃ ate. [/m-v-q-'/; CəCaCyC]
d.   qwran ki bəhwt si <u>təfsirē</u> lykhi gəi həy. [/t-f-s-r/; CəCaCiC]
e.   am ki bəhwt si <u>qysmē</u> həy. [/q-s-m/; əCCaC]
f.   yy <u>təsvirē</u> bəhwt pwrani malum hoti həy. [/t-s-v-r/; CəCaCiC]
g.   hwkumət ne pychle məhine kəi nəe <u>qanun</u> jari kie həy. [/q-v-n-n/; CəCaCiC]
h.   baryš ke bəhwt se <u>fayde</u> həy. [/f-y-d/: CəvaCyC, which becomes CəvayC here.]
i.   həmē vəhā̃ bəRi <u>təklifē</u> wThani pəRī̃. [/t-k-l-f/; CəCaCiC]
j.   davət ke bad, dostō ko kwch <u>twhfe</u> peš kie gəe. [/t-h-f/; CəCayC]
k.   həmare <u>alymō</u> ka kəhna yy həy, ky həmare nəbi pər rysalət xətm ho gəi. [/'-l-m/; CwCəCa(?)]
l.   hər ynsan ko <u>yəribō</u> ki mədəd kərni cahie. [/γ-r-b/; CwCəCa(?)]
m.   ys kam ke bwre <u>nətijō</u> se twm nəhī̃ bəc səkoge. [/n-t-j/; CəCayC]

109

n. yy kam kyn kyn <u>zəriõ</u> se kia ja səkta həy. [/z-r-'/; CəCayC; final /ay'/ = Urdu /ae/.]

o. təmam <u>nəbiõ</u> ne dwnyavalõ ko əxlaqi talim di. [The student may treat this word as though the root were /n-b-y/; see Sec. 17.111. /nb/ = Urdu /mb/.]

p. ys sal badšah ne kwch nəe <u>hwkm</u> jari kie hə̄y. [/h-k-m/; əCCaC]

q. məwlvi sahəb ke <u>xət</u> əb tək mere pas ate rəhte hə̄y. [/x-t-t/; CwCuC]

r. əyse <u>mərz</u> səfai ki mədəd se kəm ho səkte hə̄y. [/m-r-z/; əCCaC]

s. ws ne yslam se mwtəəllyq təmam <u>ylm</u> hasyl kie. [/'-l-m/; CwCuC]

t. ys ke bad, <u>vəkilõ</u> ne apəs mẽ bəhs šwru ki. [/v-k-l/; CwCəCa(ʔ)]

u. twmhẽ əpne <u>fərz</u> əda kərne cahiẽ. [/f-r-z/; CəCayC]

v. ys rəsid ki dəs <u>nəqlẽ</u> cahiẽ. [/n-q-l/; CwCuC]

w. əbhi əbhi xəbər ai həy, ky dwšmən ki <u>fəwjẽ</u> age bəRh rəhi hə̄y. [/f-v-j/; əCCaC]

x. yy <u>kytabẽ</u> zərur bhej dijie! [/k-t-b/; CwCwC]

y. meri šadi mẽ bəhwt si pwrani <u>rəsmẽ</u> əda ki gəĩ. [/r-s-m/; CwCuC + /at/]

2. Change the underlined Urdu plural nouns in the following sentences to Perso-Arabic plural forms ending in /at/ or /əjat/. The numeral "1" after the singular form indicates that the plural is made with /əjat/; "2" denotes that /ət/ in the singular form is replaced with /at/ in the plural; no numeral signifies that /at/ is added directly to the stem (minus any Type II affix).

a. səylab se, <u>məkanõ</u> ko bəhwt nwqsan pəhw̃ca.

b. yy xəbər təmam <u>əxbarõ</u> mẽ thi.

c. mə̄y ws ki <u>hərəkətõ</u>[2] se tə̄g a gəya hū̃.

d. yn <u>səvalõ</u> ke jəvab lykhie!

e. yn <u>mwqədmõ</u> ke fəysle əbhi tək nəhĩ hwe.

f. twmhari <u>šykayətẽ</u>[2] swnte swnte tə̄g a gəya hū̃.

g. mə̄y ne ədalət mẽ əpni zəmin ke <u>kaɣəz</u> peš kie.

h. ws ke sər pər əbhi tək coT ke <u>nyšan</u> baqi hə̄y.

i. hwkumət yn <u>ylaqõ</u>[1] mẽ talim phəylani cahti həy.

j. vw yn <u>mwamlõ</u> mẽ ap ki mədəd kər səkte hə̄y.

k. mwxtəlyf məzahyb mẽ, əllah ke bare mẽ mwxtəlyf <u>təsəvvwr</u> mylte hə̄y.

l. ys kytab mẽ, bəhwt se mwfid <u>nwsxe</u>[1] hə̄y.

m. ys <u>šəhr</u> mẽ, bəhwt si nəi <u>ymartẽ</u>[2] bən rəhi hə̄y.

n. yn <u>ynayətõ</u>[2] ke lie əllah ka šwkr əda kərna cahie.

o. wn ke <u>bəyanõ</u> ke mwtabyq, vw əb tək zynda həy.

p. qwran mẽ, yn <u>ybadətõ</u>[2] ka zykr kia gəya həy.

q. yn <u>kyrayõ</u> ki kwl rəqəm jəma kəro!

r. vw meri <u>hydayətõ</u>[2] pər nəhĩ cəla. ys lie wse nwqsan wThana pəRa.

s. jo šəxs ys pəhaR pər səb se pəhle cəRhega, wse kəi <u>ynam</u> mylẽge.

t. həmẽ jo <u>yttylaẽ</u> myli hə̄y, wn ke mwtabyq səylab se əRsəTh həzar rupəe ka nwqsan hwa həy.

3. Change the underlined verb forms in the following sentences to the < S + /wThna/ > construction. Retain the same tense and aspect. The instructor will discuss the connotations of each example.

a. šor nə məcao, vərna vw <u>jag jaega</u>!

b. mə̃y ne əbhi bat bhi puri nə ki thi, ky vw <u>bol pəRa</u>.

c. bəcca bap ko dekhte hi xwši se <u>cix pəRa</u>.

d. tel pəRte hi, cyraɣ <u>jəlne ləga</u>.

e. vw həmẽ dur se dekh kər <u>pwkarne ləga</u>.

f. vw meri avaz swnte hi <u>jag gəya tha</u>.

g. vw əyse məwqe pər <u>bol pəRa</u>, jəb ky wse bolna nəhĩ cahie tha.

h. mynTõ mẽ sara məkan <u>jəl gəya</u>.

i. ag dekhte hi, log <u>pwkarne ləge</u>.

j. məriz dərd se <u>cixne ləga</u>.

4. Change the underlined verb forms in the following sentences to the < S + /bəyThna/ > construction. Change any oblique subject + /ne/ to a nominative form since the < S + /bəyThna/ > construction is always intransitive. Retain the same tense and aspect. The instructor will discuss nuances of connotation.

a. mə̃y to yy <u>səmjha tha</u>, ky əb ap nəhĩ aẽge.

b. ws ne ɣələti se məwlvi sahəb se yy səval <u>pucha</u>.

c. əgər twm meri hydayət pər nəhĩ cəloge, to ys mwamle mẽ zərur ɣələti <u>kəroge</u>.

d. mə̃y ne wse hər jəga təlaš <u>kia</u>, məgər vw kəhĩ nəhĩ myla.

e. yn logõ ne əllah ke pəyɣam ko <u>bhwla dia həy</u>.

f. ws ne əpne bap ki sari zəmin <u>bec di</u>.

g. ws ne yskul mẽ daxyl hone se pəhle hi sari kytabẽ <u>xərid lĩ</u>.

h. ws ne səb ke samne yy bat <u>kəh di thi</u>.

i. maf kijie, mə̃y ne ɣələti se ap ka xət <u>khol lia həy</u>.

j. mə̃y ne sari kytab <u>pəRh li</u>, lekyn mwjhe ys mẽ koi xas bat nəzər nəhĩ ati.

k. əb to mə̃y ne <u>xərid lia həy</u>, məgər aynda ap ki dwkan se koi səwda nəhĩ xəridũga.

l. ws ki yy bat swn kər, mwjhe ɣwssa a gəya, əwr mə̃y ne wse <u>mara</u>.

m. ap ne jyn kytabõ ka zykr kia həy, mə̃y ne vw səb <u>pəRh li hə̃y</u>.

n. vw bəhwt bevwquf həy, ky ws ne ytni əcchi nəwkri <u>choR di həy</u>.

o. jyn kaɣəzat ki ap ko təlaš həy, mə̃y ne wnhẽ ɣələti se <u>phaR dia həy</u>.

17.503. Variation.

1. vw log dwnya ki bwri rwsumat mẽ Dube hwe the.

   vw log gwnahõ əwr bwraiõ mẽ Dube hwe the.

   vw qəwm ləRai jhəgRõ mẽ mwbtəla thi.

   vw xandan mwqədmat əwr dusre mwamlat mẽ phãsa hwa tha.

   vw zəxmi bəhwt bwri halət mẽ pəRa hwa tha.

   vw mwfəssyrin qwran ki təfsir pər məsruf the.

2. yy səc həy, ky vw ys nəwkri ke layq nəhĩ.

   səc to yy həy, ky vw kysi kam ke layq nəhĩ.

   yy səc həy, ky ys kam ke lie vw bəhwt layq admi həy.

   yy səc həy, ky əllah ke ylava koi dusra ybadət ke layq nəhĩ.

yy sac həy, ky həzrət mwhəmməd səlləllaho ələyhe və səlləm əllah ke axyri rəsul hə̃y.

yy sac nəhĩ, ky ws qəwm ka əxlaq gyr cwka həy.

3. ys se bəRh kər, əwr kya xwši ho səkti həy.

ys se bəRh kər, əwr kya təklif hoti!

ys se bəRh kər, mə̃y mwsəlmanõ ke lie əwr kya kər səkta hũ.

ys se bəRh kər, vw əwr kya yzzət hasyl kər səkte hə̃y!

ys se bəRh kər, ap ko əwr kya ynam cahie.

ys se bəRh kər, mə̃y wse əwr kya kəhta.

4. xa vw kytni hi xubsurət kyõ nə ho, lekyn mə̃y ws ke sath šadi nəhĩ kərũga.

xa vw kytna hi bevwquf kyõ nə ho, lekyn vw yy bat xub janta həy.

xa ws ki həysiət kwch bhi nə ho, lekyn ws mẽ bəhwt si xubiã hə̃y.

xa vw aẽ, ya nə aẽ, lekyn kəl mere hã davət zərur hogi.

xa təsvir mwkəmməl həy ya nəhĩ, mə̃y wse dekhna cahta hũ.

xa ap kam kərẽ, xa ap bekar bəyThe rəhẽ, mere lie donõ surtẽ bərabər hə̃y.

5. həmare məzhəb, təhzib, təməddwn, γərəzke pakystan ki hər ciz se wse dylcəspi həy.

jəb mə̃y jəvan tha, mə̃y ne yəhudiõ, isaiõ, mwsəlmanõ, γərəzke dwnya ke hər məzhəb ke wləma se bəhs ki.

məwlvi sahəb qwran, hədis, tarix, γərəzke hər ws ylm se vaqyf hə̃y, jo yslam se mwtəəllyq həy.

mə̃y ne mysr, šam, səudi ərəb, yraq, γərəzke hər ərəb mwlk dekha həy.

ys sal, gəndwm, sərsõ, dal, γərəzke hər fəsl baryš nə hone ki vəja se təbah ho gəi.

jəb mə̃y pakystan pəhw̃ca, mwjhe pətlunẽ, šəlvarẽ, qəmisẽ, γərəzke hər qysm ke kəpRe xəridne pəRe.

6. wnhõ ne ws məwqe pər jhuT bola.

ap ne həmare bare mẽ kyõ jhuT bola.

həmare nəbi ne kəbhi jhuT nəhĩ bola.

jhuT bolne ke xylaf bəhwt si əhadis məwjud hə̃y.

jhuT bolna həmari nəzər mẽ ek bəRa gwnah həy.

jys ke dyl mẽ jhuT həy, vw səhih təwr pər mwsəlman nəhĩ ho səkta.

7. ap ko jhuT əwr sac mẽ təmiz kərni cahie.

ys mwamle mẽ, ap ko əcchai əwr bwrai mẽ təmiz kərni cahie.

ynsan ko sidhe əwr gwmrahi ke raste mẽ təmiz kərni cahie.

kya, ap ko səhih əwr γələt ki təmiz nəhĩ?

ajkəl mə̃y ytna məsruf hũ, ky mə̃y dyn əwr rat ki təmiz nəhĩ kər səkta.

jo səfai əwr gəndəgi mẽ təmiz nəhĩ kər səkta, vw ynsan nəhĩ -- janvər həy.

8. mə̃y pərsõ ws alym ki xydmət mẽ hazyr ho jaũga.

jənab, mə̃y hər vəqt ap ki xydmət mẽ hazyr rəhna cahta hũ.

mwjrym ədalət mẽ hazyr nəhĩ tha.

vw ləRka ajkəl kylas mẽ hazyr nəhĩ hota.

mwlk ke bəRe bəRe wləma badšah ke samne hazyr kər die gəe.

ek roz aega, jəb ky əllah ke samne hazyr ho kər, həmē əpne gwnahõ ka jəvab dena pəRega.

9. wnhõ ne həmē əpna qimti vəqt ynayət fərmaya.

əllah ne ynsan ko dyl əwr dymaɣ ynayət fərmaya.

məwlvi sahəb ne mwjhe əpni təfsir ka ek nwsxa ynayət fərmaya.

əllah ne məwlvi sahəb ko ek beTa ynayət fərmaya.

mere bəRe bhai sahəb ne mwjhe əpni zəmin ka ek hyssa ynayət fərmaya.

myhrbani kər ke, do dyn ke lie mwjhe əpni kapi ynayət fərmaie!

10. yy həmare byhtərin dostõ mē se ek hõy.

yy pakystan ke məšhur wləma mē se ek hõy.

yy məšryq ki əhəmtərin kytabõ mē se ek həy.

həzrət isa ələyhyssəlam bəRe əmbia mē se ek hõy.

nəmaz həmare bwnyadi əqayd mē se ek həy.

mysr ərəb mwlkõ mē se ek həy.

11. vw bwraiõ əwr gwnahõ mē phɔ̄s gəya həy, əwr əb nəhĭ bəc səkta.

yy qəwm ləRai jhəgRõ mē phɔ̄si hwi həy, əwr ys ke bwre ənjam se nəhĭ bəcegi.

vw əysi bwraiõ mē phɔ̄s gəya həy, ky wse koi nəhĭ bəca səkta.

vw dhũē se bhəre hwe kəmre mē phɔ̄s gəya, əwr wse koi bhi nə bəca səka.

bəcce ka hath botəl mē phɔ̄s gəya, əwr wse koi nəhĭ nykal səka.

ws zəmane mē, ərəb bwri rwsumat mē phɔ̄se hwe the, əwr wnhē bəcana həmare
      rəsul hi ka kam tha.

12. əllah ke nəbiõ ne kəbhi hymmət nəhĭ hari.

həmara yskul fwTbal mē kəbhi nəhĭ harta.

həmara kalyj bəhs ke mwqable mē har gəya. [1]

vw ws mwqədme mē har gəya.

mɔ̄y ne təqribən sari rəqəm khel mē har di.

vw əpni sari dəwlət ysi khel mē har bəyTha.

[1]/harna/ is optionally treated as intransitive when there is no direct object.

13. səb nəbiõ ne yyhi pəyɣam swnaya, ky əllah ek həy.

nəmbərdar sahəb ne yy pəyɣam swnaya, ky həm səb bhai bhai hõy.

wnhõ ne yy pəyɣam swnaya, ky bwtõ ko pujna bekar həy.

rəsulõ ne yy pəyɣam swnaya, ky əllah ne surəj, səməndər, sytare, vəɣəyra pəyda
      kie.

həzrət mwhəmməd səlləllaho ələyhe və səlləm ne vwhi pəyɣam swnaya, jo dusre
      nəbiõ ne ap se pəhle swnaya tha.

məwlvi sahəb ne cənd əhadis swnaĭ, jynhõ ne logõ ke dylõ pər bəhwt əsər kia.

14. mɔ̄y ne əbhi səudi ərəb ka zykr šwru hi kia tha, ky vw bol wTha.

mɔ̄y ne wnhē səmjhana šwru bhi nəhĭ kia tha, ky vw donõ phyr ləR pəRe.

mɔ̄y ne ws ke valyd sahəb ka xət əbhi xətm bhi nəhĭ kia tha, ky vw cix wTha.

mɔ̄y ne əpni bat mwkəmməl bhi nəhĭ ki thi, ky vw cix wThi.

əbhi swba hone bhi nə pai thi, ky mɔ̄y jag wTha.

15. vw əpne məzhəb se bəhwt mwhəbbət rəkhta həy.

113

vw əpne valdəyn se bəhwt mwhəbbət kərta həy.

vw log ek dusre se bəhwt mwhəbbət kərte hə̄y.

mwjhe ws se mwhəbbət ho gəi həy.

mwjhe wrdu zəban se bəhwt mwhəbbət həy.

wse əpne valdəyn, bəhn, bhai, -- yani səb ghərvalō se bəRi mwhəbbət həy.

17.504. Response.

1. kya, ap ne yslam ke bare mē koi kytab pəRhi həy?
2. kya, yslam ke bwnyadi əqayd ap ke məzhəb ke əqayd se bəhwt mwxtəlyf hə̄y?
3. ap ke məzhəb ke mwtabyq, əllah ki ytaət zəruri həy, ya nəhī̃.
4. həzrət mwhəmməd səlləllaho ələyhe və səlləm se pəhle, ərəb ki kya halət thi.
5. qwran kys zəban mē həy.
6. ap ke məzhəb ke mwtabyq, əllah ka pəyɣam ynsan ko kəyse myla.
7. vw log, jo qwran əwr rysalət pər iman rəkhte hə̄y, kya kəhlate hə̄y.
8. əllah ke bare mē ap ka kya təsəvvwr həy.
9. kya, ap əpne məzhəb ke ylava, dusre məzahyb se bhi vaqyf hə̄y?
10. məzhəbi talimat ke təht, ek ynsan ko kya kərna cahie.
11. ap ke xyal mē, dwnya ki gwmrahi ka kya ylaj ho səkta həy.
12. kya, ap mysr ki pwrani təhzib ke bare mē kwch jante hə̄y?
13. kya, ap əpne mwlk ki pwrani rwsumat ko bekar səməjhte hə̄y?
14. wrdu sikhne se ap ka kya məqsəd həy.
15. kya, ap pakystani təhzib se dylcəspi rəkhte hə̄y?

17.505. Conversation Practice.

Mr. Smith calls on Məwlvi Sahəb again the following week.

MS: kya, ap ne vw kytab pəRhi thi, jo mə̄y ne pychle həfte di thi?

S: ji hã, bəhwt dylcəsp thi. ys kytab mē yslam ke bwnyadi əqayd ke sath sath baz dusri cizō ka bar bar zykr kia gəya həy, jəyse əxlaq vəɣəyra.

MS: əxlaq həmare məzhəb ka bəhwt əhəm hyssa həy. qwran əwr əhadis mē əksər ys ka zykr aya həy. ek dəfa həmare nəbi se kysi šəxs ne pucha, ky yslam kya həy, to ap ne fərmaya, "əxlaq."

S: əxlaq mē kəwn kəwnsi cizē šamyl hə̄y.

MS: əxlaq mē hər vw ciz šamyl həy, jo rozana ki zyndəgi se mwtəəllyq həy. mysal ke təwr pər, səc bolna, jhuT, cori, əwr dusri bwraiõ se bəcna, valdəyn əwr bəRõ ki yzzət kərna, choTõ se mwhəbbət rəkhna, ɣəribõ ki mədəd kərna -- ɣərəzke xwd nek kam kərna, əwr dusrõ ko nek kam kərne ki hydayət kərna.

S: vaqəi, əgər yn əxlaqi xubiõ ka xyal rəkha jae, to zyndəgi byhtər bən səkti həy.

MS: ji hã. baz kam əllah ke lie kie jate hə̄y, jəyse nəmaz pəRhna, ybadət kərna, vəɣəyra. dusre əyse kam hə̄y, jo am zyndəgi mē ek dusre ynsan ke lie kie jate hə̄y, jəyse ek dusre ki mədəd kərna, pəRəwsiõ ka xyal rəkhna, vəɣəyra.

S: kya, ap ke hā mərne ke bad zyndəgi ka koi təsəvvwr həy?

MS: ji hā. həmare iman əwr əqayd ke mwtabyq, ys dwnya ki zyndəgi syrf cənd dynõ ki həy. dərəsl zyndəgi vwhi zyndəgi həy, jo mərne ke bad mylegi. jo šəxs ys zyndəgi mẽ nek kam kərega, vw əgli dwnya mẽ ys ka ynam paega. əwr jo bwre kam kərega, vw əpni bwraiõ ki səza paega. cwnāce ynsan ko cahie, ky vw əllah ki ynayat ka šwkr əda kəre, əwr nek kam kəre.

S: zəra əhadis ke bare mẽ kwch fərmaie!

MS: hədis ka mətləb vw bat həy, jo həmare nəbi ne fərmai. yn batõ mẽ am zyndəgi ke hər mwamle pər rəwšni Dali gəi həy. mysal ke təwr pər, ap ne fərmaya, ky jo šəxs əllah ke raste mẽ xərc kərega, vw əgli dwnya mẽ ys se zyada paega. -- ya jəyse ap ne fərmaya, jo šəxs səc bolega, nek kam kərega, valdəyn ki ytaət kərega, vw əccha phəl paega. həmare nəbi mwxtəlyf məwqõ pər əysi batẽ fərmaya kərte the, əwr wnhẽ log yad kər lete the, ya lykh lete the. ys təra yy təmam batẽ həm tək pəhw̃c gəĩ.

S: kya, ap ko yəqin həy, ky qwran əwr əhadis wsi surət mẽ məwjud hɔ̃y, jys surət mẽ vw ws zəmane mẽ məwjud the?

MS: ji hā. əllah ka šwkr həy, ky əllah əwr ws ke rəsul ka pəyyam wsi surət əwr wsi zəban mẽ əb tək məwjud həy, jys surət əwr jys zəban mẽ vw dia gəya tha. aj bhi log həzarõ əwr lakhõ ki tadad mẽ qwran ko yad kərte hɔ̃y. ysi təra həzarõ wləma əyse məwjud hɔ̃y, jynhẽ təmam əhadis yad hɔ̃y.

S: kya, ap nəmaz ərəbi zəban mẽ pəRhte hɔ̃y, ya əpni zəban mẽ.

MS: həm nəmaz wsi zəban mẽ pəRhte hɔ̃y, jys zəban mẽ həmare nəbi pəRha kərte the. həmare bəccõ ko yskul mẽ daxyl kərane se pəhle, qwran əwr nəmaz ki talim di jati həy. ys ke ylava, yskulõ mẽ bhi yy təmam cizẽ sykhai jati hɔ̃y.

S: bəhwt xub. mera xyal həy, ky əb mwjhe yjazət dijie. ynšaəlla[h] phyr kysi vəqt hazyr ho jaũga.

MS: bəhwt əccha. xwda hafyz.

17.506. Conversation Stimulus.

Topics may include the following:
1. A visit to a religious scholar.
2. Islam.
3. One's own religion.
4. Man's social duty: manners, customs, morals.
5. The Qwran and Hədis.

Broken plurals will be listed as they occur.   They will be preceded by an asterisk and will not be counted as new vocabulary items.   Plurals and duals in /at/, /əjat/, /əyn/, and /in/ will be listed only when there is something noteworthy about their gender, number, or usage.

alym M1	learned man, scholar
axyri [common: /axri/] A1	last, final
əcchai F2	goodness, merit, virtue
*əhadis Fpl	pl. /hədis/
əhəmtərin A1	most important
ələyhyssəlam [epithet added after the names of all the Prophets except the Prophet Muhammad]	on whom be peace!
*əmbia Mpl	pl. /nəbi/
*əqayd Mpl	pl. /əqida/
əqida M2	tenet, belief
ərəb M1 A1	Arabia, Arab
ərəbi F2 [np] A1	Arabic, Arabian
əRsəTh A1	sixty-eight
əta F1	giving, benefaction, bounty
əxlaq M1 [np]	morals, ethics, manners, courtesy
əxlaqi A1	moral, ethical, relating to courtesy or manners
bəcana [C: /bəcna/: IIc]	to save, rescue, cause to escape
bəyan M1	explanation, statement, declaration, description
bekar A1	useless, futile, invalid, meaningless, unemployed
bhwlana [C: /bhulna/: IIc]	to (deliberately) forget
bwnyad F1	basis, foundation
bwnyadi A1	basic, fundamental
bwt M1	idol, image, statue
chyasəTh A1	sixty-six
dəfn PA1	buried, interred
dwnyavala M/F2	person of the world
dyl M1	heart
dylcəspi F2	interest, fascination
Dubna [IIc: /w/]	to sink, be submerged, drown
gwmrah A1	erring, lost, astray
gwmrahi F2	being astray, misguidedness, error, heresy
gwnah M1	sin
yərəzke [or /yərzeke/] Conj	in short
harna [IIIa: /ə/]	to lose (a game, war, courage, etc.)

hazyr PA1	present, attendant, in attendance
hədis F1	Tradition, a recorded saying or act of the Prophet Muhammad
həysiət F1	position, status, rank
həzrət M1	lord, sir, master (title of respect)
hydayət F1	guidance, direction
hyndostan [or /hyndwstan/] M1 [np]	India
iman M1	faith, belief
isa M1 [np]	Jesus
isai [common: /ysai/] M1 A1	Christian
jhəgəRna IIa	to quarrel
jhuT M1	lie, falsehood
kəhlana [C: /kəhna/: Ic; used both as a causative and as an intransitive]	to be called; to cause to be called
[ke] layq A1 Comp Post	suitable, proper, worthy, fit, capable; worthy of, fit for, suitable for
malumat Fpl [no sg.]	knowledge, facts, information
mane [or /mani/] Mpl [no sg.]	meaning, sense, intent
*məqasyd Mpl	pl. /məqsəd/
məqsəd M1	goal, aim, objective
məwlvi M1	Muslim religious scholar
*məzahyb Mpl	pl. /məzhəb/
məzhəb M1	religion
məzhəbi A1	religious
mwamla [common: /mamla/] M2	affair, matter, dealing
mwbtəla PA1	fallen into, suffering from, involved in, embroiled in
mwfəssyr M1	commentator (on the Qwran and Hədis)
mwhəbbət F1	love, affection
mwhəmməd M1 [np]	Muhammad
mwkəmməl A1	complete, perfected, finished
mwsəlman M1 A1	Muslim
myhrban M/F1 A1	kind, friendly, gracious
mysr M1 [np]	Egypt
nəbi M1	prophet, apostle
nəbuvvət [or /nwbuvvət/] F1 [np]	prophethood, apostleship
nyzam M1	administration, system, order, arrangement
phə̃sna [IIc: /ə̃/]	to be caught, trapped, snared, entangled
pujna [If: /w/]	to worship (as an idol)
qəwm F1	nation, tribe, people, race
qimti A1	valuable, precious
qwran M1	The Qwran, "Koran"
rəsm F1	custom, practice
rəsul M1	prophet
*rwsumat [or /rwsum/] Fpl	pl. /rəsm/

rysalət Fl [np]	prophethood
səc Ml [np]	truth
səlləllaho ələyhe və səlləm [epithet added only after the name of the Prophet Muhammad]	God's peace and blessings be upon him!
səməndər Ml	sea, ocean
səRsəTh Al	sixty-seven
səttər Al	seventy
səudi Ml Al	Saudi
surəj Ml	sun
swnana [C: /swnna/: Ic]	to relate, tell, cause to hear
sytara M2	star
šam Ml [np]	Syria
*talimat Fpl	teachings [pl. /talim/ Fl "education"]
*təfasir Fpl	pl. /təfsir/
təfsir Fl	commentary on the Qwran and Hədis
[ke] təht Comp Post	under, below, according to
təhzib Fl	culture
*təkalif Fpl	pl. /təklif/
təməddwn Ml	civilisation
təmiz Fl [np]	discrimination, discernment, distinction
təsəvvwr Ml	concept, idea, conception
valdəyn [literary: /valydəyn/] Mpl	parents
vaqyf PAl	acquainted with, knowing
*wləma Mpl	pl. /alym/
wnhəttər Al	sixty-nine
xa Conj	whether
xwšqysməti F2 [np]	good fortune
yani Conj	i.e., that is ...
yəhudi Ml Al	Jew, Jewish
ybadət Fl	worship, devotion
ylaqa M2	region, area, district
ynam Ml	reward, prize
ynayət Fl	favour, gift, benefaction, boon
ynjil Fl	The Gospels
yraq Ml [np]	Iraq
yslam Ml [np]	Islam
ytaət Fl	obedience, submission
yzzət Fl	honour, dignity, respect
zəban [or /zwban/] Fl	tongue, language
zykr Ml	mention, reference

Calligraphic mosaic tile work from the
Vazir Khan Mosque, Lahore, built in 1634.

UNIT EIGHTEEN

18.000. CONVERSATION

Mr. Smith has come again to call on Məwlvi Sahəb.

duties, obligations Mpl [pl. /fərz/]	fərayz

S: Please tell me something today about the duties of Islam.

mwjhe aj yslam ke fərayz ke bare mē kwch bətaie.

meeting, encounter, visit Fl	mwlaqat
Islamic Al	yslami
person, creature, being; humble self M2	bənda
fixing, determination, constancy; declaration; peace, tranquility Ml [np]	qərar
pillars, members Mpl [pl. /rwkn/ Ml "pillar, member"]	ərkan
Confession of Faith; phrase, sentence M2	kəlma [literary: /kəlyma/]
fasting M2	roza
pilgrimage Ml	həj
"Zəkat": poor-rate, compulsory tithe Fl [np]	zəkat
Rəmzan ["Ramadan"]: the ninth month of the Islamic calendar Ml	rəmzan [or /rəməzan/]
Mecca M2 [np]	məkka
given, bestowed, granted Al	ətakərda

MS: During [our] last meeting, I alluded to [lit. made a sign towards] the Islamic obligations. The meaning of "duties!" is [lit. are] those tasks which God has made obligatory upon His creatures. There are five important Pillars of Islam: the Confession of Faith, prayer, fasting, pilgrimage, and Zəkat. The meaning of the Confession of Faith is this, that every Muslim believe in his heart that God is One, and Muhammad (God's peace and blessings be upon him!) is His Prophet. The second duty is to pray five times in each day. The third duty is to keep the fast for a whole month during the month of Rəmzan. The fourth and fifth duties are once in [one's] life to go to Mecca for the pilgrimage, and to pay [lit. take out] the Zəkat from the property given by God [lit. from God's given property].

pychli mwlaqat ke dəwran, mɛ̄y ne yslami fərayz ki tərəf yšara kia tha. fərayz ka mətləb vw kam hɛ̄y, jo əllah ne əpne bəndɔ̄ pər zəruri qərar die. yslam ke pāc əhəm ərkan hɛ̄y. kəlma, nəmaz, roza, həj, əwr zəkat. kəlme ka mətləb yy hɛy, ky hər mwsəlman dyl se iman rəkhe, ky əllah ek hɛy, əwr həzrət mwhəmməd səlləllaho əleyhe və səlləm ws ke rəsul hɛ̄y. ek dyn mē pāc vəqt nəmaz pəRhna dusra fərz hɛy. rəmzan ke məhine mē, pure ek məhine ke roze rəkhna tisra fərz hɛy. wmr mē ek dəfa həj ke lie məkke jana, əwr əllah ke ətakərda mal mē se zəkat nykalna, cəwthe əwr pācvē fərayz hɛ̄y.

for example Adv	məslən [literary: /məsələn/]
face, appearance, image, manner, shape, form, figure, aspect, case Fl	šəkl

S: Are all these five things obligatory upon every Muslim? For example, if someone does not have such a sum that he can go to Mecca, then in this case what is the command for him?

kya, yy pācŏ cizē hər mwsəlman pər fərz hǝy? məslən əgər kysi ke pas ytni rəqəm nə ho, ky vw məkke ja səke, to ys šəkl mē ws ke lie kya hwkm həy.

compulsory, incumbent, necessary, requisite PA1

lazym

except for Comp Post

[ke] syva [or /syvae ... ke/]

compulsion, constraint, helplessness; compelling circumstance, factor which compels F2

məjburi

strength, power, energy, ability, force F1

taqət

trip, journey, travel M1

səfər

option, discretion, choice, adoption, authority, jurisdiction M1

yxtiar

question, matter, problem M2

məsla [literary: /məsyla/]

MS: The first three duties are obligatory upon every Muslim, and these are not waived [lit. forgiven] under any circumstance, except for one or two compelling exigencies. But the pilgrimage and the Zəkat are obligatory only upon that Muslim who has the power to perform them. For instance [lit. just as] if some Muslim is poor and cannot under-take the journey to Mecca, then the pilgrimage is not obligatory upon him. And the question of Zəkat is exactly the same.

pəhle tin fərayz hər mwsəlman pər lazym həy, əwr yy kysi bhi surət mē maf nəhĩ, syvae ek do məjburiŏ ke. lekyn həj əwr zəkat syrf ws mwsəlman pər fərz həy, jo yn ko əda kərne ki taqət rəkhta ho. jəyse əgər koi mwsəlman γərib həy, əwr məkka ka səfər yxtiar nəhĩ kər səkta, to ws pər həj fərz nəhĩ. əwr ysi təra zəkat ka məsla həy.

S: Is the Zəkat given according to any special rate?

kya, zəkat kysi xas hysab se di jati həy?

cash, ready money M1 [np] A1

nəqd

per, in Prep

fi

hundred, century F2

sədi

compulsory, incumbent, necessary, requisite A1

lazmi

gold M2 [np]

sona

silver F2 [np]

cādi

jewellery, ornament M1

zevər

fixed, settled, established, appointed A1

mwqərrəršwda

MS: Yes. The Zəkat is paid on various things according to various rates. For example, on cash money the payment [lit. taking out] of Zəkat [at the rate of] two and a half percent is compulsory. In the same way, upon other property such as gold and silver jewellery, etc., a fixed portion is paid out as Zəkat.

ji hā. mwxtəlyf cizŏ pər zəkat mwxtəlyf hysab se əda ki jati həy. məslən, nəqd rupəe pər Dhai fi sədi zəkat nykalna lazmi həy. ysi təra dusre mal, jəyse sone əwr cādi ke zevər vəγəyra mē se, ek mwqərrər-šwda hyssa zəkat ke təwr pər nykala jata həy.

S: To whom is the property or money of the Zəkat given, and how is it employed?

zəkat ka mal ya rupəya kyse dia jata həy, əwr kəyse ystemal mē laya jata həy.

orphan M1

yətim

other, another A1

digər

122

crippled, handicapped A1   mazur

helpless, compelled, constrained A1   məjbur

right, lot, due, portion; truth, righteous-   həq
ness; God; true M1 A1

gentlemen, companions Mpl [pl. /sahəb/]   əshab

separate, distinct, apart from A1 Adv   ələyhda

department M2   məhkma

gathered, collected, accumulated A1   jəməšwda

rightful claimant, one having a right   həqdar
M/F1

aid, assistance F1   ymdad

MS: The Zəkat property is the right of the poor, the orphans, and other handicapped and helpless people. In the time of our Prophet and his companions, there was a separate department for the Zəkat. People used to deposit [lit. caused to collect] the sum of [their] Zəkat in this department, and from this accumulated sum aid was given [lit. used to be caused to arrive] to the poor and other rightful claimants.   zəkat ka mal γəribō, yətimō, əwr digər mazur əwr məjbur logō ka həq həy. həmare nəbi əwr wn ke əshab ke zəmane mē, zəkat ka ek ələyhda məhkma tha. log zəkat ki rəqəm ys məhkme mē jəma kəra dete the, əwr ys jəməšwda rəqəm se γəribō əwr dusre həqdarō ko ymdad pəhw̃cai jati thi.

conditions, stipulations Fpl [pl. /šərt/ F1 "condition, stipulation, wager, bet"]   šərayt

S: What conditions are necessary for the fast, and what is the method of it?   roze ke lie kəwn kəwnsi šərayt zəruri hə̄y, əwr ys ka kya təriqa həy.

intention, resolve F1   niət

to set (sun), to hide [IIc: /w/]   chwpna

as much as possible, as many as possible Adv   zyada se zyada

MS: Like prayer, the fast is obligatory upon every Muslim man and woman. The method of it is this, that about an hour before the rising [lit. going out] of the sun, [one] should eat and make [one's] intention to fast, and [then] eat [or] drink nothing the whole day, and in the evening immediately after the setting [lit. hiding] of the sun [one] should break [lit. open] the fast. During the fast [one] should not do any bad thing or sin, and at night [one] should worship God as much as possible.   roza bhi nəmaz ki təra hər mwsəlman mərd əwr əwrət pər fərz həy. ys ka təriqa yy həy, ky surəj nykəlne se təqribən ek ghənTa pəhle khana khae, əwr roze ki niət kəre, əwr sara dyn kwch nə khae pie, əwr šam ko surəj chwpne ke fəwrən bad, roza khole. roze ke dəwran, koi bwrai ya gwnah nə kəre, əwr rat ko zyada se zyada əllah ki ybadət kəre.

importance F1 [np]   əhmiət

social, societal, pertaining to society A1   mwašrəti

S: Aside from their religious importance, what is the social importance of these Pillars?   məzhəbi əhmiət ke ylava, yn ərkan ki mwašrəti əhmiət kya həy.

request, petition, humble statement F1   ərz

society M2   mwašra

eastern A1   məšryqi

western A1   məγrybi

white, light-complexioned A2	gora
member, pillar M1	rwkn
side, facet, aspect M1	pəhlu
benefits, advantages Mpl [pl. /fayda/]	fəvayd
hungry A2	bhuka
thirsty A2	pyasa
feeling, perception, realisation M1	yhsas
to cause to give; to cause, create, occasion [C: /dena/: Ic]	dylana
oneself, by oneself Adv	əpne ap
perceived, felt, sensed, realised PA1	məhsus
luxury, sensuality M1 [np]	əyš
to pass [If: /ə/]	gwzarna
between, among, in the midst of Comp Post Adv	[ke] dərmyan
connection, relationship, kin M2	ryšta
to join, unite, connect, attach together [If: /w/]	joRna
deep, profound A2	gəhra
connection, concern, attachment M1	təəllwq
patience, endurance, self-restraint M1 [np]	səbr
lesson M1	səbəq
sympathy F2	həmdərdi
feeling, emotion, sentiment, enthusiasm M2	jəzba
concentration, reflection, deliberation, close attention, deep research M1 [np]	γəwr
present, existing A1	məwjuda
hard, rigid, strong, severe, intense, violent, extreme A1	səxt
clear, apparent PA1	zahyr
laws, rules Mpl [pl. /qanun/]	qəvanin
solution, solving, dissolving M1	həl
national, pertaining to the country A1	mwlki
prosperity F2 [np]	xwšhali
national, pertaining to the nation A1	qəwmi
progress, advancement F2	tərəqqi
point, dot M2 [/nwqtəe nəzər/ M1 [np] "point of view"]	nwqta
thus Adv	yū
force, strength, pressure, exertion, power M1	zor
regard, reference, point of view; consideration, respect M1 [np]	lyhaz
examination, test M1	ymtyhan

successful Al	kamyab
success F2	kamyabi

MS: Just as I have said, that Islam is not only just the name of a religion, but Islam has laid a unique society before the world, in which there is no distinction between eastern or western, white or black. Take any Pillar of Islam; aside from the religious aspect, in it there will also be social benefits. Take the example of the fast. When a man remains hungry and thirsty the whole day, then the fast gives him the realisation of those people's hunger and thirst who get nothing at all to eat. Because of this feeling, a person himself begins to realise that just passing [his] life sensually [lit. with sensuality] is no life at all. Thus, where these duties make a bond between God and creature on the one hand, on the other hand they create a profound connection with other men [lit. man]. [They] give the lesson of patience and create a feeling of sympathy. Similarly, if you look closely at the Zəkat: that if every person who has the power to pay the Zəkat would pay the Zəkat, then from it assistance for the poor people of the country would be possible. This thing is extremely necessary at the present time especially. From these things it is very clear [lit. clean clear] that the Islamic duties and laws do not serve [lit. solve] a religious objective only, but they also have great importance from the point of view of national prosperity, national progress, and [from] the social [point of view]. Rather if [it] were said thus, [it] would be better, that [these obligations] lay greater stress upon these aspects. From the religious point of view, these obligations have the status of a test. Those people who are [lit. will be] successful in this test will get the reward for this success in the next world.

jəysa ky mə̃y ne ərz kia tha, ky yslam syrf ek məzhəb hi ka nam nəhī̃ həy, bəlke yslam ne ek xas mwašra dwnya ke samne peš kia həy, jys mẽ məšryqi ya məyrybi, əwr gore ya kale ki koi təmiz nəhī̃. yslam ke kysi bhi rwkn ko le lẽ, ys mẽ məzhəbi pəhlu ke ylava, mwašrəti fəvayd bhi məwjud hõge. roze ki mysal lijie. jəb admi sara dyn bhuka əwr pyasa rəhta həy, to roza wse wn logõ ki bhuk əwr pyas ka yhsas dylata həy, jynhẽ khane ko kwch nəhī̃ mylta. ys yhsas ki vəja se, ynsan əpne ap məhsus kərne ləgta həy, ky syrf əyš se zyndəgi gwzarna hi koi zyndəgi nəhī̃. cwnãce yy fərayz, jəhã ek tərəf xwda əwr bənde ke dərmyan ryšta joRte hə̃y, to dusri tərəf ek dusre ynsan se gəhra təəllwq pəyda kərte hə̃y. səbr ka səbəq dete hə̃y, əwr həmdərdi ka jəzba pəyda kərte hə̃y. ysi tərə, əgər ap zəkat pər yəwr kərẽ, ky əgər hər šəxs jo zəkat dene ki taqət rəkhta həy, zəkat əda kəre, to ws se mwlk ke yərib logõ ki mədəd ho səkti həy. xas təwr pər, məwjuda zəmane mẽ ys ciz ki səxt zərurət həy. yn cizõ se saf zahyr həy, ky yslami fərayz əwr qəvanin syrf məzhəbi məqsəd hi həl nəhī̃ kərte, bəlke mwlk ki xwšhali, qəwmi tərəqqi, əwr mwašrəti nwqtəe nəzər še bhi bəhwt əhmiət rəkhte hə̃y. bəlke yũ kəha jae, to byhtər hoga, ky yn pəhluõ pər zyada zor dete hə̃y. məzhəbi lyhaz se, yy fərayz ek ymtyhan ki həysiət rəkhte hə̃y. jo log ys ymtyhan mẽ kamyab hõge, vw dusri dwnya mẽ ys kamyabi ka ynam paẽge.

S: Do all the people of Pakistan pay the Zəkat regularly?

kya, pakystan ke təmam log zəkat pabəndi se əda kərte hə̃y?

defect, bad point F2	xərabi
weakness F2	kəmzori
many times, repeatedly Adv	barha
to repeat [Ia]	dohrana
fixed, firm, established; steadfast PAl	qaym
great ones Mpl [pl. /bwzwrg/ Al Ml "great, venerable, respected, noble"]	bwzwrgan
faith, religion (especially Islam) Ml	din

MS: No. Not everyone pays [lit. takes out], but if everyone would pay Zəkat regularly, then many of the defects and weaknesses of the society would be done away with

ji nəhī̃. təmam log nəhī̃ nykalte, lekyn əgər təmam log pabəndi se zəkat nykalẽ, to mwašre ki bəhwt si xərabiã əwr kəmzoriã dur ho jaẽ. šayəd yy log ys ki məzhəbi əwr

[lit. would become far]. Perhaps these people [who do not pay] do not understand the religious and social importance of this. When it has been repeated so many times in the Qwran, "Establish prayers and pay the Zəkat!" In the same way, in the Hədis and the books of other great [Muslim] religious men much emphasis has been laid upon this.

mwašrəti əhmiət ko nəhf səməjhte. jəb ky barha qwran mē dohraya gəya həy, ky "nəmaz qaym kəro, əwr zəkat əda kəro!" ysi təra əhadis əwr digər bwzwrgane din ki kytabõ mē ys ciz pər bəhwt zor dia gəya həy.

wine, alcoholic beverage F1 — šərab

S: Is the drinking of wine forbidden in Islam? — kya, yslam mē šərab pina məna həy?

gambling M2 — jua

pig, swine M1 — suər

hardness, stiffness, rigidity, strength, violence, intensity, harshness, severity F2 — səxti

intoxication, addiction M2 — nəša

subject, topic M1 — məwzu

study, reading, perusal M2 [np] — mwtala [literary: /mwtalea/]

detail[s], particular[s], specification F1 — təfsil

MS: Yes. In Islam the drinking of wine, gambling, the eating of pork, and all those things which cause intoxication have been strictly forbidden. There are many books on this subject. Please read this book. Everything has been explained in it in great detail.

ji hā. yslam mē šərab pina, jua khelna, suər ka gošt khana, əwr hər vw ciz səxti se məna ki gəi həy, jo nəša lati həy. ys məwzu pər bəhwt si kytabē məwjud hāy. ys kytab ka mwtala kijie. ys mē təmam cizē bəRi təfsil se bətai gəi hāy.

S: Thank you very much. God willing, I'll come again sometime. Goodbye!

ap ka bəhwt bəhwt šwkria. māy ynšaəlla[h] phyr kysi vəqt hazyr hūga. xwda hafyz.

MS: Goodbye! — xwda hafyz!

18.101. /mwlaqat kərna/ "to meet, encounter, visit" coincides with some (though not all) of the meanings of /mylna/ IIc "to meet, mix, obtain, get." Physical connection or adjacency is denoted by /joRna/ If "to join, unite, connect, attach together, put together." E. g.

/mə̃y ne wn se mwlaqat ki. / I met them.

/mə̃y wn se myla. / I met them. [/mylna/ is, of course, intransitive.]

/mə̃y ne wnhē joR dia. / I joined them [two objects] together.

/yy phəTa hwa kaγəz joR dijie! / Please mend [lit. join] this torn paper!

/yn donõ mezõ ko joR kər, ek mez bəna dē! / Put these two tables together and make one table! [Adjacency rather than permanent connection is implied.]

18.102. /bənda/ M2 originally meant "servant," but it is no longer employed in this meaning in Urdu. /bənda/ now signifies (1) "creature, person, human being" in contrast to God or to some highly respected person, and (2) in the flowery formal style of courtly speech, /bənda/ is used for "this humble person," "your obedient servant," etc., replacing the pronoun /mə̃y/ "I." Aside from /bənda/, there are a great many other such "humble" substitutes for the first person pronoun: e. g. /əhqər/ "most contemptible," /yy naciz/ "this worthless [one]," /γwlam/ "slave," /kəmtərin/ "least," etc. Verb forms agreeing with these pronoun-substitutes are third person singular, rather than first person singular. E. g.

/həm səb əllah ke bənde hə̃y. / We are all God's creatures.

/bənda kys layq həy. / Of what use is this humble person? [Used as a deprecatory reply to a respected person's praise.]

/bənde ko əpna dost səmjhie! / Please consider this humble person [to be] your friend!

/mwjhe əfsos həy, ky bənda ərse se xət nəhī̃ lykh səka. / I regret that this humble person has not been able to write a letter for a long time.

/əgər bənde ke layq koi xydmət ho, to fərmaie! / If there is any service for [lit. worthy of] this humble person, please say [so]!

18.103. /qaym/ PA1 "fixed, established, firm, steadfast," /mwqərrər/ PA1 "fixed, settled, appointed," and /qərar/ M1 "fixing, determination, constancy, declaration; peace, tranquility" all overlap in meaning but differ in the details of their usage. Examples of /qaym/

/aj se sola sal pəhle pakystan ki pəhli hwkumət qaym hwi thi. / Sixteen years ago [lit. sixteen years before today] the first government of Pakistan was established.

/vw əpne vade pər qaym həy. / He is steadfast in [lit. upon] his promise.

/hwkumət ne mwašrəti bwraiõ ko dur kərne ke lie ek xas məhkma qaym kia həy. / The Government has set up a special department to remove [lit. make far] social evils.

Examples of /mwqərrər/:

/hwkumət ne ys kam ke lie ek əfsər mwqərrər kia həy. / The Government has appointed an officer for this task.

/aj ki davət ke lie, pāc bəje šam ka vəqt mwqərrər kia gəya həy./ Five o'clock in the evening [lit. five o'clock's evening's time] has been fixed for today's party.

/vw wn ki hydayət ke mwtabyq ys kam ke lie mwqərrər hwa./ According to their guidance, he has been appointed for this task.

/ws ki šadi ki tarix mwqərrər kər di gəi həy./ The date of his marriage has been fixed.

Examples of /qərar/:

/ws ki šadi ys məhine ki pəccys tarix ko qərar pai həy./ His marriage has been decided for the twenty-fifth of this month [lit. twenty-fifth date]. [Note that /qərar pana/ "to be fixed, decided" is treated as intransitive in spite of the fact that /pana/ is otherwise a transitive verb. See the seventh example below.]

/axyrkar yy qərar paya, ky davət ke bad həm səyr ko cəlēge./ Finally it was decided that after the party we would [lit. will] go for a stroll. [/qərar pana/ is again intransitive; its subject is /yy/.]

/wnhõ ne yə bat ko bəhwt əhəm qərar dia./ They declared this matter to be very important. [/qərar dena/ "to declare" is transitive. It may take two objects: "X declared Y [to be] Z."]

/yslam ne əyse logõ ko gwmrah qərar dia./ Islam declared such people to be misguided.

/qəwm ne wse mwlk ka dwšmən qərar dia./ The nation proclaimed [i.e. declared] him to be an enemy of the country.

/ədalət ne wse mwjrym qərar dia./ The court declared him to be a culprit.

/ws ne zyndəgi mē qərar nəhī paya./ He never found peace in life. [In this meaning /qərar/ is truly the object of /pana/ "to find," and the formation is thus transitive.]

18.104. The Five Pillars of Islam include: (1) the Confession of Faith: "I bear witness that there is no God but God and that Muhammad (God's peace and blessings be upon him!) is the Prophet of God"; (2) prayer: i.e. the five obligatory prayers performed each day (see Sec. 7.121); (3) the fast of Rəmzan: i.e. complete abstinence from all food, drink, smoking, sexual intercourse, etc. from about one hour before sunrise until just after sunset every day during this month; (4) the pilgrimage to Mecca: i.e. a visit to Mecca and presence upon the Plain of Arafat on the 9th of the month of Zwlhyj (together with various other rites); and (5) the payment of the compulsory tithe, termed /zəkat/ Fl [np]: i.e. a fixed percentage paid upon all property, income, etc. per year to a central department, which in turn uses the money to provide sustenance for the poor, funds for good works, etc. Ideally, these Five Pillars should all be part of an integrated religio-social system, based upon the Qwran and the examples and precepts provided by the Holy Prophet. The system has been at least partially rendered inoperable in modern Pakistan (as well as in most other Muslim countries) by the substitution of Western laws for the Islamic /šəriət/ in most matters, and by the establishment of secular governmental agencies (e.g. the Income Tax Department) in place of the machinery of the Islamic State. Pious Muslims still pay their Zəkat individually, however, giving it directly to the poor since there is no centralised government agency at the present time.

18.105. /məslən/ [literary: /məsələn/] Adv "for example" is synonymous with /mysal ke təwr pər/. Both are common.

18.106. /šəkl/ Fl "face, appearance, image, manner, shape, form, figure, aspect, case" is almost identical in meaning with /surət/ Fl "form, state, face, condition." /šəkl/ may be used, however, for the "appearance" of an inanimate object, while /surət/ lacks this meaning. E. g.

/kytab ki šəkl əcchi həy./ The appearance of this book is good. [/surət/ cannot be substituted.]

/ys šəkl mẽ mere lie kya hwkm həy./ In this case [matter, event] what do you want me to do [lit. for me what order is]. [/ys surət mẽ/ is synonymous and equally idiomatic.]

/vw surət se šərif admi malum hota həy./ From his face [appearance], he seems to be a noble man. [/šəkl/ is equally good.]

/šəkl surət se to vw cor nəhĩ malum hota./ From [his] face [and] appearance he doesn't seem to be a thief. [/šəkl surət/ is a noun compound like /chwri kāTa/ "knife [and] fork"; see Secs. 3.110 and 15.301.]

18.107. /lazmi/ A1 and /lazym/ PA1 both mean "necessary, compulsory, incumbent, requisite." /lazym/, however, is somewhat stronger than /lazmi/ and is often translatable as "compulsory." These words overlap /zəruri/ A1 "necessary," /zərur/ Adv "certainly," etc. The occurrence of an /i/ suffix to mark an adjective (versus a predicate adjective without /i/) is somewhat unusual. E. g.

/ap ke lie vəhā jana‘lazmi tha./ It was necessary for you to go there. [The person requiring is marked by /ke lie/ "for." Compare:]

/ap pər vəhā jana lazym tha./ Going there was obligatory upon you. [/pər/ "on, upon" is used with /lazym/; */... ke lie ... lazym/ is not idiomatic. Compare English "incumbent upon you" and "necessary for you."]

/yy lazmi bat thi, ky ys ka nətija bwra nyklega./ This was a necessary thing, that the result of it would [lit. will] turn out badly. [/lazmi/ is an adjective; */lazym bat/ is not correct.]

18.108. /məsla/ [literary: /məsyla/] M2 "question, matter, problem" cannot be used to mean "query"; this is expressed by /səval/ M1 "question, query," which also sometimes overlaps /məsla/ in the meaning of "problem." /məsla/ also denotes a question of Muslim law. E. g.

/bwzwrgane din ne ys məsle pər kafi ɣəwr kia həy./ Great religious scholars have given considerable thought [i. e. studied deeply] to this question.

/yy kam to ek məsla bən gəya./ This task has become a problem.

/əbhi tək kəšmir ka məsla həl nəhĩ ho səka./ As yet the problem of Kashmir could not be solved.

/ys təfsir mẽ yy məsla bəhwt əcchi təra bəyan kia gəya həy./ In this commentary this question [matter, problem, legal question] has been explained very well.

129

18.109. The Arabic preposition /fi/ "in" occurs as an independent word in Urdu meaning "per": /fi sədi/ "per hundred, percent." E.g.

/ek ana fi rupəe ke hysab se zəkat deni cahie./ [One] must give Zəkat at the rate of one anna per rupee.

/yy kəpRa car rupəe fi gəz mylta həy./ This cloth is available at four rupees per yard. [/car rupəe gəz/ is also correct; see Sec. 4.306. With /fi/, the sentence is stylistically a trifle more literary.]

/əcche am do rupəe fi ser myl jaẽge./ Good mangoes will be available at two rupees per seer. [Again /do rupəe ser/ is also idiomatic.]

/ys rəqəm mẽ se pəchəttər fi sədi hyssa mera həy./ Of this amount, a share [of] seventy-five percent is mine. [/fi/ cannot be omitted.]

As a noun, /sədi/ F2 means "century." E.g.

/mwyəl solhvĩ sədi mẽ hyndostan ae./ The Mughals came to India in the sixteenth century.

/fi/ is also found in a number of inseparable loan compounds. E.g.

/fylhal/ Adv presently, now, at the present time. [/hal/ M1 "state, condition." Before the Arabic article a final /i/, /u/, or /a/ becomes /y/, /w/, or /ə/ respectively; see Sec. 10.012.]

/fylhəqiqət/ Adv really, in reality. [/həqiqət/ F1 "reality."]

18.110. /sona/ M2 "gold" is homophonous with /sona/ IIc "to sleep." The similarity in sound is fortuitous.

18.111. /digər/ A1 and /dusra/ A2 both mean "other, another." The latter, however, also means "second, next," a meaning which /digər/ does not share. Stylistically, /digər/ is more literary than /dusra/. E.g.

/dusre məzahyb ke əqayd ke mwtabyq, šərab pina koi gwnah nəhĩ həy./ According to the tenets of other religions, the drinking of wine is no sin. [/digər/ is substitutable.]

/ys jhəgRe ki dusri bəRi vəja pwrani dwšməni həy./ The second major cause of this quarrel is ancient enmity. [/digər/ is not idiomatic here.]

/ys jhəgRe ki digər vwjuhat mẽ se, ek vəja yy bhi həy./ Among the other reasons for this quarrel, this is also a reason. [/vwjuhat/ Fpl is the plural of /vəja/ F1 "reason, cause"; see Sec. 17.304. /dusri/ is also idiomatic here.]

18.112. /əshab/ Mpl "gentlemen, companions" is the broken plural (Sec. 17.304) of /sahəb/ M1 "lord, sir, mister, gentleman, owner." /əshab/ is sometimes employed for the "companions" of the Prophet Muhammad: those followers and friends who joined him in the difficult task of establishing Islam. There is also a special technical term for the companions of the Prophet; /səhabi/ M1, and its plural /səhaba/ Mpl. E.g.

/kwch əshab vəhã bəyThe hwe ap ka yntyzar kər rəhe hẽy./ Some gentlemen are sitting there waiting for you.

/yy təmam əshab ədalət mẽ peš hwe./ All of these gentlemen were presented in court.

18.113. /ələyhda/ A1 Adv and /ələg/ A1 Adv both mean "apart, separate, distinct."

These two words are apparently synonymous. /ələyhda/ is a compound of the Arabic preposition /əla/ "on" + /ḥyda/ "alone, apart."

18.114. /ymdad/ Fl and /mədəd/ Fl are both from the same Arabic root, and both mean much the same thing: "help, aid, assistance." /ymdad/, however, carries the connotation of financial assistance, while /mədəd/ denotes any sort of help or aid. E.g.

/əmrika se pakystan ko ys mwamle mē bəRi mədəd myli./ Pakistan received great assistance from America in this affair. [Any sort of help may be meant. Compare:]

/əmrika ne pakystan ko dəs lakh rupəe ki ymdad di həy./ America has given Pakistan ten lakhs of rupees of aid. [Since financial assistance is specifically meant /ymdad/ is more idiomatic here.]

/ap ne ys sylsyle mē meri bəhwt mədəd ki./ You helped me a great deal in this connection. [/ ... ymdad ki/ would have the connotation of purely financial assistance.]

18.115. /zyada se zyada/ Adv means literally "more from more"; it denotes "as much as possible, as many as possible." /kəm se kəm/ (or the more Persianised form /kəm əz kəm/) Adv similarly denotes "at least, as little as possible." E.g.

/ap ko ys ymtyhan mē kəm se kəm pəcas nəmbər lene cahiē./ You must get [lit. take] at least fifty marks [lit. numbers] in this examination. [/kəm əz kəm/ is substitutable.]

18.116. /khae pie/ "may, should eat [or] drink" is another example of a pair of semantically related inflected main verbs. See Sec. 17.310.

18.117. As a noun, /ərz/ Fl means "request, petition." The Type A complex verbal formation /ərz kərna/ denotes "to (humbly) say, suggest"; it is employed for one's own "humble" utterances in honorific speech. The "honorific" counterpart of /ərz kərna/ is, of course, /fərmana/ Ia "to command, say, do." E.g.

/yyhi meri ərz həy./ This [lit. just this] is my request.

/meri ərz swnie!/ Please hear my request!

/mӟy ne əbhi ap se ərz kia tha, ky mӟy ys ke bare mē kwch nəhī̃ janta./ I have just told you that I know nothing about this. [Since /ərz kərna/ is a Type A complex verbal formation, the gender of /ərz/ does not govern the number-gender of the verb in the past tenses. See Sec. 11.306.]

/mӟy ne yy bat ərz ki thi./ I had said this thing. [/bat/ Fl "matter, word, thing" governs the number-gender of /ki thi/.]

/ys sylsyle mē, mӟy ne əpna xyal ərz kər dia tha./ In this connection I presented my own idea. [/xyal/ Ml "idea, thought" governs /kia tha/.]

/jəb mӟy ne yy ərz kia tha, to ap ne fərmaya tha, ky yy nəhī̃ ho səkta./ When I said [suggested] this, then you said that this cannot be. [Here /ərz kərna/ is contrasted with /fərmana/ in honorific speech.]

18.118. /gora/ A2 "white, light-complexioned" refers only to skin colour. Its antonym is /kala/ A2 "black, dark."

18.119. /yhsas/ M1 denotes "feeling, sensation, perception, realisation." /jəzba/ M2 also means "feeling" but in the sense of "sentiment, enthusiasm"; its Arabic plural, /jəzbat/ Mpl, means "emotions, feelings, sentiments," As well as "enthusiasm[s]." Another form from the same Arabic root as /yhsas/ is /məhsus/ PA1 "perceived, felt, sensed, realised." E.g.

/mwjhe ys bat ka yhsas həy, ky mere jane se ap ko təklif hogi./ I realise [lit. to me is this thing's realisation] that you will suffer from my going.

/mǣy ne ws ki bat məhsus ki./ I was hurt by his word[s]. [Although /məhsus kərna/ means "to perceive, realise," it also idiomatically denotes "to have one's feelings hurt."]

/mǣy ne ws ki batõ se məhsus kia, ky vw vəhā jane ke lie təyyar nəhĩ./ I realised from his words that he is not ready to go there.

/mwjhe ap ke qəwmi jəzbe ka yhsas həy./ I am aware [realise, perceive] your national sentiment.

/ws mē kam kərne ka bəhwt jəzba həy./ He has a great deal of enthusiasm for working. [Lit. In him is much feeling of doing work.]

/ap ki talimat se, ərəb qəwm mē nəya jəzba pəyda hwa./ Through his [i.e. a very respected person's] teachings, a new spirit [lit. feeling, enthusiasm] was born in the Arab nation.

/ws ne əpne jəzbat pər qabu pa lia./ He got control of his emotions.

/ap ne mere jəzbat ka xyal nəhĩ kia./ You did not consider my feelings.

18.120. /əpne ap/ Adv "self, oneself" is synonymous with /xwd/ Adv "self." /əpne ap/, however, may be followed by /ko/ to express the object of a transitive reflexive sentence, whereas */xwd ko/ is not idiomatic (see Sec. 11.122). Postpositions | other than /ko/ also occur after /əpne ap/, but they are more usually found after /əpna/ A2 "[one's] own" (see Sec. 4.311). Postpositions of any sort are very rare after /xwd/. E.g.

/mǣy ne yy kam əpne ap kər lia./ I did this work myself. [/xwd/ is substitutable here.]

/yy kam əpne ap ho gəya./ This job has become finished [lit. became] all by itself. [/xwd hi/ is also idiomatic here.]

/mǣy əpne ap ws se bat kər lūga./ I'll speak to him myself. [/xwd/ is substitutable here.]

/vw əpne ap hi naraz ho gəe./ He became angry for no reason at all. [Lit. all by himself. /xwd hi/ is also possible here.]

/mǣy ne jəb šiše mē əpne ap ko dekha, to hõs pəRa./ When I saw myself in the mirror, [I] burst out laughing.

/ap ko əpne se bəRõ ki yzzət kərni cahie./ You ought to respect those elder to yourself [lit. big from [one]self]. [Neither */əpne ap se/ nor */xwd se/ are idiomatic.]

18.121. /təəllwq/ M1, /ryšta/ M2, and /sylsyla/ M2 all denote "connection" in certain contexts. /təəllwq/ signifies "concern, attachment, connection," however, while /ryšta/ denotes a kinship relationship (and, in certain contexts, the engagement of a boy and girl previous to marriage). The basic meaning of /sylsyla/ is "chain, series," and in some sentences this is best translated as "connection." Although /sylsyla/ may mean "chain" in the sense of "chain of events," "chain of mountains," etc., it is not employed for "chain" in the sense of "fetters, iron chain."

All of the above words are rather abstract: a physical connection between two objects (e.g. a joint connecting two pipes, the joints of the body, etc.) is expressed by /joR/ M1. E.g.

/mera wn se koi təəllwq nəhī. / I have no concern with him.

/vw ek xwšhal xandan se təəllwq rəkhta həy. / He comes of [lit. keeps connection with] a prosperous family. [Compare the ninth example in this Section.]

/jəhā tək ws ki əhmiət ka təəllwq həy, to vw ys ciz se zahyr həy. / So far as its importance is concerned, it is clear from this thing.

/mera wn se koi ryšta nəhī. / I am no kin to him.

/ap ka wn se kya ryšta həy. / What relation are you to him?

/vw mere ryšte mē bhai hote hāy. / He is [classified as] a brother in relationship to me. [He is not my real brother but rather a type of cousin classified as a brother by the kinship system.]

/mera ws ləRki se ryšta qərar paya. / My engagement to that girl has been settled.

/wnhō ne ws ki beTi ka ryšta māga. / They asked for the hand of his daughter. [The boy's parents sent a message to the girl's parents requesting her hand for their son.]

/ws ka ryšta ek xwšhal xandan mē hwa həy. / He has become engaged in [i.e. engaged to a girl of] a prosperous family.

/ys sylsyle mē māy kwch nəhī kər səkta. / In this connection I can do nothing. [/[ke] sylsyle mē/ "in connection with" functions as a compound postposition. Neither /təəllwq/ nor /ryšta/ can be substituted.]

/roze ki əhmiət ke sylsyle mē, māy kwch ərz kərna cahta hū. / In connection with the importance of fasting, I wish to say something.

/yy sylsyla bəRa pwrana həy. / This series [of events] is very old. [Here /sylsyla/ denotes a connected sequence of happenings, etc. This sentence is roughly equivalent to the American expression, "This is a very old story."]

/pəhaRō ka yy sylsyla milō tək phəyla hwa həy. / This chain of mountains extends [lit. is spread] for miles.

18.122. /[ke] lyhaz se/ and /[ke] nwqtəe nəzər se/ are both compound postpositions meaning "from the point of view of ..." Although /lyhaz/ M1 has other meanings also, this is perhaps its most common usage.

18.123. /din/ M1 "faith, religion" is usually employed only in reference to Islam. /məzhəb/ M1 "religion" is used for any religion, including Islam.

18.124. /mwtala kərna/ "to read, study, peruse" is synonymous with /pəRhna/ Ic "to read, study." The former is more literary, however.

18.125. Where in English one asks for the details of something (employing the plural), in Urdu the singular is commonly used. The Arabic plurals /təfsilat/ Fpl and /təfasil/ Fpl "details" are found in literary usage, however. E.g.

/ys ki təfsil kya həy./   What are [lit. is] the detail[s] of this?

/mə̃y ne wn se təmam təfsilat bəyan kī./   I told him all the details.

/mə̃y ne yslam ke pãc ərkan ko təfsil se bəyan kia./   I explained the Five
     Pillars of Islam in [lit. with] detail.

18.126. Some Complex Verbal Formations:

A:

/ələyhda/

    /[X se] ələyhda hona/ to be, become separate, apart, distinct

    /[X ko] ələyhda kərna/ to separate [X]

    /[X ko] ələyhda rəkhna/ to keep [X] separate, apart

/ərz/

    /[X se Y] ərz kərna/ to say, suggest [Y to X]

/gəhra/

    /gəhra hona/ to be, become deep

    /[X ko] gəhra kərna/ to deepen [X]

/həl/

    /[X mẽ] həl hona/ to be, become dissolved [in X]

    /həl hona/ to be solved

    /[X ko] həl kərna/ to solve, dissolve [X]

    /[X ka] həl nykalna/ to find a solution [for X]

/lazmi/

    /[X ke lie] lazmi hona/ to be necessary [for X]

    /[X ke lie Y] lazmi kərna/ to make [Y] necessary [for X]

/lazym/

    /[X pər] lazym hona/ to be, become incumbent [upon X]

    /[X pər Y] lazym kərna/ to make [Y] incumbent, obligatory [upon X]

/mazur/

    /[X se] mazur hona/ to be, become crippled, handicapped, incapable [by X]

    /[X ko] mazur kərna/ to cripple, handicap [X], render [X] incapable

/məhsus/

    /[X ko Y] məhsus hona/ [X] to feel, sense, realise [Y]

    /[X ko] məhsus kərna/ to feel, sense, perceive, realise [X]₁ to be hurt
         [by X]. [E. g. /mə̃y ne ap ki bat məhsus ki./ "I was hurt by your word[s].]

/məjbur/

    /[X se] məjbur hona/ to be, become compelled [by X]

    /[X ko] məjbur kərna/ to compel [X]

/mwqərrər/

    /mwqərrər hona/ to be fixed, settled, appointed

    /[X pər] mwqərrər hona/ to be, become appointed [to the post of X]

    /[X ko] mwqərrər kərna/ to fix, settle, appoint [X]

    /[X ko Y pər] mwqərrər kərna/ to appoint [X to the post of Y]

/qaym/

/qaym hona/ to be, become established, fixed, steadfast

/[X ko] qaym kərna/ to establish, found, erect [X]

/səxt/

/səxt hona/ to be, become firm, hard, rigid, severe

/[X ko] səxt kərna/ to make [X] firm, hard, rigid, severe

/xwšhal/

/xwšhal hona/ to be, become prosperous

/[X ko] xwšhal kərna/ to make [X] prosperous

/yxtiar/. [See also D.]

/yxtiar hona/ to be, become adopted, chosen

/[X ko] yxtiar kərna/ to adopt, choose [X (a course of action)]

/zahyr/

/[X se] zahyr hona/ to be, become apparent [from X]

/[X ko] zahyr kərna/ to make [X] clear, plain, apparent

B:

/lyhaz/

/[X ka] lyhaz hona/ [X] to be respected, held in regard

/[X ka] lyhaz kərna/ to respect, regard, consider [X]

/mwtala/

/[X ka] mwtala hona/ [X] to be read, perused

/[X ka] mwtala kərna/ to read, study, peruse [X]

/niət/

/[X ko Y ki] niət hona/ [X] to have the intention [of doing Y]

/[X ki] niət kərna/ to resolve [to do X]

/səfər/

/[X ka] səfər kərna/ to travel [to X]

/yhsas/. [See also F.]

/[X ko Y ka] yhsas hona/ [X] to feel, perceive, realise [Y]

/[X ka] yhsas kərna/ to feel, perceive, realise [X]

/ymdad/. [See also D.]

/[X ki] ymdad kərna/ to help, aid, assist [X]

/ymtyhan/. [See also D.]

/[X ka] ymtyhan hona/ [X] to be tested, examined

/[X ka] ymtyhan kərna/ to test, examine [X (a substance, object)]

D:

/həq/. [See also F.]

/[X ko X ka] həq dena/ to give [X] his [i.e. X's] rights

/[X ko Y ka] həq dena/ to give [X] the right [to do Y]

/[X ko Y ka] həq mylna/ [X] to get the right [to Y, to do Y]

/səbəq/. [See also F.]

/[X ko Y ka] səbəq dena/ to teach [X] the lesson [of Y (experience, school lesson, etc.)]

135

/[X ko Y se] sǝbǝq mylna/ [X] to get a lesson [from Y]
/šǝkl/
   /[X ko Y ki] šǝkl dena/ to give the shape [of Y to X]
/tǝrǝqqi/. [See also F.]
   /[X ko] tǝrǝqqi dena/ to advance [X], cause [X] to progress; to promote [X] to a higher rank
   /[X ko] tǝrǝqqi mylna/ [X] to be advanced, made to progress; [X] to be promoted to a higher rank
/ymdad/
   /[X ko] ymdad dena/ to help, aid, assist [X]
   /[X ko Y se] ymdad mylna/ [X] to receive help, aid, assistance [from Y]
/ymtyhan/. [See also B.]
   /[X ka] ymtyhan dena/ to take a test, examination [in X (a subject)]
   /[X mē Y ka] ymtyhan lena/ to test, examine [Y (a student) in X (a subject)]
/yxtiar/. [See also A.]
   /[X ko Y ka] yxtiar dena/ to give [X] jurisdiction over [Y], give [X] the power [of Y]
   /[X ko Y ka] yxtiar mylna/ [X] to receive jurisdiction over [Y], power [of Y]

F:

/ǝyš/
   /ǝyš kǝrna/ to enjoy [sensual] pleasure
/bhuka/
   /[X ka] bhuka hona/ to be hungry [for X], desire [X]
/ɣǝwr/
   /[X pǝr] ɣǝwr hona/ [X] to be pondered, concentrated upon, deeply studied
   /[X pǝr] ɣǝwr kǝrna/ to ponder, consider, deeply study [X]
   /ɣǝwr se/ carefully, thoughtfully, deeply
/hǝj/
   /hǝj kǝrna/ to perform the pilgrimage to Mecca
/hǝmdǝrdi/
   /[X se] hǝmdǝrdi kǝrna/ to feel sympathy [for X]
/hǝq/. [See also D.]
   /[X ka] hǝq marna/ to deprive [X] of his right, usurp the right [of X]
/hǝqdar/
   /[X ka] hǝqdar hona/ to be the rightful claimant [to X], have a right [to X]
/jua/
   /jua khelna/ to gamble
/kamyab/
   /[X mē] kamyab hona/ to be, become successful [in X]
   /[X ko] kamyab bǝnana/ to make [X] successful
/kǝlma/
   /kǝlma pǝRhna/ to recite the Confession of Faith
/mǝsla/
   /[X ke lie] mǝsla bǝnna/ to become a problem [for X]

/[X ka] məsla wThana/ to raise the question [of X]
/mwlaqat/
    /[X se Y ki] mwlaqat hona/ [Y] to have a meeting [with X]
    /[X se] mwlaqat kərna/ to meet [X]
/nəša/
    /[X ko] nəša ana/ [X] to become intoxicated, affected by liquor, drugs, etc.
    /[X ko Y ka] nəša hona/ [X] to be, become intoxicated [by Y (a drug, etc.)]
    /nəša kərna/ to become intoxicated, addicted
    /nəša lana/ to cause intoxication
/pəhlu/
    /[X mẽ] pəhlu bədəlna/ to change sides [in the matter of X]
/qərar/
    /[X ko Y se] qərar ana, mylna/ [X] to get peace, tranquility [from Y]
    /[X ko] qərar dena/ to decide, settle [X]
    /[X ko Y] qərar dena/ to declare [X to be Y]
    /qərar pana/ to be fixed, settled, approved, established. [This formation is treated as intransitive.]
    /qərar pana/ to get peace, tranquility, contentment. [This formation is grammatically transitive.]
/roza/
    /roza kholna/ to break a fast
    /roza rəkhna/ to fast, keep a fast
/ryšta/
    /[X se Y ka] ryšta hona/ [Y] to be engaged [to X]
    /[X se] ryšta joRna, kərna/ to become engaged [to X]
    /[X se Y ka] ryšta mãgna/ to ask for the hand [of Y from X]
/səbəq/. [See also D.]
    /[X se] səbəq pəRhna/ to study a lesson [with X, under the guidance of X (a teacher)]
/səbr/
    /[X ko] səbr hona/ [X] to be patient, satisfied
    /səbr kərna/ to practice patience, be patient
/səxti/
    /[X pər] səxti hona/ [X] to be treated harshly, strictly, severely
    /[X pər] səxti kərna/ to treat [X] harshly, strictly, severely
/šərt/
    /[X pər] šərt ləgana/ to bet, wager [on X]
    /[X pər Y ki] šərt ləgana/ to lay a condition [of Y upon X]
/taqət/
    /[X ki] taqət rəkhna/ to have the power [to do X]
/təəllwq/
    /[X se] təəllwq rəkhna/ to maintain, establish a connection [with X]
/tərəqqi/. [See also D.]
    /[X mẽ] tərəqqi hona/ to progress [in X (a field, subject)]

137

/[X mē] tərəqqi kərna/ to make progress [in X]
/xərabi/
　　/[X mē] xərabi kərna/ to create a defect, cause a nuisance [in X]
/yhsas/. [See also B.]
　　/[X ko Y ka] yhsas dylana/ to cause [X] to feel, realise [Y]
/zəkat/
　　/zəkat dena, nykalna/ to pay the Zəkat
/zor/
　　/[X pər] zor dena/ to emphasise, stress, force [X]
　　/[X mē] zor dykhana/ to show one's power [in X]
　　/[X mē] zor ləgana/ to apply one's energies [in X]

18. 201. Word Recognition.

(1) Different elements in a compound tend to be written separately, although there is considerable individual variation. The student must thus learn to recognise compounds from the context rather than from the fact that they are written as "one word." E. g.

SCRIPT	PRONUNCIATION	SCRIPT	PRONUNCIATION
حقدار	həqdar	خوشحال	xwšhal
حق دار	həqdar	خوش حال	xwšhal

Compounds having /šwda/ or /kərda/ as their second member are almost always written separately. E. g.

جمع شده	jəməšwda	عطاکرده	ətakərda

(2) The following words are written with "uncommon" Arabic consonants, with final 0 = /a/, or with other special spelling conventions.

احساس	yhsas	حق	həq
اصحاب	əshab	حقدار	həqdar
امتحان	ymtyhan	حل	həl
بنده	bənda	خوشحال	xwšhal
تعلّق	təəllwq	خوشحالی	xwšhali
تفصیل	təfsil	رشته	ryšta
جذبه	jəzba	رمضان	rəmzan
جمع شده	jəməšwda	روزه	roza
جوا	jua	زکوٰة	zəkat
حج	həj	سؤر	suər

139

Decade → دہائی

SCRIPT	PRONUNCIATION	SCRIPT	PRONUNCIATION
شرائط	šərayt	لحاظ	lyhaz
شرط	šərt	مثلاً	məslən
صبر	səbr	محسوس	məhsus
صدی	sədi	محکمہ	məhkma
طاقت	taqət	مسئلہ	məsla
ظاہر	zahyr	مطالعہ	mwtala[2]
عرض	ərz	معاشرتی	mwašrəti
عطاکردہ	ətakərda	معاشرہ	mwašra
علیحدہ	ələyhda	معذور	mazur
عیش	əyš	مقررشدہ	mwqərrəršwda *(Established)*
فرائض	fərayz	مکہ	məkka
کلمہ	kəlma	موجودہ	məwjuda
گزارنا	gwzarna[1]	موضوع	məwzu
گزرنا	gwzərna[1]	نشہ	nəša
		نقطہ	nwqta *(point)*

[1]Also commonly written with ذ : گذرنا , گذارنا .

[2]This should be pronounced /mwtalea/ according to the orthography, and some speakers do indeed pronounce it this way.

18.202. Reading Drill I: Text.

The following is the text of the Conversation Section of this Unit. Read it aloud, striving for speed and accuracy.

استفتہ ۔   مجھے آج اسلام کے فرائض کے بارے میں کچھ بتایئے۔

مولوی صاحب۔ پچھلی ملاقات کے دوران میں نے اسلامی فرائض کی طرف اشارہ کیا تھا۔ فرائض کا مطلب
وہ کام ہیں جو اللہ نے اپنے بندوں پر ضروری قرار دیئے اسلام کے پانچ اہم ارکان
ہیں ۔ کلمہ ، نماز ، روزہ ، حج اور زکوٰۃ۔ کلمہ کا مطلب یہ ہے کہ ہر مسلمان دل سے
ایمان رکھے کہ اللہ ایک ہے اور حضرت محمد صلی اللہ علیہ وسلم اُس کے رسول ہیں۔
ایک دن میں پانچ وقت نماز پڑھنا دوسرا فرض ہے ۔ رمضان کے مہینے میں پورے
ایک مہینے کے روزے رکھنا تیسرا فرض ہے ۔ عمر میں ایک دفعہ حج کے لئے مکّہ جانا
اور اللہ کے عطا کردہ مال میں سے زکوٰۃ نکالنا چوتھے اور پانچویں فرائض ہیں۔

استفتہ۔   کیا یہ پانچوں چیزیں ہر مسلمان پر فرض ہیں۔ مثلاً اگر کسی کے پاس اتنی رقم نہ ہو کہ وہ مکّہ
جا سکے تو اس شکل میں اُس کے لئے کیا حکم ہے؟

مولوی صاحب۔ پہلے تین فرائض ہر مسلمان پر لازم ہیں اور یہ کسی بھی صورت میں معاف نہیں سوائے
ایک دو مجبوریوں کے ۔ لیکن حج اور زکوٰۃ صرف اُس مسلمان پر فرض ہیں جو ان کو ادا
کرنے کی طاقت رکھتا ہو۔ جیسے اگر کوئی مسلمان غریب ہے اور مکّہ کا سفر اختیار نہیں
کر سکتا تو اُس پر حج فرض نہیں ۔ اور اسی طرح زکوٰۃ کا مسئلہ ہے۔

استفتہ۔   کیا زکوٰۃ کسی خاص حساب سے دی جاتی ہے؟

مولوی صاحب۔ جی ہاں! مختلف چیزوں پر زکوٰۃ مختلف حساب سے ادا کی جاتی ہے مثلاً نقد روپیے پر
ڈھائی فیصدی زکوٰۃ نکالنا لازمی ہے۔ اسی طرح دوسرے مال جیسے سونے اور چاندی
کے زیور وغیرہ میں سے ایک مقرّرشدہ حصّہ زکوٰۃ کے طور پر نکالا جاتا ہے۔

استفتہ۔   زکوٰۃ کا مال یا روپیہ کسے دیا جاتا ہے اور کیسے استعمال میں لایا جاتا ہے؟

مولوی صاحب۔ زکوٰۃ کا مال غریبوں، یتیموں اور دیگر معذور اور مجبور لوگوں کا حق ہے۔ ہمارے نبی اور ان کے اصحاب کے زمانے میں زکوٰۃ کا ایک علیحدہ محکمہ تھا۔ لوگ زکوٰۃ کی رقم اس محکمے میں جمع کرا دیتے تھے اور اس جمع شدہ رقم سے غریبوں اور دوسرے حقداروں کو امداد پہنچائی جاتی تھی۔

استمہ۔ روزے کے لئے کون کونسی شرائط ضروری ہیں اور اس کا کیا طریقہ ہے؟

مولوی صاحب۔ روزہ بھی نماز کی طرح ہر مسلمان مرد اور عورت پر فرض ہے۔ اس کا طریقہ یہ ہے کہ سورج نکلنے سے تقریباً ایک گھنٹہ پہلے کھانا کھائے اور روزے کی نیت کرے اور سارا دن کچھ اور شام کو سورج چھپنے کے فوراً بعد روزہ کھولے۔ روزے کے دوران کوئی برائی یا گناہ نہ کرے اور رات کو زیادہ سے زیادہ اللہ کی عبادت کرے۔

استمہ۔ مذہبی اہمیت کے علاوہ ان ارکان کی معاشرتی اہمیت کیا ہے؟

مولوی صاحب۔ جیسا کہ میں نے عرض کیا تھا کہ اسلام صرف ایک مذہب ہی کا نام نہیں ہے بلکہ اسلام نے ایک خاص معاشرہ دنیا کے سامنے پیش کیا ہے، جس میں مشرقی یا مغربی اور گورے یا کالے کی کوئی تمیز نہیں۔ اسلام کے کسی بھی رکن کو لے لیں، اس میں مذہبی پہلو کے علاوہ معاشرتی فوائد بھی موجود ہوں گے۔ روزے کی مثال لیجئے۔ جب آدمی سارا دن بھوکا اور پیاسا رہتا ہے تو روزہ اسے ان لوگوں کی بھوک اور پیاس کا احساس دلاتا ہے جنہیں کھانے کو کچھ نہیں ملتا۔ اس احساس کی وجہ سے انسان اپنے آپ محسوس کرنے لگتا ہے کہ صرف عیش سے زندگی گزارنا ہی کوئی زندگی نہیں۔ چنانچہ یہ فرائض جہاں ایک طرف خدا اور بندے کے درمیان رشتہ جوڑتے ہیں تو دوسری طرف ایک دوسرے انسان سے گہرا تعلق پیدا کرتے ہیں۔ صبر کا سبق دیتے ہیں اور ہمدردی کا جذبہ پیدا

کرتے ہیں۔اسی طرح اگر آپ زکوٰۃ پر غور کریں کہ اگر ہر شخص جو زکوٰۃ دینے کی طاقت رکھتا

ہے زکوٰۃ ادا کرے تو اُس سے ملک کے غریب لوگوں کی مدد ہو سکتی ہے۔ خاص طور پر

موجودہ زمانے میں اس چیز کی سخت ضرورت ہے۔ان چیزوں سے صاف ظاہر ہے کہ

اسلامی فرائض اور قوانین صرف مذہبی مقصد ہی حل نہیں کرتے بلکہ ملک کی خوشحالی، قومی ترقی

اور معاشرتی نقطۂ نظر سے بھی بہت اہمیت رکھتے ہیں۔ بلکہ یوں کہا جائے تو بہتر ہوگا کہ

ان پہلوؤں پر زیادہ زور دیتے ہیں۔ مذہبی لحاظ سے یہ فرائض ایک امتحان کی حیثیت

رکھتے ہیں۔جو لوگ اس امتحان میں کامیاب ہوں گے وہ دوسری دنیا میں اس کامیابی

کا انعام پائیں گے۔

اسمتہ۔ کیا پاکستان کے تمام لوگ زکوٰۃ پابندی سے ادا کرتے ہیں؟

مولوی صاحب۔ جی نہیں! تمام لوگ نہیں نکالتے۔ لیکن اگر تمام لوگ پابندی سے زکوٰۃ نکالیں تو معاشرے

کی بہت سی خرابیاں اور کمزوریاں دُور ہو جائیں۔ شاید یہ لوگ اس کی مذہبی اور معاشرتی

اہمیت کو نہیں سمجھتے۔ جب کہ بارہا قرآن میں دہرایا گیا ہے " نماز قائم کرو اور زکوٰۃ

ادا کرو" اسی طرح حدیث اور دیگر بزرگانِ دین کی کتابوں میں اس چیز پہ بہت

زور دیا گیا ہے ۔

اسمتہ۔ کیا اسلام میں شراب پینا منع ہے ؟

مولوی صاحب۔ جی ہاں! اسلام میں شراب پینا، جوا کھیلنا، سؤر کا گوشت کھانا اور ہر وہ چیز سختی سے

منع کی گئی ہے جو نشہ لاتی ہے ۔ اس موضوع پر بہت سی کتابیں موجود ہیں۔اس کتاب

کا مطالعہ کیجئے۔اس میں تمام چیزیں بڑی تفصیل سے بتائی گئی ہیں۔

اسمتہ۔ آپ کا بہت بہت شکریہ ۔ میں انشاءاللہ پھر کسی وقت حاضر ہوں گا۔خدا حافظ۔

مولوی صاحب ۔ خدا حافظ ۔

18. 203. Reading Drill II: Sentences.

Read the following sentences aloud and translate them into English.

۱۔ جو اِس دنیا میں اچھائی اور نیکی کرتا ہے اور برائیوں اور گناہوں سے دور رہتا ہے وہ اللہ کے امتحان
میں کامیاب ہے اور وہ اِس کا پھل پائے گا۔

۲۔ آج کل بعض لوگوں کا خیال ہے کہ زکوٰۃ دینے میں کوئی فائدہ نہیں مگر علماتے دین کا کہنا ہے کہ یہ خیال
بالکل غلط ہے کیونکہ زکوٰۃ معاشرے کے لئے بہت مفید چیز ہے۔

۳۔ آخر کار یہ قرار پایا کہ زمین دار کی پارٹی عدالت میں چو میں تاریخ کو گواہی دے گی۔

۴۔ اُس کا بیان سُن کر مجھے یہ خیال آیا کہ یہ آدمی بیسویں صدی کا آدمی نہیں بلکہ اٹھارہویں صدی کا ہے۔

۵۔ جیسا کہ میں عرض کر چکا ہوں، سوائے ایک دو مجبوریوں کے روزہ رکھنا ہر مسلمان پر فرض ہے۔

۶۔ اُس نے ماں باپ کے انتقال کے بعد عیش کی زندگی اختیار کی اور برائیوں اور گناہوں میں مبتلا
ہو گیا۔

intention   many times

۷۔ میں نے بار ہا یہ کام کرنے کی نیت کی لیکن فرصت نہ ملنے کی وجہ سے نہ کر سکا۔

۸۔ جوا معاشرتی نقطہ نظر سے بہت بڑی برائی ہے کیونکہ بہت سے ایسے لوگ ہیں جو اِس میں اپنی زندگی
تباہ کر لیتے ہیں۔

۹۔ جب میں انگلستان میں تھا تو میں نے ایک دفعہ غلطی سے سؤر کا گوشت کھا لیا تھا لیکن اُس کے
بعد میں کھانے سے پہلے ہمیشہ لوگوں سے پوچھ لیا کرتا تھا۔

۱۰۔ مولوی صاحب کے بیان سے ظاہر ہوتا ہے کہ بنیادی طور پر اسلام اور عیسائی مذہب میں ایک گہرا

144

۱۱۔ کل رات میں نے محسوس کیا کہ کوئی میرے کمرے میں چھپا ہوا ہے۔ میں نے بہت تلاش کی مگر کسی کو

نہیں پایا۔ آج صبح میرے دوسرے دوست نے بتایا کہ اس مکان میں بھوت رہتے ہیں۔

۱۲۔ انھوں نے اسلام کے فرائض کے بارے میں بہت کچھ بیان کیا مثلاً حج، زکوٰة، نماز، روزہ

وغیرہ۔ انھوں نے مجھے ایک کتاب بھی عطا فرمائی ہے۔

۱۳۔ اللہ کی عطا کردہ عنایات میں سے قرآن ایک بہت بڑی حیثیت رکھتا ہے۔

۱۴۔ جب کہ آپ اردو نہ اچھی طرح لکھ سکتے ہیں نہ پڑھ سکتے ہیں تو پھر آپ امتحان میں کیسے کامیاب

ہو سکتے ہیں؟

۱۵۔ کیا اب بھی امریکہ پاکستان کو امداد دیتا ہے؟

18.204. Writing Drill I: Text.

Counting each speaker's part as one paragraph, write out the first six paragraphs of Sec. 18.506 (Conversation Practice) in Urdu script (i.e. down through /... ke bare mẽ malumat mylti hȳy. /).

18.205. Spelling Review and Dictionary Drill.

Write the following words in Urdu script and place them in Urdu alphabetical order.

(1) bərabər
(2) gyryftar
(3) behoš
(4) dylcəsp
(5) xubsurət
(6) hošyar
(7) bədqysməti
(8) qəydxana
(9) cəwkidar
(10) mwqərrəršwda
(11) ətakərda
(12) kamyab
(13) əfsosnak
(14) kəmzor
(15) pabənd
(16) həmdərdi
(17) həqdar
(18) rwmal
(19) zəmindar
(20) amədorəft
(21) bərdašt
(22) xwrak
(23) bəndobəst
(24) nəmbərdar

(25) abohəva

(26) bərbad

(27) əhəmtərin

(28) dərəsl

(29) xwšqysməti

(30) naraz

18.206. Persian Forms.

Using the Analysis Section of this Unit, identify the component parts of each word in Sec. 18.205. Analyse each word into (a) prefix (if any), (b) first stem element, (c) connective (if any), (d) second stem element (if the item is a compound), and (e) suffixes (if any).

18.207. Response Drill.

Answer the following questions in writing.

۱۔ کیا آپ کو جوُا کھیلنے کا شوق ہے ؟

۲۔ کیا قرآن میں نماز اور زکوٰۃ کا ذکر موجود ہے ؟ اِن کے بارے میں کیا کہا گیا ہے ؟

۳۔ کیا عیسائی مذہب میں بھی شراب پینا منع ہے ؟

۴۔ کیا آپ نے کبھی قرآن کا مطالعہ کیا ہے ؟ اگر کیا ہے تو کس زبان میں ؟

۵۔ اِسلام کے پانچ اہم ارکان کون کونسے ہیں ؟

۶۔ زکوٰۃ ادا کرنا کِن مسلمانوں پر لازم نہیں ہے ؟

۷۔ کلمہ کا مطلب کیا ہے ؟

۸۔ اگر بہت سخت گرمی ہو تو بھی روزہ رکھنا ضروری ہے یا نہیں ؟

۹۔ شراب کیوں منع کی گئی ہے ؟

۱۰۔ مذہبی لحاظ سے اِسلام کے فرائض کی کیا حیثیت ہے ؟

18.208. English to Urdu Sentences.

1. The great religious leaders [lit. greats of religion] used to pass [their] lives [lit. life] in the worship of God and the service of His creatures.

146

2. If you have the power to [lit. of] take the journey to [lit. of] Mecca, then you certainly should go for the pilgrimage.

3. In Islam, there is no distinction between [lit. in] poor and rich, white and black. All are God's creatures.

4. When the date of my marriage was settled, then my father began to make [/šwru kər dena/] all the arrangements [/yntyzam/].

5. When Rəmzan comes in the summer [lit. heats], then one becomes more hungry and thirsty [lit. hunger and thirst attach more].

6. The Government wants to establish a separate department of Zəkat [lit. Zəkat's one separate department].

7. You are the rightful claimant of this land. Why don't you start [lit. make] a lawsuit in the court?

8. It was said about him, that in the Sixteenth Century he was the greatest scholar of Egypt.

9. From the point of view of Western society, if a boy makes [his own] marriage himself, then it is not considered bad.

10. Please consider this aspect too. Along with the defects, there are some benefits also.

11. Until [lit. until when] every person keeps [lit. does not keep] the prosperity and progress of the country in view, this problem cannot be solved.

12. They stressed this matter, that there are many defects in the new laws.

13. First he explained the detail[s] of this subject, then later on [lit. in afterward] [he] gave us an examination [lit. took our examination].

14. He appointed a lawyer after [his] own father's death.

15. The sad conditions of these poor people have created a feeling [lit. emotion] of sympathy in our hearts.

18.300. ANALYSIS

18.301. Persian Plurals.

Aside from the Arabic element discussed in Unit XVII, Urdu has also made free use of Persian as a source for vocabulary and elements of grammatical structure. Persian was employed in Indian Muslim courts as the official language for several hundred years, and Indian Persian poets developed and maintained a strong local tradition. Even today there is a tendency to look to Persian (including the Arabic element, which came to Urdu through Persian) as the source for new words, for elegant modes of expression, etc. , just as an English speaker might look to Latin and Greek. Indeed, the more "high-flown" one's prose or poetry becomes in Urdu, the more it will be Persianised. Thus, in spite of the fact that much of the material given in Sections 18.301 through 18.308 may not be of immediate relevance, the student will find it useful to employ these Sections for reference.

The Persian noun is not marked for gender or for case. It does indicate two numbers: singular and plural. Plural forms are divided into "animate-rational" and "inanimate-irrational."

(1) The "animate-rational" plural is made with suffix /an/ (often pronounced /ā/ in Urdu). If the singular ends in   ٥   /a/, the form of the suffix is /gan/. If the singular ends in   ا   /a/, the suffix is /yan/. There are no other significant irregularities. E. g.

> /bwzwrgan/ Mpl great ones
> /bəcgan/ Mpl children. [Also /bəccgan/, from */bəccəgan/.]
> /danayan/ Mpl wise ones. [/dana/ Ml Al "wise, knowing, sage, wise man."]

(2) The "inanimate-irrational" plural is made with the suffix /ha/. E. g.

> /barha/ Adv repeatedly, many times. [Lit. times. This form is used only as an adverb in Urdu.]
> /salha/ Adv for years, year after year. [Lit. years. This form is also only employed as an adverb in Urdu.]

The system is not completely regular, however. A few inanimate-irrational nouns are also found with the /an/ plural. E. g.

> /cyrayan/ Ml [np] illumination. [Perhaps originally the plural of /cyray/ Ml "lamp."]
> /dərəxtan/ Mpl trees. [Rare in Urdu.]
> /sytargan/ Mpl stars. [From */sytarəgan/. Rare in Urdu.]

The /an/ plural is fairly common in literature and poetry, though rare in speech. The suffix /ha/ is rather rare, occurring chiefly in a few adverbial expressions (see above) and in highly Persianised poetry. It is also found in such constructions as the names of organisations, etc. , made entirely on the Persian model. E. g.

> /ənjwmənhae ymdade bahəmi/ Fpl Cooperative Aid Societies. [/ənjwmən/ Fl "society"; /bahəmi/ Al "cooperative, mutual."]

148

/ryasəthae mwttəhyda əmrika/ Fpl the United States [of] America.
[/ryasət/ F1 "state"; /mwttəhyda/ A1 "united."]

Many purely Persian words also occur with the Arabic plural suffix /at/ and with the Persian-Arabic suffix /əjat/ (Sec. 17.304). E.g.

/kaγəzat/ [common: /kaγzat/] Mpl papers

/zevərat/ Mpl jewellery, ornaments

/qəydxanəjat/ Mpl prisons

18.302. The /yzafət/.

Both possession and modification are indicated in Persian by the /yzafət/ F1 "addition, connection." This device consists of an enclitic /e/ added to the noun possessing, followed by a possessed noun or by a modifying adjective (i.e. a possessed quality). Thus, Noun[1]-/e/ Noun[2] denotes "Noun[1] of Noun[2]"; Noun[1]-/e/ Adjective[2] signifies "Adjective[2] Noun[1]."

If Noun[1] has a plural suffix, the /yzafət/ follows it. If Noun[1] normally ends in ɸ /a/, this is replaced by /ə/ before the /yzafət/. E.g.

/hwkumҙte pakystan/ the Government of Pakistan

/mərde jəvan/ young man

/ysme šərif/ noble name

/vəzire azəm/ prime minister. [/vəzir/ M1 "minister"; /azəm/ A1 "greatest."]

/bwzwrgane din/ great religious men. [Lit. greats of the faith.]

/ryasəthae mwttəhyda/ the United States. [/ryasət/ F1 "state"; /mwttəhyda/ A1 "united."]

/nwqtəe nəzər/ point of view. [Followed by the /yzafət/, /nwqta/ M2 "point, dot" occurs as /nwqtə/; /nəzər/ F1 sight, vision."]

The /yzafət/ construction thus has the same word order as that of the English "of" formation: e.g. /hwkumҙte pakystan/ "government of Pakistan." The Hindi-Urdu possessive construction with /ka/, on the other hand, is just the reverse: it corresponds in word order to English "-'s": e.g. /pakystan ki hwkumҙt/ "Pakistan's government." These formations must be carefully distinguished since Urdu literature abounds in examples of both -- and noun phrases containing both at once are also found. E.g.

/cyraγe yšq ki ləw/ the flame of the lamp of love. [Lit. the lamp of love's flame. /yšq/ M1 "love"; /ləw/ F1 "flame."]

/ənjwmҙne kwtwbfərošane pakystan ka jəlsa/ the meeting of the Booksellers' Association of Pakistan. [Lit. the Society of Booksellers of Pakistan's meeting. /kwtwbfəroš/ M/F1 "bookseller"; /jəlsa/ M2 "meeting, session."]

18.303. Persian Numerals.

The Persian numerals from one to ten are fairly frequent in Urdu literary usage. They are treated as A1. They are:

/yək/ one	/syh/ [or /səy/] three
/do/ two	/cəhar/ four

/pənj/ five	/həšt/ eight
/šəš/ six	/nwh/ nine
/həft/ seven	/dəh/ ten

Other cardinal numerals are rare (except for /səd/ "hundred" and /həzar/ "thousand," which have been adopted into Urdu).

Persian ordinals are formed with the suffix /wm/. A few numerals have special stem alternants before /wm/.

/yəkwm/ first	/šəšwm/ sixth
/dovwm/ [or /doyəm/] second	/həftwm/ seventh
/syvwm/ third	/həštwm/ eighth
/cəharwm/ fourth	/nəhwm/ ninth
/pənjwm/ fifth	/dəhwm/ tenth

These ordinal numerals are often employed to number the volumes of a set of books, to number chapters, etc. The Persian ordinal /yəkwm/ "first" is, however, commonly replaced by the Arabic /əvvəl/ A1 "first." E. g.

/jylde syvwm/ volume three. [/jyld/ F1 "volume; skin."]

/babe cəharwm/ chapter four. [/bab/ M1 "chapter, section, gate."]

18.304. Persian Prepositions.

Of the Persian prepositions employed in Urdu, the following are common: /əz/ "from," /ba/ "with, accompanying," /bər/ "on," /be/ "without," /by/ (usually /bə/ in Urdu) "with, by," /dər/ "in," and /ta/ "up to, until." Only /əz/, /be/, and /ta/ can be said to have any independent existence in Urdu; the others are usually so closely joined to the following element that they must be termed prefixes rather than prepositions. E. g.

/əz lahəwr ta ravəlpynDi/ from Lahore to Rawalpindi

/əz myrza γalyb/ [a book written] by Mirza Ghalib. [/myrza γalyb/ M1 "Mirza Ghalib" (1797-1869) is one of the most popular poets of Urdu.]

/əz səre nəw/ Adv all over again, from the very beginning. [Lit. from a new heading. /nəw/ "new" is purely Persian and does not occur independently in Urdu. This phrase is treated as a single unit.]

/dərəsl/ Adv really, in fact. [Lit. in origin.]

/baqayda/ A1 regular, proper, according to regulation. [/qayda/ M2 "rule, regulation."]

/bərbad/ PA1 destroyed, ruined. [Lit. on the wind. Persian /bad/ "wind" does not occur alone in Urdu.]

/bepərda/ A1 unveiled, uncovered. [Lit. without curtain.]

Persian compound prepositions consist of a simple preposition + a noun or other element. Many of these have been adapted to the Urdu compound postpositional pattern. E. g.

/[ki] bəjae/ Comp Post instead of. [/bə/ "with, by"; /ja/ F1 "place"; /e/ is the /yzafət/.]

/[ke] dərmyan/ Comp Post between, among, in the midst of. [/dər/ "in"; /myan/ "middle" is not used independently in Urdu.]

/[ke] bərxylaf/ Comp Post contrary to, opposite to. [/bər/ "on"; /xylaf/ PA1 "against, opposing." Compare /[ke] xylaf/ Comp Post "against, opposing."]

Two further prepositional formations must be noticed:

(1) Certain substantive elements occur + the /yzafət/ before a noun as a kind of compound preposition. The first element is usually an adjective or predicate adjective, and it is arguable that these formations should be termed compounds rather than prepositional phrases. They are nevertheless equivalent to an Urdu compound postpositional phrase. E. g.

/qabyle tarif/ worthy of praise. [/qabyl/ Al "capable, worthy, suitable." This is equivalent to /tarif ke qabyl/.]

/xylafe hwkm/ against the order. [Equivalent to /hwkm ke xylaf/.]

Some of these constructions also occur with a Persian preposition preceding the first element, and the whole is employed as a true preposition. E. g.

/bətəwre ymdad/ as aid, by way of aid. [/bə/ "with, by"; /bətəwre/ is equivalent to the Urdu form /[ke] təwr pər/.]

/bəzəriee həvai jəhaz/ by airplane. [/bə/ "with, by"; /bəzəriee/ is equivalent to the Urdu form /[ke] zərie [se]/. In speech, /bəzəriee/ occurs as /bəzərie/.]

A few of these formations are treated as though they were Urdu compound postpositions: i. e. the first element is preceded by /ke/, and the whole follows the noun to which it refers. E. g.

/məwlvi sahəb ke zere əsər/ under the influence of Məwlvi Sahəb. [/zer/ Ml Adv "under"; /[ke] zere əsər/ is equivalent to /[ke] əsər ke təht/. See Sec. 25. 223.]

(2) Some compound postpositions of Arabic-Persian origin admit of an alternate construction in which the postpositional element <u>precedes</u> the noun, and the noun in turn is <u>followed</u> by /ke/. Thus, one finds both /[ke] bəɣəyr/ Comp Post "without" and also /bəɣəyr ... ke/, /[ke] bərxylaf/ Comp Post "contrary to, opposite to" and also /bərxylaf ... ke/, etc. Note that it is always /ke/ which follows, even when the postposition is otherwise treated as feminine: e. g. /[ki] bəjae/ Comp Post "instead of" and also /bəjae ... ke/ (instead of */bəjae ... ki/). One compound postposition has an alternate form employed only in this construction: /[ke] syva/ Comp Post "except" but /syvae ... ke/. Of the compound postpositions introduced so far, only the following may have this laternate "split" construction: /[ke] bəɣəyr/ "without," /[ki] bəjae/ "instead of," /[ke] syva/ "except," and /[ke] ylava/ "in addition to, besides." E. g.

/ylava yn cizō ke, ɣy saman bhi mere ghər pəhw̄ca dena. / In addition to these things, take [lit. make arrive] this baggage to my house also. [Equivalent to /yn cizō ke ylava/.]

/bəjae ys kytab ke, vw kytab pəRhie! / Instead of this book, please read that book! [Equivalent to /ys kytab ki bəjae/.]

/bəɣəyr ys dəvai ke, məriz ko fayda nəhī̃ hoga. / Without this medicine, the patient will not benefit. [Equivalent to /ys dəvai ke bəɣəyr/.]

/syvae ws ke, baqi təmam ləRke kylas mē̃ hazyr the. / Except for him, all the rest of the boys were present in class. [Equivalent to /ws ke syva/.]

/bəjae ys ke, ky ap mere hā̃ yntyzar kərē, mere kalyj a jaē. / Instead of this, that you wait at my place, please come to my college. [Equivalent to /ys ki bəjae/.]

18. 305. Persian Noun and Adjective Affixes.

Unlike Arabic, Persian substantive formations are quite unsymmetrical. There is a large class of stems, a small number of prefixes, and two or three suffix classes. The occurrence of any given element or any given combination of elements is unpredictable and dependent only upon usage. The following description is not intended to be exhaustive.

There are very few true prefixes in active use in Persian noun and adjective formation. Although traditional grammarians usually give up to fifteen or twenty elements as "prefixes," most of these are also found independently in Persian as adjectives, prepositions, etc., and constructions made with them must therefore be classed as compounds (see Sec. 18.307). To the author's knowledge, only the following can be classed as real prefixes:

[In this and following Sections the meanings of all stems will be given for ease of reference, irregardless of whether or not they have been introduced as vocabulary items in this Course.]

/la/ "un-, non-, in-." This element is from Arabic.

/la/ + N = A, PA, N. E.g.

/laməzhəb/ Al irreligious. [/məzhəb/ Ml "religion."]

/na/ "non-, in-, dis-." /na/ + N = A, PA, N. See Sec. 15.302. E.g.

/navaqyf/ Al unacquainted. [/vaqyf/ PAl "acquainted, knowing."]

Other elements commonly classed as "prefixes" in Persian include: /bəd/ "bad, un-, dis-" (see Sec. 11.301); /be/ "without, -less" (see Sec. 9.302); /yəyr/ "un-, non-"; /həm/ "together, syn-, con-"; /kəm/ "less, little-"; /pwr/ "-full, full-of-"; and /xwš/ "good-, well-" (see Sec. 17.308).

Persian substantive suffixes fall into three rough order classes: (a) a large group of "derivational" suffixes used to derive an adjective from a noun stem, a noun from an adjective, a noun from a noun, etc.; (b) miscellaneous second-order suffixes (e.g. /i/-/gi/ "abstract noun formant," /ana/ "adjective formant"); and (c) the plural suffixes discussed in Sec. 18.301. The /yzafət/ (Sec. 18.302) occurs as an enclitic after this third class. Suffixes of classes (a) and (b) include:

/a/: PA + /a/ = A. This suffix, written *θ*, represents the one formal difference

in Urdu (though not in Persian, where this dichotomy does not exist) between the predicate adjective and the adjective proper. Many stems occur without /a/ only as predicate adjectives; with /a/, however, they are found before a noun as adjectives. Although this suffix does not occur with all predicate adjectives by any means, there are a great many sets like the following:

/məwjuda/ Al present. [/məwjud/ PAl "present."]

/mwtəəllyqa/ Al connected, attached. [/mwtəəllyq/ PAl "connected, attached."]

/əbraluda/ Al cloudy. [/əbralud/ PAl "cloudy." /əbr/ Ml "cloud"; /alud/ "soiled with, smeared with, covered with" is the past stem of the verb /alu/; see Sec. 18.306. It occurs only in compounds in Urdu.]

Examples of usage:

/məwjuda zəmane mẽ .yy ciz bəhwt am həy. / In the present age this thing is very common. [/məwjud/ cannot be substituted for /məwjuda/ here.]

/səb log vəhã̄ məwjud the. / Everybody was present there. [/məwjuda/ cannot occur.]

/səylab se mwtəəssyra ylaqõ ko ymdad pəhw̃c gəi həy. / Aid has reached the areas affected by the flood. [/mwtəəssyra/ A1 "affected, influenced, stricken." The PA1 form /mwtəəssyr/ is also possible here but is rather less common. Compare: j

/mə̃y wn ki batõ se bəhwt mwtəəssyr hwa. / I was much influenced by his words. [Here /mwtəəssyra/ cannot occur at all.]

/mysr əwr šam ki mwttəhyda fəwjē age bəRhī. / The united armies of Egypt and Syria advanced. [/mwttəhyda/ A1 "united. "]

/mysr əwr šam ki fəwjē mwttəhyd ho kər age bəRhī. / The armies of Egypt and Syria united and advanced [lit. having become united, advanced]. [/mwttəhyd/ PA1 "united, joined, allied. "]

/yy rwsumat ajkəl mətruk ho gəi həy. / These customs have been abandoned nowadays. [/mətruk/ PA1 "abandoned, left. "]

/yn mətruka rwsumat ko zynda kərne se koi fayda nəhī. / There is no profit in reviving [lit. making alive] these abandoned customs. [/mətruka/ A1 "abandoned, left. "]

With a numeral preceding, a noun denoting time + /a/ = A. E. g.

/do sala mənsuba/ two year project. [/sal/ M1 "year. "]

/cəwbys sala ləRki/ twenty-four year old girl. [/sal/ M1 "year. "]

/syh roza jəlsa/ three day meeting. [/roz/ M1 "day. "]

/a/: N + /a/ = N, usually with some semantic change. Again this is written ٥

In Urdu, this is treated as though it were the Type II masculine suffix /a/. E. g.

/dəsta/ M2 handle. [/dəst/ M1 "hand" is found only in very literary Urdu.]

/roza/ M2 fasting. [/roz/ M1 "day. "]

/al/: N, A + /al/ = N. Rare. E. g.

/cə̃gal/ M1 claw. [/cə̃g/ PA1 "twisted, curved." This is more commonly found as /cw̃gəl/ M1.]

/ana/: N + /ana/ = N. This is written ٌٌٍٍٍ . In Urdu, and is treated as though

it were /an/ + the Type II masculine suffix /a/. E. g.

/dəstana/ M2 glove. [/dəst/ M1 "hand. "]

/ə̃gwštana/ M2 thimble. [Persian /ə̃gwšt/ M1 "thumb" is rare in Urdu.]

/jwrmana/ M2 fine. [/jwrm/ M1 "crime. "]

/ana/ "-like, fit-for-": N + /ana/ = A. This, too is written ٌٌٍٍٍ . Adjectives

made with this suffix are employed only with nouns which denote inanimate things, abstracts, etc. and never with nouns denoting rational beings. E. g.

/šahana/ A1 kingly, king-like. [/šah/ M1 "king. "]

/mwxalyfana/ A1 opposing, opposed, contrary. [/mwxalyf/ M/F1 A1 "opponent, opposing. "]

/mərdana/ A1 man-like, manly. [/mərd/ M1 "man, male. "]

Examples of usage:

153

/ws ne yy bəRi əhməqana hərəkət ki. /   He made this very stupid move.
[/əhməqana/ A1 "stupid." If a noun denoting a rational being were
employed instead of /hərəkət/, the adjective would be /əhməq/ A1
"stupid. "]

/yslam ke yy həqiqətpəsəndana wsul ynsan ki tərəqqi ka zəria bən səkte
həy. /   These truth-loving principles of Islam can become the way
to progress for mankind. [/həqiqətpəsənd/ A1 would be the form
found before an animate rational noun: e. g. /həqiqətpəsənd admi/ truth
loving man. " See Sec. 18.307 for the compound formation
/həqiqətpəsənd/.]

/ar/: see /avər/.

/avər/-/ar/-/er/-/var/-/vər/-/yar/ "possessing": N + /avər/ (etc.) = A.   E. g.

/zoravər/ A1 strong. [/zor/ M1 "force, power, strength."]

/salar/ M1 A1 chief, leader. [/sal/ M1 "year": literally "possessing
years. "]

/dyler/ A1 brave, valiant. [/dyl/ M1 "heart."]

/wmmidvar/ M/F1 A1 candidate; hopeful, expectant. [/wmmid/ F1
"hope. "]

/taqətvər/ A1 strong, powerful. [/taqət/ F1 "power, strength, energy. "]

/hošyar/ A1 clever, intelligent. [/hoš/ M1 [np] "consciousness, aware-
ness. "]

/ək/ "diminutive": N + /ək/ = N. Rare in Urdu. E. g.

/dəstək/ F1 tapping, knocking. [/dəst/ M1 "hand": literally "little
hand. "]

/bar/ "place of": N + /bar/ = N. Rare. E. g.

/juebar/ F1 place of streams. [/ju/ denotes "stream" in Persian. "]

/ban/-/van/ "keeper of, guardian of": N + /ban/ (etc.) = N. E. g.

/bayban/ M1 gardener. [/bay/ M1 "garden. "]

/mezban/ M1 host. [/mez/ F1 "table. "]

/kocvan/ M1 coachman. [/koc/ F1 "coach. "]

/ca/-/ica/ "diminutive": N + /ca/ (etc.) = N. This suffix is treated as though it
were /c/-/ic/ + the Type II suffix /a/ in Urdu. E. g.

/kytabca/ M2 pamphlet. [/kytab/ F1 "book. "]

/bayica/ M2 little garden. [/bay/ M1 "garden. "]

/ci/ "person engaged in": N + /ci/ = N. E. g.

/əfimci/ M1 opium user. [/əfim/ F1 "opium. "]

/topci/ M1 cannoneer. [/top/ F1 "cannon. "]

/dan/ "container for": N + /dan/ = N. E. g.

/nəməkdan/ M1 salt-cellar. [/nəmək/ M1 "salt. "]

/qələmdan/ M1 pen-case. [/qələm/ M1 [or F1] "pen. "]

/er/: see /avər/.

/fam/ "-coloured": N, A + /fam/ = A. E. g.

/gwlfam/ A1 rose-coloured. [/gwl/ M1 "rose. "]

/səfəvdfam/ A1 whitish, white-coloured. [/səfəyd/ A1 "white. "]

/gah/-/gəh/ "place of": N + /gah/ (etc.) = N. Nouns made with this suffix are
always F1. E. g.

/ybadətgah/ F1 place of worship. [/ybadət/ F1 "worship. "]

/danyšgah/ F1 university. [/danyš/ F1 "knowledge, learning. "]

/gar/-/gər/-/kar/ "doing, making, person doing": N, A + /gar/ (etc.) = M/F1 A1. E. g.

/dəstkar/ M/F1 artisan, handicraftsman. [/dəst/ M1 "hand"; literally "hand-doing. "]

/xwdkar/ A1 automatic. [/xwd/ Adv "self. "]

/gwnahgar/ M/F1 sinner. [/gwnah/ M1 "sin. "]

/jadugər/ M/F1 magician. [/jadu/ M1 "magic. "]

/zərgər/ M1 goldsmith. [/zər/ M1 "gold. "]

/gā/ "worth-": N + /gā/ = A. Rare in Urdu. E. g.

/raegā/ PA1 worthless, useless. [From */rahgā/; literally "worth throwing on the road. " /rah/ F1 "road, way. "]

/gər/: see /gar/.

/gəh/: see /gah/.

/gi/: see /i/.

/gin/: see /in/.

/gū/ "-coloured": N, A + /gū/ = A. This suffix has much the same meaning as /fam/ above. E. g.

/gwlgū/ A1 rose-coloured. [/gwl/ M1 "rose. "]

/i/-/gi/ "abstract noun formant": N, A + /i/ (etc.) = N. See Secs. 7.301 and 13.301. Nouns + /i/-/gi/ are all F2 in Urdu. E. g.

/neki/ F2 virtue, goodness. [/nek/ A1 "good, virtuous. "]

/dosti/ F2 friendship. [/dost/ M/F1 "friend. "]

/zyndəgi/ F2 life. [/zynda/ A1 "alive. "]

/i/ "-ship, occupation of": N + /i/ = N. See Sec. 7.301. Nouns + this suffix are F2. E. g.

/zəmindari/ F2 landownership, post or system of landownership, estate of a landowner. [/zəmindar/ M1 "landowner. " For the analysis of /zəmindar/, see Sec. 18.307.]

/DakTri/ F2 occupation of doctor, medical practice. [/DakTər/ M/F1 "doctor. "]

/i/ "adjective formant": N, A + /i/ = A. See Sec. 7.301. E. g.

/tarixi/ A1 historic, historical. [/tarix/ F1 "history; date. "]

/yslami/ A1 Islamic. [/yslam/ M1 "Islam. "]

When this suffix occurs with a noun denoting a place, country, etc. , the construction may be M/F2 denoting "person from ... "; it may also be treated as F2 [np], signifying " ... language. " E. g.

/bəˈgali/ M1/F2 F2 [np] A1 Bengali (person from Bengal); the Bengali language; Bengali (adj.). [/bəˈgal/ M1 [np] "Bengal. "]

/əˈgrezi/ M1/F2 F2 [np] A1 English (person); the English language; English (adj.). [/əˈgrez/ A1 "English. " In Urdu /əˈgrez/ is more usually employed for "Englishman, English person. "]

/ica/: see /ca/.

/in/-/ina/-/gin/ "possessing the quality of, made of": N + /in/ (etc.) = A. In Urdu this suffix is often pronounced /ī/. E. g.

/rɔ̄gin/ A1 coloured. [/rɔ̄g/ M1 "colour."]

/nəmkin/ A1 salty. [/nəmək/ M1 "salt."]

/γəmgin/ A1 sad, sorrowful. [/γəm/ M1 "sorrow, sadness."]

/derina/ A1 lengthy. [/der/ F1 "lateness, a long time."]

Some formations with /in/ and /ina/ are nouns. A stem + /ina/ is treated as a Type II noun in Urdu (i. e. /in/ + the Type II masculine suffix /a/). Compare /derina/ above. E. g.

/postin/ M1 leather jacket. [/post/ F1 "skin, hide."]

/pəšmina/ M2 wool, woollen goods. [/pəšm/ M1 "wool."]

/ina/: see /in/.

/iza/: see /za/.

/kar/: see /gar/.

/lax/ "place of many-": N + /lax/ = N, A. Rare. E. g.

/sɔ̄glax/ M1 A1 stony place, stony, rocky. [/sɔ̄g/ M1 "stone" occurs in literary Urdu.]

/man/ "possessing the quality of": N, A + /man/ = A. Rare in Urdu. E. g.

/šadman/ A1 happy, glad. [/šad/ PA1 "happy, glad."]

/mənd/ "possessing-": N + /mənd/ = A. E. g.

/əqlmənd/ A1 wise, intelligent. [/əql/ F1 "intellect, reason, wits."]

/dəwlətmənd/ A1 wealthy. [/dəwlət/ F1 "wealth."]

/syhətmənd/ A1 healthy. [/syhət/ F1 "health."]

/nae/ "place of": N + /nae/ = N. Constructions with this suffix are F1. E. g.

/abnae/ F1 strait. [/ab/ "water" is Persian and is employed mostly in compounds in Urdu.]

/xaknae/ F1 isthmus. [/xak/ F1 "earth, dirt."]

/nak/ "-full": N + /nak/ = A. See Sec. 15.303. E. g.

/əfsosnak/ A1 sad, sorrowful. [/əfsos/ M1 "sorrow, regret."]

/dərdnak/ A1 painful. [/dərd/ M1 "pain."]

/san/ "possessing the quality of": N, A + /san/ = A. Usually pronounced /sā/ in Urdu. Rare. E. g.

/yəksā/ PA1 equal, matching. [Persian /yək/ "one."]

/sar/ "like-, possessing the quality of": N + /sar/ = A, PA. E. g.

/xaksar/ A1 humble. [Lit. like dust. /xak/ F1 "dirt, earth, dust."]

/šərmsar/ PA1 bashful, modest. [/šərm/ F1 "modesty, shame, bashfulness."]

/sar/ "place of many-": N + /sar/ = N. Rare. E. g.

/šaxsar/ M1 glen, branchy place. [/šax/ F1 "branch, bough."]

/stan/: see /ystan/.

/šən/ "place of many-": N + /šən/ = N. E. g.

/gwlšən/ M1 rose-garden. [/gwl/ M1 "rose."]

/tər/ "comparative": A + /tər/ = A. See Sec. 13.302. E. g.

/nəzdiktər/ A1 nearer. [/nəzdik/ A1 "near."]

/tərin/ "superlative": A + /tərin/ = A. This is really /tər/ + a suffix /in/. See Sec. 13.302. E. g.

/nəzdiktərin/ A1 nearest. [/nəzdik/ A1 "near."]

/ū/ "like-, possessing the quality of": N + /ū/ = N, A. Rare in Urdu. E. g.

/hwmayū/ A1 fortunate. [/hwma/ or /hwmae/ M1 "bird of happy omen."]

/van/: see /ban/.

/var/: see /avər/.

/vənd/ "possessing the quality of": N + /vənd/ = N. Rare in Urdu. E. g.

/xwdavənd/ M1 lord, master, God. [/xwda/ M1 "God."]

/vər/: see /avər/.

/vəš/ "-like": N + /vəš/ = A. Rare. E. g.

/pərivəš/ A1 fairy-like. [/pəri/ F2 "fairy."]

/yar/: see /avər/.

/ystan/-/stan/ "place of": N, A + /ystan/ (etc.) = N. /stan/ occurs after stems ending in a vowel, while /ystan/ is found elsewhere. Nouns made with this suffix are M1. E. g.

/pakystan/ M1 Pakistan. [/pak/ A1 "pure."]

/gwlystan/ M1 rose-garden. [/gwl/ M1 "rose."]

/bostan/ M1 garden. [/bo/ is an alternate form of /bu/ F1 "smell, odour."]

/za/-/iza/ "diminutive": N + /iza/ = N. In Urdu, this suffix is treated as though it were /z/-/iz/ + the Type II masculine suffix /a/. Rare. E. g.

/məškiza/ M2 small leathern bottle. [/məšk/ F1 "leather waterbag."]

/zar/ "place of": N + /zar/ = N. E. g.

/gwlzar/ M1 rose-garden. [/gwl/ M1 "rose."]

/regzar/ M1 desert. [/reg/ M1 "sand" is rare in Urdu.]

18. 306. The Persian Verb.

The Persian verb is similar to its Urdu counterpart in its basic structure: a stem ± various suffixes ± auxiliary verbs. Unlike Urdu, however, the Persian verb has a small set of prefixes, no gender distinctions, a full set of person-number suffixes, etc. Most of the details of this system are irrelevant for a knowledge of Urdu.

Each Persian verb has two possible stem forms: (1) the "past stem," used in the past tenses, the infinitive, the past participle, and the future tense (a periphrastic formation); and (2) the "present stem" which occurs in the present tenses, the imperative, the present subjunctive, the present participle, and the noun of agent. Details of these two stem forms are as follows:

(1) The "past stem" consists of the root + a suffix /t/-/d/-/id/. /t/ occurs after a root ending in a voiceless consonant (e. g. /p/, /x/, /f/, /š/); /d/ occurs after voiced consonants and vowels (e. g. /b/, /z/, /r/, /n/, /l/, /u/, /o/, etc.); /id/ may occur after any consonant. Other affixes occur after the past stem. E. g.

/pərvərd/ nourished, reared. [Root: /pərvər/ "nourish, rear."]

/nyšəst/ sat. [Root: /nyšəs/ "sit."]

/xərid/ bought. [Root: /xər/ "buy."]

/kwšt/ killed. [Root: /kwš/ "kill."]
/kənd/ dug. [Root: /kən/ "dig."]
/malid/ rubbed. [Root: /mal/ "rub."]

(2) Basically, the "present stem" consists of the root only -- without /t/-/d/-/id/. There is, however, a large class of verbs which have a present stem root alternant different from that employed for the past stem. Thus, while both the present and past stems of "kill" contain the root alternant /kwš/, the present stem of "sit" is not /nyšəs/ (the form found in the past stem) but another alternant, /nəšin/. Most such pairs of root alternants differ in only one or two sounds. One or two have completely different alternants for their two stems, however. Verbs which have the /id/ form of the past stem suffix always have just one root alternant, employed in both their present and past stems. E.g.

/pərvər/ nourish, rear. [Present stem of /pərvər/ "nourish, rear."]
/kən/ dig. [Present stem of /kən/ "dig."]
/xər/ buy. [Present stem of /xər/ "buy," an /id/ verb.]
/mal/ rub. [Present stem of /mal/ "rub," an /id/ verb.]

But compare:

/nəšin/ sit. [Present stem of /nyšəs/ "sit."]
/dar/ have. [Present stem of /daš/ "have."]
/bənd/ tie. [Present stem of /bəs/ "tie."]
/əfraz/ raise. [Present stem of /əfrax/ "raise."]
/bin/ see. [Present stem of /di/ "see."]

In Urdu, the present stem occurs only in compounds or with various suffixes (see below), but the past stems of several verbs are found as F1 nouns. E.g.

/xərid/ F1 purchase price. [/xər/ "buy."]
/fəroxt/ F1 sale. [/fəroxt/ "sell."]
/nyšəst/ F1 seat (in parliament, etc.). [/nyšəs/ "sit."]

Suffixes found with the past stem include:

/a/ "past participle": Past stem + /a/ = A, PA, Adv. This suffix is written with
ه   Before a following suffix or compound element /a/ occurs as /ə/.

The /gi/ form of the abstract noun formant /i/-/gi/ is added to many items ending in /a/. E.g.

/asuda/ A1 prosperous. [/asu/ "be satisfied, rest."]
/azwrda/ A1 melancholy. [/azwr/ "be gloomy, sad, depressed."]
/šykəsta/ A1 broken. [/šykəs/ "break."]
/danysta/ Adv knowingly, deliberately. [/danys/ "know."]
/rəfta rəfta/ Adv gradually. [/rəf/ "go." Literally "gone gone."]
/šykəstəgi/ F2 breakage, defect. [/šykəs/ "break."]

/ar/ "abstract noun formant": Past stem + /ar/ = N. E.g.

/gwftar/ F1 saying, speech. [/gwf/ "say."]
/rəftar/ F1 gait, speed. [/rəf/ "go."]
/didar/ M1 sight. [/di/ "see."]

158

/ar/ "person ... ing, agentive noun formant": Past stem + /ar/ = N. E.g.

    /xəridar/ M/F1 customer, buyer. [/xər/ "buy."]

    /pərəstar/ M/F1 worshipper. [/pərəst/"worship."]

  But note the passive sense of:

    /gyryftar/ PA1 caught, arrested, apprehended, seized. [/gyryf/ "catch, arrest, seize."]

  The /i/ form of the abstract noun formant /i/-/gi/ occurs after /ar/. E.g.

    /gyryftari/ F2 arrest, seizure. [/gyryf/ "catch, arrest, seize."]

    /xəridari/ F2 buying, purchasing. [/xər/ "buy."]

/ən/ (+ /i/) "fit for, suitable for": Past stem + /əni/ = A (?). /əni/ consists of the Persian infinitive suffix /ən/ (which is otherwise rare in Urdu) + /i/ "adjective formant." Forms ending in /əni/ are uncommon in Urdu and are usually found only after the /yzafət/. E.g.

    /xordəni/ A1 (?) fit to eat, edible. [/xor/ "eat."]

    /gwftəni/ A1 (?) worth saying. [/gwf/ "say."]

Suffixes found with the present stem include:

/a/ "noun and adjective formant": Present stem + /a/ = N, A. This suffix is

  written ا . The /i/ form of the abstract noun formant /i/-/gi/ occurs

  after this suffix. E.g.

    /dana/ M1 A1 wise, knowing, sage, wise man. [/danys/ "know"; present stem /dan/.]

    /bina/ M1 one having vision, wise, intelligent. [/di/ "see"; present stem /bin/.]

    /danai/ F2 wisdom. [/danys/ "know"; present stem /dan/.]

/a/ "noun formant": Present stem + /a/ = N. This suffix is written with ہ

  In Urdu, this suffix is treated as though it were the Type II masculine suffix /a/. E.g.

    /bosa/ M2 kiss. [/bos/ "kiss."]

    /lərza/ M2 trembling, tremor. [/lərz/ "tremble."]

    /nala/ M2 cry, lamentation. [/nal/ "cry."]

/ak/ "noun formant": Present stem + /ak/ = N. E.g.

    /təpak/ M1 warmth, enthusiasm. [/təp/ "be warm."]

    /xorak/ F1 food; dose (of medicine). [/xor/ "eat."]

    /pošak/ F1 dress, costume. [/poš/ "wear."]

    /sozak/ M1 inflammation, gonorrhea. [/sox/ "burn"; present stem /soz/.]

/an/ "abstract noun formant": Present stem + /an/ = N. This suffix is sometimes pronounced /ā/. The adjective formant /i/ may follow /an/ in some items. E.g.

    /fərman/ M1 command, edict. [/fərmu/ "order, command"; present stem /fərma/, here /fərm/.]

    /baran/ [or /barā/] F1 rain. [/bar/ "rain."]

/barani/ Al dependent upon rain (as land). [/bar/ "rain."]

/an/ "present participle": Present stem + /an/ = A, PA. This suffix is sometimes pronounced /ā/. The /i/ form of the abstract noun formant /i/-/gi/ follows /an/ in many examples. E.g.

/rəvā/ Al moving, going, in progress. [/rəf/ "go"; present stem /rəv/.]

/tabā/ Al gleaming, shining. [/taf/ "gleam, shine"; present stem /tab/.]

/sozā/ Al burning. [/sox/ "burn"; present stem /soz/.]

/rəvani/ F2 fluency. [/rəf/ "go"; present stem /rəv/.]

/tabani/ F2 brightness, shininess, gleam. [/taf/ "gleam, shine"; present stem /tab/.]

/ynda/-/ənda/-/wnda/ "noun of agent": Present stem + /ynda/ (etc.) = N, A. The last two forms of this suffix are not common. This affix is written with a final ﻩ and may be followed by the /gi/ form of the abstract noun formant /i/-/gi/ or by the /gan/ form of the plural suffix (when the form refers to persons). Before suffixes or a following element in a compound the final /a/ of this suffix occurs as /ə/. E.g.

/bəxšynda/ M/F1 giver, bestower. [/bəxš/ "give, bestow."]

/nwmaynda/ M/F1 A1 representative. [/nəmu/ or /nwmu/ "show, point out, appear"; present stem /nəma/ or /nwma/.]

/tabynda/ A1 gleaming, shining. [/taf/ "gleam, shine"; present stem /tab/.]

/nwmayndəgi/ F2 representation. [/nəmu/ or /nwmu/ "show, point out, appear"; present stem /nəma/ or /nwma/. And also:]

/nwmayndəgan/ M/Fpl representatives.

/yš/ "abstract noun formant": Present stem + /yš/ = N. Nouns made with this suffix are uniformly F1. E.g.

/xahyš/ F1 desire, wish. [/xas/ "wish, want"; present stem /xah/.]

/košyš/ F1 try, attempt. [/koš/ "try."]

/azmayš/ F1 test, trial. [/azmu/ "try, test, examine"; present stem /azma/.]

18.307. Compounding.

Persian structure is complicated by the fact that members of many grammatical classes may be juxtaposed to one another (with or without an intervening /yzafət/, the conjunction /o/ "and," etc.) to form a compound which then occurs in the same environments as a simplex noun or adjective. Many different combinations are found: noun + noun, adjective + noun, noun + adjective, present stem + past stem, adverb + adverb, etc. etc. A large number of these formations have been borrowed wholesale into Urdu, and Urdu speakers have also constructed many new compounds on Persian models. The following list is thus by no means exhaustive.

Compounds which are employed as nouns include:

N + N = N. E.g.

/qəydxana/ M2 prison. [/qəyd/ F1 "restriction, restraint, imprison-
ment"; /xana/ M2 "house of, place for; compartment."]

/roznama/ M2 daily newspaper. [/roz/ M1 "day"; /nama/ M2 "letter,
writing, document."]

N + /e/ + N = N. E. g.

/nwqtəe nəzər/ M1 point of view. [/nwqta/ M2 "point, dot"; /nəzər/
F1 "sight, vision."]

/talybe ylm/ M1 student. [/talyb/ M1 "seeker"; /ylm/ M1 "knowledge";
usually pronounced /talybylm/ in normal speech.]

N + /o/ + N = N. E. g.

/abohəva/ F1 climate. [/ab/ "water" is found mostly in compounds in
Urdu; /həva/ F1 "air, wind."]

/šoroγəwγa/ M1 noise, tumult. [/šor/ M1 "noise"; /γəwγa/ M2
"noise, tumult" is limited almost entirely to compounds in Urdu.]

A + N = N. E. g.

/xwšbu/ F1 fragrance, perfume. [/xwš/ PA1 "happy, glad, good";
/bu/ F1 "odour, smell."]

/nəwmwslym/ M1 new Muslim, new convert to Islam. [/nəw/ "new"
occurs in compounds only; /mwslym/ M1 A1 "Muslim."]

N + A = N. E. g.

/yslamabad/ M1 Islamabad. [A place name. /yslam/ M1 "Islam";
/abad/ A1 "inhabited, populated."]

N + /e/ + A = N. E. g.

/ysme šərif/ M1 illustrious name. [/ysm/ M1 "name, noun"; /šərif/
A1 "noble, illustrious."]

/tərze nəw/ F1 new style, new manner. [/tərz/ F1 "way, manner,
method"; /nəw/ "new" occurs in compounds only.]

N + Present Stem = N. E. g.

/cəwkidar/ M1 watchman. [/cəwki/ F2 "post (of a guard)"; /dar/
present stem of /daš/ "have."]

/ghəRisaz/ M1 watchmaker. [/ghəRi/ F2 "watch"; /saz/ present stem
of /sax/ "make, construct."]

/zəmindar/ M1 landowner, landlord. [/zəmin/ F1 "earth, ground, land";
/dar/ present stem of /daš/ "have."]

A + Present Stem = N. E. g.

/xwšnəvis/ M1 calligrapher, one who writes beautifully. [/xwš/ PA1
"happy, glad, good"; /nəvis/ present stem of /nəvyš/ "write."]

/durbin/ M1 telescope. [/dur/ F1 A1 "distance, far"; /bin/ present
stem of /di/ "see."]

N + Past Participle = N. E. g.

/šahzada/ M2 prince. [/šah/ M1 "king"; /zada/ past participle of
/za/ "be born."]

N + Noun of Agent = N. E. g.

/raedəhynda/ M/F1 A1 opinion-giver, voter, person polled. [/rae/ F1
"opinion"; /dəhynda/ "giver" is found in compounds only: /dəh/
present stem of /da/ "give" + /ynda/.]

/dərxastkwnynda/ M/F1 applicant. [/dərxast/ F1 "application" is
itself a compound of /dər/ "in" + /xast/, the past stem of /xas/
"wish, want"; /kwnynda/ "maker, doer" occurs in compounds only:
/kwn/ present stem of /kər/ "make, do" + /ynda/.]

Past Stem + /o/ + Past Stem = N. E.g.

/amədorəft/ F1 communication. [/aməd/ past stem of /amə/ "come"; /rəft/ past stem of /rəf/ "go."]

/gwftošwnid/ F1 conversation. [/gwft/ past stem of /gwf/ "say"; /šwnid/ past stem of /šwn/ "hear."]

Past Stem ± /o/ + Present Stem = N. E.g.

/gwftwgu/ F1 conversation. [/gwft/ past stem of /gwf/ "say"; /gu/ present stem of /gwf/ "say"; /o/ "and" is here shortened to /w/.]

/jwstwju/ F1 search. [/jwst/ past stem of /jws/ "seek, search"; /ju/ present stem of /jws/ "seek, search." Again /o/ occurs as /w/.]

Present Stem + /o/ + Past Stem = N. E.g.

/bəndobəst/ M1 arrangement. [/bənd/ present stem of /bəs/ "tie"; /bəst/ past stem of /bəs/ "tie."]

Present Stem + /o/ + Present Stem = N. E.g.

/darogir/ F1 [or M1?] catching, seizing. [/dar/ present stem of /daš/ "have"; /gir/ present stem of /gyryf/ "catch, arrest, seize."]

/sozogwdaz/ M1 burning and melting. [/soz/ present stem of /sox/ "burn"; /gwdaz/ present stem of /gwdax/ "melt."]

Adverb + N = N. E.g.

/pəsmənzər/ M1 background. [/pəs/ Adv "after, back"; /mənzər/ M1 "sight, view, scene."]

Adverb + Past Participle = N. E.g.

/pəsxorda/ M2 leavings, left-overs. [/pəs/ Adv "after, back"; /xorda/ past participle of /xor/ "eat."]

Adverb + Present Stem = N. E.g.

/pešrəw/ M1 forerunner. [/peš/ Adv "before"; /rəw/ present stem of /rəf/ "go." /rəw/ is found at the end of a word or before a consonant; /rəv/ occurs before vowels.]

Adverb + /o/ + Adverb = N. E.g.

/pəsopeš/ M1 indecision, shilly-shallying. [/pəs/ Adv "after, back"; /peš/ Adv "before."]

Preposition + Past Stem = N. E.g.

/dərxast/ F1 application. [/dər/ "in"; /xast/ past stem of /xas/ "wish, want."]

Preposition + Present Stem = N. E.g.

/dərgwzər/ F1 overlooking, ignoring. [/dər/ "in"; /gwzər/ present stem of /gwzəš/ "pass by."]

Present Stem + /a/ + Present Stem = N. E.g.

/kəšakəš/ F1 struggle, wrangle. [/kəš/ present stem of /kəš/ "pull, tug."]

Present Stem + /mə/ + Present Stem = N, Adv. /mə/ is the Persian negative imperative prefix; it is found only in compounds in Urdu. E.g.

/kəšməkəš/ F1 struggle, contention. [/kəš/ present stem of /kəš/ "pull, tug"; lit. "pull-don't-pull."]

/xahməxah/ Adv willy-nilly, all for nothing. [/xah/ present stem of /xas/ "wish, want"; lit. "want-don't-want." This is often pronounced /xaməxa/ or even /xamxa/ in normal speed speech.]

Compounds which are employed as adjectives include:

N + N = A. E.g.

/sə̄gdyl/ A1 hardhearted. [/sə̄g/ M1 "stone"; /dyl/ M1 "heart."]

/pəricyhra/ A1 beautiful, fairy-faced. [/pəri/ F2 "fairy"; /cyhra/ M2 "face."]

N + A = A. E.g.

/həqiqətpəsənd/ A1 truth-loving. [/həqiqət/ F1 "truth, reality"; /pəsənd/ PA1 F1 "pleasing, liked, choice."]

A + N = A. E.g.

/bədhal/ A1 wretched, miserable. [/bəd/ A1 "bad"; /hal/ M1 "state, condition."]

/nərmdyl/ A1 softhearted. [/nərm/ A1 "soft"; /dyl/ M1 "heart."]

/xwšqysmət/ A1 lucky, of good omen. [/xwš/ PA1 "happy, glad, good"; /qysmət/ F1 "fate, destiny."]

N + Present Stem = A. E.g.

/dylkəš/ A1 attractive. [/dyl/ M1 "heart"; /kəš/ present stem of /kəš/ "pull, tug."]

/həyrətə̄gez/ A1 wondrous, marvellous. [/həyrət/ F1 "wonder, amazement"; /ə̄gez/ present stem of /ə̄gex/ "arouse, excite."]

A + Present Stem = A. E.g.

/swstrəw/ A1 slow, slow-paced. [/swst/ A1 "slow, lazy"; /rəw/ present stem of /rəf/ "go" (see /pešrəw/ above).]

N + Past Stem = A. E.g.

/namnyhad/ A1 so-called, just for the name only. [/nam/ M1 "name"; /nyhad/ past participle of /nyha/ "put, place, apply."]

A + Past Stem = A. E.g.

/bədnyhad/ A1 ill-disposed, having bad intentions. [/bəd/ A1 "bad"; /nyhad/ past participle of /nyha/ "put, place, apply."]

N + Past Participle = A. This construction is very common in Urdu. Among those past participles most frequently employed are /kərda/ from /kər/ "make, do," /šwda/ from /šw/ "be, become," /yafta/ from /yaf/ "get, obtain," /zəda/ from /zə/ "hit, beat," etc. E.g.

/jəhādida/ A1 experienced, widely travelled. [/jəhan/ M1 "world"; /dida/ past participle of /di/ "see."]

/ətakərda/ A1 given, bestowed. [/əta/ F1 "gift, benefaction, giving"; /kərda/ past participle of /kər/ "make, do." Lit. "gift-made."]

/jəməšwda/ A1 gathered, collected, accumulated. [/jəma/ F1 "gathering, collection"; /šwda/ past participle of /šw/ "be, become." /jəməšwda/ has an intransitive connotation: "collection-became"; /jəməkərda/ also occurs and has a transitive significance: "collection-made."]

/šadišwda/ A1 married. [/šadi/ F2 "marriage"; /šwda/ past participle of /šw/ "be, become."]

/talimyafta/ A1 educated. [/talim/ F1 "education"; /yafta/ past participle of /yaf/ "get, obtain."]

/səylabzəda/ A1 flood-stricken. [/səylab/ M1 "flood"; /zəda/ past participle of /zə/ "hit, beat."]

A, PA + Past Participle = A. Adjectives are uncommon as the first element in this type of compound, but it is a frequent means of making an adjective from a predicate adjective. Again, /kərda/, /šwda/, etc. are the commonest second elements. E.g.

/mwqərrəršwda/ A1 appointed, fixed. [/mwqərrər/ PA1 "appointed, fixed, established."]

/šaekərda/ A1 published, issued. [/šae/ PA1 "published, issued."]

/nəwzayda/ A1 new-born. [/nəw/ "new" occurs in compounds only; /zayda/ past participle of /za/ "be born." /za/ occurs with both the /d/ and the /id/ alternants of the past stem formant; /zayda/ is thus from /zaida/.]

Adverb + Past Participle = A. E. g.

/pəsmanda/ A1 backward, retarded. [/pəs/ Adv "after, back"; /manda/ past participle of /man/ "remain, stay."]

/peškərda/ A1 offered, presented. [/peš/ Adv "before"; /kərda/ past participle of /kər/ "make, do."]

Preposition + N = A, PA. E. g.

/bərbad/ PA1 destroyed, ruined. [/bər/ "on"; /bad/ "wind" occurs only in compounds in Urdu: lit. "on the wind."]

/dərkar/ PA1 needed, required. [/dər/ "in"; /kar/ "work, doing" is found in compounds only in Urdu.]

Preposition + Past Stem = A, PA. E. g.

/bərxast/ PA1 dispersed, dismissed. [/bər/ "on"; /xast/ past stem of /xas/ "arise, get up."]

Preposition + Past Participle = A, PA. E. g.

/bərgəšta/ A1 rebellious, turned away. [/bər/ "on"; /gəšta/ past participle of /gəš/ "turn."]

/dərmanda/ A1 distressed, destitute. [/dər/ "in"; /manda/ past participle of /man/ "remain, stay."]

Preposition + Adverb = A, PA. E. g.

/dərpeš/ PA1 facing, confronting. [/dər/ "in"; /peš/ Adv "before."]

N, A + /a/ + N, A = A, Adv. E. g.

/bərabər/ A1 Adv equal, level, adjoining. [/bər/ "breast" is employed in compounds only in Urdu: lit. "breast-to-breast."]

/ləbaləb/ Adv brimful, to the brim. [/ləb/ M1 "lip."]

/sərapa/ Adv from head to foot. [/sər/ M1 "head"; /pa/ "foot" is found only in compounds in Urdu.]

/yəkayək/ Adv all at once. [Persian /yək/ "one."]

Many constructions contain more than one affix or consist of compounds + one or more affixes. It is not possible to deal with all of these formations in the limited space available here, however, and a few illustrative examples must suffice:

/nadanyšməndana/ A1 unwise, foolish. [/na/ "non-, in-, dis-" is a prefix; /dan/ present stem of /danys/ "know"; /yš/ is an abstract noun formant occurring with present stems; /mənd/ "possessing" is an adjective formant; /ana/ "like, fit for" is another adjective formant.]

/həqe xwdyxtiari/ F2 right of self-determination. [/həq/ M1 "right, truth"; /e/ is the /yzafət/; /xwd/ Adv "self"; /yxtiar/ M1 "option, discretion, choice, authority, jurisdiction"; /i/ "abstract noun formant." Note that /həqe xwdyxtiar/, /xwdyxtiar/, and /xwdyxtiari/ are all without meaning. This compound has been coined by Urdu newspaper writers as the translation of an English phrase.]

/qəbl əz pešəvərana/ A1 prevocational. [/qəbl/ Adv Comp Post "before" is from Arabic; /əz/ Prep "from"; /peša/ M2 "occupation"; /vər/ is one form of a suffix meaning "possessing"; /ana/ "like,

fit for" is another adjective formant suffix. Again, this is recent
newspaper coinage.]

18.308. Persian Verb Stems Employed in Compounds.

Examples of one or another form of many of the verbs given below are found in the
author's wordcount of newspaper Urdu. Others have been culled from various dictionaries
and older grammars of Urdu. The list is not exhaustive.

Alternate forms are given in square brackets.

PAST STEM	PRESENT STEM	MEANING
afrid	afrin	create, produce
alud	ala	soil, smear, defile, cover with
aməd	a	come
amext	amez	mix
amoxt	amoz	teach, learn
arast	ara	decorate, embellish, set
asud	asa	rest, be satisfied
avext	avez	hang
avwrd	avər [/ar/]	bring
azmud	azma	test, examine
azwrd	azar	grieve, disturb, vex, be gloomy, sad, depressed
əfraxt	əfraz	raise
əfroxt	əfroz	kindle
əfšanid	əfšan	scatter, diffuse
əfzud	əfza	arouse, enhance, encourage, increase
əndaxt	əndaz	throw, put down, drop, pour
əndešid	əndeš	think, meditate
ɑ̃gext	ɑ̃gez	arouse, incite, instigate
baft	baf	weave
barid	bar	rain
baxt	baz	play, lose at (game)
bəst	bənd	tie, fasten
bəxšid	bəxš	bestow, give, grant
bosid	bos	kiss
bud	baš	be
bwrd	bər	carry, bear
cəkanid	cəkan	drip, trickle
cəspid	cəsp	adhere, stick, incline to, attract
cid	cin	gather, collect, pick, pluck
dad	dəh	give
danyst	dan	know
dašt	dar	have

PAST STEM	PRESENT STEM	MEANING
did	bin	see
doxt	doz	sew, penetrate
fəhmid	fəhm	understand
fərmud	fərma	order, command, say
fəroxt	fəroš	sell
fərsud	fərsa	rub away, scratch, wear
fyreft [/fəreft/]	fyreb [/fəreb/]	deceive
fyrystad	fyryst	send
gəšt	gərd	turn, revolve
gəzid	gəzin	cut, sting, bite, be stricken by
gwdaxt	gwdaz	melt
gwft	gu [/go/]	say, tell
gwrext	gwrez	flee, run away
gwvarid	gwvar	digest, be digestible, palatable
gwzašt	gwzar	pass, experience (transitive)
gwzəšt	gwzər	pass, be experienced (intransitive)
gwzid	gwzin	choose, select, adopt
gyryft	gir	catch, arrest, seize, take
jwmbid	jwmb	move, stir
jwst	ju [/jo/]	search, look for
kašt	kar	grow, plant
kənd	kən	dig
kərd	kwn	make, do
kəšid	kəš	pull, draw, tug, attract
koft	kob	crush
kwšt	kwš	kill
kwšud	kwša	open
lərzid	lərz	tremble
lesid	les	lick
malid	mal	rub
mand	man	remain, stay
mwrd	mir	die
nalid	nal	cry, lament
nəmud [/nwmud/]	nəma [/nwma/]	show, point out, appear
nəvaxt	nəvaz	grace, bestow, cherish
nəvyšt	nəvis	write
nošt	noš	drink
nygarid [/nygaryst/]	nygar	paint, decorate, embellish, write
nyhad	nyh	place, put, apply
nyšəst [/nəšəst/]	nyšin [/nəšin/]	sit
pašid	paš	sprinkle, scatter

PAST STEM	PRESENT STEM	MEANING
pərəstid	pərəst	worship
pərdaxt	pərdaz	nourish, bring up, adorn, finish, complete, free, clean
pərvərd	pərvər	nourish, rear
pəyvəst	pəyvənd	unite, join
pəzirwft	pəzir	receive, accept, be capable of
pošid	poš	wear, clothe, dress
pwrsid	pwrs	ask
pwxt	pəz	cook
rank	ran	drive, run (transitive)
rəft	rəv	go
rəsanid	rəsan	cause to arrive
rəsid	rəs	arrive, reach
rext	rez	drop, pour, shed, spill
rwbud	rwba	snatch, seize
saxt	saz	make, construct, build
soxt	soz	burn
sypwrd	sypar	entrust
sytad	sytan	seize, carry away
šarid	šar	fall (water), flow
šənaxt [/šynaxt/]	šənas [/šynas/]	know, be acquainted with
šwd	šəv	be, become
šwmwrd	šwmar	count
šwnid [/šynid/]	šwnəv [/šynəv/]	hear
šygaft	šygaf	rupture, split, tear apart
šykəst	šykən	break
šytaft	šytab	hasten
taft [/tabid/]	tab	gleam, shine, dazzle, burn, set on fire
tərašid	təraš	cut, pare, scrape
tərsid	tərs	fear
wftad	wft	fall
vərzid	vərz	cultivate, exert oneself, endeavour, practice
xand	xan	read
xast	xez	rise, get up, arouse
xast	xah	wish, want
xəndid	xənd	laugh
xərid	xər	buy
xord	xor	eat
yaft	yab	get, obtain
zad [/zayd/]	za	be born
zəd	zən	hit, beat, strike

18. 401. Supplementary Vocabulary.

The following numerals are all Type I adjectives. See Sec. 2. 401.

ykhəttər	seventy-one
bəhəttər	seventy-two
tyhəttər	seventy-three
cəwhəttər	seventy-four
pəchəttər [or /pychəttər/]	seventy-five

Other items are:

gwzərna [I: /gwzarna/: If]	to pass, elapse, happen, transpire
mwqərrər PA1	fixed, settled, established, appointed
šərt F1	condition, stipulation; wager, bet
xwšhal A1	prosperous
kəm se kəm Adv	at least, as little as possible

18. 402. Supplementary Exercise I: Translation.

1. Employing the formula "... /rupəe/ ... /pəyse/," give the following decimal currency prices.

a.	147. 58	f.	42. 73	k.	334.69
b.	2, 535. 40	g.	5, 772. 16	l.	473. 75
c.	27. 69	h.	16. 70	m.	9,578. 25
d.	71. 75	i.	.68	n.	72. 71
e.	36. 74	j.	75. 14	o.	61. 74

2. Give the following dates in Urdu. Use the formula "... hundred [and] ... ," rather than "... thousand, ... hundred, and ...": e.g. "fifteen hundred [and] fifty," rather than "one thousand, five hundred, and fifty. "

a.	1857	c.	1771	e.	1275	g.	1968
b.	1918	d.	1874	f.	972	h.	1970

18. 403. Supplementary Exercise II: Fill the Blanks.

1. Fill the blanks in the following sentences with the appropriate form of one of the items introduced above in Sec. 18. 401.

a. vw ws kalyj mẽ ____ hwa həy.

b. vəkil sahəb ne mwjhe ek əwr ____ bətai.

c. ap ka mwlk bəhwt ____ ho gəya həy.

d. pəcas əwr ykkys ____ hote hə̄y.

e. vw əbhi yəhā̃ se ____ tha.

f. ws ne ____ ytna to kia həy.

g. ws ne ek əwr ____ ləgai, məgər phyr har gəya.

h. ek kylas mẽ chəttys ləRke əwr əRtys ləRkiã hə̄y. kwl kytne hwe. ____.

i. təqribən dəs ghənTe ____ hə̄y.

j. ys sal gərmiõ ki chwTTiã əcchi ____.

18.500. VOCABULARY AND GRAMMAR DRILL

18.501. Substitution.

1. əllah ne mwsəlmanõ pər   **həj**   zəruri qərar dia. [1]

                             fasting

                             prayer

                             the study of the Qwran

                             worship

                             the Confession of Faith

        [1]Make /dia/ agree with the number-gender of the object in each sentence.

2. yslam mẽ   **jua**   **khelna**   məna həy.

               pig   eating

               wine   drinking

               idol   worshipping

               theft   doing

               lie   speaking

3. šayəd vw yn qəvanin   **ke mwašrəti fəvayd**   nəhĩ səməjhte.

                         's national importance

                         's religious aspects

                         's other defects

                         's basic weaknesses

                         's importance

4. **roza**   **rəkhna**   hər mwsəlman pər lazym kia gəya həy.

    truth   speaking

    God   worshipping[1]

    Qwran   reading

    pilgrimage   doing

    Zəkat   giving

        [1]Lit. doing God's worship.

5. vw log   **ap ki ymdad**   ke həqdar hõy.

           one share of this land

           this property

           one share of that gold
           and silver

           this reward

           one share of this jewellery

6. səb logõ ko   **mwlk ki tərəqqi**   pər zor dena cahie.

             national prosperity

             this problem

             the Five Pillars of Islam

             [their] own religious obligations

170

education

7. ws ne   <u>əyš</u>   se zyndəgi gwzari.

           dignity

           hardship   تکلیف‌گذ

           patience

           rest

           bravery

8. <u>tāge ka kyraya</u>   <u>ek rupəya</u>   fi   <u>ghənTa</u>   həy.

     the price of these   one and a half   basket
     tomatoes   rupees

     the price of mangoes   two rupees   seer

     the price of this silken   eight rupees   yard
     cloth

     the price of qorma   twelve annas   plate

     the rent of this house   one thousand rupees   year

9. <u>ynhē</u>   dekh kər, mere dyl mē   <u>mwhəbbət</u>   ka jəzba pəyda hwa.

     poor people   sympathy

     Western countries   progress

     that great man   Islam

     this book   reading

     these gifts of God   gratitude

10. məwlvi sahəb   <u>kəl ka səbəq</u>   dohrane ləge.

                some Islamic stories

                [his] own old complaint

                [his] own point of view about
                Islam

                our Prophet's life
                [/halat/]

                the detail[s] of this
                event

11. əgər ap <u>ys məwzu</u>   pər γəwr kərē, to   <u>ys ki xubiā</u>   zahyr hōgi.

       this aspect   its weaknesses

       present society   its defects

       this decision   its errors

       these customs   their evils

       these conditions [states]   their compelling
                                     circumstances

12. vw <u>tərəqqi ka rasta</u>   yxtiar nəhī kər səkta.

      trip to [of] Mecca

      the Islamic method

      this appearance [form, shape]

      the road of severity

      the road of heresy

171

13. syvae <u>ys</u>   ke, mə̄y ap ko baqi səb <u>zevər</u>   pəhw̄ca dū̆ga.

       that cupboard   baggage

       his letter   papers

       this gun   guns

       these socks   clothing

       this last amount   amount

14. <u>mere</u>   əwr <u>ap</u>   ke dərmyan, koi <u>jhəgRa</u>   nəhī̆.

       our society   their society   difference

       Məwlvi Sahəb   our family   relationship

       white   black   distinction

       our   his department   connection

       Islam   other religions   enmity

15. <u>roza</u>   həmē <u>dusrō ki bhuk əwr pyas</u>   ka yhsas dylata həy.

       our religion   the importance of morality

       this event   the evils of wine

       his statement   national sentiment

       this story[1]   the helplessness of the poor

       the Qwran   our duties

     [1]Employ /qyssa/. If /kəhani/ is used, the verb must be made feminine.

18. 502. Transformation.

1. In the following sentences, change the Urdu possessive construction to the Persian /yzafət/ formation (see Sec. 18.302); e.g. /X <u>ka</u> Y/ to /Y-e X/.

    a. yy bəyan <u>pakystan ki hwkumət</u> ki tərəf se jari hwa həy.

    b. <u>yslam ke məzhəb</u> ke mwtabyq, ek əllah pər iman rəkhna lazmi həy.

    c. mwsəlmanō ke lie, <u>rəsul ki mwhəbbət</u> rəkhna bhi bəhwt əhəm həy.

    d. axyrkar badšah ke beTe ne <u>hwkumət ka yntyzam</u> əpne hath mē le lia.

    e. ys surət se <u>hwkumət ka nyzam</u> byhtər cəl səkega.

    f. yy qanun <u>qwran ki talimat</u> ki rəwšni mē bənaya gəya həy.

    g. <u>zəkat ke məhkme</u> ne ys bat pər zor dia, ky qəwm ke hər šəxs ko pabəndi se zəkat nykalni cahie.

    h. <u>xwda ke rəsul</u> ne fərmaya, ky əllah ek həy, əwr mə̄y ws ka bheja hwa nəbi hū̆.

    i. <u>hyndostan ke wləma</u> ka kəhna həy, ky vw jəldi hi ys məsle ko həl kərne ki košyš kərēge.

    j. əllah ke nek bənde əksər <u>xwda ke zykr</u> mē məsruf rəhte hə̄y.

    k. <u>rəsul ki əhadis</u> mē bar bar əxlaq pər zor dia gəya həy.

    l. <u>pakystan ki bwnyad</u> wnnys sə̄w sə̄ytalys mē rəkkhi gəi thi.

    m. həmē <u>yslam ke ərkan</u> ki pabəndi kərni cahie.

    n. həmē <u>mwlk ki xwšhali</u> ke lie puri košyš kərni cahie.

    o. šərab pina, jua khelna, əwr suər ka gošt khana <u>yslam ke qəvanin</u> ke xylaf həy.

2. Review: omit the subjects of the following sentences and change the underlined verb forms to the passive. Make the verb agree with the present object, wherever necessary. See Sec. 15.311.

a. wnhõ ne aj ys mwamle ki təfsil bəyan ki.

b. məɣrybi mwlkõ ne həmare mwlk ko kafi ymdad di həy.

c. ws ne həmẽ lahəwr mẽ kwch zəmin dylai həy.

d. məwlvi sahəb ne ys məsle ka ek əwr pəhlu bətaya.

e. mə̃y wn mazur əwr məjbur logõ se həmdərdi kər səkta hũ.

f. həm ne məwlvi sahəb ki hydayət pər nəmaz ki niət bãdhi.

g. ys dəwran mẽ pakystan ne zəraət mẽ kafi tərəqqi ki həy.

h. dwkandar ne mere samne wn donõ hyssõ ko joR dia.

i. əgər ap əyš se zyndəgi gwzarẽ, to ws ka ənjam bhi nəzər mẽ rəkhẽ.

j. mə̃y ne kəl ka səbəq dohraya.

k. vw log yy bat bəhwt məhsus kərẽge, ky ap ne həmare xandan se ryšta toR lia.

l. həmari qəwm ne tərəqqi ka rasta yxtiar kia həy.

m. polis ne wn sahəb ko ədalət mẽ peš kər dia.

n. badšah ne məkke mẽ cənd nəe qəvanin jari kər die həy.

o. ap ys təfsir ka mwtala kər səkte hə̃y.

18.503. Fill the Blanks.

1. Fill the blanks in the sentences below with one of the following words: /qərar/, /mwqərrər/, /mwqərrəršwda/, or /qaym/. See Sec. 18.103.

a. wse əpne mwlk mẽ bhi pəhw̃c kər ____ nə myla.

b. hwkumət ne wse ysi kam ke lie ____ kia tha.

c. pychli mwlaqat mẽ, yy ____ paya tha, ky həm donõ ykhəTTe cəlẽge.

d. jəb tək vw zynda rəhe, əpne vade pər ____ rəhe.

e. zəkat ka yy ____ hyssa syrf ɣəribõ ka həq həy.

f. ys məhine ki bays tarix ko ws ki šadi ____ pai həy.

g. bəRi košyš ke bad, hyndostan ke mwsəlmanõ ne pakystan ____ kia.

h. wn ke jane ke bad, mə̃y wn ki jəga pər ____ hwa.

i. wnhõ ne yn məwlvi sahəb ko qwran ka səb se bəRa mwfəssyr ____ dia həy.

j. ap ko hər surət se əpne mwašre ki yy rwsumat ____ rəkhni cahiẽ.

2. Fill the blanks in the sentences below with the most appropriate of the following words: /təəllwq/, /ryšta/, /sylsyla/, or /mwtəəllyq/. See Sec. 18.121.

a. ys ləRke ke ____, ap ka kya xyal həy.

b. ərse se mera wn se koi ____ nəhĩ.

c. rupəe ki kəmi ki vəja se, meri talim ka ____ TuT gəya.

d. mera ws ləRki se ____ TuT gəya.

e. vw dyhli se ____ rəkhta həy.

f. wnhõ ne mwjh se meri ləRki ka ____ mãga.

g. jəhã tək mera ____ həy, mə̃y hər surət se ap ki xydmət kərne ko təyyar hũ.

h. ys ____ mẽ, mə̃y ap ke valyd sahəb se xwd bat kərni cahta hũ.

173

3. Fill the blanks in the sentences below with the most appropriate of the following words: /əta/, /ətakərda/, /jəma/, /jəməšwda/, /məwjud/, or /məwjuda/. See Sec. 18.305 (the section dealing with the substantive suffix /a/).

   a. əllah ki ____ dəwlət mē se məjburō əwr mazurō pər bhi xərc kərna cahie.

   b. mere pas ap ki di hwi nyšani əb tək ____ həy.

   c. ys dəwran mē, māy ne do həzar rupəe ____ kie.

   d. ____ zəmane mē, ys bat ki səxt zərurət məhsus ki ja rəhi həy.

   e. ap ki bəRi ynayət həy, ky ap ne mwjhe yy ciz ____ ki.

   f. ____ rəqəm ka ek hyssa məwlvi sahəb ke pas həy.

4. Fill the blanks in the sentences below with one of the following words: /məsla/, /mwamla/, /səval/, /pərešani/, /təklif/, or /dyqqət/. See Secs. 16.117 and 18.108. In all cases more than one word is possible and idiomatic. The instructor will discuss differences in connotation.

   a. wnhō ne ys ____ mē meri bəhwt mədəd ki.

   b. səfər ke dəwran mē, mwjhe bəhwt ____ wThani pəRi.

   c. ynsan syrf ____ mē xwda ko yad kərta həy.

   d. ys ke bad, yy ____ peš ai, ky pani ka yntyzam kəwn kərega.

   e. həmare wləma ne ys ____ pər γəwr kia həy.

   f. əb yy ____ pəyda hota həy, ky ytni rəqəm kəhã se aegi.

18.504. Variation.

1. əllah ne əpne bəndō pər cənd fərayz zəruri qərar die hāy.

   yunyvərsyΓi ne ləRkō pər sal mē do ymtyhan zəruri qərar die hāy.

   jəj ne ws admi ko mwjrym qərar dia.

   wləma ne yy məsla bəhwt əhəm qərar dia həy.

   ws ki šadi əgle həfte qərar pai həy.

   yəhã a kər mwjhe qərar nəhī myla.

2. əgər mere pas ytni rəqəm nə ho, to ys šəkl mē mere lie kya hwkm həy.

   əgər māy vəhã nə jaū, to ws surət mē ap kya kərēge.

   əgər vw log kəbhi vapəs aē, to ys sylsyle mē māy wnhē kya bəta dū.

   əgər vw jue ke bare mē puchē, to ws ke mwtəəllyq māy kya jəvab dū.

   əgər māy wnhē ys ki təfsil bətaū, to kya, hər lyhaz se Thik hoga?

   əgər həm roz pãc nəmazē nə pəRhē, to kya, yy yslami nwqtəe nəzər se γələt hoga?

3. hər mwsəlman məkke ka səfər yxtiar nəhī kər səkta.

   wn ki hwkumət tərəqqi ka rasta yxtiar nəhī kərna cahti.

   mwlk ke fayde ke lie, həmē nəe raste yxtiar kərne cahiē.

   qəwmi xwšhali ke lie, zəraət ke nəe nəe təriqe yxtiar kərne cahiē.

   məzhəbi lyhaz se, əyš ki zyndəgi yxtiar kərna Thik nəhī.

4. həm log mwxtəlyf cizō pər mwxtəlyf hysab se zəkat əda kərte hāy.

   mwsəlman nəqd rupəe pər Dhai fi sədi ke hysab se zəkat dete hāy.

   mwjhe sone cãdi ke zevər pər kys hysab se zəkat deni pəRegi.

   kya, həmē digər cizō pər bhi ysi hysab se zəkat əda kərni cahie?

tāgevala ek rupəya fi ghənTe ke hysab se kyraya leta həy.

məy ne yy ənaj ek rupəya fi ser ke hysab se xərida həy.

5. zəkat ka mal ɣəribõ əwr məjbur logõ ka həq həy.

yy zəmin ap ka əwr ap ke xandan ka həq həy.

yy rəqəm yətimõ əwr mazurõ ka həq həy.

ys goʃt ka ek hyssa ɣəribõ ka həq həy.

ap ke jəməʃwda pəyse ka ek hyssa hwkumət ka həq həy.

hər fəsl mẽ se, ek mwqərrərʃwda hyssa zəraət ke məhkme ka həq həy.

6. surəj chwpne se pəhle, ap ko ys kam ka zyada se zyada hyssa xətm kər lena cahie.

cād nykəlne ke bad, ytni rəwʃni ho jaegi, ky həm kəm se kəm ek dusre ko dekh səkẽge.

ədhera hone se pəhle, kəm se kəm yy saman bādh lena cahie.

roza rəkhne ke bad, kəm se kəm jhuT nəhĩ bolna cahie.

chəy dyn kam kərne ke bad, kəm se kəm ek dyn ki chwTTi honi cahie.

yy halət dekhne ke bad, ap ko zyada se zyada hoʃyar rəhna cahie.

7. bənde ne yy ərz kia tha, ky həmare əqayd ke mwtabyq gore əwr kale mẽ koi təmiz nəhĩ.

bənda yy ərz kərna cahta həy, ky syvae ys admi ke, baqi log ys zəmin ke həqdar nəhĩ.

məy pəhle hi ərz kər cwka hū, ky məʃryqi əwr məɣrybi mwaʃrõ mẽ kafi fərq həy.

jəysa ky məy ne kəl ap se ərz kia, ky həmare mwlk mẽ zəkat ka məhkma bəhwt dynõ se qaym həy.

jəysa ky məy ərz kər cwka hū, yslam ke pāc ərkan hər admi ke lie zəruri həy.

meri ərz yy həy, ky pəhle ap ɣəwr se ys xət ka mwtala kərẽ, əwr bad mẽ ys ka jəvab dẽ.

8. roza wn logõ ka yhsas dylata həy, jynhẽ khane ko kwch nəhĩ mylta.

yy vaqea həmẽ yhsas dylata həy, ky yzzət se zyndəgi gwzarna səb se byhtər zyndəgi həy.

yy Dyrama wn logõ ki yad dylata həy, jo yslami wsulõ ke pabənd the.

yy kəhani wn logõ ki yad dylati həy, jynhõ ne kəbhi hymmət nəhĩ hari.

yy ylaqa mwjhe əpne mwlk ki yad dylata həy, jəhā ysi təra ke dərya əwr jõgəl məwjud həy.

ws ki ys bat ne mwjhe wmmid dylai, ky əb mwamla həl ho səkta həy.

9. hwkumət ne zəkat ke məsle pər xub ɣəwr kia.

həmare bwzwrgane din ne ys məsle pər bəhwt ɣəwr kia həy.

hwkumət yn ʃərayt pər ɣəwr kərne ke bad əpna fəysla degi.

məwjuda zəmane mẽ, mwaʃrəti bwraiõ pər ɣəwr kərna lazmi həy.

əgər ap ys məsle pər ɣəwr kərẽ, to ap meri bat man lẽge.

ys məwzu pər ɣəwr kia ja səkta həy.

10. ys vaqəe se saf zahyr həy, ky ajkəl yslami mwaʃre ki səxt zərurət həy.

ws ke ənjam se saf zahyr həy, ky jua khelna bəhwt bwri ciz həy.

ws ki ʃəkl se saf zahyr həy, ky vw ajkəl bəhwt pəreʃan həy.

wn ki surət se saf zahyr hota həy, ky wnhõ ne meri bat bəhwt məhsus ki həy.

175

ymtyhan ke nətije se saf zahyr həy, ky ap ne myhnət nəhī ki.

ap ke mwlk ki xwšhali se saf zahyr hota həy, ky əgər koi myhnət kərta həy, to ws
   ka phəl zərur pata həy.

11. məzhəbi lyhaz se, vw ek bəhwt bəRe bwzwrg ki həysiət rəkhte hɛ̄y.

mwašrəti lyhaz se, yy məsla bəhwt əhəm həysiət rəkhta həy.

yslami nwqtəe nəzər se, yy qəvanin bəhwt əhmiət rəkhte hɛ̄y.

mwlk ki xwšhali ke nwqtəe nəzər se, ys məhkme ka qaym rəhna bəhwt zəruri həy.

taqət ke lyhaz se, həmari fəwj dwnya ki byhtərin fəwjõ mē se ek həy.

abohəva ke lyhaz se, ap ko yy šəhr bəhwt pəsənd aega.

12. əgər ap yū kərɛ̃, to mera xyal həy, ky yy məsla həl ho jaega.

əgər ap yū kərte, to ap kamyab ho jate.

əgər vw yū kərta, jəysa ky ap ne kia həy, to vw bhi bəc jata.

əgər ap ne yū kəha, to vw log fəwrən ɣwsse mē a jaɛ̃ge.

əgər ap yse yū joRte, jəysa ky mɛ̄y ne bətaya tha, to yy phyr kəbhi nə TuTta.

əgər ap zəxm pər yū pəTTi bādhte, to kəbhi nə khwlti.

13. jəb ky qwran mē barha dohraya gəya həy, to ap log kyõ əysa nəhī kərte.

jəb ky mɛ̄y yy səbəq barha dohra cwka hū, to ap ko kyõ yad nəhī.

jəb ky nəše ki cizõ ka məwzu barha dohraya gəya həy, to ws ke phyr dohrane ki kya
   zərurət həy.

jəb ky ytne sal gwzər cwke hɛ̄y, to mɛ̄y yy ciz kəyse yad rəkh səkta hū.

jəysa ky əllah ne barha dohraya həy, ynsan ko sidhe raste pər cəlna cahie.

jys təra hwkumət cahti həy, ws təra həmari mwašrəti xərabiā dur nəhī hõgi.

14. yn halat ne həmare əwr wn ke dərmyan ek nəya təəllwq qaym kər dia həy.

ap ke beTe əwr meri beTi ki šadi həmare xandanõ mē ek bəhwt əccha ryšta qaym
   kəregi.

syrf yn cizõ se həmari qəwm ki tərəqqi əwr xwšhali qaym rəh səkti həy.

hər mwsəlman ka fərz həy, ky vw yslam ke pāc ərkan pər qaym rəhe.

əyse məhkme ke qaym kərne se, məjburõ əwr ɣəribõ ki mədəd ho səkti həy.

əgər ap yy dəvai hər roz piɛ̃, to ap ki taqət qaym rəhegi.

15. mɛ̄y ne ys məsle ko həl kərne ke lie wse vəhā mwqərrər kia.

ys məsle ki əhmiət ki vəja se, badšah ne fəwrən ek xas əfsər mwqərrər kia.

yslamia həspətal ne ys mərz pər ɣəwr kərne ke lie pāc DakTər mwqərrər kie hɛ̄y.

mere valyd sahəb ne wn se mere lie ryšta māga, əwr meri šadi ki tarix mwqərrər
   ki.

təəjjwb həy, ky həmari hwkumət ne yn bwraiõ ko dur kərne ke lie əb tək koi qədəm
   nəhī wThaya, əwr kysi ko ys kam pər mwqərrər nəhī kia.

əllah ke ətakərda mal mē se, ɣəribõ ka ek xas hyssa mwqərrər həy.

18. 505. Response.

1. mwsəlmanõ pər ek dyn mē kytni nəmazɛ̄ fərz hɛ̄y.

2. kya, ap ke xyal mē məwjuda zəmane ki bwraiā dur ki ja səkti hɛ̄y?

3. kya, ap ke məzhəb mē bhi suər khana məna həy?

176

4. kya, ap ne kəbhi kysi mwsəlman alym se mwlaqat ki həy?
5. kya, ap din əwr məzhəb ko ek dylcəsp məwzu səməjhte h̃əy?
6. kya, mwaȿrəti fəvayd ke lie, ap səxti ko lazmi səməjhte h̃əy?
7. pychle ymtyhan̄ō mē ap kamyab rəhe the, ya nəhī̃.
8. ap ki ȿadi kəb qərar pai həy.
9. ys vəqt ap ki jeb mē nəqd rupəe kytne h̃əy.
10. məwlvi sahəb ke bəyan ke mwtabyq, roza kəb se kəb tək rəkkha jata həy.
11. kya, pakystan mē zəkat kə məhkma qaym kia gəya həy?
12. kya, təklif ke məwqe pər, ap səbr se kam le səkte h̃əy?
13. kya, ap ke mwaȿre mē ȿərab pina bwra səmjha jata həy?
14. məɣrybi əwr məȿryqi pakystan ke dərmyan kytna fasyla həy.
15. məwlvi sahəb ke bəyan ke mwtabyq, zəkat kys hysab se nykali jati həy.

18. 506. Conversation Practice.

Mr. Smith has come to pay another call on Məwlvi Sahəb.

S: m̃əy ne ys kytab ka mwtala kia tha. ys mē bəRi təfsil se wn təmam cizō ka bəyan məwjud həy, jo yslami nwqtəe nəzər se məna h̃əy.

MS: ji hã. ys kytab mē təmam malumat məwjud h̃əy. yy kytab həmare ek məȿhur alym ki lykhi hwi həy.

S: aj m̃əy həj ke bare mē kwch janna cahta hū̃.

MS: həj bhi yslam ke pãc bwnyadi ərkan mē se ek həy. sal mē ek dəfa əysa məwqa ata həy, jəb ky log həj ke lie məkke jate h̃əy. pychli mwlaqat ke dəwran, m̃əy ərz kər cwka hū̃, ky həj syrf ws mwsəlman pər fərz həy, jo məkke ka səfər yxtiar kərne ki taqət rəkhta ho. hər sal dwnya ke hər mwlk se, həzarō əwr lakhō ki tadad mē mwsəlman məkke pəhw̃cte h̃əy, əwr ys fərz ko əda kərte h̃əy. mwsəlmanō ko məkke se ytni mwhəbbət həy, ky hər ȿəxs yyhi cahta həy, ky zyndəgi mē kəm se kəm ek dəfa ws jəga ko dekh le, jəhã̃ həmare nəbi ne logō ko əllah ka pəyyam swnaya tha.

S: mwaȿrəti lyhaz se, həj ke kya fəvayd h̃əy.

MS: yslam ki koi talim əwr koi rwkn əysa nəhī̃, jys mē məzhəbi pəhlu ke ylava, mwaȿrəti fəvayd məwjud nə hõ. məslən, həj ka səb se bəRa fayda yy həy, ky dwnya ke hər mwlk se mwsəlman ek jəga jəma hote h̃əy, ek dusre se mylte h̃əy, əwr əpne əpne mwlk ke halat bəyan kərte h̃əy. əysi mwlaqatē ek dusre ke dyl mē mwhəbbət əwr həmdərdi ka jəzba pəyda kərti h̃əy. ys təra həzarō mil dur bəyThe hwe mwsəlmanō ka yslami ryȿta əwr məzhəbi təəllwq qaym rəhta həy. ys ke ylava, əyse məwqō pər logō ko ek dusre ke mwlk, təhzib, əwr təməddwn ke bare mē malumat hasyl hoti h̃əy.

S: kya, nəmazō ke vəqt mwqərrər h̃əy, ya kysi vəqt bhi pəRhi ja səkti h̃əy?

MS: ji nəhī̃. nəmazō ke vəqt mwqərrər h̃əy. pəhli nəmaz swba səvere surəj nykəlne se pəhle pəRhi jati həy. dusri nəmaz dopəhr ke bad, tisri nəmaz dopəhr əwr ȿam ke dərmyan, cəwthi nəmaz surəj chwpne ke fəwrən bad, əwr pãcvī̃ nəmaz rat ke ȿwru ke hysse mē pəRhi jati həy.

S: ȿərab kyõ məna ki gəi həy.

MS: šərab əwr digər nəševali cizē ynsan ke dyl əwr dymaγ pər əsər kərti hāy. jəb ynsan nəše ki halət mē hota həy, to vw bəhwt si əysi hərkətē kərta həy, jo mwašre ke xylaf hāy. ys təra əxlaqi bwraiā bəRhti hāy. cwnāce əysi bwraiõ ka həl yyhi həy, ky šərab əwr dusri nəša lanevali cizē ystemal nə ki jaē.

S: əgər koi šəxs bimar ho, əwr ws ke mərz ka ylaj syrf šərab ho, to ws halət mē kya hwkm həy.

MS: əysi halət mē šərab ya koi dusri ciz məna nəhī həy, kyõke ys məwqe pər yy ciz ws ke lie zəruri həy. cwnāce məriz ki zyndəgi bəcane ke lie šərab ystemal ki ja səkti həy.

S: əccha, sahəb, ap ki bəRi myhrbani, ky ap ne əpna qimti vəqt həmē ynayət fərmaya. ynšaəlla[h] phyr kysi vəqt ap ki xydmət mē hazyr hūga.

MS: ap jəb cahē, təšrif la səkte hāy. xwda hafyz.

S: xwda hafyz.

18. 507. Conversation Stimulus.

Topics may include the following:

1. The Five Pillars of Islam.
2. Social problems in one's own country.
3. Should alcoholic beverages be forbidden?
4. The point of view held by one's own religion about gambling.
5. The benefits and defects of.the Zəkat system.

əhmiət Fl [np]	importance
ələyhda Al Adv	separate, distinct, apart from
əpne ap Adv	oneself, by oneself
*ərkan Mpl	pl. /rwkn/
ərz Fl	request, petition, humble statement
*əshab Mpl	pl. /sahəb/
ətakərda Al	given, bestowed, granted
əyš Ml [np]	luxury, sensuality
barha Adv	many times, repeatedly
bəhəttər Al	seventy-two
bənda M2	person, creature, being; humble self
bhuka A2	hungry
bwzwrg Al Ml	great, venerable, respected, noble
cādi F2 [np]	silver
cəwhəttər Al	seventy-four
chwpna [IIc: /w/]	to set (sun), to hide
[ke] dərmyan Comp Post Adv	between, among, in the midst of
digər Al	other, another
din Ml	faith, religion (especially Islam)
dohrana [Ia]	to repeat
dylana [C: /dena/: Ic]	to cause to give; to cause, create, occasion, obtain
*fərayz Mpl	pl. /fərz/
*fəvayd Mpl	pl. /fayda/
fi Prep	per, in
gəhra A2	deep, profound
gora A2	white, light-complexioned
gwzarna [If: /ə/]	to pass (trans.)
gwzərna [I: /gwzarna/: If]	to pass (intrans.), elapse, happen, transpire
γəwr Ml [np]	concentration, reflection, deliberation, close attention, deep research
həj Ml	the Islamic pilgrimage
həl Ml	solution, solving, dissolving
həmdərdi F2	sympathy
həq Ml Al	right, lot, due, portion; truth, righteousness; God; true
həqdar M/Fl	rightful claimant, one having a right
jəməšwda Al	gathered, collected, accumulated
jəzba M2	feeling, emotion, sentiment, enthusiasm
joRna [If: /w/]	to join, unite, connect, attach together
jua M2	gambling

kamyab A1	successful
kamyabi F2	success
kəlma [literary: /kəlyma/] M2	Confession of Faith
kəmzori F2	weakness
lazmi A1	compulsory, incumbent, necessary, requisite
lazym PA1	compulsory, incumbent, necessary, requisite
lyhaz M1 [np]	regard, reference, point of view; consideration, respect [/[ke] lyhaz se/ Comp Post "from the point of view of"]
mazur A1	crippled, handicapped
məɣrybi A1 M1	western
məhkma M2	department
məhsus PA1	perceived, felt, sensed, realised
məjbur A1	helpless, compelled, constrained
məjburi F2	compulsion, constraint, helplessness; compelling circumstance, factor which compels
məkka M2 [np]	Mecca
məsla [literary: /məsyla/] M2	question, matter, problem
məslən [literary: /məsələn/] Adv	for example
məšryqi A1 M1	eastern
məwjuda A1	present, existing
məwzu M1	subject, topic
mwašra M2	society
mwašrəti A1	social, societal, pertaining to society
mwlaqat F1	meeting, encounter, visit
mwlki A1	national, relating to the country
mwqərrər PA1	fixed, settled, established, appointed
mwqərrəršwda A1	fixed, settled, established, appointed
mwtala [literary: /mwtalea/] M2 [np]	study, reading, perusal
nəqd M1 [np] A1	cash, ready money
nəša M2	intoxication, addiction
niət F1	intention, resolve
nwqta M2	point, dot [/nwqtəe nəzər/ M1 [np] "point of view"]
pəchəttər [or /pychəttər/] A1	seventy-five
pəhlu M1	side, facet, aspect
pyasa A2	thirsty
qaym PA1	fixed, firm, established, steadfast
qərar M1 [np]	fixing, determination, constancy; declaration; peace, tranquility
*qəvanin Mpl	pl. /qanun/
qəwmi A1	national, pertaining to the nation
rəmzan [or /rəməzan/] M1	Rəmzan ["Ramadan"]: the ninth month of the Islamic calendar
roza M2	fasting

rwkn M1	member, p⋯
ryšta M2	connection,
sabaq M1	lesson
sabr M1 [np]	patience, end⋯
sadi F2	hundred, cent⋯
safar M1	trip, journey,
saxt A1	hard, rigid, st⋯ extreme, strict
saxti F2	hardness, stiffn⋯ ⋯gidity, strength, violence, intensity, harshness, severity
sona M2 [np]	gold
suar M1	pig, swine
[ke] syva [or /syvae ... ke/] Comp Post	except for
šakl F1	face, appearance, image, manner, shape, form, figure, aspect, case
šarab F1	wine, alcoholic beverage
*šarayt Fpl	pl. /šart/
šart F1	condition, stipulation; wager, bet
taqat F1	strength, power, energy, ability, force
taallwq M1	connection, concern, attachment
tafsil F1	detail[s], particular[s], specification
taraqqi F2	progress, advancement
tyhattar A1	seventy-three
xarabi F2	defect, bad point
xwšhal A1	prosperous
xwšhali F2 [np]	prosperity
yatim M1	orphan
yhsas M1	feeling, perception, realisation
ykhattar A1	seventy-one
ymdad F1	aid, assistance
ymtyhan M1	examination, test
yslami A1	Islamic
yū Adv	thus
yxtiar M1	option, discretion, choice, adoption, authority, jurisdiction
zahyr PA1	clear, apparent, plain, evident
zakat F1 [np]	"Zakat": poor-rate, compulsory tithe
zevar M1	jewellery, ornament
zor M1	force, strength, pressure, exertion, power

A Pakistani girl in one style of traditional formal dress.

UNIT NINETEEN

19.000. CONVERSATION

invitation M2

received, arrived PA1

before, previous, primary Comp Post Adv

custom, usage, tradition

S: I've received an invitation to your friend's marriage. Before [lit. before this that] I take part in the marriage, it will be better if [lit. that] you tell me something about the rites and customs here.

R: Certainly. Whatever you wish you may ask freely [lit. with great pleasure].

husband M1

to choose, select, elect, pick out, pick (fruit) [Ic: /w/]

S: Does the girl here choose her own husband, or do her parents make arrangement[s] for this?

structure, make-up F1

to search, seek [Id: /w̄/]

details Fpl [pl. /təfsil/]

both sides Mpl [dual of /tərəf/ F1 "side"]

contentment, satisfaction, confidence, reliance M1 [np]

betrothal, engagement F2

(finger) ring F2

sweets, candy F2

gifts, presents Mpl [pl. /twhfa/]

concluded, settled, decided PA1

R: Oh no, this is the custom of your country. The structure of our society is entirely different from your society. With us it is usually thus that the boy's parents look for a girl for their son. They go to the house of the girl's people and ask all of the details about the girl. In the same way, the girl's people obtain information about the boy. When both sides are satisfied with each other [lit. with each other's side], then the betrothal ceremony is performed, in which the boy's people go to the girl's house and give a ring, some candy, and various other gifts to them. After this, the date of the marriage is fixed.

circumstances, conditions Mpl [pl. /halət/ F1 "state, condition"]

davətnama

məwsul

[se] qəbl

rəvaj

mwjhe ap ke dost ki šadi ka davətnama məwsul hwa həy. ys se qəbl ky māy šadi mē šərik hū, byhtər hoga, ky ap mwjhe yəhā ki šadi ki rwsumat əwr rəvaj ke bare mē kwch bətaē.

zərur. jo kwch cahē, bəRi xwši se puch səkte hāy.

xavynd

cwnna

kya, yəhā, ləRki əpna xavynd xwd cwnti həy, ya ws ke valdəyn ys ka yntyzam kərte hāy.

bənavəT

DhūDna [or /DhūDhna/]

təfsilat

tərfəyn

ytminan

māgni

āguThi

myThai

təhayf

təy

ji nəhī̃, yy ap ke mwlk ka rəvaj həy. həmare mwašre ki bənavəT ap ke mwašre se bylkwl mwxtəlyf həy. həmare hā əksər yū hota həy, ky ləRke ke valdəyn əpne beTe ke lie ləRki DhūDte hāy. vw ləRkivalõ ke ghər ja kər, ləRki ke bare mē təmam təfsilat malum kərte hāy, ysi təra ləRkivale bhi ləRke ke bare mē malumat hasyl kərte hāy. jəb tərfəyn ko ek dusre ki tərəf se ytminan ho jata həy, to māgni ki rəsm əda hoti həy, jys mē ləRkevale ləRki ke ghər jate hāy, əwr ek āguThi, kwch myThai, əwr kwch digər təhayf wnhē peš kərte hāy. ys ke bad šadi ki tarix təy hoti həy.

halat

S: Is it also possible that an engagement may be broken off because of various [lit. several] circumstances?

kya, yy bhi mwmkyn həy, ky məgni baz halat ki vəja se TuT jae?

   basis, foundation F1 [/[ki] byna pər/ Comp Post "on the basis of"]

byna

   smallish A2

choTa moTa

   disagreement, discord, difference, opposition, variance M1

yxtylaf

R: Yes, because of some special reason such [a thing] can happen, but such [a thing] [would] happen only very rarely in case of [lit. on] some minor difference.

ji hã, kysi xas vəja ki byna pər əysa ho səkta həy, lekyn kysi choTe moTe yxtylaf pər əysa bəhwt hi kəm hota həy.

S: Does the girl meet the boy before the marriage?

kya, ləRki šadi se pəhle ləRke se mylti həy?

   fault, defect M1

əyb

   just, only Adv

məhz

   coincidence, accident; agreement, concord M1

yttyfaq

   by accident, by surprise, accidentally Adv

yttyfaqən

R: No, in our society such meetings happen very rarely. Some time ago [lit. some period before today], the girl's people used to consider this thing a great disgrace. Even now it is most often thus, that the girl does not meet her husband-to-be. And even if she does meet [him], it is only an accident, as [for example] if the meeting of the two should accidentally take place at some party or marriage.

ji nəhĩ, həmare mwašre mẽ əysi mwlaqatẽ bəhwt kəm hoti hõy. aj se kwch ərsa pəhle, to ləRkivale ys bat ko bəhwt bəRa əyb səməjhte the. əb bhi əksər əysa hi hota həy, ky ləRki əpne honevale xavynd se nəhĩ mylti. əwr əgər mylti bhi, həy, to vw məhz yttyfaq hota həy, jəyse kysi davət ya šadi pər yttyfaqən donõ ki mwlaqat ho jae.

   proved, established, firm, whole, sound, enduring A1

sabyt

   freedom F2

azadi

   theory, opinion M2

nəzərya

   habits, manners Fpl [pl. /adət/ F1 "habit"]

adat

S: It is proved from this that in our country a girl has more freedom than [lit. in comparison with] here. She generally chooses her husband herself. She can go out with her husband-to-be, because according to our theory, in this way love is created between the boy and girl, and they get a better chance to study one another's habits, etc.

ys se sabyt hota həy, ky həmare mwlk mẽ ləRki ko yəhã ke mwqable me zyada azadi hasyl həy. vw əksər əpna xavynd xwd cwnti həy. vw əpne honevale xavynd ke sath bahər ja səkti həy, kyõke həmare nəzərye ke mwtabyq, ys təra ləRke əwr ləRki ke dərmyan mwhəbbət pəyda ho jati həy, əwr wnhẽ ek dusre ki adat vəyəyra ka mwtala kərne ka byhtər məwqa mylta həy.

   occasions, opportunities Mpl [pl. /məwqa/]

məvaqe

   emotions, sentiments Mpl [pl. /jəzba/]

jəzbat

   to flow, run [IIc: /ə/]

bəhna

   basic, real; basis, root F1 A1

əsl

   responsibility F2

zymmedari

   experience, experiment M2

təjryba [common: /təjrwba/]

   offspring, children F1

əwlad

R: In this matter our conception is entirely different. According to our idea, if opportunities be given to the boy and girl to meet in this fashion, then it is possible that both may be swept away [lit. flow] in emotions only and may not realise their real responsibilities. Therefore, the parents, who have had more experience of life and the world, look for a boy or girl for their children. So far as love for one another is concerned, it is thus that with you [lit. at your place] love begins before marriage and with us [it begins] after marriage.

S: With you [lit. at your place] is the marriage ceremony performed in a mosque, as we perform [it] in a church?

ys mwamle mẽ həmara təsəvvwr bylkwl mwxtəlyf həy. həmare xyal ke mwtabyq, əgər ləRke əwr ləRki ko ys təra mwlaqat ke məvaqe de die jaẽ, to ho səkta həy, ky donõ məhz jəzbat mẽ bəh jaẽ, əwr əpni əsl zymmedariõ ko məhsus nə kərẽ. ys lie, valdəyn, jynhẽ zyndəgi əwr dwnya ka zyada təjryba hota həy, əpni əwlad ke lie ləRka ya ləRki təlaš kərte hãy. jəhã tək apəs mẽ mwhəbbət ka təəllwq həy, to vw yũ həy, ky ap ke hã mwhəbbət šadi se pəhle šwru hoti həy, əwr həmare hã šadi ke bad.

kya, ap ke hã šadi ki rəsm məsjyd mẽ əda hoti həy, jəysa ky həm log gyrja mẽ əda kərte hãy?

divorce F1	təlaq
matters, questions, problems Mpl [pl. /məsla/]	məsayl
procession, parade, accession to a throne M1	jwlus
marriage procession (of the groom's people to the bride's house) F1	bərat
magnificence, glory F1	šan
throat, front part of the neck M2	gəla
garland, wreath M1	har
instrumental music, band M2	baja
to play, make sound, ring [C: /bəjna/: IIc]	bəjana
to decorate, adorn, embellish [C: /səjna/ "to be decorated, adorned, embellished": IIc]	səjana
to be flustered, confused, worried, agitated, bewildered [IIa]	ghəbrana
guest M/F1	myhman
welcome, reception M1	ystyqbal
bride F1	dwlhən [or /dulhən/]
song M2	gana
to sing [Id: /ə/]	gana
to dance [IIc: /ə/]	nacna
to cause to believe, convince, make agree; to hold (a ceremony) [C: /manna/: Ic]	mənana
reality, truth, fact F1	həqiqət
scene, view M1	mənzər
attractive, nice, charming A1	dylkəš

R: No, because the social importance of marriage, divorce, and other matters of this sort is greater than [their] religious importance. Therefore, this ceremony is performed at the girl's house. The boy's people go to the girl's house in the form

ji nəhĩ, kyõke šadi, təlaq, əwr ys qysm ke dusre məsayl ki mwašrəti əhmiət, məzhəbi əhmiət se zyada həy. ysi lie, yy rəsm ləRki ke ghər əda ki jati həy. ləRkevale ek jwlus ki surət mẽ ləRki ke ghər jate hãy. yy jwlus bərat kəhlata həy. bərat bəhwt

of a procession. This procession is called a "bərat." The "bərat" comes with much pomp. The people wear garlands of flowers around [lit. on] their necks. In front, some people go along playing music. the girl's people also decorate their house thoroughly, and, all in a state of commotion, are busy with the arrangement[s] in order that there may be nothing lacking in the reception of their guests. The girlfriends of the bride sing songs of joy on this occasion, dance -- in short celebrate [lit. hold joys] in various ways. The fact is that this scene is very charming.

šan se ati həy. log gəle mẽ phulõ ke har pəhne hote hə̄y. age age kwch log baje bəjate cəlte hə̄y. ləRkivale bhi əpna ghər xub səjate hə̄y, əwr bəhwt ghəbrae hwe yntyzam mẽ məsruf hote hə̄y, take myhmanõ ke ystyqbal mẽ koi kəmi nə rəh jae. dwlhən ki səheliā ys məwqe pər xwši ke gane gati hə̄y, nacti hə̄y -- γərəzke mwxtəlyf təriqõ se xwšiā mənati hə̄y. həqiqət to yy həy, ky yy mənzər bəhwt dylkəš hota həy.

S: Who is included in the "bərat?"

  groom M1

  relative, kinsman M1

  father's elder brother M1

  father's younger brother M1

  father's sister's husband M1

  mother's brother M1

  mother's sister's husband M1

  distant relative; beloved, dear M1 A1

  introduction, acquaintance M1

  marriage payment made to the bride by the groom M1

  marriage ceremony, marriage contract M1

bərat mẽ kəwn kəwn log šamyl hote hə̄y.

  dulha [or /dwlha/]

  ryštedar

  taya

  cəca

  phupha

  mamū

  xalu

  əziz

  təarwf

  məhr

  nykah

R: In the "bərat" the groom's relatives are included -- for example, the father's elder brother, the father's younger brother, the father's sister's husband, the mother's brother, the mother's sister's husband, etc. Aside from these, there are also other [distant] relatives, and friends. The girl's people come forward and receive their guests and introduce themselves to one another. Then the fathers of the bride and groom discuss [lit. converse about] the bridal payment, etc. After this the marriage ceremony begins.

bərat mẽ, dulha ke ryštedar -- jəyse taya, cəca, phupha, mamū, əwr xalu vəγəyra šamyl hote hə̄y. yn ke ylava, digər əziz əwr dost bhi hote hə̄y. ləRkivale age bəRh kər əpne myhmanõ ka ystyqbal kərte hə̄y, əwr ek dusre se əpna təarwf kərate hə̄y. phyr dulha əwr dwlhən ke bap məhr vəγəyra ke bare mẽ batcit kərte hə̄y. ys ke bad nykah šwru hota həy.

  to cause to read, teach [C: /pəRhna/: Ic]

    pəRhana

S: What is the meaning of the "nykah," and how is it performed [lit. caused to be read]?

nykah ka kya mətləb həy, əwr kəyse pəRhaya jata həy.

  announcement, declaration, proclamation M1

  presence, existence F2

  O [vocative particle]

  people MVP

  prayer, invocation F1

  audience, people present Mpl [pl. /hazyr/]

  elan

  məwjudgi

  əy

  logo

  doa [or /dwa/]

  hazyrin

accepted, consented, acknowledged PA1   qwbul [or /qəbul/]

consent, admission, affirmation, acquiescence M1 [np]   yqrar

proof, testimony M1 [np]   swbut

to distribute, share [Ie: /ə/]   bāTna

turn, time F2   bari

congratulations F1   mwbarəkbad

R: The meaning of "nykah" is the proclamation of marriage that is made in the
presence of everyone. Because our
Prophet said, "O people, make the
announcement of a marriage before all!"
A Məwlvi performs [lit. causes to read]
the "nykah." In the "nykah" the praises
of God and some prayers are read. Before
all those present the boy is asked three
times whether he accepts this girl as a
wife [lit. with the position of wife] or not,
and he accepts this before all. From this
point of view this audience has the status
of witnesses or proof of the marriage.
Immediately after the "nykah," some
sweets or fruits are distributed, and
everybody offers congratulations to the
groom in turn [lit. turn turn].

nykah ka mətləb šadi ka elan həy, jo səb
logõ ki məwjudgi mẽ kia jata həy. kyõke
həmare nəbi ne fərmaya həy, ky "əy logo,
šadi ka elan səb ke samne kəro!" ek
məwlvi sahəb nykah pəRhate hə̄y. nykah
mẽ, xwda ki tarif əwr kwch doaẽ pəRhi
jati həy. təmam hazyrin ke samne ləRke
se tin dəfa pucha jata həy, ky wse yy ləRki
bivi ki həysiət se qwbul həy, ya nəhī̃, əwr
vw səb ke samne ys ka yqrar kərta həy. yy
hazyrin ys lyhaz se šadi ke gəvah ya swbut
ki həysiət rəkhte hə̄y. nykah ke fəwrən
bad kwch myThai ya phəl bāTe jate hə̄y, əwr
təmam log dulha ko bari bari mwbarəkbad
peš kərte hə̄y.

opinion, idea F1   rae

S: Is the opinion of the girl obtained before
the marriage ceremony?

kya, nykah se pəhle ləRki ki rae li jati
həy?

to cause to be read, to have (something)
taught [DC: /pəRhna/: Ic]   pəRhvana

refusal, denial, rejection M1   ynkar

permissible, allowable, valid, lawful A1   jayz

dowry M1   jəhez

departed, left, dispatched, sent PA1   rəvana

departure, leave, going, dispatch F2 [np]   rəvangi

map, chart, plan, sketch, scene M2   nəqša

changed, altered, modified PA1   təbdil

burst out crying MP   ro dete hə̄y

to cherish, raise, nurture, bring up [If: /ə/]   palna

separated, parted, apart PA1   jwda

departure, leaving, leave F1   rwxsət

sad, unhappy, gloomy A1   wdas

showing, appearance F2 [np]   dykhai

tear (lachrymal) M1   ā̃su

R: Yes. If the girl refuses to have the
marriage ceremony performed, then the
ceremony is not valid. It is for this very
reason that two or three men go to the
girl as representatives and get permission
for the "nykah" from her. After this the

ji hā̃. əgər ləRki nykah pəRhvane se ynkar
kər de, to nykah jayz nəhī̃ hota. yyhi vəja
həy, ky do ya tin admi ləRki ke pas vəkil
ke təwr pər jate hə̄y, əwr ws se nykah ki
yjazət lete hə̄y. ys ke bad, nykah pəRhaya
jata həy. nykah ke bad, ləRkivale myhmanõ

"nykah" is performed. After the "nykah"
the girl's people provide food for the guests,
and, according to their status, give [her]
a dowry. After this, the "bərat" returns
to the groom's house. On the departure
of the "bərat," this scene of joy changes
into [one of] sadness for the girl's
people. Especially the brides mother
[and] father and sister[s] [and] brother[s]
burst out crying on this occasion because
parents bring up their children with much
love. But on this occasion they separate
the girl from themselves forever. Therefore, on the departure of the bride, most
of the people appear sad. There are tears
in people's eyes and prayers for the bride's
future life in their hearts.

    tea and things, tea, etc. Fl

S: Very good. From these facts there is this
benefit that now I will be able to enjoy the
marriage customs more tomorrow at the
time of the marriage. -- It is four o'clock!
-- Come on, let's drink a little tea!

R: Fine. Come on!

ko khana khylate hə̄y, əwr əpni həysiət ke
mwtabyq jəhez dete hə̄y. ys ke bad, bərat
vapəs dulha ke ghər rəvana ho jati həy.
bərat ki rəvangi pər, yy xwši ka nəqša
ləRkivalō ke lie ɣəm mē̃ təbdil ho jata həy.
xas təwr pər, dwlhən ke mā̃ bap əwr bəhn
bhai ys məwqe pər ro dete hə̄y, kyōke
valdəyn əpni əwlad ko bəhwt mwhəbbət se
palte hə̄y. lekyn ys məwqe pər, vw ləRki
ko əpne se həmeša ke lie jwda kər dete
hə̄y. ys lie, dwlhən ke rwxsət hone pər,
əksər log wdas dykhai dete hə̄y. logō ki
ākhō mē̃ ā̃su, əwr dylō mē̃ dwlhən ki aynda
zyndəgi ke lie doaē̃ hoti hə̄y.

    cae vae

bəhwt xub. yn malumat se yy fayda hwa,
ky əb mə̄y kəl šadi ke məwqe pər šadi ki
rwsumat se zyada lwtf wTha səkŭga. --
car bəj gəe hə̄y! -- aie, zəra cae vae piē̃!

Thik həy. aie!

19.101. /[se] qəbl/ Comp Post and /[se] pəhle/ Adv Comp Post both mean "before, previous, anterior." /[se] qəbl/ is stylistically somewhat more literary. Note that the preferred postpositional construction for both of these items is made with /se/ instead of /ke/.

19.102. /rəvaj/ M1 "custom, usage, tradition" carries the sense of something prevalent, fashionable, in common practice. /rəsm/ F1 "custom, ceremony" denotes a particular item of custom: a rite, a traditional usage. /adət/ F1 "habit" signifies a personal custom, an idiosyncrasy. E. g.

/ajkəl ys ciz ka bəhwt rəvaj həy./ Nowadays this thing is very common. [I. e. prevalent, fashionable, widespread.]

/pwrane rəvaj ke mwtabyq, yy kam ys təra kia jata tha./ According to ancient practice, this task was done this way.

/ajkəl ys rəsm ka rəvaj xətm ho gəya həy./ Nowadays this custom is no longer prevalent. [Lit. Nowadays this custom's prevalency has ended.]

/šadi ki rəsm əda hwi./ The marriage ceremony was performed. [/rəvaj/ cannot be employed here since the marriage ceremony is a specific rite.]

/šərab pina bəhwt bwri adət həy./ The drinking of wine is a very bad habit.

19.103. In older Urdu, /xavynd/ M1 "husband" meant "master, lord." Another common term for "husband" is /šəwhər/ M1.

19.104. /DhūDna/ [or /DhūDhna/] Id and /tələš kərna/ both mean "to seek, search, look for." Note that /DhūD lena/ and /tələš kər lena/ may mean "to seek and find." E. g.

/zəra meri kytab DhūDie!/ Please search for my book! [/tələš kijie/ is equally correct and means the same thing. /zəra/ is used here to minimise the effort involved: "please just have a look around ... "]

/mãy ne ap ka suTkes DhūD lia./ I looked for [and found] your suitcase. [Also /tələš kər lia/. Compare:]

/mãy ne ap ka suTkes DhūDa, məgər nəhī myla./ I looked for your suitcase but did not find it. [Also /tələš kia/. /mãy ne ap ka suTkes DhūDa./ is somewhat ambiguous, although context and declarative intonation may be used to indicate that the suitcase was indeed found.]

/mãy ne ap ki kytab bəhwt DhūDi./ I looked hard [lit. much] for your book. [Also /tələš ki/. Slight emphasis on /bəhwt/, together with the fact that the verb is not the <S + /lena/> construction, indicate that the results of the search were negative.]

19.105. /tərfəyn/ Mpl "both sides, both parties" is an example of the Arabic dual formation discussed in Sec. 17.304. Note that although /tərəf/ is F1, /tərfəyn/ is treated as Mpl.

19.106. /təy/ PA1 "concluded, settled, decided, fixed" is used in many of the same senses in which /qərar/ and /mwqərrər/ occur (see Sec. 18.103). There are differences, however. E.g.

/axyrkar yy təy paya./ At last this was decided. [Also /təy ho gəya/, /qərar paya/, or /mwqərrər hwa/.]

/axyrkar yy jhəgRa təy pa gəya./ At last this quarrel was settled. [Also /təy ho gəya/. Neither /qərar/ nor /mwqərrər/ can be employed in the sense of settling a dispute.]

/ws ne ek həzar mil ka səfər do dyn mẽ təy kia./ He completed the one thousand mile journey in two days. [/təy kərna/ also means "to complete a journey." Neither /qərar/ nor /mwqərrər/ can be employed in this sense. Another example:]

/ap ne yy səfər kəyse təy kia./ How did you perform this journey?

/ys ke bad, šadi ki tarix təy pati həy./ After this the date of the marriage is fixed. [Also /təy ho jati həy/, /qərar pati həy/, and /mwqərrər ho jati həy/. All three of these words may be employed in the sense of fixing a date or settling upon a course of action. For other uses of /qərar/ and /mwqərrər/ see Sec. 18.103.]

19.107. /byna/ F1 "basis, foundation" is largely synonymous with /bwnyad/ F1. Note the compound postposition /[ki] byna pər/ "on the basis of, because of." Note also the idiomatic usages /kys byna pər/ "on which basis, on what grounds, why?" and /ys byna pər/ "on this basis, for this reason." These are analogous to /ys lie/ "therefore" and /kys lie/ "why?"

19.108. /məhz/ Adv "just, only" overlaps /syrf/ Adv "only" in most meanings. /syrf/, however, often refers to quantity (e.g. "only five rupees"), while /məhz/ is rarely used in this context. E.g.

/wn ka yəhã ana məhz ek yttyfaq tha./ His coming here was just an accident. [/məhz/ is very appropriate here, but /syrf/ is also correct.]

/vw məhz ek mamuli əfsər həy./ He is only a minor [lit. common] official. [I.e. he is not of important rank. /syrf/ is also possible here.]

/ws ka məkan yəhã se syrf do mil həy./ His house is only two miles from here. [/məhz/ is not idiomatic here since the reference is to something which can be counted or measured.]

/mere pas syrf tin rupəe hɛ̃y./ I have only three rupees. [/məhz/ is also inappropriate here.]

19.109. /yttyfaq/ M1 has two rather distinct meanings: "agreement, concord, unity" and "coincidence, accident." The adverbial form /yttyfaqən/ denotes only "by accident, by surprise, accidentally, by chance, all of a sudden." E.g.

/donõ bhaiõ mẽ bəhwt yttyfaq həy./ There is great unity between the two brothers.

/donõ dost bəRe yttyfaq se rəhte hɛ̃y./ Both friends live together amicably. [Lit. with great concord.]

/wnhõ ne ys məsle pər mwjh se yttyfaq kia./ They agreed with me upon this matter.

/mɛ̃y yttyfaq se vəhã wsi vəqt pəhw̃c gəya./ I arrived there at that very time by accident. [/yttyfaqən/ can also be used; it would connote greater suddenness and surprise.]

/meri əwr wn ki mwlaqat məhz ek yttyfaq thi. / My meeting with them
was just an accident.

/wnhõ ne mwjhe yttyfaqən dekha. / They accidentally saw me.

19. 110. The Arabic broken plural /əwlad/ is used as Fl in Urdu to denote "offspring,
children. " The singular, /vələd/ Ml "boy, " is rare in Urdu. Court and police records do
use /vəld/, an Urduised form of /vələd/, in the sense of "son of. " E. g.

/əziz vəld rəhim/ əziz, son of Rəhim

19. 111. /mənana/ is the causative form of /manna/ Ic "to believe, obey. " /mənana/
denotes "to cause to believe, cause to obey, " "to convince (generally with a sense of
compelling the other person), make agree, " and also "to hold, perform (a ceremony). " E. g.

/axyrkar mə̃y ne wnhē məna lia. / At last I convinced them. [The person
caused to believe is marked by /ko/ or an equivalent special object
form.]

/wnhõ ne ys məwqe pər bəRi xwši mənai. / On this occasion they made
a great celebration. [Lit. They on this occasion held great joy.
/xwši mənana/ is an idiom.]

/badšah ke yntyqal pər, sare mwlk mē tin dyn tək sog mənaya gəya. /
Upon the death of the king, mourning ceremonies were held in the
land for three days. [/sog/ Ml "period of mourning. "]

As seen in the first example above, when only the person[s] convinced or made to
believe are expressed, /mənana/ is employed, and the object is marked by /ko/ or its
equivalent. When the thing which the person is made to believe (i. e. the argument, matter,
etc.) is also expressed, then this thing is treated as the direct object, and the person[s]
made to believe are marked by /se/; instead of /mənana/, the double causative form of
the verb, /mənvana/, is used. E. g.

/wnhõ ne hazyrin se əpni bat mənva li. / He made the audience believe
his statement. [The direct object -- the "thing caused to be believed"
-- is /bat/; the "persons caused to believe" is marked by /se/; and
the double causative /mənvana/ is used.]

19. 112. Kinship terminology employed in Urdu-speaking areas of India and Pakistan
reflects the elaborate patterns of Indian joint family life. Most of these terms are purely
local in origin (rather than Arabic or Persian), differing from those used by Hindi-speaking
Hindus only in minor details (e. g. Muslim Urdu /mamū/ Ml "mother's brother" and
/mwmani/ or /məmani/ F2 "mother's brother's wife" versus Hindi /mama/ Ml and /mami/
F2 for these relationships).

It is not possible to deal fully with the complex structure of Indo-Pakistani family
organisation here. It will be enough for the student to note that each relationship has both
a descriptive kinship term and a proper mode of address. For example, all relatives
belonging to generations older than that of the speaker must be addressed by some special
term (and never by their personal names), and honorific language must be used in speaking
to or about them. In traditional society, the wife never takes her husband's personal name,
nor the husband his wife's; instead, there are various circumlocutions. Relatives belonging
to generations younger than oneself can generally be called by their personal names.

Various relatives play special roles: e.g. it is proper to tease and joke with one's wife's younger sister (/sali/ F2); one's mother's brother (/mamū/ M1) plays the part of a special confidant and protector (much more so than one's paternal uncles), etc. On the other hand, since Indian marriages are traditionally patrilocal (i. e. a son brings his bride to live at his father's house), the rivalry between a wife and her husband's mother may provide a basis for much domestic unhappiness.

The following charts and list of terms are given for reference only. They have been taken in modified form from an unpublished paper by Mr. Mushir ul Haque entitled "Kinship Organisation Among the Indian Muslims." Published sources include: "Kinship Organisation in India" by Mrs. Irawati Karve (Poona, 1953) and "Family and Kin in Indo-European Culture" by G. S. Ghurye (Bombay, 1955).

Numbers on the charts refer to the following list of terms.

Chart I: Consanguinity.

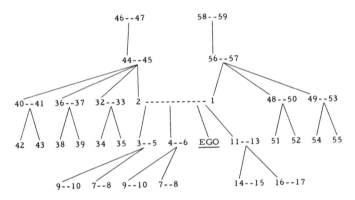

Chart II: Consanguinity (Cont.).

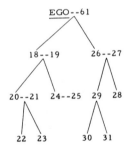

Chart III: Affinals: Husband's Relatives to Wife.

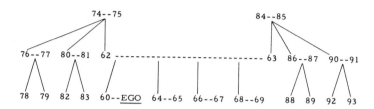

Chart IV: Affinals: Wife's Relatives to Husband.

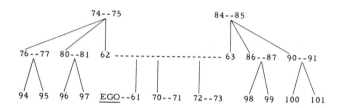

Abbreviations employed in the following list are:

B	Brother	M	Mother
D	Daughter	S	Sister
E	Elder	Sn	Son
F	Father	W	Wife
H	Husband	Y	Younger

NO.	RELATIONSHIP	KINSHIP TERM	TERM OF ADDRESS
1.	M	mã Fl	əmmã, əmmi, əmmi jan, etc.
2.	F	bap Ml	əbba, əbbi, əbba jan, etc.
3.	EB	bhai Ml	bhai, bhai jan, etc.
4.	YB	bhai Ml	By name
5.	EBW	bhabi [written /bhabhi/] F2 bhavəj Fl	bhabi jan, bhabi dwlhən, bhavəj, etc.
6.	YBW	bhəyho Fl	By name
7.	BSn	bhətija M2	By name
8.	BSnW	bhətijbəhu Fl	By name
9.	BD	bhətiji F2	By name
10.	BDH	bhətijdamad Ml	By name
11.	ES	bəhn Fl	apa, baji, bəhn, etc.
12.	YS	bəhn Fl	By name
13.	SH	bəhnoi Ml	dulha bhai. By name if Y.
14.	SSn	bhãja M2	By name

NO.	RELATIONSHIP	KINSHIP TERM	TERM OF ADDRESS
15.	SSnW	bhājbəhu F1	By name
16.	SD	bhāji F2	By name
17.	SDH	bhājdamad M1	By name
18.	Sn	beTa M2	By name
19.	SnW	bəhu F1, pətoh F1	By name
20.	SnSn	pota M2	By name
21.	SnSnW	potbəhu F1	By name
22.	SnSnSn	pəRpota M2	By name
23.	SnSnD	pəRpoti F2	By name
24.	SnD	poti F2	By name
25.	SnDH	potdamad M1	By name
26.	D	beTi F2	By name
27.	DH	damad M1	By name
28.	DD	nəvasi F2, natyn F1, or nətni F2	By name
29.	DSn	nəvasa M2, nati M1	By name
30.	DSnSn	pərnəvasa M2, pərnati M1	By name
31.	DSnD	pərnəvasi F2, pərnətni F2	By name
32.	FEB	taya M1	taya, bəRe əbba
33.	FEBW	tai F2	tai, bəRi əmmā
34.	FEBSn	tayazad bhai M1	bhai
35.	FEBD	tayazad bəhn F1	bəhn
36.	FYB	cəca M1	cəca, cəca jan, etc.
37.	FYBW	cəci F2	cəci, cəci jan, etc.
38.	FYBSn	cəcera bhai M1,[1] cəcazad bhai M1	bhai
39.	FYBD	cəceri bəhn F1, cəcazad bəhn F1	bəhn
40.	FS	phuphi F2	phuphi
41.	FSH	phupha M1	phupha
42.	FSSn	phwphera bhai M1, phuphizad bhai M1	bhai
43.	FSD	phwpheri bəhn F1, phuphizad bəhn F1	bəhn
44.	FF	dada M1	dada
45.	FM	dadi F2	dadi
46.	FFF	pərdada M1	dada
47.	FFM	pərdadi F2	dadi
48.	MB	mamū M1	mamū
49.	MS	xala F1	xala
50.	MBW	mwmani F2, məmani F2	mwmani, məmani
51.	MBSn	məmera bhai M1, mamūzad bhai M1	bhai
52.	MBD	məmeri bəhn F1, mamūzad bəhn F1	bəhn

194

NO.	RELATIONSHIP	KINSHIP TERM	TERM OF ADDRESS
53.	MSH	xalu M1	xalu
54.	MSSn	xəlera bhai M1	bhai
55.	MSD	xəleri bəhn F1	bəhn
56.	MF	nana M1	nana
57.	MM	nani F2	nani
58.	MFF	pərnana M1	nana
59.	MFM	pərnani F2	nani

AFFINALS:

NO.	RELATIONSHIP	KINSHIP TERM	TERM OF ADDRESS
60.	H	xavynd M1, šəwhər M1	---
61.	W	bivi F2	---
62.	H/WF	swsər, səswr M1, swsra M1, xwsər M1	əbba, əbbi, əbba jan, etc.
63.	H/WM	sas F1	əmmā, əmmi, əmmi jan, etc.
64.	HEB	jeTh M1	bhai, bhai jan
65.	HEBW	jyThani F2	bhabi
66.	HYB	devər M1	bhəyya
67.	HYBW	devrani F2	dwlhən
68.	HS	nənəd F1, nənd F1	bəhn, bəhni
69.	HSH	nəndoi M1	bhai
70.	WB	sala M2[2]	By name, or as one's wife addresses him
71.	WBW	sərhəj F1, səlhəj F1	" " " " " " " " "
72.	WS	sali F2	" " " " " " " " "
73.	WSH	saRhu M1, həmzwlf M1	" " " " " " " " "
74.	H/WFF	dədia swsər M1	dada
75.	H/WFM	dədia sas F1	dadi
76.	H/WFS	phwphia sas F1	phuphi
77.	H/WFSH	phwphia swsər M1	phupha
78.	HFSSn	phwphera devər M1 phwphera jeTh M1	bhai
79.	HFSD	phwpheri nənəd F1	apa, apa jan
80.	HFE/YB	cəcia swsər M1	cəca, taya
81.	HFE/YBW	cəcia sas F1	cəci, tai
82.	HFBSn	cəcera devər M1 cəcera jeTh M1	bhai
83.	HFBD	cəceri nənəd F1	apa, apa jan
84.	H/WMF	nənhya swsər M1	nana
85.	H/WMM	nənhya sas F1	nani
86.	H/WMB	məmia swsər M1	mamū
87.	H/WMBW	məmia sas F1	mwmani, məmani
88.	HMBSn	məmera devər M1, məmera jeTh M1	bhai
89.	HMBD	məmeri nənəd F1	apa, apa jan

NO.	RELATIONSHIP	KINSHIP TERM	TERM OF ADDRESS
90.	H/WMS	xəlia sas Fl	xala
91.	H/WMSH	xəlia swsər M1	xalu
92.	HMSSn	xəlera devər M1, xəlera jeTh M1	bhai
93.	HMSD	xəleri nənəd Fl	apa, apa jan
94.	WFSSn	phwphera sala M2	bhai
95.	WFSD	phwpheri sali F2	apa
96.	WFE/YBSn	cəcera sala M2	bhai
97.	WFE/YBD	cəceri sali F2	apa
98.	WMBSn	məmera sala M2	bhai
99.	WMBD	məmeri sali F2	apa
100.	WMSSn	xəlera sala M2	bhai
101.	WMSD	xəleri sali F2	apa

[1]The adjectival forms /cəcera/, /phwphera/, /məmera/, and /xəlera/ are
all A2. Those ending in /ia/ (e.g. /nənhya/, /dədia/) are A1.

[2]The term /sala/ M2 "wife's brother" has come to be a term of abuse. If
one addresses a person as /sala/ when this relationship does not apply, it
would be taken as a serious insult. Even one who is in fact one's wife's
brother would not like to be introduced as one's /sala/; instead, the Persian
term /bəradəre nysbəti/ "brother by relation" would be employed. According
to one theory, the derogatory connotation of /sala/ goes back to a time when
the husband carried his bride off by force. Her brothers' failure to prevent
her abduction caused them to "lose face" and appear weak.

Four terms denoting kinship residence may be added to the preceding list:

/dədhyal/ Fl [or M1] home of one's father's people

/nənhyal/ Fl [or M1] home of one's mother's poeple

/swsral/ Fl [or M1] home of one's in-laws

/məyka/ M2 or /nəyhər/ Fl [or M1] original home of a married woman,
her parents' home.

19.113. As an adjective, /əziz/ M1 A1 denotes "dear, beloved. " When employed as
a noun, it means "distant relative" -- a distant member of the joint family. E.g.

/yy mera əziz dost həy. / This is my dear friend.

/vw mwjhe bəhwt əziz həy. / He is very dear to me.

/vw mera əziz həy. / He is my distant kinsman.

19.114. Aside from the very considerable expenses of the wedding itself, the bride's
family must also provide a dowry commensurate with their status: the /jəhez/ M1 "dowry"
may consist of money, jewels, clothing, and such items as household furniture, etc. All
of this must be agreed upon by both families before the wedding, and it must be as
extravagant and lavish as the bride's family can manage. The Government of Pakistan has
repeatedly tried to discourage lavish expenditure upon weddings and /jəhez/, but the current
of social tradition runs deep, and a man with several daughters still has reason to consider
himself a most unfortunate individual indeed.

The groom's family must provide gifts as well, but on a much less luxurious scale. The /bərat/ itself brings certain traditional gifts: raisins and nuts to be distributed during the wedding, clothing for the bride and her immediate family, jewellery, etc. This is called /bəri/ F2. The groom's people must also agree to the amount of /məhr/ M1 "groom's gift to the bride" before the wedding. According to the practice of the Prophet Muhammad, the groom must pay the bride a sum of money at the time of the marriage. This money is to be totally hers, and no one can rightfully take it from her. The original purpose of this gift was to provide subsistence for a girl in the event of divorce -- somewhat similar in intent to the modern practice of alimony. Many families, however, defer the actual payment of the /məhr/, demanding it for the bride only in the event of a divorce. Since divorce is quite rare in Indo-Pakistani Muslim culture, it has become customary to agree upon very large amounts of /məhr/ simply as a matter of prestige and with no intention of ever having to pay it.

19.115. /pəRhana/ is the causative form of /pəRhna/ Ic "to read, study." It normally means "to teach." /nykah pəRhana/ "to perform the marriage ceremony" is thus an idiom. Compare /nəmaz pəRhna/ "to perform one's prayers" and /nəmaz pəRhana/ "to lead the prayers."

The double causative, /pəRhvana/ "to cause to be read, to have taught" can be employed with /nykah/ to mean "to have someone perform the marriage ceremony." Similarly, /nəmaz pəRhvana/ means "to have someone lead the prayers." E. g.

/məwlvi sahəb ne nykah pəRhaya./   The Məwlvi performed the marriage ceremony.

/mə̃y ne məwlvi sahəb se əpni beTi ka nykah pəRhvaya./   I had the Məwlvi perform my daughter's marriage ceremony.

/məwlvi sahəb ne nəmaz pəRhai./   The Məwlvi led the prayers.

/vw wrdu pəRhata həy./   He teaches Urdu.

/rəhim sahəb ne wn məwlvi sahəb se əpni beTi ko qwran pəRhvaya./   Mr. Rəhim had that Məwlvi teach the Qwran to his daughter.

19.116. /qwbul/ [or /qəbul/] PA1 "accepted, consented, acknowledged" and /yqrar/ M1 "consent, admission, affirmation, acquiescence" differ in that the former has the sense of acceptance (e. g. of an object, a concept), while the latter carries connotations of admission (e. g. of a crime), acceptance (of a suggestion), acquiescence (to a plan of action), affirmation (of one's promise), etc. E. g.

/meri doa qwbul hwi./   My prayer was granted [lit. accepted].

/mə̃y ne wn ki rae qwbul kər li./   I accepted his opinion. [I. e. came to agree with him.]

/mə̃y ne wn ki yy šərt qwbul ki./   I accepted this condition of his.

/ws ne yslam qwbul kia./   He accepted Islam. [Also /... yslam ko qwbul kia./.]

/ws ne əpne gwnah ka yqrar kia./   He confessed [admitted, owned up to] his sin.

/ws ne səb ki məwjudgi mẽ ys bat ka yqrar kia./   He admitted this matter in the presence of all.

197

/mə̄y yqrar kərta hū, ky mə̄y yy rəqəm jəldi hi əda kər dū̃ga. / I promise
that I will pay this amount very quickly. [I.e. affirm, avow, declare.]

19.117. /bari bari/ Adv "by turns, in turn, turn by turn" must be distinguished from
/bar bar/ Adv "repeatedly, again and again, from time to time"; see Sec. 14.115. Alone,
/bari/ F2 means "turn (as in a game), " while /bar/ F1 denotes "time, occasion." E.g.

/əb ap ki bari həy. / Now it's your turn.

/yy pəhli bar həy, ky mə̄y ne š̌ərab pi. / This is the first time that I
have drunk [lit. drank] wine.

/vw bar bar ae. / They came again and again.

/vw bari bari ae. / They came by turns.

19.118. /mwbarəkbad/ F1 "congratulations" is a compound consisting of Arabic
/mwbarək/ A1 "blessed, fortunate, auspicious" + /bad/ "may [it] be, let [it] be, " a
Persian subjunctive form from the root /bu/ "be, become."

19.119. Both /rae/ F1 and /xyal/ M1 mean "idea, thought, opinion." Informants
felt that /rae/ may be somewhat more specific than /xyal/ -- i.e. /rae/ might be preferred
in reference to some particular idea, plan, etc., while /xyal/ is employed for a less
definite, broader concept. This distinction does not seem to be important from the point
of view of practical usage, however.

There is one semantic area, nevertheless, in which these two words do not overlap:
/xyal/ is employed in the sense of "thought for, care for, vigilance over, " while /rae/
never has this meaning. E.g.

/ys ke bare mē ap ki kya rae həy. / What is your opinion about this?
[Or:/ ... ka kya xyal həy. /. Here /rae/ and /xyal/ appear to be
quite interchangeable.]

/zəra ys ka xyal kəro! / Just take care of it! [Or: "look out for it, watch
out for it, keep watch over it, " etc. /rae/ cannot be substituted.]

19.120. /rəvana/ PA1 "departed, left, dispatched, sent" is employed with /hona/ to
mean "to go, depart, leave" and with /kərna/ to mean "to send, cause to leave." /rwxsət/
F1 "departure, leaving, leave" is similarly employed with /hona/ meaning "to take one's
leave, depart" and with /kərna/ signifying "to see off, say goodbye to." Complex verbal
formations made with both /rəvana/ and /rwxsət/ are Type A (see Sec. 19.123).

/rwxsət/ does not occur as a noun meaning "departure"; instead, /rwxsəti/ F2 [np]
"departure" is employed, almost always in the meaning of "departure of the bride for the
groom's house after the marriage ceremony." /rəvangi/ F2 [np] "departure, leave, going,
dispatch" has a much broader range of uses.

/rwxsət/ is employed as a true noun, however, in the sense of "vacation, holiday,
leave." It is thus synonymous in this context with /chwTTi/ F2. E.g.

/vw swba rəvana ho gəya. / He left this morning.

/aj vw rwxsət ho gəya. / He left today. [/rəvana hona/ and /rwxsət hona/
are almost synonymous: rather like "to leave" and "to depart" in
English.]

/səb myhman šam ko pāc bəje rwxsət ho jaẽge. / All the guests will
depart this evening at five o'clock. [/rəvana ho jaẽge/ is substitutable.]

/axyrkar vw ys dwnya se rwxsət ho gəya. / At last he died. [Lit. At
last he departed from this world. An idiomatic use of /rwxsət hona/.]

/mə̃y ne ap ki kytabẽ rəvana kər dī. / I sent off your books. [/rwxsət
kərna/ cannot be employed in this sense.]

/mə̃y ne wn logõ ko ysTešən pər rwxsət kia. / I saw those people off at
the station. [/rəvana kərna/ cannot be employed here.]

/ap ki rəvangi kəb həy. / When is your departure? [/rwxsəti/ is not
substitutable.]

/dwlhən ki rwxsəti hwi. / The bride took her departure [for the groom's
home]. [/rəvangi/ does not have this sense.]

/mə̃y rwxsət pər hū̃. / I am on leave. [/chwTTi/ may be substituted
here.]

/mə̃y ne pāc dyn ki rwxsət li. / I took five days' leave. [/chwTTi/ is
equally correct.]

19.121. /təbdil/ PA1 "changed, altered, modified" occurs with /hona/ and /kərna/
meaning "to change, be altered, be modified" and "to change, alter, modify" respectively.
These formations are synonymous with /bədəlna/ IIIa "to change" (which is both transitive
and intransitive; see Secs. 9.306 and 11.303). As might be expected, forms with /təbdil/
are more literary in style than /bədəlna/.

19.122. /ələg/ A1 Adv and /ələyhda/ A1 Adv both mean "apart, separate, distinct"
(see Sec. 18.113). /jwda/ PA1 "separated, parted, apart" is usually used of persons or
things which are separated but not of their own will: i.e. "apart, but wanting to be
together. " E.g.

/donõ bhai ələyhda ho gəe. / The two brothers have separated. [I.e.
they have parted and no longer wish to be together. /ələg/ can be
substituted here.]

/mera dost mwjh se jwda ho gəya. / My friend has become separated
from me. [The separation was not desired by either party. If /ələg/
or /ələyhda/ is substituted here, the sense becomes one of permanent
and deliberate parting.]

19.123. Some Complex Verbal Formations.

A:

/azad/

/azad hona/ to be, become free

/[X ko] azad kərna/ to free [X]

/jayz/

/jayz hona/ to be permissible, allowable, valid, lawful

/[X ko] jayz kərna/ to make [X] permissible, allowable, valid, lawful

/jwda/

/[X se] jwda hona/ to be parted, separated [from X]

/[X ko Y se] jwda kərna/ to separate [X from Y]

/məwsul/

    /məwsul hona/ to be received (letter, parcel, message)

/qwbul/

    /qwbul hona/ to be accepted

    /[X ko] qwbul kərna/ to accept [X]

/rəvana/

    /rəvana hona/ to go, leave, depart

    /[X ko] rəvana kərna/ to send, dispatch [X]

/rwxsət/. [See also F.]

    /rwxsət hona/ to depart, leave

    /[X ko] rwxsət kərna/ to see [X] off, say goodbye [to X]

/sabyt/

    /sabyt hona/ to be proved, established

    /[X ko] sabyt kərna/ to prove, establish [X]

/təbdil/

    /təbdil hona/ to change, be altered, modified

    /[X ko] təbdil kərna/ to change, alter, modify [X]

/təy/

    /təy hona, pana/ to be decided, determined, fixed, settled

    /[X ko] təy kərna/ to decide, determine, fix, settle [X]. [Also "to complete [X (a journey)]. "]

/wdas/

    /wdas hona/ to be, become sad, unhappy, gloomy

    /[X ko] wdas kərna/ to make [X] sad, unhappy, gloomy

B:

    /elan/

        /[X ka] elan hona/ [X] to be announced, proclaimed

        /[X ka] elan kərna/ to announce, proclaim [X]

    /təarwf/

        /[X ka Y se] təarwf hona/ [X] to be introduced [to Y]

        /[X se Y ka] təarwf kərana/ to introduce [Y to X]

    /təjryba/

        /[X ko Y ka] təjryba hona/ [X] to have experience [of Y]

        /[X ka] təjryba kərna/ to experience [X]; to experiment [with X]

        /[X pər Y ka] təjryba kərna/ to experiment [with Y on X]

    /yqrar/

        /[X ka] yqrar hona/ [X] to be confessed, admitted, consented to

        /[X ka] yqrar kərna/ to confess, admit to, affirm, acquiesce [to X]

    /ystyqbal/

        /[X ka] ystyqbal hona/ [X] to be welcomed, received

        /[X ka] ystyqbal kərna/ to welcome, receive [X]

D:

    /azadi/

/[X ko] azadi dena/ to free, liberate [X]

/[X se] azadi lena/ to take one's independence [from X]

/[X ko Y se] azadi mylna/ [X] to receive one's independence [from Y]

/doa/. [See also F.]

/[X ko] doa dena/ to bless [X], pray [for X], wish [X] well

/[X ki] doa lena/ to patronise [X], do good [to X]. [I.e. to obtain the prayers of X.]

/[X se] doa mãgna/ to pray [to X (God)]

/mwbarəkbad/

/[X ko] mwbarəkbad dena/ to congratulate [X]

/rae/

/[X ko] rae dena/ to express one's opinion [to X]

/[X se] rae lena/ to obtain the opinion [of X]

/rəvaj/. [See also F.]

/[X ko] rəvaj dena/ to popularise [X], make [X] prevalent, fashionáble

/swbut/

/[X ko Y ka] swbut dena/ to give proof [of Y to X]

/[X se Y ka] swbut mãgna/ to demand proof [of Y from X]

/[X ko Y se Z ka] swbut mylna/ [X] to get proof [of Z from Y]

/təlaq/

/[X ko] təlaq dena/ to divorce [X]

/[X ki] təlaq hona/ [X] to be divorced

/[X se] təlaq lena/ to get a divorce [from X]

/[X se] təlaq mãgna/ to ask for a divorce [from X]

F:

/əyb/

/[X mẽ] əyb nykalna/ to find fault [with X], point out defect[s] [in X]

/əziz/

/[X ko] əziz rəkhna/ to hold [X] dear

/baja/

/baja bəjana/ to play music

/bari/

/[X ki] bari ana/ [X's] turn to come

/bari lena/ to take one's turn

/doa/. [See also D.]

/[X ke lie] doa kərna/ to pray [for X]

/dykhai/

/dykhai dena/ to appear, be visible. [This formation is intransitive. See Sec. 19.307.]

/har/

/[gəle mẽ] har pəhnna/ to wear a garland [around the neck]

/jəhez/

/[X ko] jəhez dena/ to give [X] a dowry

/jəhez lana/ to bring a dowry. [The subject of this formation is usually the bride.]
/jwlus/
    /jwlus nykalna/ to take out a procession, parade
/məhr/
    /[X ka] məhr bādhna/ to agree to a "məhr" [of X (an amount)]
/māgni/
    /[X se] māgni hona/ to be, become engaged [to X]
    /[X ki] māgni TuTna/ [X's] engagement to be broken
/myhman/
    /[X ka] myhman hona/ to stay as [X's] guest
/nəqša/
    /[X ka] nəqša khēcna/ to sketch, outline, map [X]
/nykah/
    /[X ka] nykah hona/ [X's] marriage ceremony to take place
    /[X ka] nykah pəRhana/ to perform [X's] marriage ceremony
/rəvaj/. [See also D.]
    /[X ka] rəvaj hona/ [X] to be prevalent, fashionable, customary, popular
    /rəvaj pana/ to be, become prevalent, fashionable, customary, popular
/rwxsət/. [See also A.]
    /rwxsət lena/ to take leave, holiday
/swnai/
    /swnai dena/ to be heard, be audible. [This formation is intransitive. See Sec. 19.307.]
/šan/
    /šan dykhana/ to make a display of pomp
/ynkar/
    /[X se] ynkar kərna/ to deny [X (an accusation, etc.)]
    /[X se] ynkar kərna/ to refuse [X]. [Here X is usually a verbal infinitive (+ an object): e.g. /māy ne pani pine se ynkar kia./ "I refused to drink water."]
/ytminan/
    /[X ko Y se] ytminan hona/ [X] to be confident [about X], satisfied [with Y]
/yttyfaq/
    /[X ko Y se] yttyfaq hona/ [X] to be in agreement [with Y]
    /[X se Y pər] yttyfaq kərna/ to agree [with X about Y]
    /yttyfaq se/ by accident, suddenly
/yxtylaf/
    /[X əwr Y ka Z pər] yxtylaf hona/ [X and Y] to have a disagreement [about Z]
    /[X se Y pər] yxtylaf kərna/ to disagree [with X about Y]
/zymmedari/
    /[X ki] zymmedari lena, wThana/ to take on the responsibility [for X]

19.200. SCRIPT

19.201. Word Recognition.

(1) The following words are written with "uncommon" Arabic consonants, with final
ه = /a/, or with other special spelling conventions.

SCRIPT	PRONUNCIATION	SCRIPT	PRONUNCIATION
اتّفاقاً	yttyfaqən	رخصت	rwxsət
اصل	əsl	رشته دار	ryštedar
اطمینان	ytminan	روانہ	rəvana
اعلان	elan	تحالف	təhayf
تجربہ	təjryba	طرفَین	tərfəyn
تعارف	təarwf	طلاق	təlaq
تفصیلات	təfsilat	طَے	təy
ثابت	sabyt	عادات	adat
ثبوت	swbut	عادت	adət
جذبات	jəzbat	عزیز	əziz
حالات	halat	عَیب	əyb
حاضرین	hazyrin	محض	məhz
حقیقت	həqiqət	منظر	mənzər
دعا	doa	مواقع	məvaqe
دعوت نامہ	davətnama	موصول	məwsul
ذمّہ داری	zymmedari	نظریہ	nəzərya

203

SCRIPT	PRONUNCIATION	SCRIPT	PRONUNCIATION
نقشہ	nəqša	نکاح	nykah

19.202. Reading Drill I: Text.

The following is the text of the Conversation Section of this Unit. Read it aloud, striving for speed and accuracy.

اسمتھ۔   مجھے آپ کے دوست کی شادی کا دعوت نامہ موصول ہوا ہے ۔ اِس سے نبل کہ میں شادی میں شریک ہوں بہتر ہوگا کہ آپ مجھے یہاں کی شادی کی رسومات اور رواج کے بارے میں کچھ بتائیں ۔

رحیم۔   ضرور ۔ جو کچھ چاہیں بڑی خوشی سے پوچھ سکتے ہیں ۔

اسمتھ۔   کیا یہاں لڑکی اپنا خاوند خود چنتی ہے ۔ یا اُس کے والدین اِس کا انتظام کرتے ہیں؟

رحیم۔   جی نہیں ۔ یہ آپ کے ملک کا رواج ہے ۔ ہمارے معاشرے کی بناوٹ آپ کے معاشرے سے بالکل مختلف ہے ۔ ہمارے ہاں اکثریوں ہوتا ہے کہ لڑکے کے والدین اپنے بیٹے کے لئے لڑکی ڈھونڈتے ہیں ۔ وہ لڑکی والوں کے گھر جاکر لڑکی کے بارے میں تمام تفصیلات معلوم کرتے ہیں ۔ اسی طرح لڑکی والے بھی لڑکے کے بارے میں معلومات حاصل کرتے ہیں ۔ جب طرفین کو ایک دوسرے کی طرف سے اطمینان ہو جاتا ہے تو منگنی کی رسم ادا ہوتی ہے جس میں لڑکے والے لڑکی کے گھر جاتے ہیں اور ایک انگوٹھی، کچھ مٹھائی اور کچھ دیگر تحائف اُنہیں پیش کرتے ہیں ۔ اِس کے بعد شادی کی تاریخ طے ہوتی ہے ۔

اسمتھ۔   کیا یہ بھی ممکن ہے کہ منگنی بعض حالات کی وجہ سے ٹوٹ جائے ؟

رحیم   جی ہاں ۔ کسی خاص وجہ کی بنا پر ایسا ہو سکتا ہے ۔ لیکن کسی کسی چھوٹے موٹے اختلاف

204

پر ایسا بہت ہی کم ہوتا ہے .

اسمتھ ۔   کیا لڑکی شادی سے پہلے لڑکے سے ملتی ہے ؟

رحیم ۔   جی نہیں ۔ ہمارے معاشرے میں ایسی ملاقاتیں بہت کم ہوتی ہیں ۔ آج سے کچھ عرصہ پہلے
تو لڑکی والے اس بات کو بہت بڑا عیب سمجھتے تھے ۔ اب بھی اکثر ایسا ہی ہوتا ہے
کہ لڑکی اپنے ہونے والے خاوند سے نہیں ملتی ۔ اور اگر ملتی بھی ہے تو وہ محض
اتّفاق ہوتا ہے جیسے کسی دعوت یا شادی پر اتّفاقاً دونوں کی ملاقات ہو جائے ۔

اسمتھ ۔   اس سے ثابت ہوتا ہے کہ ہمارے ملک میں لڑکیوں کو یہاں کے مقابلے میں زیادہ آزادی
حاصل ہے ۔ وہ اکثر اپنا خاوند خود چنتی ہے ۔ وہ اپنے ہونے والے خاوند کے ساتھ باہر
جا سکتی ہے ۔ کیونکہ ہمارے نظریہ کے مطابق اس طرح لڑکے اور لڑکی کے درمیان محبّت
پیدا ہو جاتی ہے اور اُنہیں ایک دوسرے کی عادات وغیرہ کا مطالعہ کرنے کا بہتر موقعہ
ملتا ہے ۔

رحیم ۔   اس معاملے میں ہمارا تصوّر بالکل مختلف ہے ۔ ہمارے خیال کے مطابق اگر لڑکے اور لڑکی
کو اس طرح ملاقات کے مواقع دے دئے جائیں تو ہو سکتا ہے کہ دونوں محض جذبات میں
بہہ جائیں اور اپنی اصل ذمّہ داریوں کو محسوس نہ کریں ۔ اس لئے والدین جنہیں زندگی اور دنیا کا
زیادہ تجربہ ہوتا ہے اپنی اولاد کے لئے لڑکا یا لڑکی کی تلاش کرتے ہیں ۔ جہاں تک آپس میں
محبّت کا تعلق ہے تو وہ یوں ہے کہ آپ کے ہاں محبّت شادی سے پہلے شروع ہوتی
ہے اور ہمارے ہاں شادی کے بعد ۔

اسمتھ ۔   کیا آپ کے ہاں شادی کی رسم مسجد میں ادا ہوتی ہے جیسا کہ ہم لوگ گرجا میں ادا کرتے
ہیں ؟

رحیم۔ جی نہیں۔ کیونکہ شادی، طلاق اور اس قسم کے دوسرے مسائل کی معاشرتی اہمیت مذہبی اہمیت
سے زیادہ ہے۔اسی لئے یہ رسم لڑکی کے گھر ادا کی جاتی ہے۔ لڑکے والے ایک جلوس کی صورت
میں لڑکی کے گھر جاتے ہیں۔ یہ جلوس برات کہلاتا ہے۔ برات بہت شان سے آتی ہے۔
لوگ گلے میں پھولوں کے ہار پہنے ہوتے ہیں۔ آگے آگے کچھ لوگ باجے بجاتے چلتے ہیں۔ لڑکی
والے بھی اپنا گھر خوب سجاتے ہیں اور بہت گھبراتے ہوئے انتظام میں مصروف ہوتے ہیں
تاکہ مہمانوں کے استقبال میں کوئی کمی نہ رہ جائے۔دلہن کی سہیلیاں اس موقعہ پر خوشی کے
گانے گاتی ہیں، ناچتی ہیں، غرض کہ مختلف طریقوں سے خوشیاں مناتی ہیں۔ حقیقت تو یہ ہے
کہ یہ منظر بہت دلکش ہوتا ہے۔

اسمتھ۔ برات میں کون کون لوگ شامل ہوتے ہیں؟

رحیم۔ برات میں دولہا کے رشتہ دار جیسے تایا، چچا، پھوپھا، ماموں اور خالو وغیرہ شامل ہوتے ہیں۔
ان کے علاوہ دیگر عزیز اور دوست بھی ہوتے ہیں۔ لڑکی والے آگے بڑھ کر اپنے مہمانوں کا
استقبال کرتے ہیں اور ایک دوسرے سے اپنا تعارف کراتے ہیں۔ پھر دولہا اور دلہن کے
باپ مہر وغیرہ کے بارے میں بات چیت کرتے ہیں۔ اس کے بعد نکاح شروع ہوتا ہے۔

اسمتھ۔ نکاح کا کیا مطلب ہے اور کیسے پڑھایا جاتا ہے؟

رحیم۔ نکاح کا مطلب شادی کا اعلان ہے جو سب لوگوں کی موجودگی میں کیا جاتا ہے کیونکہ ہمارے
نبیّ نے فرمایا ہے " اے لوگو! شادی کا اعلان سب کے سامنے کرو" ایک مولوی
صاحب نکاح پڑھاتے ہیں۔ نکاح میں خدا کی تعریف اور کچھ دعائیں پڑھی جاتی ہیں۔ تمام
حاضرین کے سامنے لڑکے سے تین دفعہ پوچھا جاتا ہے کہ اسے یہ لڑکی بیوی کی حیثیت سے
قبول ہے یا نہیں۔ اور وہ سب کے سامنے اس کا اقرار کرتا ہے۔ یہ حاضرین اس لحاظ

سے شادی کے گواہ یا ثبوت کی حیثیت رکھتے ہیں ۔ نکاح کے فوراً بعد کچھ مٹھائی یا پھل بانٹے

جاتے ہیں ۔ اور تمام لوگ دولہا کو باری باری مبارک باد پیش کرتے ہیں ۔

اسمتہ ۔ کیا نکاح سے پہلے لڑکی کی رائے لی جاتی ہے ؟

رحیم ۔ جی ہاں ۔ اگر لڑکی نکاح پڑھوانے سے انکار کر دے تو نکاح جائز نہیں ہوتا ۔ یہی وجہ ہے

کہ دو یا تین آدمی لڑکی کے پاس وکیل کے طور پر جاتے ہیں اور اُس سے نکاح کی اجازت لیتے

ہیں ۔ اِس کے بعد نکاح پڑھایا جاتا ہے ۔ نکاح کے بعد لڑکی والے مہمانوں کو کھانا کھلاتے ہیں ۔

اور اپنی حیثیت کے مطابق جہیز دیتے ہیں ۔ اِس کے بعد برات واپس دولہا کے گھر روانہ ہو

جاتی ہے ۔ برات کی روانگی پر یہ خوشی کا نقشہ لڑکی والوں کے لئے غم میں تبدیل ہو جاتا ہے ۔

خاص طور پر دلہن کے ماں باپ اور بہن بھائی اِس موقعہ پر رو دیتے ہیں ۔ کیونکہ والدین اپنی

اولاد کو بہت محبت سے پالتے ہیں لیکن اِس موقعہ پر وہ لڑکی کو اپنے سے ہمیشہ کے لئے جدا کر

دیتے ہیں ۔ اِس لئے دلہن کے رخصت ہوتے ہونے پر اکثر لوگ اداس دکھائی دیتے ہیں ۔ لوگوں کی

آنکھوں میں آنسو اور دلوں میں دلہن کی آئندہ زندگی کے لئے دعائیں ہوتی ہیں ۔

اسمتہ ۔ بہت خوب ۔ اِن معلومات سے یہ فائدہ ہوا کہ اب میں کل شادی کے موقعہ پر شادی کی

رسومات سے زیادہ لطف اٹھا سکوں گا ــــــ چار بج گئے ہیں ۔ آئیے ذرا چائے وائے پئیں ۔

رحیم ۔ ٹھیک ہے ۔ آئیے ۔

19. 203. Reading Drill II: Sentences.

Read the following sentences aloud and translate them into English.

١ ۔ جب اُسے اطمینان ہو گیا کہ یہی اُس کا بڑا بھائی ہے تو خوشی سے اُس کی آنکھوں میں آنسو آ گئے اور

کہنے لگا کہ اے میرے بھائی، کیا آپ مجھے بھول گئے؟ بیس سال ہوئے کہ ہم ایک دوسرے سے
جدا ہو گئے تھے لیکن یقین جانئے کہ ہر وقت میرے دل میں آپ کی یاد رہتی تھی۔

۲۔ جب سب رشتہ دار انتظام میں مصروف تھے تو ایک چور کمرے میں گھس گیا اور جہیز میں سے کچھ زیور
نکال کر بھاگ گیا۔

۳۔ آخر کار اُنہوں نے حاضرین سے اپنی بات منوا لی اور سب لوگ ایک جلوس کی صورت میں اُن کے پیچھے
ہو لئے۔

۴۔ ہمارے معاشرے کی بناوٹ ایسی ہے کہ اگر کسی مرد کو کسی عورت سے محبت ہو جائے اور یہ اُن کے والدین
کو پسند نہ ہو تو اُن کی شادی ہونا مشکل ہے۔

۵۔ سب لوگوں نے اِس بات پر اتّفاق کیا کہ شراب پینا ایک بہت بُری عادت ہے۔ اِسے کسی نہ کسی
طرح روکنا چاہئے۔

۶۔ اگرچہ اُس نے دولہا کو مبارکباد پیش کی، لیکن اُس کی شکل سے صاف پتہ چلتا تھا کہ وہ اِس شادی
سے خوش نہیں ہے۔

۷۔ اسمتھ صاحب کو پاکستانی رسومات دیکھنے کے ایسے مواقع ملے ہیں جو کسی دوسرے باہر والے کو کبھی نہیں
ملے۔

۸۔ میری رودائگی کے وقت میرے عزیزوں اور رشتہ داروں نے مجھے بہت سے تحائف دئے۔

۹۔ جب ہم سب لوگوں نے اسمتھ صاحب کو رخصت کیا، تو اُن کے گلے میں پھولوں کے ہار تھے اور اُن
کے ہاتھوں میں دوستوں کے دئے ہوئے تحائف۔ مسز اسمتھ بھی ہار پہنے ہوئے تھیں اور اُن کے ہاتھ
میں مٹھائی کا ایک بڑا ڈبّہ تھا جو مسز رحیم نے اُنہیں پیش کیا تھا۔

۱۰۔ ایسا دکھائی دیتا ہے کہ امریکہ کی حکومت ہماری یہ شرط نہیں مانے گی۔

۱۱۔ پروفیسروں نے بہت اچھی طرح میرا استقبال کیا۔اُنہوں نے مجھے خوب چائے دائے پلائی اور ہم کافی دیر تک آپس میں بات چیت کرتے رہے۔

۱۲۔ جب میرے تعارف کی باری آئی تو میں آگے بڑھا۔اتّفاقاً رحیم صاحب بھی اُسی وقت آگے بڑھے۔اِس طرح ہم دونوں ٹکرا گئے۔اِس پر سب حاضرین ہنس پڑے۔

۱۳۔ سب لوگ جذبات میں آکر چیخنے لگے اور پتھر پھینکنے لگے۔

۱۴۔ برات کا انتظام کرنا آپ کی ذمّہ داری ہے کیونکہ آپ کو ایسے کاموں کا کافی تجربہ ہے۔

۱۵۔ اِس مسئلے پر علمائے دین میں اختلاف ہے۔

19. 204. Reading Drill III: Unseen Text.

Vocative

اِس شخص نے چھت پر چڑھ کر کہا۔ اسے بھائیو اور بہنو۔ ذرا میری بات سنو، ہم لوگ کوئی جانور نہیں ہیں اور نہ ہی یہ بادشاہ کوئی خدا ہے کہ جب کا ہر حکم مانا جائے۔ ہم اِنسان ہیں اور اِس ملک کی

Deserving

دولت کے حقدار ہیں۔ آزادی ہر اِنسان کا بنیادی حق ہے اور اِسے حاصل کرنے کے لئے ہم مرنے کے

aftuwall

لئے بھی تیّار ہیں۔ ہمیں ہر چھوٹی موٹی بات پر بادشاہ کی پولیس گرفتار کر لیتی ہے۔ سخت سزائیں دیتی ہے۔ ہم عدالت میں جاتے ہیں تو وہاں بھی کوئی ہماری بات نہیں سنتا۔ آخرکار ہم اِنسان ہیں کب تک اِس حال میں پڑے رہیں اور کب تک یہ برداشت کرتے رہیں؟ ہمیں پتہ ہے کہ بادشاہ کی فوج کے پاس بحری جہاز ، بندوق اور پستول وغیرہ ہیں لیکن ہمیں یہ نہیں بھولنا چاہئے کہ ہم ایسا دل رکھتے ہیں جس

courage

میں ہمّت ، بہادری اور آزادی کا جذبہ ہے اور ہم تعداد میں بھی اُن سے بہت زیادہ ہیں۔اگر ہم

hurry

ہمّت کریں اور پوری طاقت سے لڑیں تو اِنشا۔اللہ ہم کبھی نہیں ہاریں گے۔ کیونکہ خدا اُن لوگوں کی مدد کرتا ہے جو سچ حق کے لئے لڑتے ہیں۔ آؤ اور آگے بڑھ کر یہ ثابت کر دو کہ اب بھی دنیا میں ایسے لوگ موجود ہیں جو خدا کے سوا کسی سے نہیں ڈرتے۔

یہ سنتے ہی لوگ اِس شخص کے پیچھے ہولئے اور قلعے پر پہنچ گئے ۔ قلعے کے دروازے بند تھے اور

چاروں طرف بادشاہ کی فوج بندوقیں لئے ہوئے کھڑی تھی لیکن اِن لوگوں نے اِس کا کوئی خیال نہ کیا اور

برابر آگے بڑھتے گئے ۔ بادشاہ کی فوج نے اُنہیں روکنے کی کوشش کی لیکن وہ اُنہیں روکنے میں کامیاب نہ

ہو سکی ۔ آخرکار لڑائی شروع ہوگئی ۔ لڑائی میں طرفین کے کوئی دو سو آدمی مارے گئے اور تین سو زخمی

ہوئے ۔ سڑکیں خون سے لال ہوگئیں لیکن اِن لوگوں نے ہمّت نہ ہاری اور بہادری سے لڑتے رہے ۔

کچھ دیر بعد آہستہ آہستہ بادشاہ کی فوج بھاگنے لگی ۔ اور یہ لوگ قلعے کا دروازہ توڑ کر اندر گھس گئے ۔ بادشاہ

یہ دیکھ کر بہت گھبرایا ۔ اور اپنے ہوائی جہاز میں بیٹھ کر مُلک سے بھاگ گیا ۔

19.205.   Writing Drill I: Text.

Counting each speaker's part as one paragraph, write out the first twelve paragraphs of Sec. 19.506 (Conversation Practice) in Urdu script (i. e. down through /kya, ap ke məzhəb mẽ bhi təlaq jayz həy?/).

19.206.   Spelling Review and Dictionary Drill.

Write out the following words in Urdu script and place them in Urdu alphabetical order.

(1)	myThai	(11)	pyas
(2)	bənavəT	(12)	gana
(3)	swnai	(13)	bhuki
(4)	hyndostan	(14)	jhəgRa
(5)	bəcpən	(15)	pyasa
(6)	dwlhən	(16)	beTi
(7)	cəwRai	(17)	jhaRu
(8)	ghoRa	(18)	mar
(9)	əkela	(19)	əcchai
(10)	ələg	(20)	chwri

19.207.   Hindi Forms.

Using Secs. 19.302 and 19.303, identify the component elements of each word in Sec. 19.206.

19.208. Response Drill.

Answer the following questions in writing.

۱۔ آپ کے ملک میں منگنی کی رسم کس طرح ادا کی جاتی ہے ؟

۲۔ مہر کسے کہتے ہیں اور اس کی کیا بنیاد ہے ؟

۳۔ کیا ہندوستان اور پاکستان میں جہیز دینا لازمی سمجھا جاتا ہے ؟

۴۔ عزیز صاحب کے کہنے کے مطابق محبت شادی کے بعد شروع ہوتی ہے ۔کیا آپ کو اس سے اتفاق ہے؟

۵۔ اس کا کیا ثبوت ہے کہ طلاق سے معاشرے میں خرابیاں پیدا ہوتی ہیں ؟

۶۔ کیا آپ ثابت کر سکتے ہیں کہ صفائی صحت کے لئے ضروری ہے ؟

۷۔ کیا آپ کو پاکستانی کھانوں کا تجربہ ہے ؟

۸۔ اگر دلہن نکاح پڑھوانے سے انکار کرے تو کیا نکاح جائز ہوگا ؟

۹۔ کیا آپ کے ملک میں بھی لڑکی والے شادی کے موقع پر گھر سجاتے ہیں ؟

۱۰۔ کیا نکاح سے قبل لڑکی سے نکاح کی اجازت لینی ضروری ہے؟

19.209. English to Urdu Sentences.

1. God accepts the prayers of virtuous people.
2. I disagreed [differed] with [/se/] his opinion, but he did not change his opinion.
3. When your letter arrived [lit. became received], I at once made preparation[s] for [lit. of] departure.
4. At first Mr. Smith refused, but I finally made him agree.
5. The culprit confessed that he was the one who had stolen [lit. he-emphatic had stolen] the map from my room.
6. I have been [lit. am] separated from my wife for [/se/] eleven years. She lives in Pakistan, and I do not have enough [lit. this much] money that I can bring [lit. call] her.
7. I have much experience of life. Therefore, I can say this, that divorce is a very bad thing, and if you divorce [lit. will give divorce] your wife, your entire family

211

will be caught in fighting [and] quarreling.

8. Having heard this thing, all the audience became excited [lit. came into emotions], and carrying guns and pistols [they] went to the office of the newspaper.

9. In our country [lit. our place] in the beginning of the cold season [lit. season of cold], we all together take out a procession. This procession goes with great pomp to [lit. on] the seashore [lit. bank of the sea], and there everyone sings songs and dances.

10. This scene is very nice, but from here the sound of the singing cannot be heard [lit. does not give audibility].

11. It is the responsibility of the parents that they choose a suitable bridegroom or bride for their children.

12. After the death of my father, I got the largest [lit. more than all] share of [lit. from in] his land.

13. The conditions of that country have become so [lit. this much] bad, that now every evil is permitted there. In my opinion the reason for this [lit. of this] is the weakness of the government.

14. My coming was just an accident. If I had known before [lit. if to me from before [it] had been known] that some guests were staying with you [lit. at your place], then I would not have come.

15. After the marriage ceremony all the relatives congratulated the groom in turn.

19.300. ANALYSIS

19.301. The Hindi Element in Urdu.

Urdu relies upon three major sources for its grammar and lexicon: Hindi, Persian, and Arabic. (A fourth, English, is also of growing importance.) From the viewpoint of the basic structure of the language, Hindi must be considered the most fundamental element in Urdu: much of the "grammar" (noun and verb paradigms, postpositions, word order, etc.) and also a large percentage of the lexicon (common nouns and adjectives, pronominal roots, verb stems, adverbs, etc.) are of local origin, rather than imports from external sources.

As the student has no doubt gathered, the native Hindi element is not prominent in literary Urdu. Not only grammar and lexicon but also similes, metaphors, and concepts have been borrowed wholesale from the Perso-Arabic heritage. The Hindi element becomes predominant only when one turns to contexts related to the "grassroots" of Indo-Pakistani life: agriculture, domestic life, the village, handicrafts, animals and plants, the family, marriage, etc.

This is to ignore the recent development of "High Hindi, " of course. This Sanskritised form of Hindi-Urdu is written in the Deva Nagari character and is employed as one of the official languages of post-Partition India. Since this variety of the language is not used at all in Pakistan it will be omitted from the discussion which follows.

The Hindi element (or rather "the local Indo-Aryan base") is rather more difficult to describe in terms of a concise, comprehensive system than were Arabic and Persian. The Indo-Aryan dialect which forms the "base" for Urdu is derived from one or another form of Sanskrit through various Prakrit and Middle Indic developments. If one may speak impressionistically for the moment, this Indo-Aryan element is "harder to segment" into component stems and affixes: they are "more closely fused together, " with more modifications of both stem and affix than were found in either Arabic or Persian. Since Sanskrit and its various daughter languages are similarly complex, this is certainly not a new phenomenon.

The question that now arises is this: just how much of this segmentation (i.e. word analysis) is relevant to a modern, descriptive Hindi-Urdu grammar, and how much should be left to the philologist? In many cases it is difficult to decide whether two rather different looking forms can be descriptively analysed in the modern language, although they may be traceable to the same Sanskrit source. In the discussion which follows, the author has tried to avoid analyses which are too complex or esoteric to be of use to the beginning student of modern Hindi-Urdu. The objective of these reference Sections is to provide the student with the tools to analyse (relatively) frequent constructions and compounds and thus increase his passive vocabulary. Uncommon formations have thus been omitted, as have the Sanskritised constructions of "High Hindi. " A good, thorough reference grammar is still a desideratum.

19.302. Hindi Prefixes.

The following prefixes are fairly frequent:

/ə/-/ən/ "un-, non-, in-": /ə/ (etc.) + Verb stem, Past Participle, etc. = A,
N, Adv. E. g.

/əmyT/ A1 indelible, ineffaceable, not erasable. [/myTna/ "to be
erased." Also /ənmyT/.]

/əmər/ A1 immortal. [/mərna/ "to die."]

/ənpəRh/ A1 illiterate. [/pəRhna/ "to read."]

/əndekha/ A2 unseen, unexperienced. [/dekhna/ "to see."]

/ələg/ A1 Adv apart, separate, distinct. [/ləgna/ "to be fastened,
attached."]

/əchuta/ A2 untouched, undefiled, pure, new. [/chut/ F1 "touch,
defilement" from /chuna/ "to touch."]

/byn/ "un-, without-": /byn/ + Past Participle, N, etc. = A, Adv. E. g.

/byndhyan/ Adv unthinkingly. [/dhyan/ M1 thought, meditation."]

/bynjwta/ A2 unploughed. [/jwtna/ "to be ploughed."]

/bynsyla/ A2 unsewn. [/sylna/ "to be sewn."]

/kw/-/kə/ "dis-, ill-": /kw/ (etc.) + N = N, A. E. g.

/kwDhəb/ A1 ugly, ill-shaped. [/Dhəb/ M1 shape, form."]

/kwDhāg/ M/F1 A1 ill-behaved, ill-mannered. [/Dhāg/ M1 "manner,
way, style."]

/kwpəth/ M1 evil way, immorality. [/pəth/ M1 "path, course, road."]

/kwput/ [or /kəput/ or /kwpwtr/] M1 disobedient son. [Hindi /pwtr/ M1
"son."]

/ny/-/nyr/ "-less": /ny/ (etc.) + V stem, N = A. E. g.

/nyDər/ A1 fearless. [/Dər/ M1 "fear."]

/nyhətta/ A2 weaponless. [/hətta/ M2 means "handle" and is not used
for "weapon" in Urdu.]

/nykəmma/ A2 shiftless, worthless, idle, useless. [Cf. /kam/ M1
"work."]

/nyrasa/ A2 having no hope, hopeless. [Hindi /as/ F1 "hope."]

/nyrbəl/ A1 powerless, weak. [/bəl/ M1 "power, strength."]

/nyrgwn/ A1 unskilled, having no good quality. [/gwn/ M1 "quality,
skill."]

/pər/ "another-, next-": /pər/ + N = N. E. g.

/pərdes/ M1 foreign land. [/des/ M1 "country."]

/pərlok/ M1 [np] the next world, the hereafter. [/lok/ M1 "world."]

/sw/-/sy/-/sə/ "good-, well-": /sw/ (etc.) + N = N, A. E. g.

/swDəwl/ [or /syDəwl/] A1 well-shaped. [/Dəwl/ M1 shape, form,
appearance."]

/swcet/ A1 thoughtful, attentive, heedful. [/cet/ M1 "thought."]

/swphəl/ A1 fruitful, beneficial, propitious. [/phəl/ M1 "fruit."]

/swput/ [or /səput/] M1 good son. [Cf. /kwput/ under /kw/ above.]

19.303. Hindi Substantive Suffixes.

Common inflectional affixes (e. g. the MOP affix /ō/) are omitted in the list given below.

Verb Stem + /∅/ = N. E. g.

    /har/ F1 loss. [/harna/ "to lose."]

    /khel/ M1 game. [/khelna/ "to play."]

    /jit/ F1 winning, victory. [/jitna/ "to win."]

    /mar/ F1 beating. [/marna/ "to beat."]

    /rok/ F1 hindrance, obstacle, check. [/rokna/ "to stop."]

/a/ "Type II msc. noun formant": Noun stem + /a/ = M2; Verb stem + /a/ = M2. E. g.

    /ləRka/ M2 boy. [Stem /ləRk-/.]

    /beTa/ M2 son. [Stem /beT-/.]

    /bəkheRa/ M2 mess, clutter. [/bəkherna/ "to scatter, disperse" (?).]

    /chapa/ M2 printing, stamp, dye. [/chapna/ "to print."]

    /ghera/ M2 siege, encirclement, fence. [/gherna/ "to surround, encircled."]

    /jhəgRa/ M2 quarrel, dispute. [/jhəgRna/ "to quarrel."]

    /mela/ M2 fair, festival. [The stem is the same as that of /mylna/ "to meet, mix, get."]

    /phera/ M2 turn, time, circuit. [/pherna/ "to turn, turn away, bend, twist."]

/a/ "Type II msc. adjective formant": Adjective stem + /a/ = A; Noun + /a/ = A. E. g.

    /bhuka/ A2 hungry. [/bhuk/ F1 "hunger."]

    /jhuTa/ A2 lying, false. [/jhuT/ M1 "lie."]

    /məyla/ A2 dirty, filthy. [/məyl/ M1 "filth."]

    /gerva/ A2 saffron-coloured. [/geru/ M1 "red ochre, reddish stone."]

    /choTa/ A2 small. [Stem /choT-/.]

/a/ "abstract noun formant": Adjective or Verb stem + /a/ + the abstract noun formant /i/ = abstract noun. E. g.

    /bəRai/ F2 bigness. [Stem /bəR-/ "big."]

    /golai/ F2 roundness. [/gol/ A1 "round."]

    /sylai/ F2 sewing. [/sylna/ "to be sewn."]

/ahəT/-/avəT/ "abstract noun formant": Adjective or Verb stem + /ahəT/ (etc.) = N. Nouns formed with this suffix are F1. In the Deccani dialect /ahəT/ and /avəT/ are both represented by /aT/. E. g.

    /cyknahəT/ F1 greasiness, slipperiness. [/cykna/ A2 "greasy, slippery" (stem /cykn-/).]

    /ghəbrahəT/ F1 worry, upset, distress, fluster. [/ghəbrana/ "to be worried, upset, flustered."]

    /kəRvahəT/ F1 bitterness. [/kəRva/ A2 "bitter-tasting" (stem /kəRv-/).]

    /nilahəT/ F1 blueness. [/nil/ M1 "blue colouring"; /nila/ A2 "blue."]

    /bənavəT/ F1 structure, form, shape. [/bənna/ "to be made, built."]

    /mylavəT/ F1 adulteration, mixing. [/mylna/ "to meet, mix, get."]

    /rwkavəT/ F1 obstacle, hindrance. [/rwkna/ "to stop (intrans.)."]

    /səjavəT/ F1 decoration, adornment, embellishment. [/səjna/ "to be decorated, adorned, embellished."]

/ak/ "formant for nouns of agency": Verb stem or Noun stem + /ak/ = N, A. This affix is followed in some words by the Type II affix /a/. E. g.

/calak/ A1 clever, sharp, deceitful. [/cal/ F1 "move, strategem." Here the original sense of "one who moves" is obscured.]

/ləRak/ M1 [or /ləRaka/ M2 A2] quarrelsome person, fighter. [/ləRna/ "to fight. "]

/pəyrak/ M/F1 swimmer. [/pəyrna/ "to swim. " Also:]

/təyrak/ M/F1 swimmer. [/təyrna/ "to swim. " /təyrna/ is now more common than /pəyrna/.]

/al/-/alu/-/əl/-/əyl/-/el/-/er/-/il/-/l/-/ol/-/oR/-/yəl/ "adjective formant": Noun, Verb, or Adjective stem + /al/ (etc.) = A. Of these variants, /al/, /el/, /er/, /il/, /l/, and /oR/ are obligatorily followed by the Type II affixes /a/, /e/, /i/, etc. (at least in the corpus which the author has used as the basis of this description). /əyl/ occurs in some words as the last affix in the word and in others followed by the Type II affixes. /əl/, /alu/, and /yəl/ occur only as the last affix in the word. E. g.

/məTyala/ A2 dust-coloured. [/myTTi/ F2 "dirt, dust, earth" is from the same root.]

/kəwRyala/ A2 spotted. [/kəwRi/ F2 "cowry shell. "]

/jhəgRalu/ A1 quarrelsome. [/jhəgRna/ "to quarrel. "]

/bojhəl/ A1 burdensome. [/bojh/ M1 "burden. "]

/dəbəyl/ M/F1 A1 weak, subordinate. [/dəbna/ "to be pressed down. "]

/kəsəyla/ [or /kəsila/] A2 coppery-tasting, metallic in flavour. [/kəs/ M1 "the bitter taste of something sour kept in a metal container, astringency. "]

/əkela/ A2 alone. [The root is the same as that of /ek/ A1 "one. "]

/kəmera/ A2 hard-working, industrious. [/kam/ M1 "work, job. "]

/cəcera/ A2 pertaining to the father's younger brother. [/cəca/ M1 "father's younger brother" (stem /cəc-/).]

/bwhtera/ A2 Adv many, much, a lot. [The stem is the same as that of /bəhwt/ A1 "many, much, very. "]

/pəthrila/ A2 stony, rocky. [/pətthər/ M1 "stone, rock. "]

/rə̄gila/ A2 colourful, lively, gay. [/rə̄g/ M1 "colour. "]

/əgla/ A2 next, forthcoming, ahead, previous. [The stem is the same as that of /age/ Comp Post Adv "on ahead, in front. "]

/pychla/ A2 back, behind, latter. [The stem is the same as that of /picha/ M2 "hind portion, back. "]

/dhw̄dla/ A2 hazy, misty. [/dhw̄d/ F1 "haze, mist. "]

/ThəThol/ M1 A1 jesting, jester. [The stem is the same as that of /ThəTTha/ M2 "loud laughter, guffaw. "]

/hə̄soRa/ A2 laughing. [/hə̄sna/ "to laugh. "]

/mwtoRa/ A2 urinating, one who urinates a lot. [/mut/ M1 "urine"; /mutna/ "to urinate. "]

/DəRhyəl/ M1 A1 bearded person, bearded. [The stem is the same as that of /DaRhi/ F2 "beard. "]

/ghayəl/ A1 wounded, injured. [The stem is the same as that of /ghao/ M1 "wound. "]

/al/: see /šal/.

/alu/: see /al/ "adjective formant."

/an/ "abstract noun formant": Adjective or Verb stem + /an/ = N. Most of these are F1. This suffix may well be grouped together with /ən/, q.v. E.g.

/cəwRan/ F1 width. [/cəwRa/ A2 "wide."]

/ləgan/ M1 assessment of land tax. [/ləgna/ "to be fastened, attached." (?)]

/ləmban/ F1 length, tallness. [/ləmba/ A2 "long, tall."]

/ūcan/ F1 height. /ūca/ A2 "high."

/wRan/ F1 flight. [/wRna/ "to fly."]

/wThan/ F1 upbringing, growth, height. [/wThna/ "to rise, get up."]

/an/: see /stan/.

/an/: see /ən/.

/ao/ "abstract noun formant": Verb stem + /ao/ = N. All of these are M1. See also /ahəT/ and /av/ for possibly related elements. E.g.

/bəcao/ M1 escape, protection, refuge. [/bəcna/ "to escape"; /bəcana/ "to rescue, save."]

/bəhao/ M1 flow. [/bəhna/ "to flow."]

/cəRhao/ M1 ascent, steep slope. [/cəRhna/ "to climb, ascend, go up."]

/jhwkao/ M1 bending, inclination, leaning. [/jhwkna/ "to bend, bow, incline, lean."]

/ləgao/ M1 connection, link, relation, attachment, affection. [/ləgna/ "to be fastened, attached."]

/ap/ "abstract noun formant": Verb stem + /ap/ = N. Only one example is found in the corpus:

/mylap/ M1 connection, harmony, mutual good relations, reconciliation. [/mylna/ "to meet, get, mix." This affix may possibly be related to /pən/, q.v.]

/ar/: see /har/ "noun of occupation."

/ari/-/aRi/ "agentive noun": Verb stem (or possibly noun stem?) + /ari/ (etc.) = N. All of these are M1. It is possible to treat this suffix as another variety of /har/, q.v. E.g.

/bhykari/ M1 beggar. [/bhik/ F1 "alms."]

/khylaRi/ M1 player. [/khelna/ "to play"; /khel/ M1 "game."]

/pwjari/ M1 worshipper, devotee (Hindu). [/pujna/ "to worship"; /puja/ M2 "worship, prayer."]

/aRi/: see /ari/.

/as/-/vas/ "abstract noun formant": Adjective or Verb stem + /as/ (etc.) = N. All of these seem to be F1. In many cases, the Type II affixes may be added after /as/ to produce a Type II adjective. E.g.

/bhəRas/ F1 explosion of anger, burst of rage, fury. [Probably the same stem as /bhəR/ M1 [or F1?] "sound of an explosion, pop, bang."]

/khəTas/ F1 sourness. [The stem is the same as that of /khəTTa/ A2 "sour."]

/myThas/ F1 sweetness. [The stem is the same as that of /miTha/ A2 "sweet."]

/pyas/ F1 thirst. [The stem is the same as that of /pina/ "to drink."]

/bəkvas/ F1 nonsense. [/bəkna/ "to talk nonsense."]

Examples of Stem + /as/ + /a/ = A2:

/bəkvasa/ A2 nonsensical. [Archaic; mostly obsolete.]

/nȳdasa/ A2 sleepy, drowsy. [The stem is the same as that of /nīd/ F1 "sleep, doze." /nȳdas/ F1 "sleepiness, drowsiness" also occurs but is less common.]

/pyasa/ A2 thirsty

/rwāsa/ [or /rwasa/] A2 ready to weep, tearful. [The stem is the same as that of /rona/ "to cry." No */rwās/ or */rwas/ are found.]

/at/ "abstract noun formant": Adjective stem + /at/ = N. The only example recorded is:

/bwhtat/ F1 plenty, abundance. [The stem is the same as that of /bəhwt/ A1 "much, many, very."]

/au/ "adjective formant": Verb stem + /au/ = A1. E.g.

/bykau/ A1 for sale, saleable. [/bykna/ "to sell (intrans.), to be sold."]

/cəlau/ A1 common, ordinary. [/cəlna/ "to go, move."]

/dəbau/ A1 oppressing, suppressive, pressing. [/dəbna/ "to be pressed down."]

/av/ "noun formant": Verb stem + /av/ + the Type II affixes = M2. Cf. also /ao/ and /ahəT/. E.g.

/bəRhava/ M2 encouragement, incitement. [/bəRhna/ "to advance, expand, enlarge."]

/bwlava/ M2 invitation. [/bolna/ "to speak"; /bwlana/ "to call, invite."]

/cəRhava/ M2 offerings made to a saint, etc. [/cəRhna/ "to climb, ascend, go up": i.e. "what has been elevated, raised."]

/dykhava/ M2 ostentation, outward pomp and show. [/dekhna/ "to see"; /dykhana/ "to show."]

/avəT/: see /ahəT/

/əhl/: see /har/ "adjective formant."

/əhr/: see /har/ "adjective formant."

/ək/ "abstract noun formant": Adjective stem + /ək/ = N. Examples in the corpus are F1. E.g.

/kalək/ F1 blackness, soot. [The stem is the same as that of /kala/ A2 "black."]

/ThənDək/ F1 coldness. [/ThənD/ F1 "cold, coldness"; also /ThənDa/ A2 "cold."]

/ək/-/k/ "diminutive": N + /ək/ (etc.) = N. The /k/ variant is obligatorily followed by the Type II affixes. The diminutive sense is greater when the feminine affix /i/ occurs. E.g.

/Dholək/ F1 small drum. [/Dhol/ M1 "drum." Also:]

/Dholki/ F2 very small drum

/balək/ M1 small boy. [Hindi /bal/ M1 "boy."]

/məTka/ M2 small earthen vessel. [/maT/ M1 "large earthen vessel." Also:]

/məTki/ F2 very small earthen vessel

/ək/: see /yk/.

/əkkəR/ "agentive noun": Verb stem + /əkkəR/ = N. Rare. E.g.

    /bhwləkkəR/ M1 forgetful person. [/bhulna/ "to forget."]

    /bwjhəkkəR/ M1 guesser, one who pretends to be wise. [/bujhna/ "to think."]

/əl/: see /al/ "adjective formant."

/ən/-/n/-/an/ "feminine noun formant": Noun + /ən/ (etc.) = N. The variants /n/ and /an/ are obligatorily followed by the Type II feminine suffix /i/. Noun stems often display alternant forms before this affix. E.g.

    /cəmarən/ F1 leatherworker's wife. [/cəmar/ M1 "leatherworker."]

    /dhobən/ F1 washerman's wife. [/dhobi/ M1 "washerman."]

    /dwlhən/ F1 bride. [Cf. /dulha/ M2 "groom"; stem /dulh-/ or /dwlh-/.]

    /gəvalən/ F1 cowherd's wife. [/gəvala/ M2 "cowherd"; see /val/.]

    /malən/ F1 gardener's wife. [/mali/ M1 "gardener."]

    /nayən/ F1 barber's wife. [/nai/ M1 "barber."]

    /DakTərni/ F2 female doctor. [/DakTər/ M1 "doctor."]

    /həthni/ F2 female elephant. [Cf. /hathi/ M1 "male elephant."]

    /šerni/ F2 female tiger. [/šer/ M1 "tiger."]

    /mwmani/ F2 mother's brother's wife. [/mamū/ M1 "mother's brother" -- a modified stem.]

    /myhtərani/ F2 sweeper's wife, female sweeper. [/myhtər/ M1 "sweeper."]

    /mwllani/ F2 Muslim religious scholar's wife. [/mwlla/ M1 "Muslim religious scholar."]

    /pənDytani/ F2 Hindu scholar's wife. [/pənDyt/ M1 "Hindu scholar." /pənDytayən/ F1 is also found.]

    /wstani/ F2 female teacher. [/wstad/ M1 "teacher, master" is originally Persian.]

/ən/-/n/ "noun formant": Verb stem + /ən/ (etc.) = N. After the variant /n/, the Type II msc. affix /a/ often occurs. See also /an/. E.g.

    /cələn/ M1 deportment, character, habit, custom. [/cəlna/ "to go, move."]

    /ləgən/ F1 affection, enthusiasm, time. [/ləgna/ "to be attached, fastened."]

    /kətrən/ F1 small swatch of cloth left over from cutting. [/kətərna/ "to cut."]

    /mylən/ M1 meeting. [/mylna/ "to meet, get, mix."]

    /thəkən/ F1 weariness, fatigue. [/thəkna/ "to be tired, fatigued."]

    /phəbən/ F1 decoration, embellishment. [/phəbna/ "to suit, fit, look well on, adorn."]

    /gana/ M2 song. [/gana/ "to sing."]

    /khana/ M2 food. [/khana/ "to eat."]

    /wtrən/ F1 hand-me-down clothing. [/wtərna/ "to go down, descend, alight, get off."]

/ən/: see /n/ "noun of instrument."

/ət/-/t/ "abstract noun formant": Verb stem (etc.) + /ət/ (etc.) = N. The variant /t/ is obligatorily followed by the abstract noun formant /i/. Nouns ending in /ət/ are F1, and those ending in /t/ + /i/ are F2. E.g.

219

/bəcət/ F1 residue, saving. [/bəcna/ "to escape, be left over."]

/khəpət/ F1 consumption. [/khəpna/ "to be consumed."]

/rə̄gət/ F1 complexion, colouring. [/rə̄gna/ "to colour, dye"; /rə̄g/ M1 "colour."]

/bəRhti/ F2 increase, excess. [/bəRhna/ "to increase, expand, enlarge, advance."]

/bhərti/ F2 filling, completion, additional or irrelevant material ("filler"), conscription, enlistment. [/bhərna/ "to fill, be filled."]

/kəmti/ F2 deficiency. [/kəm/ A1 "less, little."]

/phəbti/ F2 simile which fits one, jest. [/phəbna/ "to suit, fit, etc." See the sixth example under /ən/ above.]

/əyl/: see /al/ "adjective formant."

/əyt/ "agentive noun": Noun or Verb stem + /əyt/ = N. Examples found in the corpus are M1. E.g.

/Dəkəyt/ M1 robber, bandit. [Cf. /Daku/ M1 "robber" and /Daka/ M2 "robbery" (stem /Dak/-/Dək/).]

/kəRkəyt/ M1 herald (one who walks in front of the king's procession announcing his coming); war-herald (officer whose duty it is to exhort the soldiers in battle). [/kəRək/ F1 "peal of thunder"; /kəRka/ or /kəRkha/ M2 "war-song, exhortation, paean."]

/phykəyt/ M1 spear thrower; expert at quarterstaves. [/phēkna/ "to throw."]

/pycəyt/ M1 wrestler; one who employs stratagems. [/pec/ M1 "twist, stratagem, screw."]

Many of these formations can be followed by the abstract noun formant /i/:

/Dəkəyti/ F2 robbery, banditry

/pycəyti/ F2 wrestling

/baR/-/vaR/-/var/ "noun of place": N + /baR/ (etc.) = N. Of these variants, /baR/ always seems to be followed by the Type II affixes /a/ or /i/ (with no apparent distinction in size); /vaR/ is also followed by these affixes but may also occur as the last suffix in the word; /var/ is rather less common and is followed by /i/, at least in examples found in the author's corpus. E.g.

/ymambaRa/ M2 building where services are held for Ali, Hasan, and Husayn (the son-in-law and grandsons of the Prophet Muhammad) by the Shia sect of Islam. [/ymam/ M1 "guide, leader" is from Arabic.]

/bāsbaRi/ F2 bamboo grove. [/bās/ M1 "bamboo."]

/həDvaR/ M1 boneyard, place of bones. [The stem is the same as that of /həDDi/ F2 "bone."]

/pychvaRa/ M2 back part, back-yard. [Cf. /picha/ M2 back portion, hind part.]

/phwlvaRi/ [or /phwlvari/] F2 flower-bed, garden. [Cf. /phul/ M1 "flower."]

/el/: see /al/ "adjective formant."

/el/: see /r/ "diminutive."

/er/: see /al/ "adjective formant."

/er/: see /har/ "noun of profession."

/eru/: see /har/ "noun of profession."

/han/: see /stan/ "noun of place."

/har/-/əhl/-/əhr/ "adjective formant": Verb stem + /ən/ (q. v.) + /har/ (etc.) = A. Noun stem + /har/ (etc.) = A. /əhl/ and /əhr/ are obligatorily followed by the Type II affixes; /har/ is optionally followed by these affixes. Cf. also /al/ "adjective formant, " which may be identifiable as the same affix. E. g.

/honhar/ A1 promising, hopeful, about to be. [/ho/ "be, become" + /n/ (variant of /ən/ "noun formant. ")]

/mərənhar/ A1 dying, mortal, perishable, moribund. [/mər/ "die" + /ən/ + /har/.]

/janhar/ A1 one who risks his life, adventurer. [/jan/ F1 "life. "]

/swnəhra/ A2 golden. [/sona/ M2 "gold" (stem /son-/).]

/rupəhla/ A2 silvery, silver. [/rup/ M1 [or /rupa/] M2 "silver. "]

/har/-/ar/-/er/-/eru/-/yar/ "noun of occupation, noun of agent": Noun or (rarely) Verb stem + /har/ (etc.) = N. The variants /er/ and /yar/ seem to be obligatorily followed by the Type II affixes; /eru/ is never followed by these affixes, and the other variants are followed by the Type II affixes in some examples and not in others. E. g.

/ləkəRhara/ M2 woodcutter. [The stem is the same as that of /ləkRi/ F2 "stick, wood"; cf. /ləkkəR/ M1 "big piece of wood, log. "]

/pənhara/ M2 water-carrier. [The stem is the same as that of /pani/ M1 "water. "]

/kwmhar/ M1 potter. [The stem is the same as that of /kwmbh/ M1 "water-pot. "]

/bənjara/ M2 nomadic trader, merchant. [Hindi /bənəj/ [or /bənyj/] M1 "trading, mercantile transactions. "]

/lohar/ M1 blacksmith. [The stem is the same as that of /loha/ M2 "iron. "]

/lwTera/ M2 bandit, looter. [The stem is the same as that of /luT/ F1 "spoil, pillage, booty. "]

/səpera/ M2 snake charmer. [The stem is the same as that of /sãp/ M1 "snake. "]

/pəkheru/ M1 bird. [/pəkh/ M1 "wing, feathers. "]

/ghəsyara/ M2 grass-cutter. [The stem is the same as that of /ghas/ F1 "grass. "]

/hyal/: see /šal/ "noun of place. "

/i/-/ya/ "feminine-diminutive noun formant": Noun stem + /i/ = F2; Noun + /ya/ =F1. In one or two cases, where the semantic referent of a noun requires a masculine gender, diminutives ending in /ya/ are M1. E. g.

/beTi/ F2 daughter. [Stem /beT-/.]

/ləRki/ F2 girl. [Stem /ləRk-/.]

/hyrni/ F2 female deer, doe. [/hyrən/ M1 "male deer. "]

/cəmari/ F2 leatherworker's wife. [Also /cəmarən/, see /ən/. Stem /cəm-/ + /ar/ (variant of /har/ "noun of profession").]

/bərəhməni/ F2 Brahmin's wife. [Cf. /bərəhmən/ M1 "Brahmin. "]

/pəThani/ F2 female Pathan. [/pəThan/ M1 "Pathan (ethnic group living in Afghanistan and Northwestern Pakistan). "]

/kwtya/ F1 bitch. [Cf. /kwtta/ M2 "male dog. "]

/kəTya/ F1 female water-buffalo calf. [/kəTTa/ [or /kəTra/] M2 "male water-buffalo calf. "]

221

/pəhaRi/ F2 hillock, small mountain. [/pəhaR/ M1 "mountain."]

/kəTari/ F2 small dagger (type). [/kəTar/ F1 "type of dagger."]

/Dybya/ F1 small box. [Cf. /Dybba/ M2 "box."]

/lwTya/ F1 small brass vessel. [Cf. /loTa/ M2 "'lota': a small brass vessel."]

/phwRya/ F1 pimple. [Cf. /phoRa/ M2 "boil."]

/bhəyya/ M1 brother. [/bhai/ M1 "brother." /bhəyya/ is employed as a term of affection.]

/i/-/ya/ "noun of profession": N + /i/ (etc.) = N. Occasionally a Verb stem + /ən/ + /ya/ = N also. E.g.

/həlvai/ M1 sweetmeat maker. [/həlva/ M2 "type of sweetmeat" is from Arabic.]

/beopari/ M1 businessman. [/beopar/ M1 "business."]

/teli/ M1 oil merchant. [/tel/ M1 "oil."]

/gəDərya/ M2 shepherd. [/gaDər/ F1 "sheep, ewe."]

/nəcənya/ M2 dancer. [The stem is the same as that of /nacnà/ "to dance" + /ən/ "noun formant."]

/bəkheRya/ M2 quarrelsome person. [Cf. /bəkheRa/ M2 "mess, clutter" under /a/ "Type II msc. noun formant" above.]

/i/ "abstract noun formant": N + /i/ = F2. Many adjective stems, verb stems, and a few nouns occur with /a/ (q.v.) before the /i/ suffix. It is possible that the /a/ in Verb stem + /a/ + /i/ formations could be analysed as the causative affix /a/, although this does not seem to be historically correct. Segmentation, in any case, is only provisional. E.g.

/cori/ F2 theft. [/cor/ M1 "thief."]

/Thəgi/ F2 robbery, cheating, deception. [/Thəg/ M1 "deceiver, cheater, robber."]

/golai/ F2 roundness. [/gol/ A1 "round."]

/ləmbai/ F2 longness, tallness. [Stem /ləmb-/ "long, tall."]

/bəRai/ F2 bigness. [Stem /bəR-/ "big."]

/pənDytai/ F2 punditry, being a Hindu scholar. [/pənDyt/ M1 "Hindu scholar."]

/kəmai/ F2 earning. [/kəmana/ "to earn." This would seem to be /kəma-/ + /i/.]

/sylai/ F2 sewing. [/sylna/ "to be sewn"; /sylana/ "to cause to be sewn."]

/rəgai/ F2 colouring, dyeing. [/rəg/ M1 "colour, dye"; /rəgna/ "to colour, dye."]

Often a Verb stem + /a/ + /i/ construction denotes "the price paid for ... ing". E.g.

/dhwlai/ F2 price paid for washing. [/dhwlna/ "to be washed"; /dhwlana/ "to cause to be washed."]

/cərai/ F2 wages paid for cattle grazing; grazing. [/cərna/ "to graze"; /cərana/ "to cause (cattle) to graze."]

/pysvai/ F2 wages paid for grinding. [Cf. /pisna/ "to grind"; /pysvana/ "to cause to be ground, etc."]

/i/ "Type II feminine adjective formant": Adjective stem + /i/ = A; Noun + /i/ = A. Cf. /a/ "Type II masculine adjective formant." E.g.

/bəRi/ A2 big. [Stem /bəR-/ "big."]

/choTi/ A2 small. [Stem /choT-/ "small."]

/bhuki/ A2 hungry. [/bhuk/ F1 "hunger."]

/i/ "Type I adjective formant": Noun stem + /i/ = A. Possibly identifiable with the last above? E. g.

/desi/ A1 local, native, country-made, indigenous. [/des/ M1 "country."]

/pəhaRi/ A1 mountainous. [/pəhaR/ M1 "mountain." Homophonous with the diminutive form; see above.]

/uni/ A1 woollen. [/un/ F1 [or M1] "wool."]

/il/: see /al/ "adjective formant."

/k/ "noun formant": Verb stem + /k/ + the Type II feminine suffix /i/ = N. Possibly identifiable as a variant of /ək/ "abstract noun formant" or of /ək/-/k/ "diminutive?" E. g.

/cwski/ F2 suck, sip. [The stem is the same as that of /cusna/ "to suck."]

/cwTki/ F2 snap of the fingers, pinch, handful. [Apparently from a stem /cwT/ which occurs now only in various derived forms.]

/Dwbki/ F2 dip, dive, plunge. [/Dubna/ "to dive, sink, be immersed, submerged."]

/k/: see /ək/ "diminutive."

/k/: see /yk/ "adjective formant."

/l/: see /al/ "adjective formant."

/l/: see /r/ "diminutive."

/man/: see /vənt/ "adjective-noun formant."

/n/-/ən/ "instrumental noun": Noun stem or Verb stem + /n/ (etc.) = N. The variant /n/ is obligatorily followed by the Type II affixes. Possibly relatable to /ən/-/n/ "noun formant?" E. g.

/belən/ M1 rolling pin. [/belna/ "to roll out flat." Also:]

/belna/ M2 rolling pin. [And the diminutive form:]

/belni/ F2 small rolling pin

/dhə̄wkni/ F2 bellows. [/dhə̄wkna/ "to blow upon, to puff, pant."]

/cādna/ M2 light, brilliance. [Cf. /cād/ M1 "moon" and /cādni/ F2 "moonlight." The instrumental significance is not clear, but the identification of an /n/ suffix seems obvious.]

/kətərni/ F2 scissors. [/kətərna/ "to cut."]

/oRhni/ F2 small scarf. [/oRhna/ "to wrap (as a shawl, scarf)."]

/phūkni/ F2 blowpipe. [/phūkna/ "to blow."]

/n/ "adjective formant": Verb stem + /n/ + the Type II affixes = A2. Rare in the corpus. E. g.

/physəlna/ A2 slippery. [/physəlna/ "to slip, slide."]

/n/: see /ən/ "noun formant."

/o/ "ending for feminine proper names": Noun stem, etc. + /o/ = F1. In rural areas, personal names often consist of a stem + /u/ to denote a male or a stem + /o/ to denote a female. Such formations are also common among the lower classes in urban areas. Persons of the middle and upper classes may

223

also have such names, but these are then simply pet names, household names, or intimate nicknames, in contradistinction to the person's formal name (derived from Arabic or Persian). See also /u/. E. g.

/nəjjo/ F1 girl's personal name

/rəmzano/ F1 girl's personal name. [/rəmzan/ M1 "Rəmzan, the month of fasting. " This may denote that the girl was born in the month of Rəmzan.]

/ol/: see /al/ "adjective formant. "

/ol/: see /r/ "diminutive. "

/oR/: see /al/ "adjective formant. "

/oR/: see /r/ "diminutive. "

/p/: see /pən/ "abstract noun formant. "

/pən/-/p/-/pət/ "abstract noun formant": Noun stem or Adjective stem + /pən/ (etc.) = N. The variant /p/ is obligatorily followed by the Type II masculine suffix /a/, and the variant /pən/ may also be optionally followed by /a/. /pət/ is word-final. Constructions ending in /pən/ are M1; those in /p/ + /a/ or /pən/ + /a/ are M2; those ending in /pət/ are F1. Occasional minor semantic differences are observed between a stem + /pən/ versus the same stem + /pən/ + /a/. The variant /pət/ is rather rare and is becoming obsolete. E. g.

/bəcpən/ M1 childhood. [/bəcca/ M2 "child" is originally from Persian.]

/chwTpən/ M1 smallness, childhood. [The stem is the same as that of /choTa/ A2 "small. "]

/ləRəkpən/ M1 boyhood, childhood. [The stem is the same as that of /ləRka/ M2 "boy. "]

/əcpəlapən/ M1 restlessness, fickleness, mischievousness. [Cf. /əcpəla/ A2 "mischievous, restless. " The /a/ in /əcpəlapən/ is identifiable as /a/ "abstract noun formant. "]

/bəcpəna/ M2 childishness, childhood. [This is used as a less common alternant for /bəcpən/, and it also has a derogatory sense which /bəcpən/ lacks: "childishness. "]

/chwTpəna/ M2 smallness, childhood, childishness. [Cf. /chwTpən/ above.]

/mwTapa/ M2 fatness. [The stem is the same as that of /moTa/ A2 "fat. " Again, the /a/ in /mwTapa/ can be identified as the abstract noun formant /a/, q. v.]

/bwRhapa/ M2 old age. [The stem is the same as that of /buRha/ A2 "old, aged. "]

/gə̄varpət/ F1 rusticity. [The stem is a construction of /gað/ M1 "village" + /ar/ (variant of /har/ "noun of profession, etc. "): /gə̄var/ M1 means "villager, peasant, boor. " /gə̄varpət/ is less common than /gə̄varpən/ M1.]

/syanpət/ F1 astuteness, wisdom, sagacity. [/syan/ M1 "wisdom, sagacity" is archaic in Urdu; /syanpən/ M1 is common.]

/pət/: see /pən/ "abstract noun formant. "

/r/-/el/-/l/-/ol/-/oR/-/R/-/T/ "diminutive": N + /r/ (etc.) = N. All of these variants except /oR/ are obligatorily followed by the Type II affixes. /oR/ and /T/ are rare. E. g.

/Thikra/ M2 small potsherd. [/Thik/ is obsolete.]

/bəghela/ M2 tiger cub. [The stem is the same as that of /bagh/ M1
"tiger."]

/hətheli/ F2 palm of the hand. [The stem is the same as that of /hath/
M1 "hand."]

/khwjli/ F2 minor itch. [The stem is the same as that of /khaj/ F1
"itch."]

/khəTola/ M2 small cot. [The stem is the same as that of /khaT/ F1
"cot, bed."]

/bəndoR/ F1 bad-mannered girl. [The stem is the same as that of /bādi/
F2 "female slavegirl, bondmaid."]

/TwkRa/ M2 piece, portion, part. [The stem is the same as that of
/Tuk/ M1 "piece, part," now mostly obsolete.]

/pələgRi/ F2 small bed. [/pələg/ M1 "bed."]

/jōkTi/ F2 small leech, stomach worm. [/jōk/ F1 "leech."]

/R/: see /r/ "diminutive."

/sal/: see /šal/ "noun of place."

/šal/-/sal/-/al/-/hyal/ "noun of place": Noun or Noun stem + /šal/ (etc.) = N.
The variant /šal/ is always followed by the Type II masculine affix /a/; /sal/
occurs as the last affix in the word, as does /hyal/; the variant /al/ may
occur as the last affix or it may be followed by the Type II affixes. E. g.

/paThšala/ M2 school. [/paTh/ M1 "lesson."]

/dhərmšala/ M2 alms-house, place of rest for travellers. [/dhərm/
M1 "religion, piety."]

/Təksal/ M1 mint, assay office. [The stem is the same as that of /Təka/
M2 "copper coin."]

/hymala/ M2 place of cold weather, the Himalayas. [/hyma/ F1 "the
cold season, cold weather."]

/šyvala/ M2 temple dedicated to Siva. [The stem is the same as that
of /šiv/ M1 "Siva."]

/swsral/ F1 [or M1] home of one's father-in-law. [/swsər/ M1 "father-
in-law."]

/mwtali/ F2 runnel for animal urine in a stable. [The stem is the same
as that of /mut/ M1 "urine."]

/dədhyal/ F1 [or M1] home of one's paternal grandparents. [/dada/ M1
"paternal grandfather," /dadi/ F2 "paternal grandmother."]

/nənhyal/ F1 [or M1] home of one's maternal grandparents. [/nana/ M1
"maternal grandfather," /nani/ F2 "maternal grandmother."]

/stan/-/-/an/-/han/-/ystan/ "noun of place": Noun or Noun stem + /stan/ (etc.)
= N. The older Hindi form of this affix, which also occurs in Persian, is
/sthan/ (and /ysthan/). The variants /stan/ and /ystan/ are always word-final,
while /an/ and /han/ are followed by the Type II masculine affix /a/. Constructions ending in /stan/ or /ystan/ are M1, and those ending in /an/ or /han/ +
/a/ are M2. E. g.

/rajəstan/ [or /rajəsthan/] M1 Rajastan. [Lit. king's place; Hindi
/raja/ M1 "king."]

/hyndostan/ M1 India. [/hyndu/ M1 A1 "Hindu."]

/ghərana/ M2 family, home. [/ghər/ M1 "house, home."]

/səmdhyana/ M2 house of one's father-in-law. [/səmdhi/ M1 "father-
in-law" is Hindi.]

/syrhana/ M2 head-place, head-rest. [/sər/ M1 "head."]

/t/: see /ət/ "abstract noun formant."

/T/: see /r/ "diminutive."

/u/-/v/-/vah/-/vəyy/ "agentive noun": Noun stem or Verb stem + /u/ (etc.) = N. The variants /v/, /vah/ and /vəyy/ are obligatorily followed by the Type II affixes. The variant /u/ is word-final. After noun stems, only the variants /u/ and /v/ occur in the corpus, while after verb stems all of the variants are found. E. g.

/Daku/ M1 bandit, robber. [The stem is the same as that of /Daka/ M2 "robbery." Cf. also under /əyt/ above.]

/pyTThu/ M1 puppet, yes-man. [The stem is probably the same as that of /pəTTha/ M2 "young (of an animal), young man, pupil (as of a wrestler)."]

/məchva/ M2 fisherman. [The stem is the same as that of /məchli/ F2 "fish."]

/bhəRva/ M2 pimp. [The stem is the same as that of /bhaR/ M1 "wages of prostitution."]

/bygaRu/ M1 A1 spoiler, destroyer, spoiling. [/bygaRna/ "to spoil, ruin, destroy."]

/bhwlau/ M1 A1 misleader, deceiver, misleading, deceiving. [/bhwlana/ "to cause to forget."]

/kəmau/ M1 A1 earner, earning. [/kəmana/ "to earn."]

/kətru/ M1 cutter. [Hindi. /kətərna/ "to cut."]

/khau/ M1 A1 eater, glutton, bribe-taker. [/khana/ "to eat."]

/deva/ M2 giver. [/dena/ "to give."]

/leva/ M2 taker. [/lena/ "to take."]

/cərvaha/ M2 herdsman. [/cərna/ "to graze," /cərana/ "to cause (cattle) to graze."]

/bāTvəyya/ M2 sharer. [/bāTna/ "to distribute, share."]

/gəvəyya/ M2 singer. [/gana/ "to sing."]

/u/-/va/ "adjective or noun formant": Noun or Noun stem + /u/ (etc.) = A1 (and also sometimes = N). See also /au/, which might be identified as the same suffix. E. g.

/bazaru/ A1 cheap, common. [/bazar/ M1 "market."]

/calu/ A1 going, moving, operating. [/cal/ F1 "move, strategem, gait."]

/Dhalu/ A1 slanting, sloping. [/Dhal/ M1 "slope, inclination."]

/pwrva/ F1 A1 eastern, east wind. [The stem is the same as that of /purəb/ M1 "east."]

/pychva/ [or /pəchva/] F1 A1 western, west wind. [The stem is the same as that of /pəcchym/ M1 "west."]

/u/ "ending for masculine proper names": Noun stem, etc. + /u/ = M1. See /o/ for details. E. g.

/kəjju/ M1 man's proper name

/rəmzanu/ M1 man's proper name

/v/-/va/ "diminutive": Noun stem or Noun + /v/ (etc.) = N. The variant /v/ is obligatorily followed by the Type II masculine affix /a/. Wherever the

226

construction is feminine, the variant /va/ occurs, and then no oblique or plural forms can usually be made. Most words made with this suffix have a rustic-humorous connotation. In many cases the diminutive connotation has been lost. E. g.

/ghərva/ M2 little house, hut, toy house. [/ghər/ M1 "house."]

/jwrva/ F1 (little) wife. [/joru/ F1 "wife" (rustic, low-class language).]

/mərdva/ M2 (little) man, mannikin, husband. [/mərd/ M1 "man, male."]

/TəTva/ M2 (little) pony. [The stem is the same as that of /TəTTu/ M1 "pony."]

/v/: see /u/ "agentive noun."

/va/: see /u/ "adjective formant."

/va/: see /v/ "diminutive."

/vah/: see /u/ "agentive noun."

/val/ "agentive noun": Noun stem or Verb stem + /val/ = N. Aside from such substantive constructions, /val/ has a great many other uses (see Secs. 14.301 and 15.312). In noun constructions, however, /val/ may occur as the last affix in the word, or it may be followed by the Type II affixes. E. g.

/deval/ M/F1 giver. [The stem is the same as that of /dena/ "to give." Constructions with this word are peculiar: e.g. /vw yy ciz deval nəhĩ./ "He is not the giver of this thing." = "He will not give this thing."]

/kotval/ M1 city guardian, head of the city police. [The stem is probably /koT/ M1 "fort" + /val/. An alternate explanation is that the firearms kept in the police headquarters were called /kota/ M2, and the person who was in charge of these was called /kotəval/ > /kotval/.]

/gəvala/ M2 cowherd. [/gae/ F1 "cow"; also /gao/ F1.]

/rəkhval/ M/F1 keeper, guard, custodian. [Also /rəkhvala/ M2. /rəkhna/ "to keep, place, put."]

/van/: see /vənt/ "adjective-noun formant."

/var/: see /baR/ "noun of place."

/vaR/: see /baR/ "noun of place."

/vas/: see /as/ "abstract noun formant."

/vā/: see /vənt/ "adjective-noun formant."

/vənt/-/man/-/van/-/vā/ "adjective-noun formant": Noun stem or Verb stem + /vənt/ (etc.) = M1 or A1. In some cases the same stem may occur with more than one of the variants of this suffix, and there is apparently some slight difference in meaning. The problem of segmentation and identification of these variants as one suffix or as more than one suffix is left for later research. E. g.

/bəlvənt/ [or /bəlvan/] M1 A1 courageous, brave, powerful. [/bəl/ M1 "strength, force, power."]

/bhəgvənt/ [or /bhəgvan/] M1 A1 saintly, godly, worshipful. [/bhəg/ F1 "divine power, omnipotence." The form /bhəgvan/ is commonly reserved for "God."]

/bwddhiman/ M1 A1 scholarly, wise, sagacious. [/bwddh/ F1 "wisdom." This is also found as /bwddhi/ F2.]

/gwnman/ [or /gwnvan/ or /gwnvənt/] M/F1 A1 skilled, clever, accomplished, possessed of good qualities. [/gwn/ M1 "quality, art, skill."]

/dhənvan/ A1 rich, wealthy. [/dhən/ M1 "wealth."]

/Dhəlvan/ [or /Dhəlvā/] F1 A1 slope, sloping. [/Dhəlvan/ is treated as an F1 noun meaning "slope, incline," and /Dhəlvā/ as A1 meaning "sloping, slanting."]

/physəlvā/ A1 slippery. [/physəlna/ "to slip, slide."]

/gəThvā/ A1 [or A2?] tightly knitted, sturdy (as someone's body). [The stem is the same as that of /gāTh/ F1 "knot, bale, bundle."]

/vəyy/: see /u/ "agentive noun."

/ya/ "adjective formant": Verb stem + /ya/ = A1. E.g.

/bəRhya/ A1 superior, excellent, surpassing. [/bəRhna/ "to increase, expand, enlarge, advance."]

/dwkhya/ A1 painful, hurtful, causing suffering. [/dwkhna/ "to pain, hurt, cause suffering."]

/ghəTya/ A1 low-class, cheap, inferior, base. [/ghəTna/ "to lessen, decrease, be deficient, abate."]

/ya/: see /i/ "feminine-diminutive noun formant."

/ya/: see /i/ "noun of profession."

/yar/: see /har/ "noun of occupation, noun of agent."

/yəl/: see /al/ "adjective formant."

/yət/ "abstract noun formant": Noun or Adjective stem + /a/ "abstract noun formant" + /yət/ = F1. Rare in the corpus. E.g.

/əpnayət/ F1 kinship, familiarity, intimacy. [The stem is the same as that of /əpna/ A2 "one's own."]

/pə̃cayət/ F1 village council. [/pə̃c/ M1 "head, chief." The stem is the same as that of /pā̃c/ A1 "five," according to the dictionaries.]

/yk/-/ək/-/k/ "adjective formant": Noun or Verb stem + /yk/ (etc.) = A1 (and sometimes N). The variant /k/ is followed by the Type II affixes. E.g.

/phuTək/ A1 cracked, crushed, broken (as corn, rice). [/phuTna/ "to break, shatter." /phuTək/ is also used as F1 to denote any broken grain.]

/pəkka/ A2 cooked, ripe, ready, mature. [The stem is the same as that of /pəkna/ "to be cooked, ripen, mature."]

/səmajyk/ A1 belonging to a society, societal. [/səmaj/ M1 "society." /səmajyk/ is also used as M/F1 to denote "member of a society."]

/vəydyk/ A1 Vedic. [/ved/ M1 [or /veda/ M2] "Hindu scriptures." /vəydyk/ may also be employed as M1 to denote "Brahman who knows the Vedas."]

/ystan/: see /stan/ "noun of place."

19.304. Hindi Compounds.

Hindi compounds are divisible into (a) those compounds which are in use in everyday speech, and (b) "High Hindi" Sanskrit-derived compounds. The latter are generally unnecessary for those who wish to study literary Urdu.

Just as in Persian, Hindi compounds consist of a variety of elements: stems, independent nouns, independent adjectives, participles, adverbs, etc. Examples of almost any given combination of these elements can be found in the dictionaries, and the following lists are thus presented only as a superficial survey.

N + N = N, Adv. This type of formation is really "copulative": the two elements are both equally "heads" of the construction, and a conjunction "and" seems to be understood. E.g.

/mā bap/ Mpl parents. [/mā/ Fl "mother"; /bap/ Ml "father."]

/lykhət pəRhət/ Fl reading and writing. [/lykhət/ Fl "writing" (/lykh/ "write" + /ət/ "abstract noun formant"); /pəRhət/ Fl "reading" (/pəRh/ "read" + /ət/).]

/dyn rat/ Mpl Adv night and day. [/dyn/ Ml "day"; /rat/ Fl "night."]

N + N = N. In this type of construction, the two components are not equal partners, but one appears to modify or define the other. E.g.

/bagDor/ Fl reins, bridle. [/bag/ Fl "bridle"; /Dor/ Fl "rope, string, cord." /bagDor/ is now used mostly in a metaphorical sense: e.g. "reins of government."]

/rajhəns/ Ml large sp. of goose. [/raj/ Ml "king" (a form of /raja/ Ml "king"); /həns/ Ml "goose."]

/relgaRi/ F2 railway train. [/rel/ Fl "railway, train"; /gaRi/ F2 "vehicle, cart, car, carriage."]

/bhumidan/ Ml the giving of land as a charity. [/bhumi/ F2 "earth, land"; /dan/ is found only in compounds, being a variant of the same stem as that of /dena/ "to give" + /n/ (variant of /ən/ "abstract noun formant").]

/targhər/ Ml telegraph office. [/tar/ Ml "wire, telegram, telegraph"; /ghər/ Ml "house, home."]

N + /a/ + N = N, Adv. Cf. Sec. 18.307 for a similar formation in Persian. E.g.

/dhəRadhəR/ Fl Adv repeated sharp sounds, loud and continuous noise (as of heavy rain, falling logs, etc.). [/dhəR/ Fl "sound of something heavy striking, thump, bang, bump."]

/chənachən/ Fl Adv clinking, jingle. [/chən/ Fl "clinking sound, jingle, metallic noise."]

N + V stem = N, A. E.g.

/dylphĕk/ Ml Al one who falls in love with any passing girl, lover. [/dyl/ Ml "heart"; /phĕkna/ "to throw."]

/mw̃hphəT/ Ml Al rude, ill-mannered person, outspoken. [/mw̃h/ Fl "mouth, face"; /phəTna/ "to tear, break."]

/sərphoR/ Al head-breaking, headache-causing (as difficult work). [/sər/ Ml "head"; /phoRna/ "to break, shatter, burst (trans.)."]

/pətjhəR/ Fl autumn, the season of falling leaves. [/pət/ is from the same stem as /pətta/ M2 "leaf"; /jhəRna/ "to be swept away, shed, drop off, fall."]

N + PasP = N, A. E.g.

/desnykala/ M2 expulsion, exile. [/des/ Ml "country"; /nykala/ PasP of /nykalna/ "to take out, remove."]

/dyljəla/ M2 A2 sufferer. [/dyl/ Ml "heart"; /jəla/ PasP of /jəlna/ "to burn."]

/məncəla/ M2 A2 romantic minded, zealous, distracted, mad. [/mən/ Ml "mind, heart"; /cəla/ PasP of /cəlna/ "to go, move."]

/sərphyra/ M2 A2 crackpot, insane person. [/sər/ Ml "head"; /phyra/ PasP of /phyrna/ "to turn."]

A + N = N, A. E.g.

/bhəlmənsai/ F2 humanity, benignity, humanitarianism, gentlemanliness.
[/bhəl/ has the same root as /bhəla/ A2 "good, well"; /mənsai/
F2 "humanity" (stem /məns-/) is from the same origin as Hindi
/mənwš/ M1 "man, person."]

/məharaja/ M1 great king, king. [/məha/ "great" is mostly found in
compounds; /raja/ M1 "king."]

/dopəTTa/[or /dwpəTTa/] M2 kind of scarf worn by women having two
ends hanging back down over the shoulders. [/do/ A1 "two";
/pəTTa/ M2 "breadth (of cloth, etc.)."]

/kəroRpəti/ M1 multi-millionaire. [/kəroR/ A1 "ten million"; /pəti/
M1 "master."]

/cəwmasa/ M2 rainy season. [/cəw/ is a variant of /car/ A1 "four"
used only in compounds; /mas/ M1 "moon, month": i.e. "four
months (of rain)."]

/barasỹgha/ [or /barasỹga/] M2 stag, antlered deer. [/bara/ A1
"twelve"; /sĩg/ or /sỹg/ M1 "horn."]

/donali/ A1 double-barreled. [/do/ A1 "two"; /nali/ F2 "tube,
barrel."]

/baramasa/ A2 twelve-monthly, perennial. [/bara/ A1 "twelve";
/mas/ M1 "moon, month."]

A stem + A = N. E.g.

/ūcnic/ F1 ups and downs, vicissitudes. [/ūc/ occurs only in compounds
and is from the same origin as /ūca/ A2 "high, tall"; /nic/ A1
"low, base."]

A + PasP = A. Both members of this compound end in the Type II affixes. Only
one example occurs in the corpus:

/rukha sukha/ A2 common, dry, ordinary, plain, flat, insipid, blunt.
[/rukha/ A2 "dry, flat, blunt, sullen, laconic"; /sukha/ PasP of
/sukhna/ "to become dry."]

V stem + V stem = N. E.g.

/bhagdəwR/ F1 haste, hurry, effort, struggle. [/bhagna/ "to run away,
flee"; /dəwRna/ "to run."]

/dekhbhal/ F1 care, looking after, concern for. [/dekhna/ "to see";
/bhalna/ "to see, look" is now mostly obsolete.]

/luTmar/ F1 rapine, pillage, chaos. [/luTna/ "to loot, rob"; /marna/
"to beat, hit, kill."]

/marpiT/ F1 fighting, beating. [/marna/ "to beat, hit, kill"; /piTna/
"to beat, hit."]

/wləTpələT/ F1 reversal, upset, turning topsyturvy. [/wləTna/ "to
turn over, upside down, reverse"; /pələTna/ "to turn over, upset,
return, change."]

V stem[1] + (V stem[1] + /ao/) = N. E.g.

/cəlcəlao/ M1 haste, hurry, time of departure, old age (i.e. "time to
go"). [/cəlna/ "to go, move."]

/rəkhrəkhao/ M1 ostentation, pomp and show, care, nurture. [/rəkhna/
"to keep, put, place."]

V stem[1] + /əm/ + V stem[1] = N, Adv. E.g.

/bhagəmbhag/ F1 Adv haste, hurry, rush, in haste, in a hurry. [/bhagna/
"to run away, flee."]

V stem[1] + /əm/ + PasP[1] (?) = A, Adv. Only one example occurs:

/khwlləmkhwlla/ A1 Adv open, openly. [The stem is the same as that
of /khwlna/ "to open." The stem variation is unique.]

PreP + N = A. Again, this compound differs in that it appears to be less closely
joined than the others described here. E. g.

/cəlta pwrza/ A2 clever, mischievous, smart. [/cəlta/ PreP of /cəlna/
"to go, move"; /pwrza/ M2 "part, piece, component."]

PasP + N = A, Adv. E. g.

/ləgatar/ A1 Adv continuous, incessant, in succession, incessantly.
[/ləga/ PasP of /ləgna/ "to be attached, fastened"; /tar/ M1
"thread, line, succession, wire, telegraph, telegram."]

PasP + (Persian) Past Participle = A. E. g.

/thəka manda/ A2 fatigued, tired out. [/thəka/ PasP of /thəkna/ "to be
tired, fatigued"; /manda/ Past Participle of Persian /man/ "to
stay, remain" (see Sec. 18.306). Note that both components of this
compound end in the Type II affixes (i. e. /thəki mandi/, /thəke
mande/ are correct), although in purely Persian compounds /manda/
is treated as though it were Type I.]

N, Adv¹ + /ō/ + N, Adv¹ = Adv, Comp Post. E. g.

/bicōbic/ Adv Comp Post right in the middle, in the heart of. [/bic/
occurs in the Comp Post /[ke] bic mẽ/ "between, in the middle of";
/[ke] bicōbic/ is also a common Comp Post.]

/hathōhath/ Adv warmly received, welcomed, hand over hand, quickly.
[/hath/ M1 "hand."]

/ratōrat/ Adv overnight. [/rat/ F1 "night."]

19.305. Echo Compounds.

One of the commonest features of spoken Urdu is the frequent occurrence of "echo
compounds": compounds which consist of a word preceded or followed by a jingling, rhyming
repetition of itself. The repeated portion is always modified in some fashion: the first
consonant may be replaced by another, the first vowel of the word may be substituted by
another, or the whole stem may be altered in some other manner. There are several
common patterns, as well as a great many unique and idiomatic constructions. These
formations are reminiscent of the Yiddish-American echo compounds in which a normal
word is followed by a jingling repetition beginning with /šm-/: e. g. "work-shmerk,"
"school-shmool," etc.

The connotations of the Urdu echo compound include (1) vague inclusiveness (e. g. /cae
vae/ "tea and things, tea and all that goes with it, tea etc. etc. "), (2) light or humorous
style (i. e. echo compounds will be rare in serious discourse). A great many echo compounds have, however, become part of "normal" Urdu and are to be found in all types of
discourse.

Common patterns include:

(1) The normal word is followed by a repetition beginning with /v/ (i. e. omitting the
first consonant of the word and substituting /v/ instead). E. g.

/cae vae/ F1 tea and things. [/cae/ F1 "tea."]
/roTi voTi/ F2 bread, etc.; food. [/roTi/ F2 "bread."]
/am vam/ M1 mangoes, etc. [/am/ M1 "mango."]

/mez vez/ F1 tables and things. [/mez/ F1 "table."]

/šərab vərab/ F1 wine and things, alcoholic beverages. [/šərab/ F1 "wine, liquor."]

/kytab vytab/ F1 books and things. [/kytab/ F1 "book."]

(2) The rhyming portion precedes the normal word and begins with a vowel (usually the same as the first vowel of the normal word). E. g.

/əRos pəRos/ M1 neighbourhood, environs. [/pəRos/ M1 "neighbour-hood, vicinity."]

/ədla bədla/ M2 Adv [or /ədəl bədəl/ M1] exchange, interchange, in exchange, mutatis mutandis. [/bədla/ M2 "exchange, revenge"; /bədəlna/ "to change."]

/amna samna/ M2 confrontation. [/samna/ M2 "facing, front part, opposing." Note that both elements of this type of compound are M2: i.e. /amne samne se .../, etc. Echo compounds almost never occur in the plural, however.]

/əntər məntər/ M1 spells, charms. [/məntər/ M1 "incantation, spell, religious formula."]

/əTvaTi khəTvaTi/ F2 sulking, feigning illness. [/khəTvaTi/ F2 "feigning illness, sullenness, sulking."]

/ystər bystər/ M1 bedding and things. [/bystər/ M1 "bedding."]

/əta pəta/ M2 whereabouts, address. [/pəta/ M2 "trace, clue, informa-tion, address."]

/aspas/ M1 surroundings, environment. [Usually used as a Comp Post: /[ke] aspas/ "all around, in the environs of." /[ke] pas/ Comp Post Adv "near."]

/yrd gyrd/ Adv Comp Post surroundings, environs, vicinity. [/gyrd/ M1 "orbit, circuit, environs." Again, /[ke] yrd gyrd/ is mostly found as a Comp Post.]

(3) The rhyming portion follows the normal word and has a different vowel. Normal words occurring in this pattern always seem to have a C(h)VC structure: i.e. no two- or three-syllable words occur in this pattern. E. g.

/Thik Thak/ PA1 Adv completely all right, tip-top, well. [/Thik/ A1 "good, well, O.K."]

/bhiR bhaR/ F1 crowd, mob. [/bhiR/ F1 "crowd."]

/cheR chaR/ F1 teasing, taunting. [/cheR/ F1 "molesting, annoying, jesting."]

/Tip Tap/ F1 pomp and show, ostentation, magnificence, splendour. [/Tip/ F1 "splendour, etc."]

(4) Many verb stems of the pattern C(h)VC may be repeated as seen above under (3). They are followed by /ke/ (the conjunctive participle enclitic) and the whole functions as a kind of conjunctive participle or as an adverb. E. g.

/khol khal ke .../ having opened, etc. ... [/kholna/ "to open"; e.g. /ws ne səb saman khol khal ke phēk dia./ "He opened up all the luggage and threw it away."]

/soc sac ke/ Adv thoughtfully. [/socna/ "to think"; e.g. /ws ne soc sac ke kəha .../ "He said after much thought ..."]

/toR taR ke .../ having broken to pieces. [/toRna/ "to break."]

/ghum gham ke .../ having strolled around. [/ghumna/ "to wander, stroll, revolve."]

/gher ghar ke .../ having besieged, surrounded. [/gherna/ "to encircle, besiege, surround."]

232

(5) The normal word is followed by a repetition beginning with /m/. The stem may undergo still further modifications. E.g.

/jhuT muT/ Adv lyingly, falsely. [/jhuT/ M1 "lie, falsehood."]

/choTa moTa/ A2 smallish. [/choTa/ A2 "small"; /moTa/ A2 means "fat," but most of the informants agreed that /choTa moTa/ is an echo compound rather than a sequence of two meaningful adjectives.]

/sɔc mwc/ Adv really, in fact. [/sɔc/ M1 "truth." Here the vowel of the repeated portion is also modified."]

/Tal məTol [or /Tal Tol/ or /Tal əmTol/ or /Tal məTal/] F1 evasion, postponement, making excuses. [/Talna/ "to delay, postpone, make excuses. Some dictionaries also give /Tal/ as an F1 noun meaning "evasion, postponement."]

/gol məTol/ [or /gol mol/] A1 round, plump, lump shaped. [/gol/ A1 "round."]

A few examples of unique patterns may also be given:

/əkela dwkela/ A2 all alone. [/əkela/ A2 "alone, only, unique."]

/ənap šənap/ Adv meaninglessly, nonsensically, for no reason at all. [/ənap/ A1 "without.measure" (prefix /ə/ "un-, non-" + /nap/ F1 "measure") is now mostly obsolete.]

/ənT šənT/ A1 Adv irrelevant, inappropriate. [/ənT/ F1 "knot, twist, contrariness, opposition."]

/baja gaja/ M2 band, instrumental accompaniment, music. [/baja/ M2 "band, music." Note that both elements have Type II endings: /baje gaje se .../, etc.]

/cori cəkari/ F2 theft, robbery. [/cori/ F2 "theft."]

/dana dwnka/ M2 crumbs, pickings, grains, bird food. [/dana/ M2 "a grain."]

/gali gəloc/ F1 profanity, cursing, abuse, swearing. [/gali/ F2 "swearing, abuse."]

/gəp šəp/ F1 gossip, chit-chat. [/gəp/ F1 "gossip."]

/kəbhi kəbhar/ Adv rarely, seldom, only occasionally. [/kəbhi/ Adv "sometime, ever."]

/log bag/ Mpl people. [/log/ Mpl "people."]

/moTa jhoTa/ A2 tough, rough, coarse. [/moTa/ A2 "fat."]

/səwda sələf/ M1 groceries, provisions. [/səwda/ M2 "provisions, merchandise, wares, purchases."]

There are also examples of echo compounds in which neither component seems to have any independent meaning:

/gəRbəR/ [or /gəR bəR/] F1 confusion, chaos, disorder, muddle, mix-up. [Neither /gəR/ nor /bəR/ has any independent usage, and /gəRbəR/ itself may occur as the "meaningful" element in a further echo compound: /gəRbəR səRbəR/ F1 Adv "confusion, muddle, mess, confusedly."]

/lət pət/ PA1 splattered, drenched. [This is probably relatable to /lythəRna/ or /ləthəRna/ "to soak, drench, be smeared, daubed."]

19.306. The Vocative.

The vocative form is employed when one uses a noun as part of a direct address to some second person(s): e.g. "O boy!" "Hey, lady!" "My brethren!" The forms of the vocative are as follows:

MASCULINE

	TYPE I			TYPE II	
MVS	∅	/mərd/	MVS	e	/ləRke/
MVP	o	/mərdo/	MVP	o	/ləRko/

FEMININE

	TYPE I			TYPE II	
FVS	∅	/əwrət/	FVP	∅[1]	/ləRki/
FVP	o	/əwrto/	FVP	o[1]	/ləRkio/

[1]The vocative affixes occur after the Type II feminine affix /i/, just as the plural affixes do.

Adjectives modifying a vocative noun have the following endings:

MASCULINE

	TYPE I			' TYPE II	
MVS	∅	/nek/	MVS	e	/mere/
MVP	∅	/nek/	MVP	e	/mere/

FEMININE

	TYPE I			TYPE II	
MVS	∅	/nek/	MVS	∅[1]	/meri/
MVS	∅	/nek/	MVP	∅[1]	/meri/

[1]Again, the vocative /∅/ occurs after the Type II feminine affix /i/.

Various particles are employed with the vocative, the commonest of which are /əy/ "O!" and /əre/ "O!" The latter has endings like those of a Type II adjective: /əre/ before a masculine vocative noun, and /əri/ before a feminine vocative noun. E.g.

/əy ləRke!/ O boy!

/əre ləRko!/ O boys!

/əy beTi!/ O daughter!

/əri beTio!/ O daughters!

/bhaio əwr bəhno!/ Brothers and sisters!

/əy xwda ke nek bəndo!/ O virtuous servants of God!

/əy meri bəhno!/ O my sisters!

/sahbo!/ Gentlemen!

19.307. /dykhai dena/ and /swnai dena/.

Two special verbal noun forms, /dykhai/ F2 [np] "appearance, showing" and /swnai/ F2 [np] "hearing, audibleness," are employed with /dena/ (and sometimes with /pəRna/ "to fall") to mean "to appear, be visible, come to view" and "to be audible, be heard," respectively. Neither /dykhai/ nor /swnai/ are used elsewhere as independent nouns in modern Urdu. The most important point about these constructions is that, although the main verb is transitive (/dena/ "to give"), the subject is NOT marked by /ne/ in the past tenses. E.g.

/māy əkela jāgəl mē ja rəha tha, ky samne se ek rəwšni dykhai di./
I was going along all alone in the forest, when a light appeared before
[me]. [NOT */rəwšni ne dykhai dia/.]

/həm kəmre mē bayThe batē kər rəhe the, ky bərabərvale məkan se rone
ki avaz swnai di./   We were sitting [and] talking in the room, when
from the neighbouring house the sound of weeping was heard.

/cād əbhi tək dykhai nəhī dia./   The moon has not appeared as yet.

/ws kəmre mē rat ke vəqt mwxtəlyf qysm ki avazē swnai dene ləgī./
During the night various kinds of noises [lit. voices] began to be
heard in that room.

/mwjhe dykhai de rəha həy, ky twm ymtyhan mē kamyab nəhī hoge./   It
appears to me that you will not be successful in the examination.

/əgər ap ys pəhaR pər khəRe hõ, to sara šəhr dykhai dega./   If you stand
on this mountain, the whole city will be visible. [Here /dykhai dega/
= /nəzər aega/.]

/ys minar pər se sara gaõ dykhai deta həy./   The whole village is visible
from on [top of] this minaret.

/dykhai pəRna/ and /swnai pəRna/ have an impersonal and a conjectural sense:

/əysa swnai pəRta həy, ky vw log bərat mē nəhī aēge./   It is heard [i.e.
rumour has it, they say ...] that those people will not come in the
wedding procession.

/əysa dykhai pəRta həy, ky dwšmən ko əpni fəwj vapəs bwlani pəRegi./
It appears [i.e. it looks as though ...] that the enemy will have to
call their army back.

19.308.   The Verb: Intransitive Verb Stem + /dena/ and /lena/.

Compound verb formations made with a transitive stem + /dena/ "to give" and /lena/
"to take" were discussed in Sec. 13.303. A few intransitive stems also occur with these
auxiliaries, but these formations are idiomatic and often have rather unusual meanings.

   (1) Intransitive stem + /dena/: of the vocabulary so far introduced, only /cəlna/
"to go, move," /hãsna/ "to laugh," and /rona/ "to cry" may occur with /dena/. Here,
/dena/ gives the sense of "suddenly, violently." The most noteworthy feature of all of
these formations is that the subject is not marked by /ne/ in the past tenses.
   Most of the restrictions described for compound verbal formations in Sec. 13.303 apply
to these forms as well: e.g. they are rarely found in negative sentences, etc.
   /cəl dena/ "to start off, depart." Here the idea of suddenness and violence is not
great, but a connotation of immediate action remains. E.g.
       /khana khane ke bad, vw səb səyr ko cəl die./   After eating, they all
       started off on a stroll.
       /surəj nykəlne se pəhle hi, həm gaõ se cəl dēge./   Even before sunrise,
       we will start off from the village.
   /hãs dena/ "to burst out laughing." The sense of immediate, spontaneous action
is greater even than with /hãs pəRna/. E.g.
       /māy ws ki yy hərəkət dekh kər hãs dia./   I burst out laughing on seeing
       this action of his.
       /jəb bhi māy ws se koi bat kərta hū, to vw hãs deta həy./   Whenever I
       say anything to him, he bursts out laughing.
   /ro dena/ "to burst out weeping." Again, the connotation of violence and spontaneity

235

is stronger than with /ro pəRna/. E. g.

/vw əpne bap ke mərne ki xəbər swn kər ro dia. / On hearing the news of the death of his father, he burst out weeping.

/jəb vw yy swnega, to vw ro dega. / When he hears this, he'll burst out weeping.

(2) Formations with an intransitive stem + /lena/ are less common and more idiomatic in meaning. The following are treated as intransitive (i. e. the subject is not marked by /ne/ in the past tenses):

/cəl lena/ "to walk, to complete a walk. " E. g.

/ytna cəl lia hū, ky əb əwr cəlne ki hymmət nəhī̃. / I have walked so much that I have not the courage to walk any more.

/ho lena/ "to accompany, go along, join. " E. g.

/bəccō ko nə jəgao, vərna vw bhi mere sath ho lēge. / Don't wake up the children, or else they'll accompany [i. e. follow along after] me!

/vw mere sath ho lia. / He joined me. [Or: "He accompanied me, " "He came along with me, " etc.]

/jəb həmare nəbi ne logō se šəhr ke bahər cəlne ke lie kəha, to səb log wn ke piche piche ho lie. / When our Prophet said to the people to go out of the city, then everyone followed along after him.

The following are treated as transitive (i. e. the subject is marked by /ne/ in the past tenses), and they can also be considered "conjunct verbs. " E. g.

/a lena/ "to come and take: to overtake, catch up with. " The sense of "coming" and then "taking" is perhaps still present, and this formation might thus be considered "conjunct" rather than "compound. " E. g.

/əbhi mə̄y ghər se nykəlne bhi nə paya tha, ky baryš ne a lia. / I had not yet managed to leave [my] house, when the rain overtook [me].

/ja lena/ "to go and take: to overtake, catch up with. " The sense is like that of /a lena/, except that the action is _away_ from the speaker or centre of discussion. E. g.

/həmari fəwj ne dwšmən ki fəwj ko ja lia. / Our army overtook the army of the enemy.

236

19.400. SUPPLEMENTARY VOCABULARY

19.401. Supplementary Vocabulary.

The following numerals are all Type I adjectives. See Sec. 2.401.

chəyhəttər	seventy-six
səthəttər	seventy-seven
əThəttər	seventy-eight
wnasi	seventy-nine
əssi	eighty

Other items are:

adət F1	habit, idiosyncrasy
azad A1	free, independent
mənvana [DC: /manna/: Ic]	to cause to be believed, to cause to be obeyed, to convince (someone of something); to cause (a ceremony) to be held, performed
nac M1	dance
swnai F2 [np]	hearing, audibleness

19.402. Supplementary Exercise I: Substitution.

1. ws ke valyd ne ws ki šadi pər   <u>əssi</u>   həzar rupəe xərc kie.

    seventy-nine
    seventy-six
    forty-six
    seventy-seven
    seventy-eight

2. ləRai mẽ   <u>ykyavən</u>   admi mare gəe.

    seventy-seven
    eighty
    seventy-two
    sixty-four
    seventy-eight

19.403. Supplementary Exercise II: Fill the Blanks.

1. Fill the blanks in the following sentences with the appropriate form of one of the items introduced above in Sec. 19.401.

    a. həmara mwlk wnnys səw səytalys mẽ _____ hwa tha.
    b. kya, meri avaz _____ nəhĩ de rəhi?
    c. mə̃y ne bəRi mwškyl se wn se yy bat _____.
    d. gyara bəje tək sona ap ki bəhwt bwri _____ həy.
    e. həmare məzhəb mẽ _____ məna həy.

237

19.500. VOCABULARY AND GRAMMAR DRILL

19.501. Substitution.

1. mere taya   bhi bərat mẽ šərik the.
   father's younger
   brother
   mother's brother
   father's sister's
   husband
   mother's sister's
   husband
   relative

2. ap ne jwlus   ki tarix təy ki həy, ya nəhĩ.
   marriage
   betrothal
   marriage ceremony
   dance
   party

3. mãy ne wn logõ se yttyfaq   kia.
   opposition
   quarrel
   mention
   introduction
   request

4. mere valyd ne wse pala həy.
   has decorated
   has selected
   has taught
   has convinced [lit. caused
   to believe]
   has joined

5. ws ke xavynd   ne wse təlaq   di.
   America   freedom
   groom   ring
   my father's younger   prayer
   brother
   doctor   medicine
   guest   candy

6. šadi   ka mənzər bəhwt dylkəš   hota həy.
   marriage procession   beautiful
   funeral   sad
   Pilgrimage   interesting
   prison   frightening

238

Pakistani marriage   different

7. səb log əpne əpne mwlk ke   <u>ganc</u>   <u>ga</u>   rəhe the.
                                   dances   dance
                                   (band)   play
                                   music [s]
                                   games   play
                                   foods   cook
                                   clothing   show

8. əgər vw <u>ws ka ryšta</u>   qwbul kərē, to mwjhe xwši hogi.
            my gifts
            this much dowry
            my congratulation[s]
            this theory
            his opinion

9. ys mwamle mē <u>həmara</u>   <u>təsəvvwr</u>   bylkwl mwxtəlyf həy.
                   Arabs'   habit
                   my husband's   opinion
                   our country's   custom
                   our relatives'   experience
                   Məwlvi Sahəb's   theory

10. jəhā̃ tək <u>apəs mē mwhəbbət</u>   ka təəllwq həy, to vw yū həy.
             singing and dancing
             our society's structure
             its proof
             your responsibility
             divorce

11. age age kwch log <u>baja bəjate</u>   cəlte hə̄y.
                       making noise
                       singing songs
                       making announcement
                       distributing candy
                       showing [a] dance

12. <u>vw</u>   bari bari <u>mwbarəkbad</u>   peš kərne ləge.
    my relatives   gifts
    all the servants   proof
    the girl's people   sweets
    all the friends   garlands of flowers
    all the commentators   their own opinions

13. mə̄y <u>wn ke ylm</u>   se ynkar nəhī̃ kərta.
          [my] own faults
          [my] own responsibilities
          this theory of yours
          this proof
          their experience

14. əy bəcco, zəra meri ə̃guThi   DhũD kər lao!

    sons   our map

    girls   the guest's hat

    brothers   my book

    daughter   our invitation

    boy   my horse

15. mə̃y ne yy ə̃guThi   cwni həy. [1]

    song   have sung

    marriage ceremony   have read

    two dogs   have raised

    happiness   have caused to believe[2]

    candy   have distributed

[1] The verb must agree with the object in number-gender in each sentence.

[2] "To cause to believe happiness" = "to celebrate."

16. mere mamũ   ne əpna nəzərya   təbdil   kər lia həy. [1]

    my family   this [kinship]   accepted
                    connection

    their scholars   wine   legal

    my relatives   quarrel   settled

    villagers   their leader   appointed

    Məwlvi Sahəb   his commentary   completed

[1] The verb must agree with the object in number-gender in each sentence.

19.502. Transformation.

1. Change the underlined verb forms in the following sentences to the <S + /dena/>
or <S + /lena/> formations (see Sec. 19.308). Retain the same tense. The
instructor will discuss the connotations of each sentence.

    a. vw kəl yəhã se cəla gəya.

    b. jəb ws ne yy mənzər dekha, to vw ro pəRa.

    c. ys gane ko swnte hi, səb log hə̃s pəRe.

    d. aj həm bəhwt cəle hə̃y!

    e. səb ryštedar mere sath the. [1]

    f. mere phupha naraz ho kər fəwrən cəle gəe.

    g. jəb mə̃y ap ko vəhã ke əfsosnak halat swnaũga, to ap ro pəRẽge.

    h. jəb ws ne wn ka nac dekha, to vw hə̃s pəRa.

    i. gaRi kəl swba aTh bəje cəlegi.

    j. mera kwtta bhi mere sath hoga.

    [1] The stem of /the/ is, of course, /ho/.

2. After each of the following sentences an English word is given. Translate this into
an Urdu vocative form and place it at the beginning of its sentence. It may be
preceded by a vocative particle (/əy/, /əre/, or /əri/) if desired.

a. səb logõ se kəho, ky dwlhən rwxsət ho rəhi həy.   [boys]
b. əpne jəzbat pər qabu rəkhna cahie.   [sister]
c. əysa gana nəhĩ gana cahie!   [daughters]
d. mə̃y ap ke hwkm pər cəlne ko təyyar hũ.   [my husband]
e. əb həmare səfər ka qyssa bhi swno!   [people]
f. mə̃y ap ke samne ek əysa vaqea bəyan kərne vala hũ, ky ap səb ro dẽge!   [audience]
g. jao, mamũ sahəb ka ystyqbal kəro!   [son]
h. həm əpne dwšmənõ se zərur bədla lẽge!   [brothers]
i. əbhi to bij bone ka vəqt nəhĩ aya.   [farmers]
j. yslam ke qəvanin ki pabəndi kərna twmhara fərz həy.   [Muslims]

3. Change the underlined word in each of the following sentences to an "echo compound" formation in which the meaningful word is repeated with /v/ substituted for its first consonant. See Sec. 19.305.

a. zəra khana nykal kər, mez pər rəkh dijie!
b. wnhõ ne mere hath pər pəTTi bãdhi.
c. bəs, mə̃y ne syrf pətlun xəridi.
d. xansamã, zəra yy jəle hwe kayəz bahər phẽk ao!
e. vw log pərda nəhĩ kərte.
f. wse šərab ki adət pəR gəi, əwr ws ki zyndəgi bərbad ho gəi.
g. jəb šadi ki rəsmẽ xətm ho cwkẽ, to mwjhe bəta dẽ!
h. ləRkiã saRi bãdhne mẽ məsruf thĩ.
i. bazar ja kər, kwch kəbab xərid laẽ!
j. meri kyrae ki səb rəsidẽ ysi ryjysTər mẽ hə̃y.
k. ap ki mez pər Dak pəRi hwi həy.
l. kwch ləkRiã le ao, take ag jəlaẽ.
m. ws yərib ke pas koi khet nəhĩ.
n. yy məsla ləRai se həl nəhĩ hoga.
o. mwxalyf parTi yy bat swn kər ywsse mẽ a gəi, əwr laThiã le kər nəmbərdar sahəb ke ghər pəhw̃c gəi.

19.503. Fill the Blanks.

1. Fill the blanks in the sentences below with the most appropriate of the following words: /təy/, /qərar/, or /mwqərrər/. In some sentences more than one of these can be employed. See Secs. 18.103 and 19.106.

a. məwjuda zəmane mẽ, həm pãc ghənTe mẽ car həzar mil ka səfər ___ kər səkte hə̃y.
b. ynšaəlla[h], həmara əwr wn ka jhəgRa ___ ho jaega.
c. jəb davət ki tarix ____ ho jae, to mwjhe bəta dijie!
d. ws ne səb ke samne ws buRhe ko mwjrym ____ dia.
e. jəb tərfəyn ko ytminan ho jata həy, to šadi ki tarix ___ pati həy.
f. ws thəke hwe mwsafyr ne axyrkar yy fasyla ____ kər lia.

241

g. həm ne ____ kia həy, ky həm pərsõ jwlus nykalēge.

h. jəb yy məsla ____ ho gəya, to wnhõ ne ys ka elan kəra dia.

i. həqiqət yy həy, ky yy jhəgRa kəbhi ____ nəhī ho səkta.

j. məwlvi sahəb ne do admi vəkil ke təwr pər ____ kie.

2. Fill the blanks in the sentences below with the most appropriate of the following words: /rəvaj/, /rəsm/ (or its broken plural, /rwsumat/), or /adət/. In some sentences more than one of these can be employed. See Sec. 19. 102.

a. ajkəl choTe bal rəkhne ka ____ həy.

b. jəb mãgni ki ____ əda ho cwkti həy, to səb ko myThai khylai jati həy.

c. synima mē bat kərna ws ki bəhwt bwri ____ həy.

d. šadi ke bad, ãguThi pəhnna ek məɣrybi ____ həy.

e. jəj sahəb ki ____ həy, ky našta kərne ke bad ek pyali kəwfi zərur pite hãy.

f. mera əndaza yy həy, ky dəs sal ke əndər šadi ki bəhwt si pwrani ____ xətm ho jaēgi.

g. ajkəl ləRkiõ mē, tãg šəlvar pəhnne ka ____ həy.

h. hyndostan əwr pakystan mē, log gəle mē phulõ ke har pəhnte hãy, lekyn həmare hã ys ka ____ nəhī.

i. yy ____ bəhwt pwrani həy.

j. həmare mwlk mē ys nac ka bəhwt ____ tha.

19. 504. Variation.

1. pāc sal hwe, ky meri bivi mwjh se jwda ho gəi.

tin həfte hwe, ky mãy əpne xavynd se jwda ho gəi hū.

pāc məhine hwe, ky meri səheli mwjh se ələg ho gəi həy.

car sədiã hwī, ky həmara mwlk ws mwlk se ələyhda hwa tha.

dəs sal hwe, ky ys jhəgRe ne wnhē jwda kər dia.

koi tin məhine hwe, ky vw əpni bivi ko tələq de kər ələg rəhne ləga həy.

2. mere valdəyn ne meri šadi ki tarix təy ki həy.

wn ke ryštedarõ ne mãgni ke lie jwme ka dyn təy kia həy.

həm ne bəRi mwškylõ se yy rasta təy kia həy.

həvai jəhaz ne Dhai ghənTe mē yy fasyla təy kia.

ws ka məhr dəs həzar rupəe təy paya həy.

hyndostan əwr pakystan ke dərmyan səb jhəgRe təy ho gəe.

3. mwjhe yn hoTlõ ka xub təjryba həy.

həmē məɣrybi təhzib ka xub təjryba həy.

valdəyn ko zyndəgi ki zymmedario ka zyada təjryba hota həy.

ysmyth sahəb ko pakystan ki rwsumat ka koi təjryba nəhī.

mãy ne əyš ki zyndəgi ka bhi təjryba kia həy.

DakTərõ ne məriz pər ek nəi dəvai ka təjryba kia.

4. mãy ne pakystan vapəs jane ke lie doa mãgi.

mã əpni əwlad ke lie doaē kərti rəhi.

mwjrym ne xwda se doa ki, ky gəvahõ ke bəyan ɣələt sabyt ho jaē.

242

ws buRhe admi ne mwjhe bəhwt doaē dī.

vw ləRki dyn rat əllah se doa māga kərti thi, ky ws ki māgni TuT jae.

məwlvi sahəb əyse nek ynsan hǣy, ky hər γərib admi ki doa lete hǣy.

5. mera məwlvi sahəb se təarwf hwa.

kya, mere phupha se ap ka təarwf həy?

ys vəqt səb hazyrin se ap ka təarwf nəhī ho səkta.

māy ne ap ke mamū ka əpne taya se təarwf kəraya.

mere xalu ne dulha se mera təarwf kəraya.

zəra wn sahəb se mera təarwf kəra dijie!

6. yəhā se šəhr dykhai deta həy.

vw ajkəl bəhwt wdas dykhai dete hǣy.

əb tək bərat dykhai nəhī di, məgər ane hi vali hogi.

ws ki šəkl əysi dykhai de rəhi thi, jəyse ws ne koi bhut dekha ho.

əysa dykhai deta həy, ky ys yxtylaf ki byna pər wn ki māgni TuT jaegi.

mwjhe əysa dykhai de rəha həy, ky donō bhaiō mē yttyfaq nəhī rəhega.

7. ws ki səheliō ne vapəs jane se ynkar kia.

badšah ne həmē azadi dene se ynkar kia.

ləRki nykah pəRhvane se ynkar kər degi.

jəj sahəb ne mere təhayf qwbul kərne se ynkar kər dia.

wnhō ne sərdar ki əcchaiō se ynkar kia.

ws ne əpne xavynd se təlaq māgi thi, məgər ws ne ynkar kər dia.

8. yəhā se wn ki avaz swnai degi.

bərat ke bajō ki avaz swnai de rəhi thi.

upər se ws ka gana əcchi təra swnai dega.

šor ki vəja se kwch swnai nəhī deta.

məkkhi ki avaz to swnai de rəhi həy, məgər vw dykhai nəhī deti.

vw kūē ke əndər se cixta rəha, məgər həmē swnai nəhī dia.

9. bərat əksər rat ko rwxsət hoti həy.

jəb vw həm logō se rwxsət hwa, to ws ki ākhō mē āsu the.

meri beTi aj rwxsət hone vali həy.

kya, ap ke myhman kəl rwxsət ho gəe?

dostō əwr əzizō ne dwlhən ko rwxsət kia.

mwjhe ek həfte ki rwxsət leni pəRegi.

10. māy ap ka yy fəysla qwbul nəhī kər səkta.

yəhudiō ne ərəbō ki šərayt qwbul nəhī kī.

təəjjwb ki bat həy, ky ap wn ki rae fəwrən qwbul kər lete hǣy.

ys mwamle mē, təmam mwfəssyrin pwrane zəmane ke wləma ka nəzərya qwbul kərte hǣy.

mwjhe wmmid həy, ky meri doa qwbul hogi.

əy əllah, māy əpne gwnahō ka yqrar kərta hū!

11. mere valyd sahəb ne mere xalu ko məna lia.

axyrkar dwlhən ne əpne mā bap ko məna lia.

mere ryštedarō ne meri šadi ke məwqe pər bəhwt xwši mənai.

sal mẽ ek dəfa ws bwzwrg ki yad mənai jati həy.

ləRkõ ne yunyvərsyTi se əpni šərayt mənva lĩ.

axyrkar mãy ne ws se mənva lia, ky vw vəqt ki pabəndi nəhĩ kərta.

12. səb logõ ne myl kər ws ki ãguThi DhũDi, məgər nəhĩ myli.

mwfəssyrin ne ys səval ka jəvab DhũDa, məgər kysi kytab mẽ nəhĩ myla.

mãy əpna davətnama tin ghənTe tək DhũDta rəha, məgər nəhĩ myla.

həm ne axyrkar pakystan ka nəqša DhũD lia, əwr masTər sahəb ko dykha dia.

jəb sare kysanõ ne myl kər meri gae DhũDi, to myl gəi.

vw becari, əgər sari zyndəgi xavynd DhũDti rəhe, to bhi nəhĩ mylega.

13. ap ka xət aj hi mwjhe məwsul hwa həy.

šadi ka davətnama əbhi əbhi Dak mẽ məwsul hwa həy.

ap ka məni arDər kəl məwsul hwa tha.

jənab ke sare təhayf bənde ko məwsul ho gəe hõy, əwr bənda wn ka šwkria əda
     kərta həy.

ərse se wn ka koi pəyyam məwsul nəhĩ hwa.

ap fykr nə kərẽ. šayəd kəl tək koi jəvab məwsul ho.

14. wn ka vəhã jana məhz ek yttyfaq tha.

yy to məhz ek rəsm həy. yslam ke əqayd se ys ka koi təəllwq nəhĩ.

yy məhz ek choTi si ɣələti thi.

məhz ek mamuli se yxtylaf ki byna pər ləRna nəhĩ cahie.

məhz əyš se zyndəgi gwzarna to koi zyndəgi nəhĩ.

məhz bəhs kərne se məsla həl nəhĩ hoga.

15. pakystan əwr hyndostan ne əmrika ki ys rae se yttyfaq kia.

pakystan əwr hyndostan ne əpni fəwjõ ki məwjuda tadad kəm kərne pər yttyfaq kia.

šam əwr səudi ərəb ke dərmyan, yn šərayt pər yttyfaq ho gəya həy.

sari dwnya ke mwsəlmanõ mẽ yttyfaq hona cahie.

mera vəqt se pəhle pəhw̃cna məhz ek yttyfaq tha.

mãy yttyfaqən ws vəqt vəhã pəhw̃ca, jəb vw log jwlus nykalne vale the.

19. 505. Response.

1. kya, ap pakystani šadiõ ki rwsumat se vaqyf hõy?

2. jəhez ki rəsm ke bare mẽ ap ka kya xyal həy.

3. kya, ap ke hã šadi ke məwqe pər təmam ryštedarõ ki məwjudgi zəruri həy?

4. ap ka nykah kəhã hwa tha -- gyrja mẽ ya ghər pər.

5. ap ke məzhəb mẽ təlaq jayz həy, ya nəhĩ.

6. əgər jayz həy, to kya, xavynd əwr bivi donõ ko ek dusre se təlaq mãgne ka həq
   hasyl həy?

7. ap ke hã təlaq kys kys byna pər ho səkti həy.

8. kya, ap ke mwlk mẽ ləRka əwr ləRki ek dusre ko dekhe bəɣəyr šadi kərte hõy?

9. ap ke nəzərye ke mwtabyq, mwhəbbət səhih təwr pər šadi se qəbl ya šadi ke bad
   šwru hoti həy?

10. kya, ap ke hã šadi ke məwqe pər gana bəjana hota həy?

244

11. əgər šadi se pəhle ləRka əwr ləRki donō əkele synima ya kysi parTi vəγəyra mē
jaē, to kya, ap ke mwašre mē yy ciz bwri səmjhi jaegi?

12. kya, ap ko kwtta ya koi əwr janvər palne ka šəwq həy?

13. əgər ap ke hā bəhwt se myhman a jaē, to kya, ap ghəbra jaēge.

14. ap ke hā šadi ke məwqe pər dulha kəyse kəpRe pəhnta həy.

15. kya, ap ke mwlk mē ek se zyada šadi kər səkte hōy?

19. 506. Conversation Practice.

Mr. Smith and Dr. Rəhim have arrived at the house where the marriage is taking
place.

S: vaqəi, ghər bəhwt əcche təriqe se səjaya gəya həy!

R: ji hā. bərat ka yntyzar həy. ysi lie səb log yntyzam mē məsruf hōy.

S: bajō ki avaz swnai de rəhi həy. šayəd ydhər se bərat a rəhi həy.

R: əysa hi malum hota həy, kyōke yy log bhi ystyqbal ke lie bəRh rəhe hōy. aie, həm bhi
yəhā khəRe ho jaē. yəhā səb logō se təarwfi kəraya jaega.

S: lijie, bərat a gəi! yy age age kəwn log hōy.

R: yy dulha ke ryštedar hōy, jəyse taya, cəca, phupha vəγəyra, əwr wn ke piche piche dulha
ke dost vəγəyra hōy.

S: ap ne kəl Thik fərmaya tha. bərat ka mənzər vaqəi bəhwt dylkəš həy. əgərce həmare
mwlk mē bhi log parTi ki surət mē gyrja jate hōy, lekyn yy šan nəhī hoti.

R: əpne əpne mwlk ka rəvaj həy. kya, ap ke hā šadi ke məwqe pər ys təra bərat nəhī ati,
əwr ys təra baje vəγəyra bəjae jate?

S: ji nəhī. həmare hā dulha ke ryštedar əwr dost, əwr dwlhən ki səheliā əwr wn ke valdəyn
mwxtəlyf parTiō mē gyrja jate hōy, jəhā šadi ki rəsm əda hoti həy. həmare mwlk mē
gəle mē phulō ke har pəhnne ka bhi rəvaj bəhwt kəm həy, lekyn šadi ke məwqe pər dwlhən
ke hath mē phul hote hōy, əwr vw əksər səfəyd kəpRe pəhnti həy. kya, ap ke hā dwlhən
ys məwqe pər kysi xas rōg ke kəpRe pəhnti həy?

R: əgərce yy zəruri nəhī, lekyn əksər dwlhən šadi ke məwqe pər lal kəpRe pəhnti həy.

S: ap ke mwašre mē təlaq ko kəysa səmjha jata həy.

R: əgərce təlaq həmare məzhəb əwr mwašre mē jayz həy, əwr kysi əhəm vəja ki byna pər
təlaq di ja səkti həy, lekyn təlaq ko əccha nəhī səmjha jata. həmare nəbi ne fərmaya
həy, "jayz cizō mē se, səb se bwri ciz təlaq həy." kya, ap ke məzhəb mē bhi təlaq jayz
həy?

S: jəysa ky ap jante hōy, ky isai məzhəb mwxtəlyf mwlkō mē phəyla hwa həy, cwnāce ys ke
bare mē hər mwlk ke qəvanin mwxtəlyf hōy. baz mwlkō mē to əb bhi təlaq nəhī di ja
səkti, əwr nə hi dusri šadi ho səkti həy. lekyn baz mwlkō mē log təlaq bhi dete hōy, əwr
dusri šadi bhi kərte hōy.

R: aie, nykah šwru ho rəha həy. məwlvi sahəb a gəe hōy.

S: yy do admi əbhi bərabərvale kəmre mē gəe the, əwr ynhō ne vapəs a kər məwlvi sahəb
se kwch kəha həy.

R: yn mē se ek sahəb vəkil hōy, əwr dusre sahəb gəvah hōy. bərabərvale kəmre mē dwlhən
bəyThi hwi həy. yy donō admi ləRki se yjazət lene gəe the, ky wse yy ləRka xavynd ki

245

həysiət se pəsənd həy, ya nəhĩ. cwnãce əgər ws ne yjazət de di hogi, to nykah əbhi šwru ho jaega.

S: kya, ləRki xwd nykah mẽ šərik nəhĩ hoti?

R: ji nəhĩ. əksər vw dusre kəmre mẽ ryštedar əwrtõ əwr səheliõ ke sath bəyThti həy, lekyn ws ki mərzi nykah mẽ šamyl hoti həy.

S: nykah to šayəd xətm ho gəya, kyõke log ləRke ko mwbarəkbad de rəhe hãy.

R: ji hã. aie, həm bhi wse mwbarəkbad dẽ.

After Mr. Smith and Dr. Rəhim have presented their congratulations to the groom, they wander about among the guests.

S: yy log ws kəmre mẽ kyõ ja rəhe hãy.

R: ws kəmre mẽ jəhez rəkkha hwa həy. yy bhi həmari šadi ki rwsumat mẽ se ek rəsm həy, ky nykah ke bad hazyrin ko jəhez dykhaya jata həy. aie, həm bhi dekhẽ, ky jəhez mẽ kya kya cizẽ di gəi hãy.

S: kya, yy səb saman jəhez hi ka həy?

R: ji hã. həmare dost bəhwt əmir admi hãy. wnhõ ne əpni beTi ko təqribən tis həzar rupəe ka saman jəhez mẽ dia həy.

S: kya, yy hər šəxs ke lie zəruri həy, ky ytna hi saman jəhez mẽ de?

R: ji nəhĩ. yy zəruri nəhĩ. log əpni əpni həysiət ke mwtabyq jəhez dete hãy. əgər ytni hi rəqəm ka jəhez hər šəxs ko dena pəRe, to əksər ləRkiõ ki šadi hi nə ho!

S: ji hã, mãy bhi yyhi soc rəha tha.

R: aie, khane ke kəmre mẽ cəlẽ!

S: bəhwt əccha!

19. 507. Conversation Stimulus.

Topics may include the following:

1. Marriage in one's own country.
2. The custom of giving a dowry.
3. Divorce.
4. One's own marriage.
5. Differences of customs connected with the selection of a mate.

Echo compounds are preceded by an asterisk in this and following Vocabulary Sections. They are not counted as new words.

*adat Fpl	pl. /adət/
adət F1	habit, idiosyncrasy
azad A1	free, independent
azadi F2	freedom, independence
āsu M1	tear (lachrymal)
əsl F1 A1	basis, root, source, origin; basic, real, genuine
əssi A1	eighty
əThəttər A1	seventy-eight
əwlad F1	offspring, children
əy Vocative Particle	O!
əyb M1	fault, defect
əziz M1 A1	distant relative; beloved, dear
āguThi F2	(finger) ring
baja M2	instrumental music, band
bari F2	turn, time
bāTna [Ie: /ə/]	to distribute, share
bəhna [IIc: /ə/]	to flow, run (liquid)
bəjana [C: /bəjna/: IIc]	to play, make sound, ring
bənavəT F1	structure, make-up
bərat F1	marriage procession (of the groom's people to the bride's house)
byna F1	basis, foundation [/[ki] byna pər/ Comp Post "on the basis of"]
*cae vae F1	tea and things, tea etc.
cəca M1	uncle: father's younger brother
chəyhəttər A1	seventy-six
*choTa moTa A2	smallish
cwnna [Ic: /w/]	to choose, select, elect, pick out, pick (fruit)
davətnama M2	invitation
doa [or /dwa/] F1	prayer, invocation
dulha [or /dwlha/] M1	groom
dwlhən [or /dulhən/] F1	bride
dykhai F2 [np]	showing, appearance
dylkəš A1	attractive, nice, charming
DhūDna [or /DhūDhna/] [Id: /w̄/]	to search, seek, look for
elan M1	announcement, declaration, proclamation
gana M2	song
gana [Id: /ə/]	to sing

247

gəla M2	throat, front part of the neck
ghəbrana [IIa]	to be flustered, confused, worried, agitated, bewildered
*halat Mpl	pl. /halət/ Fl
har Ml	garland, wreath
hazyrin Mpl	pl. /hazyr/: audience, people present
həqiqət Fl	reality, truth, fact
jayz Al	permissible, allowable, valid, lawful, legal
jəhez Ml	dowry
*jəzbat Mpl	pl. /jəzba/
jwda PA1	separated, parted, apart
jwlus Ml	procession, parade, accession to a throne
mamū Ml	uncle: mother's brother
məhr Ml	marriage payment made to the bride by the groom
məhz Adv	just, only
mənana [C: /manna/: Ic]	to cause to believe, convince, make agree; to hold (a ceremony)
mənvana [DC: /manna/: Ic]	to cause to be believed, to cause to be obeyed, to convince (someone of something); to cause (a ceremony) to be held, performed
mənzər Ml	scene, view
*məsayl Mpl	pl. /məsla/
*məvaqe Mpl	pl. /məwqa/
məwjudgi F2	presence, existence
məwsul PA1	received, arrived
məgni F2	betrothal, engagement
mwbarəkbad Fl	congratulations
myhman M/Fl	guest, visitor
myThai F2	sweets, candy
nac Ml	dance
nacna [IIc: /ə/]	to dance
nəqša M2	map, chart, plan, sketch, scene
nəzərya M2	theory, opinion
nykah Ml	marriage ceremony, marriage contract
palna [If: /ə/]	to cherish, raise, nurture, bring up
pəRhana [C: /pəRhna/: Ic]	to cause to read, teach
pəRhvana [DC: /pəRhna/: Ic]	to cause to be read, to have (something) taught
phupha Ml	uncle: father's sister's husband
[se] qəbl Comp Post Adv	before, previous, primary
qwbul [or /qəbul/] PA1	accepted, consented, acknowledged
rae Fl	opinion, idea
rəvaj Ml	custom, usage, tradition
rəvana PA1	departed, left, dispatched, sent
rəvangi F2 [np]	departure, leave, going, dispatch

248

rwxsət F1	departure, leaving, leave
ryštedar M1	relative, kinsman
sabyt A1	proved, established, firm, whole, sound, enduring
səjana [C: /səjna/: IIc]	to decorate, adorn, embellish
səthəttər A1	seventy-seven
swbut M1 [np]	proof, testimony
swnai F2 [np]	hearing, audibleness
šan F1	magnificence, glory, pomp
taya M1	uncle: father's elder brother
təarwf M1	introduction, acquaintance
təbdil PA1	changed, altered, modified
*təfsilat Fpl	pl. /təfsil/
*təhayf Mpl	pl. /twhfa/
təjryba [common: /təjrwba/] M2	experience, experiment
təlaq F1	divorce
tərfəyn Mpl	both sides, both parties
təy PA1	concluded, settled, decided, fixed
wnasi A1	seventy-nine
wdas A1	sad, unhappy, gloomy
xalu M1	uncle: mother's sister's husband
xavynd M1	husband
ynkar M1	refusal, denial, rejection
yqrar M1 [np]	consent, admission, affirmation, acquiescence
ystyqbal M1	welcome, reception
ytminan M1 [np]	contentment, satisfaction, confidence, reliance
yttyfaq M1	coincidence, accident; agreement, concord
yttyfaqən Adv	by accident, by surprise, accidentally, by chance, all of a sudden
yxtylaf M1	disagreement, discord, difference, opposition, variance
zymmedari F2	responsibility

The Provincial Assembly Chambers, Lahore.

UNIT TWENTY

20.000. CONVERSATION

political science F1 [np]

syasiat

student M1

talybylm [or /talybe ylm/]

politics F1

syasət

constitution, code of laws, statutes M1

ain

S: Mr. əziz, you have been [lit. have ceased remaining] a student of political science. You must know a lot [lit. much something must come to you] about politics. Please just tell me something about the constitution and government of Pakistan. I mean [lit. my meaning is] how the government is formed in your country.

əziz sahəb, ap to syasiat ke talybylm rəh cwke hɔy. ap ko to syasət ke bare mẽ bəhwt kwch ata hoga. zəra mwjhe pakystan ke ain əwr hwkumət ke mwtəəllyq kwch bətaie! mera mətləb həy, ky ap ke hã hwkumət kys təra bənti həy.

democratic A1

jəmhuri [or /jwmhuri/]

existence, being M1

vwjud

parliamentary A1

parlimani

public, common people Mpl

əvam

political A1

syasi

action, operation, practice, deed, work M1

əməl

presidential A1

sədarti

manner, mode, way, kind, type, style F1

tərz

to adopt, make one's own [Ia]

əpnana

president M/F1

sədr

realm, state, kingdom F1

mwmlykət [lit. /məmlykət/ or /məmlwkət/]

most high, supreme, superior A1

ala

ruler, sovereign; ruling M1 A1

hwkmran

minister, vizier M/F1

vəzir

highest, greatest A1

azəm

post, position, rank M2

whda

powers Mpl

yxtiarat

democracy F1

jəmhuriət [or /jwmhuriət/]

representative M/F1 A1

nwmaynda

ə: Yes, I certainly can tell you something or other about my country. Our constitution is democratic. When Pakistan came into existence, we adopted the parliamentary system, but after fourteen [or] fifteen years of experience, we came to this conclusion, that this system is not suitable for the Pakistani public. Instead, we need that sort of political system which the public can understand and upon which [they] can act. With this in view [lit. under this idea], a new constitution was made, in

ji hã, mɛ̃y əpne mwlk ke bare mẽ ap ko kwch nə kwch zərur bəta səkta hū. həmara ain jwmhuri həy. pakystan, jəb vwjud mẽ aya, to həm ne parlimani nyzam yxtiar kia, lekyn cəwda pəndra sal ke təjrybe ke bad, həm ys nətije pər pəhw̃ce, ky y nyzam pakystani əvam ke lie mwfid nəhĩ. bəlke həmẽ ek əyse syasi nyzam ki zərurət həy, jyse əvam səməjh səkẽ, əwr jys pər əməl kər səkẽ. ys xyal ke təht, ek nəya ain bənaya gəya, jys mẽ sədarti tərze hwkumət əpnaya gəya həy. yani sədre mwmlykət

251

which the presidential form of government was adopted; i.e. the president of the state was declared the supreme ruler. Thus the post of prime minister was abolished. Now the president alone holds all the powers. In the present constitution a new system of Basic Democracies has also been established, in order that a representative government of the common people can be set up in the country.

ala hwkmran qərar paya. ys təra vəzire azəm ka whda xətm kər dia gəya. əb sədr hi ko təmam yxtiarat hasyl hote həy. məwjuda ain mē bwnyadi jwmhuriətõ ka ek nəya nyzam bhi qaym kia gəya həy, take mwlk mē əvam ki nwmaynda hwkumət qaym ho səke.

   assembly F2

   cabinet F1

S: Then does the president rule all by himself? Is there no assembly or cabinet?

   əsəmbli

   kabina

to kya, sədr xwd hwkumət kərta həy? koi əsəmbli ya kabina nəhĩ?

   province M2

   provincial A1

   member M/F1

   ministers Mpl [pl. /vəzir/]

   election, selection, choice M1

ə: And why not? According to the constitution, there is a National Assembly. For the provinces of East and West Pakistan, there are two provincial assemblies. The president chooses his ministers from among the members of the National Assembly and rules the country with their help.

   suba

   subai

   mymbər

   vwzəra

   yntyxab

kyõ nəhĩ həy! ain ke mwtabyq ek qəwmi əsəmbli həy. məšryqi əwr məyrybi pakystan ke subõ ke lie do subai əsəmbliã həy. sədr qəwmi əsəmbli ke mymbərõ mē se əpne vwzəra ka yntyxab kərta həy, əwr wn ki mədəd se hwkumət kərta həy.

   majority F1

   minority A1

   sect, party M2

   rights Mpl [pl. /həq/]

S: There are people of various religions living in your country, among whom the majority are Muslims. In your constitution, do the people of minority sects also have the same rights which have been given to Muslims?

   əksəriət

   əqliəti [or /əqəlliəti/]

   fyrqa

   hwquq

ap ke mwlk mē mwxtəlyf məzahyb ke log rəhte həy, jyn mē əksəriət mwsəlmanõ ki həy. kya, ap ke ain mē əqliəti fyrqõ ke logõ ko bhi vwhi hwquq hasyl həy, jo mwsəlmanõ ko die gəe həy?

   non-Muslim M1 A1

   inhabitant, resident, native, dweller M2

   yəyrmwsəlman

   bašynda

ə: Yes. There is no distinction made in our constitution between Pakistan's Muslim and non-Muslim residents. Every resident of Pakistan has equal rights.

S: What are the Basic Democracies?

ji hã. həmare ain mē pakystan ke mwsəlman əwr yəyrmwsəlman bašyndõ ke dərmyan koi təmiz nəhĩ ki gəi həy. pakystan ke hər bašynde ko bərabər ke hwquq hasyl həy.

yy bwnyadi jwmhuriətē kya hãy.

   administrative A1

   piece, part, portion M2

   division, partition, sharing F1

   stage, destination, goal, level, tier, storey (of a house) F1

   union F1 A1

   council F1

   yntyzami

   TwkRa

   təqsim

   mənzyl

   yunyən

   kəwnsəl

elected, selected, chosen A1 [usually PA1]	mwntəxəb
chairman M/F1	cermeyn
"təhsil," a small administrative unit, subdivision of a district F1	təhsil
police station; small administrative unit equal to the "təhsil" (East Pakistan only) M2	thana
district M2	zyla
division (large administrative unit) M1	Dyvižən
automatically, spontaneously, all by oneself Adv	xwdbəxwd
selected, appointed, fixed A1	mwqərrərkərda
service Fp1 [pl. /xydmət/]	xydmat
government, governmental, official A1	sərkari

ə: The Basic Democracies are a system under which the country has been divided into very small administrative sections, in order that the public may take part in the tasks of the government. There are four tiers in this system. The first tier is the Union Council. At this stage the common man takes part in the election and selects his representative for the Council. The elected representatives of this Council choose their chairman themselves. The "təhsil" or "thana" [is] the second tier; the district and the division are the third and fourth tiers. The chairmen of the councils of the first level automatically become members of the second level councils. These people send their representatives to the third level council. The same method is [used] for the fourth tier. The government also appoints some of its own members to all of these tiers of councils in order that the public may profit from the experience and services of these appointed members. Some government officers are also members of these councils.

bwnyadi jwmhuriətē ek əysa nyzam həy, jys ke təht mwlk ko choTe choTe yntyzami TwkRō mē təqsim kər dia gəya həy, take əvam hwkumət ke kamō mē hyssa le səkē. ys nyzam ki car mənzylē hōy. pəhli mənzyl yunyən kəwnsəl həy. ys mənzyl pər, am admi yntyxab mē hyssa leta həy, əwr kəwnsəl ke lie əpna nwmaynda mwntəxəb kərta həy. ys kəwnsəl ke mwntəxəb nwmaynde əpna cermeyn xwd cwnte hōy. təhsil ya thana dusri mənzyl, zyla əwr Dyvižən tisri əwr cəwthi mənzylē hōy. pəhli mənzyl ki kəwnsəlō ke cermeyn xwdbəxwd dusri mənzyl ki kəwnsəlō ke mymbər bən jate hōy. yy log tisri mənzyl ki kəwnsəl ke lie əpne nwmaynde bhejte hōy. yyhi təriqa cəwthi mənzyl ke lie bhi həy. hwkumət yn təmam mənzylō ki kəwnsəlō mē əpne bhi kwch mymbər mwqərrər kərti həy, take əvam yn mwqərrər-kərda mymbərō ke təjrybe əwr xydmat se fayda wTha səkē. kwch sərkari əfsər bhi yn kəwnsəlō ke mymbər hote hōy.

S: Do the members of the fourth level councils automatically become members of the Provincial Assembly?

kya, cəwthi mənzyl ki kəwnsəl ke ərkan xwdbəxwd subai əsəmbli ke mymbər bən jate hōy?

ə: No, the members of the Union Council elect the members of the Provincial and National Assemblies.

ji nəhī, subai əwr qəwmi əsəmbli ke mymbərō ka yntyxab yunyən kəwnsəl ke mymbər kərte hōy.

S: Do you mean that the common man does not elect the members of the Provincial or National Assemblies?

kya, ap ka mətləb yy həy, ky am admi subai ya qəwmi əsəmbli ke mymbərō ko mwntəxəb nəhī kərta?

candidate; expecting, hopeful M/F1

wmmidvar

ə: Yes, this is true. He only picks his representative for the Union Council of his own region. These representatives elect the members of the Provincial and National Assemblies. Being a member of some Union Council is not necessary to become a member of the National or

ji hã, yy səhih həy. vw syrf əpne ylaqe ki yunyən kəwnsəl ke lie əpna nwmaynda cwnta həy. yy nwmaynde subai əwr qəwmi əsəmbli ke mymbərō ka yntyxab kərte hōy. qəwmi ya subai əsəmbli ka mymbər bənne ke lie, kysi yunyən kəwnsəl ka mymbər hona zəruri nəhī. koi bhi pakystani

Provincial Assemblies. Any Pakistani
can become a candidate.

governor M/F1

S: Who elects the president and the governors
of the provinces?

to remove, take away, move aside
[C: /həTna/ "to move away,
withdraw": IIc]

ə: The members of the National Assembly
elect the president. The governors are
not elected, but instead the president
afterwards appoints governors for the
provinces. He can also remove these
governors from their posts.

S: When there is a National Assembly, what
do the Basic Democracies do?

local, resident Al

therefore Conj

necessities, requirements, needs Fpl

project, scheme, plan M2

officers Mpl [pl. /əfsər/]

lecture, speech Fl

centre Ml

eighty-five Al

population, settlement F2

advice, consultation, counsel M2

tax Ml

received, acquired, realised, levied
(as funds) PAl

central Al

law-maker, law-making Ml Al

institute, institution, body, department,
organisation M2

reform, improvement, emendation Fl

plans, proposals, suggestions, schemes
Fpl [pl. /təjviz/ Fl "plan, suggestion"]

industrial Al

commercial Al

economic Al

policy F2

peace, security, safety Ml [np]

war Fl

foreign countries Mpl

connections, relations Mpl [pl.
/təəllwq/]

affairs, matters Mpl [pl. /mwamla/]

wmmidvar bən səkta həy.

gəvərnər

sədr əwr subõ ke gəvərnərõ ka yntyxab
kəwn kərta həy.

həTana

qəwmi əsəmbli ke mymbər sədr ka yntyxab
kərte hə̃y. gəvərnərõ ka yntyxab nəhĩ hota,
bəlke sədr bad mẽ subõ ke lie gəvərnər
mwqərrər kərta həy. vw yn gəvərnərõ ko
wn ke whdõ se həTa bhi səkta həy.

jəb qəwmi əsəmbli məwjud həy, to bwnyadi
jwmhuriətẽ kya kərti hə̃y.

mwqami

lyhaza

zəruriat

mənsuba

əfsəran

təqrir

mərkəz

pycasi [or /pəcasi/]

abadi

məšvəra

Təyks

vwsul

mərkəzi

qanunsaz

ydara

yslah

təjaviz

sənəti

tyjarti

məaši

palisi

əmn

jə̃g

ɣəyrmwmalyk

təəllwqat

mwamlat

254

ə: The fundamental objective of the Basic Democracies is to work for the progress and prosperity of their own regions. Since these people are local residents, therefore they know their own needs, and [they] prepare projects according to this. The government officials of this region assist in the completion of these projects. Our president recently said in one of his speeches, "The centre of this system is the village, because eighty-five percent of the population of the country lives in the village. Therefore the prosperity of the village is the prosperity of the country." It is for this very reason that [we] call this system "Basic Democracy," because the people of several [lit. two-four] villages solve their problems by consulting among themselves [lit. having consulted ... solve]. They have also been given the power of collecting various minor taxes. On the other hand, the National Assembly is the central law-making body of Pakistan, which presents proposals for the progress of the country and the prosperity of the society, and makes laws for them. It frames the industrial, commercial, economic and administrative policy of the country. Aside from this, it decides upon peace and war, relations with foreign countries, and other such important matters.

bwnyadi jwmhuriətõ ka əsl məqsəd əpne əpne ylaqõ ki tərəqqi əwr xwšhali ke lie kam kərna həy. cũke yy log mwqami bašynde hote hõy, lyhaza vw əpni zəruriat jante həy, əwr wsi ke mwtabyq mənsube bənate hõy. ys ylaqe ke sərkari əfsəran yn mənsubõ ko mwkəmməl kərne mẽ mədəd dete hõy. həmare sədr ne hal hi mẽ əpni ek təqrir mẽ kəha tha, ky "ys nyzam ka mərkəz gaõ həy, kyõke mwlk ki pycasi fi sədi abadi gaõ mẽ rəhti həy. ys lie gaõ ki xwšhali mwlk ki xwšhali həy." yyhi vəja həy, ky ys nyzam ko bwnyadi jwmhuriət kəhte hõy, kyõke do car gaõ ke log əpəs mẽ məšvəra kər ke əpne məsayl ko həl kərte hõy. ynhẽ choTe moTe Təyks vwsul kərne ka bhi yxtiar dia gəya həy. dusri tərəf, qəwmi əsəmbli pakystan ka mərkəzi qanunsaz ydara həy, jo mwlk ki tərəqqi əwr mwašre ki yslah ki təjaviz peš kərta həy, əwr wn ke lie qanun bənata həy. mwlk ki sənəti, tyjarti, məəši, əwr yntyzami palisi təyyar kərta həy. ys ke ylava, əmn əwr jãg, γəyrmwmalyk ke sath təəllwqat, əwr əyse hi digər əhəm mwamlat ke fəysle kərta həy.

S: How are the central and provincial governments formed?

mərkəzi əwr subai hwkumtẽ kys təra qaym hoti hõy.

ə: The president chooses his ministers from the members of the party having the majority in the National Assembly, these being [lit. which is] called his cabinet. In the same way, the governor selects his minister[s] from the members of the party having the majority in the Provincial Assembly.

sədr qəwmi əsəmbli mẽ əksəriət rəkhnevali parTi ke mymbərõ mẽ se vəzirõ ka yntyxab kərta həy, jo ws ki kabina kəhlati həy. ysi təra, gəvərnər subai əsəmbli mẽ əksəriət rəkhnevali parTi ke mymbərõ mẽ se vəzir cwnta həy.

S: Is there freedom in your country to form political parties?

kya, ap ke hã syasi parTiã bənane ki azadi həy?

society, group, association, organisation, company Fl

ənjwmən

foreign, foreigner Ml Al

γəyrmwlki

ə: According to our constitution people are free to form their own political and other social associations. You must have had an idea [lit. to you must have been an estimate] from the newspapers that in our country there are many political parties, which each have their own points of view about national and foreign matters.

həmare ain ke mwtabyq, log əpni syasi əwr digər mwašrəti ənjwmənẽ bənane mẽ azad hõy. ap ko əxbarõ se əndaza hwa hoga, ky həmare mwlk kəi syasi parTiã hõy, jo mwlki əwr γəyrmwlki mwamlat pər əpna əpna nwqtəe nəzər rəkhti hõy.

S: Are there opposition parties too in the Provincial and National Assemblies?

kya, subai əwr qəwmi əsəmbliõ mẽ mwxalyf parTiã bhi hoti hõy?

minority Fl

əqliət [or /əqəlliət/]

criticism Fl

tənqid

255

ə: Yes, the members of those parties who are in the minority form the opposition party, and they criticise those policies of the government which they think [are] bad for the country.

ji hā, jys parTi ke mymbər əqliət mē hote hǝy, vw mwxalyf parTi qaym kərte hǝy, əwr hwkumət ki wn palisiõ pər tənqid kərte hǝy, jynhē vw mwlk ke lie bwra səməjhte hǝy.

elections Mpl [pl. /yntyxab/]

yntyxabat

vote Ml

voT

S: Can women also vote in the elections?

kya, yntyxabat mē əwrtē bhi voT de səkti hǝy.

individual, person Ml

fərd

employment, job, service Fl

mwlazmət

ə: Yes, in our country every individual has the right to vote whose age is twenty-one years or over. Therefore women have the same rights as men do. They also can hold government jobs.

ji hā, həmare hā hər ws fərd ko voT dene ka həq hasyl həy, jys ki wmr ykkys sal ya ws se zyada həy. cwnāce əwrtõ ko vwhi hwquq hasyl həy, jo mərdõ ke hǝy. vw sərkari mwlazmət bhi kər səkti hǝy.

office holder, official M/Fl

S: Are judges, police officers, and other high government officials also elected?

kya, jəjõ, polis ke əfsərõ, əwr digər ala sərkari whdedarõ ka bhi yntyxab hota həy?

employees, workers Mpl [pl. /mwlazym/ Ml "worker, employee"]

mwlazymin

civil Al

syvyl

service Fl

sərvys

regular, according to rule Al

baqayda

examinations, tests Mpl [pl. /ymtyhan/]

ymtyhanat

training, instruction, upbringing Fl

tərbiət

ruler, governor Ml

hakym

ə: No, in our country those who work at government posts are not elected, but instead there are regular Civil Service examinations for high government employees, and those who are successful in these examinations are given training in order that they may perform their duties well in the capacity of court judges, police officers, or district rulers.

ji nəhī, həmare mwlk mē sərkari whdõ pər kam kərnevalõ ka yntyxab nəhī hota, bəlke ala sərkari mwlazymin ke lie syvyl sərvys ke baqayda ymtyhanat hote hǝy, əwr yn ymtyhanat mē kamyab honevalõ ko tərbiət di jati həy, take vw ədalət ke jəj, polis ke əfsər, ya zyle ke hakym ki həysiət se əpne fərayz əcchi təra əda kər səkē.

brother, friend [vocative particle]

bhəi

S: My friend, I am feeling thirsty. Could you please get me a little water [lit. cause a little water to be requested].

bhəi, mwjhe pyas ləg rəhi həy. zəra pani māgva dē!

ə: Yes, certainly. -- Here, tea is also coming!

ji hā, zərur! -- yy lijie, cae bhi a rəhi həy!

20.100. WORD STUDY

20.101. Although /syasiat/ F1 [np] "political science" is historically an Arabic plural, it is treated as singular in Urdu. As stated in Sec. 17.305, the names of various branches of knowledge are often made from what appears to be an adjective ending in /i/ + /at/. Other examples:

/lysaniat/ F1 [np] linguistics. [/lysani/ A1 "relating to language."]

/məašiat/ F1 [np] economics. [/məaši/ A1 "economic."]

/yslamiat/ F1 [np] Islamic Studies. [/yslami/ A1 "Islamic."]

The student should also note /syasət/ F1 "politics, diplomacy" and /syasi/ A1 "political."

20.102. /talybylm/ M1 "student" is a common contraction for /talybe ylm/, lit. "seeker of knowledge" (/talyb M/F1 "seeker"). The plural of /talybylm/ is /twləba/ or /tələba/ Mpl; a feminine student is termed /talyba/ F1, and the plural of /talyba/ is /talybat/. Note that these latter items occur always WITHOUT /ylm/, while /talyb/ alone never means "student."

20.103. /ana/ IIa "to come" idiomatically denotes "to know (a subject, a language, an art), to have proficiency in." The person knowing is marked with /ko/ or its equivalent: /X ko Y ata həy./ "X knows Y." E.g.

/mwjhe wrdu əcchi təra ati həy./ I know Urdu very well.

/mwjhe gana ata həy./ I know [how] to sing.

/mwjhe aj ka səbəq ata həy./ I know today's lesson.

/vw jhuT bolta həy. dərəsl wse kwch nəhĩ ata./ He lies. In fact he knows nothing.

/ws ke xyal mẽ, mwjhe bəhwt kwch ata həy./ In his opinion I know a lot.

20.104. /vwjud/ M1 "existence, being" is used with /[mẽ] ana/ "to come [into]" and /[mẽ] lana/ "to bring [into]" to denote "to come into being" and "to bring into being" respectively. Note that /vwjud/ means "being" in the existential sense; physical presence is denoted by /məwjudgi/ F2 "presence." Both words are derived from the Arabic root v-j-d, which means "to find." E.g.

/pakystan wnnys səw sãytalys mẽ vwjud mẽ aya./ Pakistan came into existence in 1947.

/mwyəl hwkumət kəb vwjud mẽ ai./ When did the Mughal government come into existence?

/ynsan ko vwjud mẽ lane ka məqsəd yy tha, ky vw əllah ki ybadət kəre, əwr nek kam kəre./ The object of bringing Man into existence was this, that he should worship God and do good works.

/meri məwjudgi mẽ ws ka nykah pəRhaya gəya./ His marriage ceremony was performed in my presence. [Here, where "being in a certain location" is meant, /vwjud/ cannot be used.]

/kya, davət mẽ meri məwjudgi zəruri həy./ Is my presence necessary at the party./ [/vwjud/ cannot be substituted here.]

20.105. /əvam/ Mpl "public, common people" is the broken plural of /amma/ M2 "commonality, the crowd." /amma/ is uncommon in Urdu, being employed mostly in compounds.

20.106. /əməl/ Ml "action, operation, practice, deed, work" has two important usages: /X pər əməl kərna/ "to practice X" and /X [ko] əməl mẽ !ana/ "to bring X into practice, put X into operation." E.g.

/ws ne mere kəhne pər əməl kia, əwr kamyab rəha./ He acted upon my statement [lit. saying], and was successful.

/pakystan əmn ki palisi pər əməl kərta həy./ Pakistan follows [lit. acts upon] a policy of peace.

/ys mənsube ko əməl mẽ lane ke lie, dəs həzar rupəe ki zərurət həy./ In order to put this project into operation, ten thousand rupees are needed.

/wnnys səw əTThavən mẽ yy ain pəhli dəfa əməl mẽ laya gəya./ This constitution was put into effect for the first time in 1958.

20.107. /tərz/ "manner, mode, way, kind, type, style" may be treated as both Ml and Fl. The author's informants tended to lean towards the feminine gender for this word, although various older dictionaries state that the preference is for the masculine. It must be noted that constructions of /tərz/ + /yzafət/ + a noun ("manner of ..., style of ...") are treated as masculine by all of the author's sources. E.g.

/ws ne ek nəi tərz ki hwkumət qaym ki./ He established a new form of government. [/nəe tərz ki .../ was also felt to be correct, though less idiomatic for the author's informants.]

/əmrika ka tərze hwkumət jwmhuri həy./ America's form of government is democratic. [/tərze hwkumət/ "form of government" is generally Ml.]

/ws ka tərze bəyan dusrõ se bylkwl mwxtəlyf həy./ His style of expression is entirely different from others. [/tərze bəyan/ "style, mode of expression" is Ml.]

/mwjhe ap ka tərze zyndəgi bəhwt pəsənd həy./ I like your way of life very much. [/tərze zyndəgi/ "way of life" is Ml, although /zyndəgi/ is feminine and /tərz/ alone is also usually feminine.]

20.108. /əpnana/ "to adopt, make one's own" is a denominative verb stem made from the same root as that of /əpna/ A2 "one's own". /əpnana/ has neither a causative nor a double causative form.

20.109. Most Indo-Pakistani speakers use the pronunciation /mwmlykət/ Fl "realm, state, kingdom," although Urdu dictionaries recommend /məmlykət/ or /məmlwkət/ in accordance with the Arabic original. Note that /mwmalyk/ Mpl is really the broken plural of /məmlykət/, but Urdu speakers treat it as the plural of /mwlk/ Ml "country."

20.110. /ala/ Al "most high, superior, supreme" is made on the Arabic comparative-superlative pattern əCCəC from the root '-l-y "to be high." */ə'ləy/ occurs as /ə'la/ in Arabic according to the regular pattern for root-final y, and as /ala/ in Urdu.

/azəm/ Al "greatest" is also made on the same pattern from the root '- z̧-m "to be great": /ə'zəm/ occurs in Urdu as /azəm/. This word is of very limited use in Urdu, being employed only after a noun + the /yzafət/: e.g. /vəzire azəm/ Ml "prime minister," /qayde azəm/ Ml "greatest leader" (/qayd/ Ml "leader"), etc. /ala/ is not so limited; it is often found as a regular Type I adjective. E.g.

/vəzire ala/ Ml chief minister. [This is also a technical term.]

/hwkmrane ala/ Ml supreme ruler, head of state. [Compare:]

/ala hwkmran/ Ml superior ruler. [Here /ala/ may have the sense of "excellent."]

/yy kəpRa bəhwt ala dərje ka həy./ This cloth is of very superior quality.

/həmare məhkməe zəraat ke nwmaynde ne kəha həy, ky "əcchi fəsl wgane ke lie, ala qysm ki khad ystemal kərni cahie."/ The representative of our Department of Agriculture stated that "In order to grow a good crop, [one] must employ a superior type of fertiliser."

/ala whdõ pər əksər wn logõ ko hi mwqərrər kia jata həy, jo syvyl sərvys ke ymtyhan mẽ kamyab hote hãy./ Generally those people are appointed to the highest posts, who have been successful in the Civil Service examination.

/polis ke ala əfsərõ ka kəhna həy, ky "əvam qəvanin ki pabəndi nəhĩ kərte."/ It is the statement of the highest police officers that the public does not obey the laws.

20.111. In the meaning of "member (of a party, organisation, etc.)," /mymbər/ M/Fl is synonymous with /rwkn/ M/Fl. /rwkn/ may also be used in the sense of "pillar" (though not in the architectural sense), and in this meaning /mymbər/ cannot occur. In passing, it may also be noted that /mymbər/ occurs with a Persian plural suffix, although it is of English origin: /mymbəran/ Mpl "members". E.g.

/vw ys ənjwmən ka mymbər həy./ He is a member of this society. [Here /rwkn/ may be freely substituted.]

/yslam ke pãc bwnyadi ərkan hãy./ There are five basic pillars of Islam. [/mymbər/ cannot be substituted here.]

20.112. /hwquq/ Mpl "rights" is the broken plural of /həq/ Ml Al "right, lot, due, portion, God; true." The Arabic root is ḥ-q-q, and the singular should be /həqq/. Arabic final doubled consonants are borrowed into Urdu as single consonants, however: /həq/.

20.113. /mənzyl/ Fl has several meanings: "goal (of a journey), destination" and hence "objective"; "stage (of a journey), stopping place" and hence "stage, level, tier"; and also "level, storey (of a house)." E.g.

/pəhli mənzyl pər pəhw̃c kər, Thəyr jaẽ əwr mera yntyzar kərẽ!/ On reaching the first stage [of the journey], stop and wait for me!

/ys mənsube ki car mənzylẽ hãy./ There are four stages to this project.

/axyrkar vw əpni mənzyl pər pəhw̃c gəya./ At last he reached his destination. [Here /mənzyl/ may refer to the destination of a journey or to a non-physical objective or goal.]

/ws ne əpni mənzyl pa li./ He obtained his objective. [Here /mənzyl/ overlaps with /məqsəd/ Ml "goal, objective," and one could also say:]

259

/ws ne əpna məqsəd pa lia./ He obtained his goal.

/həm ys ymarət ki cəwthi mənzyl pər rəhte hɔ̄y./ We live on the fourth
floor of this building.

20.114. Pakistan is divided into two provinces (/suba/ M2), each ruled by a governor
(/gəvərnər/ M/F1). Each province is divided into divisions (/Dyvižən/ M1), administered
by a Commissioner (/kəmyšnər/ M/F1). Each division in turn is composed of districts
(/zyla/ M2), administered by a Deputy Commissioner (/DypTi kəmyšnər/ M/F1 or /hakym/
M1). The /zyla/ is composed of /təhsil/ F1, each administered by a /təhsildar/ M/F1.
In East Pakistan there is no /təhsil/ unit; instead a similar administrative unit is termed
/thana/ M2, a term which means only "police station" in West Pakistan. A /thana/ is
administered by a /thanedar/ M1.

High officials in the Pakistani governmental system may be chosen from the ranks with-
in their respective services, or they may be directly recruited through a nation-wide system
of Civil Service examinations. In the latter case, those who pass these examinations with
the highest marks are given training for the Foreign Service; other successful candidates
are trained for the Civil Service, the Police, the Post and Telegraphs Department, etc. etc.

Civil cases and other lower court cases are tried by magistrates selected via the Civil
Service examinations. Although the /təhsil/ is mostly a tax collecting and land registration
unit, there may be a /təhsil/ court, which is empowered to try minor cases, land disputes,
etc. There are also District Courts, High Courts, and finally the Supreme Court. Justices
of the High Court need not necessarily have passed the Civil Service examinations; they
are directly appointed from the ranks of the legal profession by the Governor and a panel
of justices. Supreme Court Justices are similarly appointed by the President and his
advisors.

The Police function also as a province-wide organisation, rather than as distinct city,
county, state, and federal police systems, as in the United States.

All of the Civil Services (and the Army) are quite separate from the Provincial and
National Assemblies and the Basic Democracies. Members of the Basic Democracies are
elected directly by the populace. These electees alone have the right to vote in elections
for the Provincial and National Assemblies. Any Pakistani citizen may, however, stand
for election to these latter bodies.

20.115. /xwdbəxwd/ Adv "automatically, spontaneously, all by [one's] self" is a
Persian compound meaning literally "self with self." It may be noted that whenever /əpne
ap/ and /xwd/ denote "by [one's] self, automatically," then /xwdbəxwd/ may be substituted
for them. When /xwd/ and /əpne ap/ mean "self" in the reflexive sense, then /xwdbəxwd/
cannot occur. E.g.

/mɔ̄y əpne ap cəla jaūga./ I'll go myself. [Here /xwd/ may be substituted,
but /xwdbəxwd/ may not.]

/mwjhe əpne ap ys ciz ka yhsas həy./ I myself feel this thing. [Here
again /xwd/ is possible, but not /xwdbəxwd/.]

/mɔ̄y ne wse əpne ap əpni ākhɔ̄ se dekha./ I saw him myself with my
own eyes. [Here again /xwdbəxwd/ is not possible, although /xwd/
alone may be substituted.]

/mə̄y xwd ys γələti pər šərmynda hū./ I myself am ashamed of this
mistake. [/əpne ap/ is possible, but not /xwdbəxwd/.]

/mə̄y ne xwd yy kam kia./ I myself did this work. [/əpne ap/ is possible
but not /xwdbəxwd/.]

/yy dərəxt mə̄y ne nəhī̃ ləgaya, bəlke vw xwdbəxwd wg aya./ I did not
plant this tree; instead it came up all by itself. [/əpne ap/ may
occur here also, but /xwd/ -- though correct -- is less preferable.]

/yy dərvaza xwdbəxwd bənd ho gəya./ This door went shut all by itself.
[Again, although /əpne ap/ is possible, /xwd/ is somewhat less
preferable.]

/mə̄y ne ys məšin ko hath nəhī̃ ləgaya. vw xwdbəxwd cəl pəRi./ I didn't
lay a hand on this machine. It started up all by itself. [As above,
/əpne ap/ is possible, but /xwd/ is less preferable.]

20.116. /mwqərrərkərda/ A1 "appointed, selected" has a transitive sense which is
lacking in /mwqərrəršwda/ A1 "appointed, selected." The former lays stress upon the
transitive act of appointing; the latter does not. See Sec. 18.307.

20.117. /lyhaza/ Conj "therefore" is synonymous with /ys lie/. /lyhaza/ is, however,
markedly more literary in style. When analysed into its Arabic components, it will be seen
that /lyhaza/ and /ys lie/ both have the same literal meaning: "for this" (/ly-/ "to, for"
+ /haza/ "this").

20.118. In the true sense of the word, /zəruriat/ Fpl "necessities, needs, requirements"
has no singular form. It appears to be an Arabic plural of /zəruri/ A1 "necessary," but
/zəruri/ is never used as a singular noun. This type of formation was discussed in Sec.
17.304.

20.119. /mənsuba/ M2 "project, scheme, plan" denotes something considerably more
concrete than /təjviz/ F1 "plan, scheme, suggestion, proposal." The former word
connotes almost exactly what "project" connotes in English. /təjviz/, however, means
only a suggestion, a proposed course of action, a proposal. E.g.

/məwlvi sahəb ne yy təjviz peš ki, ky bəccō ke lie qwran ki talim zəruri
qərar di jae./ Məwlvi Sahəb suggested that the teaching of the Qwran
be declared essential for children.

/məwlvi sahəb ki ys təjviz pər, yunyən kəwnsəl ne əpne ylaqe ke yskulō
mē qwran pəRhane ka ek mənsuba təyyar kia./ On Məwlvi Sahəb's
suggestion, the Union Council prepared a project for the teaching of
the Qwran in the schools of its district.

/yunyən kəwnsəl ne mərkəzi hwkumət ko əpne ylaqe mē səRkē əwr pwl
vəγəyra bənane ka mənsuba peš kia./ The Union Council presented
a project to the Central Government for the building of roads, schools,
etc. in its region.

/mere dada ne yy nam təjviz kia./ My Grandfather proposed this name
[for the baby].

20.120. /vwsul/ PA1 "received, acquired, realised, levied" is usually employed only
for physical objects and particularly for sums of money. /məwsul/ PA1 "received, arrived,"
on the other hand is used for nonphysical objects and for letters, telegrams, and other items

sent by mail or other conveyance. These two words are both constructed from the same
Arabic root: v-ṣ-l "to arrive, be joined, connect." At times they overlap in usage. E.g.

/mə̃y wn se yy rəqəm vwsul kər lūga./ I will collect this amount from
them. [/məwsul/ cannot occur here.]

/mə̃y ne Təyks ki sari rəqəm vwsul pai./ I realised the entire amount
of the tax. [Again /məwsul/ would not be idiomatic.]

/mwjhe kyrae ki səb rəqəm vwsul ho gəi./ I received the whole amount
of the rent. [/vwsul pana/ and /vwsul hona/ are nearly synonymous.
Again /məwsul/ would not be preferred here.]

/meri səb myhnət vwsul ho gəi./ I have received all the fruits of my
labour. [Idiomatic: lit. All my labour has been received.]

/ap ke məni arDər ki rəsid vwsul hwi./ The receipt for your money order
has been received. [/vwsul pai/ is also possible, and /məwsul hwi/
is acceptable as well, since a receipt is something which is sent by
mail. etc.]

/səvere ki Dak se ap ke məni arDər ki rəsid məwsul hwi./ The receipt
for your money order was received in this morning's mail. [Here
/məwsul hwi/ is better than /vwsul hwi/ or /vwsul pai/, since /Dak/
is mentioned.]

/ap ka xət aj məwsul hwa./ Your letter was received today. [/vwsul
hwa/ or /vwsul paya/ could also be used but would be somewhat less
usual.]

/ap ka pəyɣam məwsul hwa./ Your message was received. [/vwsul/ is
not idiomatic here, since /pəyɣam/ is not a physical object.]

20.121. /hal hi mē/ Adv "at present, recently" literally means "in this very state."
/hal mē/ (without /hi/) is also found but rather less commonly. Both of these expressions
usually refer to the past, but /hal mē/ may also refer to the future: "very soon, in the
immediate future." E.g.

/vw hal hi mē ɣəyrmwmalyk ka səfər kər ke vapəs aya həy./ He has
recently returned from making a trip to foreign lands.

/mə̃y ne hal hi mē yy məkan xərida həy./ I bought this house just
recently.

/sədre pakystan hal mē məšryqi pakystan jaēge./ The President of
Pakistan will soon go to East Pakistan.

20.122. /məhkma/ M2 denotes "department (of a government, institution, etc.)";
/ydara/ M2 may also mean "department" in some contexts but generally can be translated
"institute, institution, organisation" and also "body" (e.g. /qanunsaz ydara/ "law-making
body"). /ənjwmən/ F1 also means "organisation" but in the sense of a smaller, less
formalised group: "society, association" and also "assembly, company."

20.123. /fərd/ M1 "individual, person" is employed only when one wishes to emphasise
the separateness of the individual. It is thus less common than /šəxs/ M1 "person" or
/admi/ M1 "man, person." /fərd/ is also used in the sense of "member" but only in the
context of "member of a family."
   The Arabic broken plural of /fərd/ is /əfrad/ Mpl. This word is employed for "persons"
and is thus synonymous with /əšxas/ Mpl "persons," the broken plural of /šəxs/. /əfrad/
is more common than the singular form /fərd/. E.g.

/hər fərd pər lazym həy, ky yn qəvanin ki pabəndi kəre./ It is incumbent upon every individual that [he] obey these laws. [Here /fərd/ stresses the distinct identity of each individual.]

/mə̃y ys xandan ka fərd hū./ I am a member of this family.

/polis ne kəl rat car əfrad kȯ gyryftar kia həy./ The police arrested four persons last night. [/əšxas/ or /admiõ/ could also occur here.]

/ys ənjwmən mẽ dəs əfrad əwr bhi šamyl kər lie gəe hə̃y./ Ten more persons have been taken into [lit. included] this society. [Again /əšxas/ or /admi/ could have been substituted.]

20.124. /mwlazmət/ F1 and /nəwkri/ F2 both mean "employment, service, job." The former is more literary and also perhaps a trifle more honorific in connotation. The most honorific term for "job, occupation" has not yet been introduced: /šəɣl/ M1 "occupation." This term should be employed when asking an equal or a superior about his employment:

/ap ka kya šəɣl həy./ What is your occupation?

20.125. /hakym/ M1 denotes "ruler, administrator, official." The broken plural is /hwkkam/ Mpl "rulers, officials."

The term /hwkmran/ M1 "ruler" is also made from the same Arabic root: ḥ-k-m "to order, command." It denotes a somewhat more elevated status than /hakym/: "sovereign, ruler (of a country)." It also has connotations of royalty, monarchy, or one man rule. Thus, while one may speak of /səudi ərəb ke hwkmran/ "the ruler of Saudi Arabia," /əmrika ke hwkmran/ "the ruler of America" would sound strange unless one wished to imply that the American president was a monarch or a despot. /hwkmran/ is also employed as an adjective in Urdu newspaper prose to mean "ruling." E.g.

/zyle ke hakym ka dəftər ws ymarət mẽ həy./ The office of the Deputy Commissioner is in that building.

/sube ke hakym ko gəvərnər kəhte hə̃y./ [We] call the ruler of a province "governor".

/gəvərnər ne sube ke təmam hwkkam ko hydayət ki həy, ky vw ys mənsube ko jəldi xətm kərne ki košyš kərẽ./ The Governor instructed the officials of the province to try to complete this project quickly.

/mysr ke pwrane hwkmran fyrəwn kəhlate the./ The ancient rulers of Egypt were called "Pharoah." [/fyrəwn/ M1 "Pharoah".]

/həmari parTi ajkəl pakystan ki hwkmran parTi həy./ These days our party is the ruling party of Pakistan. [Here /hwkmran/ is employed as an adjective.]

20.126. /bhəi/ "friend, brother" is used as a vocative particle by equals who are on familiar terms, by a superior to an inferior, or by non-familiar equals among the lower classes. Although, for example, two students of equal age may address each other with this term, a young student would not address an elderly well-dressed stranger with /bhəi/. /bhəi/ is, of course, a shortened form of /bhai/ M1 "brother," but it may be used to women as well: a man may address his wife with /bhəi/; two women friends may sometimes employ it for each other (although /bəhn/ F1 "sister" is commoner), etc. /bhəi/ often has the sense of drawing the hearer's attention to a forthcoming request or command: e.g.

/bhəi, zəra meri bat swn lijie!/   Friend, just listen to what I have to say!

20.127. Some Complex Verbal Formations.

A:
   /mwntəxəb/
      /[Y] mwntəxəb hona/ to be elected [to the post of Y]
      /[X ko Y] mwntəxəb kərna/ to elect [X to the post of Y]
   /təjviz/
      /təjviz hona/ to be proposed
      /[X ko] təjviz kərna/ to propose [X]
   /təqsim/
      /[Y mẽ] təqsim hona/ to be divided [into Y]
      /[X ko Y mẽ] təqsim kərna/ to divide [X into Y]
   /vwsul/
      /vwsul hona/ to be received, realised, levied
      /[X ko] vwsul kərna/ to collect, realise, receive [X]
      /[X ko] vwsul pana/ to collect, realise, receive [X]

B:
   /nwmayndəgi/
      /[X ki] nwmayndəgi kərna/ to represent [X]
   /yntyxab/
      /[X ka] yntyxab hona/ [X] to be elected
      /[X ka] yntyxab kərna/ to elect [X]
   /yslah/
      /[X ki] yslah hona/ [X] to be reformed, improved
      /[X ki] yslah kərna/ to reform, improve [X]

D:
   /tərbiət/
      /[X ko] tərbiət dena/ to train [X]
      /[X se] tərbiət lena/ to receive, take training [from X]
      /[X se] tərbiət mylna/ to receive training [from X]
      /[X se] tərbiət pana/ to receive training [from X]
   /voT/
      /[X ko] voT dena/ to vote [for X]
      /[X mẽ] voT lena/ to receive a (large, small, etc.) vote [in X]

F:
   /əməl/
      /[X pər] əməl hona/ [X] to be put into practice, followed, made use of
      /[X pər] əməl kərna/ to practice, follow [X]
      /[X ko] əməl mẽ lana/ to bring [X] into operation, put [X] into practice

/jə̄g/

    /[X əwr Y mẽ] jə̄g hona/ to be a war [between X and Y]

    /[X se] jə̄g kərna/ to fight a war [with X]

/mənzyl/

    /mənzyl mylna/ to attain one's goal

    /mənzyl pana/ to attain one's goal

/məšvəra/

    /[X ko Y ke bare mẽ] məšvəra dena/ to give advice [to X about Y]

    /[X se Y ke bare mẽ] məšvəra hona/ to take council, consult [with X about Y]

    /[X se Y ke bare mẽ] məšvəra kərna/ to consult, take the advice [of X about Y]

    /[X se Y ke bare mẽ] məšvəra lena/ to take advice [from X about Y]

/mwlazmət/

    /[X mẽ] mwlazmət kərna/ to have a job [in X]

/mwlazym/

    /[X mẽ] mwlazym hona/ to be an employee [in X]

/sərvys/

    /[X mẽ] sərvys kərna/ to have a job [in X]

/tənqid/

    /[X pər] tənqid hona/ [X] to be criticised

    /[X pər] tənqid kərna/ to criticise [X]

/təqrir/

    /[X pər] təqrir hona/ to be a speech, lecture [upon X]

    /[X pər] təqrir kərna/ to give a speech [about X]

/Təyks/

    /[X pər] Təyks ləgana/ to tax [X], put a tax [on X]

/TwkRa/

    /[X ke] TwkRe hona/ [X] to be divided, broken, etc. into pieces. [/TwkRe/ only occurs in the plural.]

    /[X ke] TwkRe kərna/ to divide, break, etc. [X] into pieces. [/TwkRe/ only occurs in the plural.]

/vwjud/

    /[X] vwjud mẽ ana/ [X] to come into existence

    /[X ko] vwjud mẽ lana/ to bring [X] into existence

20.201. Word Recognition.

(1) The following compounds are usually written as two separate units:

SCRIPT	PRONUNCIATION	SCRIPT	PRONUNCIATION
خود بخود	xwdbəxwd	غیر ملکی	ɣəyrmwlki
طالب علم	talybylm	غیر ممالک	ɣəyrmwmalyk
عہدے دار	whdedar	قانون ساز	qanunsaz
غیر مسلمان	ɣəyrmwsəlman	مقرر کردہ	mwqərrərkərda

(2) The following words are written with "uncommon" Arabic consonants, with final ٥ = /a/, or with other special spelling conventions.

ادارہ	ydara	تھانہ	thana
اصلاح	yslah	چیپیرمین	cerməyn
اعظم	azəm	حاکم	hakym
اعلیٰ	ala	حقوق	hwquq
اکثریت	əksəriət	حکمران	hwkmran
اکثریتی	əksəriəti	صدارتی	sədarti
امتحانات	ymtyhanat	صدر	sədr
انتظامی	yntyzami	صنعتی	sənəti
باشندہ	bašynda	عوام	əvam
باقاعدہ	baqayda	فرقہ	fyrqa
تحصیل	təhsil	کابینہ	kabina
تعلّقات	təəllwqat	لہٰذا	lyhaza

266

SCRIPT	PRONUNCIATION	SCRIPT	PRONUNCIATION
مشوره	məšvəra	طلباء	twləba [or /tələba/]
معاشی	məaši	عمل	əməl
صوبائی	subai	عہدہ	whda
صوبہ	suba	معاملات	mwamlat
ضروریات	zəruriat	منصوبہ	mənsuba
ضلع	zyla	نمائندہ	nwmaynda
طرز	tərz	وزراء	vwzəra[1]
		وصول	vwsul

[1] The /həmza/ at the end of /vwzəra/ is optional in Urdu.

20. 202. Reading Drill I: Text.

The following is the text of the Conversation Section of this Unit. Read it aloud, striving for speed and accuracy.

اِستّہ۔   عزیز صاحب ، آپ تو سیاسیات کے طالب علم رہ چکے ہیں ۔ آپ کو تو سیاست کے بارے میں بہت کچھ آتا ہوگا ۔ ذرا مجھے پاکستان کے آئین اور حکومت کے متعلّق کچھ بتائیے ۔ میرا مطلب ہے کہ آپ کے ہاں حکومت کس طرح بنتی ہے ۔

عزیز۔   جی ہاں، میں اپنے ملک کے بارے میں آپ کو کچھ نہ کچھ ضرور بتا سکتا ہوں ۔ ہمارا آئین جمہوری ہے ۔ پاکستان جب وجود میں آیا تو ہم نے پارلیمانی نظام اِختیار کیا ۔ لیکن چودہ پندرہ سال کے تجربے کے بعد ہم اِس نتیجے پر پہنچے کہ یہ نظام پاکستانی عوام کے لئے مفید نہیں۔ بلکہ ہمیں ایک ایسے سیاسی نظام کی ضرورت ہے جسے عوام سمجھ سکیں اور جس پر عمل کر سکیں ۔ اِس خیال کے تحت ایک نیا آئین بنایا گیا ، جس میں صدارتی طرزِ حکومت اپنایا

گیا ہے ۔یعنی صدرِ مملکت اعلیٰ حکمران قرار پایا ۔ اِس طرح وزیرِ اعظم کا عہدہ ختم کر دیا گیا ۔ اب صدر ہی کو تمام اختیارات حاصل ہوتے ہیں ۔ موجودہ آئین میں بنیادی جمہوریتوں کا ایک نیا نظام بھی قائم کیا گیا ہے ۔تاکہ ملک میں عوام کی نمائندہ حکومت قائم ہو سکے ۔

اسمتھ ۔ تو کیا، صدر خود حکومت کرتا ہے ؟کوئی اسمبلی یا کابینہ نہیں ؟

عزیز ۔ کیوں نہیں ہے ! آئین کے مطابق ایک قومی اسمبلی ہے ۔ مشرقی اور مغربی پاکستان کے صوبوں کے لئے دو صوبائی اسمبلیاں ہیں ۔ صدر قومی اسمبلی کے ممبروں میں سے اپنے وزرا کا انتخاب کرتا ہے ۔ اور اُن کی مدد سے حکومت کرتا ہے ۔

اسمتھ ۔ آپ کے ملک میں مختلف مذاہب کے لوگ رہتے ہیں ، جن میں اکثریت مسلمانوں کی ہے ۔ کیا آپ کے آئین میں اقلیتی فرقوں کے لوگوں کو بھی وہی حقوق حاصل ہیں جو مسلمانوں کو دیئے گئے ہیں ؟

عزیز ۔ جی ہاں ۔ ہمارے آئین میں پاکستان کے مسلمان اور غیر مسلمان باشندوں کے درمیان کوئی تمیز نہیں کی گئی ہے ۔ پاکستان کے ہر باشندے کو برابر کے حقوق حاصل ہیں ۔

اسمتھ ۔ یہ بنیادی جمہوریتیں کیا ہیں ؟

عزیز ۔ بنیادی جمہوریتیں ایک ایسا نظام ہے ، جس کے تحت ملک کو چھوٹے چھوٹے انتظامی ٹکڑوں میں تقسیم کر دیا گیا ہے ، تاکہ عوام حکومت کے کاموں میں حصہ لے سکیں ۔ اِس نظام کی چار منزلیں ہیں ۔ پہلی منزل یونین کونسل ہے ۔ اِس منزل پر، عام آدمی انتخاب میں حصہ لیتا ہے اور کونسل کے لئے اپنا نمائندہ منتخب کرتا ہے ۔ اِس کونسل کے منتخب نمائندے اپنا چیئرمین خود چنتے ہیں ۔ تحصیل یا تقانہ دوسری منزل ، ضلع اور ڈویژن تیسری اور چوتھی منزلیں ہیں ۔ پہلی منزل کی کونسلوں کے چیئرمین خود بخود دوسری منزل کی کونسلوں کے ممبر

بن جاتے ہیں۔ یہ لوگ تیسری منزل کی کونسل کے لئے اپنے نمائندے بھیجتے ہیں۔ یہی طریقہ چوتھی منزل کے لئے بھی ہے۔ حکومت اِن تمام منزلوں کی کونسلوں میں اپنے بھی کچھ ممبر مقرّر کرتی ہے، تاکہ عوام اِن مقرّر کردہ ممبروں کے تجربے اور خدمات سے فائدہ اٹھا سکیں۔ کچھ سرکاری افسر بھی اِن کونسلوں کے ممبر ہوتے ہیں۔

استھہ۔ کیا چوتھی منزل کی کونسل کے ارکان خود بخود صوبائی اسمبلی کے ممبرین بن جاتے ہیں؟

عزیز۔ جی نہیں، صوبائی اور قومی اسمبلی کے ممبروں کا انتخاب یونین کونسل کے ممبر کرتے ہیں۔

استھہ۔ کیا، آپ کا مطلب یہ ہے، کہ عام آدمی صوبائی یا قومی اسمبلی کے ممبروں کو منتخب نہیں کرتا؟

عزیز۔ جی ہاں، یہ صحیح ہے۔ وہ صرف اپنے علاقے کی یونین کونسل کے لئے اپنا نمائندہ چنتا ہے۔ یہ نمائندے صوبائی اور قومی اسمبلی کے ممبروں کا انتخاب کرتے ہیں۔ قومی یا صوبائی اسمبلی کا ممبر بننے کے لئے کسی یونین کونسل کا ممبر ہونا ضروری نہیں۔ کوئی بھی پاکستانی امیّدوار بن سکتا ہے۔

استھہ۔ صدر اور صوبوں کے گورنروں کا انتخاب کون کرتا ہے؟

عزیز۔ قومی اسمبلی کے ممبر صدر کا انتخاب کرتے ہیں۔ گورنروں کا انتخاب نہیں ہوتا۔ بلکہ صدر بعد میں صوبوں کے لئے گورنر مقرّر کرتا ہے۔ وہ اِن گورنروں کو اُن کے عہدوں سے ہٹا بھی سکتا ہے۔

استھہ۔ جب قومی اسمبلی موجود ہے، تو بنیادی جمہوریتیں کیا کرتی ہیں؟

عزیز۔ بنیادی جمہوریتوں کا اصل مقصد اپنے اپنے علاقوں کی ترقی اور خوشحالی کے لئے کام کرنا ہے۔ چونکہ یہ لوگ مقامی باشندے ہوتے ہیں، لہٰذا وہ اپنی ضروریات جانتے ہیں اور اُسی کے مطابق منصوبے بناتے ہیں۔ اِس علاقے کے سرکاری افسران اِن منصوبوں کو مکمل کرنے میں مدد دیتے ہیں۔ ہمارے صدر نے حال ہی میں اپنی ایک تقریر میں کہا تھا کہ "اِس نظام کا مرکز گاؤں ہے، کیونکہ ملک کی پچاسی فیصدی آبادی گاؤں میں رہتی ہے۔ اِس لئے

گاؤں کی خوشحالی ملک کی خوشحالی ہے۔" یہی وجہ ہے کہ اِس نظام کو بنیادی جمہوریت کہتے ہیں۔ کیونکہ دو چار گاؤں کے لوگ آپس میں مشورہ کرکے اپنے مسائل کو حل کرتے ہیں۔ اُنہیں چھوٹے موٹے ٹیکس وصول کرنے کا بھی اختیار دیا گیا ہے۔ دوسری طرف، قومی اسمبلی پاکستان کا مرکزی قانون ساز ادارہ ہے۔ جو ملک کی ترقی اور معاشرے کی اصلاح کی تجاویز پیش کرتا ہے اور اُن کے لئے قانون بناتا ہے۔ ملک کی صنعتی، تجارتی، معاشی اور انتظامی پالیسی تیار کرتا ہے۔ اِس کے علاوہ امن اور جنگ، غیر ممالک کے ساتھ تعلقات اور ایسے ہی دیگر اہم معاملات کے فیصلے کرتا ہے۔

استاد۔ مرکزی اور صوبائی حکومتیں کس طرح قائم ہوتی ہیں؟

عزیز۔ صدر قومی اسمبلی میں اکثریت رکھنے والی پارٹی کے ممبروں میں سے وزیروں کا انتخاب کرتا ہے جو اُس کی کابینہ کہلاتی ہے۔ اِسی طرح گورنر صوبائی اسمبلی میں اکثریت رکھنے والی پارٹی کے ممبروں میں سے وزیر چنتا ہے۔

استاد۔ کیا آپ کے ہاں سیاسی پارٹیاں بنانے کی آزادی ہے؟

عزیز۔ ہمارے آئین کے مطابق، لوگ اپنی سیاسی اور دیگر معاشرتی انجمنیں بنانے میں آزاد ہیں۔ آپ کو اخباروں سے اندازہ ہوا ہوگا کہ ہمارے ہاں کئی سیاسی پارٹیاں ہیں، جو ملکی اور غیر ملکی معاملات پر اپنا اپنا نقطۂ نظر رکھتی ہیں۔

استاد۔ کیا، صوبائی اور قومی اسمبلیوں میں مخالف پارٹیاں بھی ہوتی ہیں؟

عزیز۔ جی ہاں، جس پارٹی کے ممبر اقلیت میں ہوتے ہیں وہ مخالف پارٹی قائم کرتے ہیں۔ اور حکومت کی اُن پالیسیوں پر تنقید کرتے ہیں جنہیں وہ ملک کے لئے بُرا سمجھتے ہیں۔

استاد۔ کیا انتخابات میں عورتیں بھی ووٹ دے سکتی ہیں؟

عزیز۔ جی ہاں ، ہمارے ہاں ہر اُس فرد کو دوٹ دینے کا حق حاصل ہے جس کی عمر اکیس سال یا اِس سے زیادہ ہے ۔ چنانچہ عورتوں کو وہی حقوق حاصل ہیں ، جو مردوں کے ہیں ۔ وہ سرکاری ملازمت بھی کر سکتی ہیں ۔

اسمتھ۔ کیا ججوں ، پولیس کے افسروں اور دیگر اعلیٰ سرکاری عہدیداروں کا بھی انتخاب ہوتا ہے ؟

عزیز۔ جی نہیں ، ہمارے ملک میں سرکاری عہدوں پر کام کرنے والوں کا انتخاب نہیں ہوتا۔ بلکہ اعلیٰ سرکاری ملازمین کے لئے سِول سروس کے باقاعدہ امتحانات ہوتے ہیں اور اِن امتحانات میں کامیاب ہونے والوں کو تربیت دی جاتی ہے تاکہ وہ عدالت کے جج ، پولیس کے افسر یا ضلع کے حاکم کی حیثیت سے اپنے فرائض اچھی طرح ادا کر سکیں ۔

اسمتھ۔ بھئی ، مجھے پیاس لگ رہی ہے ۔ ذرا پانی منگوا دیں!

عزیز۔ جی ہاں ، ضرور! ... یہ لیجئے ، چائے بھی آ رہی ہے ۔

20.203. Reading Drill II: Sentences.

Read the following sentences aloud and translate them into English.

۱۔ جب ہمارا ملک وجود میں آیا ، تو ہم نے صدارتی طرز حکومت اختیار کیا ۔ ہمارا خیال تھا کہ یہ نظام ہمارے عوام کے لئے مفید ہو گا۔

۲۔ میں سیاست بالکل نہیں سمجھتا ۔ جب کوئی انتخاب ہوتا ہے تو میں آنکھ بند کرکے دوٹ دے دیتا ہوں۔

۳۔ ہمارے ملک کا انتظام چار منزلوں میں تقسیم کیا گیا ہے ۔ بنیادی منزل تحصیل ہے ۔ دوسری ضلع ، تیسری ڈویژن اور چوتھی منزل صوبہ ہے ۔ ہر منزل کو مختلف اختیارات حاصل ہیں ۔

۴۔ میرے خیال میں پرانی انتظامی پالیسی اچھی تھی ۔ حکومت کے لئے نئی پالیسی پر عمل کرنا مشکل ہو گا۔

۵۔ تحصیل کونسل کے آدھے ممبر منتخب کئے جاتے ہیں اور باقی پچاس فیصدی ممبر حکومت کے مقرّرکردہ ہوتے

271

ہیں۔ یہ مقررکردہ ارکان ووٹ نہیں دے سکتے ۔ مگر وہ کونسل کے تمام کاموں میں مشورہ اور مدد دیتے ہیں۔

۶۔ ہمارے ملک میں اکثریت غیر مسلمانوں کی ہے ۔ مسلمان وہاں بہت ہی کم ہیں۔ پھر بھی ہماری قومی اسمبلی میں اُن کے ایک دو نمائندے موجود ہیں ۔

۷۔ اِن ممالک کے ساتھ ہمارے تعلّقات بہت اچّھے ہیں۔ تقریباً سات سال سے ہماری اور اُن کی پالیسیوں میں کوئی اختلاف نہیں ہوا۔

۸۔ ہماری انجمن کے چیئرمین نے جو تجویز پیش کی تھی اُسے ممبروں نے پسند نہیں کیا۔

۹۔ کیا کوئی غیر مسلمان انتخاب میں امیدوار بن سکتا ہے ؟ جی ہاں ،کسی بھی فرقے کا فرد انتخاب لڑ سکتا ہے۔ وہ سرکاری ملازمت بھی حاصل کر سکتا ہے ۔ مذہب کی بنیاد پر ملک کے باشندوں میں کوئی تمیز نہیں کی جاتی۔

۱۰۔ کیا یونین کونسل کے ممبروں کی اکثریت اپنے چیئرمین کو ہٹا سکتی ہے ؟ جی ہاں ، اگر وہ اچّھا آدمی نہیں تو وہ اُسے اُس کے عہدے سے ہٹا سکتے ہیں ۔

۱۱۔ حکومت نے اِس سال کئی معاشرتی منصوبے شروع کئے ہیں ۔تاکہ عوام کی ضروریات کو پورا کیا جا سکے۔

۱۲۔ گورنر صاحب نے اپنی ایک تقریر میں فرمایا کہ پاکستان میں قالینوں کا مرکز لاہور ہے ۔ اُنہوں نے یہ بھی کہا کہ صوبائی حکومت اپنی نئی صنعتی پالیسی کے تحت قالین بنانے والوں کو ہر طرح کی مدد دے گی۔

۱۳۔ جب ٹیکس کی تمام رقم وصول نہ ہوئی تو پولیس نے اُسے گرفتار کر لیا۔

۱۴۔ اِس ادارے کے آئین میں اصلاح کی ضرورت ہے ۔

۱۵۔ دونوں فرقے کے لوگوں نے آپس میں بات چیت کرکے اپنا جھگڑا طے کر لیا۔

20. 204. Reading Drill III: Unseen Text.

جب تین سال کی جنگ کے بعد بھی ہم دشمنوں کو اپنے ملک سے نہ نکال سکے تو ہمارے صدر نے اپنی کابینہ کے تمام وزرا ٕ کو بلایا اور اُن کے سامنے تقریر کرتے ہوئے کہا کہ " جیسا کہ آپ لوگ جانتے ہیں

کہ ہم لوگ اس وقت بہت کمزور ہیں اور ہماری فوج دشمنوں کو ملک سے نہیں نکال سکتی۔بعض پڑوسی ممالک جو ہمارے دوست ہیں اس سلسلے میں ہماری مدد کرنے کے لئے تیار ہیں ۔ میرے خیال میں ہمیں اُن کی مدد لینے سے انکار نہیں کرنا چاہئے کیونکہ اس میں کوئی نقصان نہیں ہے بلکہ اس میں ہمارا ہی فائدہ ہے ۔ میں نے اسی خیال سے آپ لوگوں کو جمع کیا ہے تاکہ آپ اس اہم سوال پر اپنی رائے دیں ۔"

صدر کی یہ تجویز سن کر ایک وزیر نے کہا کہ ہمارے صدر مملکت نے جو کچھ کہا ہے وہ بنیادی طور پر ٹھیک ہے مگر ہمیں اِن ممالک کی امداد کے بعض پہلوؤں پر ضرور غور کر لینا چاہئے ۔ مثلاً یہ ممالک ہمارے دوست ضرور ہیں مگر ہماری خاطر اس لڑائی میں کیوں شریک ہوں گے کیونکہ دوسرے ملک کے لئے لڑنا کوئی آسان کام نہیں ہے ۔ اس جنگ میں اُن کے بہت سے آدمی مارے جائیں گے۔ممکن ہے کہ اُن کے بعض شہر بھی تباہ ہو جائیں اور پھر یہ کہ اُنہیں اس لڑائی پر کافی رقم بھی خرچ کرنی پڑے گی۔میرے خیال میں وہ ہماری مدد کرنے کے لئے ایسی شرائط ضرور لگائیں گے جو شاید ہم قبول نہ کر سکیں۔ کیا آپ کو اندازہ ہے کہ ہمیں اُن کی اس امداد کی کیا قیمت دینی ہو گی ؟

صدر نے اس کے جواب میں وزرا کو بتایا کہ میں نے ان دوست ممالک کے اعلیٰ حکمرانوں سے خود بات چیت کی ہے۔اُنہوں نے مجھے اطمینان دلایا ہے کہ وہ اس امداد کے ساتھ کوئی شرط نہیں لگا رہے ہیں ۔ وہ کہتے ہیں کہ آپ کے ملک سے ہمارے تعلقات کئی صدیوں سے قائم ہیں ۔ اور آج بھی آپ کے ملک کے ساتھ ہمارے سیاسی، معاشی، تجارتی اور صنعتی تعلقات بہت گہرے ہیں ۔ ایسی صورت میں اگر آپ کا ملک لڑائی میں ہار گیا تو ہمارے ملکوں کی معاشی ، تجارتی اور صنعتی ترقی کو بہت نقصان پہنچے گا۔ ان حالات میں ہمارا یہ فرض ہے کہ ہم آپ کی مدد کریں تاکہ آپ کے ملک میں امن قائم ہو۔کیونکہ یہ ہمارے اور آپ کے عوام کی خوشحالی کے لئے ضروری ہے۔ان حکمرانوں نے کہا کہ پریشانی کے وقت دوست کی مدد کرنا ہمارا اخلاقی فرض

273

هے ۔اُنہوں نے کہا کہ اگرچہ ہم نے ہمیشہ امن کی پالیسی اختیار کی ہے گرراب حالات اِتنے خراب ہو گئے

ہیں کہ اگر ہم نے مل کر جنگ نہ کی تو ہمارے ملک تباہ ہو جائیں گے ۔

صدر کا یہ جواب سن کر ایک دوسرے وزیر نے کہا کہ اِن باتوں سے تو یہی معلوم ہوتا ہے کہ ہمارے

اِن دوست ممالک کے اِرادے نیک ہیں پھر بھی یہ ایسا معاملہ نہیں کہ اِس کا فیصلہ ہم خود ہی کر لیں۔

میرے خیال میں اِس پر قومی اسمبلی کا اِتّفاق ضروری ہے ۔

صدر نے کہا، مجھے آپ کی رائے سے اِتّفاق ہے ۔ میں کل ہی یہ مسئلہ قومی اسمبلی میں پیش کر دوں گا ۔ اگر

اکثریت نے اِسے مان لیا تو اِمداد قبول کر لی جائے گی ۔ ورنہ پھر جیسا اسمبلی چاہے گی ویسا ہی کروں گا۔

20. 205.   Writing Drill I: Text.

Counting each speaker's part as one paragraph, write out the first ten paragraphs of Sec. 20. 506 (Conversation Practice) in Urdu script (i. e. down through /hwkumət ne yn kəwnsəlõ ko kwch Təyks bhi ləgane ka yxtiar dia həy. /).

20. 206.   Spelling Review and Dictionary Drill.

Write out the following words in Urdu script and place them in Urdu alphabetical order.

(1) ynjil	(11) ysm
(2) ybadət	(12) ystemal
(3) isa	(13) yslah
(4) ystri	(14) ydara
(5) yqrar	(15) yrada
(6) ỹc	(16) yšara
(7) ylm	(17) yhtiat
(8) ylaj	(18) ytminan
(9) ymarət	(19) yzzət
(10) ytvar	(20) yraq

20. 207.   Response Drill.

Answer the following questions in writing:

274

۱۔ آپ نے پچھلے انتخاب میں ووٹ دیا تھا یا نہیں ؟

۲۔ کیا، آپ کے ہاں وزیرِ اعظم کا عہدہ ہے ؟

۳۔ آپ نے کسی سرکاری ادارے میں ملازمت کی ہے یا نہیں ؟

۴۔ کیا آپ یہ سمجھتے ہیں کہ آپ کے ملک میں بھی بنیادی جمہوریت کا نظام عوام کے لئے مفید ثابت ہو سکتا ہے ؟

۵۔ کیا، آپ سیاسی موضوع پر تقریر کر سکتے ہیں ؟

۶۔ کیا آپ کے ہاں مقامی باشندوں اور غیر ملکیوں کو برابر کے حقوق حاصل ہیں ؟

۷۔ کیا آپ کے ملک کی سول سروس میں ملازمت کے لئے امتحانات ہوتے ہیں ؟

۸۔ کیا آپ تجارتی، صنعتی اور دیگر معاشی معاملات میں دلچسپی لیتے ہیں ؟

۹۔ آپ کن کن یونیورسٹیوں میں طالبِ علم رہ چکے ہیں ؟

۱۰۔ کیا آپ کے ملک میں ججوں، پولیس کے افسروں اور دیگر عہدیداروں کا انتخاب ہوتا ہے ؟

20. 208. English to Urdu Sentences.

1. In the National Assembly the minority party criticised the policies of the President.

2. For the highest government posts there are regular Civil Service examinations.

3. Our Union Council is preparing a new project in this connection which will be presented before the District Council [lit. Council of the District] on [lit. to] Thursday.

4. Reform of this policy is necessary, because much harm is being done to the nation because of it [lit. from it to the nation much loss is arriving].

5. It has been stated in an announcement of the Government that this year only two weeks of leave will be given to government officials and employees.

6. Mr. əziz has been successful in the Union Council election. Now he will contest [/ləRna/] the provincial election next year.

7. Such a [ytni] large amount of tax cannot be realised from this division because people here [lit. here's people] are very poor.

8. Our form of government is not presidential but parliamentary. In our country [lit. our place] the Prime Minister is chosen from the majority party.

9. Today the representatives of the minority party are meeting with the President of the State. They will present their point of view upon the new commercial policy before the President.

10. When the officers of the department became sure [lit. when to the officers of the department this became certain], that he was the one who had committed the theft [lit. that he-emphatic did this theft], then they removed him from [his] employment.

11. Before this new system, our common people could not take any part in the tasks of the Government.

12. When our country came into existence, then our army numbered [lit. our army's number was] only ten thousand, but inside of seventeen years this number has become eighty thousand.

13. Friend, such matters become solved of themselves. There is no necessity of consulting [our] father in this connection.

14. Nowadays the National Assembly is investigating the details of this project.

15. I have heard that in some countries women do not have the right to vote.

20.300. ANALYSIS

20.301. Substantive Composition: the Prefix /ba/.

The Persian preposition /ba/ "with" occurs as the first member of a great many loan compounds. Although /ba/ is a separate word in Persian, it never occurs alone in Urdu and may thus be considered a sort of prefix for all practical purposes. /ba/ occurs with nouns, the resulting construction then being an adjective, predicate adjective, or adverb. Many of these may again become nouns through the addition of the noun formant suffix /i/ (or /gi/). See also Sec. 18.304. E.g.

/baqayda/ A1 regular, orderly, according to rule. [/qayda/ M2 "rule, regulation." Compare:]

/baqaydəgi/ F2 regularity, orderliness, conformity to rule.

/bavəfa/ A1 faithful, loyal. [/vəfa/ F1 "faithfulness, fidelity, fulfilment (of a promise)". Cf.]

/bavəfai/ F2 [np] faithfulness, sincerity

/bavwzu/ PA1 ceremonially clean; in a state of having performed one's ablutions for prayer. [/vwzu/ M1 "ablutions for prayer"]

/bayxtiar/ A1 authorised, having power. [/yxtiar/ M1 "choice, power, authority"]

/baxəbər/ A1 well informed, aware. [/xəbər/ F1 "news"]

/bayzzət/ A1 honourable, respectable. [/yzzət/ F1 "respect, dignity"]

20.302. Substantive Composition: /γəyr/ "Other."

/γəyr/ "other" may occur alone as M1 or A1 denoting "stranger, outsider, foreigner" or "strange, different, other." It also occurs as the first element of a great compounds with the meaning "un-, non-." For a similar case, cf. /bəd/ A1 and prefix meaning "bad-" (Sec. 9.302). See also Sec. 18.305.

Examples of /γəyr/ as M1 or A1:

/ws ne mwjhe γəyr səməjh kər əpne ghər se nykal dia./ He thought me to be a stranger and turned me out of his house.

/axyrkar əTThara səw səttavən mẽ həmara mwlk γəyrõ ke hath mẽ cəla gəya./ At last in 1857 our country passed into the hands of strangers.

/mə̃y ap ka bhai hū̃ -- koi γəyr nəhī̃ hū̃!/ I'm your brother -- not some stranger!/

Literally hundreds of compounds with /γəyr/ are possible, especially constructions with the adjective formant suffix /i/ (e.g. like /γəyrmwlki/ A1 "foreign"). Some examples are:

/vw ləRki γəyrmamuli təwr pər xubsurət həy./ That girl is unusually beautiful. [/mamuli/ A1 "ordinary, common": /γəyrmamuli/ A1 "uncommon"]

/ek γəyrsərkari yttyla ke mwtabyq, bənd TuTne se cəwrasi admi mər gəe./ According to unofficial information [lit. an unofficial information], eighty four people died from the breaking of the dike. [/sərkari/ A1 "governmental, official": /γəyrsərkari/ A1 "unofficial"]

/pakystan ne γəyrmwlki ymdad qwbul kərne se ynkar kər dia./ Pakistan
refused to accept foreign aid. [/mwlki/ Al "national, country":
/γəyrmwlki/ Al "foreign"]

/həmare ain ke mwtabyq, pakystan ke mwsəlman əwr γəyrmwsəlman
bašynde bərabər ke hwquq rəkhte hǝy./ According to our constitution,
Pakistan's Muslim and non-Muslim citizens have equal rights.
[/mwsəlman/ Ml Al "Muslim": /γəyrmwsəlman/ Ml Al "non-
Muslim"]

/ap ne əysa kər ke, γəyrzymmedari ka swbut dia./ [By] doing thus, you
have given proof of [your] irresponsibility. [/zymmedari/ F2
"responsibility"; /γəyrzymmedari/ F2 "lack of responsibility"]

/γəyrmwmalyk ke nwmaynde bhi ys mē šərik the./ Representatives of
foreign countries also took part in this. [/mwmalyk/ Mpl "countries,
nations"; /γəyrmwmalyk/ Mpl "foreign countries." The singular
form also occurs but is less common:]

/ys jhəgRe mē kysi γəyrmwlk ka hath həy./ There is the hand of some
foreign country in this dispute. [/mwlk/ Ml "country": /γəyrmwlk/
Ml "foreign country". "Foreign country," however, is not commonly
expressed by /γəyrmwlk/; instead some other expression would be
used.]

20.303. Adverbs as Noun Modifiers.

One method of employing an adverb before a noun as a modifier was discussed above in
Unit XIV. This was done by adding the suffix /val/ (+ the Type II ending) to the adverb and
using the resulting construction as an adjective: e.g.

/vw upərvale kəmre mē rəhta həy./ He lives in the room above. [Lit.
the above-one room.]

Another method, introduced in this Unit, is to follow the adverb with the postposition
/ka/ "of, 's" and thus "possess" the following noun. E.g.

/vw upər ke kəmre mē rəhta həy./ He lives in the room above. [Lit.
above's room. This is semantically identical to the example just
given above.]

/əndər ki kwrsiā ys vəqt nəhĩ cahiē./ The chairs inside [lit. inside's
chairs] are not needed now. [/əndərvali kwrsiā/ would also be
possible.]

/bahər ke log əndər a jaē!/ All the people outside come in! [/bahərvale
log/ is also possible, though redundant, since / -vale/ itself means
/log/ "people."]

/vw bərabər ke kəmre mē sota həy./ He sleeps in the adjoining room.
[/bərabərvale kəmre/ is also possible.]

As is clear from the foregoing examples, whenever reference to a <u>physical</u> <u>location</u> is
made, both of these constructions are semantically identical: i.e. one may say /upər ka
kəmra/ or /upərvala kəmra/ with no distinction in meaning. Whenever the relationship is
<u>non-physical</u>, however, only the possessive construction seems to be idiomatic, according
to the author's informants. E.g.

/səb ko bərabər ke hwquq hasyl həy./ Everyone has equal rights. [Lit.
equal's rights. Here */bərabərvale hwquq/ is just not idiomatic.]

/ap pər bhi bərabər ki zymmedari həy./ You too have an equal responsibility. [Never */bərabərvali zymmedari/.]

/yy mere bad ki bat həy./ This is something that happened after my
departure. [Lit. This is my after's matter. Never */badvali bat/.]

/ys ke bad ke halat ke bare mē kwch pəta nəhī./ [I] don't know about conditions after this. [Lit. this's after's conditions. Never */badvale halat/.]

There are cases of semantic overlapping, however: e.g.

/bahər ke ləRkō ko kəmre se nykal do!/ Turn those boys [who are] outsiders out of the room! [I.e. those boys who are not members of our organisation. Although the relationship is not purely one of physical location, /bahərvale ləRkō/ is possible here. Compare, however:]

/ys davət mē, bahər ke mwlkō ke bhi kwch nwmaynde šamyl the./ Some representatives of foreign [lit. outside's] countries were also included in this party. [Here /bahərvale mwlkō/ was felt to be unidiomatic.]

Whenever an adjective may be formed from the adverbial root by the addition of the suffix /l/ + the Type II affixes (Sec. 19.303), this will be preferred to the /val/ form (though not necessarily to the possessive formation with /ka/). E.g.

/vw ys məkan ke nycle hysse mē rəhta həy./ He lives in the lower part of this house. [/nycla/ A2 "lower, nether." /nice ke hysse/ would also be idiomatic, but /nicevale hysse/ was felt to be less correct.]

/ys ymarət ka pychla hyssa xali həy./ The back portion of this building is vacant. [/pychla/ A2 "back, behind, rear." /piche ka hyssa/ is possible, but /pichevala hyssa/ would be less idiomatic.]

/səylab se məkan ke əgle hysse ko nwqsan pəhw̃ca./ The front portion of the house was damaged by the flood. [/əgla/ A2 "front, fore, ahead." Again /age ke hysse/ is possible; /agevale hysse/ is less idiomatic.]

When no adjective form is possible, then the /val/ form is considered idiomatic. E.g.

/ws ne samnevali dwkan xərid li həy./ He has bought the shop in front. [Or: /samne ki dwkan/; */samənli/ does not occur.]

20.400. SUPPLEMENTARY VOCABULARY

20.401. Supplementary Vocabulary.

The following numerals are all Type I adjectives. See Sec. 2.401.

ykasi [or /ykkyasi/]	eighty-one
beasi [or /bəyasi/]	eighty-two
tyrasi	eighty-three
cəwrasi	eighty-four

Other items are:

*əfrad Mpl	persons, individuals [pl. /fərd/]
əksəriəti Al	majority [adj.]
həTna [IIc: /ə/]	to move away, withdraw, get out of the way
mwlazym Ml	employee, worker
*mwmalyk Mpl	countries [pl. /mwlk/]
nwmayndəgi F2	representation
təjviz Fl	plan, scheme, suggestion, proposal
*twləba [or /tələba/] Mpl	students [msc.]

20.402. Supplementary Exercise I: Substitution.

1. ys mwlk ki abadi syrf <u>pycasi</u> həzar həy.

       eighty-four
       eighty-one
       eighty-two
       seventy-six
       eighty-three

2. ys məhkme ke <u>pycasi</u> mwlazymin əpne whdõ se həTa die gəe hãy.

       seventy-nine
       eighty-one
       sixty-two
       fifty-six
       eighty-three

20.403. Supplementary Exercise II: Fill the Blanks.

1. Fill the blanks in the following sentences with the most appropriate word from those given in Sec. 20.401.

 a. _____ ko qəwmi kamõ mẽ dylcəspi leni cahie.
 b. dərvaze ke samne se _____ jao!
 c. vw ajkəl məɣrybi _____ ki səyr kər rəha həy.
 d. baz mwmalyk mẽ əwrtõ ko _____ hasyl nəhĩ.

280

e. vw kəl se məhkmae zəraət mē ____ ho gəya həy.

f. yunyvərsyTi ke ____ ek jwlus ki šəkl mē qəwmi əsəmbli jaēge, əwr vəhā
ərkane əsəmbli ke samne əpni šykayətē peš kərēge.

g. ys sylsyle mē ap bhi əpni ____peš kərē!

h. kəmre mē bəhwt se ____ bəyThe hēy.

i. yy jhəgRa ____ fyrqe ke logō ne kəraya həy.

j. baz log əyse bhi hēy, jo kəhte hēy, ky əwrtõ ko hwkumət mē ____ nəhī̃ deni
cahie.

20.500. VOCABULARY AND GRAMMAR DRILL

20.501. Substitution.

1. kya, ap ko   <u>syasiat</u>   ati həy?
                  Urdu
                  history
                  agriculture
                  Arabic
                  our language

2. həm <u>ys qanun</u>   pər əməl nəhĩ kər səkte.
         this policy
         this advice
         this plan
         this principle
         these teachings

3. <u>həmari kəwnsəl</u>   <u>yy nəi tyjarti palisi</u>   əpnaegi.
    our government   a new political policy
    our cabinet   a democratic constitution
    the central government   a new industrial policy
    our university   a new system of education
    our nation   the Western way of life

4. aj əvam ne   <u>sədr</u>   ka yntyxab kia.
                  the prime minister
                  their representatives
                  the governor
                  some important officers
                  their supreme ruler

5. <u>həmare sube</u>   se pãc <u>əfrad</u>   mwntəxəb kie gəe hãy.
    their division   persons
    this district   representatives
    our təhsil   Christians
    my institute   members
    these regions   new chairmen

6. <u>həmara məzhəb</u>   <u>bəhəttər fyrqõ</u>   mẽ təqsim həy.
    this province   thirteen districts
    this project   six portions
    my district   four təhsils
    India   seventeen provinces
    this land   five pieces

7. <u>həmari parTi</u>   mẽ se, sədr <u>ek mymbər</u>   mwntəxəb kərẽge.
    the National Assembly   prime minister

282

minority
non-Muslims
minority party
army

some representatives
a minister
chairman
some officers

8. sədr ne vəzire azəm ko whde se həTa dia.
   Governor   judge
   Union Council   chairman
   ruler of the district some officers
   president   those ministers
   government   nəmbərdar

9. baz mwqami bašyndõ ne   ys palisi   pər tənqid ki.
                           administrative policy
                           Məwlvi Sahəb's speech
                           this economic project
                           the presidential system of
                           government
                           these suggestions

10. yəyrmwmalyk   bhi ys mənsube mẽ hyssa le səkte hə̃y.
    the chairman of the
    Union Council
    local residents
    appointed members
    government employees
    high officers

11. meri rae mẽ, ys təra həm   əcche təəllwqat   qaym kər səkte hə̃y.
                                peace
                                a new institute
                                the parliamentary form of
                                government
                                a new society
                                a new system

12. kya, yntyxabat mẽ   əqliəti fyrqe ke log   bhi voT de səkte hə̃y?
                        government officials
                        foreign people
                        students
                        members of the cabinet
                        appointed representatives

13. həmare hwkmran ne ys   ke bare mẽ vwzəra   se məšvəra kia.
    president   war   National
                                           Assembly
    chairman   our   Central
                     necessities   Government
    ministers   constitution   religious
                                           scholars
    governor   this policy   non-Muslims

283

	teacher	examinations	students

14. həmare twləba   ko baqayda tərbiət di jati həy.

officers of the army
members of the Union Council
government office-holders
employees
nurses

15. məhkməe talim məwjuda nyzame talim pər ɣəwr kərega.

Department of agriculture	these questions
our institution	those conditions
our department	these matters
law-making body	these laws
governor	this industrial policy

20.502. Transformation.

1. Change the underlined verb forms in the following sentences to the simple past tense. Make all other necessary changes.

 a. həmari hwkumət ek nəi palisi yxtiar <u>kəregi</u>.

 b. yunyən kəwnsəl ka nwmaynda zyle ki kəwnsəl ke samne həmari yy təjviz peš <u>kərega</u>.

 c. həmari fəwj bəhadri se kam <u>legi,</u> əwr əpni jəga se nəhī <u>həTegi</u>.

 d. polis wn do əfrad ko thane <u>le jaegi</u>.

 e. ap ki košyšõ se, yy sari rəqəm vwsul <u>ho jaegi</u>.

 f. jõg ke bad, yy mwlk tin hyssõ mẽ təqsim <u>kər dia jaega</u>.

 g. sədr əwr wn ke vwzəra syasi mwamlat ke bare mẽ məšvəra <u>kərēge</u>.

 h. yy məšin xwdbəxwd cəl <u>pəRegi</u>.

 i. syrf sərkari mədəd ke zərie hi se, yy palisi əməl mẽ lai <u>ja səkegi</u>.

 j. əvam sədr ka yntyxab <u>kərte hə̄y</u>.

 k. mərkəzi hwkumət yunyən kəwnsəlõ ke cerməynõ ko tərbiət deni šwru <u>kəregi</u>.

 l. həmara zyla hwkumət ke yn mwqərrərkərda əfsəran ke təjrybe əwr xydmat se bəhwt fayda <u>wThaega</u>.

 m. ys məhine mẽ həmari sənəti palisi təbdil <u>ho jaegi</u>. lyhaza həmẽ bəhwt sa mal ɣəyrmwmalyk se fəwrən <u>mãgva lena cahie</u>.

 n. qəwmi əsəmbli mwašre ki yslah ke lie nəe qəvanin <u>bənaegi</u>.

 o. ys mənsube pər bəhwt xərc <u>hoga</u>.

2. Change the underlined verb forms in the following sentences to the <PasP + /kərna/> (i.e. "habitual action") formation. See Sec. 14.306.

 a. mərkəzi hwkumət həmẽ mədəd <u>degi</u>.

 b. wn ki fəwj həmeša əysi hərəkat <u>kərti həy</u>.

 c. bwzwrgõ ke təjrybe se fayda <u>wThaie!</u>

 d. vw əpni əwlad ki syhət əwr xwšhali ke lie doaẽ <u>kərti həy</u>.

e. mwjhe ytminan həy, ky ap vəqt pər Təyks əda kərēge.

f. həmari yunyən kəwnsəl hwkumət ko mənsube peš kərti həy.

g. vw fyrqa həmare əqayd se yxtylaf kərta həy.

h. kam kərte vəqt, vw həmeša gati həy.

i. mere taya mwjhe bəhwt marte the.

j. yy talybylm syasiat mē həmeša əcche nəmbər hasyl kərta həy. [1]

  [1]/nəmbər hasyl kərna/ means "to get (good) marks."

3. Change the underlined verb forms in the following sentences to the <PreP + /rəhna/ (i.e. the "iterative" or "repeated action") formation. See Sec. 14.305.

a. həmare cermoyn hər məhine ek nəi təjviz peš kərte the.

b. ws mwlk mē hər roz nəi hwkumtē bənti həy.

c. əgər həmare hwkmran hər roz əpni palisi bədlē, to mwlk tərəqqi nəhī kər səkta.

d. šadi ke məwqe pər, ləRkiā dyn rat nacti həy.

e. kəhā tək səbr kərū!

f. sərdi ke məwsəm mē bhi, yy dərya ysi təra bəhta həy.

g. vw donō mwlk apəs mē həmeša jōg kərte həy.

h. yy məšin xwdbəxwd cəlti həy.

i. həmare sədr əyse əhəm mwamlat mē kabina se məšvəra kərte hōy.

20.503. Fill in the Blanks.

1. Fill the blanks with the proper Type II adjective suffix to make the adjective agree with the noun it modifies.

a. mwjhe ys xət k__ nəql cahie.

b. həmare gaō k__ jwnub mē, ek əwr choTa sa gaō həy.

c. yy jəhaz bəhwt hi pwran__ həy.

d. əgle sal, māy sərsō k__ fəsl ləgaūga.

e. masTər sahəb ne ws talybylm k__ kan pəkəRte hwe kəha, ky "twm əys__ šərarət kəbhi nə kəro!"

f. ap k__ lyfafe pər pur__ TykəT nəhī.

g. māy ap k__ nap lūga.

h. əys__ hədisō se, həmē həzrət mwhəmməd səlləllaho ələyhe və səlləm k__ talimat ke bare mē malumat hasyl hoti həy.

i. həm log ap k__ nykah mē šərik nəhī the.

j. yy ys məwzu k__ ek əjib pəhlu həy.

k. māy bazar se ap k__ səwda xərid laya hū.

l. yy ek bəhwt əcch__ təjviz həy.

m. ys vəqt həmar__ thane mē koi əfsər məwjud nəhī.

n. māy ek əys__ ənjwmən qaym kərūga, jo ky ylm k__ xydmat kər səke.

o. əys__ nyzam həmar__ əvam ke lie mwfid nəhī.

p. pychl__ jōg ke bad, hyndostan əwr pakystan ko azadi myli thi.

q. ys janvər k__ šəkl ws janvər se mwxtəlyf həy.

285

r. yy bəhwt əcch__ sabwn həy.

s. yy mer__ səməjh mē nəhī́ ata.

t. hwkumət k__ mədəd kərna ap k__ fərz həy.

2. Fill the blanks with the proper verbal affixes to make the verb agree with its subject. In some cases Type II adjective suffixes must also be supplied.

a. mwjhe wmmid th__, ky ws ka peT Thik ho jaega.

b. yy pələ̄g TuT__ hw__ həy.

c. mera xyal həy, ky kəbab təyyar ho gə__ hə̄y.

d. swba səb logō ne naš̌ta k__.

e. kya, ap ko sina ata həy? yy jeb kwch phəT__ hw__ həy.

f. mə̄y ne ate hwe səb Dak dekh__ th__, məgər ap k__ koi xət nəhī́ th__.

g. həmari polis ne təmam ylaqō mē əmn qaym kər d__ həy.

h. wnhō ne ys sylsyle mē ek mysal d__.

i. kəl mwjhe pecyš̌ th__. ys lie mə̄y dəftər nə a səka.

j. ws vəqt mere pas rezgari nəhī́ th__.

k. səudi ərəb ki xwš̌hali ke lie, tel bəhwt əhmiət rəkht__ həy.

l. həmare nwmaynde ne swbai əsəmbli ke samne mənsuba peš̌ k__.

m. əgər həm əysa kərē̌, to həmar__ təmam məaš̌i məsayl həl ho jaə̄g__.

n. aj həmare nəwkər ne ek nə__ jhaRu xərid__.

o. ws zəmane mē, həmare mwaš̌re k__ bənavəT kwch mwxtəlyf th__.

p. vəzire azəm ne sədr se mer__ təarwf kəra__.

q. dwlhən ne š̌əlvar pəhn__.

r. zyle ki kəwnsəlō ke cerməynō ko baz əhmiət yxtiarat d__ gə__ hə̄y.

s. mə̄y ne pakystan ke tərze hwkumət ke bare mē kwch malumat hasyl k__.

t. həmare sədr ne hyndostan ke nwmayndō k__ ystyqbal k__.

20.504. Variation Drill.

1. həm ys nəi palisi pər əməl kərē̌ge.

yunyən kəwnsəl ke ərkan meri təjviz pər əməl kərē̌ge.

Dyviž̌ən ke hakym ys nəi palisi pər əməl nəhī́ kərna cahte.

nəe hwkmranō ne bhi pwrani yntyzami palisi pər əməl kia.

ap ne mere məš̌vəre pər əməl nəhī́ kia, vərna əysa nə hota.

həmari hwkumət jəldi hi yy nəi palisi əməl mē laegi.

2. sədre mwmlykət ne məaš̌i mwamlat ke mwtəəllyq qəwmi əsəmbli se məš̌vəra kia.

hwkmrane ala ne nyzame talim ke bare mē həm logō se məš̌vəra kia.

əwrtō ki kəwnsəl ki cerməyn ne əwrtō ke hwquq ke mwtəəllyq əsəmbli ke mymbərō
se məš̌vəra kia.

vəzire azəm əmn əwr jə̄g ke bare mē qəwmi əsəmbli se məš̌vəra kərte hə̄y.

mə̄y əpne mamū se əpni š̌adi ke bare mē məš̌vəra kərna cahta hū.

kabina ko ys qanun ke bare mē qanunsazō se məš̌vəra kərna pəRa.

3. pakystani əvam ne aj sədre mwmlykət ka yntyxab kia.

hər sal yunyən kəwnsəl ke ərkan ka yntyxab hota həy.

286

əksəriəti parTi ne əpna cerməyn mwntəxəb kia.

yunyən kəwnsəl ne əziz sahəb ko əpna sədr mwntəxəb kia.

əqliəti fyrqe ke dəs nwmaynde mwntəxəb hwe hə̃y.

aj ke yntyxabat mẽ, həmare do wmmidvar kamyab rəhe hə̃y.

4. sədre mwmlykət ne əpni təqrir mẽ kəha, ky "mwlk ka mərkəz gaõ həy."

həmare nwmaynde ne əpni təqrir mẽ kəha, ky "parlimani tərze hwkumət həmare
əvam ke lie mwfid nəhĩ."

vəzire zəraət ne hal hi mẽ əpni ek təqrir mẽ bətaya, ky "khad ki kəmi ki vəja se ys
sal fəsl əcchi nəhĩ hogi."

vəzire azəm ne təqrir kərte hwe kəha, ky "gaõ ki xwšhali mwlk ki xwšhali həy."

vəzire talim əpni kəi təqrirõ mẽ kəh cwke hə̃y, ky "nyzame talim ki yslah kərni
cahie."

vəzire ala ki təqrir se zahyr hota həy, ky γəyrmwmalyk ke sath həmare təəllwqat
byhtər hote ja rəhe hə̃y.

5. mə̃y əpni jəga se kəbhi nəhĩ həTũga.

vw admi xwdbəxwd vəhã se həT jaega.

həmari fəwj ko ws pəhaR se həTna pəRa.

sədr ne aj vəzire azəm ko ws ke whde se həTa dia həy.

polis ne badšah ke məhl ke samne se logõ ko həTa dia.

ys əlmari ko yəhã se həTa dẽ!

6. vw gaRi xwdbəxwd cəl pəRi.

həvai jəhaz əpne ap cəl pəRa.

səylab ka pani xwdbəxwd ghəT gəya.

əysi bwraiã xwdbəxwd xətm ho jati hə̃y.

əgər ap səbr kərẽ, to əyse məsayl xwdbəxwd həl ho jaẽge.

vw xwdbəxwd ys ydare ka sədr bən bəyTha həy.

7. ys sal Təyks ki kwl rəqəm vwsul nəhĩ ho səkti.

ap ke məni arDərõ ki rəsidẽ vwsul paĩ.

ys sal yunyən kəwnsəl ne Təyks ki sari rəqəm vwsul kər li.

nəmbərdar sahəb ne yn məkanõ ka kyraya vwsul kər lia.

hər ghər se cəwrasi rupəe ka Təyks vwsul kərna həy.

aj Dak se do xət məwsul hwe.

8. əndər ke logõ ko bahər bwlaie!

piche ki kwrsiã həTa do!

age ke dərəxtõ ko kaT dena cahie.

nice ke sare kəpRe nykal kər swkhane cahiẽ.

hər fərd ko bərabər ke hwquq hasyl hə̃y.

vw əbhi samne ke məkanõ ko toR Dalẽge.

9. mə̃y ne sari myThaiã bəccõ mẽ təqsim kər dĩ.

yy məsla həmari parTi ko choTe choTe TwkRõ mẽ təqsim kər dega.

ə̃grezõ ne hyndostan ko do TwkRõ mẽ təqsim kər dia.

ws ki sari zəmin ws ki əwlad mẽ təqsim kər di gəi.

dusri jə̃g ke bad, vw mwlk kəi hyssõ mẽ təqsim kər dia gəya.

10. jəb həmara mwlk vwjud mẽ aya, to həmare pas kwch nəhĩ tha.

jəb bwnyadi jwmhuriətõ ka nyzam vwjud mẽ aya, to həmare əvam hwkumət ke kamõ mẽ hyssa lene ləge.

wnnys səw sāytalys, mẽ, jəb pakystan vwjud mẽ aya, to həm ne parlimani tərze hwkumət əpnaya.

jwmhuri nyzam ke vwjud mẽ ane se pəhle, əksər mwlkõ mẽ badšah hwkumət kərte the.

əllah ne dwnya ko vwjud mẽ lane ke sath sath, ynsan ko bhi pəyda kia.

11. həmare hwkmran ne ys mənsube pər tənqid ki.

vəzire azəm ne məɣrybi mwmalyk ki ys palisi pər tənqid ki.

zyle ke hakym ne ws ydare ke kamõ pər tənqid ki.

əvam ke nwmayndõ ne parlimani tərze hwkumət pər tənqid ki.

həmare nyzame talim pər bəhwt tənqid ki gəi həy.

ys hərəkət ki vəja se, yunyən kəwnsəl pər bəhwt tənqid hwi.

20.505. Response.

1. pakystan ki abadi təqribən kytni həy.
2. ap ke əpne mwlk ki abadi kya həy.
3. ap ke hã, kys qysm ka nyzame hwkumət həy.
4. kya, ap ka mwlk subõ mẽ təqsim həy?
5. kya, ap ke hã vəzire azəm ka whda həy?
6. voT dene ka həq kys ko hasyl hona cahie.
7. kya, ap ne kəbhi syasiat pəRhi həy?
8. kya, ap kəbhi kysi yntyxab mẽ wmmidvar bəne hə̃y?
9. kya, ap ke hã qəwmi əwr subai əsəmbliõ mẽ fərq həy?
10. pakystan ki qəwmi əsəmbli mẽ kwl kytne mymbər hə̃y.
11. kya, ap ke mwlk mẽ əqliəti fyrqõ ko bərabər ke hwquq hasyl hə̃y?
12. ap ke hã sədre mwmlykət ka əgla yntyxab kəb hoga.
13. ap ki rae mẽ jwmhuri tərze hwkumət ke kya fəvayd hə̃y.
14. kya, ap ko əpne mwlk ki əksər palisiõ se yttyfaq həy?
15. kya, ap ke mwlk mẽ bhi ala sərkari whdedarõ ka yntyxab hota həy?

20.506. Conversation Practice.

After tea, Mr. Smith questions Mr. əziz further about Pakistan's political system.

S: qəwmi əsəmbli mẽ kwl kytne mymbər hote hə̃y.

ə: qəwmi əsəmbli ke mymbərõ ki kwl tadad ek səw chəppən hoti həy. yn mẽ se məšryqi pakystan se pəchəttər mərd əwr tin əwrtẽ. ysi təra məɣrybi pakystan se pəchəttər mərd əwr tin əwrtẽ mwntəxəb ki jati hə̃y.

S: kya, qəwmi əsəmbli mẽ syrf chəy əwrtẽ mwntəxəb ho səkti hə̃y?

ə: ji nəhĩ! ys se zyada tadad mẽ bhi əwrtẽ mymbər bən səkti hə̃y, lekyn kəm se kəm chəy əwrtõ ka mymbər hona zəruri həy. yy tadad mwqərrər kərne ka məqsəd yy həy, ky

288

əwrtõ ko bhi əvam ke nwmaynde ki həysiət se mwntəxəb kiə jae, take vw bhi mərdõ ke sath hwkumət ke kamõ mẽ hyssa le səkẽ.

S: qəwmi əsəmbli əwr sədre mwmlykət ka yntyxab kytne ərse ke lie hota həy.

ə: sədr ka yntyxab pãc sal ke lie kia jata həy. ysi təra qəwmi əwr subai əsəmbli ke mymbər bhi pãc pãc sal ke lie cwne jate həy.

S: subai əsəmbli mẽ kytne mymbər hote hẽy.

ə: subai əsəmbli mẽ ek səw pəcas mymbər hote hẽy, jyn mẽ kwch tadad əwrtõ ki bhi hoti həy.

S: kya, bwnyadi jwmhuriətõ ko kwch yxtiarat bhi hasyl hẽy?

ə: ji hã. cũke ys nyzam ko vwjud mẽ lane ka məqsəd hi yy həy, ky əvam ko hwkumət ke kamõ mẽ hyssa lene ka məwqa dia jae, ys lie yunyən kəwnsəlõ əwr digər mənzylõ ki kəwnsəlõ ko baz choTe moTe yxtiarat bhi die gəe hẽy, take vw əpni zəruriat ke mwtabyq əpne ylaqe ka nyzam əcchi təra cəla səkẽ. mysal ke təwr pər, yunyən kəwnsəlẽ əpne ylaqe ke yntyzam əwr ws ki tərəqqi, ədalət se mwtəəllyq baz mwamlat, əwr logõ mẽ qəwmi jəzba pəyda kərne ke kam mẽ mədəd deti hẽy. hwkumət ne yn kəwnsəlõ ko kwch Təyks bhi ləgane ka yxtiar dia həy.

S: əccha, yunyən kəwnsəlõ ko Təyks ləgane ka bhi yxtiar həy? məgər vw kys qysm ka Təyks ləgati hẽy.

ə: yunyən kəwnsəlẽ əpne ylaqe mẽ honevali šadiõ əwr əyse hi digər məvaqe pər ek rupəya ya DeRh rupəya ka Təyks vwsul kərti hẽy.

S: to əmrika ki təra ap ke hã bhi qədəm qədəm pər Təyks dena pəRta həy!

ə: ji hã, yy səhih həy. məgər həmare hã Təyks ki rəqəm bəhwt mamuli hoti həy, jyse əvam asani se əda kər səkte hẽy.

S: jəysa ky ap ne bətaya, ky bwnyadi jwmhuriətẽ əpne ylaqe ke lie xwd mənsube bənati hẽy, to vw kys qysm ke mənsube hote hẽy.

ə: bwnyadi jwmhuriətẽ hər vw mənsuba təyyar kər səkti hẽy, jys ki wn ke ylaqe ko zərurət ho, məslən kysi yunyən kəwnsəl ke ylaqe mẽ səylab ki vəja se koi pwl TuT gəya ho, ya vəhã ke log koi nəya pwl ya səRək bənana cahte hõ, to yn kamõ ke lie ys ylaqe ki yunyən kəwnsəl mənsuba bəna səkti həy, əwr əgər yy kam ws ki taqət se bahər həy, to vw əpne mənsube ko təhsil kəwnsəl ke samne peš kər səkti həy. təhsil ya thana, zyle əwr Dyvižən ki kəwnsəlẽ yunyən kəwnsəl ke mwqable pər bəRe mənsube bənati hẽy.

S: məgər pwl əwr səRkẽ vəɣəyra bənane pər to kəroRõ rupəe xərc hote hẽy. yunyən kəwnsəl ya dusri kəwnsəlẽ ytni rəqəm kəhã se xərc kər səkti hẽy.

ə: yunyən kəwnsəlẽ tərəqqi ke choTe moTe kamõ ko xwd ənjam deti hẽy, lekyn jo mənsube zəra bəRe hote hẽy, wnhẽ əgli mənzyl ki kəwnsəl ke samne peš kərti hẽy. mwlk mẽ pwl, səRkẽ, əwr nəhrẽ bənane ka kam mərkəzi hwkumət ka həy, əwr ys sylsyle mẽ kabina fəysla kərti həy.

S: təmam mwlk mẽ bwnyadi jwmhuriətõ ke kytne mymbər hẽy.

ə: yn ki kwl tadad əssi həzar həy.

S: yunyən kəwnsəl ka ek mymbər kytne admiõ pər cwna jata həy, əwr ek kəwnsəl mẽ kytne mymbər hote hẽy.

ə: yunyən kəwnsəl ke lie təqribən ek həzar əfrad pər ek mymbər cwna jata həy. ek kəwnsəl mẽ am təwr pər dəs mwntəxəb əwr pãc hwkumət ke mwqərrərkərda ərkan hote hẽy.

S: kya, hwkumət ke mwqərrərkərda mymbərõ ko bhi vwhi yxtiarat hasyl hote hə̃y, jo
mwntəxəb mymbərõ ke hə̃y?

ə: mwqərrərkərda mymbərõ ko digər yxtiarat to hasyl hote hə̃y, məgər wnhẽ kəwnsəl ke
fəyslõ mẽ voT dene ka həq hasyl nəhĩ hota, kyõke vw əvam ki nwmayndəgi nəhĩ kərte.

S: yunyən kəwnsəl ki tərа, kya, hwkumət təhsil ya thana, zyla əwr Dyvižən ki kəwnsəlõ mẽ
bhi əpne mymbər mwqərrər kərti həy?

ə: ji hã. hwkumət hər mənzyl ki kəwnsəl mẽ əpne mymbər mwqərrər kərti həy. yunyən
kəwnsəl ke ylava, digər kəwnsəlõ mẽ hwkumət ke mwqərrərkərda mymbərõ ki tadad
mwntəxəb mymbərõ ke bərabər hoti həy.

S: hwkumət kyn logõ ko əpna mymbər mwqərrər kərti həy, əwr ys se ws ka kya məqsəd
hota həy.

ə: hwkumət wn logõ ko mymbər mwqərrər kərti həy, jo mwxtəlyf qysm ka təjryba rəkhte
hə̃y. cũke əyse log am təwr pər syasət mẽ hyssa nəhĩ lete, ys lie hwkumət wn ko əpni
tərəf se mwqərrər kər deti həy, take əvam wn ki xydmat se fayda wTha səkẽ. ys ka
məqsəd yy həy, ky sərkari əwr mwntəxəb mymbər ek dusre ke məšvəre se mənsube
vəɣəyra təyyar kərẽ, əwr yn ko əməl mẽ laẽ.

S: kya, ap ke hã sərkari whdõ ko syvyl sərvys ke zərie hi hasyl kia ja səkta həy?

ə: mwlk ke təmam bəRe yntyzami whdõ pər əksər wn logõ ko hi mwqərrər kia jata həy, jo
syvyl sərvys ke ymtyhanat mẽ kamyab hote hə̃y.

S: kya, əwrtẽ bhi yn ymtyhanõ mẽ bəyTh səkti hə̃y?

ə: ji hã, əwrtõ ko bhi mərdõ ke bərabər hwquq hasyl hə̃y. vw bhi am təwr pər hwkumət ke
təmam whdõ ko hasyl kər səkti hə̃y.

S: kya, sərkari mwlazymin bhi yntyxab mẽ hyssa le səkte hə̃y?

ə: ji nəhĩ! lekyn əgər vw syasət mẽ hyssa lena cahẽ, to pəhle wnhẽ sərkari mwlazmət
choRni hogi. ys ke bad vw azadi se bwnyadi jwmhuriət, subai əsəmbli, ya qəwmi əsəmbli
ka yntyxab ləR səkte hə̃y.

S: kya, pakystan ke əqliəti fyrqõ se təəllwq rəkhnevale log bhi vəzire azəm ya vəzir ka whda
hasyl kər səkte hə̃y?

ə: kyõ nəhĩ! jəysa ky mə̃y ərz kər cwka hũ, həmara ain jwmhuri həy. pakystan ka koi bhi
bašynda yn whdõ ko hasyl kər səkta həy, xa ws ka təəllwq kysi bhi məzhəb se kyõ nə ho.

S: əccha, əb yjazət dijie. bəhwt vəqt ho gəya həy. ynšaəlla[h] kəl mwlaqat hogi.

ə: bəhwt əccha. xwda hafyz.

20.507. Conversation Stimulus.

Topics may include the following:
1. The political system of one's own country.
2. The Basic Democracies.
3. Women's rights.
4. The feasibility of various political systems for a country like Pakistan.
5. One's own political views or experiences.

abadi F2	population, settlement
ain M1	constitution, code of laws, statutes
ala A1	most high, greatest, superior, supreme
azəm A1	highest, greatest
*əfrad Mpl	individuals, persons. [pl. /fərd/]
*əfsəran Mpl	pl. /əfsər/
əksəriət F1	majority
əksəriəti A1	majority (adj.)
əməl M1	action, operation, practice, deed, work
əmn M1 [np]	peace, security, safety
ənjwmən F1	society, group, association, organisation, company
əpnana [Ia]	to adopt, make one's own
əqliət [or /əqəlliət/] F1	minority
əqliəti [or /əqəlliəti/] A1	minority (adj.)
əsəmbli F2	assembly
əvam Mpl	public, common people
baqayda A1	regular, according to rule
bašynda M2	inhabitant, resident, native, dweller
beasi [or /bəyasi/] A1	eighty-two
bhəi Vocative Particle	brother, friend
cəwrasi A1	eighty-four
cerməyn M/F1	chairman
Dyvižən M1	division (administrative unit)
fərd M1	individual, person, member
fyrqa M2	sect, party
gəvərnər M/F1	governor
yəyrmwsəlman M1 A1	non-Muslim
yəyrmwlki M1 A1	foreigner, foreign
yəyrmwmalyk Mpl	foreign countries
hakym M1	ruler, governor
həTana [C: /həTna/: IIc]	to remove, take away, move aside
həTna [IIc: /ə/]	to move away, withdraw, get out of the way
hwkmran M1 A1	ruler, sovereign; ruling
*hwquq Mpl	pl. /həq/
jə̃g F1	war
jwmhuri [or /jəmhuri/] A1	democratic
jwmhuriət [or /jəmhuriət/] F1	democracy
kabina F1	cabinet (of a president)
kəwnsəl F1	council
lyhaza Conj	therefore

məaši A1	economic
mənsuba M2	project, scheme, plan
mənzyl F1	stage, destination, goal, level, tier, storey (of a house)
mərkəz M1	centre
mərkəzi A1	central
məšvəra M2	advice, counsel, consultation
*mwamlat Mpl	pl. /mwamla/
mwlazmət F1	employment, job, service
mwlazym M1	employee, worker
*mwlazymin Mpl	pl. /mwlazym/
*mwmalyk Mpl	pl. /məmlykət/, but treated in Urdu as though pl. of /mwlk/ M1 "country"
mwmlykət [lit. /məmlykət/ or /məmlwkət/] F1	realm, state, kingdom
mwntəxəb A1	elected, selected, chosen
mwqami A1	local, resident
mwqərrərkərda A1	appointed, selected, fixed
mymbər M/F1	member
nwmaynda M/F1 A1	representative
nwmayndəgi F2	representation
palisi F2	policy
parlimani A1	parliamentary
pycasi [or /pəcasi/] A1	eighty-five
qanunsaz M1 A1	law-maker, law-making
sədarti A1	presidential
sədr M/F1	president
sənəti A1	industrial
sərkari A1	governmental, government, official
sərvys F1	service
suba M2	province
subai A1	provincial
syasət F1	politics
syasi A1	political
syasiat F1 [np]	political science
syvyl A1	civil
talybylm [or /talybe ylm/] M1	student
*təəllwqat Mpl	pl. /təəllwq/
təhsil F1	"təhsil," a small administrative unit
*təjaviz Fpl	pl. /təjviz/
təjviz F1	plan, scheme, suggestion
tənqid F1	criticism
təqrir F1	lecture, speech
təqsim F1	division, partition, sharing

tərbiət F1	training, instruction, upbringing
tərz F1	manner, mode, way, kind, type, style
thana M2	police station; small administrative unit equal to the "təhsil" (East Pakistan only)
*twləba [or /tələba/] Mpl	pl. /talybylm/
tyjarti A1	commercial, relating to business
tyrasi A1	eighty-three
Təyks M1	tax
TwkRa M2	piece, part, portion
vəzir M1	minister, vizier
voT M1	vote
vwjud M1	existence, being
vwsul PA1	received, acquired, realised, levied (as funds)
*vwzəra Mpl	pl. /vəzir/
whda M2	post, position, rank
whdedar M/F1	office holder, official
wmmidvar M/F1	candidate; hopeful, expectant
xwdbəxwd Adv	automatically, spontaneously, all by oneself
*xydmat Fpl	pl. /xydmət/
ydara M2	institute, institution, body, department, organisation
ykasi [or /ykkyasi/] A1	eighty-one
*ymtyhanat Mpl	pl. /ymtyhan/
yntyxab M1	election, selection, choice
*yntyxabat Mpl	pl. /yntyxab/
yntyzami A1	administrative
yslah F1	reform, improvement, emendation
yunyən F1 A1	union
*yxtiarat Mpl	pl. /yxtiar/
zəruriat Fpl	necessities, requirements, needs
zyla M2	district

Mohenjo Daro, the ruins of the oldest civilization on the Subcontinent.

UNIT TWENTY-ONE

21.000. ESSAY

From this point on, each Unit will begin with an essay in the Urdu script. This will be followed by a vocabulary of new words introduced in the essay arranged in order of their occurrence. Other sections will be the same as before, except that the Script Section will now be omitted, and script exercises will be included in the Vocabulary and Grammar Drill Section.

تاریخِ ہند و پاکستان

ہندوستان یعنی موجودہ پاکستان اور ہندوستان دُنیا کے قدیم ترین ملکوں میں سے ایک ہے ۔ اِس کی قدیم تاریخ کے بارے میں کوئی مستند کتاب نہیں ملتی ۔ لیکن موّرخین نے مختلف ذرائع سے اِس ملک کی تاریخ پر تحقیق کی ہے ۔ آج سے تقریباً پچاس سال پہلے یہاں کی پرانی تہذیب کے بارے میں بہت کم معلومات حاصل تھیں ۔ لیکن موجودہ دَور میں ہڑپّہ اور موہنجودارو جیسے شہروں کی دریافت کے بعد تاریکی کے بہت سے پردے اٹھ گئے ہیں ۔ اِن شہروں کی کھدائی سے سونے ، چاندی اور تانبے کے زیورات ، سکّے ، ٹُہریں ، پتھر کے برتن ، کھلونے اور ہتھیار وغیرہ برآمد ہوئے ہیں ۔ ماہرین نے اِن چیزوں پر بڑی محنت سے تحقیق کی ہے اور اِس نتیجے پر پہنچے ہیں کہ سندھ کی وادی میں آج سے تقریباً ساڑھے چار ہزار برس پہلے بھی ایک تہذیب یافتہ قوم آباد تھی ۔ یہ لوگ کون تھے ؟ اِس کے متعلّق موّرخین مختلف رائے رکھتے ہیں ۔ لیکن اکثر کا خیال یہی ہے کہ یہ لوگ دراوڑ تھے اور ایک مہذّب زندگی بسر کرتے تھے موہن جو دارو اور ہڑپّہ میں اِن لوگوں کے مکان برآمد ہوئے ہیں ۔ جن سے پتہ چلتا ہے کہ یہ لوگ پکّے مکان تعمیر کرتے تھے ۔ مکانوں کے آگے چوڑی چوڑی گلیاں رکھتے تھے ۔ گندے پانی کو شہر سے باہر پھینکنے کے لئے باقاعدہ نالیاں بناتے تھے اور شہر میں نہانے کے لئے غسل خانوں کا انتظام تھا ۔ یہ لوگ کنویں کھودتے تھے

295

پتھر کے ہتھیار اور برتن استعمال کرتے تھے ۔ بعض چیزوں پر کچھ تحریریں بھی پائی گئی ہیں ۔ جن سے ظاہر ہوتا ہے کہ یہ لوگ رسم الخط سے بھی واقف تھے ۔ ان تحریروں کو ابھی تک پڑھا نہیں جا سکا ہے لیکن ان پر مزید تحقیق جاری ہے ۔

جس زمانے میں دراوڑ ایک خوش حال اور مہذب زندگی بسر کر رہے تھے تو انہیں ایک بیرونی حملے کا سامنا کرنا پڑا ۔ ان حملہ آوروں نے دراوڑوں کو شکست دے کر ان کے علاقے پر قبضہ کرلیا ۔ یہ لوگ تاریخ میں آریا کے نام سے یاد کئے جاتے ہیں ۔ ان کے اصلی وطن کے بارے میں مورخین کی رائے مختلف ہے ۔ آریا دراصل خانہ بدوش تھے ۔ وہ مویشی جیسے گائے ، بھیڑ ، بکری وغیرہ پالتے تھے ۔ اور لڑائی میں گھوڑے اور رتھ استعمال کرتے تھے ۔ انہوں نے مقامی باشندوں کو شکست دے کر جنوب کی طرف دھکیل دیا اور رفتہ رفتہ تمام شمالی ہندوستان پر چھا گئے ۔ ان کے مذہب کے بارے میں کہا جاتا ہے کہ یہ لوگ ہندو مذہب سے تعلق رکھتے تھے اور مختلف دیوتاؤں کو پوجتے تھے ۔ جیسے آسمان کا دیوتا ، بارش کا دیوتا وغیرہ ۔ انہوں نے دراوڑوں کو شکست ہی نہیں دی بلکہ ان کی تہذیب کو بھی تباہ کر ڈالا ۔ پرانی کتابوں جیسے وید اور مہا بھارت سے آریاؤں کے حالات ، مذہب اور تہذیب پر روشنی پڑتی ہے ۔

چھ سو سال قبل از مسیح ہندوستان میں ایک نئے مذہب کا آغاز ہوا جو بدھ مذہب کے نام سے مشہور ہے ۔ اس مذہب کا بانی گوتم بدھ تھا جو ہندوستان کی ایک ریاست کا شہزادہ تھا ۔ لوگوں کو بیماری اور تکلیف میں دیکھ کر اس کا دل دنیا سے بیزار ہوگیا اور اپنا تخت اور تاج چھوڑ کر جنگلوں میں نکل گیا ۔ جہاں برسوں عبادت میں مصروف رہا ۔ اس کے بعد اس نے اپنے مذہب کی تبلیغ شروع کی ۔ یہ مذہب جلد ہی ہندوستان بھر میں پھیل گیا ۔

آریاؤں کے بعد کئی دوسرے بیرونی قبیلوں نے ہندوستان پر حملے کئے اور چھوٹی چھوٹی ریاستوں

پر حکومت کرتے رہے۔ اسی طرح یونانیوں اور ایرانیوں نے بھی حملے کئے۔ خاص طور پر یونانی بادشاہ سکندر اعظم کے حملے نے ہندوستان کی تہذیب پر بہت گہرا اثر ڈالا۔ یہ وہ زمانہ تھا کہ ہندوستان میں کوئی منظم حکومت نہ تھی اور ملک چھوٹی چھوٹی ریاستوں میں بٹا ہوا تھا اور بیرونی حملہ آور حملے کرتے رہتے تھے۔ ہندوستان پر آئے دن حملوں کو دیکھ کر مقامی راجاؤں کے دل میں ایک مضبوط حکومت قائم کرنے کا جذبہ پیدا ہوا۔ چنانچہ چندرگپت موریہ نے چھوٹی چھوٹی ریاستوں کو ختم کر کے ایک مضبوط حکومت کی بنیاد رکھی۔ اس نے بیرونی حملوں کو روکنے کے لئے ایک بہت بڑی فوج تیار کی۔ یونانیوں کو شکست دی۔ ملک کا اندرونی انتظام بہتر بنایا۔ سڑکیں بنوائیں۔ کنویں کھدوائے اور مسافروں کے لئے سرائیں تعمیر کرائیں۔ ملک کو مختلف صوبوں میں تقسیم کیا۔ ہر صوبہ کئی ضلعوں پر مشتمل ہوتا تھا۔ چندرگپت کی طرح راجہ اشوک نے بھی سلطنت کا انتظام شاندار طریقے سے چلایا۔ ملک کی خوشحالی کے لئے سینکڑوں کام کئے۔ اشوک بدھ مذہب کا پیرو تھا۔ اس نے بدھ مذہب کے اصول اور قوانین ملک بھر میں پھیلائے۔ مگر اشوک کی وفات کے بعد ملک پھر کمزور حکمرانوں کے ہاتھ میں چلا گیا اور چھوٹے چھوٹے ٹکڑوں میں بٹ گیا۔ سوائے راجہ کنشک اور ہرش کی حکومت کے، اور کسی مضبوط حکومت کے آثار نہیں تھے۔

ساتویں صدی عیسوی کے شروع میں عرب میں ایک نیا مذہب شروع ہوا جو اسلام کے نام سے مشہور ہے اور اس مذہب کے پیرو مسلمان کہلاتے ہیں۔ اس مذہب نے پچاس سال کے عرصے میں اتنی ترقی کی کہ آج تک کسی دوسرے مذہب نے نہیں کی۔ مسلمانوں نے ایران اور روم جیسی بڑی بڑی سلطنتوں کو شکست دے کر وہاں اسلامی جھنڈا لہرایا۔ اسلامی فتوحات کا سلسلہ ایران اور روم تک ہی محدود نہیں رہا بلکہ یہ لوگ برابر آگے بڑھے گئے۔ اور انہوں نے اپنی سلطنت کی حدیں افریقہ اور ایشیا تک بڑھا لیں۔

کہا جاتا ہے کہ عربوں کے کچھ جہاز دیبل کی بندرگاہ پر مقامی لیڈروں نے لوٹ لئے تھے۔

مسلمان خلیفہ نے ہندوستان کے حکمران راجہ داہر سے اس کے بارے میں شکایت کی مگر اُس نے اس سلسلے میں کوئی قدم نہ اٹھایا بلکہ خلیفہ کو سخت جواب دیا۔ چنانچہ سات سو بارہ عیسوی میں اسلامی فوج ایک سترہ سالہ نوجوان سپہ سالار محمد بن قاسم کی قیادت میں ہندوستان پر حملہ آور ہوئی۔ مسلمانوں نے راجہ داہر کو شکست دے کر سندھ اور ملتان کے صوبوں پر قبضہ کر لیا۔ اس فتح کے بعد اسلامی تہذیب رفتہ رفتہ ہندوستان میں پھیلنے لگی۔ ایران اور افغانستان کے مسلمان بادشاہوں جیسے محمود غزنوی اور محمد غوری وغیرہ نے ہندوستان کے راجاؤں سے مختلف وجوہات کی بنا پر لڑائیاں کیں۔ اگرچہ ان لڑائیوں سے کوئی منظم حکومت تو وجود میں نہ آسکی لیکن ہندو راجہ کمزور پڑ گئے اور آئندہ حملہ آوروں کے لئے راستہ صاف ہو گیا۔ محمد غوری نے شمالی ہندوستان کی فتح کے بعد اپنے ایک غلام کو وہاں اپنا نائب مقرر کیا۔ اُس کے اس قدم سے ہندوستان میں ایک باقاعدہ اسلامی حکومت قائم ہو گئی۔ ہندوستان کے تخت پر پہلا مسلمان خاندان غلاموں کے خاندان کے نام سے مشہور ہے۔ قطب الدین ایبک ، شمس الدین التمش اور غیاث الدین بلبن اس خاندان کے مشہور بادشاہ گذرے ہیں۔ خاص طور پر بلبن نے ملک کا اندرونی انتظام بہتر بنایا اور لوگوں کی خوشحالی کے لئے بہت سی اصلاحات کیں۔ سرحد پر منگل اکثر حملے کرتے رہتے تھے۔ بلبن نے ان حملوں کو بھی روکے رکھا۔ مگر اُس کی وفات کے بعد حکومت اُس کے کمزور جانشینوں کے ہاتھ میں چلی گئی۔ چنانچہ خلجی قبیلے کے ایک سردار نے غلاموں کے خاندان کو ختم کرکے خلجی خاندان کی بنیاد رکھی۔ علاؤالدین خلجی اس خاندان کا سب سے مشہور بادشاہ ہے۔ اُس نے ملک میں ایسی ایسی اصلاحات کیں جو اُس سے پہلے کبھی کسی نے نہیں کی تھیں۔ اُس نے اپنی سلطنت جنوبی ہندوستان میں دکن تک بڑھائی۔ ملک کی حفاظت کے لئے سرحدوں پر مضبوط قلعے تعمیر کرائے۔

خلجی خاندان کے بعد تغلق خاندان کے بادشاہ تقریباً نوے سال تک حکومت کرتے رہے۔

298

محمد شاہ تغلق نے چند نئی اصلاحات کرنے کی کوشش کی جس میں وہ ناکام رہا۔ جیسے اُس نے سونے چاندی کے سکوں کے بدلے تانبے کے سکّے اور بعض مورّخین کے مطابق کاغذ کے نوٹ جاری کرائے ۔ جنہیں لوگوں نے لینے سے انکار کر دیا۔ جس سے حکومت کو بہت نقصان پہنچا ۔

تغلق خاندان کے بعد سادات خاندان اور لودھی خاندان نے حکومت کی ۔ لودھی خاندان کے پہلے دو بادشاہ بہلول لودھی اور سکندر لودھی نے حکومت کا انتظام اچھی طرح چلایا لیکن اس خاندان کا آخری بادشاہ ابراہیم لودھی حکومت کے کاموں میں دلچسپی نہیں لیتا تھا۔ چنانچہ عوام تنگ آگئے اور پنجاب کے گورنر نے کابل کے بادشاہ ظہیرالدین بابر کو ہندوستان پر حملہ کرنے کی دعوت دی ۔ بابر بارہ ہزار سپاہیوں کو ساتھ لے کر پندرہ سو چھبیس عیسوی میں ہندوستان پر حملہ آور ہوا۔ ابراہیم لودھی ایک لاکھ سپاہیوں کی فوج لے کر آگے بڑھا اور پانی پت کے تاریخی میدان میں جنگ ہوئی جس میں بابر کو فتح ہوئی اور اُس نے ہندوستان میں مغل سلطنت کی بنیاد رکھی ۔

21.100. SERIAL VOCABULARY

New vocabulary items are listed here in order of their occurrence in Sec. 21.000. All personal names, place names, book titles, etc. are included, but the student is expected to treat as "active vocabulary" only those place names which denote countries, provinces or other large regions, names of major cities, etc.

Names of persons are singular, of course, and depend for their grammatical gender upon the gender of the person to whom they refer. They are thus marked only by "PN" ("personal name"). Book titles similarly depend for their gender upon whether the speaker is treating them as a "book" (/kytab/ F1), a "story" (/qyssa/· M2 or /kəhani/ F2), a "novel" (/navəl/ M1), etc. -- i.e. their gender does not depend upon the gender of the words in the title. Usage differs from speaker to speaker, and thus book titles are simply left unmarked.

In the third column a "modified English spelling" has been adopted for the transliteration of personal names and uncommon place names. Many names admit of several spellings in English (e.g. "Haq," "Haqq," "Huq," "Huqq," "Haque," etc. all for /həq/!), and it thus seems better to reduce all of these names to a single system. This system is rather similar to that employed by many orientalists for Urdu, except that no diacritics are used, thus ignoring such differences as /d/ versus /D/, /u/ versus /w/, etc. Such phonemic matters are, of course, clear from the second column.

"Active vocabulary" -- the vocabulary to be learned and used by the student -- is listed again in alphabetical order in Sec. 21.600.

ہِند	hynd M1 [np]	India [alternate for /hyndostan/]
و	o Conj	and. [See Secs. 15.301 and 18.307]
قدیم ترین	qədimtərin A1	oldest, most ancient
قدیم	qədim A1	old, ancient
مستند	mwstənəd A1	authentic, genuine, reliable
مورّخین	*mwvərryxin Mpl [pl. /mwvərryx/]	historians
ذرائع	*zərae Mpl [pl. /zəria/]	ways, methods, means, sources, agencies
تحقیق	təhqiq F1	research, investigation
دَور	dəwr M1	age, epoch, period

300

ہڑپہ	həRəppa M2 [np]	Harappa, the ruins of a city of the Indus Valley Civilisation. About 100 miles southwest of Lahore
موہن جو دارو	mohənjo daro M1 [np]	Mohenjo Daro, the ruins of a city of the Indus Valley Civilisation. About 200 miles north of the mouth of the Indus
دریافت	dəryaft F1	discovery, ascertainment, inquiry
تاریکی	tariki F2	darkness
کھدائی	khwdai F2	digging, excavation
تانبا	tāba M2 [np]	copper
زیورات	*zevərat Mp1 [pl. /zevər/]	jewellery, ornaments
سکہ	sykka M2	coin
مہر	mwhr F1	seal
کھلونا	khyləwna M2	toy
ہتھیار	həthyar M1	weapon
برآمد	bəraməd F1 PA1	recovered, discovered, found; export
ماہرین	*mahyrin Mp1 [pl. /mahyr/]	experts, skilled persons, masters (of a craft)
سندھ	syndh M1 [np]	Sindh
وادی	vadi F2	valley
برس	bərəs M1	year
تہذیب یافتہ	təhzibyafta A1	cultured, civilised
آباد	abad A1	populated, inhabited
دراوڑ	dəravəR M1 A1	Dravidian, the inhabitants of India before the Aryan invasion, now dwelling mostly in South India

مہذّب	mwhəzzəb A1	cultured, civilised
بسر	bəsər PA1	passing, spending (time), living
تعمیر	tamir F1	building, construction, erection
نالی	nali F2	tube, drain, channel
نہانا	nəhana [IIb: /ə/]	to bathe
کھودنا	khodna [If: /w/]	to dig, excavate
تحریر	təhrir F1	writing, inscription, document
رسم الخط	rəsmwlxət M1	script, system of writing
مزید	məzid A1	further, more
بیرونی	beruni A1	external, exterior, outside
حملہ	həmla M2	attack, assault, invasion
سامنا	samna M2	confrontation, encounter
شکست	šykəst F1	defeat
قبضہ	qəbza M2	power, possession, grasp, seizure, holding
آریا	arya M1 A1	Aryan, the invaders of India in approx. 1500 B.C.
اصلی	əsli A1	original, genuine, pure
وطن	vətən M1	homeland, native country
خانہ بدوش	xanəbədoš M1 A1	nomadic, wandering, nomad
مویشی	məveši Mpl	cattle
بھیڑ	bheR F1	sheep, ewe

302

رتھ	rəth M1	chariot
دھکیلنا	dhəkelna [Ia]	to shove, push away, repel
شمالی	šymali [or /šwmali/] A1	northern, north
چھانا	chana [IIa]	to spread out over, diffuse, overshadow, make shade
ہندو	hyndu M/F1 A1	Hindu
دیوتا	deota M1	deity, god
وید	ved M1	the Vedas, the earliest of the Hindu scriptures
مہا بھارت	məhabharət M1 [np]	the Mahabharata, the great Hindu religious epic, parts of which may date back to the Tenth Century B.C. This work is traditionally ascribed to Vyasa
قبل از مسیح	qəbl əz məsih A1 [after a numeral denoting a year]	Before Christ, B.C.
آغاز	aɣaz M1	beginning, start, inception
بدھ	bwdh M1 [np]	Buddha
بانی	bani M/F1	founder, originator
گوتم بدھ	gəwtəm bwdh PN	Gawtama Buddha; 518-488 B.C.
ریاست	ryasət F1	state, small kingdom, rule, sovereignty
شہزادہ	šəhzada [or /šahzada/] M2	prince
بیزار	bezar PA1	disgusted with, sick of, fed up with
تخت	təxt M1	throne
تاج	taj M1	crown

برسوں	bərsõ Adv	for many years, for years and years
تبلیغ	təbliɣ F1	spreading (of a doctrine), preaching, missionary work
جَلد	jəld Adv	soon, quickly
بھر	bhər Enclitic Particle	whole, entire, complete, full, throughout
قبیلہ	qəbila M2	tribe, clan
یونانی	yunani M/F1 A1	Greek
ایرانی	irani M/F1 A1	Persian
سکندر	sykəndər PN	Alexander the Great; 356-323 B.C.
منظم	mwnəzzəm A1	well-organised, ordered, systematised, well-administered
بٹنا	bəTna [I: /bāTna/: Ie]	to be divided, distributed, shared
حملہ آور	həmləavər M1 A1	attacking, invading, attacker, invader
آئے دن	ae dyn Adv	every day, constantly
راجہ	raja M1	king, Raja (usually Hindu)
چندر گپت موریہ	cəndər gwpt morya PN	Chandra Gupta Mawrya, founder of the Mawrya Dynasty; ruled approx. 321-296 B.C.
اندرونی	əndəruni A1	internal, interior, inside
کھدوانا	khwdvana [DC: /khodna/: If]	to cause to be dug
سرائے	sərae F1	sarai, inn, way station for travellers
مشتمل	mwštəmyl PA1	comprising, consisting of, including

اشوک	əšok PN	Ashoka, the great Buddhist king of India; approx. 274-? B.C.
سلطنت	səltənət F1	kingdom, sultanate, sovereignty, dominion, empire
شاندار	šandar A1	glorious, splendid, majestic
سینکڑہ	səykRa [or /səykRa/] A2	hundred
پیرو	pəyrəw M/F1	follower, devotee
وفات	vəfat F1	death
کنشک	kənyšk PN	Kanishka, a king of India; ruled c. 78 A.D.
ہرش	hərš PN	Harsha, a king of India; ruled 605-646 (-47) A.D.
آثار	*asar Mpl [pl. /əsər/]	remains, ruins, indications
عیسوی	isvi A1 [usually after a numeral denoting a year]	After Christ, A.D.
ایران	iran M1 [np]	Iran, Persia
روم	rum M1 [np]	Rome, the Byzantine Empire
جھنڈا	jhənDa M2	flag, banner
لہرانا	ləhrana [IIIa]	to wave, make wave
فتوحات	*fwtuhat Fpl [pl. /fəta/ (/fətəh/)]	victories
محدود	məhdud A1	limited, bounded, confined
بڑھتے گئے	bəRhe gəe MP	kept on advancing, kept expanding
حد	həd F1	limit, boundary, edge, border

305

افریقه	əfriqa M1 [np]	Africa
ایشیا	ešya M1 [np]	Asia
دیبل	debəl M1 [np]	Debal, an ancient port on the coast of what is now West Pakistan near Karachi Karachi
بندرگاه	bəndərgah F1	seaport, harbour
لٹیرا	lwTera M2	looter, bandit
لوٹنا	luTna [Ie: /w/]	to loot, rob, plunder
خلیفه	xəlifa M1	Caliph
داہر	dahyr PN	Dahir, king of Sindh and the Panjab in 712 A.D.
ساله	sala A1 [follows a numeral]	-yeared, -year-old
نوجوان	nəwjəvan M1 A1	youth, young
سپه سالار	sypəsalar [or /sypehsalar/] M1	general, commander
محمد بن قاسم	mwhəmməd byn qasym PN	Muhammad bin Qasim, the first Muslim conqueror of Sindh (712 A.D.)
قیادت	qəyadət F1	leadership, command
فتح	fəta [or /fətəh/] F1	victory, conquest
افغانستان	əfɣanystan M1 [np]	Afghanistan
محمود غزنوی	məhmud ɣəznəvi PN	Mahmud Ghaznavi, king of Ghazna; ruled 998-1030
محمد غوری	mwhəmməd ɣəwri PN	Muhammad Ghawri, king of Ghawr; ruled 1174-1206
وجوہات	*vwjuhat Fpl [pl. /vəja/ (/vəjəh/)]	reasons, càuses

غلام	ɣwlam M1	slave
نائب	nayb M/F1 A1	deputy, regent, viceroy
قطب الدّین ایبک	qwtbwddin əybək PN	Qutb-ud-din Aybak; ruled 1206-1210
شمش الدّین التمش	šəmswddin yltəməš PN	Shams-ud-din Iltamash; ruled 1210-1236
غیاث الدّین بلبن	ɣyaswddin bəlbən PN	Ghias-ud-din Balban; ruled 1266-1287
اصلاحات	* yslahat Fpl [pl. /yslah/]	reforms, improvements
سرحد	sərhəd F1	border (of a country), frontier, boundary line
روکے رکّھا	roke rəkkha MS	held in check, stopped
جانشین	janəšin M/F1	successor
خلجی	xylji PN	Khilji, name of a Turkic tribe
علاؤالدّین خلجی	əlawddin xylji PN	Ala-ud-din Khilji; ruled 1296-1316
جنوبی	jwnubi A1	southern, south
دکن	dəkən [or /dəkkhən/, or /dəkkhyn/] M1 [np]	the Deccan, central south India
حفاظت	hyfazət F1	safeguard, protection, safety, guarding
تغلق	twɣlwq [or /twɣləq/] PN	Tughluq, name of a Turkic tribe
نوّے	nəvve A1	ninety
محمّد شاه تغلق	mwhəmməd šah twɣlwq PN	Muhammad Shah Tughluq; ruled 1325-1351
ناکام	nakam A1	unsuccessful, failed

[میں] بدلے [کے]	[ke] bədle [± mẽ] Comp Post	in exchange for
نوٹ	noT M1	note, currency note
سادات	* sadat Mpl [pl. /səyyəd/ M1 "descendant of the Prophet Muhammad"]	the Sayyid Dynasty; ruled 1414-1451
لودھی	lodhi PN	Lodhi, name of a Pathan tribe; ruled 1451-1526
بہلول لودھی	bəhlol lodhi PN	Bahlol Lodhi, a king of the Lodhi Dynasty; ruled 1451-1488
سکندر لودھی	sykəndər lodhi PN	Sikandar Lodhi, a king of the Lodhi Dynasty; ruled 1488-1518
ابراہیم لودھی	ybrahim lodhi PN	Ibrahim Lodhi, the last king of the Lodhi Dynasty; ruled 1518-1526
پنجاب	pənjab M1 [np]	the Panjab
کابل	kabwl M1 [np]	Kabul, the present capital of Afghanistan
ظہیرالدین بابر	zəhirwdin babər PN	Zahir-ud-din Babar, the first king of the Mughal Dynasty; ruled India 1526-1530
سپاہی	sypahi M1	soldier (also used for "police constable")
پانی پت	panipət M1 [np]	Panipat, a small city in India
تاریخی	tarixi A1	historic, historical

21.201. /pwrana/ A2 and /qədim/ A1 both mean "old, ancient," and both are mutually substitutable in many contexts. /qədim/, however, is somewhat more literary and carries a sense of greater antiquity. Neither of these two words may be used to denote "old (age)"; this is expressed by /buRha/ A2. See Sec. 7.110. E.g.

> /yy ek bəhwt qədim kytab həy./ This is a very ancient book. [/pwrani/ could be substituted here, but it would not carry as great a connotation of antiquity.]

> /yy həmara pwrana nəwkər həy./ This is our old [i.e. long-time] servant. [/qədim/ cannot be substituted here.]

> /yy nəwkər bəhwt buRha həy./ This servant is very old. [Neither /pwrana/ nor /qədim/ may occur here.]

21.202. /dəryaft/ F1 denotes "discovery, ascertainment" and also "inquiry." /bəraməd/ F1 PA1 signifies "recovered, discovered, brought to light, found" and also "export." Although these two words may be substituted in many contexts, /bəraməd/ has a sense of "ferreting out, digging out" which /dəryaft/ does not. Note that /bəraməd/ is used as a true noun only in the sense of "export." E.g.

> /šymali pakystan mē hal hi mē khwdai ke bad ek qədim šəhr bəraməd hwa həy./ Recently in northern Pakistan an ancient city has been discovered after an excavation. [Compare:]

> /do nəe šəhr dəryaft hwe./ Two new cities were discovered. [/bəraməd hwe/ is also possible here: the difference is like that between "discovered" and "recovered."]

> /mwjrym ke ghər se cori ka sara mal bəraməd ho gəya./ All of the stolen property [lit. property of the theft] was recovered from the home of the culprit. [Here /bəraməd/ is appropriate since the sense is that of "finding something hidden."]

> /ys sal gəndwm ki bəraməd bəRh gəi həy./ This year the export of wheat has increased.

> /ws ne pəndərvĩ sədi mē əmrika dəryaft kia./ In the fifteenth century he discovered America. [/bəraməd/ cannot occur here since America was not hidden, buried, etc.]

> /səb se pəhle ws ne yy wsul dəryaft kia./ He was the first [lit. first from all, he ...] to discover this principle.

> /rəhim sahəb se ys məsle ke bare mē dəryaft kərē!/ Find out about this matter from Mr. Rəhim!

> /ap wn se dəryaft kərē, ky vw kəb təšrif la rəhe hõy./ Find out from them when they are coming.

21.203. /tariki/ F2 and /ãdhera/ M2 A2 both mean "darkness." The former is rather more literary, however, and may be used metaphorically. E.g.

> /wn ke ãkhõ se tariki ke pərde wTh gəe./ The curtains of darkness have lifted from his eyes. [I.e. he has become aware, cognizant.]

> /b>dəl ate hi, tariki cha gəi./ The moment the clouds came, darkness fell [lit. overspread]. [/ãdhera cha gəya/ is equally substitutable.]

21.204. /bərəs/ M1 and /sal/ M1 both mean "year." They are almost completely interchangeable. /bərəs/ is of Hindi origin, while /sal/ is from Persian. "For years and years" may be expressed by /bərsõ/, /salõ/, or in a more literary way, by /salha/. See Secs. 7.305 and 18.301. E. g.

/vw bərsõ ləRai jhəgRe mẽ məsruf rəha. / He was busy in fighting [and] quarrelling for years and years. [Also /salõ/ or /salha/.]

/ys kam mẽ salõ ləg gəe. / This work took years and years. [Lit. In this work years attached.]

21.205. /təhzibyafta/ Al and /mwhəzzəb/ Al both mean "cultured, civilised. " The former is composed of the Arabic Form II verbal noun /təhzib/ Fl "culture" (from the root /h-d-b/) + the past participle of the Persian verb /yaf/ "to get, obtain": hence "culture-gotten. " See Sec. 18.307. /mwhəzzəb/ is an Arabic Form II passive participle also made from /h-d-b/; see Sec. 17.301. If there is any semantic distinction between these two words, it may be said that /mwhəzzəb/ has the same connotation found in English "cultured, " while /təhzibyafta/ has these and also those of "civilised. " In many contexts these two words are mutually substitutable.

21.206. /bəsər/ PAl "passing, spending (time), living" consists of Persian /bə/ (or /by/) + /sər/ "head. " This form once had meanings like "at an end (i. e. at a head), finished, accomplished, " but in modern Urdu it is employed only with /kərna/ and /hona/ meaning "to pass (time). " Although formations with /bəsər/ are often mutually substitutable with forms of /gwzarna/ "to spend, pass (time), " the latter may denote the passing of a specific period of time (e. g. a week, two years, etc.), while /bəsər kərna/ or /bəsər hona/ cannot be so employed. E. g.

/vw bəhwt xwšhal zyndəgi bəsər kər rəha həy. / He leads a very prosperous life. [Also /gwzar rəha həy. /]

/yn halat mẽ zyndəgi bəsər kərna bəhwt mwškyl həy. / It is very difficult to live [lit. pass life] in these circumstances.

/ws ki sari zyndəgi pərešaniõ mẽ bəsər hwi. / His whole life was passed in tribulations.

/vw əyš ki zyndəgi bəsər kər rəha həy. / He is living a life of pleasure.

/mãy ne pakystan mẽ do sal gwzare. / I spent two years in Pakistan. [/bəsər kie/ cannot be substituted here since a specified period of time is expressed.]

21.207. /tamir/ Fl "building, construction, erection" is often found in complex verbal constructions with /kərna/ and /hona/, and these are substitutable for /bənana/ IIc "to make, build" when the context is one of physical construction (e. g. the building of a mosque, etc.). In a metaphorical sense, however, /bənana/ is less common than /tamir/. E. g.

/mãy ajkəl əpne məkan ki tamir mẽ məsruf hũ. / These days I'm busy building my new house. [/əpna nəya məkan bənvane mẽ/ is substitutable. The double causative form is required since one does not usually build one's own house but instead has it built by carpenters.]

/mãy ne pychle sal ek nəya məkan tamir kəraya. / Last year I had a new house built. [Also /bənvaya/.]

/qəwm ke hər fərd ko qəwm ki tamir mẽ hyssa lena cahie. / Every individual of the nation should take part in the building of the nation. [Here /bənane/ is less appropriate.]

21.208. /nəhana/ IIb "to bathe" is synonymous with the complex verbal construction /ɣwsl kərna/. Like other verbs with stems ending in /əh/, the causative of /nəhana/ is made with /l/: /nəhlana/ "to bathe (someone). "

21.209. /samna/ M2 "confrontation, encounter" is the noun form of /[ke] samne/ "in front of, opposite, facing. " E. g.

> /qəwm ko əhəm məsayl ka samna həy. / The nation is facing important problems.

> /mwjhe bəcpən mẽ bəRi pərešaniõ ka samna kərna pəRa. / In my childhood I had to face great tribulations.

21.210. /əsli/ A1 denotes "original, genuine" and also "pure, unadulterated. " /əsl/ F1 A1 is from the same Arabic root and denotes "origin, root, source" and also "real, true. " Although there are many contexts in which these two words overlap, there are points of difference. E. g.

> /yy əsli ghi həy. / This is pure [i. e. genuine, unadulterated] ghi. [/əsl/ is less appropriate here.]

> /wn ke əsli vətən ke bare mẽ pəta nəhī̃ cəlta. / There is no information about their original homeland. [/əsl vətən/ means "true, real homeland. "]

> /ws ka əsl məqsəd yy tha. / This was his real objective. [/əsli/ here would denote "original. "]

> /yy ys kytab ki əsl həy. / This is the original [original copy] of this book. [/əsli/ can never occur as a noun.]

21.211. /məveši/ Mpl "cattle" is a mass noun and is always treated as plural. Although English "cattle" usually includes only cows, oxen and other bovine quadrupeds, /məveši/ includes these and also horses, goats, sheep, and other large domesticated animals.

21.212. /qəbl əz məsih/ "Before Christ, B. C. " is also found as /qəble məsih/ (with

the Persian /yzafət/). This formula is usually abbreviated in writing to ق . م

As in English, /qəbl əz məsih/ follows the numeral denoting the year. /isvi/ A1 "Christian, A. D. " is similarly employed, although it may also be found as an adjective denoting "Christian (year). " /isvi/ is thus limited only to time expressions; the normal adjective

for "Christian" is /isai/ A1. /isvi/ is abbreviated in writing to a tiny ع written after

the numeral. E. g.

> /tin səw səttər qəbl əz məsih/ three hundred and seventy B. C. [Also /qəble məsih/.]

> /tin səw əTThasi isvi/ three hundred and eighty-eight A. D.

> /isvi kəylənDər ke mwtabyq, yy vaqea əTThara səw səttavən mẽ peš aya. / According to the Christian calendar, this event took place in 1857. [/kəylənDər/ M1 "calendar"]

311

21.213. /aɣaz/ M1 "beginning, start, inception" is nearly synonymous with /šwru/ M1 "beginning, start, inception, commencement. " /aɣaz/ is somewhat rare in complex verbal formations, while /šwru/ is extremely common. Conversely, /šwru/ is infrequent as a true noun, while /aɣaz/ is most common in this usage. E. g.

/ys ke bad ws ne əpni təqrir ka aɣaz kia. / After this he began his lecture. [/šwru ki/ is more common.]

/pācvī sədi ke aɣaz mē, hyndostan choTi choTi ryasətõ mē bəTa hwa tha. / At the beginning of the fifth century, India was divided into various small states. [Here /šwru/ is less likely.]

21.214. /bwdh/ M1 "Buddha" is homophonous with /bwdh/ M1 "Wednesday. " According to most dictionaries, the first word should be /bwddh/, but there is no audible contrast between final /ddh/ and /dh/, and both are thus written /bwdh/. In Hindi /bwdh/ is used in its original meaning as a feminine noun: "intelligence, comprehension, sagacity. "

21.215. /jəld/ Adv "soon, quickly" and /jəldi/ F2 Adv "speed, quickness, hurry, rapidly, quickly" differ slightly in usage. /jəld/ denotes temporal proximity only: "soon. " /jəldi/ carries a connotation of hurry, haste, rapidity, etc. Examples of /jəld/:

/mãy jəld hi vapəs ləwTũga. / I'll return soon. [If /jəldi/ is substituted here, it will signify "rapidly. "]

/tariki ke pərde jəld hi wTh jaẽge. / The curtains of darkness soon will lift.

/vw mamuli si bat pər bəhwt jəld ghəbra jata həy. / He very soon becomes upset over just a minor matter.

/ap ki rəqəm ap ko bəhwt jəld vapəs myl jaegi. / Your sum [of money] will be returned to you very soon.

Examples of /jəldi/:

/mwjhe jəldi həy. / I'm in a hurry. [Lit. to me hurry is. /jəldi/ here is a noun.]

/ws ne yy kam jəldi kia. / He did this work quickly. [Synonymous with:]

/ws ne yy kam jəldi se kia. / He did this work quickly. [Compare:]

/ws ne yy kam jəldi mē kia. / He did this work in a hurry. [/jəldi mē/ "in a hurry" has the connotation of "too hurriedly for good results. "]

/jəldi se yy kam kərẽ! vw anevale hõge. / Do this work quickly. They must be coming.

/ws ne yy qədəm wThane mē jəldi ki. / He took this step hurriedly. [/jəldi kərna/ "to act hurriedly"]

/ws ne cəlne ki jəldi ki. / He was impatient to leave. [Lit. He made haste of going.]

/vw jəldi jəldi əpne ghər ki tərəf ja rəha tha. / He was going along hurriedly towards his house. [/jəldi jəldi/ Adv "in a hurry, in a rush, hurriedly"]

/jəld/ also occurs in /jəld əz jəld/ [or less preferably /jəld se jəld/] Adv "as soon as possible. " /jəldi/ cannot occur in this construction. E. g.

/ap ki rəqəm jəld əz jəld əda kərne ki košyš kərūga. / I'll try to return your sum [of money] as soon as possible.

21.216. /bhər/ "whole, entire, complete, full, throughout" always follows the noun it modifies. It is thus technically an enclitic particle (like /hi/, /bhi/), although it is translatable in English as an adjective, etc. E. g.

/ys məwqe pər mwlk bhər mẽ xwšiā mənai gəī. / On this occasion celebrations were held throughout the country. [/mwlk bhər mẽ/ "throughout the country" is the proper order; never */bhər mwlk mẽ/.]

/yy bat dwnya bhər mẽ məšhur həy. / This matter is famous throughout the world.

/mwjhe pyali bhər aTa do! / Give me a cupful of flour!

/dərd ki vəja se, vw rat bhər jagta rəha. / Because of the pain, he remained awake the whole night.

/swnaie, ap dyn bhər kəhā rəhe. / Tell [me], where have you been all day?

21.217. As was stated in Sec. 7.305, when one wishes to express "hundreds of ..., " the oblique plural form of /səw/ A1 "hundred" cannot be used (whereas one may employ /həzarõ/ "thousands, " /lakhõ/ "hundreds of thousands, " etc.). Instead, the oblique plural form of /sãykRa/ (or /səykRa/) A2 "hundred" is employed. E. g.

/sãykRõ admi mər gəe. / Hundreds of men died. [Never */səwõ/ or */səvõ/.]

/sãykRõ ka nwqsan hwa. / There was a loss of hundreds [of rupees].

/sãykRa/ (or /səykRa/) is also used for "per hundred, " and in this usage /sãykRa/ is always MNS in form. /fi sãykRa/ may also occur. /sãykRa/ may also denote "unit of a hundred" in the purchase of commodities sold by the hundred and in mathematical terminology. E. g.

/am car rupəe sãykRa mylte hãy. / Mangoes can be had for four rupees per hundred. [/car rupəe fi sãykRa/ is also correct.]

/ek sãykRe ki kya qimət həy. / What is the price of [an aggregate of] one hundred?

21.218. Note that the oblique plural of /pəyrəw/ M/F1 "follower, devotee" is /pəyrəvõ/.

21.219. /vəfat/ F1 "death" is synonymous with /yntyqal/ M1 "death. " The latter also means "transfer, " however, a meaning which /vəfat/ does not have. Both of these terms are equally honorific. Note that /vəfat pana/ may be both transitive and intransitive. E. g.

/ws ne vəfat pai. / He died. [Or: /vw vəfat pa gəya. /]

/ws ki vəfat ho gəi. / He died.

/ws ne yntyqal kia. / He died.

/ws ka yntyqal ho gəya. / He died.

21.220. /asar/ Mpl is the Arabic broken plural of /əsər/ M1 "effect, trace, influence. " /asar/ does not denote "effects, " however, but rather "ruins, remains" and also "traces, indications. " /əsər/ has another Arabic plural form, /əsrat/ Mpl, which denotes "effects, influences. " E. g.

/asar kəh rəhe hãy, ky ymarət bəhwt šandar thi. / The ruins show [lit. are saying] that the building was very grand.

/aj baryš ke asar hõy. / There are indications of rain today.

/əmrika ke sədarti yntyxab ke syasi əsrat ərse tək məhsus kie jaẽge. /
The effects of the American presidential elections will be felt for a
long time.

21.221. /həd/ F1 denotes "limit, edge, border, boundary, extreme" in an abstract
sense, while /sərhəd/ F1 denotes a physical boundary: "frontier, boundary line, border
(of a country). " /sərhəd/ is a compound of /sər/ "head" + /həd/.

/həd/ is derived from the Arabic root /ḥ-d-d/, and the broken plural of /həd/ is
/hwdud/ Fpl "borders, limits" (but not */sərhwdud/ -- only /sərhədẽ/ and /sərhədõ/). The
Arabic passive participle of Form I of this root is /məhdud/ (see Sec. 17.301), and this
occurs as A1 in Urdu meaning "limited, bounded, confined. " E.g.

> /pakystan ki šymali sərhədẽ əfɣanystan se mylti hõy. / Pakistan's
> northern borders join with [those of] Afghanistan.

> /ws ne sərhədõ pər məzbut qəle tamir kərae. / He caused strong forts
> to be built on the frontiers.

> /ys mwamle mẽ vw həd se zyada bəRh gəya həy. / In this matter he has
> exceeded the limit [of propriety, etc.].

21.222. /sala/ A1 "-yeared, -year-old" is really the second member of a large
number of loose compounds, the first members of which are numerals. Since this type of
compound is of Persian origin, the Persian numerals are sometimes employed. See Sec.
18.303. E.g.

> /yy ek pācsala mənsuba həy. / This is a five year project. [The Persian
> form /pãjsala/ is also found.]

> /iran ki sat həzarsala tarix mẽ əysa koi vaqea nəhĩ hwa. / Such an event
> has not occurred in the seven thousand year history of Iran.

> /ws ne ek pəndrəsala ləRki se šadi ki. / He married a fifteen year old
> girl.

21.223. /sadat/ Mpl is the Arabic plural of /səyyəd/ M1 "Sayyid, a descendant of
the Prophet Muhammad. " In Sec. 21.000 the term refers to a dynasty of rulers of northern
India.

21.224. Some Complex Verbal Formations. See Sec. 7.123.

A:

/abad/
> /abad hona/ to be settled, populated, inhabited
> /[X ko] abad kərna/ to settle, populate [X]

/bəraməd/
> /bəraməd hona/ to be discovered, found, dug out, brought to light, exported
> /[X ko] bəraməd kərna/ to find, discover, recover, bring to light, export [X]

/bəsər/
> /[X] bəsər hona/ [X] to pass, be spent, be lived
> /[X ko] bəsər kərna/ to spend, pass [X]

/bezar/

    /[X se] bezar hona/ to become sick of, fed up with, disgusted [with X]

    /[X ko] bezar kərna/ to cause [X] to become disgusted, sick (of something)

/dəryaft/

    /dəryaft hona/ to be discovered, found out, ascertained

    /[X ko] dəryaft kərna/ to discover, find out [X]

    /[X ke bare mẽ] dəryaft kərna/ to inquire [about X]

/fəta/

    /fəta hona/ to be conquered

    /[X ko] fəta kərna/ to conquer [X]

    /[X pər] fəta pana/ to gain the victory [over X]

/məhdud/

    /məhdud hona/ to be limited, bounded

    /[X ko] məhdud kərna/ to limit, bound [X]

/mwnəzzəm/

    /mwnəzzəm hona/ to be well-administered, systematically organised

    /[X ko] mwnəzzəm kərna/ to administer [X] well, establish an orderly administration for [X]

/nakam/

    /[X mẽ] nakam hona/ to be unsuccessful [in X]

    /[X ko] nakam kərna/ to render [X] unsuccessful

/tamir/

    /tamir hona/ to be built, erected, constructed

    /[X ko] tamir kərna/ to construct, build, erect [X]

/təhrir/

    /təhrir hona/ to be written, inscribed

    /[X ko] təhrir kərna/ to write, inscribe [X]

B:

/aɣaz/

    /[X ka] aɣaz hona/ [X] to be begun, started

    /[X ka] aɣaz kərna/ to begin [X]

/hyfazət/

    /[X ki] hyfazət kərna/ to protect, safeguard [X]

/khwdai/

    /[X ki] khwdai hona/ [X] to be excavated

    /[X ki] khwdai kərna/ to excavate, dig [X]

/qəyadət/

    /[X ki] qəyadət kərna/ to lead [X]

/samna/

    /[X ka] samna hona/ [X] to be faced, confronted

    /[X ka] samna kərna/ to confront, face, encounter [X]

/təbliɣ/

    /[X ki] təbliɣ hona/ [X] to be spread, preached

/[X ki] təbliɣ kərna/ to spread [X (a doctrine, religion, etc.)], preach [X]

/təhqiq/
   /[X ki] təhqiq hona/ [X] to be investigated
   /[X ki] təhqiq kərna/ to investigate [X]
   /[X pər] təhqiq kərna/ to do research [upon X]

D:

/šykəst/
   /[X ko] šykəst dena/ to defeat [X]
   /[X ko] šykəst hona/ [X] to be defeated
   /šykəst khana/ to be defeated
   /šykəst wThana/ to be defeated

F:

/həd/
   /həd ho jana/ to exceed the limits (of propriety, expectation, etc.)
   /həd kər dena/ to exceed the limits (of propriety, expectation, behaviour, etc.)

/həmla/
   /[X pər] həmla hona/ [X] to be attacked, an attack to be made [upon X]
   /[X pər] həmla kərna/ to attack, assault [X]

/həmləavər/
   /[X pər] həmləavər hona/ to attack [X], invade [X]

/həthyar/
   /həthyar Dal dena/ to surrender

/mwhr/
   /[X pər] mwhr ləgana/ to seal [X]

/mwštəmyl/
   /[X pər] mwštəmyl hona/ to consist [of X], be composed [of X]

/qəbza/
   /[X ka Y pər] qəbza hona/ [X] to have possession [of Y]
   /[X pər] qəbza kər lena/ to take possession [of X], seize [X]
   /[X pər] qəbza pa lena/ to gain possession [of X]

/ryasət/
   /[X pər] ryasət kərna/ to rule [X (a small state)]

/səltənət/
   /[X pər] səltənət kərna/ to rule [X (an empire, kingdom)]

/vəfat/
   /[X ki] vəfat hona/ [X] to die
   /vəfat pana/ to die

21.300. ANALYSIS

21.301. Substantive Composition.

Various Arabic-Persian compounds have been introduced in this Unit. These will be briefly analysed here as an aid to understanding the compounding patterns of literary Urdu.

/bəndərgah/ F1 "seaport, harbour": Persian /bənd/ "closed, dammed, dike" and also present stem of /bəs/ "close"; /dər/ "in, door"; /gah/ "place." All compounds ending in /gah/ are F1.

/bəraməd/ F1 PA1 "recovered, discovered, found; export": Persian preposition /bər/ "on"; /aməd/ past stem of /amə/ "come."

/bəsər/ PA1 "passing, spending (time), living": see Sec. 21.206.

/dəryaft/ F1 "discovery, ascertainment, inquiry": Persian preposition /dər/ "in, door"; /yaft/ past stem of /yaf/ "get, obtain."

/həmləavər/ M1 A1 "attacking, invading, attacker, invader": Arabic /həmla/ "attack"; Persian /avər/ present stem of /avwr/ "bring."

/janəšin/ M/F1 "successor": Persian /ja/ "place"; /nəšin/ present stem of /nyšəs/ "sit."

/nəwjəvan/ M1 A1 "youth, young": Persian /nəw/ "new"; /jəvan/ "young."

/pəyrəw/ M/F1 "follower, devotee": Persian /pəy/ "foot"; /rəw/ present stem of /rəf/ "go."

/rəsmwlxət/ M1 "script, writing system": Arabic /rəsm/ "drawing, sketch, inscription, writing, custom"; /wl/ the Arabic definite article; /xət/ "writing, line" (Arabic /xəṭṭ/).

/sərhəd/ F1 "boundary, frontier, border": see Sec. 21.221.

/sypəsalar/ M1 "general, commander": Persian /sypah/ or /sypəh/ "army"; /salar/ "leader." See Sec. 18.305 for /salar/.

/šandar/ A1 "glorious, majestic": Arabic /šan/ "thing, matter, rank" used as "glory, majesty" in Persian; Persian /dar/ present stem of /daš/ "have."

/šəhzada/ [or /šahzada/] M2 "prince": Persian /šah/ "king"; /zada/ past participle of /za/ "be born."

/təhzibyafta/ A1 "cultured, civilised": see Sec. 21.205.

/xanəbədoš/ M1 A1 "nomad, nomadic": Persian /xana/ "house"; /bə/ (or /by/) "with, by"; /doš/ "shoulder": "carrying one's house on one's back."

21.302. The Verb: the OPasP + /rəkhna/ and /rəhna/.

The oblique past participles of a limited number of transitive verbs occur with inflected forms of /rəkhna/ "to keep, put, place" and /rəhna/ "to stay, live." These two formations are nearly synonymous: both mean "retaining in a state of having performed the action." In English these forms are usually translatable with "keep"; e.g. "keeps holding his hand," "keeps a bandage tied on his head." If there is any difference between <OPasP + /rəkhna/> and <OPasP + /rəhna/>, it seems to lie in the transitive nature of the former versus the

317

intransitiveness of the latter: i. e. the former connotes conscious, continued effort, while the latter simply connotes the continued maintenance of a state. In the case of <OPasP + /rəkhna/>, if the object of the action is animate, the construction may denote "maintaining the object in a state against the object's will. "

Both of these formations are found mainly in the simple past tense. Future tense and present general tense example also occur, but the present and past perfect, the continuative, etc. are very rare. Both of these constructions are also extremely rare in the negative. E. g.

/ws ne dwšmənõ ko həmla kərne se roke rəkkha. / He kept the enemies from attacking. [I. e. he stopped them and held them in that state.]

/polis ne mwjhe do ghənTe tək roke rəkkha. / The police held [lit. stopped and kept] me for two hours.

/mə̃y ne ərse tək wse šərab pine se roke rəkkha. / I kept him from drinking liquor for a long time.

/mə̃y ne wnhẽ der tək roke rəkkha, lekyn jəb ap nə ae, to vw cəle gəe. / I detained them for a long time, but when you did not come, they left.

/ap ke ane tək mə̃y wnhẽ roke rəkhũga. / I'll detain them until you come.

/jəb tək həm səyr kərte rəhe, ws ne mera hath pəkRe rəkkha. / As long as we kept strolling, he kept hold of my hand.

/əysi pabəndiã hi yn bwraiõ ko roke rəkkhti hə̃y. / Only such restrictions keep these evils in check. [Also /roke rəhti hə̃y/.]

/mə̃y wse roke rəha, vərna vw gyr pəRta. / I held him [lit. stayed him stopped], otherwise he would have fallen.

/vw bərsõ əpne jəzbat ko roke rəha. / He kept his emotions pent up for years. [Also: /ws ne ... roke rəkkha. / Remember that <OPasP + /rəkhna/> is transitive, while <OPasP + /rəhna/> is intransitive.]

/jəb tək mə̃y vapəs aũ, yy kytabẽ əpne pas rəkkhe rəhie! / Please keep these books with you until I return! [* /rəkkhe rəkhie/ is not possible because the repetition of the verb stem is incongruous.]

/vw kəi həftõ tək əpni ākhõ pər pəTTi bãdhe rəha. / He kept a bandage tied on his eyes for many weeks. [Also /ws ne ... bãdhe rəkkhi/. The latter connotes more transitive action, the former just the maintenance of a state.]

/vw həmeša əpni jeb mẽ səw rupəe rəkkhe rəhta həy. / He always keeps a hundred rupees in his pocket.

/əyse səxt qəvanin yn bwraiõ ko roke rəhe. / Such strict laws kept these evils in check. [Also /... qəvanin ne ... roke rəkkha/]

Both of these formations may be compared with the <S + /rəkhna/> construction, which denotes deliberate action with lasting effects. See Sec. 16.301. It may be noted that the <S + /rəkhna/> construction is commonest in the perfect and past perfect tenses, and it is so rare as to be nonexistent in the simple past tense. The <OPasP + /rəkhna/, /rəhna/> constructions, on the other hand, are rare in the perfect and past perfect tenses but are very common in the simple past tense. In some examples all three of these constructions appear to be interchangeable, but in most cases the <S + /rəkhna/> formation cannot be substituted for the other two. E. g.

/ap ka jəvab ane tək, mə̃y ap ka yy mal roke rəkhũga. / I'll keep these goods of yours until your answer comes. [Also /roke rəhũga/ and /rok rəkhũga/. Informants stated that although all three are here interchangeable, /rok rəkhũga/ is less appropriate.]

/əyse səxt qəvanin ne yn bwraiõ ko rok rəkkha həy. / Such strict laws have checked these evils. [Also /... qəvanin ne ... roke rəkkha/ or / ... qəvanin ... roke rəhe/. The latter two emphasise the

318

maintenance of the state; the former emphasises the action of
checking. Note that one cannot employ [*]/rok rəkkha/ without /həy/
here.]

/həmari fəwjõ ne dwšmənõ ko sərhəd pər rok rəkkha həy./ Our armies
have stopped the enemies on the border. [Again /roke rəkkha/ and
/roke rəhĩ/ are possible.]

/əb tək to bənd ne səylab ke pani ko roke rəkkha həy./ Up until now the
dike has kept the floodwater in check. [An example of the <OPasP +
/rəkhna/> construction in the perfect tense. /roke rəha həy/ and
/rok rəkkha həy/ are also possible.]

21.303. The Verb: the OPasP + Various Other Auxiliaries.

Oblique past participles of various transitive verbs (and less commonly of certain
intransitive stems as well) may be found with various inflected auxiliaries: /dena/, /Dalna/,
/khana/, and /lena/. These constructions denote emphatic action to be performed in the
immediate future. /dena/ has its expected sense of "action away from the actor"; /lena/
of "action to or for the actor"; /Dalna/ of "violent action"; /khana/ is rare and idiomatic
in this formation. Note that all of these constructions occur principally in the present
general tense: e.g. /kəhe deta hũ/, /khae leta həy/, etc. Examples in the past tenses are
not found, and these formations are also not employed in negative sentences. E.g.

(1) /dena/:

/məy wn se kəhe deta hũ, ky vw ap ka yntyzar kərẽ./ I'll just tell him
that he should wait for you.

/məy ap se kəhe deta hũ, ky ap vəhã nə jaẽ, vərna ys ka ənjam bwra hoga./
I am telling you that you should not go there; otherwise the result
of it will be bad. [Here the connotation of emphasis is predominant.]

/məy əbhi ap ka saman khole deta hũ./ I'll just open your luggage. [Here
the connotation is one of immediacy, together with a slight degree of
emphasis.]

/məy əbhi ap ke lie našta təyyar kie deti hũ./ I'll just prepare breakfast
for you.

/məy əbhi hoTəl se ap ke lie khana lae deta hũ./ I'll just bring food for
you from the restaurant. [If /la deta hũ/ were substituted, the
connotation of immediacy would not be as great.]

/əgər ap ki yyhi mərzi həy, to məy yy səb saman wse die deta hũ./ If
this is your pleasure, I'll just give him all this luggage.

(2) /Dalna/:

/dərya ka tez pani bənd ko toRe Dalta həy./ The swift water of the river
is breaking the dike. [The process of breaking has begun, and the
actual breakthrough will occur in the immediate future.]

/yy šor mere kan phaRe Dalta həy./ This noise is breaking [lit. tearing]
my ears.

/yy γəm mwjhe mare Dalta həy./ This sorrow is killing me.

(3) /khana/:

/ws ki yy batẽ mwjhe kaTe khati hãy./ These words of his trouble me
greatly. [/kaTe khana/ is almost the only common example of OPasP
+ /khana/. It denotes "tease, taunt, overwhelm with gloom, bad
memories, sadness, loneliness, etc."]

/yy məkan mwjhe kaTe khata həy./ This house overwhelms me [with
gloom, etc.].

(4) /lena/:

/yy dəvai əbhi khae leta hū. / I'll just take [lit. eat] this medicine.

/ap kəhte hǣy, to zəhr pie leta hū. / [If] you say [so], I'll just drink poison.

/mǣy ap ki rəqəm wn se aj hi vapəs lie leta hū. / I'll just get your amount [of money] back from him today.

/mǣy əbhi wn se myle leta hū. / I'm just going to meet him. [/mylna/ is an example of an intransitive verb in this construction.]

21.304. The Verb: the OPasP + /jana/.

The <OPasP + /jana/> construction is quite different in meaning from any of the above. It denotes a type of continuous action. This formation is sometimes almost synonymous with the <PreP + /rəhna/> construction (Sec. 14.305) and occasionally with the <PreP + /jana/> formation (Sec. 15.310). E.g.

/həmari fəwjē bərabər bəRhti rəhī. / Our armies kept on advancing. [<PreP + /rəhna/>.]

/həmari fəwjē bərabər bəRhti gəī. / Our armies kept on advancing. [<PreP + /jana/>.]

/həmari fəwjē bərabər bəRhe gəī. / Our armies kept on advancing. [<OPasP + /jana/>.]

The differences between the above examples and the "continuative" (<S + /rəha həy/>) and the "habitual" (<PasP + /kərna/>) are rather obvious. See Secs. 5.311 and 14.306. E.g.

/həmari fəwjē bərabər bəRh rəhi thī. / Our armies were continuously advancing.

/vw həmare hā əksər aya kərta tha. / He [habitually] used to come to our place.

There is a slight semantic difference between the first three sentences above. /bəRhti rəhī/ indicates simple iteration: a single act performed over and over again. /bəRhti gəī/ denotes a gradual modification of the state of the subject. With transitive verbs, this formation denotes "persevering, doing deliberately, doing against obstacles nevertheless, " etc. The third form, /bəRhe gəī/, has the meaning "continuing to do willy-nilly, continuing out of control, unstoppably. " All of these formations are interchangeable in certain contexts, and the very slight amount of semantic difference between them makes them very difficult for a beginner. E.g.

/dərya mē pani bəhta rəhta həy. / Water keeps flowing in the river. [Here only the connotation of simple iteration is desired, and thus /bəhta jata həy/ and /bəhe jata həy/ are idiomatically less correct.]

/DakTər ne bəhwt košyš ki, lekyn məriz ke zəxmō se xun bəhe gəya. / The doctor tried hard, but blood kept flowing from the patient's wounds. [Here the sense of uncheckable continuity is desired. /bəhta rəha/ is also correct but would imply only simple continuance. /bəhta gəya/ is not idiomatic here.]

/do do ghənTe ke bad ek xwrak khylate rəho! / Go on giving [lit. feeding] [him] one dose after every two hours! [This denotes simple iteration. /khylae jao! / would denote "willy-nilly -- no matter what, " while /khylate jao! / would indicate perseverance.]

/vw əksər kytabē xəridta rəhta həy. / He keeps on buying books. [Simple iteration.]

/vw rəfta rəfta yskul ki kytabẽ xəridta jata həy. / He gradually goes on buying [his] school books. [Gradual, persevering action.]

/vw kytabẽ xəride jata həy. / He goes on buying books. [Any books -- he buys books continually and indiscriminately.]

/mə̃y swn rəha hū. twm kytab pəRhte rəho! / I am listening. You keep on reading! [Simple iteration without pause.]

/mə̃y swn rəha hū. twm kytab pəRhte jao! / I am listening. You keep on reading the book! [Persevere, keep at it!]

/mə̃y swn rəha hū. twm kytab pəRhe jao! / I am listening. You go on reading the book. [Keep on, whether you want to or not, no matter what. Do not stop!]

The sense of continuity is not as intense in the <PreP + /jana/> construction: the action may be extended over a longer period. E.g.

/vw mera rupəya əpne ryštedarõ ko deti rəhti həy. / She keeps giving away my money to her relatives. [Simple repetition: the individual acts of giving are quite close to one another in time.]

/vw mera rupəya əpne ryštedarõ ko die jati həy. / She keeps giving away my money to her relatives. [Here the sense is "indiscriminately, no matter what."]

/vw mera rupəya əpne ryštedarõ ko deti jati həy. / She keeps giving away my money to her relatives. [Over a longer period of time, perseveringly, deliberately, against my opposition.]

21.400. SUPPLEMENTARY VOCABULARY

21..401. Supplementary Vocabulary.

The following numerals are all Type I adjectives. See Sec. 2.401.

chyasi [or /cheasi/ or /chəyasi/]	eighty-six
səttasi	eighty-seven
əTThasi	eighty-eight
nəvasi	eighty-nine

Other items are:

mahyr M/F1	expert, artisan, skilled person, master-craftsman
mwvərryx M1	historian

21.402. Supplementary Exercise I: Substitution.

1. ys mwvərryx ke mwtabyq, yy vaqea <u>sətra səw nəvve</u> mē peš aya.

 fourteen hundred and eighty-nine

 seven hundred and eighty-seven

 twelve hundred and sixty-eight

 eighteen hundred and eighty-six

 fifteen hundred and eighty-eight

21.403. Variation.

1. vw tarix ka mahyr həy.

 yy log syasiat ke mahyr hə̄y.

 vw əpne kam mē mahyr həy.

 vw ləRki khana pəkane mē mahyr həy.

 ys mwamle mē, kysi mahyre syasiat se rae leni cahie.

 təjryba ynsan ko mahyr bəna deta həy.

21.500. VOCABULARY AND GRAMMAR DRILL

21.501. Substitution.

1. khwdai ke bad, vəhā se kwch bərtən   bəraməd hwe.
                                        toys
                                        idols
                                        weapons
                                        coins
                                        ancient ornaments

2. məɣrybi mahyrin   ne   hyndostan ki qədim təhzib   pər təhqiq ki həy.
    our religious scholars   the Buddhist religion
    that historian   the life of the nomadic people
    our professor   the life of the third Caliph
    many historians   the ancient history of the Valley of Sindh
    an English scholar   the customs of this tribe

3. ws badšah   ne   syndh   pər qəbza kər lia.
    his successor   the Deccan
    that prince   Kabul
    the Aryans   India
    that young general   the throne of Delhi
    the looters   the seaport

4. ɣwlamõ   ne   badšah ke məhl   pər həmla kia.
    the external tribe   our state
    the looters   the inn
    our army   the Mughal army
    the Raja   their borders
    the Aryans   the Dravidians

5. xanəbədoš qəbilõ   ne   šəhr   ko fəta kər lia.
    the enemies   our country
    the Mughals   the Panjab
    the British   this seaport
    the king's deputy   Afghanistan
    a twenty-one year old   Rome
    general

6. šəhzade   ne   sərhəd pər   ek məzbut qəla   tamir kəraya.
    the Raja   in the city   a glorious palace
    the king   on the river   a bridge
    the government   the shore of the a lighthouse [lit. a
                         sea   tower of light]
    the ruler of the   in the village   a hospital
    district
    the village elder   outside the   a well
                         village

7.   <u>yy suba</u>   <u>nəw zylõ</u>   pər mwštəmyl həy.

      our army   eleven thousand soldiers

      Islam   different sects

      the National   one hundred and fifty-six
      Assembly   members

      his empire   four big provinces

      this district   twelve təhsil

8.   <u>səza ke Dər</u>   ne   <u>logõ ko gwnahõ se</u>   rok rəkkha həy.

      the dike of the river   the water of the flood

      religious teachings   these evils

      our army   the enemies

      this policy   our industrial progress

      the landowners   all the grain[1]

         1/ko/ should be used to mark the object in the first four sentences, but not in
      the fifth.

9.   <u>hynduõ</u>   ne   <u>həmləavərõ</u>   ko šykəst di.

      the Raja   his enemies

      the Caliph   the armies of Rome

      the Persian general   the nomads

      the Greeks   the Persians

      the Dravidians   the Aryans

10. <u>həmẽ</u>   <u>bəhwt se əndəruni məsayl</u> ka samna kərna pəRa.

           hundreds of troubles

           many external problems

           the attacks of looters

           these circumstances

           the army of the enemy

11. <u>mẽy ne</u> <u>əziz sahəb</u>   se   <u>pakystani jəjõ ke yxtiarat</u>   ke bare mẽ dəryaft kia.

            the Hindus   their gods

            Məwlvi Sahəb   the Arabic script

            historians   the original homeland of the Aryans

            experts   these ancient coins

            local residents   these ancient ruins

12. <u>mẽy</u>   <u>ap ke məšvərõ</u>   se bezar ho gəya hũ.

           the world

           his leadership

           the people of the present era

           your projects

           politics

13. <u>ws ne</u> <u>əpne vətən ki sərhədõ</u>   ki hyfazət ki.

           his cattle

           the throne of Iran

           his empire

           his sheep

the valuable jewellery

14. wnhõ ne əTThara səw səttavən   mẽ vəfat pai.
three hundred and eighty-
nine B.C.
southern Iran
West Africa
northern India
eastern Pakistan

15. vw   dyn bhər   rota rəha.
the whole night
[his] whole life
for years
the whole year
for months

21.502. Transformation.

1. Change the underlined verb forms in the following sentences to the OPasP +
auxiliary verb construction: e.g. /kəhe deta həy/, /khae leta həy/, etc. This
involves the following changes: (a) change all future tense verbs to the present
general tense; (b) change the main verb to the OPasP; (c) retain the auxiliary
given in the original, or, if no auxiliary occurs, insert the auxiliary given in
brackets, at the end of the sentence. Thus, /kha lũga/ becomes /khae leta hũ/.
In some cases other appropriate auxiliaries are given at the end of the sentence in
brackets, and the sentence may have two correct transformations.
   a.   mə̃y kəhta hũ, ky əysa kərne se ap ko nwqsan wThana pəRega. [/dena/]
   b.   ap fykr nə kijie, mə̃y ap ka səb saman əbhi bhyjva dũga.
   c.   mə̃y yy rəqəm vapəs kər dũga.
   d.   əgər ap ko həva bwri ləg rəhi həy, to mə̃y dərvaza bənd kər deta hũ.
   e.   mə̃y əbhi wn se əpni kytab le lũga.
   f.   mə̃y ap ke lie yy mal rok lũga.
   g.   mə̃y sara khana əbhi pəka dũga. [Also /Dalna/]
   h.   khane ke sath, dəva bhi pi leta hũ. [Also /Dalna/]
   i.   mə̃y əbhi bəccõ ke kəpRe bədəl dũgi. [Also /Dalna/]
   j.   əgər ap yy khyləwna dəs rupəe mẽ dẽ, to xərid lũga.

2. Letters in brackets after the following sentences indicate that the underlined verb
forms may be changed to (a) <OPasP + /rəkhna/>, (b) <OPasP + /rəhna/>, or (c)
<S + /rəkhna/>. It should be remembered that the <OPasP + /rəhna/> construction
is intransitive, and the subject must thus be nominative; this will require changes
in all of the following sentences.
   a.   bimari ne mwjhe vəhã jane se rok dia.   [a, b, c]
   b.   ap ki yn batõ ne meri hymmət bəRhai.   [a, b, c]
   c.   yn halat ne əvam ko Dəraya.   [a, c]

325

d. ws ne əpne γwsse ko <u>roka</u>. [a, b, c]

e. məcchərõ ke ǒor ne mwjhe <u>jəga dia</u>.   [a, c]

f. qwli ne aluõ ki Tokri <u>wTha li</u>.   [a, b, c]

g. ws ne əpne ghər mẽ mera sara saman <u>rəkh lia</u>. [b, c]

h. həmare nəbi ki talimat ne logõ ko bwraiõ se <u>bəcaya</u>.   [a, b, c]

i. ws ne dwlhən ke yntyzar mẽ əpna ghər <u>səjaya</u>. [a, b, c]

j. coT ki vəja se, ws ne hath pər pəTTi <u>bãdhi</u>.   [a, b, c]

3. Change the underlined verb forms in the following sentences to the <OPasP + /jana/> formation. Retain the same tense. Sentences (h), (m), and (o) may also be changed to the <PreP + /jana/> construction, but informants generally felt that this formation was less preferable, weak, or impossible for the remaining sentences.

a. kafi der tək ws ke zəxmõ se xun <u>bəhta rəha</u>.

b. vw ghənTõ ws təsvir ko bəRe γəwr se <u>dekhta rəha</u>.

c. ws ne meri bat nə swni, əwr əpni hi bat <u>kəhta rəha</u>.

d. əfsər ne sypahiõ ko bəhwt məna kia, phyr bhi vw goli <u>cəlate rəhe</u>.

e. mẽy ne wse bəhwt səmjhaya, məgər vw yyhi <u>dohrata rəha</u>, ky vw səhih raste pər həy.

f. mẽy ne wse bətaya, ky vw ghər pər nəhĩ həy, phyr bhi vw <u>pwkarta rəha</u>.

g. xa ap ko pəsənd ho, ya nə ho, mẽy to yyhi gana <u>gata rəhũga</u>.

h. əgərce rasta bəhwt mwškyl tha, phyr bhi vw pəhaR pər <u>cəRhta rəha</u>.

i. xa ys jəga se kwch bəraməd ho, ya nə ho, həm <u>khodte rəhẽge</u>.

j. məriz rat bhər <u>khãsta rəha</u>.

k. ãdhera ho gəya, phyr bhi vw ãguThi <u>DhũDti rəhi</u>.

l. ap jəvab dẽ, ya nə dẽ, mẽy xət <u>lykhti rəhũgi</u>.

m. əgərce wnhẽ sãykRõ təkalif ka samna kərna pəRa, phyr bhi vw mənzyl ki tərəf <u>bəRhte rəhe</u>.

n. əgərce wn ke bəhwt se admi mare gəe, phyr bhi vw <u>ləRte rəhe</u>.

o. jəb tək yy səbəq əcchi təra yad nə ho jae, <u>pəRhte rəhie</u>!

21.503. Variation.

1. asman pər bədəl cha gəe.
   arya qəbile hyndostan pər ahysta ahysta cha gəe.
   wn ki fəwjẽ bəhwt jəld sare iran pər cha gəĩ.
   yslami fəwjẽ əpne layq sypəsalar ki qəyadət mẽ məγrybi ešya pər cha gəĩ.
   baryš se pəhle, asman pər cha jati həy.
   badšah ke mərne se, mwlk pər γəm ke bədəl cha gəe.

2. vw səb log, bivi əwr bəccõ ke sath, pənjab mẽ abad ho gəe.
   kwch yunani xandan əpna mwlk choR kər šam mẽ abad ho gəe.
   ys təra, yy xanəbədoš qəbile ahysta ahysta šymali pakystan mẽ abad hote gəe.
   hwkuməte pakystan ne hyndostan se anevalõ ke lie kəi choTe choTe šəhr abad kie.
   yn ylaqõ ko abad kərne ke lie, hwkuməte pakystan ne əmrika ki mədəd se ek pãcsala mənsuba təyyar kia.

3. šəhzade ne əpne choTe bhai ki hyfazət ki.

həmari fəwj həmari sərhədõ ki hyfazət kərti həy.

rat ko həmara kwtta məvešiõ ki hyfazət kərta həy.

ləRai ke vəqt, yn tin sypahiõ ne həmare jhənDe ki hyfazət ki.

šəhzade ne əpne valyd ki mwhr hyfazət se rəkkhi.

mwjhe wmmid həy, ky ap meri nyšani hyfazət se rəkhēgi.

4. ap ke xət ka jəvab jəld hi təhrir kərūga.

yy xəbər swnte hi, mãy ne jəldi se wse ek xət təhrir kia.

ws ne yy yttyla pəhw̃cane ke lie jəldi jəldi kəi xət təhrir kie.

ws ne təhrir kia tha, ky vw jəld hi kəraci aega.

mãy ne yy xət jəldi mē təhrir kia həy. əgər ys mē koi ɣələti ho, to maf fərmaē.

ys təhrir se to ys bat ka koi swbut nəhĩ mylta.

5. vw əyš ki zyndəgi bəsər kər rəhe the.

dəravəR ek mwhəzzəb zyndəgi bəsər kər rəhe the.

vw qəbila jãgəl mē aram ki zyndəgi bəsər kər rəha tha.

ys šəhr ke log ek xwšhal zyndəgi bəsər kərte the.

ws ne əpni adhi zyndəgi ỹglystan mē bəsər ki.

kwch to bəsər ho gəi həy, əwr baqi bhi kysi nə kysi təra bəsər ho jaegi.

6. wnhõ ne dwšmənõ ko šykəst de kər, jwnubi hyndostan ki tərəf dhəkel dia.

iraniõ ne wn qəbilõ ko šykəst di, əwr wnhē šymal ki tərəf dhəkel dia.

aryaõ ne wnhē šykəst de kər, dəkən ki tərəf dhəkel dia.

ys təra ərəb yn qəbilõ ko šykəst dete gəe, əwr məɣryb ki tərəf dhəkelte gəe.

šykəst ke bad, yunaniõ ko məšryq ki tərəf dhəkel dia gəya.

gaRi ko dhəkel kər, dərvaze ke samne khəRi kər do!

7. wnnysvĩ sədi ke aɣaz mē, yy ylaqa choTi choTi ryasətõ mē bəTa hwa tha.

pychle sal ke aɣaz hi mē, həmari sari zəmin xandan mē bəT gəi thi.

cəwdəvĩ sədi ke aɣaz mē, šymali hyndostan choTe choTe TwkRõ mē bəTa hwa tha.

wnnys səw sãytalys isvi mē, hyndostan do azad mwlkõ mē bəT gəya.

fəta ke bad, jo mal myla, vw sypahiõ mē bəT gəya.

gaõ ke nəmbərdar ki vəfat ke bad, ws ki sari zəmin əwr məveši ws ki əwlad mē
         bəT gəe.

8. ys šəhr ki khwdai se, bəhwt si mwhrē əwr sykke bəraməd hwe hãy.

kəraci ke nəzdik, khwdai ke bad, ek qədim təhzib ke asar bəraməd hwe hãy.

kūā khodte vəqt, myTTi ke bəhwt se khyləwne əwr bərtən bəraməd hwe.

polis ne mwjrym ke qəbze se sara mal bəraməd kər lia.

sypahiõ ne mwjrym ki jeb se zəhr ki botəl bəraməd kər li.

polis ne cor ke ghər se sare pəyse əwr noT bəraməd kər lie.

9. mãy ap se ys həd tək yttyfaq kər səkta hū̃.

həmari parTi ap logõ se syrf ys həd tək yttyfaq kər səkti həy.

həmara mənsuba bəRi həd tək kamyab rəha həy.

vw qəbile əb kysi həd tək mwhəzzəb ho gəe hãy.

ws dəwr mē, mwɣəl səltənət bəRi həd tək kəmzor ho cwki thi.

ys mwamle mē, vw həd se bəRh gəya həy.

327

10. ys raja ne zyndəgi bhər əpne mwlk ki xydmət ki.

ys raja ne mwlk bhər mẽ talim phəylai.

ys dəvai ki dəryaft se, dwnya bhər ko fayda pəhw̃ca həy.

DakTər ne rat bhər koŝyŝ ki, .məgər xun bərabər bəhe gəya.

kysanõ ne sal bhər myhnət ki, məgər səylab ne wn ki fəslõ ko təbah kər dia.

mẽy ne dyn bhər təlaŝ kia, məgər əsli ghi kəhĩ nəhĩ myla.

11. mẽy ap se yy dəryaft kərna cahta hũ, ky pakystan ke məwjuda əhəm məsayl kya hẽy.

mẽy ne mwvərryxin se dəryaft kia, ky dwnya ki qədimtərin təhzib kəwnsi həy.

mẽy ap se yy dəryaft kərna cahta hũ, ky ap kys həd tək həmari mədəd kər səkte hẽy.

mẽy ne əpne profesər sahəb se dəryaft kia, ky mohənjo daro kəb abad hwa tha.

kysi mwstənəd mwvərryx se dəryaft kijie, ky dusri jõg ki əsl vwjuhat kya thĩ.

mwjhe bwdh məzhəb ke mwtəəllyq ap se kwch batẽ dəryaft kərni hẽy.

12. ws ne pakystan ja kər isai məzhəb ki təbliɣ ki.

wn ke nwmaynde ɣəyrmwmalyk mẽ ja kər əpne syasi nəzəryõ ki təbliɣ kərte hẽy.

yəhã ke cənd əfrad əmrika ja kər yslam ki təbliɣ kərni cahte hẽy.

am təwr pər, hyndu dusre mwmalyk mẽ əpne məzhəb ki təbliɣ nəhĩ kərte.

dusre mwlk mẽ ja kər əpne məzhəb ki təbliɣ kərna koi asan kam nəhĩ.

ys dəwr mẽ, eŝya bhər mẽ bwdh məzhəb ki təbliɣ jari thi.

13. rum ki təhzib ne õgrezõ pər bəhwt gəhra əsər Dala həy.

hynduõ ki rwsumat ne həmare mwaŝre pər bəhwt gəhra əsər Dala həy.

gəwtəm bwdh ki talimat ne təmam eŝya pər bəhwt gəhra əsər Dala həy.

yunani həmle ne hyndostan ki təhzib pər kafi əsər Dala həy.

ys ŝykəst ne yslami tarix pər gəhra əsər Dala həy.

mysr ke pwrane məzhəb ka məwjuda mysr pər koi əsər baqi nəhĩ.

14. kysanõ ne ek nəya kũã khod lia.

zyle ke hakym ne kwch nəe kũẽ khwdvae hẽy.

DakTərõ ne səfai ke lie pwrane ŝəhr mẽ bəhwt si naliã khwdvai hẽy.

ys məwsəm mẽ, kysan nəi naliã khod lete hẽy.

kysanõ ne bəhwt si myTTi khod kər, ek nəya bənd bənaya.

sãykRõ admi ys ŝəhr ki khwdai mẽ məsruf hẽy.

15. wnhõ ne nəhane ke lie ŝəhr mẽ ɣwslxane bənvae.

bədqysməti se, ws ŝəhr mẽ nəhane ka yntyzam syrf bəRe bəRe hoTlõ tək məhdud
həy.

həmare məzhəb ke mwtabyq, ybadət se pəhle nəhana lazmi həy.

syhət ke lie, nəhana bəhwt zəruri həy.

ɣwslxane mẽ təwlia, sabwn vəɣəyra rəkh dẽ. mẽy thoRi der mẽ a kər nəhata hũ.

mwrde ko ɣwsl dene ke bad dəfn kər dia gəya.

21. 504. Translation.

1. Write out the following sentences in the Urdu script. Then translate them into
English.

328

a. jəb babər hyndostan pər həmləavər hwa, to ybrahim lodhi ne ws ka mwqabla kia, əwr panipət ke tarixi məydan mē donõ ke dərmyan jõg hwi, jys mē babər ko fəta əwr ybrahim lodhi ko šykəst hwi.

b. jəb ws qədim šəhr ke asar myle, to hwkumət ne ws ki baqayda khwdai šwru kərai.

c. yn pətthərõ pər kwch təhrirē pai gəi hõy, məgər əb tək wnhē koi nəhĩ pəRh səka.

d. ws ki vəfat ke bad, ws ke janəšin ne səltənət ka yntyzam šandar təriqe se cəlaya.

e. həmē, jyn məsayl ka samna həy, əgər wnhē həl nə kia gəya, to həmari təhzib xətm ho jaegi.

f. jəb xəlifa ko mwxtəlyf zərae se yy xəbər pəhw̄ci, to ws ne əpne sypəsalarõ ko bwlaya əwr kəha, ky "dwšmənõ ka jhənDa həmari səltənət pər nəhĩ ləhrana cahie. "

g. həmare rəsmwlxət mē, jo xərabiã thĩ, mahyrin ne wnhē dur kər dia həy.

h. məhabharət əwr ved hynduõ ki əhəmtərin məzhəbi kytabē hõy. wn se pəta cəlta həy, ky ek həzar sal qəbl əz məsih, hyndostan ke bašynde ek mwhəzzəb əwr xwšhal zyndəgi bəsər kərte the.

i. əgərce wn ke əsli vətən ka pəta nəhĩ cəlta, lekyn əksər mwvərryxin ka xyal həy, ky vw məɣrybi ešya ke rəhnevale the.

j. jəb sykəndəre azəm sərhəd se age bəRha, to mwqami fəwj Dər kər bhag gəi, əwr ws ne ləRai kie bəɣəyr, mwlk fəta kər lia.

k. yy choTe choTe qəbile hyndostan pər ae dyn həmləavər hote rəhte the. bad mē yn mē se əksər qəbile hyndostan hi mē abad ho gəe.

l. vw bis sal tək əpne məzhəb ki təbliɣ kərte rəhe.

m. rəfta rəfta ws ne əpni səltənət ki hədē kəšmir tək bəRha lĩ.

n. jwnubi ylaqe mē nəhrē khwdvane ka mənsuba subai əsəmbli ke samne peš kər dia gəya həy.

o. məɣrybi əfriqa mē, baz qədim šəhr bəraməd hwe hõy, jyn se pəta cəlta həy, ky wn ke bašynde təhzibyafta the.

2. Translate the following sentences into Urdu. Write them out in the Urdu script.

a. Having become disgusted with the constant [lit. every day] attacks of the nomads, they formed [lit. made] a large army.

b. Chariots and weapons of copper were used in ancient Egypt.

c. He solved the external problems of the country, and also improved [lit. made better] the internal administration.

d. This country consists of fourteen provinces. Each province is divided into three districts.

e. That raja destroyed [lit. finished] the [various] small states, and established an orderly government.

f. In exchange for that horse, that peasant gave me four sheep.

g. The followers of the Buddhist religion built [lit. inhabited] a glorious city in this valley.

h. Further research is necessary upon this period [lit. further research's necessity is], because no reliable history of it is available [lit. about it some reliable history is not gotten].

i. [At] this time our means are somewhat [lit. some] limited. Otherwise we would certainly have helped you.

j. That young chief conquered the fort and took possession of the entire northern region.

k. In the cities notes and coins both are used [lit. /cəlte hə̄y/], but the villagers prefer [lit. like more] coins.

l. After the excavation of this city, many curtains have lifted from the history of that period [i. e. much more has become known ...].

m. When he left the throne and crown and went off into the jungle [lit. having left the throne and crown went out in the jungle (/nykəl gəya/)], then his brothers began to fight among themselves for the throne.

n. At [lit. in] the beginning of the thirteenth century A.D., the Muslims laid [lit. placed, put] the foundation of a systematic government in India.

o. Babar was the founder of the Mughal Empire in India. This family ruled on the throne of India [for] approximately three hundred and fifty years.

21.505. Script.

1. Write out the following words in the Urdu script and place them in Urdu alphabetical order.

a. zərae
b. aɣaz
c. pəyrəw
d. səltənət
e. hyfazət
f. mwnəzzəm
g. fəta
h. bəndərgah
i. sərhəd
j. təhzibyafta
k. khyləwna
l. təhqiq
m. mwhəzzəb
n. rəsmwlxət
o. həmla
p. qəbila
q. məhdud
r. asar
s. fwtuhat
t. xəlifa

21.506. Response.

1. Answer the following questions verbally:

a. kya, ap ne kəbhi sykke ya Dak ke TykəT jəma kie hə̄y?
b. kya, ap ko tarix se dylcəspi həy?
c. ap ki rae mē, ə̄grezi rəsmwlxət mē yslah ki zərurət həy, ya nəhī̃.
d. kya, jwnubi əmrika mē bhi qədim təhzib ke asar bəraməd hwe hə̄y?
e. pakystan ki məɣrybi sərhədē kyn kyn mwmalyk se mylti hə̄y.
f. ap ka mwlk kytne subō pər mwštəmyl həy.
g. ap ke xandan ka əsli vətən kəhā̃ həy.
h. kya, rum ki fəwjō ne ỹglystan pər bhi həmla kia tha?

330

i.   gəwtəm bwdh kəwn tha.

j.   kya, əšok hyndu məzhəb ka pəyrəw tha?

2.   Write out the answers to the following questions in Urdu. Answers to most of these may be found in Sec. 21. 000.

۱۔   سکندرِ اعظم نے ہندوستان پر کب حملہ کیا ؟

۲۔   جب محمد بن قاسم سندھ پر حملہ آور ہوا تو اُس کی عمر کیا تھی ؟

۳۔   ہندوستان میں مغل سلطنت کی بنیاد کس نے ڈالی ؟

۴۔   کیا ، محمود غزنوی نے ہندوستان میں کوئی منظم حکومت قائم کی ؟

۵۔   اکثر مؤرخین کے خیال کے مطابق ہڑپہ اور موہن جو دارو کے باشندے کون تھے۔

۶۔   کیا ، سکندرِ اعظم نے ہندوستان میں وفات پائی ؟

۷۔   آریا کس قسم کی زندگی بسر کرتے تھے ؟

۸۔   آریاؤں کا مذہب کیا تھا ؟

۹۔   چندر گپت موریہ نے اپنے ملک میں کیا کیا اصلاحات کیں ؟

۱۰۔   غلاموں کے خاندان کے مشہور بادشاہ کون کون تھے ؟

۱۱۔   غیاث الدین بلبن کی وفات کے بعد اُس کی سلطنت کس کے ہاتھ آئی ؟

۱۲۔   کیا، ہڑپہ اور موہن جو دارو کی تحریریں اب پڑھی جا سکتی ہیں ؟

۱۳۔   پانی پت کا میدان کیوں مشہور ہے ؟

۱۴۔   محمد شاہ تغلق نے سونے اور چاندی کے سکوں کے بدلے کیا چیز جاری کی۔

۱۵۔   تغلق خاندان نے ہندوستان پر کتنے سال حکومت کی۔

21. 507. Conversation Practice.

Mr. Smith has read the essay given in Sec. 21, 000, and he has drawn up a list of questions and points of interest which he now wishes to discuss with Dr. Rəhim.

اسمتھ
کیا دراوڑ اب بھی ہندوستان یا پاکستان کے کسی حصے میں موجود ہیں؟

رحیم
جی ہاں ، پاکستان کے مغربی حصے اور جنوبی ہندوستان کے کچھ حصوں میں آج بھی دراوڑ قوم کے بہت سے لوگ آباد ہیں۔

اسمتھ
موہن جو دارو اور ہڑپّہ کے علاوہ اور بھی کہیں کھدائی ہوئی ہے یعنی کسی دوسری جگہ سے بھی پرانی تہذیب کے آثار برآمد ہوتے ہیں؟

رحیم
جی ہاں ۔ ملک کے کئی دوسرے حصوں میں بھی کھدائی کا کام جاری ہے ۔ اور حال ہی میں بعض جگہوں سے قدیم تہذیب کے کچھ آثار بھی برآمد ہوتے ہیں ۔ اِس کے علاوہ اُن تحریروں پر بھی کام جاری ہے جو اِن جگہوں سے برآمد ہوئی ہیں ۔ اُمّید ہے کہ اِن تحریروں کو پڑھنے کے بعد بہت سی نئی معلومات حاصل ہوں گی ۔

اسمتھ
بیرونی قبیلوں کے آئے دن ہندوستان پر حملہ کرنے کی کیا وجہ تھی؟

رحیم
ہندوستان اُس زمانے میں ایک امیر ملک تھا ۔ یہاں کے لوگ ایک مہذّب اور خوشحال زندگی بسر کرتے تھے ۔ چونکہ اِن بیرونی قبیلوں کی زندگی اِتنی خوشحال نہ تھی ۔ اِس لئے وہ اکثر ہندوستان پر حملے کرتے رہتے تھے ۔ تاکہ یہاں آباد ہوکر یہاں کے لوگوں کی طرح آرام کی زندگی گذار سکیں ۔

اسمتھ
گوتم بدھ نے اپنا تخت اور تاج کیوں چھوڑ دیا تھا؟

رحیم
کہتے ہیں کہ ایک دن گوتم بدھ بازار میں جا رہا تھا ۔ اُس نے سڑک کے کنارے ایک بیمار آدمی کو دیکھا ۔ بدھ نے اپنے نوکر سے پوچھا کہ یہ آدمی کون ہے ۔ اور یہ کیوں

رو رہا ہے؟ ذکر نے بتایا کہ یہ آدمی بیمار ہے ۔ جب کوئی آدمی بیمار ہوتا ہے تو اُسے تکلیف

ہوتی ہے ۔ دوسرے دن بدھ نے ایک بوڑھے آدمی کو دیکھا۔ اُس کے پوچھنے پر لوگوں نے

بتایا کہ یہ آدمی ہمیشہ ایسا نہ تھا۔ اب یہ بوڑھا ہو گیا ہے ۔ اور اس عمر میں ہر آدمی کو تکلیف

ہوتی ہے ۔ اسی طرح ایک دن بدھ نے ایک جنازہ دیکھا جس کے پیچھے بہت سے لوگ

روتے ہوئے جا رہے تھے ۔ گوتم نے لوگوں سے پوچھا کہ یہ لوگ کیوں رو رہے ہیں؟ تو

اُنہوں نے بتایا کہ ایک آدمی مر گیا ہے ۔ اور یہ لوگ جو رو رہے ہیں اُس کے دوست

اور رشتہ دار وغیرہ ہیں۔ اُسے یہ بھی پتہ چلا کہ ہر شخص کو ایک دن ضرور مرنا ہے ۔ اِن

باتوں نے بدھ کے دماغ پر بہت اثر ڈالا. اور وہ اکثر پریشان رہنے لگا ۔ اُس

کے دل میں بار بار یہ خیال آتا تھا کہ آدمی کیوں بیمار ہوتا ہے، اور اُسے کیوں تکلیف

ہوتی ہے۔ آدمی کس لئے پیدا ہوتا ہے، اور کیوں مرتا ہے ۔ اِن سوالوں کا جواب

حاصل کرنے کے لئے اُس نے اپنے وطن ، تخت اور تاج کو چھوڑ دیا اور جنگلوں میں نکل

گیا۔ جہاں برسوں عبادت میں لگا رہا ۔ جب اُسے اُس کے سوالوں کا جواب مل گیا تو

اُس نے دنیا والوں کے سامنے اپنی تعلیمات پیش کیں ۔

اسمتہ   یہ واقعہ بہت دلچسپ ہے ۔ میں بدھ کی زندگی اور اُس کی تعلیمات کے بارے میں کچھ

پڑھنا چاہتا ہوں۔ کیا آپ میرے لئے کوئی کتاب لا سکتے ہیں؟

رحیم   جی ہاں ۔ میں انشاء اللہ کل آپ کے لئے اس موضوع پر چند کتابیں لاؤں گا۔

اسمتہ   شکریہ! ہاں ذرا یہ بھی بتائیے کہ ہندوستان کے پہلے مسلمان خاندان کو غلاموں کا خاندان

کیوں کہتے ہیں؟

رحیم   اِس کی وجہ یہ تھی کہ اِس خاندان کے بادشاہ یا تو خود غلام تھے یا غلاموں کے خاندان سے

تعلق رکھتے تھے۔ اُس زمانہ میں غلاموں کو خریدنے اور بیچنے کا عام رواج تھا۔ امیر لوگ اپنی
خدمت کے لئے بہت سے غلام خرید لیا کرتے تھے۔ بعض لوگ اپنے غلاموں کو اولاد کی طرح
رکھتے تھے۔ یہاں تک کہ اپنی بیٹیوں کی شادیاں بھی اُن سے کر دیتے تھے۔ جیسے
قطب الدّین ایبک نے اپنی بیٹی کی شادی اپنے غلام شمس الدّین التمش سے کی۔ اِسی
طرح مشہور ہے کہ محمّد غوری کے کوئی اولاد نہ تھی۔ ایک دفعہ کسی نے کہا کہ بڑے
افسوس کی بات ہے کہ آپ کے کوئی بیٹا نہیں، جو آپ کے بعد آپ کی سلطنت کا بادشاہ
بن سکے اور آپ کا نام زندہ رکھ سکے۔ اس پر محمّد غوری نے جواب دیا کہ کون کہتا ہے
کہ میرے اولاد نہیں۔ میرے تو چار بیٹے ہیں جو بہت قابل اور لائق ہیں، اور یہ کہہ کر اُس
نے اپنے چار غلاموں کی طرف اشارہ کیا جِس میں قطب الدّین ایبک بھی تھا۔ واقعی یہ
چاروں غلام محمّد غوری کی وفات کے بعد بہت قابل حکمران ثابت ہوئے۔ خاص طور پر
قطب الدّین۔ وہ پہلا بادشاہ ہے جس نے ہندوستان میں اسلامی حکومت کی بنیاد رکھی۔

اسمتھ   بہت خوب ۔۔۔۔۔۔ میرا خیال ہے کہ اب مجھے اجازت دیجئے کیونکہ مجھے یونیورسٹی جانا
ہے۔ انشاءاللہ کل شام کو کہا نے پر ملاقات ہوگی۔ خدا حافظ ۔

رحیم   خدا حافظ ۔

21. 508. Conversation Stimulus.

Topics may include:

1. Mohenjo daro.
2. The Aryan conquest of India.
3. Buddhism and Hinduism.
4. The first Muslim conquerors of India.
5. The achievements of the Muslims in India.

Although common place names have been included in this section as usual, personal
names and less useful place names have been omitted.

abad A1	populated, inhabited
ae dyn Adv	every day, constantly
aɣaz M1	beginning, start, inception
arya M1 A1	Aryan
*asar Mpl	remains, ruins, indications [pl. /əsər/ M1 "effect, trace, influence. "]
əfɣanystan M1 [np]	Afghanistan
əfriqa M1 [np]	Africa
əndəruni A1	internal, interior
əsli A1	original, genuine, pure
əTThasi A1	eighty-eight
bani M/F1	founder, originator, builder
[ke] bədle [± /mẽ/] Comp Post	in exchange for
bəndərgah F1	seaport, harbour
bəraməd F1 PA1	recovered, discovered, found; export
bərəs M1	year
bərsō Adv	for many years, for years and years
bəsər PA1	passing, spending (time), living
bəTna [I: /bāTna/: Ie]	to be divided, distributed, shared
beruni A1	external, exterior
bezar PA1	disgusted with, sick of, fed up with
bhər Enclitic Particle	whole, entire, complete, full, throughout
bheR F1	sheep, ewe
bwdh M1 [np]	Buddha
chana [IIa]	to spread out over, diffuse, overshadow, make shade
chyasi [or /cheasi/ or /chəyasi/] A1	eighty-six
dəkən [or /dəkkhən/ or /dəkkhyn/] M1 [np]	the Deccan
dəravəR M1 A1	Dravidian
dəryaft F1	discovery, ascertainment, inquiry
dəwr M1	age, epoch, period, era
deota M1	god, deity
dhəkelna [Ia]	to shove, push away, repel
ešya M1 [np]	Asia
fəta [or /fətəh/] F1	victory, conquest
*fwtuhat Fpl	pl. /fəta/
ɣwlam M1	slave
həd F1	limit, boundary, edge, border
həmla M2	attack, assault, invasion

həmləavər M1 A1	attacking, invading, attacker, invader
həRəppa M2 [np]	Harappa
həthyar Mİ	weapon
hyfazət F1	safeguard, protection, safety, guarding
hynd M1 [np]	India
hyndu M/F1 A1	Hindu
iran M1 [np]	Iran, Persia
irani M/F1 A1	Persian
isvi A1 [after a numeral denoting a year]	After Christ, A.D.
janəšin M/F1	successor
jəld Adv	soon, quickly
jhənDa M2	flag, banner
jwnubi A1	southern, south
kabwl M1 [np]	Kabul
khodna [If: /w/]	to dig, excavate
khwdai F2	digging, excavation
khwdvana [DC: /khodna/: If]	to cause to be dug
khyləwna M2	toy, plaything
ləhrana [IIIa]	to wave, make wave
luTna [Ie: /w/]	to loot, rob, plunder
lwTera M2	looter, bandit
mahyr M/F1	expert, artisan, skilled person
*mahyrin Mpl	pl. /mahyr/
məhabharət M1 [np]	the Mahabharata
məhdud A1	limited, bounded, confined
məveši Mpl	cattle
məzid A1	further, more
mohənjo daro M1 [np]	Mohenjo Daro
mwhəzzəb A1	cultured, civilised
mwhr F1	seal
mwnəzzəm A1	well-organised, ordered, systematised, well-administered
mwstənəd A1	authentic, genuine, reliable
mwštəmyl PA1	comprising, consisting of, including
mwvərryx M1	historian
*mwvərryxin Mpl	pl. /mwvərryx/
nakam A1	unsuccessful, failed
nali F2	tube, drain, channel
nayb M/F1 A1	deputy, regent, viceroy
nəhana [IIb: /ə/]	to bathe
nəwjəvan M1 A1	youth, young
nəvasi A1	eighty-nine
nəvve A1	ninety

noT M1	note
o Conj	and [See Secs. 15.301 and 18.307]
pənjab M1 [np]	Panjab
pəyrəw M/F1	follower, devotee
qəbila M2	tribe, clan
qəbl əz məsih A1 [after numeral denoting a year]	Before Christ, B.C.
qəbza M2	power, possession, grasp, seizure, holding
qədim A1	old, ancient
qədimtərin A1	most ancient, oldest
qəyadət F1	leadership, command
raja M1	king, Raja
rəsmwlxət M1	script, system of writing
rəth M1	chariot
rum M1 [np]	Rome, the Byzantine Empire
ryasət F1	state, small kingdom, rule, sovereignty
sala A1 [follows a numeral]	-yeared, -year-old
samna M2	confrontation, encounter
səltənət F1	kingdom, sultanate, sovereignty, dominion, empire
sərae F1	sarai, inn, way station for travellers
sərhəd F1	border (of a country), frontier, boundary line
səttasi A1	eighty-seven
sə̄ykRa [or /səykRa/] A2	hundred
sykka M2	coin
syndh M1 [np]	Sindh
sypahi M1	soldier, trooper
sypəsalar M1	general, commander
šandar A1	glorious, splendid, majestic
šəhzada [or /šahzada/] M2	prince
šykəst F1	defeat
šymali [or /šwmali/] A1	northern, north
taj M1	crown
tamir F1	building, construction, erection
tariki F2	darkness
tarixi A1	historic, historical
tāba M2 [np]	copper
təbliɣ F1	spreading (of a doctrine), preaching, missionary work
təhqiq F1	research, investigation
təhrir F1	writing, inscription, document
təhzibyafta A1	cultured, civilised
təxt M1	throne
vadi F2	valley
vəfat F1	death

vətən M1	homeland, native country
ved M1	Veda
*vwjuhat Fpl	pl. /vəja/
xanəbədoš M1 A1	nomadic, wandering, nomad
xəlifa M1	Caliph
*yslahat Fpl	pl. /yslah/
yunani M/F1 A1	Greek
*zərae Mpl	pl. /zəria/
*zevərat Mpl	pl. /zevər/

The tomb of the Mughal Emperor Humayun, Delhi, built in 1564.

تاریخِ ہند و پاکستان

مغلوں کی آمد سے ہندوستان کی تاریخ کا ایک نیا باب شروع ہوتا ہے۔ مغل خاندان کے بانی بابر کو پانی پت کے میدان میں فتح تو ہوگئی لیکن اُس کے سامنے اور بھی مشکلات تھیں۔ مقامی راجہ اِس غیر ملکی بادشاہ کے غلاف مستعد ہو گئے۔ چنانچہ کنواہا کے مقام پر بابر اور مقامی راجاؤں کی فوجوں میں جنگ ہوئی۔ اگرچہ بہادر راجپوت اپنے سردار رانا سانگا کی قیادت میں بڑی بہادری سے لڑے اور اُن کی فوج بھی بابر کی فوج سے کئی گنا زیادہ تھی، اِس کے باوجود بابر کو فتح ہوئی۔ اِس فتح کے بعد تمام شمالی ہندوستان بابر کے قبضے میں آگیا۔ لیکن اُس کو حکومت منظم کرنے اور سلطنت کا انتظام بہتر بنانے کا موقع نہ ملا۔ کیونکہ چار سال کے بعد وہ وفات پاگیا۔ بابر ایک جنگجو اور بہادر سپاہی ہونے کے ساتھ ساتھ ایک بہت اچھا شاعر اور ادیب بھی تھا۔ وہ بڑی سے بڑی مصیبت سے بھی نہ گھبراتا تھا۔ اُس نے اپنی زندگی کے حالات خود لکھے ہیں۔ جو بہت دلچسپ ہیں۔

بابر کے بعد اُس کا بیٹا ہمایوں بادشاہ بنا۔ جو مغل سلطنت کے لئے بہت کمزور ثابت ہوا۔ وہ بہت نیک انسان تھا لیکن شراب اور افیون کے استعمال نے اُس کی طبیعت سے استقلال چھین لیا تھا۔ اُس کے زمانے میں ایک شخص شیر شاہ نے بہت طاقت پکڑی۔ شیر شاہ صوبہ بہار کے ایک جاگیردار کا بیٹا تھا۔ وہ ایک اچھا سپاہی، قابل سیاست دان، فارسی عربی کا عالم اور اعلیٰ درجہ کا منتظم تھا۔ یہ شخص ابتدا ہی سے مغلوں کا دشمن تھا۔ اُس کی خواہش تھی کہ کسی نہ کسی

طرح منگلوں کو ہندوستان سے نکال دیا جائے ۔ چنانچہ وہ اس مقصد میں کامیاب ہوگیا۔ اُس نے ہمایوں کو شکست دے کر ہندوستان کے تخت پر قبضہ کر لیا۔ ہمایوں شکست کھا کر ایران چلا گیا ۔ اور وہاں کے بادشاہ کے پاس پناہ لی۔

شیر شاہ نے حکومت سنبھالتے ہی ملک میں اصلاحات کیں۔ اُس نے تقریباً چھ سال حکومت کی۔ اور اس عرصے میں عوام کی خوشحالی کے لئے وہ کام کئے جو اُس سے پہلے کسی دوسرے بادشاہ نے نہیں کئے تھے۔ اُس نے ملک میں جگہ جگہ سڑکیں بنوائیں، زمین کی پیمائش کرائی اور باقاعدہ ٹیکس وصول کرنے کا نظام رائج کیا ۔ وہ عوام کی شکایات خود سنتا تھا۔ بڑے عہدے داروں پر سختی رکھتا تھا۔ تاکہ وہ اپنی ذمہ داری محسوس کریں اور حکومت کے کام اچھی طرح سرانجام دیں ۔ اُس کے عدل و انصاف اور اعلیٰ انتظام سلطنت کی وجہ سے اُس کا نام تاریخ میں ہمیشہ سنہرے حروف سے لکھا جائے گا۔ دہلی سے آگرہ تک اور پشاور سے کلکتہ تک کی سڑکیں اسی بادشاہ کی یادگار ہیں ۔ شیر شاہ زیادہ عرصہ زندہ نہ رہا ورنہ ممکن تھا کہ ہندوستان کی تاریخ موجودہ تاریخ سے مختلف ہوتی ۔ شیر شاہ کی وفات کے بعد اُس کے جانشین کمزور ثابت ہوئے ۔ اور حکومت نہ سنبھال سکے ۔ دوسرے، ہمایوں ایران سے فوجی امداد لے کر ہندوستان پر حملہ آور ہوا ۔ اور شیر شاہ کے جانشینوں کو شکست دے کر اپنا کھویا ہوا تاج واپس لے لیا۔

ہمایوں کی وفات کے بعد اُس کا بیٹا اکبر تخت پر بیٹھا جو اپنے باپ کے بالکل برعکس تھا۔ اکبر مغل خاندان کا سب سے اعلیٰ حکمران گنا جاتا ہے ۔ اُس نے پچاس سال حکومت کی اور اس عرصے میں سلطنت کا انتظام بہتر بنایا۔ اور حکومت کے ہر شعبے میں شاندار اصلاحات کیں۔ وہ ہندو، مسلمان، عیسائی، بدھ۔ غرض کہ ہر مذہب کے لوگوں سے یکساں سلوک کرتا تھا۔ اُس نے ایک نیا مذہب بھی شروع کیا جو دینِ الٰہی کے نام سے مشہور ہے ۔ اس مذہب میں اُس نے ہر مذہب

لے اچھے اصول شامل کئے۔ لیکن یہ مذہب اُس کی وفات کے ساتھ ہی ختم ہوگیا۔ اکبر کے زمانہ میں
علم و ادب نے بھی بہت ترقی کی۔ اُس کا دربار شاعروں، ادیبوں، سائنس دانوں، مؤرخوں اور
موسیقاروں کا مرکز تھا۔ اکبر نے جب حکومت سنبھالی تو سلطنت بہت کمزور تھی، لیکن اُس کی وفات
پر ایک بہت وسیع اور مضبوط سلطنت وجود میں آچکی تھی۔ اِسی وجہ سے اُسے تاریخ میں اکبرِ اعظم کے
نام سے یاد کیا جاتا ہے۔ دوسرے الفاظ میں اگر یوں کہا جائے تو غلط نہ ہوگا کہ اکبر ہی مغل
سلطنت کا بانی تھا۔

اکبر کی وفات کے بعد اُس کا بیٹا جہانگیر تخت پر بیٹھا۔ جہانگیر نے بھی اپنے باپ کی طرح سلطنت کا
انتظام اچھی طرح چلایا۔ وہ اپنے انصاف کی وجہ سے آج بھی مشہور ہے۔ جہانگیر شعر و شاعری کا
بہت اچھا ذوق رکھتا تھا۔ خود بھی شاعر تھا اور شعراء اور اُدباء کی بہت قدر کرتا تھا۔ اُس نے بھی
اپنی زندگی کے حالات خود لکھے ہیں۔ جن سے اُس زمانے کی تہذیب اور دیگر حالات کے بارے
میں بہت سی اہم باتوں کا پتہ چلتا ہے۔ اُس کی وفات کے بعد اُس کا بیٹا شاہجہاں بادشاہ بنا۔
اُسے عمارتیں بنوانے کا بہت شوق تھا۔ چنانچہ ہندوستان اور پاکستان میں ایسی سینکڑوں مسجدیں
باغ اور مزار آج بھی موجود ہیں جو اُس نے تعمیر کرائے تھے۔ دہلی کی جامع مسجد، لاہور اور کشمیر کے
شالامار باغ اور آگرہ کا تاج محل اسی بادشاہ کی یادگاریں ہیں۔ شاہجہاں کی زندگی میں ہی اُس کے
بیٹوں کے درمیان تخت حاصل کرنے کے لئے جنگ ہوئی۔ جس میں اُس کے تیسرے   بیٹے
اورنگ زیب کو فتح ہوئی۔ اورنگ زیب ایک بہادر سپاہی، اعلیٰ درجے کا عالم اور پکا مسلمان
تھا۔ اُس کی طبیعت میں ضد اور سختی اس قدر تھی کہ جس کام کا ارادہ کرتا تھا اُسے کرکے ہی
چھوڑتا تھا۔ اور کسی کی پروا نہ کرتا تھا۔ یہ بادشاہ حکومت کے خزانے سے ایک پیسہ بھی نہ
لیتا تھا۔ وہ ٹوپیاں بنا کر اور قرآن شریف لکھ کر اپنی روزی کماتا تھا۔ اور بہت سادہ زندگی

بسر کرتا تھا۔اُس کے زمانے میں ملک میں چاروں طرف بغاوتیں ہوئیں۔یہی وجہ ہے کہ اُس کی عمر کا
زیادہ حصہ لڑائیوں ہی میں گزر گیا۔ اُس کی وفات کے بعد اُس کے کمزور جانشین اتنی بڑی سلطنت
نہ سنبھال سکے۔ کیونکہ یہ لوگ حکومت کے کاموں پر عیش کو ترجیح دیتے تھے، عوام پر ظلم کرتے تھے
اور حکومت کے انتظام سے بالکل واقف نہ تھے۔ اِن باتوں کا نتیجہ یہ نکلا کہ انگریزوں اور فرانسیسیوں نے
ہندوستان پر قبضہ کرنے کی کوششیں شروع کیں۔ اگرچہ مغل بادشاہ ۵۵۸۱ء تک ہندوستان پر
حکومت کرتے رہے۔ لیکن یہ حکمران محض نام کے بادشاہ تھے۔ اصل میں بیرونی طاقتیں ہی حکومت
کرتی تھیں۔ پرتگالی، فرانسیسی اور انگریز شروع میں تجارت کی غرض سے ہندوستان آئے تھے لیکن یہاں
کے حالات اور حکمرانوں کی کمزوری سے فائدہ اٹھاکر اِن لوگوں نے ملکی معاملات میں بھی دخل دینا شروع
کر دیا۔اِن بیرونی طاقتوں میں انگریزوں کو سب سے زیادہ کامیابی ہوئی اور اُنہوں نے رفتہ رفتہ حکومت اور
بادشاہوں پر اتنا اثر ڈالا کہ مغل بادشاہ اُن کی مرضی کے بغیر کچھ نہ کر سکتے تھے۔ مقامی راجاؤں اور
نوابوں نے انگریزوں کے اِس بڑھتے ہوئے اثر کو دیکھ کر ۷۵۸۱ء میں اُن کے خلاف بغاوت کی۔
اِس بغاوت کی اور بھی بہت سی وجوہات تھیں۔ جن میں سے ایک وجہ یہ بھی تھی کہ مقامی نواب
اور راجہ انگریزوں کو اپنے وطن سے نکالنا چاہتے تھے۔ لیکن اِس وقت اُنہیں ملک سے نکالنا
آسان نہ تھا کیونکہ اُن کے قدم ملک میں جم چکے تھے۔اور اُنہیں بہت سے مقامی امراء کی حمایت
بھی حاصل تھی۔ اِس بغاوت کے بعد انگریزوں نے ہندوستان کے تخت پر باقاعدہ قبضہ کر لیا۔
انگریزوں نے اپنے دورِ حکومت میں ملک کے لئے بہت سے اچھے کام کئے تعلیم، زراعت، مالیات
اور دیگر شعبوں میں اصلاحات کیں،جگہ جگہ سڑکیں بنوائیں، ڈاک خانے اور بینک قائم کئے، ملک
میں بجلی اور ریل جیسی ضروری چیزیں اِسی عہد کی یادگار ہیں۔ کچھ عرصے بعد ہندوستان کے لوگوں
میں بیداری کا جذبہ پیدا ہوا اور اُنہیں یہ احساس ہونے لگا کہ وہ ایک آزاد قوم ہیں ۔اور اپنی

کمزوریوں کی وجہ سے غلام بن گئے ہیں ۔

چنانچہ شعراء نے اپنی شاعری کے ذریعے قوم کو بیدار کرنے کی کوشش کی ۔ رسالوں اور اخباروں میں ایسے مضامین شائع ہونے شروع ہوئے، جن سے مردہ قوم کو آزادی کا پیغام ملا ۔ اس سلسلے میں سرسیّد احمد خان اور اُن کے ساتھیوں کی خدمات قابلِ ذکر ہیں ۔ سرسیّد نے محسوس کیا کہ ہندوستانی مسلمان صرف مغربی علوم حاصل کرکے ہی ترقّی کر سکتے ہیں ۔ چنانچہ اُنہوں نے علی گڑھ میں ایک یونیورسٹی قائم کی ۔ وہ خود انگلستان گئے ۔ اور وہاں کے تعلیمی اداروں اور تعلیمی نظام کا جائزہ لیا اور واپس آکر   اپنی یونیورسٹی میں ویسا ہی نظام جاری کیا ۔ اکثر مسلمان سیاست دان اسی یونیورسٹی نے پیدا کئے ۔

شاعروں میں مولانا الطاف حسین حالی پہلے شاعر ہیں جنہوں نے اپنی نظموں میں مسلمانوں کی گذشتہ عظمت کے واقعات بیان کئے ۔ اسی طرح ڈاکٹر محمّد اقبال نے اپنی شاعری میں آزادی اور بیداری کا فلسفہ پیش کرکے ہندوستان کے سوئے ہوئے مسلمانوں کو جگایا ۔ رفتہ رفتہ ہندوستانی مسلمان بیدار ہونے شروع ہوئے ۔ ملک میں تعلیم بڑھی اور اچھے اچھے سیاستدان میدان میں آئے ۔ ان میں محمّد علی جوہر، ابوالکلام آزاد ، حسرت موہانی ، محمّد علی جناح اور لیاقت علی خان قابل ذکر ہیں ۔

مسلمانوں کی طرح ہندو بھی بیدار ہوتے اور آزادی کا جھنڈا لے کر آگے بڑھے ۔ ہندو سیاستدانوں میں گاندھی ، موتی لال نہرو ، سوبھاش چندر بوس ، راجندر پرشاد اور جواہر لال نہرو قابل ذکر ہیں ۔

ان ہندو اور مسلمان سیاستدانوں نے مل کر انڈین نیشنل کانگریس کے تحت آزادی کی تحریک شروع کی اور یہ ان ہی لوگوں کی کوششوں کا نتیجہ تھا کہ انگریز ہندوستان کو آزاد کرنے پر مجبور ہوگئے ۔ شروع میں تو ہندو اور مسلمان سیاست دانوں کا مطالبہ متّحدہ ہندوستان کی آزادی تھا ۔ لیکن کچھ مسلمان سیاست دانوں نے یہ محسوس کیا کہ کانگریس کے ہندو لیڈر ہندوستان کی آزادی کی بجائے ہندو راج کے لئے کوشش کر رہے ہیں ۔ چنانچہ بہت سے مسلمان سیاست دانوں نے

کانگریس کو چھوڑ دیا اور مسلم لیگ میں شامل ہو گئے۔

محمد علی جناح کے آنے سے پہلے مسلم لیگ کوئی طاقت در جماعت نہ تھی لیکن اُنہوں نے اپنی کوششوں سے اُسے ایک منظم جماعت بنا دیا۔ اس جماعت نے ہندوستان کی آزادی کے ساتھ ساتھ ہندوستان کی تقسیم کا بھی مطالبہ کیا۔ آخرکار اِن سیاسی جماعتوں کی کوششیں ۱۴؍ اگست ۱۹۴۷ء کو پھل لائیں۔ جبکہ ہندوستان کو آزادی مل گئی۔ اور پاکستان کے نام سے دنیا کے سیاسی نقشے پر ایک نیا ملک وجود میں آیا۔ تقسیم اِس اصول پر ہوئی کہ مسلم اکثریتی علاقے پاکستان کے حصّے میں آئے۔ اور ہندو اکثریتی علاقے ہندوستان میں چلے گئے۔

آمد	aməd F1 [np]	coming, advent, arrival
باب	bab M1	chapter; door, gate
مشکلات	*mwškylat Fpl [pl. /mwškyl/]	difficulties, problems
متحد	mwttəhyd PA1	united, unified
کنواہا	kənvaha M1 [np]	Kanvaha (or Khanua), a place about 40 miles from Agra
مقام	mwqam M1	place, position, location, rank, level, station
بهادر	bəhadwr M1 A1	hero, heroic, courageous
راجپوت	rajput M1 A1	Rajput, a warrior caste
رانا سانگا	rana sāga PN	Rana Sanga, also called Sangrama, a Rajput chieftain
گنا	gwna Enclitic A2	-fold, times
[کے] باوجود	[ke] bavwjud Comp Post	nevertheless, in spite of
جنگ جو	jə̄gju A1	warlike, war-loving
شاعر	šayr M1	poet
ادیب	ədib M1	prose writer, literateur
مصیبت	mwsibət F1	difficulty, trouble, adversity, affliction, calamity
ہمایوں	hwmayū PN	Humayun, Mughal ruler; reigned 1530-1539, 1555-1556
افیون	əfyun F1 [np]	opium

استقلال	ystyqlal M1 [np]	determination, resolution, firmness, independence
چھینا	chinna [Id: /y/]	to seize, take away, snatch, grab, pluck
شیرشاہ	šer šah PN	Sher Shah, a king of Afghan descent settled in Bihar; ruled India 1539-1545
بہار	byhar M1 [np]	Bihar, a province in northeastern India
جاگیردار	jagirdar M1	holder of a "jagir," an estate or fief awarded by the government for services rendered
سیاست دان	syasətdan [or /syasətdā/] M/F1	politician
فارسی	farsi F2 [np] A1	Persian (language)
منتظم	mwntəzym M/F1 A1	administrator, manager, organiser
ابتدا	ybtyda M1 [np]	beginning, commencement
خواہش	xahyš F1	desire, wish
پناہ	pənah F1	refuge, sanctuary, shelter
سنبھالنا	sə̄bhalna [Ig: /ə/]	to set right, look after, take care of, sustain, catch (something falling), hold onto, take over, curb, keep in check
پیمائش	pəymayš F1	measuring, survey
رائج	rayj PA1	current, in force, prevailing, prevalent
شکایات	*šykayat Fpl [pl. /šykayət/]	complaints
سرانجام	sərənjam PA1	completed, accomplished
عدل	ədl M1 [np]	justice, rectitude

348

انصاف	ynsaf Ml [np]	justice, fairness, righteousness
سنہرا	swnəhra A2	golden, golden-coloured
حروف	*hwruf Mpl [pl. /hərf/]	letters (of the alphabet)
آگرہ	agra M2 [np]	Agra, a city in north-central India
پشاور	pyšavər Ml [np]	Peshawar, a city in Pakistan on the Northwest Frontier
کلکتہ	kəlkətta M2 [np]	Calcutta
یادگار	yadgar Fl	memorial, memento, souvenir, relic
فوجی	fəwji Ml Al	soldier; military (adj.)
کھونا	khona [IIIa]	to lose
اکبر	əkbər PN	Akbar, Mughal ruler, reigned 1556-1605
[کے] برعکس	[ke] bərəks Comp Post	contrary to, in contrast with, opposite to
شعبہ	šoba M2	department, division, section
یکساں	yəksā Al	equal, uniform, identical, alike
سلوک	swluk Ml [np]	treatment, behaviour, usage
الٰہی	ylahi Al	divine, God-like
ادب	ədəb Ml [np]	literature; courtesy, etiquette
دربار	dərbar Ml	court (of a ruler)
سائنس دان	saynsdan [or /saynsdā/] M/Fl	scientist
موسیقار	məwsiqar M/Fl	musician

349

وسیع	vəsi A1	broad, vast, spacious, wide
الفاظ	*əlfaz Mpl [pl. /ləfz/]	words
جہانگیر	jəhāgir PN	Jahangir, Mughal ruler; reigned 1605-1628
شعر	šer M1	couplet, verse
شاعری	šayri F2 [np]	poetry, the art of poetry
ذوق	zəwq M1 [np]	taste (for something), hobby
شعراء	*šwəra Mpl [pl. /šayr/]	poets
اُدباء	*wdəba Mpl [pl. /ədib/]	writers, literary men
قدر	qədr F1	value, amount, appreciation
شاہ جہاں	šah jəhā PN	Shah Jahan, Mughal ruler; reigned 1628-1659
مزار	məzar M1	tomb (usually of a saint or revered person)
جامع مسجد	jame məsjyd F1	Jami Masjid, the great mosque of Delhi, built in 1658
تاج محل	taj məhl M1 [np]	the Taj Mahal, built in 1654
اورنگ زیب	əwrãgzeb PN	Aurangzeb, Mughal ruler; ruled 1659-1707
ضد	zyd F1 [np]	contrariness, obstinacy, stubbornness
پروا	pərva [or /pərvah/] F1	care, concern
خزانہ	xəzana M2	treasury
روزی	rozi F2	livelihood, employment

كمانا	kəmana [Ia]	to earn
بغاوت	bəɣavət F1	revolt, revolution, uprising
ترجیح	tərjih F1	preference, precedence
ظلم	zwlm M1	tyranny, oppression, cruelty
فرانسیسی	fəransisi M1 F2 [np] A1	French(man); French (language); French (adj.)
پرتگالی	pwrtəgali M1 F2 [np] A1	Portuguese (person); Portuguese (language); Portuguese (adj.)
تجارت	tyjarət F1	commerce, business
غرض	ɣərəz F1	objective, aim, design, intention
دخل	dəxl M1 [np]	entrance, intrusion, concern, influence, jurisdiction, competence, grasp
نواب	nəvab M1	Navab, title of a ruler of a Muslim state
جمنا	jəmna [IIc: /ə/]	to become set, firm, hard, fixed, congealed, frozen, take root
امراء	*wməra Mpl [pl. /əmir/]	influential people, wealthy people
حمایت	hymayət F1	support, protection, defence
غدر	ɣədr M1	mutiny, rebellion, chaos
مالیات	maliat F1 [np]	finance, financial matters, revenue
بجلی	byjli F2	lightning, electricity
عہد	əhd M1	period, reign, era; promise, contract, undertaking
بیداری	bedari F2	awakening, wakefulness
بیدار	bedar PA1	awake, watchful, vigilant

رساله	rysala M2	magazine, journal
مضامین	*məzamin Mpl [pl. /məzmun/]	articles; subjects
شائع	šae [or /šaya/] PA1	published, issued
سرسید احمد خان	sər səyyəd əhməd xan [or /xā/] PN	Sir Sayyid Ahmad Khan, Urdu writer and social reformer; 1817-1898
ساتھی	sathi M/F1	companion, colleague, comrade
علوم	*wlum Mpl [pl. /ylm/]	sciences, branches of knowledge
علی گڑھ	əligəRh M1 [np]	Aligarh, a city in north-central India
تعلیمی	talimi A1	educational
جائزہ	jayza M2	examination, survey, scrutiny, checking
الطاف حسین حالی	əltaf hwsəyn hali PN	Altaf Husayn Hali, poet and prose writer; 1837-1914
نظم	nəzm F1	poem
گذشتہ	gwzəšta A1	past (adj.)
عظمت	əzmət F1	greatness, glory, might
واقعات	*vaqəyat Mpl [pl. /vaqea/]	events, occurrences, incidents
ڈاکٹر محمد اقبال	DakTər mwhəmməd yqbal PN	Dr. Muhammad Iqbal, poet and philosopher; 1873-1938
فلسفہ	fəlsəfa M2	philosophy
محمد علی جوہر	mwhəmməd əli jəwhər PN	Muhammad Ali Jawhar, journalist and politician; 1878-1931
ابوالکلام آزاد	əbwlkəlam azad PN	Abu-l-Kalam Azad, scholar and politician; 1889-1958

حسرت موہانی	həsrət mohani PN	Fazl-ul-Hasan Hasrat Mohani, poet, literateur, and politician; 1878-1951
محمد علی جناح	mwhəmməd əli jynah PN	Muhammad Ali Jinnah, the founder of Pakistan; 1876-1948
لیاقت علی خان	lyaqət əli xan PN	Liaqat Ali Khan, politician; 1896-1951
گاندھی	gādhi PN	Mohandas Karamchand Gandhi, politician and reformer; 1869-1948
موتی لال نہرو	moti lal nyhru PN	Motilal Nehru, politician; 1861-1931
سبھاش چندر بوس	subhaš cəndər bos PN	Subhash Chandra Bos, politician; 1897-1942(?)
راجندر پرشاد	rajəndər pəršad PN	Rajendra Prashad, politician; 1884-1962
جواہر لال نہرو	jəvahyr lal nyhru PN	Javahirlal Nehru, politician; 1889-1964
انڈین نیشنل کاگریس	ynDyən nešnəl kāgres F1 [np]	Indian National Congress
تحریک	təhrik F1	movement, incitement, encouragement
مطالبہ	mwtaləba M2	demand, claim
متحدہ	mwttəhyda A1	united, unified
کاگریس	kāgres F1	congress
لیڈر	liDər M/F1	leader
راج	raj M1	rule, government
مسلم لیگ	mwslym lig F1 [np]	Muslim League
طاقتور	taqətvər A1	strong, powerful
جماعت	jəmat [literary: /jəmaət/] F1	party, society, group, organisation, class (in school)

مسلم   mwslym M1 A1   Muslim

22.201. /aməd/ Fl "coming, advent, arrival" occurs only in the singular. Stylistically, it is more literary than the Urdu infinitive /ana/ "to come, " for which it may often be substituted. E. g.

/hyndostan mẽ, mwɥlõ ki aməd se yəhã ki mwqami təhzib pər kafi əsər pəRa. / In India due to [lit. from] the coming of the Mughals, the local culture was considerably affected. [/mwɥlõ ke ane se/ could also be employed here.]

22.202. In Arabic, /bab/ Ml has the basic meaning "door, gate" but also means "chapter. " It is this latter meaning which has become common in Urdu, and /bab/ is employed for "door" only in certain literary "set phrases. " E. g.

/ys kytab ke tisre bab ko pəRhẽ. / Please read the third chapter of this book!

/axyrkar əllah ne mwjh pər əpna babe rəhmət khola. / At last God opened His Gate of Compassion [i. e. took pity] upon me. [/babe rəhmət/ Ml "(God's) Gate of Compassion" is a set phrase. /rəhmət/ Fl "compassion, mercy. "]

22.203. /mwttəhyd/ PA1 and /mwttəhyda/ A1 are another example of the adjective - predicate adjective pattern discussed in Sec. 18.305. Both of these words are Arabic in origin, being participles of Form VIII of v-ḥ-d "to be one, to unite"; see Sec. 17.301. E. g.

/ys təra, mwlk ki təmam syasi parTiã məwjuda hwkumət ke xylaf mwttəhyd ho gəĩ. / Thus, all the political parties of the country became united against the present government. [/mwttəhyda/ cannot occur here.]

/yy kytab həmari mwttəhyda košyšõ ka nətija həy. / This book is the result of our united efforts. [/mwttəhyd/ cannot be substituted here.]

22.204. /mwqam/ Ml "place, position, location" overlaps /jəga/ Fl "place. " The former is, of course, more literary in style. /mwqam/ also means "level, rank, station. " E. g.

/yy əysa mwqam həy, ky yəhã dur dur tək pani nəhĩ mylta. / This is such a place that for a very great distance [lit. up to far, far] water is unavailable. [/jəga/ can be substituted here.]

/donõ fəwjõ mẽ kənvaha ke mwqam pər jõg hwi. / A battle between the two armies took place at a place [called] Kanvaha. [/jəga/ cannot occur here, since a particular place is mentioned, and /jəga/ is too general in connotation.]

/həmari nəzər mẽ, wn ka bəhwt bəRa mwqam həy. / In our view he holds a very high position.

/əfsos ka mwqam həy, ky ap mere kəhne pər əməl nəhĩ kərte. / It is a matter [lit. place] of regret, that you do not act upon my advice [lit. saying]. [This use of /mwqam/ is idiomatic. /jəga/ cannot be substituted.]

22.205. /mwsibət/ Fl denotes a bad turn of fortune, an event which causes sorrow, unfortunate circumstances, etc. and may best be translated as "adversity, calamity, trouble. " This word contrasts with /təklif/ Fl "trouble, hardship, pain, " /dyqqət/ Fl

"problem, perplexity, dilemma, " /mwškyl/ Fl Al "difficulty, problem, difficult, " and
/pərešani/ F2 "distress, anxiety, upset, " see Sec. 16.117. E. g.

/mɛ̃y ne zyndəgi mɛ̃ bəRi bəRi mwsibtõ ka samna kia. /　I faced great
hardships in [my] life.

/ek dəm təmam xandan pər mwsibət a pəRi. /　All at once a calamity
came and fell upon the whole family.

/əjib mwsibət mɛ̃ phɛ̃s gəya hũ. /　[I] have become ensnared in a strange
[turn of] ill fortune.

22.206.　/halat/ Mpl "states, conditions, circumstances" is sometimes found in the
sense of "biography" or "autobiography" in certain specific contexts. E. g.

/wnhõ ne əpne halat xwd lykhe hɛ̃y. /　He has written his autobiography
himself.

/əkbər ki zyndəgi ke halat bəhwt dylcəsp hɛ̃y. /　The biography [lit.
circumstances of the life] of Akbar is very interesting.

22.207.　/əfyun/ Fl [np] "opium" is the common written form; in spoken Urdu /əfim/
Fl [np] is often heard. E. g.

/ws ne əfim khai. /　He ate opium. [Written /əfyun/.]

22.208.　Used alone, /ystyqlal/ Ml denotes "resolution, determination, firmness" in
a good sense. In certain set phrases, however, this word may retain its original Arabic
meaning of "freedom, independence. " /ystyqlal/ may be contrasted with /zyd/ Fl, which
denotes "obstinacy, stubbornness" in a bad sense. E. g.

/ws ke myzaj mɛ̃ ystyqlal nəhĩ. /　There is no firmness in his temperament.

/yəwme ystyqlale pakystan ke məwqe pər, mwlk bhər mɛ̃ xwšiã mənai
jaɛ̃gi. /　On Pakistan's Independence Day celebrations will be held
throughout the country. [/yəwm/ Ml "day" is from Arabic and is
not very common in Urdu.]

/mɛ̃y ys pər zərur zyd kərũga. /　I'll certainly be stubborn about this.

22.209.　/jagir/ Fl denotes a large grant of land made by a ruler (or, more recently,
by the British Government) to some individual in return for services rendered. The holder
of a /jagir/ is termed a /jagirdar/ Ml. These words carry a connotation of feudalism, and
/jagirdar/ is thus a more splendid title than /zəmindar/ M/Fl "landholder. " The /jagir/
system has been abolished in both India and Pakistan, and the remaining large estates are
being divided up into smaller holdings.

22.210.　/ybtyda/ Fl "beginning, start, commencement" is almost entirely synonymous
with /aɣaz/ Ml "beginning. " See Sec. 21.213. /aɣaz/ may, however, be used for the
first part of a book (i. e. the first chapter, the introduction, etc.), while /ybtyda/ cannot.
E. g.

/wnnys səw sɛ̃ytalys mɛ̃ ys ciz ka aɣaz hwa. /　The beginning of this thing
was in 1947. [Or: / ... ki ybtyda hwi/.]

/ys təhrik ka aɣaz iran mɛ̃ hwa. /　The beginning of this movement was
in Iran. [Or: / ... ki ybtyda ... hwi/.]

/ys kytab ka ayaz dekhie!/   Please see the first part of this book!
[/ybtyda/ cannot be substituted here.]

22.211. /xahyš/ F1 denotes "wish, desire," while /yrada/ M2 carries a connotation
of greater resolution: "desire, intent, resolve." E. g.

/meri xahyš həy, ky mɛ̃y yy nəwkri choR dũ./   I desire [lit. my desire
is] to leave [lit. that I may leave] this job. [This is my wish, but
there is not much likelihood of my actually doing so.]

/mera yrada həy, ky mɛ̃y yy nəwkri choR dũga./   I want [lit. my intention
is] to leave [lit. that I will leave] this job. [There is considerable
likelihood of my doing so.]

/yy kam meri xahyš ke mwtabyq hwa./   This work was done [lit. happened]
according to my wish.

/əysa dykhai deta həy, ky meri yy xahyš puri nəhĩ hogi./   It appears that
this wish of mine will not be fulfilled.

/mere yrade ko, dwnya ki koi taqət nəhĩ bədəl səkti./   No power in [lit.
of] the world can change my resolve.

22.212. /rayj/ PA1 "current, in force; prevailing, prevalent" differs somewhat from
/jari/ PA1 "in force, continuing, issuing." /rayj/ indicates that something has become
(or is being made) common, widespread, prevalent; /jari/ simply denotes that the action
or state is continuing, or, in some cases, that the action or state is issuing, emerging and
continuing. E. g.

/yy rwsumat əb tək rayj hɛ̃y./   These customs are still prevalent.
[/jari/ here would denote that these customs are continuing but not
necessarily that they are widespread.]

/hyndostan mɛ̃, rel əwr byjli əgrezõ ke zəmane mɛ̃ rayj hwĩ./   In India,
the railway and electricity were introduced [lit. became common] in
the British period. [/jari/ could not be substituted here.]

/yy qanun aj se səw sal pəhle bhi rayj tha./   This law was current a
hundred years ago too. [/jari/ can be substituted here but was
considered less good by the informants.]

/šer šah ne zəminõ pər baqayda Təyks ləgane ka sylsyla rayj kia./   Sher
Shah introduced [lit. made current] a system [lit. chain, connection]
of assessing regular taxes upon land. [/jari/ can be substituted here,
meaning "issued, promulgated."]

Both /rayj/ and /rəvaj/ M1 "custom, usage, prevalence" come from the same Arabic
root: r-v-j "to be current." These may sometimes overlap in meaning. See Sec. 19.102.
E. g.

/yy rəsm rayj hwi./   This custom became current. [Or:]

/ys rəsm ne rəvaj paya./   This custom gained currency.

/ajkəl ys qysm ki məšin ka rəvaj nəhĩ./   Nowadays this kind of machine
is not common. [Or:]

/ajkəl ys qysm ki məšin rayj nəhĩ./   Nowadays this kind of machine is
not common.

22.213. /sərənjam/ PA1 "accomplishing, completing (a task)" is a compound of
Persian /sər/ "head, chief" + /ənjam/ M1 "end, termination." /sərənjam/, however, is
not a noun. In some senses this word overlaps /əda/ PA1 "performed, paid, accomplished,
fulfilled"; /əda/, however, has the sense of performing a duty or an act which is compulsory,

357

while /sərənjam/ simply denotes the accomplishment of some task. E. g.

/ys ka ənjam bəhwt bwra hoga. / The end of this will be very bad. [/sərənjam/ cannot be substituted here.]

/ws ne əpni zymmedariā bəhwt əcchi təra sərənjam dī. / He carried out his responsibilities in a very good fashion.

/ws ne yy kam sərənjam dia. / He accomplished this task.

/pāc sal mē yy kam sərənjam paya. / In five years this work reached completion.

/ws ne əpne fərayz əda kie. / He performed his duties. [/sərənjam/ is not proper here, since /fərayz/ denotes something which must obligatorily be performed rather than just accomplished.]

22.214. /ədl/ M1 and /ynsaf/ M1 are synonymous. Both mean "justice, fairness, rectitude. " /ynsaf/ is somewhat more common. Both words are often found together in a loose compound made with the Persian conjunction /o/ "and": /ədl o ynsaf/ M1 [np] "justice. " E. g.

/ws ka ədl aj bhi məšhur həy. / His justice is still famous today. [/ynsaf/ may be substituted.]

/vw badšah ədl o ynsaf se kam leta tha. / That king used to act justly [lit. used to make use of justice-and-justice].

22.215. The meaning of /šoba/ M2 overlaps that of /məhkma/ M2: both denote "department. " /šoba/, however, may refer to a department of a school or university (e. g. Department of Arabic) or to "department" in the sense of "field, sphere, area. " /məhkma/ is usually restricted to "department (of a government)": e. g.

/vw pənjab yunyvərsyTi ke šobəe farsi mē profesər həy. / He is a professor in the Department of Persian of Panjab University.

/vw maliat ke məhkme mē ek ala əfsər həy. / He is a high officer in the Department of Finance.

/wnhõ ne hər šobe mē yslahat kī. / He made reforms in every sphere [field, area].

/həmare rəsul ki talimat zyndəgi ke hər šobe mē mədəd deti həy. / The teachings of our Prophet give aid in every sphere of life.

22.216. /ylahi/ A1 "divine, God-like" is extremely rare as an ordinary adjective (i. e. preceding the noun it modifies): it usually occurs after a preceding noun + the /yzafət/. E. g.

/rəhməte ylahi/ F1 [np] Divine Mercy. [/rəhmət/ F1 "compassion, mercy"]

22.217. /ədəb/ M1 has two meanings: (1) "literature" and (2) "respect, honour, courtesy, etiquette. " In the former meaning, /ədəb/ has no plural, but in the latter sense it has the Arabic plural /adab/ Mpl "respects, salutations, forms of address, " introduced to the student in Unit I in /adab ərz/, the common greeting form. In the sense of "respect, honour, " /ədəb/ overlaps the meaning of /yzzət/ F1 "respect, honour, dignity. " E. g.

/farsi ədəb mē əysi səykRõ mysalē məwjud həy. / In Persian literature there are hundreds of such examples.

/həmē əpne bəRõ ka ədəb kərna cahie. / We ought to respect our elders. [Or: / ... ki yzzət kərni cahie/.]

22.218. Technically, /šer/ M1 "verse, couplet" denotes a verse consisting of two lines having the same metre (but not necessarily the same rhyme). /šayri/ F2 "poetry" is an abstract noun made from the word for "poet": /šayr/ M1. The Arabic plural of /šayr/ is /šwəra/ Mpl "poets, " and the Arabic plural of /šer/ is /əšar/ Mpl "verses. " A poetess is termed /šayra/ F1, and the plural of this word is /šayrat/ Fpl, following the Arabic pattern. All of these forms are made from the Arabic root š-'-r "to feel, perceive. " The Persian compound /šer o šayri/ F1 denotes "poetry" in the abstract aggregate.

A /nəzm/ F1 "poem" is composed of more than one /šer/. The /əšar/ of a /nəzm/ must be of the same metre and must be connected in meaning (i. e. tell a story, describe a scene, express a connected idea, etc.). The rhyme scheme of the /nəzm/ is rather free: commonly the pattern is AA, BB, CC, etc. ("A" representing the first line of the first couplet, the second "A" representing the second line of the first couplet, "B" representing the first line of the second couplet, etc.). The pattern may also be AB, CB, DB, or even AA, AA, AA, etc. There is no restriction on the number of couplets in a /nəzm/, nor upon the type of subject which the /nəzm/ may treat.

22.219. /šəwq/ M1 "pleasure, fondness, enjoyment" contrasts with /zəwq/ M1 "taste (for something), hobby. " E. g.

/vw šayri ka əccha zəwq rəkhta həy. / He has good taste in poetry.

/mwjhe təsvirē jəma kərne ka bəhwt šəwq həy. / I enjoy collecting pictures very much.

/mwjhe ys ciz se koi zəwq nəhī. / I have no taste for this thing.

/mwjhe ys ciz ka koi šəwq nəhī. / I don't enjoy this thing. [I. e. I am not fond of it, have no liking for it.]

22.220. /qədr/ F1 denotes "amount, value, sum" and also "appreciation, regard. " Before a noun or adjective, /ys qədr/ (lit. "this amount") is synonymous with /ytna/ A2 "this much, " /ws qədr/ (lit. "that amount") with /wtna/ A2 "that much, " /jys qədr/ (lit. "which amount") with /jytna/ A2 "as much, " and /kys qədr/ (lit. "which amount? ") with /kytna/ A2 "how much. " E. g.

/vw meri bəhwt qədr kərte hēy. / He holds me in high esteem. [Roughly synonymous with /vw meri bəhwt yzzət kərte hēy. /]

/əfsos həy, ky wn ki zyndəgi mē wn ki koi qədr nə hwi. / It is too bad that in his lifetime he was not appreciated at all. [Lit. ... his some value did not become.]

/ws ka yy kam qabyle qədr həy. / This work of his is commendable [lit. worthy of value].

/ys mənsube pər, kys qədr rəqəm xərc hwi. / On this project how much money [lit. which amount sum?] was spent?

/ys mənsube pər, jys qədr rəqəm xərc hogi, vw əmrikən hwkumət əda kəregi. / On this project, whatever amount will be spent, the American Government will pay it. [/jytni/ can be substituted here.]

/ys qədr myhnət ke bad bhi, yy kam mwkəmməl nə ho səka. / Even after so much labour this task could not be completed. [/ytni/ can be substituted here.]

/vw ajkəl kysi qədr pərešan həy. / These days he is somewhat upset. [Here /kwch/ can be substituted for /kysi qədr/.]

359

22.221. The following idiom should be noted:

/vw jys kam ka yrada kərta tha, wse kər ke choRta tha./ Whatever task
he decided upon, he never left it until it was finished. [Lit. Which
task's decision [he] resolved, [he] having done it left [it].]

Here the conjunctive participle followed by /choRna/ "to leave, abandon, let go" has the
sense of "to leave in a finished state, " "to do completely, " or "not to leave undone. "
Further examples:

/xa kwch ho, mə̄y yy kam kər ke choRū̃ga./ Whatever may be, I'll
complete this task.

/mə̄y ws se bədla le ke choRū̃ga./ I'll get my complete revenge from him.
[I.e. I won't leave him alone until I've had my revenge.]

/mə̄y ne ws se əpni rəqəm vwsul kər ke choRi./ I didn't leave him alone
until I had obtained my money from him. [Lit. I left [him] having
realised my amount from him. Note that /choRi/ agrees with the
object, /rəqəm/ F1 "amount, sum. "]

/mə̄y wse səbəq de ke choRū̃ga./ I'll give him a good lesson. [Lit. I'll
leave [him] alone having given him a lesson.]

22.222. /pərva/ F1 denotes "concern (with something), care (for something, for
someone's opinion)" while /fykr/ F1 denotes "worry, mental anguish, concern. " E.g.

/mwjhe ys ki koi pərva nəhī̃./ I don't care about it at all. [Compare:]

/mwjhe ys ki koi fykr nəhī̃./ I am not worried about it at all.

/əgər vw meri pərva nəhī̃ kərta, to mwjhe bhi ws ki pərva nəhī̃./ If he
does not care about me, then I have no concern for him either.

/mə̄y həmešа ysi fykr mē̃ rəhta hū̃, ky kysi təra bəccō̃ ko ala talim dylai
jae./ I always worry [lit. I always remain in this worry] that the
children should be given the best education somehow [or other].

/mwjhe ymtyhan ki fykr rəhti həy./ I keep worrying about the examination.

/mwjhe ymtyhan ki kwch pərva nəhī̃./ I don't care at all about the
examination.

22.223. When mentioning the Qwran, Muslims usually append some adjective denoting
"glorious, " "noble, " etc. Grammatically, these adjectives should be connected to /qwran/
by the Persian /yzafət/, but in speech the /e/ of the /yzafət/ is usually omitted. E.g.

/qwran šərif/ M1 [np] the Noble Qwran. [Grammatically: /qwrane̲
šərif/.]

/qwran məjid/ M1 [np] the Glorious Qwran. [Grammatically: /qwrane̲
məjid/. /məjid/ A1 "glorious, noble, exalted. "]

22.224. The following idiom should be noted:

/wn ke qədəm mwlk mē̃ jəm cwke the./ They had already become firmly
established in the country. [Lit. Their feet had already become
fixed in the country.]

The basic meaning of /jəmna/ IIc is "to congeal, become frozen, fixed, solidified, take
root. " Other examples:

/pani jəm gəya./ The water froze.

/dəhi jəm gəya./ The curds congealed. [/dəhi/ M1 "curds"]

22.225. /γədr/ M1 originally meant (1) "chaos, anarchy, turmoil" and (2) "mutiny (of troops). " In the latter meaning, however, /γədr/ has come to have the specific meaning of "the Mutiny" (the so-called "Sepoy Mutiny" of 1857, which Indians and Pakistanis prefer to think of as their first war of independence), and /γədr/ is thus no longer used in the general sense of "mutiny, " /bəγavət/ F1 "rebellion, uprising, revolution, mutiny" being employed instead. /γədr/ is, however, still found in the meaning of "chaos, turmoil. " E. g.

/sypahiõ ne badšah ke xylaf bəγavət ki. / The soldiers revolted against the king. [Here /γədr/ can no longer be used.]

/γədr mẽ bəhwt se log mare gəe. / Many people were killed in the Mutiny [of 1857].

/vəhã γədr sa məca hwa tha. / It was all chaos there. [In the meaning of "chaos, " /γədr/ is usually found with /məcna/ "to be raised, produced (noise)" or /məcana/ "to raise, produce (noise). "]

22.226. /əhd/ M1, /dəwr/ M1, and /zəmana/ M2 are all employed for "period, era, epoch, reign. " /əhd/ also means "undertaking, promise, giving of one's word. " It is thus considerably stronger in connotation than /vada/ M2 "promise. " E. g.

/yy ymarət əwrãgzeb ke əhd mẽ tamir hwi thi. / This building was built in the reign of Aurangzeb. [Or: /... ke dəwr mẽ/ or /... ke zəmane mẽ/.]

/mãy ne əhd kər lia həy, ky mãy kəbhi šərab nəhĩ piũga. / I have under- taken that I will never drink liquor. [I. e. given my word, made a solemn resolve.]

/mãy ne vada kia tha, ky mãy šam ko pãc bəje vəhã pəhwc jaũga. / I had promised that I would arrive there at five o'clock in the evening. [In the meaning of "(simple) promise" /əhd/ cannot occur.]

/hwkuməte əmrika ne məzid fəwji ymdad dene ka vada kia həy. / The American Government has promised to give more military aid. [Here again /əhd/ cannot occur.]

/nəe sədr ne əhd kia həy, ky vw mwašrəti bwraiõ ko xətm kərne ki puri košyš kərẽge. / The new president has undertaken that he will make every [lit. complete] attempt to end social evils. [/vada/ can also occur here but is much less forceful.]

/həmare əwr wn ke dərmyan yy əhd hwa həy, ky həm zərurat ke vəqt ek dusre ki mədəd kərẽge. / Between them and us it has been resolved that at the time of need [we] will help one another.

/mãy ne wn se ys bat ka əhd lia həy. / I have taken an undertaking from him in [lit. of] this matter.

22.227. /bedar/ PA1 "awake, watchful, vigilant" is used in complex verbal formations with /hona/ and /kərna/. These are generally synonymous with /jagna/ "to awaken (intrans.)" and /jəgana/ "to awaken (trans.), " although much more literary in style. E. g.

/wse bedar nə kərẽ. vw əbhi soya həy. / Don't awaken him. He has just gone to sleep. [/wse nə jəgaẽ/ can be substituted here but is less literary.]

22.228. /məzmun/ M1 means "contents (of a book, letter), article (in a journal, news- paper), " and also "subject, course of study (in school). " /məwzu/ M1 may also be translated as "subject, " but always in the sense of "topic. " E. g.

361

/ys xət ka məzmun kya həy. /   What are the contents of this letter?

/mə̃y ys məwzu pər ek məzmun lykhna cahta hū. /   I want to write an
article on this topic. /məwzu/ and /məzmun/ cannot be interchanged
here.]

/mə̃y ne car məzamin le rəkkhe hə̃y. /   I have taken four subjects [in
school].

/kalyj mē ap ke pas kəwn kəwnse məzamin the. /   In college what courses
did you have?

/ws ki šayri mē nəe nəe məzamin mylte hə̃y. /   [One] finds new subjects
in his poetry. [The use of /məzmun/ for the "topic, thought, idea"
of a poem is a technical usage.]

22.229. /qabyle zykr/ "worthy of mention" is another loose compound made with the
/yzafət/. Such formations are quite common. E. g.

/qabyle tarif/ praiseworthy

/qabyle qədr/ commendable, worthy of appreciation

/qabyle bəyan/ worthy of statement, worth describing

22.230. /jayza/ M2 denotes "survey, examination, scrutiny, analysis, " contrasting
with /mwayna/ M2 "examination (of a physical object), inspection (of a school, factory,
etc.)" and with /ymtyhan/ M1 "(school) test, examination, " and also occasionally "(physical)
examination. " E. g.

/vəzire talim ne pychle məhine təmam talimi ydarō ka mwayna kia. /
The Minister of Education inspected all of the educational institutions
last month.

/wnhō ne mere xun ka mwayna kia. /   They examined my blood. [/ymtyhan
kia/ is also correct, although rather less common.]

/hwkuməte əmrika ne həmari sənəti zəruriat ka jayza lene ke bad yy
ymdad di. /   After surveying our industrial needs, the American
Government gave [us] this aid.

/wnhō ne halat ka jayza lia, əwr əpni fəwjē sərhəd pər bhej dī. /   They
took stock of the situation [lit. circumstances] and sent their armies
to the border.

/mahyrine zəraət ne həmari fəslō ka jayza lene ke bad kwch əhəm təjaviz
peš kī. /   After surveying our crops, the agricultural experts presented
some important suggestions.

22.231. /fəlsəfa/ M2 "philosophy" and /məwsiqar/ M/F1 "musician" are originally
of Greek origin, borrowed into Arabic and from thence through Persian to Urdu. /məwsiqar/
contains the Persian suffix /ar/ (see Sec. 18.305)ı the word for "music" is /məwsiqi/ F2.

22.232. /təhrik/ F1 denotes "(political, religious, etc.) movement" and also "incitement,
encouragement. " In the meaning of "movement, " /təhrik/ contrasts with /hərəkət/ F1,
which also means "movement" but in the sense of "(physical) movement" and also "act,
action, (mischievous) act. " Both words are derived from the Arabic root ḥ-r-k "to move. "
E. g.

/ys ke bad həmari fəwjē bhi hərəkət mē a gəī. /   After this our armies
also came into action.

/ws ki ys hərəkət ne sare xandan ko mwsibət mẽ Dal dia./ This
[mischievous, bad] act of his put the whole family into trouble.

/yy təhrik səb se pəhle agre mẽ šwru hwi./ This movement first began
in Agra.

/ap ko dekh kər, mwjhe bhi ys kam ki təhrik hwi./ Seeing you, I was
also encouraged [to do] this job. [Lit. this work's incitement became.]

/ap ke ys kam ne dusrõ ko bhi təhrik di./ This work of yours also
encouraged others.

22.233. /raj/ Ml means "rule (of a country, etc.)"; /hwkumət/ Fl denotes a
particular government. E. g.

/mwylõ ke raj mẽ əysa nəhĩ hota tha./ Under [lit. in] the Mughal rule,
such [a thing] did not happen.

/sədr ne vəzire azəm ko nəi hwkumət bənane ka hwkm dia./ The president
ordered the prime minister to form a new government. [/raj/ cannot
occur here since a specific government is meant.]

22.234. The difference between /taqətvər/ Al "strong, powerful" and /məzbut/ Al
"stout, sturdy, strong" was discussed in Sec. 7.122.

22.235. Both /jəmat/ [literary: /jəmaət/] Fl and /parTi/ F2 mean "party, group."
/jəmat/ also means "grade, class (in school)," a meaning which /parTi/ does not share.
E. g.

/mwlk mẽ ek nəi syasi jəmat vwjud mẽ ai./ A new political party has
come into existence in the country. [/parTi/ can be substituted here.]

/ajkəl wləma ki ek jəmat ys gaõ mẽ Thəyri hwi həy./ These days a group
of scholars is staying in this village. [/parTi/ can also be substituted
here.]

/meri bəcci pācvĩ jəmat mẽ pəRhti həy./ My daughter studies in the fifth
class. [I. e. in American terminology, the "fifth grade." /parTi/
cannot occur here, but /kylas/ Fl "class" can indeed be substituted
for /jəmat/.]

22.236. The following idiom should be noted:

/axyrkar yn syasi jəmatõ ki košyšẽ phəl laĩ./ At last the efforts of these
political parties bore fruit. [Lit. brought fruit.]

Another example:

/car sal ke bad ws ki myhnət phəl lai./ After four years his effort bore
fruit.

22.237. /mwslym/ Ml Al is roughly synonymous with /mwsəlman/ Ml Al "Muslim."
The former, however, is not very common in Urdu. A male member of the Islamic faith
is usually termed a /mwsəlman/, and the adjective "Muslim" (as in "Muslim duties,"
"Muslim customs") is usually rendered by /yslami/ Al "Islamic." A Muslim woman may
be referred to by the special Arabic term /mwslyma/ Fl or by /mwsəlman əwrət/.

22.238. Some Complex Verbal Formations:

/bedar/

    /bedar hona/ to wake up

    /[X ko] bedar kərna/ to awaken [X]

/mwttəhyd/

    /[X əwr Y] mwttəhyd hona/ [X and Y] to be united

    /[X ko] mwttəhyd kərna/ to unite [X]

/rayj/

    /[Y mẽ] rayj hona/ to become current [in Y]

    /[X ko] rayj kərna/ to make [X] current, to promulgate [X]

/šae/

    /šae hona/ to be published, issued

    /[X ko] šae kərna/ to publish, issue [X]

/vəsi/

    /vəsi hona/ to become broad, wide, spacious

    /[X ko] vəsi kərna/ to make [X] broad, wide, spacious

/ədəb/

    /[X ka] ədəb hona/ [X] to be respected

    /[X ka] ədəb kərna/ to respect, honour [X]

/əhd/

    /[X ka Y se] əhd hona/ [X] to have an undertaking [with Y]

    /[X se Y ka] əhd kərna/ to promise [Y to X]

/hymayət/. [See also F.]

    /[X ki] hymayət hona/ [X] to be supported

    /[X ki] hymayət kərna/ to support [X]

/mwtaləba/

    /[X ka] mwtaləba hona/ [X] to be demanded

    /[X se Y ka] mwtaləba kərna/ to demand [Y of X]

/pərva/

    /[X ki] pərva hona/ [X] to be cared for

    /[X ki] pərva kərna/ to care for, have concern [for X]

/pəymayš/

    /[X ki] pəymayš hona/ [X] to be measured, surveyed

    /[X ki] pəymayš kərna/ to measure, survey [X]

/qədr/

    /[X ki] qədr hona/ [X] to be valued, appreciated

    /[X ki] qədr kərna/ to value, appreciate [X]

/tyjarət/

    /[X ki] tyjarət hona/ [X] to be traded, to have commerce [in X]

    /[X ki] tyjarət kərna/ to trade [in X]

/xahyš/

    /[X ki] xahyš hona/ [X] to be desired, wished for

/[X ki] xahyš kərna/ to wish [for X]
/ybtyda/
    /[X ki] ybtyda hona/ [X] to begin
    /[X ki] ybtyda kərna/ to begin, commence [X]

D:

/pənah/
    /[X ko] pənah dena/ to give sanctuary [to X]
    /[X se] pənah lena/ to take refuge [with X]
    /[X se] pənah māgna/ to seek refuge [from X]
    /[X ko] pənah mylna/ [X] to be given refuge
/sərənjam/
    /[X ko] sərənjam dena/ to complete, accomplish [X]
    /[X] sərənjam pana/ [X] to attain completion, be accomplished
/tərjih/
    /[X ko Y pər] tərjih dena/ to prefer [X to Y]
    /[X ko Y pər] tərjih mylna/ [X] to be preferred [to Y]

F:

/bəɣavət/
    /bəɣavət hona/ to be a rebellion, revolt
    /[X ke xylaf] bəɣavət kərna/ to revolt [against X]
/byjli/
    /byjli gyrna/ lightning to strike
/dərbar/
    /dərbar hona/ court to be held
    /dərbar kərna, ləgana/ to hold a court
/dəxl/
    /[X mē] dəxl dena/ to intrude, interfere [in X]
    /[X ko Y mē] dəxl hasyl hona/ [X] to have a grasp of, command [of Y]
    /[X ka Y mē] dəxl hona/ [X] to have a hand [in Y]
/ɣədr/
    /ɣədr məcana/ to create chaos, turmoil
    /ɣədr məcna/ turmoil, chaos to be created
/hymayət/. [See also B.]
    /[X ki] hymayət lena/ to take the part [of Y]
/jayza/
    /[X ka] jayza lena/ to survey, scrutinise, take a survey [of X]
/nəzm/
    /nəzm kəhna/ to compose a poem
    /[X ko] nəzm kərna/ to put [X] into verse
/raj/
    /[X pər] raj kərna/ to rule [over X]
/swluk/

365

/[X se Y ka] swluk hona/ [X] to receive [Y] treatment. [Note: "Y" here may also be an adjective: /əccha swluk/, /bwra swluk/, etc.]

/[X se Y ka] swluk kərna/ to give [X Y] treatment. [Again "Y" here may be an adjective.]

/šer/

/šer kəhna/ to compose a verse

/šer pəRhna/ to recite a verse

/təhrik/

/təhrik wThana, cəlana/ to begin a movement

/[X ko Y ki] təhrik dena/ to encourage [X to do Y]

/təhrik hona/ to be a movement

/ynsaf/

/[X se] ynsaf hona/ [X] to be treated justly

/[X se] ynsaf kərna/ to act justly [with X]

/zəwq/

/[X ko Y ka] zəwq hona/ [X] to have a taste [for Y]

/[X ka] zəwq pana/ to get a taste [for X]

/zwlm/

/[X ka] zwlm wThana/ to bear [X's] tyranny

/[X se Y pər] zwlm hona/ [Y] to be tyrannised [by X]

/[X pər] zwlm kərna/ to oppress, tyrannise [X]

/zyd/

/[X ko Y ki] zyd hona/ [X] to become stubborn [about Y]

/[X pər] zyd kərna/ to be stubborn [about X]

22.300. ANALYSIS

22.301. Substantive Composition.

The analysis of various Arabic-Persian compounds introduced in this Unit is as follows:

/[ke] bərəks/ Comp Post "contrary to, in contrast with, opposite to": Persian /bər/ "on"; Arabic /əks/ M1 "reflection, image, shadow. "

/jagir/ F1 "estate, fief": Persian /ja/ "place"; /gir/ present stem of /gyryf/ "take, seize": i.e. "place-taking. "

/jagirdar/ M1 "fief-holder, 'jagirdar'": see above; /dar/ present stem of /daš/ "have. "

/jāgju/ A1 "war-like, war-loving": Persian /jāg/ F1 "war"; /ju/ present stem of /jws/ "seek. "

/saynsdan/ M/F1 "scientist": English /sayns/ F1 "science"; Persian /dan/ present stem of /danys/ "know. "

/sərənjam/ PA1 "completed, accomplished": Persian /sər/ "head, chief"; /ənjam/ M1 "end, conclusion. "

/syasətdan/ M/F1 "politician": Arabic /syasət/ F1 "politics"; see /saynsdan/ above.

22.302. Substantives Occurring Both as Noun and Adjective.

As has been seen, Urdu substantives fall into four large categories: (1) those occurring only as nouns (e.g. /ghər/ M1 "house"); (2) those occurring as adjectives and predicate adjectives (e.g. /bəRa/ A2 "big"); (3) those occurring as predicate adjectives only (e.g. /maf/ PA1 "forgiven"); and (4) those occurring as both nouns and adjectives. An example of this latter type is /γəyrmwlki/ M1 A1. Compare:

> /ek γəyrmwlki mere hā Thəyra hwa həy. / A foreigner is staying at my place. [Here /γəyrmwlki/ is used as a noun.]

> /wnhō ne γəyrmwlkiõ ko hyndostan se nykal dia. / They turned the foreigners out of India. [Here again /γəyrmwlki/ is a noun, this time with the OP ending.]

> /əb həmē γəyrmwlki ymdad ki zərurət nəhī. / Now we have no need of foreign aid. [Here /γəyrmwlki/ is an adjective modifying /ymdad/ F1 "aid. "]

Except for the necessity of learning which substantives can occur in this dual role, the problem is relatively simple so far. It is important to note that such dual-role substantives occur either as adjectives or as MASCULINE nouns; they are only rarely found as feminine nouns. E. g.

> /ek mwsəlman aya. / A Muslim came.

> /do isai ap ka yntyzar kər rəhe hāy. / Two Christians are waiting for you.

> /ek γəyrmwlki ws hoTəl mē Thəyra hwa həy. / A foreigner is staying in that hotel.

But NOT:

> */ek mwsəlman ai. / A [fem.] Muslim came.

367

*/do isai ap ka yntyzar kər rəhi̱ hə̃y. / Two [fem.] Christians are
waiting for you.

*/ek γəyrmwlki ws hoTəl mē Thəyri̱ hwi̱ həy. / A [fem.] foreigner is
staying in that hotel.

In such cases it is necessary to employ the substantive as an adjective and include some
word denoting "woman, " "girl, " etc. as the context demands. In some cases there are also
special feminine forms for the substantive in question. E. g.

/ek mwslyma ai. / A [fem.] Muslim came. [/mwslyma/ Fl is the
technical term for a female Muslim. One may also say /mwsəlman
əwrət/. See Sec. 22.237.]

/do isai əwrtē ap ka yntyzar kər rəhi hə̃y. / Two Christian ladies are
waiting for you.

/ek γəyrmwlki əwrət ws hoTəl mē Thəyri hwi həy. / A foreign woman is
staying in that hotel.

Similarly:

/ws nəwjəvan ki šadi hwi həy. / That young [man]'s marriage has taken
place. [Compare:]

/ws nəwjəvan ləRki ki šadi hwi həy. / That young girl's marriage has
taken place.

/ləRai mē do irani mare gəe. / In the fight two Iranis [men] were killed.
[Compare:]

/ləRai mē do irani əwrtē mari gəĩ. / In the fight two Irani women were
killed.

/vw yunani naraz ho gəya. / That Greek [man] became angry. [Compare:]

/vw yunani əwrət naraz ho gəi. / That Greek woman became angry.

There are, of course, a great many substantives which may have either masculine or
feminine reference. These are usually nouns only, however, denoting a post, etc. , which
can be held by either a man or woman, and they are not often found as adjectives as well.
Examples do occur, however:

/wn ka nwmaynda pəhw̃c gəya. / Their representative arrived.

/wn ki nwmaynda pəhw̃c gəi. / Their [fem.] representative arrived.

/pakystan mē ek nwmaynda hwkumət qaym hwi həy. / In Pakistan a
representative government has been established. [The use of /nwmaynda/
as an adjective is rather limited.]

22. 303. "Times" and "-Fold. "

The enclitic /gwna/ A2 is employed after a cardinal number to express "times" (or
"double, " "triple, " "quadruple, " etc.). /gwna/ is treated as a Type II adjective and agrees
in number-gender-case with its noun.

In three cases, /gwna/ has "fused" with the cardinal numeral to produce new forms.
These are:

/dwgna/ A2 two times, double. [Also /do gwna/.]

/tygna/ A2 three times, triple. [Also /tin gwna/.]

/cəwgna/ A2 four times, quadruple. [Also /car gwna/.]

Examples:

/ys mənsube ke lie, ys se dwgni rəqəm cahie. / For this project double this amount [lit. from this two-times amount] is required.

/ys sal, pychle sal ke mwqable mẽ, dwgni fəsl hwi həy. / This year, compared with last year, double the crop has been produced [lit. two-times crop has become.]

/mə̃y ne yy ciz tygni qimət pər xəridi həy. / I bought this thing at triple the price. [I. e. at a price three times its normal selling price.]

/həmari fəwj ki tadad dwšmən ki fəwj ki tadad se cəwgni həy. / The number [of troops] of our army is quadruple the number of the army of the enemy.

/hyndostan ki abadi pakystan ki abadi se kəi gwna zyada həy. / The population of India is many times [larger] than the population of Pakistan. [/gwni/ is expected here since /abadi/ "population" is F2. /gwni/ is indeed also found, but /gwna/ as an independent word in the predicate adjective position tends to become invariable.]

/ys šəhr ki abadi ws šəhr ki abadi se koi chəy gwna zyada həy. / The population of this city is about six times the population of that city. [Again, /gwni/ should occur.]

"Doubled, folded twice, " "tripled, folded three times, " etc. are expressed for the first four cardinal numerals by the numeral + a suffix /əhr/ or /hr/ + the Type II adjective endings:

/ykəhra/ A2 single, unfolded, having no fold

/dohra/ A2 doubled, folded once

/tyhra/ A2 tripled, folded twice

/cəwhra/ A2 quadrupled, folded thrice

After /cəwhra/, "folded four times, " etc. must be expressed with the word /təh/ F1 "fold. " E. g.

/yy kəpRa dohra həy. ys lie moTa ləg rəha həy. yse ykəhra kər ke dekhẽ. / This cloth is doubled. Therefore it seems thick. Unfold it and look at it. [/moTa/ A2 "fat, thick. " /ykəhra kərna/ literally means "to make a folded thing single: to make into a single surface. "]

/ys kayəz ko dohra kijie. / Please fold this paper [once].

/ys kəpRe ko tyhra kər lẽ. / Fold this cloth twice [i. e. make three folds].

/cadər ko cəwhra kər ke pələ̃g pər Dal do! / Fold the sheet thrice and put it on the bed [i. e. make four folds]!

/ys kəpRe ki pãc təh kijie! / Please fold this cloth four times [i. e. make five folds]!

/ykəhra/ and /dohra/ are also used idiomatically to mean "thin, slenderly built (body)" and "stout, well-built (body)" respectively. Note that /ykəhra/ cannot be employed to mean "single" in the sense of "only one" (e. g. "a single boy, " "a single book"): this must be expressed by /ek hi/ or /ek bhi/.

/vw ykəhre bədən ka admi həy. / He is a man of slender build. [/bədən/ M1 "body. "]

/vw dohre bədən ka admi həy. / He is a well-built man.

22.304. Complex Verbal Formations with /khana/ and /marna/.

/khana/ "to eat" and /marna/ "to hit, beat, kill" are often employed in a rather periph-eral type of complex verbal formation.

(1) Formations with /khana/: Here /khana/ means "to undergo, suffer. " In the past tenses the gender of the noun of the complex verbal formation governs the number-gender of the occurring form of /khana/. E. g.

> /dhoka khana/ to be deceived. [/dhoka/ M2 "deceit, trick, deception. "]
>
>> /ws ne tyjarət mẽ dhoka khaya. / He suffered a deception [i. e. someone misled him, tricked him] in business.
>
> /jute khana/ to be beaten with shoes. [/juta/ M2 "shoe. " To be beaten with a shoe is among the most humiliating forms of insult.]
>
>> /ap əpni yn hərkətõ ki vəja se zərur jute khaẽge!/ Because of these acts of yours you will certainly be beaten with shoes! [Metaphorically: you will be despised and treated with contempt.]
>
> /mar khana/ to get a beating. [/mar/ F1 "beating. "]
>
>> /ws ne aj yskul mẽ bəhwt mar khai. / He really got a beating today in school.
>
> /šykəst khana/ to be defeated. [/šykəst/ F1 "defeat. "]
>
>> /dwšmən ki fəwj ne šykəst khai. / The army of the enemy was defeated.
>
> /Thokər khana/ to stumble, run into an obstacle, suffer a loss, make a blunder.
>
> [/Thokər/ F1 "stumble, mistep. "]
>
>> /mãy raste mẽ Thokər kha kər gyra. / I stumbled and fell on the road.
>>
>> /əgərce vw məšhur mwvərryx həy, lekyn ws ne bhi ys jəga Thokər khai. / Although he is a famous historian, he too made a blunder at this place.
>>
>> /ws ne tyjarət mẽ Thokər khai. / He suffered a loss in business.

(2) Formations with /marna/: /marna/ retains its usual meaning of "to hit, strike, " but the instrument with which the striking is done occurs as the noun of the complex verbal formation: e. g. /laThi marna/ "to hit [with] a stick" rather than /laThi se marna/. In the past tenses the number-gender of the noun of the complex verbal formation governs the number-gender of the occurring form of /marna/. Another point is that the object of the striking is usually marked by /ke/ instead of /ko/: i. e. one says /[X ke] laThi marna/ "to hit [X] with a stave, " and not *\/[X ko] laThi marna/. The author's informants felt that some portion of the body was understood here: i. e. that /[X ke] laThi marna/ stood for /[X ke bədən pər] laThi marna/, /[X ke sər pər] laThi marna/, etc. E. g.

> /goli marna/ to hit with a bullet. [/goli/ F2 "bullet, pellet. "]
>
>> /ws kwtte ko goli mar di gəi. / That dog was shot with a bullet.
>
> /juta [or /jute/] marna/ to beat with a shoe. [See above under /jute khana/.]
>
>> /mãy ne ws ke sər pər juta mara. / I struck [him] on the head with a shoe.
>
> /laThi marna/ to hit with a stave, stick. [/laThi/ F2 "stave, stick. "]
>
>> /ləRke ne bhẽys ke laThi mari. / The boy struck the buffalo with a stave. [Or:]
>>
>> /ləRke ne bhẽys ke sər pər laThi mari. / The boy struck the buffalo on the head with a stave.
>
> /təlvar marna/ to strike with a sword. [/təlvar/ F1 "sword. "]
>
>> /ws ne ws ka hath təlvar mar ke kaT Dala. / He struck his hand with a sword and cut [it] off.
>
> /thəppəR marna/ to slap. [/thəppəR/ M1 "slap. "]
>
>> /zəmindar ne kysan ke thəppəR mara. / The landowner slapped the farmer.

22.401. Supplementary Vocabulary.

The following numerals are all Type I adjectives. See Sec. 2.401.

ykanve	ninety-one
banve	ninety-two
tyranve	ninety-three
cəwranve	ninety-four
pycanve	ninety-five

Other items are:

hərf M1	letter (of the alphabet)
jagir F1	estate, fief, lands given by the government as a reward for services
ləfz M1	word
məzmun M1	article; subject, contents

21.402. Supplementary Exercise I: Substitution.

1. ys məzmun mē, <u>nəvve</u>   qədim šwəra ka zykr kia gəya həy.
   ninety-one
   seventy-six
   ninety-two
   ninety-four
   sixty-one

2. ys səbəq mē, <u>pycanve</u>   nəe əlfaz ystemal kie gəe hə̄y.
   fifty-four
   ninety-three
   eighty-one
   forty-two
   eighty-nine

3. wn ki jagir mē, <u>pəchəttər</u>   gaõ šamyl hə̄y.
   thirty-seven
   sixty-nine
   ninety
   eighty-eight
   ninety-two

22.501. Substitution.

1. ə̃grezõ   ki aməd se ek nəya dəwr šwru hota həy.
   French
   Portuguese
   Persians
   Aryans
   Dravidians

2. mə̃y ys məzmun   mə̃   ek nəya fəlsəfa   peš kərũga.
         story   some events of the Mutiny
         poem   [a] scene of Indian life
         lecture   the theory of Pakistan
         journal   the Government's new
                                    political policy
         book   the history of the Congress
                                    Party

3. ws zəmane mə̃   yn šwəra   ki qədr nəhĩ ki gəi.
                      these writers
                      this poet
                      this musician
                      this writer
                      these politicians

4. wnhõ ne əpne beTe   ko vəzir   pər tərjih di.
         your poem   my poem
         that word   this word
         tyranny   justice
         poetry   the tasks of the
                              country
         my companion   me

5. həmare liDər   iraniõ   ki hymayət kərni cahte the.
   our President   this party
   the Minister of   this project
   Education
   these scientists   this theory
   the Jagirdar   the demand of
                           the farmers
   the Navabs   the British

6. cerməyn   ne   həmare mənsube   ka jayza lia.
   the Irani poet   Urdu poetry
   the President of   our educational system
   the State
   our politicians   this new movement
   the Raja   his treasury

the Prime Minister   the military strength

7. <u>ys məzmun</u>   ke šae hone ke bad, həmari qəwm bedar honi šwru hwi.

    this journal

    this lecture

    these poems

    these words

    these events

8. <u>sərdar</u>   ne   <u>xanəbədošõ</u>   se əccha swluk nəhĩ kia.

    the Governor   the Muslims

    the Department   this student
    of Persian

    the soldiers   the Greeks

    the king   the poets of his court

    the Caliph   the non-Muslims

9. wnhẽ   <u>syasi mwamlat</u>   mẽ dəxl nəhĩ dena cahie.

        these religious problems

        our educational policies

        the politics of Pakistan

        the Union Councils

        his brother's marriage

10. <u>əwrãgzeb</u>   ne   <u>mwlk</u>   mẽ ek nəya talimi nyzam ...

    Sher Shah   his empire   a new method of realising tax

    Muhammad   India   [currency] notes
    Tughluq

    the king   his reign   coins of gold

    the English   the world   these customs

    the President   this province   this new law

                  ... rayj kərne ki košyš ki.

11. vw <u>yy whda</u>   nə sə̃bhal səka.

    such a big responsibility

    the administration of the
    government

    such a big family

    such a big empire

    his duties

12. <u>meri təjviz</u>   <u>ap ki təjviz</u>   ke bylkwl bərəks həy.

    our philosophy   your philosophy

    this result   our hopes

    this custom   our ancient customs

    the policy of the its promise
    the Government

    his life   the life of Muslims

13. vw <u>šer o šayri</u>   ka bəhwt əccha zəwq rəkhti thi.

    clothes

jewellery

songs

dramas

Persian literature

14. wse   <u>məsajyd</u>   <u>bənvane</u>   ka bəhwt šəwq tha.

             pictures   taking

             couplet   saying

             opium   eating

             football   playing

             dogs   raising

15. vw   <u>qwran šərif</u>   <u>lykh kər</u>   əpni rozi kəmata tha.

             Persian   having taught

             newspaper   having sold

             fish   having caught

             toys   having made

             manure   having sold

16. <u>nəi hwkumət</u>   ne   <u>əvam</u>   ko mwttəhyd kər dia.

     the Mutiny   Hindus and
                             Muslims

     this event   the nation

     this law   political parties

     the prince   both tribes

     this attack   both countries

22.502. Transformation.

1.   Review of the present participle as an adjective: follow the instructions given in
Sec. 16.502 (2). E. g.

         /ləRki hɛ̃s rəhi thi. ləRki əcanək rone ləgi. / [This becomes:]

         /hɛ̃sti hwi ləRki əcanək rone ləgi. /

   a.   xun bəh rəha tha. DakTər xun ko nə rok səka.

   b.   ləRke nac rəhe the. mɛ̃y ne ləRkõ ki təsvir khɛ̃ci.

   c.   vəqt gwzər rəha həy. vəqt ko kəwn rok səkta həy.

   d.   wn ka sərdar so rəha tha. kysi ne wn ke sərdar ke goli mari.

   e.   sypahi bhag rəhe hɛ̃y. sypahiõ ko kysi nə kysi təra rok dijie!

   f.   ləRkiã ga rəhi thĩ. ləRkiõ ne masTər sahəb ko yšara kia, ky wn ka gana xətm
hone vala həy.

   g.   dwšmənõ ka jhənDa ləhra rəha tha. həmare sypahiõ ne dwšmənõ ke jhənDe pər
goli cəlai.

   h.   pani bəh rəha həy. pani ko rok do!

   i.   yy musibtẽ bəRh rəhi hɛ̃y. yn musibtõ se tɛ̃g a gəya hũ.

   j.   dwšmən ki fəwj bəRh rəhi thi. həm ne dwšmən ki fəwj ko sərhəd pər rok dia.

2. Review of the present participle as a predicate complement: follow the instructions given in Sec. 16. 502 (3) and (4). In all of the following sentences except (i) and (j) the present participle refers to the object; in nos. (i) and (j) it refers to the subject (although (i) is possibly ambiguous). E. g.

/mwsafyr ro rəha tha. ws ne mwsafyr ko dekha. / [This becomes:]
/ws ne mwsafyr ko rote hwe dekha. /

a. vw yy šer pəRh rəha tha. məy ne wse swna.

b. byjli gyr rəhi thi. məy ne byjli dekhi.

c. dwlhən ro rəhi thi. wnhõ ne dwlhən ko rwxsət kia.

d. vw jhuT bol rəha tha. həmare mwntəzym ne wse pəkRa.

e. vw mwsibət se ghəbra rəha tha. kya, ap ne wse dekha?

f. məy gyr rəha tha. ws ne mwjhe səbhala.

g. yy ədib šykayət kər rəha tha. məy ne ys ədib ko swna.

h. vw bwtõ ko puj rəha tha. ws ke pəyrəvõ ne wse paya.

i. mymbər šor məca rəhe the. mymbərõ ne wse əsəmbli se nykal dia.

j. vw bəh rəha tha. vw dur tək pani mẽ cəla gəya.

3. Review of the present participle + /hi/ "as soon as ..., while ... ": follow the instructions given in Sec. 16. 502 (7). E. g.

/ws ne hwkumət səbhali. ws ne yslahat šwru kĩ. / [This becomes:]
/ws ne hwkumət səbhalte hi yslahat šwru kĩ. / [Or:]
/hwkumət səbhalte hi, ws ne yslahat šwru kĩ. /

a. cor ne mere hath se pəyse chine. cor bhag gəya.

b. ws ne halat ka jayza lia. ws ne cənd əcchi təjaviz peš kĩ.

c. məy pyšavər pəhw̃ca. mera saman cwra lia gəya.

d. ws ne kytab kholi. ws ne həmare rəsul ka nam swnəhre hwruf mẽ lykha hwa dekha.

e. dysəmbər šwru hwa. dərya ka pani jəm gəya.

f. vw ləRai ke məydan mẽ pəhw̃ca. vw əpne bhai ko təlaš kərne ləga.

g. vw jəhaz se wtra. ws ne hwkuməte pakystan se syasi pənah mãgi.

h. məzar pər pəhw̃ca. wn ki ãkhõ mẽ ãsu a gəe.

i. ws ne taj o təxt pər qəbza kia. ws ne zwlm šwru kər dia.

j. ws ne šykəst khai. ws ne əpni fəwj ko piche həTaya.

k. məy ne məzmun lykha. məy ne wse rəvana kər dia.

l. ws ne šərab nə pine ka əhd kia. ws ne toR dia.

m. ws ne xəzane ko khola. ws ne dekha, ky cori ho gəi həy.

n. wnhõ ne ys kam ko sərənjam dia. wnhõ ne hwkumət ko ek nəya mənsuba peš kia.

o. badšah ne yy halat dekhe. badšah ne sərhəd pər fəwjẽ bhej dĩ.

4. Review of the past participle as an adjective: follow the instructions given in Sec. 16. 502 (8). E. g.

/ləRka ghəbraya hwa həy. ləRke ki mədəd kəro! / [This becomes:]
/ghəbrae hwe ləRke ki mədəd kəro! /

a. dərəxt gyr gəya həy.   dərəxt ko wˈThao!
b. dyl TuT gəya həy.   dyl ko kəwn joR səkta həy.
c. bəcci kho gəi həy.   bəcci ko DhŭD kər lao!
d. zəmana gwzər gəya.   zəmane ko koi vapəs nəhĭ la səkta.
e. hwmayŭ ne əpna taj kho dia tha.   hwmayŭ ne əpna taj vapəs le lia.
f. yy kytabē bādh gəi hāy.   yn kytabõ ko Dak ke zərie bhej dijie!
g. kwtta mər gəya həy.   kwtte ko phēk ao!
h. qəmis phəT gəi həy.   qəmis ko wtaro!
i. zevər bykhər gəe hāy.   māy ne zevərõ ko wThaya.
j. pətlun sukh gəi həy.   pətlun ko əndər laie!

22. 503. Variation.

1. hwmayŭ ne iran ja kər pənah li.
    pychli ləRai ke zəmane mē, bəhwt se fəransisiõ ne ȳglystan mē pənah li thi.
    hwmayŭ iran ke badšah ke pas pənah leni cahta tha.
    iran ke badšah ne hwmayŭ ko pənah di.
    pwrtəgaliõ ne wse pənah dene se ynkar kər dia.
    sədr ne wse pənah dene ka vada kia.

2. wn ki xahyš thi, ky wnhē hyndostan se nykal dia jae.
    həmari xahyš həy, ky pwrtəgaliõ ko əfriqa se nykal dia jae.
    wn ki xahyš həy, ky mwntəzym ko whde se həTa dia jae.
    šer šah ki xahyš thi, ky mwɣlõ se hwkumət chin li jae.
    ybtyda hi se, wn ki yy xahyš rəhi həy, ky yy kam jəld sərənjam dia jae.
    sypəsalar ki xahyš thi, ky ys mwqam pər ləRai hoti.

3. əvam ne badšah ke məhl ke samne azadi ka mwtaləba kia.
    ɣəribõ ne badšah se ynsaf ka mwtaləba kia.
    wməra ne badšah se vəzir ko həTane ka mwtaləba kia.
    vwzəra ne sədr ke pas ja kər vəzire azəm ko nykalne ka mwtaləba kia.
    gaõvalõ ne yunyən kəwnsəl se səfai ka yntyzam Thik rəkhne ka mwtaləba kia.
    baz mymbərõ ne qəwmi əsəmbli mē vəzire maliat se Təyksõ mē kəmi kərne ka
      mwtaləba kia.

4. nəvab sahəb ne saynsdanõ se əccha swluk nəhĭ kia.
    wnhõ ne əqliəti fyrqõ se yəksā swluk kia.
    wn ki hərkətõ ke bavwjud, kāgres ke liDərõ ne wn se bəhwt əccha swluk kia.
    ws ke ys šer ki vəja se, badšah ne ws se dərbar mē əccha swluk nəhĭ kia.
    ws ke əhd mē, šwəra o wdəba se bəhwt əccha swluk kia jata tha.
    māy ne əpne məzmun mē əqliətõ se əccha swluk kərne ka mwtaləba kia.

5. āgrez dərəsl tyjarət ki ɣərəz se hyndostan ae the.
    mera sathi ymtyhan dene ki ɣərəz se agre aya həy.
    yy mwvərryx ɣədr pər təhqiq kərne ki ɣərəz se dyhli aya həy.
    bəhwt se mwsəlman pənah lene ki ɣərəz se pakystan ae the.
    yn wdəba ne mwrda qəwm ko bedar kərne ki ɣərəz se yy məzamin lykhne šwru kie
    the.

həmari jəmat təbliɣ ki ɣərəz se ȳglystan jane vali həy.

6. ap əpni ys hərəkət pər mar khaēge.

məhz ap ki vəja se, həmē mar khani pəRi.

dwšmən ki fəwj ne šykəst khai.

rana sãga šykəst khane ke bad pəhaRõ mē ja kər chwp gəya.

ws ne pəhaR se gyr kər bəhwt coT khai.

axyrkar ap ne ys mwamle mē ɣələti khai.

7. sare wmǝra ne dərbar mē vəzir ki hymayət ki.

həmari parTi ne qəwmi əsəmbli mē wn ki hymayət ki.

ɣədr mē, baz rajaõ əwr nəvabõ ne ēgrezõ ki hymayət ki.

ws šəhzade ne kəlkətte ja kər ēgrezõ ki hymayət hasyl ki.

ybtyda mē, mwslym lig əwr kãgres parTi ek dusre ki hymayət kərti thī.

jagirdar ne ys jhəgRe mē kysan ki hymayət li.

8. mȳy ne ys kytab ke pəhle bab ko sari kytab pər tərjih di.

šwəra ne wn ki ys nəzm ko dusrõ ki nəzmõ pər tərjih di.

wn ke kəmzor janəšinõ ne əyš ki zyndəgi ko hwkumət ke kamõ pər tərjih di.

ys jəga, əksər wdəba ys ləfz ko ws ləfz pər tərjih dēge.

wnhõ ne ēgrezõ ke tərze zyndəgi ko əpne tərze zyndəgi pər tərjih de rəkkhi həy.

zyndəgi ke hər šobe mē, ynsaf ko zwlm pər tərjih deni cahie.

9. mȳy ap ke ɣwsse ki pərva nəhī̆ kərta.

vw wdəba əwr šwəra ki pərva nəhī̆ kərta.

ap ko syrf əpne ymtyhan ki pərva kərni cahie.

əfsos həy, ky vw əpne məzhəbi fərayz ki pərva nəhī̆ kərta.

xa vw kytne hi taqətvər kyõ nə hõ, mȳy wn ki pərva nəhī̆ kərta.

ybtyda hi se, mwjhe yn cizõ ki koi pərva nəhī̆.

10. šalymar baɣ mwɣəl raj ki ek šandar yadgar həy.

yy gyrja pwrtəgaliõ ke dəwre hwkumət ki yadgar həy.

yy məzar əwr məsjydē šah jəhã ke əhd ki yadgar hɔ̄y.

yy qəla əwr qəydxana ws ke zwlm ke dəwr ki yadgar hɔ̄y.

pakystan mwslym lig ke liDərõ ki košyšõ ki yadgar həy.

yy kytab mere wsi dost ki yadgar həy, jys ka zykr mȳy əbhi kər rəha tha.

11. ys mənsube ke lie, ys se dəs gwni rəqəm cahie.

wnhē šykəst dene ke lie, həmē ys se tin gwni fəwj cahie.

ws vəqt se, həmari jəmat ki tadad tin gwni bəRh gəi həy.

wn logõ ki aməd se, həmari tadad pãc gwni bəRh gəi həy.

ys sal fəsl gwzəšta sal ki fəsl se təqribən car gwni həy.

meri pərešaniã pəhle se do gwni ho gəi hɔ̄y.

12. mahyrine maliat ne həmare sənəti mənsubõ ka jayza lia.

həmare mwntəzym ne kəmpni ke hysab ka jayza lia.

ys kytab mē, mwvərryx ne ws əhd ka səhih jayza lia həy.

ws ədib ne ys məzmun mē mwašre ki bwraiõ ka jayza lia həy.

mahyrine maliat həmare halat ka jayza le kər kwch təjaviz peš kərēge.

wnhõ ne Təyks ke nyzam ka jayza lene ke bad yy təjaviz peš kī̆.

13. yy əfsər həmeša hwkumət ke mwamlõ mē dəxl dete hə̄y.

ap wn ki šadi mē kyõ dəxl dete hə̄y.

jəb bwzwrg batē kər rəhe hõ, to dəxl nə dena cahie.

ap ke dəxl dene se sara kam xərab ho gəya.

ap ko həmare ys fəysle mē dəxl dene ka həq hasyl nəhĩ.

wse məhkməe maliat mē bəhwt bəRa dəxl hasyl həy.

14. šəhzada ws šayr ki bəhwt qədr kərta tha.

dwnya həmeša ap ki qədr kəregi.

mə̄y dyl se ap ki qədr kərta hũ.

ws ki zyndəgi mē, kysi ne ws ki qədr nəhĩ ki.

ws šayr ke mərne ke bad, ws ki qədr hwi.

meri nəzrõ mē ws ki bəhwt qədr həy.

15. ap ko jys qədr fəwj ki zərurət ho, həm bhej səkte hə̄y.

mwjhe ys qədr təklif thi, ky mə̄y bəyan nəhĩ kər səkta.

yy bat swn kər, vw ys qədr naraz hwe, ky phyr wnhõ ne mwjh se koi bat nə ki.

dərya ys qədr jəm gɔya həy, ky ws pər gaRiā cəl səkti hə̄y.

əb həmari qəwm kysi qədr bedar ho gəi həy.

ap ko məkan bənvane ke lie kys qədr rəqəm cahie.

22. 504. Translation.

1. Write out the following sentences in the Urdu script. Then translate them into English.

   a. jəb wn ka sara mal səylab mē bəh gəya, to wnhē əxbar bec kər rozi kəmani pəRi.

   b. əkbər ne dine ylahi ko rayj kərne ki bəhwt košyš ki, məgər əvam ne wse qwbul nəhĩ kia. cwnāce yy məzhəb ws ke əpne dərbar tək hi məhdud rəha.

   c. mwɣəl badšahõ ke dərbar mē bəhwt se šwəra, wdəba, əwr məwsiqar rəhte the. yy badšah wnhē bəhwt əziz rəkhte the, əwr wnhē bəRe bəRe ynam dete the.

   d. bəñda ap ka ɣwlam həy. ap jo bhi kam fərmaēge, ynšaəlla[h] yy bəñda wse sərənjam dega.

   e. wnhõ ne mwlk ki jo xydmət ki həy, ws se tarix mē wn ka nam, əwr həmare dylõ mē wn ki yad baqi rəhegi.

   f. əgər ap wn logõ se ysi təra bwra swluk kərte rəhe, to ap kysi nə kysi roz zərur mar khaēge.

   g. yy mwlk wn ki yadgar həy. wn ki košyšõ se vwjud mē aya. vw hi ys ke bani the, əwr wn ki košyšõ ne hi ys ko tərəqqi di.

   h. ys təhsil ki yunyən kəwnsəl ka yntyzam bəhwt əccha həy. ys ke mymbər bəRi myhnət se kam kərte hə̄y. yy wn ki myhnət hi ka nətija həy, ky aj təqribən hər gaõ mē byjli məwjud həy.

   i. šəhzade ne ynsaf se kam nəhĩ lia, əwr əpne sypahiõ ko hwkm dia, ky ws ɣərib admi ko phyr qəydxane mē Dal dia jae.

   j. aj ws ne zəmin ki pəymayš kərai həy. kəl ya pərsõ tək tamir ka kam šwru ho jaega. mera əndaza həy, ky ys məzar ki tamir mɛ̃ do tin sal ləgɛ̃ge.

k. vəzire talim əpni zyd pər qaym rəhe, əwr wnhõ ne twləba ka mwtaləba swnne
    se ynkar kər dia.

l. həmare wləma ne əpni təqrirõ əwr məzamin ke zərie logõ mɛ̃ azadi ka jəzba
    pəyda kia. cwnãce log rəfta rəfta bedar hone šwru hwe, əwr ek vəqt əysa aya,
    ky mwlk mɛ̃ azadi ki ek mwnəzzəm təhrik šwru hwi.

m. liDərõ ke gyryftar hote hi, əvam ne hwkumət ke xylaf bəɣavət kər di.

n. məwjuda saynsdanõ ki rae həy, ky həm cãd ke ɣlava dusre sytarõ tək bhi pəhw̃c
    səkte hɛ̃y.

o. həmare šwəra ne ylm o ədəb ke sath sath qəwm ki bhi bəhwt xydmət ki həy.
    wnhõ ne əpni šayri ke zərie logõ ko azadi ka pəyɣam dia.

2. Translate the following sentences into Urdu. Write them out in the Urdu script.

a. When his elder [lit. big] brother seized the throne and crown from him, he
    fled [lit. having fled] and took refuge with [lit. at the place of] the king of
    Egypt.

b. In our country every individual is treated alike, whether he is a Muslim or
    non-Muslim.

c. Our chieftain took stock of the situation [lit. made a survey of the circumstances]
    and, having called us all to him, he presented some important suggestions.

d. There is no firmness in his nature. In my opinion, he will not be able to
    manage his responsibilities.

e. At that time the Congress Party was very weak, but after the elections it has
    become very strong.

f. He is a professor in the Department of Persian, and he has excellent [lit.
    good] taste in [lit. of] Persian poetry [lit. couplet and poetry].

g. The Rajputs fought with great heroism under their heroic leader, but Mughal
    military power was greater. Therefore they had to accept defeat [lit. they
    had to eat defeat].

h. I am ready to publish your article in my magazine, but our government will
    not like it.

i. If you will not support our party, then we will certainly lose.

j. He did not care for his father's words and kept on living a life of pleasure.

k. The empire of the Mughals lasted [lit. remained established] for [lit. up to]
    three hundred and fifty years, and after them the British ruled India for about
    one hundred years.

l. I praised this verse of his very much, but the other poets did not like it.

m. In the Mutiny, the Hindus and Muslims, having become united, revolted against
    the British.

n. At last our efforts bore fruit, and our country also became independent.

o. Master Sahəb prefers this red book to that green book. In his opinion, the
    exercises of the green book are better.

379

22. 505. Script.

1. Write out the following words in the Urdu script and place them in Urdu alphabetical order.

   a. təhrik
   b. wlum
   c. əlfaz
   d. məzamin
   e. əzmət

   f. jayza
   g. zyd
   h. zwlm
   i. xahyš
   j. šoba

22. 506. Response.

1. Answer the following questions verbally:

۱۔ آپ اپنی روزی کیسے کماتے ہیں ؟

۲۔ کیا، آپ شعر و شاعری سے بھی ذوق رکھتے ہیں ؟

۳۔ ہندوستان کی آبادی آپ کے ملک کی آبادی سے کتنے گنا زیادہ ہے ؟

۴۔ کیا، آپ کسی سیاسی جماعت کے رکن ہیں ؟

۵۔ اردو کے لئے آپ کن سے رسم الخط کو ترجیح دیں گے ؟

۶۔ کیا آپ بھی شعر کہتے ہیں ؟

۷۔ جب پانی جم جاتا ہے تو کیا کہلاتا ہے ؟

۸۔ کیا آپ نے کبھی افیون کھائی ہے ؟

۹۔ تاج محل جو ہندوستان کی سب سے مشہور عمارت ہے، کس شہر میں واقع ہے ؟

۱۰۔ آپ کی رائے میں مختلف مذاہب کے لوگوں سے یکساں سلوک کرنا چاہئے یا نہیں ؟

۱۱۔ کیا آپ کی یونیورسٹی میں اردو کا کوئی شعبہ ہے ؟

۱۲۔ آپ کے شہر میں بجلی کب آئی ؟

۱۳۔ کیا آپ ایران جانے کی خواہش رکھتے ہیں ؟

۱۴۔ کیا آپ محکمہ مالیات میں کسی کو جانتے ہیں ؟

۱۵۔ کیا ، آپ شعر و شاعری کے موضوع پر کوئی مضمون لکھ سکتے ہیں ؟

2. Write out the answers to the following questions in Urdu. Answer to these may be found in Sec. 22.000.

۱۔ ہمایوں اپنے باپ کے برعکس تھا۔ کیسے ؟

۲۔ ہندوستان میں زمین کی پیمائش کا نظام کس نے رائج کیا ؟

۳۔ کیا غدر میں کسی مسلمان نواب یا ہندو راجہ نے انگریزوں کی مدد کی تھی ؟

۴۔ اورنگ زیب کی زندگی کا زیادہ حصہ کس کام میں بسر ہوا ؟

۵۔ علی گڑھ یونیورسٹی کا بانی کون تھا ؟

۶۔ اورنگ زیب اپنی روزی کس طرح کمایا کرتا تھا ؟

۷۔ ہمایوں نے کہاں پناہ لی تھی ؟

۸۔ کیا ، اب تک ہندوستان کے کسی علاقے پر پرتگالیوں کا قبضہ ہے ؟

۹۔ ہندوستانی تہذیب پر کس کا اثر زیادہ تھا ؟ انگریزوں کا یا فرانسیسیوں کا ؟

۱۰۔ ہندوستان کی اکثر بڑی بڑی سڑکیں (مثلاً کلکتہ سے پشاور تک) کس کی یادگار ہیں ؟

22.507. Conversation Practice.

Mr. Smith is discussing the essay given in Sec. 22.000 with Dr. Rəhim.

اسمتھ۔   میں نے بابر کی زندگی کے حالات پڑھے ۔ بہت ہی دلچسپ ہیں۔ بابر کی زندگی
سے ہر انسان کو ہمت اور بہادری کا سبق ملتا ہے ۔ واقعی مصیبتوں سے نہ گھبرانا
اور اپنے مقصد کے لئے کوشش کئے جانا ہی زندگی ہے ۔

381

رحیم ۔   میں نے پہلے ہی عرض کیا تھا کہ آپ اُس کی زندگی کے حالات بہت دلچسپ
پائیں گے۔

اسمتھ ۔   ایک بات میری سمجھ میں نہیں آئی کہ شیر شاہ مغلوں کے خلاف کیوں تھا؟

رحیم ۔   شیر شاہ مغلوں کی فوج میں معمولی ملازم تھا۔ اُن میں رہ کر اُن کی اچھائیوں
اور برائیوں سے واقف ہو گیا تھا۔ وہ مغلوں کو غیر ملکی باشندے سمجھتا تھا۔
اور کہا کرتا تھا کہ " میں نے مغلوں کو بہت قریب سے دیکھا ہے ۔ وہ نہ تو اچھے
لڑنے والے ہیں اور نہ ہی اچھے منتظم ۔ اگر خدا نے کبھی مجھے موقع دیا تو میں
اُنہیں اُن کے وطن واپس بھیج دوں گا "

اسمتھ ۔   واقعی اُس نے ثابت بھی کر دیا کہ وہ مغلوں سے بہتر منتظم تھا۔

رحیم ۔   جی ہاں! اُس نے پانچ چھ سال کے عرصے میں وہ کام کئے جو عام بادشاہ تیس
سال کے عرصے میں بھی نہیں کر پاتے۔

اسمتھ ۔   اکبر کو ایک نیا مذہب شروع کرنے کا خیال کیوں پیدا ہوا؟

رحیم ۔   دراصل اکبر کے دربار میں مختلف مذاہب کے علماء موجود تھے ۔ یہ علماء آپس میں مذہبی
بحثیں کرتے رہتے تھے ۔ اکبر ان بحثوں میں بہت دلچسپی لیتا تھا ۔ چنانچہ اُس کے
دل میں یہ خیال پیدا ہوا کہ کیوں نہ ایک ایسا مذہب شروع کیا جائے ۔ جس میں
تمام مذاہب کے اچھے اچھے اصول شامل ہوں۔ دوسرے، اکبر ایک ایسی سلطنت
کی بنیاد رکھنا چاہتا تھا۔ جس میں ہر شخص کا مذہب ایک ہو۔

اسمتھ ۔   کیا اکبر کے دربار کے شعراء اردو میں شعر کہتے تھے؟

رحیم ۔   جی نہیں ۔ اردو نے ابھی اتنی ترقی نہیں کی تھی ۔ اُس زمانے تک مغلوں کے دربار

کی زبان فارسی تھی۔ چنانچہ اُس زمانے کا اکثر ادب فارسی میں ہے۔

اسمتھ۔ آخری مغل بادشاہوں کے زمانے میں اِتنی بغاوتیں ہونے کی کیا وجہ تھی؟

رحیم۔ اُس زمانے میں مغل سلطنت بہت وسیع ہو چکی تھی۔ مگر اِس دَور کے تقریباً تمام بادشاہ بہت کمزور ثابت ہوئے۔ اِن میں کوئی بھی ایسا نہ تھا جو اِتنی بڑی سلطنت کو سنبھال سکتا۔ اِن کا زیادہ وقت حکومت کے کاموں کی بجائے عیش میں گذرتا تھا۔ جس کا نتیجہ یہ ہوا کہ مختلف علاقوں میں مقامی راجاؤں اور نوابوں نے بغاوتیں شروع کردیں۔ بیرونی طاقتوں نے جو اُس وقت ہندوستان میں تجارت کی غرض سے آئی ہوئی تھیں، موقع سے فائدہ اٹھا کر ملک کو اپنے قبضے میں لینے کی کوششیں شروع کردیں۔

اسمتھ۔ کیا علی گڑھ مسلم یونیورسٹی سے پہلے اِس قسم کی کوئی اور یونیورسٹی ہندوستان میں نہیں تھی؟

رحیم۔ جی نہیں۔ یہ پہلی یونیورسٹی تھی جو صرف مسلمانوں میں تعلیم پھیلانے کی غرض سے کھولی گئی تھی۔ کیونکہ اِس سے پہلے عام طور پر ہندوستانی مسلمان مغربی علوم اور زبانیں پڑھنی اور پڑھانی بُری سمجھتے تھے۔ لیکن سرسید احمد خان اور اُن کے ساتھیوں نے اِس بات پر زور دیا کہ ہندوستانی مسلمان مغربی تعلیم حاصل کئے بغیر ترقی نہیں کرسکتے۔ چنانچہ رفتہ رفتہ مسلمانوں نے مغربی تعلیم کی اہمیت محسوس کرنی شروع کی اور اِس کا نتیجہ یہ نکلا کہ مسلمانوں میں بھی بہت سے قابل سیاست دان، موّرخ اور ماہرینِ تعلیم پیدا ہوئے جنہوں نے ہندوستانی مسلمانوں کو ترقی کا راستہ دکھایا۔

اسمتھ۔ آپ کے خیال میں ہندوستان کی تقسیم سے فائدہ ہوا یا نقصان؟

رحیم۔ ہر کام کے فائدے بھی ہوتے ہیں اور نقصان بھی۔ میرے خیال میں ملک کی تقسیم ضروری

تھی۔ کیونکہ اِن دونوں قوموں۔یعنی ہندوؤں اور مسلمانوں۔میں اِتنا اختلاف تھا کہ اُس کا

حل صرف تقسیم ہی ہو سکتا تھا۔دونوں قوموں کی آپس میں دُشمنی کا اندازہ اِس بات سے

ہو سکتا ہے کہ تقسیم کے موقع پر لاکھوں آدمی مارے گئے۔ اب بھی ہندوستان اور پاکستان

کے درمیان بہت سے مسائل پر اختلاف ہے۔ جنہیں دونوں حکومتیں دُور کرنے کی

کوشش کر رہی ہیں۔ بہتر ہے کہ یہ جھگڑے ختم ہو جائیں اور ہم اچھے پڑوسیوں کی

طرح زندگی بسر کریں۔

اِستَہ۔   آپ نے صحیح فرمایا۔ امن اور دوستی کی زندگی سب سے اچھی زندگی ہے۔

رحیم۔   آئیے، کھانے کے کمرے میں چلیں۔ شاید کھانا تیار ہے۔

اِستَہ۔   بہت اچّھا۔

22. 508. Conversation Stimulus.

Topics may include the following:

1. British innovations in India.
2. Sher Shah.
3. An essay on one of the Mughal Emperors.
4. The making of Pakistan.
5. The causes of the decline of Mughal power in India.

agra M2 [np]	Agra
aməd F1 [np]	coming, advent, arrival
ədəb M1 [np]	literature; etiquette, courtesy
ədib M1	writer, literateur
ədl M1 [np]	justice, rectitude
əfyun F1 [np]	opium
əhd M1	period, reign, era; promise, contract
*əlfaz Mpl	pl. /ləfz/
əligəRh M1 [np]	Aligarh
əzmət F1	greatness, glory, might
bab M1	chapter; door, gate
banve A1	ninety-two
[ke] bavwjud Comp Post	nevertheless, in spite of
bəɣavət F1	revolt, revolution, uprising
bəhadwr M1 A1	hero; heroic, courageous
[ke] bərəks Comp Post	contrary to, in contrast with, opposite to
bedar PA1	awake, watchful, vigilant
bedari F2	awakening, wakefulness
byhar M1 [np]	Bihar
byjli F2	lightning; electricity
cəwranve A1	ninety-four
chinna [Id: /y/]	to seize, snatch, grab, pluck, take away
dərbar M1	court (of a ruler)
dəxl M1 [np]	entrance, intrusion, concern, influence, jurisdiction, competence, grasp
farsi F2 [np] A1	Persian (language)
fəlsəfa M2	philosophy
fəransisi M1 F2 [np] A1	French(man), French (language), French
fəwji M1 A1	soldier; military
gwna A2 Enclitic	-fold, -times
gwzəšta A1	past (adj.)
ɣədr M1	mutiny, rebellion, chaos
ɣərəz F1	objective, aim, design, intention
hərf M1	letter (of the alphabet)
*hwruf Mpl	pl. /hərf/
hymayət F1	support, protection, defence
jagir F1	estate, fief, lands given by the government as a reward for services
jagirdar M1	holder of a jagir
jayza M2	examination, survey, scrutiny, checking
jəmat [literary: /jəmaət/] F1	party, society, group, organisation, class

jəmna [IIc: /ə/]	to become set, firm, hard, fixed, congealed, frozen, take root
jõgju A1	warlike, war-loving
kãgres F1	congress
kəlkətta M2 [np]	Calcutta
kəmana [Ia]	to earn
khona [IIIa]	to lose
ləfz M1	word
liDər M/F1	leader
maliat F1 [np]	finance, financial matters, revenue
məwsiqar M/F1	musician
*məzamin Mpl	pl. /məzmun/
məzar M1	tomb (usually of a saint or revered person)
məzmun M1	article; subject; contents
mwntəzym M/F1 A1	administrator, manager, arranger
mwqam M1	place, location, position, station, rank
mwsibət F1	difficulty, trouble, affliction, adversity, calamity
mwslym M1 A1	Muslim
*mwškylat Fpl	pl. /mwškyl/
mwtaləba M2	demand, claim
mwttəhyd PA1	united, unified
mwttəhyda A1	united, unified
nəvab M1	Navab, title of a ruler of a Muslim state
nəzm F1	poem
pənah F1	refuge, sanctuary, shelter
pərva F1	care, concern
pəymayš F1	measuring, survey
pwrtəgali M1 F2 [np] A1	Portuguese (person), Portuguese (language), Portuguese
pycanve A1	ninety-five
pyšavər M1 [np]	Peshawar
qədr F1	value, amount, appreciation
raj M1	rule, government
rayj PA1	current, in force, prevailing, prevalent
rozi F2	livelihood, employment
rysala M2	magazine, journal
sathi M/F1	companion, colleague, comrade
saynsdan [or /saynsdã/] M/F1	scientist
sərənjam PA1	completed, accomplished
sõbhalna [Ig: /ə/]	to set right, look after, take care of, sustain, catch (something falling), hold onto, take over, curb, keep in check
swluk M1 [np]	treatment, behaviour, usage
swnəhra A2	golden, golden-coloured

syasətdan [or /syasətdā/] M/F1	politician
šae [or /šaya/] PA1	published, issued
šayr M1	poet
šayri F2	poetry, the art of poetry
šer M1	couplet, verse
šoba M2	department, division, section
*šwəra Mpl	pl. /šayr/
*šykayat Fpl	pl. /šykayət/
talimi A1	educational
taqətvər A1	strong, powerful
təhrik F1	movement, incitement, encouragement
tərjih F1	preference, precedence
tyjarət F1	commerce, business
tyranve A1	ninety-three
*vaqəyat Mpl	pl. /vaqea/
vəsi A1	broad, vast, spacious, wide
*wdəba Mpl	pl. /ədib/
*wlum Mpl	pl. /ylm/
*wməra Mpl	pl. /əmir/
xahyš F1	desire, wish
xəzana M2	treasury
yadgar F1	memorial, memento, souvenir, relic
yəksā A1	equal, uniform, identical, alike
ybtyda M1 [np]	beginning, commencement
ykanve A1	ninety-one
ylahi A1	divine, Godlike
ynsaf M1 [np]	justice, fairness, righteousness
ystyqlal M1 [np]	determination, resolution, firmness, independence
zəwq M1 [np]	taste (for something), hobby
zwlm M1	tyranny, oppression, cruelty
zyd F1 [np]	contrariness, obstinacy, stubbornness

The Sakkhar Barrage, one of Pakistan's new dams.

تاریخِ پاکستان

۱۹۴۷ء میں ہندوستان کو دو آزاد ملکوں میں تقسیم کر دیا گیا ۔ یہ ملک آج ہندوستان اور پاکستان کے نام سے مشہور ہیں ۔ حکومتِ انگلستان نے ۱۴ اگست ۱۹۴۷ء کو پاکستان کی حکومت کے اختیارات مسلم لیگ کے سپرد کرتے اور اِسی طرح ۱۵ اگست ۱۹۴۷ء کو ہندوستان کی حکومت کے اختیارات کانگریس کو دے دیے گئے ۔

پاکستان کے دو حصے ہیں ۔ مشرقی پاکستان اور مغربی پاکستان ۔ ان دونوں حصوں کے درمیان تقریباً ایک ہزار میل کا فاصلہ ہے ۔ جس میں ہندوستان کا شمالی علاقہ پھیلا ہوا ہے ۔ پاکستان کی کُل آبادی تقریباً گیارہ کروڑ ہے ۔ مشرقی پاکستان کی آبادی تقریباً چھ کروڑ اور مغربی پاکستان کی آبادی تقریباً پانچ کروڑ ہے ۔

ہندوستان کے تقسیم ہوتے ہی ہندوستان اور پاکستان کے بہت سے صوبوں میں فرقہ وارانہ فسادات شروع ہوگئے ۔ اس گڑ بڑ میں لاکھوں افراد کی جانیں ضائع ہوئیں ۔ یہ ہندوستان اور پاکستان کی تاریخ کا بدترین باب ہے ۔ حالات کچھ ایسے بدلے کہ وہی لوگ جو سینکڑوں برس سے اکٹھے دوستوں کی طرح رہتے تھے ایک دوسرے کو قتل کرنے لگے ۔

پاکستان کے وجود میں آتے ہی مسلم لیگ کے صدر محمد علی جناح پاکستان کے پہلے گورنر جنرل مقرر ہوئے ۔ پاکستان کی پہلی حکومت مسٹر لیاقت علی خان کی قیادت میں بنی ۔ پاکستان کے بانی مسٹر محمد علی جناح زیادہ عرصے تک زندہ نہ رہ سکے ۔ اُنہوں نے ۱۱ ستمبر ۱۹۴۸ء کو

میں اُس موقع پر وفات پائی جب کہ قوم کو اُن کی سخت ضرورت تھی ۔ قوم آج بھی اُنہیں قائدِ اعظم
کے نام سے یاد کرتی ہے ۔ اُن کی وفات کے بعد مسلم لیگ کے ایک پرانے لیڈر خواجہ ناظم الدّین
گورنر جنرل مقرّر ہوئے ۔ ۱۶؍ اکتوبر ۱۹۵۱ء کو مسٹر لیاقت علی خان کو گولی مار کر شہید کردیا گیا۔
آپ راولپنڈی کے ایک جلسے میں تقریر کر رہے تھے کہ ہجوم میں سے کسی نے گولی چلا دی۔
اُن کی شہادت کے بعد گورنر جنرل خواجہ ناظم الدّین نے وزیرِ اعظم کا عہدہ سنبھالا اور اُن
کی جگہ وزیر مالیات ملک غلام محمّد گورنر جنرل مقرّر ہوئے ۔ اس عرصے میں پاکستان کی پارلیمنٹ ایک
نیا آئین بنانے میں مصروف رہی ۔ اس نے انگریزی دَور کے بعض قوانین پر دوبارہ غور کرکے اُن
کی منظوری دی ۔ اور بہت سے نئے قوانین بھی منظور کئے ۔ کچھ عرصے بعد مسٹر غلام محمّد نے
وزیرِ اعظم خواجہ ناظم الدّین کی جگہ محمّد علی بوگرہ کو وزیرِ اعظم مقرّر کیا ۔ مسٹر بوگرہ اُس وقت امریکہ میں
پاکستان کے سفیر تھے ۔ گورنر جنرل نے پارلیمنٹ بھی توڑ دی ۔ اور نئی پارلیمنٹ منتخب کرنے کا
حکم جاری کیا ۔ اُس وقت تک پاکستان میں کئی سیاسی جماعتیں وجود میں آچکی تھیں ۔ مگر حکومت
مسلم لیگ ہی کے ہاتھوں میں رہی ۔ مسٹر غلام محمد کے بعد مسٹر اسکندر مرزا نے گورنر جنرل کا
عہدہ سنبھالا ۔ ۱۹۵۶ء میں پاکستان کا پہلا آئین نافذ کیا گیا ۔ اس آئین کے تحت پاکستان کو اسلامی
جمہوریہ قرار دیا گیا ۔ اور آخری گورنر جنرل مسٹر اسکندر مرزا کو جمہوریۂ پاکستان کا پہلا
صدر چنا گیا۔

یہ حقیقت ہے کہ مسٹر لیاقت علی خان کے بعد پاکستان میں کوئی مضبوط حکومت قائم نہ
ہو سکی ۔ کیونکہ تقریباً ہر سال حکومت بدل جاتی تھی ۔ جس کی وجہ سے ملک کی سیاسی حالت
خراب تھی ۔ اقتصادی اور سماجی ترقّی کے کاموں کی رفتار سست پڑ گئی تھی اور ملک کی
ترقّی رُکی ہوئی تھی ۔ کیونکہ جو بھی حکومت آتی ایک نئی پالیسی اختیار کرتی ۔ ان حالات میں

کمانڈر انچیف محمد ایوب خان نے فوجی انقلاب کے ذریعہ حکومت کو اپنے ہاتھوں میں لے لیا اور
آئین کو ختم کر کے ملک میں مارشل لاء نافذ کردیا۔ ۷ اکتوبر ۱۹۵۸ء کو مسٹر اسکندر مرزا کو صدر کے
عہدے سے ہٹا کر اُنہوں نے یہ عہدہ بھی خود سنبھال لیا۔ صدر ایوب کے حکومت سنبھالتے ہی
ملک کے حالات میں انقلاب آگیا۔ مختلف قسم کی اشیاء کو زیادہ قیمت پر فروخت کرنے اور
اُن کا ذخیرہ کرنے والوں کو گرفتار کر لیا گیا۔ کھانے پینے کی چیزوں میں ملاوٹ کرنے والوں پر بھاری
جرمانے کئے گئے۔ اور اسمگلنگ کی روک تھام کے لئے سخت قدم اٹھایا گیا۔ مارشل لاء حکومت
نے زندگی کے مختلف شعبوں میں بھی اصلاحات کیں۔ چنانچہ شادی ، طلاق اور تعلیمی نظام وغیرہ
کی اصلاح کے لئے کمیشن مقرر کئے گئے۔ جن کی سفارشات پر ان شعبوں میں بہت سے نئے اقدامات
کئے گئے۔ حکومت نے سرکاری ملازمین کی تنخواہوں میں اضافہ کیا اور مالک و مزدور کے تعلقات
بہتر بنانے کے لئے بھی قدم اٹھایا۔ صدر ایوب نے ملک کے سیاسی نظام کو بھی ایک نئی شکل دی۔
اُنہوں نے پارلیمانی نظام کی بجائے صدارتی طرز حکومت اختیار کیا۔ اور بنیادی جمہوریتوں کا نظام
رائج کیا۔ بنیادی جمہوریتوں کے پہلے انتخاب کے بعد ۸ جون ۱۹۶۲ء کو مارشل لاء ختم کر دیا
گیا۔ اس طرح چار سال کے بعد ملک میں پھر جمہوریت قائم ہو گئی۔ ۲ جنوری ۱۹۶۵ء کو
ملک میں پہلی دفعہ عام انتخابات ہوتے ۔ جس میں صدر محمد ایوب خان دوبارہ پانچ سال
کے لئے صدر منتخب ہوتے۔

پاکستان ایک امن پسند ملک ہے ۔ وہ اقوامِ متحدہ ، دولتِ مشترکہ اور دیگر بہت سے
بین الاقوامی اداروں کا ممبر ہے ۔ اس کے علاوہ پاکستان بعض دفاعی معاہدوں کا بھی رکن ہے ۔
دنیا کے اکثر ممالک سے پاکستان کے دوستانہ تعلقات ہیں ۔ جن میں کمیونسٹ ممالک بھی شامل
ہیں ۔ اور ان ممالک میں اس کے باقاعدہ سفارت خانے کھلے ہوتے ہیں ۔ ہندوستان ،چین، برما،

افغانستان اور ایران، پاکستان کے پڑوسی ملک ہیں ۔ ہندوستان سے اس کے تعلقات زیادہ خوشگوار نہیں ۔ اس کا سبب کشمیر کا مسئلہ ہے ۔ یہ مسئلہ اقوامِ متحدہ کے سامنے پیش کیا جا چکا ہے ۔ مگر اس سلسلے میں ابھی تک کوئی موثر کارروائی نہیں ہو سکی ہے ۔

جہاں تک پاکستان کی خارجہ پالیسی کا تعلق ہے وہ تمام ممالک سے دوستی اور تعاون چاہتا ہے ۔ وہ تمام ملکوں کی آزادی کا احترام کرتا ہے اور اسی کی امید دوسرے ممالک سے بھی رکھتا ہے ۔ پاکستان ایٹمی ہتھیاروں اور ہر قسم کی جنگ کے خلاف ہے ۔ لیکن اگر کوئی ملک پاکستان کو لڑنے پر مجبور کر دے تو وہ اپنی آزادی کی حفاظت کے لیے خاموش نہیں رہے گا ۔

پاکستان جب وجود میں آیا تو اس کے سامنے بہت سے مسائل تھے ۔ اس کے داخلی مسائل میں سب سے اہم مسئلہ ان مہاجرین کو آباد کرنا تھا ۔ جو ہندوستان سے آئے تھے ۔ حکومت نے ان لوگوں کے لیے چھوٹے چھوٹے نئے شہر آباد کئے ۔ اب یہ لوگ اپنے نئے وطن میں ذمہ دار شہریوں کی طرح زندگی بسر کر رہے ہیں ۔

اگرچہ پاکستان بنیادی طور پر ایک زرعی ملک ہے اور اس کی آبادی کے تین چوتھائی حصہ کا پیشہ زراعت ہے ، اس کے باوجود ملک کو اناج کی کمی کا سامنا ہے ۔ اناج کی اس کمی کو دُور کرنے کے لیے زرعی پیداوار بڑھانے کی کوشش کی جا رہی ہے ۔ اس مقصد کو حاصل کرنے کے لیے نئے بڑے بڑے بند تعمیر کئے گئے ہیں ۔ زراعت کے نئے نئے طریقے بھی اختیار کئے جا رہے ہیں اور کھیتوں کو پانی پہنچانے کے لیے نہروں کا انتظام بہتر بنایا جا رہا ہے ۔

پاکستان دنیا کے بہت سے ممالک سے تجارت کرتا ہے ۔ وہ ان ملکوں کو چاول ، چائے ، پٹ سن ، روئی ، اونی اور سوتی کپڑا ، کھالیں ، چمڑا اور کھیلوں کا سامان برآمد کرتا ہے ۔ اسی طرح دوسرے ممالک سے مزدوری سامان جیسے مشینیں اور دوائیاں وغیرہ درآمد کرتا ہے ۔ اگرچہ ملک میں چینی ، پٹ سن ، سیمنٹ اور اونی و سوتی کپڑے کے کارخانے قائم ہو چکے ہیں ۔ اس

کے باوجود پاکستان کو نئی نئی مشینوں، کارخانوں اور بھاری صنعت کی سخت ضرورت ہے کیونکہ
پاکستان کے حصے میں جو علاقے آئے وہ ترقی یافتہ نہ تھے۔ دوسرے پاکستان میں لوہے اور کوئلے
کی کمی ہے۔ ملک کے مختلف حصوں میں ان چیزوں کی دریافت کی کوششیں کی جا رہی ہیں۔ اس
کے علاوہ ملک میں تعلیم کی بھی کمی ہے۔ خاص طور پر فنی تعلیم کی سخت ضرورت ہے۔ اگر ملک
میں فنی تعلیم بڑھ جائے تو کارخانے اور فیکٹریاں بھی بڑھ جائیں گی جن سے زیادہ سے زیادہ
لوگوں کو ملازمتیں ملیں گی۔ اور وہ چیزیں جو آج کل پاکستان دوسرے ملکوں سے منگواتا ہے ملک
میں ہی بننی شروع ہو جائیں گی۔ اس طرح ملک اپنے پیروں پر کھڑا ہو جائے گا۔

جن حالات میں پاکستان وجود میں آیا اور جن جن مشکلات کا اُسے سامنا کرنا پڑا، ان کو
دیکھ کر کہا جا سکتا ہے کہ پاکستان نے سترہ اٹھارہ سال کے مختصر عرصے میں زبردست ترقی کی
ہے۔ اور توقع ہے کہ اِس کا مستقبل اِس کے ماضی سے زیادہ روشن اور شاندار ہوگا۔

سپرد [کے]	[ke] swpwrd PA1 Comp Post	entrusted to, committed to, handed over to, in the care of
فرقہ وارانہ	fyrqəvarana A1	sectarian, communal
فسادات	*fəsadat Mpl [pl. /fəsad/]	disturbances, riots, strife
گڑبڑ	gəRbəR F1 [np]	confusion, mix-up, disorder, mess
جان	jan F1	life, soul, spirit
ضائع	zae [common: /zaya/] PA1	wasted, lost, spoiled
بدترین	bədtərin A1	worst
قتل	qətl M1 [np]	killing, slaying, murder
جنرل	jənrəl M1 A1	general (common), general (military)
مسٹر	mysTər M1	mister
عین	əyn A1	exact, precise
قائد	qayd M1	leader
خواجہ ناظم الدین	xaja nazymwddin PN	Khvaja Nazim-ud-din; Governor General 1948-1951; Prime Minister 1951-1953; died 1964
شہید	šəhid M/F1	martyr
جلسہ	jəlsa M2	meeting, gathering, assembly
ہجوم	hwjum M1	crowd, throng, mob
شہادت	šəhadət F1	martyrdom; witnessing
ملک غلام محمد	məlyk ɣwlam mwhəmməd PN	Malik Ghulam Muhammad; Governor General 1951-1955; died 1955

پارلیمنٹ	parlimǝyT Fl	parliament
انگریزی	ǝgrezi F2 [np] Al	English (language), English (adj.)
دوباره	dwbara Adv	a second time, again
منظوری	mǝnzuri F2	consent, approval, sanction, acceptance
منظور	mǝnzur PAl	accepted, sanctioned, approved, agreed to
محمد علی بوگره	mwhǝmmǝd ǝli bogra PN	Muhammad Ali Bogra; Prime Minister 1953-1955; died 1963
سفیر	sǝfir M/Fl	ambassador, envoy
اسکندر مرزا	yskǝndǝr myrza PN	Iskandar Mirza; Governor General 1955-1956; President 1956-1958
نافذ	nafyz PAl	enforced, put into effect, promulgated
جمہوریہ	jwmhuria [or /jǝmhuria/] Fl [np]	republic
اقتصادی	yqtysadi Al	economic
سماجی	sǝmaji Al	social, societal
رفتار	rǝftar Fl	speed, pace
سست	swst Al	slow, sluggish, lazy
رکنا	rwkna [I: /rokna/: If]	to stop (intrans.)
کمانڈر انچیف	kǝmāDǝr yncif Ml	commander in chief
محمد ایوب خان	mwhǝmmǝd ǝyyub xan PN	Muhammad Ayyub Khan; President 1958- to date
انقلاب	ynqylab Ml	revolution, upheaval, change, vicissitude
مارشل لار	maršǝl la Ml [np]	martial law

395

اشیار	*əšya Fpl [pl. [pl. /šəy/]	things, articles, commodities
فروخت	fəroxt F1	selling, sale
ذخیره	zəxira M2	stock, store, hoard
ملاوٹ	mylavəT F1	mixture, adulteration
بھاری	bhari A1	heavy, weighty
اسمگلنگ	ysməglyg F1 [np]	smuggling
روک تھام	roktham F1 [np]	stop, check, restraint
کمیشن	kəmišən M1	commission
سفارشات	*syfaryšat Fpl [pl. /syfaryš/]	recommendations, intercessions
اقدامات	*yqdamat Mpl [pl. /yqdam/]	steps
تنخواہ	tənxa[h] F1	salary
اضافہ	yzafa M2	addition, increase, augment
مالک	malyk M1	owner, master, proprietor
مزدور	məzdur M1	labourer, worker
صدارت	sədarət F1	presidency, chairmanship
امن پسند	əmnpəsənd A1	peace-loving
اقوام	əqvam Fpl [pl. /qəwm/]	nations [/əqvame mwttəhyda/ F1 [np] "United Nations"]
مشترکہ	mwštərka [literary: /mwštərəka/] A1	shared, in common, joint [/dəwləte mwštərka/ F1 "Commonwealth"]
بین الاقوامی	bəynwləqvami A1	international

396

دفاعی	dyfai A1	pertaining to defence
معاہدہ	mwahyda [literary: /mwahəda/] M2	treaty, contract, alliance
دوستانہ	dostana A1	friendly, amicable
کمیونسٹ	kəmyunysT M/F1 A1	Communist
سفارت خانہ	syfarətxana M2	embassy
چین	cin M1 [np]	China
برما	bərma M1 [np]	Burma
خوشگوار	xwǐgəvar A1	pleasant, delightful
سبب	səbəb M1	reason, cause
مؤثر	mwəssyr A1	effective, efficacious
کاروائی	karəvai F2	proceeding, working, action, operation
خارجہ	xaryja A1	external, exterior, foreign
دوستی	dosti F2	friendship
تعاون	təavwn M1 [np]	cooperation, mutual aid
احترام	yhtyram M1 [np]	respect, honour, veneration, reverence
ایٹمی	əyTmi A1	atomic
خاموش	xamoš A1	silent, quiet
داخلی	daxyli A1	interior, internal
مہاجرین	*mwhajyrin [or /məhajyrin/] Mpl [pl. /mwhajyr/ or /məhajyr/ M1 "refugee"]	refugees

397

ذمّہ دار	zymmedar A1	responsible, answerable
شہری	šəhri M/F1 A1	citizen; urban
زرعی	zərəi A1	agricultural
چوتھائی	cəwthai F2	quarter, one fourth part
پیشہ	peša M2	occupation, profession
پیداوار	pəydavar F1	produce, yield, production
پٹ سن	pəTsən M1 [np]	jute
روئی	rui F2 [np]	cotton wool
اُونی	uni A1	woollen
سُوتی	suti A1	made of cotton
کھال	khal F1	skin, hide
چمڑا	cəmRa M2	leather, skin
درآمد	dəraməd F1	import
سیمنٹ	siməyT M1 [or F1]	cement
کارخانہ	karxana M2	factory, workshop
صنعت	sənət F1	industry
ترقّی یافتہ	tərəqqiyafta A1	progressive, advanced
لوہا	loha M2 [np]	iron
فنّی	fənni A1	technical
فیکٹری	fəykTri F2	factory
پَیر	pəyr M1	foot

398

زبردست	zəbərdəst A1	vigorous, powerful, strict
توقّع	təvəqqo F1	expectation, hope
مستقبل	mwstəqbyl M1 [np]	the future
ماضی	mazi M1 [np]	the past
روشن	rəwšən A1	illuminated, splendid, bright

23.201. /jan/ F1 denotes "life" in the sense of "spirit, vigour, vitality." /zyndəgi/ F2 means "life[time]," and /wmr/ F1 also means "life[time], lifespan" but has the further meaning of "age (of a person)." Although these three words may overlap in certain contexts, their semantic ranges are generally quite distinct. Occasionally /jan/ may also mean "soul, life, person" (see the first example below), but "soul" in the religious sense is expressed by /ruh/ F1 (not yet introduced). E. g.

> /ys fəsad mē həzarō janē zae hwī. / In this riot thousands of lives [souls] were lost.
>
> /ws ki jan nykəl gəi. / His life went out. [I. e. he died. Or, metaphorically: he was overcome by fear.]
>
> /ws mē bəRi jan həy. / He has a great deal of vitality.
>
> /ws ki təqrir ne qəwm mē jan pəyda kər di. / His lecture created a [new] spirit in the nation.
>
> /ws ne zyndəgi bhər aram nə paya. / He found no rest throughout [his] life. [/wmr/ may be substituted here but not /jan/.]
>
> /wse sari wmr yyhi təklif rəhi. / He had this same trouble all [his] life. [/zyndəgi/ may be substituted here but not /jan/.]
>
> /ap ki kya wmr həy. / What is your age? [Neither /zyndəgi/ nor /jan/ may occur here.]
>
> /vw ys ydare ki ruh the. / He was the soul of this institution. [I. e. the guiding spirit, /jan/ may also occur here in the sense of "vitality. "]
>
> /meri doa həy, ky əllah wn ki ruh ko jənnət mē jəga de. / It is my prayer that God may give his soul a place in Paradise. [/jan/ cannot be substituted here. /jənnət/ F1 "Paradise. "]

23.202. The usage of /əyn/ A1 "exact, precise," is very limited: it occurs only before a few nouns. Examples should be carefully noted. E. g.

> /polis ne cor ko əyn məwqe pər gyryftar kia. / The police caught the thief redhanded. [Lit. on the exact occasion.]
>
> /vw əyn vəqt pər mere pas pəhw̃ca. / He arrived at my place [lit. to me] at the exact time.
>
> /əgər ap mera yy kam kər dē, to əyn myhrbani hogi. / If you do this task for me [lit. my this task], [it] will be a real favour [lit. precise kindness].

23.203. /qayd/ M1 and /liDər/ M/F1 both mean "leader," the latter being particularly frequent in the modern context of political parties, etc. The title /qayde azəm/ "greatest leader" is reserved for Muhammad Ali Jinnah, the founder of Pakistan.

23.204. /šəhid/ M/F1 "martyr" and /šəhadət/ F1 "martyrdom" are employed only in reference to Muslims who have been killed in the cause of Islam, or, in an expanded sense, in any noble cause.

23.205. Both /parlimə̃yT/ F1 "parliament" and /simə̃yT/ M1 [or F1] "cement" are spelled as though their last syllables were /-mənT/ or /-mynT/ (i. e. with no ی to represent the /əy/). An alternate form, /parliman/ Fl, is also found for "parliament. "

23. 206.   /nafyz/ PA1 "enforced, put into effect, promulgated" is employed only for laws, rules, etc.   Compare /jari/ PA1 "issued, continuing" and /rayj/ PA1 "made current"; see Sec. 22. 212.   E. g.

> /hwkumət ne maršəl la nafyz kia. /   The government promulgated [i. e. declared] martial law.

> /wnhõ ne yy qanun nafyz kia. /   They enforced this law.   [/jari kia/ here would mean "issued. "]

> /wnhõ ne talim ka yy nəya nyzam rayj kia. /   They introduced [i. e. made current] this new system of education.   [/jari kia/ could be employed here if the system were "issued" as a separate unit, but it is not something which one "enforces"; hence /nafyz kia/ is not substitutable here.]

> /talimi yslahat nafyz ki gəĩ. /   The educational reforms were put into effect.   [I. e. specific regulations.   /jari/ is also substitutable here.]

23. 207.   /jwmhuria/ [or /jəmhuria/] Fl [np] denotes "republic, " while /jwmhuriət/ [or /jəmhuriət/] Fl denotes "democracy. "

23. 208.   /yqtysadi/ A1 and /məaši/ A1 are synonyms: both mean "economic" in Urdu.   The Arabic root q-ṣ-d means "to act purposefully, moderately, sparingly, " and in Form VIII means "to save money" (see Sec. 17. 301).   /məaš/ is a noun of place (see Sec. 17. 305) from the root '-y-š "to live, " and means "livelihood, means of life. "   "Economics" is either /yqtysadiat/ Fl [np] or /məašiat/ Fl [np].

23. 209.   Similarly, /səmaji/ A1 and /mwašrəti/ A1 are synonyms of different origins: both mean "social, societal. "   The former is from Hindi /səmaj/ M1 "society, group, " and the latter is from the Arabic root '-š-r, which in Form III has meanings like "to seek someone's society, social intercourse. "   See Sec. 17. 301.

23. 210.   /ynqylab/ M1 "revolution, upheaval, change, vicissitude" contrasts with /bəγavət/ Fl "revolt, mutiny, revolution. "   The latter usually denotes an unsuccessful uprising, while /ynqylab/ has good connotations and signifies a successful revolution or a sweeping change.   E. g.

> /ys mwlk mẽ ynqylab a gəya. /   There has been a revolution [or a radical change] in this country.

> /ws ne mwlk mẽ fəwji ynqylab lane ke bad, hwkumət sõbhal li. /   After bringing about the military revolution, he took charge of the government.   [/bəγavət/ is not possible here since it would imply an unsuccessful attempt to overthrow the government.]

> /wn ki yn yslahat ne mwlk ke məaši, səmaji, talimi, əwr sənəti halat mẽ ynqylab pəyda kər dia. /   These reforms of his brought about a revolution in the economic, social, educational, and industrial conditions of the country.

401

23.211. The English loanword /maršəl la/ Ml [np] "martial law" is often written

with a final /həmza/ in Urdu script, perhaps to distinguish /la/ "law" from the Arabic

negative particle /la/ "not" used in compounds: مارشل لا ء   The /həmza/ is optionally

omitted.

23.212. /šəy/ Fl "thing, commodity" (and its Arabic broken plural /əšya/ Fpl) overlap the semantic range of /ciz/ Fl "thing." /šəy/ and /əšya/, however, are rather
literary, while /ciz/ is colloquial and common. See also Sec. 5.109 for the difference
between /ciz/ and /bat/ Fl "thing, matter." E.g.

> /yy səb əšya ws dwkan se myl jaẽgi./ All these things [commodities] will
> be available from that shop. [/ciz/ is more common and colloquial
> here.]
>
> /yy kya šəy həy./ What is this thing? [Again /ciz/ is more common.]
>
> /ap kys bat pər naraz həy./ What [lit. on what thing] are you angry·
> about? [/šəy/ and /ciz/ are both rather inappropriate here since the
> context demands an inanimate, abstract thing; this is expressed by
> /bat/.]
>
> /ys kytab mẽ yy ciz mwjhe pəsənd nəhĩ./ In this book this thing is not
> pleasing to me. [Again /bat/ may be substituted but not /šəy/.]

23.213. /fəroxt/ Fl "selling, sale" is used in complex verbal formations with /kərna/
and /hona/ to mean "to sell" and "to be sold" respectively. These formations are synonymous
with /becna/ "to sell" and its intransitive form /bykna/ "to be sold" (not yet introduced),
but the latter are less literary. /fəroxt/ is also used as a noun meaning "sale." E.g.

> /məy ne wn ke hath səb kytabẽ fəroxt kər dĩ./ I sold all the books to him.
> [Or: /bec dĩ/.]
>
> /əfyun ki fəroxt jayz nəhĩ./ The sale of opium is not permitted.

23.214. /mylavəT/ Fl "mixing, adulteration" is almost always employed in a bad
sense: the mixing of some undesirable substance into some commodity. See Sec. 19.303.
E.g.

> /ws ne dudh mẽ pani ki mylavəT ki./ He mixed water into the milk.

23.215. /qədəm/ Ml means "step, footstep" both in the physical and metaphorical
senses, and in some contexts it also denotes "foot" (although the physical foot is expressed
by /pəyr/ Ml or /paõ/ Ml; see Sec. 15.127). /yqdam/ Ml is another form from the same
Arabic root, but it is used for "step" in the metaphorical sense only. Note that /qədəm
wThana/ "to take a step" (lit. "to lift a foot") and /yqdam kərna/ are almost synonymous.
E.g.

> /hwkumət ne ys sylsyle mẽ qədəm wThaya həy./ The government has
> taken a step in this connection. [/yqdam kia həy/ is substitutable here.
> The plural of the latter would be /yqdamat kie hãy/.]
>
> /hwkumət ke ys yqdam ki vəja se, mwlk ki syasi halət byhtər ho gəi./
> Because of this step the political condition of the country has become
> better. [Plural /yqdamat/. /qədəm/ here is considered somewhat

unidiomatic.]

/ws ne mere kəmre mẽ qədəm rəkkha hi tha, ky gyr pəRa. / He had only
just set foot in my room when [he] fell down. [/yqdam/ cannot occur
here in the sense of "(physical) step. "]

/ws ne əpni sari zyndəgi ws bwzwrg ke qədmõ mẽ gwzari. / He spent all
[his] life in the humble service [lit. in the steps of] that great [man].
[Again, /yqdam/ cannot occur.]

23.216. /məzdur/ M1 denotes "labourer, worker" in the sense of a manual labourer
or a common factory worker. It is not usually applied to skilled technicians or other classes
of employees.

23.217. /dəwlət/ F1 was introduced in Unit XV in its common meaning of "wealth,
riches. " The Arabic root d-v-l means "to alternate, rotate, turn (as time, fortune), " and
in Arabic thus /dəwlət/ means "change, alternation, turn of fortune, " and hence "dynasty, "
and hence "state, power, " and finally "wealth. " /dəwlət/ is used for "state" in Urdu only
in a few constructions. In this meaning, the broken plural of /dəwlət/ is /dwvəl/ Fpl. E. g.

/ws ke pas bəhwt dəwlət həy. / He has much wealth.

/dəwləte pakystan/ the State of Pakistan. [/mwmlykəte pakystan/ is more
common.]

/dwvəle mwštərka/ the Commonwealth. [A less common alternate for
/dəwləte mwštərka/.]

23.218. /mwštərka/ A1 "shared, in common, joint" is derived from the Arabic root
š-r-k "to share. " In Arabic itself, there are two distinct participles for each verbal form,
and in Form VIII the active participle should mean "sharing" (/mwštəryk/), while the
passive participle should mean "shared" (/mwštərək/). See Sec. 17.301. This clear
difference has been obscured in Urdu, and if one examines the examples given in the
preceding Section, one will see that /dəwləte mwštərka/ seems to mean "shared state, "
while /dwvəle mwštərka/ appears to mean "sharing states. " In fact, the adjective form
/mwštərka/ most often occurs in the meaning "shared, in common, joint, " and there is a
corresponding predicate adjective form /mwštəryk/ with the same meaning. For "sharing,
sharer, " another form from the same root, /šərik/ M/F1 PA1, is used. E. g.

/donõ bhaiõ ne mwštərka tyjarət šwru ki. / Both the brothers started a
joint business.

/yy kytab həmari mwštərka košyšõ ka nətija həy. / This book is the result
of our joint efforts.

/donõ dostõ mẽ yy bat mwštəryk həy. / This thing is common to both the
friends.

/mə̃y ap ke ɣəm mẽ šərik hū. / I share your sorrow. [Lit. I am a sharer
in your sorrow. Neither /mwštəryk/ nor /mwštərka/ may occur here.]

/həm ne wse bhi əpni xwši mẽ šərik kər lia. / We included him also in
our happiness. [Neither /mwštəryk/ nor /mwštərka/ is substitutable.]

23.219. /mwahyda/ [literary /mwahəda/] M2 denotes a written treaty or contract.
/əhd/ M1 is from the same Arabic root, but it means "contract" only in the sense of a
verbal commitment or undertaking. E. g.

/donõ mwlkõ ke dərmyan yy mwahyda tha, ky mwsibət ke vəqt ek dusre
ki mədəd kərēge. / There was a treaty [lit. this treaty was] between
the two countries that they would aid one another in time[s] of trouble.
[Compare:]

/donõ bhaiõ ne əhd kia, ky mwsibət ke vəqt ek dusre ki mədəd kərēge. /
Both the brothers undertook that they would aid one another in time[s]
of trouble.

23.220. /səbəb/ M1 "reason, cause" is almost entirely synonymous with /vəja/ F1.
In compound postpositional form, /[ke] səbəb/ (and also /[ke] səbəb se/) is synonymous with
-- but less frequent than -- /[ki] vəja se/ "because, for the reason that. " E. g.

/ys səbəb se, mɔ̃y wn ke hã nəhĩ gəya. / For this reason I did not go to
their place. [/ys vəja se/ is perhaps commoner.]

23.221. /xaryja/ A1 "external, exterior" (and an alternate form, /xaryji/ A1) is
derived from the Arabic root x-r-j "to go out. " Informants felt that both of these could be
substituted in most contexts for /beruni/ A1 "external, exterior, " although there were
individual differences of preference in many cases. E. g.

/beruni məsayl/ external problems. [Or: /xaryja məsayl/ or /xaryji
məsayl/.]

23.222. /yhtyram/ M1 [np] "respect, honour, veneration, reverence" denotes a somewhat higher plane of reverence than /yzzət/ F1 "respect, honour. " The former has
connotations of "placing on a high plane, holding sacred, esteeming, " and it is more often
employed for abstracts (e. g. freedom, beliefs, constitution, etc.) than /yzzət/. E. g.

/mɔ̃y əpne valyd sahəb ka yhtyram kərta hũ. / I hold my father in high
esteem. [/... ki yzzət kərta hũ/ can be substituted here but denotes
a somewhat lesser degree of respect. Some informants felt that
/yhtyram kərna/ here means "to venerate, mentally place on a plane
of high esteem, " while /yzzət kərna/ means "to show respect, act
respectfully towards. "]

/pakystan dusre mwlkõ ki azadi ka yhtyram kərta həy. / Pakistan respects
the freedom of other countries. [/... ki yzzət kərta həy/ is not
possible here since /azadi/ F2 "freedom" is an abstract noun.]

/mɔ̃y wn ke əqayd ka yhtyram kərta hũ. / I respect their beliefs. [/...
ki yzzət kərta hũ/ is not possible.]

23.223. /daxyli/ A1 "interior, internal" (and an alternate form /daxyla/ M2 A1) is
derived from the Arabic root d-x-l "to go in. " These forms are substitutable in many
environments for /əndəruni/ A1 "interior, internal. " Again there were differences of
individual preference, but no clear semantic pattern could be adduced. Note that /daxyla/
also occurs as an M2 noun meaning "entrance, admission. " E. g.

/daxyli palisi/ internal policy. [Also /daxyla palisi/ and /əndəruni
palysi/.]

/daxyli məsayl/ internal problems. [/əndəruni məsayl/ and /daxyla
məsayl/ are considered correct but are less preferable.]

/əndəruni halat/ internal conditions. [Also /daxyli halat/, but not */daxyla
halat/.]

/əndəruni ylaqe/ interior areas. [But not */daxyla ylaqe/ or */daxyli ylaqe/. Compare the case of /beruni/, /xaryja/, and /xaryji/ in Sec. 23.221: only the first of these may occur with /ylaqe/ meaning "outer areas."]

23.224. /rui/ F2 [np] denotes carded, cleaned cotton wool. While /sut/ M1 [np] means "cotton thread." Uncarded, raw cotton is termed /kəpas/ F1 [np]. Note that /sut/ is not the common word for "thread": this is /taga/ or /dhaga/ M2.

23.225. /khal/ F1 is used for "hide, (untanned) skin," while /cəmRa/ M2 denotes "leather, tanned skin." Human skin is called /jyld/ F1.

23.226. /karxana/ M2 "factory, workshop" and the English loanword /fəykTri/ F2 are roughly synonymous. A /fəykTri/, however, is usually a large establishment, while a /karxana/ may denote either a large place or just a small private workshop.

23.227. /fən/ M1 "art, craft" is derived from the Arabic root f-n-n "to adorn, beautify," and the broken plural of /fən/ is thus /fwnun/ Mpl. The translation of "fine arts," for example, is /fwnune lətifa/ (/lətifa/ A1 "pleasing, delicate, fine"). In searching for a translation of the term "technical" (as in "technical training," "technical education"), Urdu writers have adopted the adjective /fənni/ A1, although this might have been selected just as logically as the translation of "artistic."

23.228. /təvəqqo/ F1 "expectation, hope" denotes a greater likelihood of realisation than /wmmid/ F1 "hope." E.g.

/mwjhe təvəqqo həy, ky vw vəqt pər pəhw̃c jaẽge./ I expect [lit. to me expectation is] that he will arrive on time. [/mwjhe wmmid həy .../ "I hope ..." denotes a lesser degree of certainty on the part of the speaker.]

23.229. Some Complex Verbal Formations.

A:

/dəraməd/
    /dəraməd hona/ to be imported
    /[X ko] dəraməd kərna/ to import [X]
/fəroxt/
    /fəroxt hona/ to be sold
    /[X ko] fəroxt kərna/ to sell [X]
/gəRbəR/
    /gəRbəR hona/ to become a mess, confused
    /[X ko] gəRbəR kərna/ to make a mess [of X]
/mənzur/
    /mənzur hona/ to be accepted, approved, sanctioned
    /[X ko] mənzur kərna/ to approve, sanction [X]

/nafyz/

    /nafyz hona/ to be promulgated, enforced

    /[X ko] nafyz kərna/ to promulgate, enforce [X]

/qətl/

    /qətl hona/ to be killed, murdered

    /[X ko] qətl kərna/ to kill, murder [X]

/rəwšən/

    /rəwšən hona/ to be illuminated, bright

    /[X ko] rəwšən kərna/ to illuminate, brighten [X]

/swpwrd/. [See also under F.]

    /[X ko Y] swpwrd kərna/ to entrust [Y to X]

/swst/

    /swst hona/ to be slow, sluggish, lazy

    /[X ko] swst kərna/ to slow [X] down

/šəhid/

    /šəhid hona/ to become a martyr

    /[X ko] šəhid kərna/ to make [X] a martyr

/xamoš/

    /xamoš hona/ to be, become silent

    /[X ko] xamoš kərna/ to silence [X]

/zae/

    /zae hona/ to be wasted

    /[X ko] zae kərna/ to waste [X]

B:

/mylavəT/

    /[X mẽ Y ki] mylavəT hona/ [Y] to be mixed [in X]

    /[X mẽ Y ki] mylavəT kərna/ to mix [Y into X]

/roktham/

    /[X ki] roktham hona/ [X] to be checked, stopped

    /[X ki] roktham kərna/ to check, stop, restrain [X]

/sədarət/

    /[X ki] sədarət kərna/ to act as chairman [of X]

/syfaryš/

    /[X ki Y se] syfaryš hona/ [X] to be recommended [to Y]

    /[X se Y ki] syfaryš kərna/ to recommend [Y to X]

/təvəqqo/

    /[X ko Y se Z ki] təvəqqo hona/ [X] to have expectation [of Z from Y]

    /[X se Y ki] təvəqqo kərna/ to expect [Y from X]

/yhtyram/

    /[X ka] yhtyram kərna/ to respect [X]

/yqdam/

    /[X ka] yqdam kərna/ to take a step [(consisting) of X]

/ysməglȳg/

   /[X ki] ysməglȳg hona/ [X] to be smuggled
   /[X ki] ysməglȳg kərna/ to smuggle [X]
/yzafa/

   /[X ka] yzafa hona/ [X] to be added
   /[X ka] yzafa kərna/ to add [X]
/zəxira̅/

   /[X ka] zəxira kərna/ to store, hoard [X]

D:

/mənzuri/

   /[X ko Y ki] mənzuri dena/ to give approval, sanction, grant [Y to X]
   /[X se Y ki] mənzuri lena/ to take approval [for Y from X]
   /[X ko Y ki] mənzuri mylna/ [X] to get approval [for Y]

F:

/dosti/

   /[X se] dosti kərna/ to make friends [with X]
/fəsad/

   /fəsad hona/ to be a riot, strife
   /fəsad kərna/ to riot
/jan/

   /[X se Y mē] jan ana/ life (vitality) to be created [in Y because of X]
   /[X mē] jan dena/ to give one's life [in, for X]
   /[X pər] jan dena/ to give one's life [for X], to sacrifice one's life [for X], to love [X] greatly
   /[X ki] jan lena/ to take the life [of X]
   /[X mē Y se] jan pəRna/ [X] to get life (vitality) [from Y]
   /[X ki Y se] jan nykəlna/ [X] to die [because of Y], [X] to be frightened to death [of Y]
/jəlsa/

   /jəlsa hona/ to be a meeting, a meeting to be held
   /jəlsa kərna/ to hold a meeting
/karəvai/

   /[X mē] karəvai hona/ action, proceedings to be taken [in X]
   /[X ke xylaf] karəvai kərna/ to take (legal) action [against X]
/khal/

   /khal wtarna/ to skin
/maršəl la/

   /maršəl la ləgana/ to impose martial law
/mwahyda/

   /[X se] mwahyda hona/ to be a treaty [with X]
   /[X se] mwahyda kərna/ to make a treaty [with X]
/swpwrd/. [See also under A above.]

   /[X Y ke] swpwrd hona / [X] to be entrusted [to Y]

407

/[X ko Y ke] swpwrd kərna/ to hand [X] over [to Y]

/təavwn/

    /[X se Y mē] təavwn kərna/ to cooperate [with X in Y]

/ynqylab/

    /[X mē] ynqylab ana/ to be a revolution, sweeping change [in X], a revolution
    to come about [in X]

    /[X mē] ynqylab hona/ to be a revolution, sweeping change [in X]

    /[X mē] ynqylab lana/ to bring about a revolution, sweeping change [in X]

/zəbərdəsti/

    /[X pər] zəbərdəsti kərna/ to tyrannise [X], force [X]

23.301. Substantive Composition.

The analysis of various compounds introduced in this Unit is as follows:

/əmnpəsənd/ A1 "peace-loving": Arabic /əmn/ "peace"; Persian /pəsənd/ "pleasing, liking. "

/bəynwləqvami/ A1 "international": Arabic /bəyna/ "between"; /wl/, the Arabic definite article; /əqvam/ "nations, " the broken plural of /qəwm/ F1 "nation"; /i/, an adjective formant suffix. According to Arabic rules, this should be /bəynələqvami/, but this pronunciation is not retained in Urdu.

/dəraməd/ F1 "import": Persian /dər/ "in"; /aməd/ the past stem of /amə/ "come. "

/gəRbəR/ F1 "confusion, disorder, mess": Hindi echo compound in which neither element has any independent meaning. See Sec. 19.305, end.

/karəvai/ F1 "proceeding, action, working, operation": Persian /kar/ "work, deed, act"; /rəv/ present stem of /rəf/ "go"; /a/, a noun and adjective formant; /i/, abstract noun formant suffix. See Sec. 18.306. Note that in

the Urdu script this is spelled as though it were /kar rəvai/:   It

is always pronounced /karəvai/, however.

/karxana/ M2 "factory, workshop": Persian /kar/, see above; /xana/ "house, room for, building for. "

/pəTsən/ F1 "jute": Hindi /pəT/ M1 "coarse cloth"; /sən/ F1 "hemp. " This compound is more often written as two separate words in Urdu, but occasionally it is found joined as one word.

/roktham/ F1 [np] "stop, check, restraint": Hindi /rokna/ If "to stop"; /thamna/ Ie "to check, hold. " See Sec. 19.304.

/syfarətxana/ M2 "embassy": Arabic /syfarət/ F1 "ambassadorship, mission"; Persian /xana/, see above under /karxana/.

/tənxa[h]/ F1 "salary, wages": Persian /tən/ "body"; /xah/ present stem of /xas/ "wish, want": "[what-the]-body-desires. "

/tərəqqiyafta/ A1 "advanced, progressive": Arabic /tərəqqi/ "progress"; Persian /yafta/, past participle of /yaf/ "get, obtain. "

/xwšgəvar/ A1 "pleasant, delightful": Persian /xwš/ "happy, glad"; /gəvar/ present stem of /gəvaš/ "digest, pass upon. "

/zəbərdəst/ A1 "vigorous, forceful, strict": Persian /zəbər/ "above, upon"; /dəst/ "hand. " Compare English "high-handed. "

/zəbərdəsti/ F2 "vigour, power, force, tyranny": the same as above + /i/, the abstract noun formant.

/zymmedar/ A1 "responsible, answerable": Arabic /zymma/ "protection, care, custody, responsibility"; Persian /dar/ present stem of /daš/ "have. "

23.302. Fractions.

Fractions are expressed in the following ways:

(1) A separate word denoting a fraction. These are restricted to /cəwthai/ F2 [np] Al "one quarter," and /tyhai/ F2 [np] Al "one third." E.g.

/mere mal ka tin cəwthai hyssa fəroxt ho gəya. / Three quarters of my stock [lit. my stock's three quarter part] has been sold.

/meri bəhn ko zəmin ka ek cəwthai hyssa myla həy. / My sister has received a quarter share of the land [lit. the land's one quarter part].

/mwlk ki ek tyhai abadi ka peša zəraət həy. / The occupation of one third of the country's population is agriculture.

/ys parTi ke do tyhai mymbər kəmyunysT hə̄y. / Two thirds of this party's members are Communists.

(2) The MNS past participle of /bəTna/ "to be divided" treated as indeclinable: /bəTa/. This is inserted between the two digits of the fraction: e.g. /tin bəTa pāc/ "three fifths," /nəw bəTa dəs/ "nine tenths," etc. E.g.

/ys mwlk ke car bəTa pāc hysse mē pəhaR phəyle hwe hə̄y. / Mountains occupy [lit. are spread out in] four fifths [lit. a four-divided-five part] of this country.

/mwlk ka do bəTa dəs hyssa jə̄gəl həy. / Two tenths of this country are forest.

/ys sube ki abadi ka pāc bəTa chəy hyssa hyndu həy. / Five sixths of the population of this province are Hindu.

(3) When one speaks of only one part of a whole, the ordinal number can be employed as a fraction: e.g. /chəTa hyssa/ "[one] sixth part." In some older Urdu grammars this formation was shown to be possible for the plural also (i.e. one could say /do pācvē hysse/ "two fifth parts" = "two fifths"), but the author's informants stated that this is now obsolete. E.g.

/kwl abadi ka dəsvā hyssa isai həy. / [One] tenth of the total population is Christian.

/ws ne əpni zəmin ka satvā hyssa bəRe beTe ko dia. / He gave a seventh part of his land to his eldest son. [This may be ambiguous: if the land were divided into ten sections of which the eldest son received section number seven, it might still be expressed this way. The usual implication is, however, that there are only seven sections of which the eldest son received one.]

(4) Another common method is to give the number of parts in the whole subtracting the required number of fractional parts: /X ke Y hyssō mē se, Z hysse .../ "from [lit. from in] Y parts of X, Z parts ..." E.g.

/abadi ke pāc hyssō mē se, do hyssō ka peša zəraət həy. / From [a total] of five parts of the population, the occupation of two parts is agriculture. [= The occupation of two fifths of the population is agriculture.]

/fəsl ke sat hyssō mē se, do hysse kəT gəe hə̄y. / From [a total] of seven parts of the crop, two parts have been cut. [= Two sevenths of the crop have been harvested.]

Note that for "one half of" one must employ /adha/ A2 "half." See Sec. 4.307. E.g.

/mera adha zəxira fəroxt ho gəya həy. / Half [of] my stock has been sold.

23.303. "A Second Time," Etc.

The numeral /do/ "two" occurs in a compound with /bar/ F1 "time, turn" + the adjective formant suffix /a/ (written ﻭ). See Sec. 18.305. Usually /do/ has an alternate form, /dw/ in this compound, but /dobara/ is also found. This compound is employed as an adverb meaning "again, a second time." E.g.

/əgər ap ne dwbara yy hərəkət ki, to səza mylegi. / If you do such a thing again, [you] will be punished.

/əysi bat dwbara nə kəhna! / Don't say such a thing again!

Another form, /tybara/ Adv "thrice, three times," is also found, but it is comparatively rare. Compare /tygna/ A2 "threefold" and /tyhra/ A2 "tripled" in Sec. 22.303.

Note that /dwbara/ is synonymous with /phyr/ Conj Adv "then, again" when the latter is used for "a second time." /phyr/, however, may denote "a third time," "a fourth time," etc. depending upon the context, and then /dwbara/ cannot, of course, be substituted. E.g.

/kəl məy phyr wn ke hā gəya. / Yesterday I went to his place again. [If the context indicates that /phyr/ here really means "a second time," then /dwbara/ may be substituted.]

/aj məy wn ke hā jaūga. əgər vw nə myle, to kəl dwbara jaūga, əwr əgər kəl bhi nə myle, to məy pərsõ phyr jaūga. / I'll go to his place today. If [I] don't meet him, then I'll go again [lit. a second time] tomorrow, and if he is not at home at that time, I'll go again the day after tomorrow. [Here /phyr/ means "a third time" in the context, and /dwbara/ cannot be substituted.]

If the action is repeated more than three times, this must be expressed by a numeral + /dəfa/ F1 "time," or + /bar/ F1 "time, turn." See Sec. 14.115. E.g.

/məy car dəfa ap ke ghər gəya tha, məgər ap məwjud nəhī the. / I went to your house four times, but you were not present.. [Here /car bar/ is substitutable.]

23.304. The Verb: the <PreP> as the Main Verb of Its Clause.

As was shown in Sec. 11.307, the present participle is employed alone for the "past conditional" (or "irrealis"). E.g.

/əgər ap jate, to əccha hota. / If you had gone, [it] would have been well.

Compare the following sentence from Sec. 23.000:

/ ... əwr mwlk ki tərəqqi rwki hwi thi, kyõke jo bhi hwkumət ati, ek nəi palisi yxtiar kərti. / ... And national progress was stopped because whichever government came, [it] adopted a new policy.

In this example /ati/ and /kərti/ have much the same meaning as /ati thi/ "used to come" and /kərti thi/ "used to do" since they express a general past condition. The present participle is idiomatic here, however, whereas the <PreP + /tha/> construction is not. Usually such sentences consist of two clauses: a relative clause introduced by /jo/ "who, which," /jəysa/ "as, such as," /jəhā/ "where," etc., followed by a correlative clause. Examples of non-relative-correlative sentences do occur, however. In all cases the reference is to a general state or action in the past. E.g.

/jo bhi ata, ek nəi təjviz peš kərta. / Whoever came, used to present a new suggestion.

/jo koi ata, yyhi kəhta, ky məy rəhim sahəb se phyr dosti kər lū. /

411

Whoever came, used to say this very [thing], that I should make friends again with Mr. Rəhim.

/jo bhi divar pər cəRhta, fəwrən gyr jata. / Whoever climbed the wall, immediately fell down.

/jəyse hi tənxah mylti, fəwrən xərc ho jati. / As soon as [lit. just as-emphatic] [one] got [one's] salary, [it] was spent at once.

/vw jəhā̃ bhi jata, yyhi qyssa swnata. / Wherever he used to go, [he] used to tell this same tale.

/jəb vəzire azəm logō̃ ki yy halət dekhta, to bar bar yyhi socta, ky ys badšah ko kəyse həTaya jae. / When the prime minister saw this condition of the people, he used to think this, that how can this king be removed.

/vw badšah ae dyn ek nəya hwkm jari kərta, jys ki vəja se log tāg a gəe the. / Every day that king used to issue a new command, because of which the people became distressed.

Note that if this type of sentence refers to present time, the verb must be the <PreP + /həy/> construction. Similarly, if the context requires future time, the verb must be in the future tense. E. g.

/jo bhi badšah bənta həy, yyhi hwkm jari kərta həy. / Whatever new king comes, [he] issues this same order.

/jo bhi aega, yyhi qyssa swnaega. / Whoever will come, will tell this same story.

The present participle alone may also stand for the <PreP + /həy/> or <PreP + /tha/> constructions in a multi-clausal sentence containing a series of main verbs. In this case, the auxiliary verb is omitted in every clause in the series except the last one. This usage must be kept distinct from that just discussed above. E. g.

/mā̃y aTh bəje wThta, dəs bəje dəftər jata, do bəje khana khata, car bəje cae pita, əwr chəy bəje ghər vapəs ata tha. / I used to get up at eight o'clock, go to the office at ten o'clock, eat lunch at two o'clock, drink tea at four o'clock, and come back home at six o'clock. [Here /wThta/ stands for /wThta tha/, /jata/ for /jata tha/, etc. The last verb in the series, /ata tha/, must contain the auxiliary. To change the above sentence to present time one need only substitute /ata hū̃/ for /ata tha/.]

23.400. SUPPLEMENTARY VOCABULARY

23.401. Supplementary Vocabulary.

The following numerals are all Type I adjectives. See Sec. 2.401.

chyanve [or /cheanve/ or /chəyanve/]	ninety-six
səttanve	ninety-seven
əTThanve	ninety-eight
nynnanve	ninety-nine

Other items are:

fən M1	art, craft
fəsad M1	disturbance, riot, strife
mwhajyr [or /məhajyr/] M1	refugee
sut M1 [np]	cotton thread
syfaryš F1	recommendation, intercession
šəy F1	thing, article, commodity
un F1 [np]	wool
xamoši F2	silence, quiet
yqdam M1	step
zəbərdəsti F2 Adv	vigour, power, strictness, tyranny, force; by force

23.402. Supplementary Exercise I: Substitution.

1. ys sal pakystan <u>pəchəttər lakh</u> rupəe ki <u>un</u> bəraməd kərega.
   ninety-eight thousand   skins
   forty-seven lakhs   sugar
   ninety-nine lakhs   cotton wool
   forty-six lakhs   tea
   ninety-six thousand   pulses

2. ys zyle mẽ, <u>əTThanve həzar</u> mwhajyr abad kie gəe hə̃y.
   seventy-three thousand
   ninety-six thousand
   three hundred and ninety-seven
   two thousand, four hundred and ninety-nine
   only ninety-four

23.403. Supplementary Exercise II: Translation.

1. Translate the following sentences into Urdu.
   a. He is a master of this art.

413

b. This riot took place [/hwa tha/] because of this step of the Government's.

c. This factory makes cotton thread.

d. The police used force [/zəbərdəsti kərna/] in this affair.

e. He recommended that the house be given to that refugee.

23.501. Substitution.

1. ys sal, həm <u>gəndwm ki pəydavar</u>   <u>əmrika</u>   ke hath fəroxt kərēge.
     jute   the French
                                 government
     cotton cloth   England
     cement   foreign countries
     woollen cloth   Afghanistan
     skins and sugar   Communist China

2. qəwmi əsəmbli   šayəd əgle məhine   <u>ys qanun</u>   ko mənzur kəre.
     the United Nations   these recommendations
     the Commonwealth   these reforms
     the union of labourers   these suggestions
     the Provincial Assembly   these laws
     the Cabinet   this project

3. baryš ke səbəb   <u>ənaj ka sara zəxira</u>   zae ho gəya həy. [1]
               all the silken cloth
               all the stock of mustard
               seed
               all the melons
               all the watermelons
               all the potatoes

[1]Make the verb agree with the subject in each case.

4. həmari hwkumət ne   <u>ysməglȳg ki roktham</u>   ke sylsyle mē baz yqdamat kie hēy.
                  foreign [/beruni/] trade
                  the protection of the border
                  technical education
                  import of medicines
                  export of jute

5. məhkməe maliat   ne   <u>yn əšya</u>   ki dəraməd pər baz nəi pabəndiā ləgai hēy.
     the Cabinet   leather
     the new commission   English cloth
     the Government of Burma   guns
     the Department of   barley and rice
     Commerce
     the Central Government   woollen cloth

6. sədre mwmlykət   ne   <u>yy yxtiarat</u>   <u>vəzire azəm</u>   ke swpwrd kər die.
     the Provincial   these projects   the Union Councils
     Assembly
     the Jagirdar   his sons   the teacher
     the soldiers   all the cattle   their owners
     the tailor   my clothes   another tailor

	the Caliph		these duties	the general
7.	yn fəsadat	mẽ	lakhõ admi	mare gəe.
	the last war		thousands of soldiers	
	these communal quarrels		hundreds of people	
	this fight		many refugees	
	1948		lakhs of Hindus and Muslims	
	this confusion		scores [twenties] of travellers	

8.	mwjrym ne	ghi	mẽ	tel	ki mylavəT ki.
		cement		dirt	
		gold		copper	
		medicine		water	
		wheat		barley	
		opium		other things	

9.	dwšmənõ	ne	gəvərnər jənrəl	ko goli mar kər šəhid kər dia.
	a member of the opposition party		our leader	
	a member of the minority party		the president	
	local residents		our ambassador	
	the owner of the factory		that labourer	
	someone from in the crowd		Məwlvi Sahəb	

10.	pychle sal	sərkari mwlazymin ki tənxahõ	mẽ kafi yzafa hwa.
		the production of this factory	
		our defense strength	
		the number of our army	
		the production of jute	
		the export of skins	
		the import of iron	

11.	wn ki yn yslahat	se	mwlk ke halat	mẽ ynqylab a gəya.
	these steps of his		Iran	
	this new industrial policy		our industry	
	the new external policy		our external relations	
	these efforts of his		our educational system	
	this step		international politics	
	the advent of the Mughals		our social system	

12.	ysməglyg	ki roktham ke lie səxt qədəm wThana cahie.
	cholera	

416

these social evils
these quarrels
atomic war
these riots

13. <u>pakystan</u>   <u>dusre mwmalyk ki azadi</u>   ka yhtyram kərta həy.
    our country   neighbour countries' borders
    a good citizen   the laws of the country
    every individual   the constitution of the country
    a good husband   the rights of his wife
    a good ruler   the rights of the public

14. həm   <u>hər əmnpəsənd mwlk</u>   se dostana təəllwqat qaym kərne ko təyyar hõy.
        Muslim countries
        all nations of the world
        Communist countries
        Burma and China
        Egypt and Syria
        Afghanistan and India

15. <u>səmaji bwraiõ ko dur kərne</u>   ke lie

	<u>əvam</u>	<u>hwkumət</u>	se . . .
stopping atomic war	all countries	the United Nations	
increasing agricultural production	farmers	the Department of Agriculture	
national prosperity	Egypt and Iraq	one another	
establishing peace in the world	all free countries	America	
making the educational system better	all educational institutions	the Department of Education	

. . . təavwn kərẽge.

23.502. Variation.

1. ys sal sərkari mwlazymin ki tənxahõ mẽ pəndra fi sədi yzafa hwa həy.
  məwlvi sahəb ki təfsir pəRhne se, meri malumat mẽ kafi yzafa hwa.
  yn dəs salõ mẽ simãyT ki fəykTriõ ki tadad mẽ kafi yzafa hwa həy.
  wnhõ ne əpne məkan ke əgle hysse mẽ do kəmrõ ka yzafa kia.
  ys sal donõ mwlkõ ne əpne əyTmi həthyarõ ke zəxire mẽ koi yzafa nəhĩ kia.
  məhkməe zəraət gəndwm ke məwjuda zəxire mẽ yzafa kərne ki košyš kər rəha həy.

2. ys šəhr ke DakTərõ ne həyze ki roktham ke lie baz zəruri yqdamat kie hõy.
  məhkməe zəraət pəydavar bəRhane ke lie bəhwt se nəe yqdamat kər rəha həy.
  hwkumət ne ysməglỹg ki roktham ke lie yy bəhwt əhəm yqdam kia həy.
  məhkməe xwrak ne khane ki cizõ mẽ mylavəT ki roktham ke lie səxt qədəm wThaya
  həy.

417

mwmlykəte pakystan digər mwmalyk se dosti ke lie hər zəruri qədəm wThaegi.

əqvame mwttəhyda əyTmi jŏg rokne ke lie hər qədəm wThane ko təyyar həy.

3. kəmišən ne ys mənsube ki mənzuri ki syfaryš ki.

məhkməe polis ne əpne mwlazymin ki tənxahē bəRhane ki syfaryš ki həy.

sənəti kəmišən ne yy syfaryš ki həy, ky yy mənsuba mənzur kia jae.

meri syfaryš se, ws ki tərəqqi hwi.

məhkməe talim ne həmare ydare ki syfaryšat mənzur kər li hēy.

yy kam məhz ap ki syfaryš se hwa

4. ap ki košyš se, ys kam ki rəftar kafi bəRh gəi həy.

ys nəi məšin ki vəja se, fəsl kaTne ki rəftar bəhwt bəRh gəi həy.

yn yslahat ke səbəb, mwlk ki tərəqqi ki rəftar kafi tez ho gəi həy.

šor swn kər, ghoRe ki rəftar əwr tez ho gəi.

əysi məšinŏ ki kəmi ki vəja se, həmari tərəqqi ki rəftar ghəT gəi həy.

ys gəRbəR ki vəja se, həmare mənsube ki rəftar swst pəR gəi thi.

5. polis ne ys kes mē cerməyn ke xylaf karəvai ki.

wnhŏ ne ədalət mē mere xylaf karəvai šwru kər di.

əb tək ysməglỹg ki roktham ke sylsyle mē koi mwəssyr karəvai nəhī̃ ho səki.

aj ədalət mē karəvai der se šwru hwi.

əxbar mē kəl ke jəlse ki karəvai šae ho cwki həy.

qəwmi əsəmbli ki karəvai kytab ki surət mē šae kər di jaegi.

6. ws ləRki ne sari rəqəm kəpRŏ pər zae kər di.

jagirdar ne əpni sari dəwlət-jue mē zae kər di.

ləRkŏ ne sara vəqt khel mē zae kər dia.

ys sal jəw ka təmam zəxira zae ho gəya.

ləRai mē səykRŏ janē zae hwī̃.

ys baryš ki vəja se, sari fəsl zae ho jaegi.

7. yy həmari tarix ka ek rəwšən bab həy.

yy həmare mwašre ka rəwšən pəhlu həy.

cyraɤ jəlne se, sara kəmra rəwšən ho gəya.

həmara mazi rəwšən tha, əwr ynšaəlla[h] mwstəqbyl ys se bhi zyada rəwšən hoga.

ys təhqiq se, ws dəwr ke mwašre pər rəwšni pəRti həy.

həmare rəsul ki talimat ne dymaɤŏ ko rəwšən kər dia.

8. pakystan dusre mwmalyk ki azadi ka yhtyram kərta həy.

həmara mwlk əpne bəynwləqvami mwahydŏ ka yhtyram kərta həy.

ap ko dusre məzahyb ka yhtyram kərna cahie.

bəRŏ ka yhtyram kərna cahie.

mɛ̄y ap ke dostŏ ka bhi yhtyram kərta hū̃.

wn ki xydmat qabyle yhtyram hēy.

9. həmari hwkumət dəwləte mwštərka se ys mənsube mē təavwn kəregi.

əqliəti parTi hwkmran parTi se daxyli məsayl həl kərne mē təavwn kərne ko təyyar həy.

pəTsən ki pəydavar bəRhane ke lie, zəmindarŏ ko məhkməe zəraət se təavwn kərna cahie.

suti əwr uni kəpRõ ki bəraməd ke sylsyle mẽ, məhkmǝe tyjarət se karxanõ ka

təavwn kərna lazmi həy.

yn fyrqəvarana fəsadat ko rokne ke lie, fəwj əwr polis se šəhriõ ka təavwn zəruri

həy.

fənni talim bəRhane ke sylsyle mẽ, baz γəyrmwlki ydarõ ka təavwn bhi cahie.

10. hwkumət ne hal hi mẽ do nəe qəvanin nafyz kie hə̃y.

badšah ne jwrmanõ əwr səzaõ se mwtəəllyq baz nəe qəvanin nafyz kie hə̃y.

subai əsəmbli ki mənzuri ke bad, hwkumət ne ys qanun ko nafyz kər dia.

ysməglỹg ki roktham ke lie, hwkumət səxt qəvanin nafyz kəregi.

khane ki əšya mẽ mylavəT ki roktham ke lie maršəl la hwkumət ne səxt qəvanin

nafyz kie hə̃y.

gəndwm, cavəl, əwr digər əšya ki dəraməd ke sylsyle mẽ, kwch nəe qəvanin nafyz

kie gəe hə̃y.

11. məhkmǝe tyjarət ne rui ka təmam zəxira γəyrmwmalyk mẽ fəroxt kər dia.

ws ne əpne zəxire ka ek cəwthai hyssa fəroxt kər dia.

bhari sənətẽ qaym hone ke bad, pakystan bhi əpne pəRəwsiõ ke hath məšinẽ, gaRiã,

vəγəyra fəroxt kər səkega.

ys sal zərəi pəydavar ka ek bəRa hyssa bərma, cın, əwr əfγanystan ke hath fəroxt

kia gəya həy.

zərəi yslahat ke təht, γərib kysanõ ko səsti qimət pər zəminẽ fəroxt ki jaẽgi.

həmari tyjarti palisi ke təht, dusre mwlkõ ke hath yn əšya ki fəroxt məna həy.

12. kəmišən ne yy kam mere swpwrd kər dia həy.

mwayne ke bad, polis ne mwrde ko ws ke ryštedarõ ke swpwrd kər dia.

mwqədme ke bad, yy məkan ws mwhajyr ke swpwrd kər dia gəya.

meri rae mẽ, ap yy mənsuba kysi zymmedar šəxs ke swpwrd kər dijie.

meri rae mẽ, yy kam ek bədtərin admi ke swpwrd ho gəya həy.

ek dyn həm səb ko əpni jan əllah ke swpwrd kərni hogi.

13. pakystan ne hal hi mẽ səttanve lakh rupəe ka ənaj dəraməd kia həy.

ys dyfai mwahyde ke təht, həmara mwlk əmrika se fəwji saman dəraməd kərega.

hyndostan əfγanystan se hər sal lakhõ rupəe ke phəl dəraməd kərta həy.

həmare mwlk ko pakystan se bəhwt si əšya dəraməd kərni pəRti hə̃y.

mazi ke mwqable mẽ, mwstəqbyl mẽ həmẽ zyada tel əwr koyla dəraməd kərna

pəRega.

pychle sal se əb tək, təqriban sə̃ytys həzar gaRiã dəraməd hwi hə̃y.

14. jəb sədre mwmlykət təqrir ke lie khəRe hwe, to hwjum xamoš ho gəya.

jəb mə̃y ne wse yy bətaya, ky yy šərarət wsi ke ləRke ki həy, to vw xamoš ho gəya.

jəb vw mere bare mẽ əysi batẽ kəhte rəhte həy, to mə̃y kəyse xamoš rəhũ!

jəb masTər sahəb dusri tərəf dekh rəhe the, to vw xamoši se wTh kər kəmre se

cəla gəya.

jəb ws ne yy elan kia, to jəlse pər xamoši cha gəi.

əgər vw phyr bola, to mə̃y wse zərur xamoš kər dũga!

15. mwjhe təvəqqo həy, ky vw vəqt pər pəhw̃c gəya hoga.

təvəqqo həy, ky aj ke jəlse mẽ zəbərdəst hwjum hoga.

419

həmẽ təvəqqo nəhĩ, ky hwkumət tənxahē bəRhaegi.

mãy ap se əysi hərəkət ki təvəqqo nəhĩ rəkhta tha.

jəysa ky təvəqqo thi, həmari fəwjõ ne dwšmən ki fəwjõ ko sərhədõ hi pər rok dia.

yy kam meri təvəqqo ke mwtabyq hwa.

23. 503. Translation.

1. Translate the following sentences from Urdu to English:

١۔ اس سال پاکستان کو اناج درآمد نہیں کرنا پڑے گا ۔کیونکہ مشینوں کے استعمال کے سبب
پچھلے سال سے اناج کی پیداوار تین گنی ہوگئی ہے ۔ اور اب ہر ضلع میں اس کا کافی
ذخیرہ موجود ہے ۔

٢۔ چونکہ اُس کے اِن اقدامات سے عوام کو تکلیف پہنچی تھی لہٰذا حکومت نے اُسے عہدے سے
ہٹا دیا۔

٣۔ آج موسم بہت خوشگوار ہے ۔ میرے دفتر کے اکثر لوگ سیر کرنے گئے ہوئے ہیں جس کے
سبب دفتر میں کام کی رفتار سست پڑ گئی ہے ۔ شہر میں بھی زیادہ تر دُکانیں بند
ہیں مگر باغوں میں ہجوم ہے ۔ اگر آپ کو فرصت ہو تو ہم لوگ بھی تھوڑی دیر کے لئے
کسی باغ میں چلیں ۔

٤۔ اس فیکٹری میں صرف سوتی کپڑا بنتا ہے ۔ یہ کپڑا غیر ممالک کے ہاتھ فروخت کیا جاتا ہے ۔
ہماری حکومت سوتی کپڑے کی پیداوار بڑھانے کی کوشش کر رہی ہے ۔ تاکہ بیرونی تجارت میں
اضافہ ہو۔

٥۔ پہلے مزدوروں کو بہت کم تنخواہ ملتی تھی۔ مگر جب سے اُنہوں نے یونین بنائی ہے اُن کی
تنخواہیں تقریباً دوگنی ہوگئی ہیں۔

٦۔ کمیشن نے جن اصلاحات کی سفارش کی تھی قومی اسمبلی نے اُنہیں منظور نہیں کیا ۔اب صدر

مملکت ان سفارشات کی منظوری کے سلسلے میں کابینہ سے مشورہ کریں گے ۔

۷۔ دو سال سے پاکستان کی بیرونی تجارت بڑھ گئی ہے ۔ خاص طور پر کھالوں، چمڑوں اور کپڑوں کی برآمد میں کافی اضافہ ہوا ہے ۔ پاکستان اپنا زیادہ تر سوتی اور اُونی کپڑا انگلستان کے ہاتھ فروخت کرتا ہے ۔

۸۔ پاکستان میں اب تک اعلیٰ تعلیم یعنی یونیورسٹی اور کالجوں میں تعلیم انگریزی ہی میں دی جاتی ہے ۔ مگر حال ہی میں کراچی یونیورسٹی نے طلبا کو امتحان کے جوابات اردو میں بھی لکھنے کی اجازت دے دی ہے ۔

۹۔ اگر آپ مصر جانا چاہتے ہیں تو پہلے آپ کو مصر کے سفارت خانے سے اجازت لینی پڑے گی۔ مصر کے سفیر میرے دوست ہیں ۔ اگر آپ فرمائیں تو میں اُنہیں ٹیلیفون کر دوں ۔

۱۰۔ اس ملک کو سب سے پہلے اپنے داخلی مسائل حل کرنے چاہئیں ۔ اگر سیاسی پارٹیاں اسی طرح جھگڑوں میں مصروف رہیں تو ملک ترقّی نہیں کر سکے گا ۔ اور یہاں کے عوام خوش حال نہیں ہو سکیں گے ۔

۱۱۔ آج پولیس کی ایک پارٹی اُس کی دکان پر گئی اور ایسی تمام کتابوں کو جو حکومت کے خلاف تھیں اپنے قبضے میں لے لیا ۔ میرا خیال ہے کہ عدالت ان کتابوں کا سارا ذخیرہ ضائع کر دینے کا حکم جاری کرے گی۔

۱۲۔ اسمگلنگ کی روک تھام کے لئے کئی نئے قوانین نافذ کئے گئے ہیں ۔ سرحدوں پر پولیس کی تعداد بھی دوگنی کر دی گئی ہے ۔ اور اب پولیس والے مسافروں کا سامان باقاعدہ کھول کر دیکھتے ہیں ۔

۱۳۔ صدر کے ان اقدامات سے قوم کی حالت میں انقلاب آگیا ہے ۔ اب لوگوں میں قومی جذبات

پیدا ہو رہے ہیں ۔ اور وہ اچھے اور برے میں تمیز کرنے لگے ہیں ۔

۱۴۔ ہر ملک کو صنعتی ترقی کے لئے تین چیزوں کی ضرورت ہوتی ہے ۔ یہ چیزیں لوہا ، کوئلہ اور تیل ہیں ۔ اِن کے بغیر فیکٹریاں اور مشینیں نہیں چل سکتیں ۔ یہی وجہ ہے کہ ہمارے ماہرین اِن چیزوں کو دریافت کرنے کی کوشش کر رہے ہیں ۔

۱۵۔ اِس شاعر کے صرف چند شعر اردو ادب میں رہ گئے ہیں ۔ غدر میں اُس کی شہادت کے ساتھ ہی اُس کی شاعری بھی ختم ہوگئی ۔ کیونکہ غدر میں جو گڑ بڑ ہوئی اُس میں اِس کی ساری تحریریں ضائع ہو گئیں ۔

۱۶۔ جیسے ہی یہ خبر پھیلی کہ اُن کی پارٹی انتخاب میں ہار گئی ہے شہر میں فسادات شروع ہو گئے ۔ فسادات کی اطلاع ملتے ہی پولیس اُن جگہوں پر پہنچ گئی اور فوراً ہی امن قائم کر دیا ۔ چند گھنٹوں کے اِن فسادات میں دو افراد قتل اور گیارہ زخمی ہوئے ۔ پولیس نے اِس سلسلے میں سَو سے زیادہ افراد کو گرفتار کر لیا ہے ۔

۱۷۔ جب ملک میں فسادات شروع ہوئے تو وزیرِ اعظم نے حکومت سے علیٰحدہ ہونے کا اعلان کر دیا ۔ اُن کے اِس اقدام پر صدر نے حکومت کمیونسٹ لیڈروں کے سپرد کر دی کیونکہ اگر وہ ایسا نہ کرتے تو ملک میں بغاوت ہو جاتی ۔

۱۸۔ اِن تین ملکوں میں اناج کی سخت کمی ہے ۔ اِس کمی کو دُور کرنے کے لئے زرعی پیداوار میں اضافے کی کوششیں کی جا رہی ہیں ۔ اِس مقصد کے لئے اُس بڑے دریا پر جو اِن تینوں ملکوں سے گزرتا ہے ۔ ایک زبردست بند تعمیر کرنے کا منصوبہ بنایا گیا ہے تاکہ زیادہ سے زیادہ علاقہ میں فصلیں اگائی جائیں ۔ توقع ہے کہ اِس منصوبے میں اِن تینوں ممالک کے علاوہ دیگر ممالک بھی تعاون کریں گے ۔

۱۹۔ مولانا صاحب نے جلسے میں بہت زبردست تقریر کی ۔ اُنہوں نے بتایا کہ مہاجرین کیسی بُری حالت میں زندگی بسر کر رہے ہیں ۔ مولانا صاحب نے حکام سے مہاجرین کے ساتھ انصاف کا مطالبہ کیا۔

۲۰۔ پولیس عین اُس وقت پہنچی جب کہ چور دیوار پر چڑھ کر بھاگنے کی کوشش کر رہے تھے۔ چور پولیس کو دیکھ کر گھبرا گئے ۔ چنانچہ ایک چور دیوار سے گر پڑا ۔ اُس کے پَیر میں سخت چوٹ آئی ۔ پولیس نے تھوڑی دیر کی کوشش کے بعد تمام چوروں کو گرفتار کر لیا۔

۲۱۔ جب امن کا معاہدہ ہوا تو ملک بھر میں خوشیاں منائی گئیں ۔ شہر میں جگہ جگہ چراغوں کی روشنی کی گئی ۔ دفتروں ، اسکولوں اور کالجوں میں چھٹی رہی ۔ شہر میں ہر جگہ لوگوں کا ہجوم تھا۔ جہاں لوگ خوشی میں ناچ رہے تھے ۔ شام کو ملک کے سیاسی لیڈر اور امرا مجلس کی شکل میں صدر کے محل کے پاس گئے جہاں اُنہوں نے اِس معاہدے پر صدر کو مبارکباد دی۔

۲۲۔ پٹ سن کی پیداوار پچھلے دس سال میں تقریباً چار گنی ہو گئی ہے ۔ ہماری موجودہ فیکٹریاں اب اِس کے لئے کافی نہیں ہوں گی ۔ ہمیں کم سے کم تین نئی فیکٹریاں اور بنانی پڑیں گی۔ دوسرے چاول اور گندم کی پیداوار بھی کافی بڑھ گئی ہے ۔ جس سے اناج کی کمی تو ختم ہو گئی ہے لیکن اگر ہم اُونی اور سوتی کپڑے کی حالت دیکھیں تو ہمیں ماننا پڑے گا کہ ہم نے اِس میدان میں کوئی خاص ترقی نہیں کی ۔

۲۳۔ اُس کی اِن حرکات سے ہمارے منصوبے میں بہت گڑ بڑ ہوئی ۔ اگر ایک آدمی سست ہو اور اپنی ذمّہ داریاں سرانجام نہ دے تو باقی آدمیوں کا کام بھی خراب ہوتا ہے ۔ اِس لئے ہمیں اُسے اُس کے عہدے سے ہٹانا پڑا۔

۲۴۔ اِن کی تقریر بہت مؤثّر تھی کیونکہ اُنہوں نے جو باتیں کہیں وہ بالکل صحیح تھیں اور اِس

423

موقعہ کے لئے جو الفاظ استعمال کئے اُن میں بڑی جان تھی ۔جس سے لوگوں پر بڑا اثر ہوا۔ توقع ہے کہ اب اِس سلسلے میں ضرور کوئی مفید کارروائی کی جائے گی ۔

۲۵۔ اُن کی شہادت سے ہمیں یہ سبق ملتا ہے کہ تبلیغ کا کام کوئی آسان کام نہیں ہے۔ جو لوگ اِس کے لئے اپنا وطن اور گھر چھوڑنے اور دوسرے ممالک میں جا کر اسلام کے لئے جان دینے کو تیار ہیں۔ اللہ کے نزدیک اُن کا مقام بہت اعلیٰ ہوگا اور اللہ اُنہیں اِس کا انعام دے گا۔ اسلام کی خدمت کے اِس راستے میں آرام نہیں ہے ۔ اِس کے برعکس سینکڑوں مصیبتوں کا سامنا کرنا پڑتا ہے ۔

۲۶۔ اقوامِ متحدہ کے تحت بہت سے ادارے ہیں جو نیک کام کرتے ہیں ۔ اِن میں سے ایک ادارہ بچوں کو خوراک اور دوائیاں پہنچاتا ہے ، دوسرا بڑوں کی تعلیم میں مدد دیتا ہے ، تیسرا ہیضہ اور دیگر بیماریوں کی روک تھام کے لئے اقدامات کرتا ہے ، چوتھا غریب ملکوں کی زرعی پیداوار بڑھانے کی کوشش کرتا ہے ۔ اِسی طرح اِس کے دوسرے ادارے بھی لوگوں کی بھلائی اور خوشحالی کے کام کرتے ہیں ۔ میری رائے میں اقوامِ متحدہ کی حمایت کرنا اپنی مدد کرنا ہے۔

۲۷۔ اگر ہم اِن ممالک سے دوستانہ تعلقات قائم کرنا چاہتے ہیں تو ہمیں اپنی خارجہ پالیسی تبدیل کرنی پڑے گی ۔ یہ اقدام ہماری تجارت کے لئے بھی مفید ثابت ہوگا ۔ کیونکہ پھر ہم اِن ملکوں کے ہاتھ روئی، کھالیں اور چمڑا وغیرہ فروخت کر سکیں گے ۔ اور اِن سے سیمنٹ، لوہا، اُون، اور دیگر ضروری اشیاء خرید سکیں گے ۔ اِس طرح طرفین کو کافی فائدہ ہوگا۔

۲۸۔ چین کی آبادی کے تین چوتھائی حصے کو پڑھنا لکھنا نہیں آتا ۔ اور فنی تعلیم کے لحاظ سے تو وہ بہت ہی پیچھے ہیں ۔ چین کی حکومت لوگوں میں تعلیم پھیلانے کے لئے پوری کوشش کر رہی ہے۔ اِس سلسلے میں اب تک ہزاروں نئے اسکول کھولے جا چکے ہیں ۔

۲۹ ۔ انقلاب کے بعد انہوں نے ہر معاملے میں زبردستی سے کام لیا۔ لوگوں کی مرضی کے خلاف پرانے تعلیمی نظام کو ختم کر دیا اور نیا غیر ملکی تعلیمی نظام رائج کیا۔ اسی طرح عربی رسم الخط کی جگہ انگریزی حروف کو اپنا لیا گیا۔ بعض قدیم رسومات کو بھی ختم کر دیا گیا اور لوگوں کو ملکی کپڑوں کی بجائے انگریزی کپڑے پہننے پر مجبور کیا گیا۔

۳۰ ۔ ہم قائدِ اعظم محمد علی جناح کا بہت احترام کرتے ہیں۔ انہوں نے اپنی تمام زندگی مسلمانوں کی خدمت میں بسر کی۔ پاکستان قائدِ اعظم ہی کی کوششوں کا نتیجہ ہے۔ اور وہی صحیح طور پر اس ملک کے بانی ہیں۔

2. Translate the following sentences into Urdu and write them out in the Urdu script.

   a. Today the Commander in Chief has issued an order that an increase of twenty rupees be made in the salary of each soldier.

   b. The Commission has presented a new project to Parliament, under which heavy industries will be established in Pakistan.

   c. [It] is expected that every peace-loving country will cooperate in the tasks of the United Nations.

   d. Because of these steps of his, a revolution took place [lit. came] in our social conditions.

   e. Burma also shares in this defense treaty. If ever [/kəbhi/] we need her help, she will certainly send her army.

   f. Three quarters of the population of this city are very poor. [Lit. This city's three-quarter population. Or: This city's population's three-quarter part.]

   g. Because of this verse, the king had him killed [/qətl kəra dena/]. Now people call him a martyr, and many people go to [lit. on] his tomb.

   h. Our Government has established friendly relations with the Government of China. Now we soon [/jəld hi/] will begin to import many things from China, and [we] will export jute, skins, and sugar to them.

   i. The villagers handed over the culprit to the police.

   j. J expect that next year our Government will sell fifty lakhs [of] rupees of cement to Afghanistan.

   k. Although we respect your goal, we cannot cooperate in this connection.

   l. Their armies have attacked our neighbour country, because of which we will have to change our foreign policy.

   m. Because of the lack of such machines, the speed of our industrial development has become sluggish.

n. The Commission has settled the refugees in various small cities [/choTe choTe šəhrõ mẽ/] in the Panjab. They have been given houses, shops, and lands, and now they are living [/zyndəgi bəsər kərna/] like other citizens of Pakistan.

o. This year there has been an increase of twelve percent in our agricultural production. We now èxport wheat, rice, and cotton wool to various countries.

23.504. Script.

1. Write out the following words in the Urdu script and place them in Urdu alphabetical order.

a.	sənət	k.	məzmun
b.	xaryja	l.	rəsmwlxət
c.	karəvai	m.	zwlm
d.	zae	n.	zyd
e.	dyfai	o.	šərt
f.	əyn	p.	əvam
g.	mənzuri	q.	pyaz
h.	mwahyda	r.	əta
i.	zymmedar	s.	ytaət
j.	zərəi	t.	mənzur

23.505. Response.

1. Answer the following questions verbally:

۱۔ کیا آپ کے ملک اور پاکستان کے درمیان کوئی دفاعی معاہدہ ہے ؟

۲۔ آپ کے ملک میں کس طرز کی حکومت ہے ۔ جمہوری ، صدارتی یا پارلیمانی ؟

۳۔ کیا آپ کے ملک میں کبھی فوجی انقلاب آیا ہے ؟

۴۔ کیا آپ نے کبھی کسی جلسے کی صدارت کی ہے ؟

۵۔ اقوام متحدہ کے بارے میں آپ کی کیا رائے ہے ؟

۶۔ کیا آپ نے کبھی عدالت میں کسی کے خلاف کارروائی کی ہے ؟

۷۔ زرعی پیداوار کن کن طریقوں سے بڑھائی جا سکتی ہے ؟

426

۸۔ کیا موجودہ دَور میں ہر شہری کو فنی تعلیم حاصل کرنی چاہیے ؟

۹۔ آپ کے ملک میں کون کون سی اشیاء درآمد ہوتی ہیں ؟

۱۰۔ کیا آپ کے ہاں مالک و مزدور کے تعلقات اچھے ہیں ؟

۱۱۔ کیا آپ کا ملک کمیونسٹ ممالک سے تعاون کرنے کو تیار ہے؟

۱۲۔ کیا آپ دوسرے مذاہب کے عقائد کا احترام کرتے ہیں ؟

۱۳۔ ایک اچھے شہری کے کیا کیا فرائض ہیں ؟

۱۴۔ آپ اپنے ملک کی خارجہ پالیسی کے بارے میں کیا رائے رکھتے ہیں؟

۱۵۔ آپ کے ملک میں اکثریت کا پیشہ کیا ہے ؟

2. Write out the answers to the following questions in Urdu. Answers to these may be found in Sec. 23.000, and Sec. 23.506.

۱۔ پاکستان دوسرے ملکوں سے کون کون سی اشیا درآمد کرتا ہے ؟

۲۔ کیا پاکستان دولتِ مشترکہ کا رکن ہے ؟

۳۔ پاکستانیوں کی نظر میں قائدِاعظم محمّد علی جناح کی کیا حیثیت ہے ؟

۴۔ ہندوستان اور پاکستان نے کب آزادی حاصل کی؟

۵۔ پاکستان کی حکومت کے اختیارات کس سیاسی پارٹی کے سپرد کئے گئے تھے ؟

۶۔ پاکستان کے بانی قائدِاعظم محمّد علی جناح کا مزار کس شہر میں ہے ؟

۷۔ لیاقت علی خان کا انتقال کیسے ہوا ؟

۸۔ گورنر جنرل بننے سے پہلے ملک غلام محمّد کا کیا عہدہ تھا؟

۹۔ صدر محمّد ایوب خان نے مارشل لاء کیوں نافذ کیا ؟

427

۱۰۔ مارشل لاء حکومت نے ملک کے حالات بہتر بنانے کے لئے کیا کیا اقدامات کئے ؟

۱۱۔ ہندوستان کی تقسیم سے جو علاقے پاکستان میں آئے ۔ کیا اُن میں نیکلڑیاں اور بھاری صنعتیں پہلے سے موجود تھیں ؟

۱۲۔ کیا پاکستان کے سفارت خانے کیونٹ ممالک میں موجود ہیں ؟

۱۳۔ کیا کشمیر کا مسئلہ اقوامِ متّحدہ میں پیش ہو چکا ہے؟

۱۴۔ پاکستان کی زیادہ آبادی کا کیا پیشہ ہے ؟

۱۵۔ پاکستان کے پہلے صدر کون تھے ؟

23. 506. Conversation Practice.

Mr. Smith is discussing the essay given in Sec. 23. 000 with Dr. Rǝhim.

اسمتھ۔ پاکستان نے زندگی کے ہر شعبے میں کافی ترقی کی ہے مگر اِس کی کیا وجہ ہے کہ وہ ابھی تک اناج کی کمی کو دُور نہیں کر سکا؟

ریم۔ پاکستان میں اناج کی کمی کا مسئلہ انشاء اللہ بہت جلد حل ہو جائے گا۔ کیونکہ ہماری زرعی پیداوار کافی بڑھ گئی ہے جس سے اُمید ہے کہ اب ہمیں باہر سے اناج منگانے کی ضرورت نہیں رہے گی۔ اب تک اِس مسئلے کے حل نہ ہونے کی وجہ تو آپ کو معلوم ہی ہے ۔ یعنی ہمارے کسان ابھی تک سینکڑوں سال پرانے طریقے استعمال کرتے ہیں۔ مگر پچھلے چند سالوں میں محکمۂ زراعت نے موجودہ طریقوں کو سامنے رکھ کر مختلف تجربے کئے جو کامیاب رہے۔ چنانچہ اب کسان نئے طریقے سے تیار کی ہوئی کھاد اور اچھے بیجوں کے ذریعہ بھاری فصلیں حاصل کرنے لگے ہیں ۔ اِس کے علاوہ اب ایسی زمینوں پر بھی کھیت

428

بوئے جاتے ہیں جو پہلے زراعت کے قابل نہ تھیں ۔

اسمتھ۔ میرے خیال میں پاکستانی کسانوں کو کھیتوں میں مشینیں استعمال کرنی چاہئیں ۔ اس سے کام کی رفتار تیز ہو جائے گی اور انہیں اتنی سخت محنت بھی نہیں کرنی پڑے گی ۔ مثلاً آج کل اگر یہ لوگ ایک کھیت کو دو دن میں کاٹتے ہیں تو مشین سے اسی کھیت کو چند گھنٹوں میں کاٹ لیں گے ۔ اسی طرح دوسرے کام بھی آسان ہو جائیں گے ۔

رحیم۔ حکومت اس سلسلے میں بھی اقدامات کر رہی ہے ۔ محکمۂ زراعت نے کئی جگہ ایسے مرکز کھولے ہیں جہاں کسانوں کو بعض مشینوں کے استعمال کا طریقہ بتایا جاتا ہے ۔ یہ مرکز ان مشینوں کو خریدنے میں بھی مدد دیتے ہیں ۔ حکومت پوری کوشش کر رہی ہے کہ کسان بہت جلد کھیتوں میں مشینوں سے کام لینے لگیں ۔

اسمتھ۔ حکومت کا یہ اقدام بہت اچھا ہے مگر اس کے لئے کسانوں میں تعلیم بڑھانے کی بھی ضرورت ہے ۔ کیونکہ فصلیں بوئے، کھاد بنانے اور کھیتوں میں مختلف قسم کی مشینوں کے استعمال کے بارے میں اچھی اچھی کتابیں شائع ہوتی رہتی ہیں ۔ اگر کسانوں کو پڑھنا لکھنا آتا ہو تو ان کتابوں سے فائدہ اٹھا کر اپنی اور ملک کی حالت بہتر بنا سکتے ہیں ۔

رحیم۔ واقعی کسانوں کی ایک بڑی تعداد کو پڑھنا لکھنا نہیں آتا ۔ ہمارے ملک میں عام طور پر تعلیم کی کمی ہے ۔ چنانچہ حکومت نہ صرف کسانوں بلکہ عام لوگوں میں بھی تعلیم پھیلانے کے لئے جگہ جگہ اسکول کھول رہی ہے ۔ بچوں کے اسکولوں کے علاوہ ایسے مرکز بھی قائم کئے گئے ہیں جہاں بڑی عمر کے لوگوں کو تعلیم دی جاتی ہے ۔ حکومت فنی تعلیم دینے کے لئے بھی خاص اسکول کھول رہی ہے ۔

اسمتھ۔ ہر حکومت کو ایسے اقدامات ضرور کرنے چاہئیں ۔ خاص طور پر آپ کے ہاں زرعی پیداوار میں

429

اضافہ بہت ضروری تھا۔ کیونکہ جو روپیہ اناج کی درآمد پرخرچ ہوتا تھا اُسے اب نئی صنعتیں قائم کرنے اور عوام کی خوشحالی کے کاموں پر خرچ کیا جا سکتا ہے۔

رحیم۔ آپ بالکل صحیح فرماتے ہیں۔ پاکستان صنعتی ترقی کو بھی ضروری سمجھتا ہے۔ اِس سلسلے میں حکومت کے سامنے بہت سے منصوبے ہیں۔ مثال کے طور پر پاکستان کے سمندروں سے کافی مچھلی حاصل ہوتی ہے۔ چنانچہ حکومت کوشش کر رہی ہے کہ ایسے کارخانے قائم کئے جائیں جو اِن مچھلیوں کو ڈبوں میں بند کرکے غیر ممالک کے ہاتھ فروخت کریں۔ اِس سے ایک طرف تو ملک کی مالی حالت بہتر ہوگی۔ دوسری طرف سینکڑوں لوگوں کو کام ملے گا۔

اسمتھ۔ یہ منصوبہ تو بہت اچھا ہے کیونکہ مغربی ممالک میں کھانے کی اشیاء عام طور پر بند ڈبوں میں فروخت ہوتی ہیں۔ پاکستان میں مختلف قسم کے پھل ہوتے ہیں۔ وہ اِسی طرح اِن پھلوں کی بھی تجارت کرسکتا ہے۔

رحیم۔ جی ہاں۔ حکومت تجارت، صنعت، زراعت۔غرض کہ ہر شعبے میں ترقی کے لئے قدم اٹھا رہی ہے۔

اسمتھ۔ کشمیر کے متعلق آپ کا کیا خیال ہے۔ کیا اِس مسئلے کے حل ہونے کی کوئی اُمید ہے؟

رحیم۔ دنیا کا کون سا ایسا مسئلہ ہے جس کا کوئی حل نہ ہو۔ ہمیں اُمید ہے کہ دونوں ملکوں کے بڑے لیڈر آپس میں بات چیت کے ذریعہ دوستانہ طریقے پر یہ مسئلہ ضرور حل کر لیں گے کیونکہ جب تک یہ مسئلہ حل نہیں ہو جاتا، ہندوستان اور پاکستان دونوں اپنی فوجوں پر بھاری رقم خرچ کرتے رہیں گے۔ لیکن اگر یہ مسئلہ حل ہو جائے تو یہی رقم ملک کی اقتصادی اور سماجی ترقی کے کاموں پر خرچ کرسکتے ہیں۔

اسمتھ۔ کیا پاکستان کے مزدور اپنی یونین بنا سکتے ہیں؟

رحیم۔ کیوں نہیں ۔ ہمارے آئین میں بنیادی حقوق کا ایک مکمل باب موجود ہے ۔ جس میں پاکستانیوں

کو ساجی،معاشی اور پیشے سے متعلق انجمنیں بنانے کی پوری آزادی دی گئی ہے۔

اسمتھ۔ آپ کے ہاں مزدوروں سے متعلق جو قوانین ہیں، کیا وہ مزدوروں کے حقوق کی حفاظت کرتے ہیں؟

رحیم۔ جی ہاں، یہ قوانین مزدوروں کے حقوق کے ساتھ ساتھ مالکوں کے حقوق کی بھی حفاظت کرتے

ہیں۔ مثلاً ان قوانین میں مزدوروں کے روزانہ کام کرنے کے وقت، اُن کی تنخواہ، چھٹی اور بیماری

وغیرہ کا صاف الفاظ میں ذکر کیا گیا ہے۔ دوسری طرف مالکوں کے حقوق کا بھی خیال رکھا گیا

ہے ۔ یہ لوگ اپنی مرضی کے مطابق لوگوں کو ملازمت دے سکتے ہیں۔ مزدوروں کو پہلے سے

بتا کر اُنہیں ملازمت سے ہٹا سکتے ہیں۔اُنہیں اِسی قسم کے اور بہت سے اِختیارات بھی حاصل ہیں۔

اسمتھ۔ قائدِ اعظم محمد علی جناح کے مزار کی عمارت کا کیا ہوا؟ کیا یہ عمارت تیار ہوگئی ہے؟ کچھ عرصہ

ہوا میں نے اخباروں میں اِس کا نقشہ دیکھا تھا۔

رحیم۔ جی ہاں،اُن کے مزار کی عمارت تیار ہوگئی ہے۔ یہ بہت خوبصورت ہے۔ روزانہ بہت سے

لوگ اِسے دیکھنے کے لئے جاتے ہیں ۔ مزار کی عمارت کے چاروں طرف ایک خوبصورت باغ

لگایا گیا ہے۔ یہاں شام کو لوگ سیر کے لئے بھی آتے ہیں۔ آپ بھی اِس عمارت کو ضرور دیکھیں۔

اسمتھ۔ میں اگلے مہینے کراچی جا رہا ہوں۔ انشاءاللہ یہ عمارت ضرور دیکھوں گا ۔ اچّھا رحیم صاحب، اب

مجھے اجازت دیجئے ۔ انشا۔اللہ جلد ہی پھر ملاقات ہوگی۔

رحیم۔ ضرور ۔ ضرور! مجھے ہمیشہ آپ سے مل کر خوشی ہوتی ہے۔ آپ کو جب فرصت ملے ضرور

تشریف لائیں ۔

اسمتھ۔ خدا حافظ ۔

رحیم۔ خدا حافظ ۔

431

23.507.   Conversation Stimulus.

Topics may include:
1.   Pakistan's imports and exports.
2.   The division of India and Pakistan.
3.   The needs of a developing economy.
4.   The work of the United Nations.
5.   Problems faced by the United Nations.

əmnpəsənd A1	peace-loving
*əqvam Fpl	pl. /qəwm/
*əšya Fpl	pl. /šəy/
əTThanve A1	ninety-eight
əyn A1	exact, precise
əyTmi A1	atomic
əgrezi F2 [np] A1	English (language), English
bədtərin A1	worst
bərma M1 [np]	Burma
bəynwləqvami A1	international
bhari A1	heavy, weighty
cəmRa M2	leather, skin
cəwthai F2 [np] A1	quarter, one fourth part
cheanve [or /chyanve/ or /chəyanve/] A1	ninety-six
cin M1 [np]	China
daxyli A1	interior, internal
dəraməd F1	import
dostana A1	friendly, amicable
dosti F2	friendship
dwbara Adv	a second time, again
dyfai A1	pertaining to defence
fən M1	art, craft
fənni A1	technical
fəroxt F1	selling, sale
fəsad M1	disturbance, riot, strife
*fəsadat Mpl	pl. /fəsad/
fəykTri F2	factory
fyrqəvarana A1	sectarian, communal
gəRbəR F1 [np]	confusion, mix-up, disorder, mess
hwjum M1	crowd, throng, mob
jan F1	life, soul, spirit
jəlsa M2	meeting, gathering, assembly
jənrəl M1 A1	general (common), general (military)
jwmhuria [or /jəmhuria/] F1 [np]	republic
karəvai F2	proceeding, action, working, operation
karxana M2	factory, workshop
kəmāDər yncif M1	commander-in-chief
kəmišən M1	commission
kəmyunysT M/F1 A1	Communist
khal F1	skin, hide

loha M2 [np]	iron
malyk M1	owner, master, proprietor
maršəl la M1 [np]	martial law
mazi M1 [np]	the past
mənzur PA1	accepted, sanctioned, approved, agreed to
mənzuri F2	consent, approval, sanction, acceptance
məzdur M1	labourer, worker
mwahyda [literary: /mwahəda/] M2	treaty, contract, alliance
mwəssyr A1	effective, efficacious
mwhajyr [or /məhajyr/] M1	refugee
*mwhajyrin [or /məhajyrin/] Mpl	pl. /mwhajyr/
mwstəqbyl M1 [np]	the future
mwštərka [literary: /mwštərəka/] A1	shared, in common, joint
mylavəT F1	mixture, adulteration
mysTər M1	mister
nafyz PA1	enforced, put into effect, promulgated
nynnanve A1	ninety-nine
parliməyT F1	parliament
pəTsən M1 [np]	jute
pəydavar F1 [np]	produce, yield, production
pəyr M1	foot
peša M2	occupation, profession
qayd M1	leader
qətl M1 [np]	killing, slaying, murder
rəftar F1	speed, pace
rəwšən A1	illuminated, splendid, bright
roktham F1 [np]	stop, check, restraint
rui F2 [np]	cotton wool
rwkna [I: /rokna/: If]	to stop (intrans.)
səbəb M1	reason, cause
sədarət F1	presidency, chairmanship
səfir M1	ambassador, envoy
səmaji A1	social, societal
sənət F1	industry
səttanve A1	ninety-seven
siməyT M1 [or F1]	cement
sut M1 [np]	cotton thread
suti A1	made of cotton
[ke] swpwrd PA1 Comp Post	entrusted to, committed to, handed over to, in the care of
swst A1	slow, sluggish, lazy
syfarətxana M2	embassy
syfaryš F1	recommendation, intercession

*syfaryšat Fpl	pl. /syfaryš/	
šəhadət F1	martyrdom	
šəhid M/F1	martyr	
šəhri M/F1 A1	citizen, urban	
šəy F1	thing, article, commodity	
təavwn M1 [np]	cooperation, mutual aid	
tənxa[h] F1	salary	
tərəqqiyafta A1	progressive, advanced	
təvəqqo F1	expectation, hope	
un F1 [np]	wool	
uni A1	woollen	
xamoš A1	silent, quiet	
xamoši F2	silence, quiet	
xaryja A1	external, exterior, foreign	
xwšgəvar A1	pleasant, delightful	
yhtyram M1 [np]	respect, honour, veneration, reverence	
ynqylab M1	revolution, upheaval, change	
yqdam M1	step	
*yqdamat Mpl	pl. /yqdam/	
yqtysadi A1	economic	
ysməglȳg F1 [np]	smuggling	
yzafa M2	addition, increase, augment	
zae [common: /zaya/] PA1	wasted, lost, spoiled	
zəbərdəst A1	vigorous, powerful, strict	
zəbərdəsti F2 Adv	vigour, power, strictness, tyranny, force; by force	
zərəi A1	agricultural	
zəxira M2	stock, store, hoard	
zymmedar A1	responsible, answerable	

A page from a manuscript of Mir Hasan's narrative
poem "Sihru-l-Bayan." This copy is dated 1797.

24.000. ESSAY

اُردو ادَب کی مختصر تاریخ

(پہلا حصہ)

اُردو آریائی زبانوں میں سے ایک زبان ہے ۔ اِس کی ابتدا کب ، کیسے اور کہاں ہوئی یہ ایک طویل بحث ہے ۔ بعض محققین کے خیال کے مطابق یہ زبان غزنویوں کے دَورِ حکومت میں پنجاب میں شروع ہوگئی تھی ۔ لیکن اکثر محققین اِس رائے سے اتفاق کرتے ہیں کہ اُردو مغربی ہندی کی نئی شکل کا نام ہے ۔ جو دِلّی اور میرٹھ کے علاقوں میں بولی جاتی تھی اور جس کا تعلّق شورسینی پراکرت سے ہے ۔ اُردو کی قواعد اور اِس میں ہندی الفاظ کی کثرت اِس بات کا ثبوت ہے کہ اِس کی اصل ہندی ہے ۔ اگرچہ بعد میں یہ زبان فارسی اور عربی سے بہت متاثر ہوئی۔ چونکہ ہندوستان پر عربوں اور ترکوں نے حملے کئے ۔ چنانچہ اِن حملہ آور فوجوں کی زبان اور مقامی لوگوں کی زبان ایک دوسرے سے متاثّر ہونے لگی ۔ اِس طرح ایک نئی زبان وجود میں آنی شروع ہوئی۔ جس نے رفتہ رفتہ اُردو کی شکل اختیار کرلی ۔ غالباً اِسی وجہ سے اِس زبان کا نام اُردو ہے ۔ کیونکہ ترکی زبان میں اُردو لشکر کو کہتے ہیں ۔

تیرہویں صدی عیسوی میں ترکوں نے شمالی ہندوستان میں اپنی سلطنت قائم کی ۔ اُن کا دارالحکومت دِلّی تھا ۔ چنانچہ دِلّی اور اُس کے آس پاس کے علاقوں کی زبان حملہ آوروں کی زبان سے متاثّر ہوئی ۔ امیر خسرو جو ایک زبردست عالم اور شاعر تھے، اِسی دَور سے تعلّق رکھتے ہیں۔ اُنہوں نے فارسی ، ہندی ، عربی اور ترکی کے علاوہ اُس زمانے کی اُردو میں بھی شعر کہے ۔

چودھویں صدی عیسوی میں گجرات اور دکن کا علاقہ بھی سلطنتِ دہلی کے تحت آگیا۔ اس طرح یہ
زبان وہاں بھی پھیلنی شروع ہوئی۔ چودھویں صدی کے آخر میں دہلی کی سلطنت کا قبضہ حیدرآباد اور
گجرات پر کمزور پڑ گیا۔ چنانچہ یہ ریاستیں آزاد ہوگئیں۔ یہاں کے بادشاہوں کی سرپرستی کی وجہ سے
اس زبان نے رفتہ رفتہ ادبی حیثیت اختیار کرلی۔ سولہویں صدی عیسوی میں نثر اور نظم کا آغاز
ہوا۔ اس دور کی اردو موجودہ اردو سے کافی ملتی جلتی ہے۔

اس سے پہلے کہ ہم اس دور کی شاعری کا جائزہ لیں اور اردو زبان کے شعراء کا ذکر کریں،
یہ بتا دینا ضروری سمجھتے ہیں کہ ان چند صفحوں میں اردو کے صرف بڑے بڑے شعراء کا تعارف
کرانے کی کوشش کی گئی ہے۔ ان شاعروں کے علاوہ اور بھی سینکڑوں اچھے شاعر موجود ہیں
جن کا ذکر نہیں کیا گیا۔ کیونکہ اردو کے تمام شعراء کا یہاں ذکر کرنا بہت مشکل ہے۔

دکن کے ابتدائی شعراء میں قلی قطب شاہ، نصرتی، وجہی، غواصی اور ولی دکنی بہت
مشہور ہیں۔ ان میں ولی دکنی نے حقیقتاً اردو شاعری کی بنیاد رکھی۔ اٹھارہویں صدی عیسوی
کے شروع میں ولی، دکن سے دہلی چلے آئے۔ جہاں علم و ادب کے بہت سے قدردان موجود
تھے۔ ولی کا کلام دہلی میں بہت مقبول ہوا۔ ان کے کلام میں سادگی اور روانی ہے۔ ان
کی زبان دوسرے دکنی شعراء کے مقابلے میں فارسی اور عربی سے زیادہ متاثر ہے۔ جس وقت
ولی دہلی آئے تو وہاں گلشن، آرزو اور فقیر جیسے بڑے شعراء موجود تھے۔ دہلی کی شاعری
پر ابتدا ہی سے فارسی کا اثر تھا۔ جس کی وجہ یہ معلوم ہوتی ہے کہ مغل دربار کی زبان
فارسی تھی۔ شاہ حاتم اور مظہر جان جاناں اس دور کے دو بڑے استاد ہیں جنہوں نے
اردو کو فارسی کے قریب لانے کی کوشش کی۔

اردو شاعری کا دوسرا دور اٹھارہویں صدی کے وسط سے شروع ہوتا ہے۔ اس دور

438

میں زبان اور شاعری دونوں نے بہت ترقی کی ۔ اس دَور میں میر جیسے غزل گو اور سودا جیسے قصیدہ گو اساتذہ پیدا ہوئے ۔ میر کی زبان بہت سادہ اور پُر اثر ہے ۔ بات اس سادگی سے کہتے ہیں کہ ایک معمولی آدمی بھی اُن کا کلام پڑھ کر لطف اٹھاتا ہے ۔ اُن کی شاعری میں بہت درد ہے ۔ سودا نے زبان اور خیالات کے لحاظ سے قصیدے کو ایک بلند مقام بخشا۔ اِن دونوں اساتذہ کے علاوہ درد ، سوز اور قائم بھی اس دَور کے بڑے شاعر ہیں ۔ یہ تمام شعراء غزل کے استاد ہیں ۔ اِن سے زبان اور شاعری کو بہت عروج حاصل ہوا۔ میر حسن کی مثنوی "سحرالبیان" بھی اِسی دَور کی یادگار ہے ۔ یہ مثنوی آج بھی اردو زبان کا شاہکار سمجھی جاتی ہے ۔ اِس کی زبان بہت آسان اور افکار بہت سادہ ہیں ۔ اردو کے کئی تذکرے بھی اِسی دَور میں لکھے گئے ۔ جن میں میر اور قائم کے تذکرے خاص طور پر قابل ذکر ہیں ۔

اِس زمانے میں مغل سلطنت کا زوال شروع ہو چکا تھا ۔ چنانچہ دہلی کے اکثر شعراء دہلی چھوڑ کر لکھنؤ جانے لگے ۔ جہاں کے نواب اور اُن کے امراء شعراء کی بہت قدر کرتے۔ اِس دَور میں بڑے بڑے شاعر پیدا ہوئے ، جنہوں نے غزل ، قصیدہ ، ہجو ، رباعی ۔ غرض کہ ہر صنفِ سخن میں شعر کہے ۔ اُن کی شاعری سے زبان کو بہت ترقی ہوئی ۔ اِن میں بعض شعراء ایسے بھی ہیں جنہوں نے اپنی شاعرانہ صلاحیتوں کو غلط طریقے سے استعمال کیا۔ مثلاً انشا اور مصحفی اِس دَور کے دو بڑے استاد ہیں ۔ وہ ایک دوسرے سے شعروں میں مذاق کرتے تھے ۔ رفتہ رفتہ یہ مذاق اِس قدر بڑھا کہ وہ اپنی شاعرانہ اہمیت کھو بیٹھے اور اُنہوں نے زبان و ادب کی وہ خدمت نہ کی، جو وہ کر سکتے تھے ۔ انشا زبان کے بادشاہ تھے ۔ اردو اور فارسی کے علاوہ عربی ، ترکی اور دوسری بہت سی زبانوں میں بھی شعر کہتے تھے ۔ مصحفی کی عظمت اِس بات سے ظاہر ہے کہ وہ اردو زبان کے کئی بڑے شعراء کے استاد تھے ۔

439

جرأت اور رنگین بھی اس دور کے دو بڑے شاعر ہیں۔ اُنہوں نے معشوق کے حُسن کی تعریف اس
کھلے انداز سے کرنی شروع کی کہ بعض اوقات تو بات عریانی کی حد تک پہنچ جاتی تھی۔ مختصر یہ کہ
اس دور کی شاعری اُس زمانے کے معاشرے کی پوری تصویر کھینچتی ہے۔ اس زمانے کے شعراء
نے مختلف اصنافِ سخن میں نئے نئے تجربے کئے جن میں سے کچھ کامیاب بھی رہے۔

اسی زمانے میں اردو کے ایک اور بڑے شاعر بھی گذرے ہیں۔ جن کا نام نظیرؔ اکبر آبادی
ہے۔ نظیرؔ کسی دربار سے تعلّق نہ رکھتے تھے۔ اُن کے دوستوں کے حلقے میں امیر، غریب،
جاہل ، عالم ، ہندو، مسلمان۔ سب ہی شامل تھے ۔ وہ گلیوں بازاروں میں گھومتے پھرتے
تھے۔ نظیرؔ معمولی اور عام موضوعات پر شعر کہتے تھے ۔ اُن کے پاس الفاظ کا ذخیرہ اتنا تھا کہ
شاید ہی کسی دوسرے شاعر کے پاس ہو ۔ وہ خالص ہندوستانی شاعر تھے ۔ وہ معمولی معمولی باتوں
کو بڑے دلچسپ انداز میں بیان کرتے تھے ۔ اُنہوں نے مختلف میلوں اور تہواروں جیسے عید
وغیرہ اور دیگر چھوٹے چھوٹے عام موضوعات پر نظمیں لکھی ہیں ۔ اُن کے کلام میں عریانی سے
سے کر نصیحتوں تک ہر موضوع ملے گا۔ وہ مناظرِ قدرت کا نہایت دلکش نقشہ کھینچتے ہیں۔

جیسا کہ پہلے بیان کیا گیا ہے کہ دہلی کی سلطنت زوال پر تھی اور لکھنؤ کا دربار شعراء کا مرکز
بن گیا تھا۔ کیونکہ وہاں شعراء کے بہت سے قدردان موجود تھے ۔ یہی وجہ تھی کہ دہلی کے
شعراء بھی لکھنؤ کھنچے چلے آ رہے تھے ۔ لکھنؤ کے شعراء نے خیالات اور انکار کی بجائے
زبان پر زیادہ زور دیا ۔ ناسخؔ اس اسکول کے بانی ہیں ۔ ناسخؔ کا کلام محاوروں اور نئی نئی اصطلاحات
سے بھرا ہوا ہے۔ اگرچہ بعض اوقات پیچیدہ محاوروں کی وجہ سے شعر کے معنی سمجھنے میں
مشکل ہوتی ہے لیکن اس میں کوئی شک نہیں کہ اُن کی شاعری نے زبان اور قواعد کی بہت
خدمت کی ۔ اس اسکول کے دوسرے بڑے شاعر آتشؔ کا کلام ناسخؔ کے مقابلے میں آسان

اور پُر اثر ہے۔ وہ محاورات کا استعمال بہت خوبصورتی سے کرتے ہیں۔ روز مرّہ کی زبان آتش

کے کلام میں ایک خاص لطف پیدا کرتی ہے۔ نسیم اس عہد کے ایک اور مشہور شاعر ہیں

جن کی مثنوی "گلزارِ نسیم" اردو ادب میں خاص مقام رکھتی ہے۔ اس کی زبان بہت آسان

اور کہانی بہت دلچسپ ہے۔

لکھنؤ کے اس دور کے ساتھ ساتھ دہلی کی شاعری کا بھی ایک نیا دور شروع ہوتا ہے۔

اس دور کو اردو ادب میں بہت اہمیت حاصل ہے۔ اس دور میں غزل اپنے عروج کو پہنچی۔

قصیدے نے بھی خوب ترقی کی۔ اس دور کی زبان اور شاعری فارسی سے بہت متأثر ہے۔ فلسفے

اور تصوّف کے مضامین نے غزل کو ایک نیا رنگ بخشا۔ غالب جو اردو شاعری کے سب سے

بڑے شاعر مانے جاتے ہیں اس دور سے تعلق رکھتے ہیں۔ غالب کی سب سے بڑی خوبی اُن

کا اندازِ بیان ہے۔ وہ معمولی سی بات بھی اس انوکھے انداز سے بیان کرتے ہیں کہ لطف

آجاتا ہے۔ ساری اردو شاعری میں یہ فنی کسی دوسرے شاعر کو حاصل نہیں۔ اپنے اندازِ بیان

کے بارے میں وہ خود فرماتے ہیں ؎

ہیں اور بھی دنیا میں سخنور بہت اچھے

کہتے ہیں کہ غالب کا ہے اندازِ بیاں اور

غالب فارسی اور اردو کے مستند عالم تھے۔ نثر اور نظم دونوں پر مہارت حاصل تھی۔ فارسی

زبان میں بھی ان کا پورا دیوان موجود ہے۔ قصیدہ، مرثیہ، غزل، رباعی-غرض کہ ہر صنف سخن

میں شعر کہے۔ لیکن ان کا اصل میدان غزل ہی ہے۔ غزل میں فلسفیانہ خیالات و افکار بہت

خوبصورتی سے بیان کرتے ہیں۔ بڑے سے بڑے موضوع کو ایک شعر میں اس انداز سے پیش

کردیتے ہیں کہ حیرت ہوتی ہے۔ غالب کا مطالعۂ زندگی اتنا وسیع اور گہرا ہے کہ جو بات

بھی کہتے ہیں اُس کی صحیح تصویر کھینچ دیتے ہیں ۔ اُن کے خیالات اِتنے بلند اور مضامین اِس قدر ہیں کہ شاید ہی کسی دوسرے شاعر کے ہاں مل سکیں ۔ اُن کی مقبولیت اِس بات سے ظاہر ہے کہ تقریباً ہر اُردو پڑھنے والے کو اُن کے بیسیوں اشعار یاد ہوں گے ۔

غالب کے علاوہ ذوق ، مومن ، شاہ نصیر اور ظفر بھی اِس عہد کے مشہور شاعر ہیں ۔ اِن میں ذوق کو قصیدے میں وہی مقام حاصل ہے جو غالب کو غزل میں ۔ ذوق کی زبان بہت آسان اور سادہ ہے ۔ الفاظ کا انتخاب اِتنا اچھا ہے کہ شعروں میں موسیقی محسوس ہوتی ہے ۔ مومن غزل کے شاعر ہیں اور اپنا خاص مقام رکھتے ہیں ۔ عشق و محبت کی باتیں بہت خوبصورتی سے بیان کرتے ہیں ۔

اِس سے پہلے کہ ہم اُردو کے اگلے دَور کا ذکر کریں، مرثیے کا ذکر کرنا ضروری ہے ۔ غزل کی طرح مرثیہ بھی تھوڑا ہی سے اُردو شاعری میں موجود تھا ۔ دکنی شعراء سے لے کر میر ، سودا اور غالب تک سب ہی نے مرثیے لکھے ۔ لیکن اِن کے مرثیوں کو کوئی بلند مقام حاصل نہ ہوا بلکہ مرثیہ گو شاعر کے بارے میں کہا جاتا تھا کہ " بگڑا شاعر مرثیہ گو" ۔

لیکن انیس اور دبیر نے مرثیے لکھ کر یہ ثابت کر دیا کہ صرف بہترین شاعر ہی مرثیہ گو ہو سکتا ہے ۔ انیس کو زبان پر جو قدرت حاصل تھی وہ کسی دوسرے شاعر کو نہیں تھی ۔ زبان اور الفاظ انیس کے غلام معلوم ہوتے ہیں ۔ اُن کی زبان نہایت ہی آسان ہے ۔ ایک ہی واقعہ کو دس مختلف انداز سے پیش کرتے ہیں ۔ لیکن کہیں بھی دلچسپی کم نہیں ہوتی اور شاعری کا معیار بھی گرنے نہیں پاتا ۔ انیس جذبات کے مصّور ہیں ۔ اُن کے اشعار سے کردار کی پوری تصویر سامنے آجاتی ہے ۔ دریا ، جنگل ، شام اور دوپہر وغیرہ کا منظر اِس خوبصورتی سے کھینچتے ہیں کہ کسی مصّور کا قلم بھی ایسی تصویر نہیں بنا سکتا ۔ میدانِ جنگ اور لڑائی کے مناظر کو ایسے بیان کرتے ہیں ۔ جیسے وہ خود میدانِ جنگ میں موجود ہوں ۔ وہ مشکل سے مشکل مضمون کو

442

نہایت آسان زبان میں بیان کرتے ہیں۔ انیس کے مقابلے میں دبیر کی شاعری اور زبان مشکل ہے۔

وہ اپنے رنگ کے استاد ہیں۔ لیکن زبان کی روانی اور مشکل بات کو آسان انداز میں پیش کرنے میں

وہ مہارت نہیں رکھتے جو انیس کو حاصل ہے۔ لیکن دونوں مرثیہ گوئی کے بادشاہ ہیں۔ ان کی شاعری

ہمّت، صبر، بہادری اور ایسی ہی دیگر اخلاقی باتوں کا سبق دیتی ہے۔

۱۸۵۷ء میں لکھنؤ کی حکومت کو زوال آگیا۔ ۱۸۵۷ء میں غدر کے بعد دہلی کی سلطنت بھی

ختم ہوگئی اور آخری مغل بادشاہ بہادر شاہ ظفر کو قید کرکے برما بھیج دیا گیا۔ اس طرح دہلی اور

لکھنؤ دونوں جگہ شعراء کی سرپرستی ختم ہوگئی۔ چنانچہ اب شعراء قریب کی ریاستوں میں جانے لگے۔

بعض ریاستوں نے اُن کی بہت سرپرستی کی۔ خاص طور پر رام پور کے نوابوں نے شعراء اور علماء

کی بہت قدر کی۔ داغ دہلوی، امیر مینائی، جلال لکھنوی اس دور کے بڑے شاعر ہیں۔ اس

دور میں زبان بھی آسان ہوگئی۔ مشکل تشبیہات اور پیچیدہ محاورات کم ہوگئے۔ انیس اور

دبیر کے مرثیوں نے شاعری کا میدان بہت وسیع کر دیا تھا۔ جس کا اثر یہ ہوا کہ حسن و عشق کے

علاوہ شاعری کو اب اور بھی بہت سے مضامین مل گئے۔ جیسے ماں باپ کی محبت، مناظرِ قدرت

اور میدانِ جنگ وغیرہ۔ داغ دہلوی اس دور کے سب سے بڑے غزل گو ہیں۔ اُن کی زبان

بہت اچھی اور آسان ہے۔ چنانچہ آج بھی اُن کی زبان مستند مانی جاتی ہے۔ امیر مینائی شاعر

ہونے کے ساتھ ساتھ ایک زبردست عالم بھی تھے۔ اُن کی شاعری داغ کے مقابلے میں مشکل

ہے۔ مگر اُن کے قصیدے داغ کے قصیدوں سے بہتر ہیں۔ شاعری کے علاوہ "امیر اللغات" سے

بھی اُن کے علم کا اندازہ ہوتا ہے۔

۱۸۵۷ء کے غدر کے بعد ملک غیر ملکیوں۔ یعنی انگریزوں۔ کے ہاتھ میں چلا گیا۔ غدر نے جہاں

ملک کی سیاسی، اقتصادی اور معاشی حالت پر اثر ڈالا وہاں علمی اور ادبی دنیا کو بھی متأثر کیا۔

انگریزی تعلیم کا رواج ہوا۔ شعراء میں گل و بلبل کی شاعری کی بجائے قومی شاعری کا رجحان پیدا ہوا۔ انہوں نے قوم کو بیدار کرنے اور اپنے ملک کو آزاد کرانے کے لئے نظمیں لکھنی شروع کیں۔ آزاد اور حالی نے اپنی شاعری سے قوم میں ایک نئی روح پھونک دی۔

حالی ، آزاد ، اسمٰعیل میرٹھی اور اکبر الہ آبادی اس دور کے بڑے شعراء میں سے ہیں۔ حالی نے اپنی نظموں میں مسلمانوں کی گذشتہ عظمت کے واقعات دوہرائے۔ اسمٰعیل میرٹھی نے بچوں کے لئے چھوٹی چھوٹی آسان نظمیں لکھیں۔ اکبر الہ آبادی طنز و مزاح کے بادشاہ تھے۔ انگریزی افعال کو اپنی نظموں میں بہت خوبصورتی سے استعمال کرتے تھے۔ اس دور کے اکثر شعراء کا مقصد معاشرے کی اصلاح اور قوم کو آزادی کا احساس دلانا تھا۔ کیونکہ انہوں نے محسوس کیا کہ شاعری کو محض گل و بلبل کے افسانوں تک محدود رکھنا قوم کو گمراہی کا سبق دینا ہے۔ چنانچہ انہوں نے پرانے طرز کو چھوڑ کر نیا انداز اختیار کیا۔ اس دور کی شاعری نے اردو کے آنے والے دور پر بھی بہت اثر ڈالا۔ اس دور میں اقبال اور چکبست جیسے شاعر پیدا ہوئے۔ اقبال بنیادی طور پر فلسفی شاعر ہیں۔ وہ زندگی کے ہر پہلو پر فلسفیانہ نظر ڈالتے ہیں۔ حالی کی طرح ان کی شاعری بھی مسلمانوں کی گذشتہ عظمت ، اسلام کے فلسفۂ زندگی اور موجودہ زمانے کے حالات سے تعلق رکھتی ہے۔ ان کے دل میں قوم کا درد تھا۔ یہی وجہ ہے کہ ان کی شاعری ایک خاص مقصد رکھتی ہے۔ ان کی اس قومی محبت کی وجہ سے آج بھی ساری قوم ان کا احترام کرتی ہے۔ قومی شاعری کے علاوہ اس دور میں غزل نے بھی بہت ترقی کی۔ حضرت موہانی ، فانی بدایونی ، ریاض خیر آبادی ، اصغر گنڈوی ، جگر مراد آبادی ، جوش ملیح آبادی اور فراق گورکھپوری اس دور کے بڑے شاعر ہیں۔ ان شعراء نے پرانے اساتذہ کے رنگ میں غزلیں کہیں۔ لیکن بے شمار نئے مضامین بھی شامل کئے۔ ان کی غزلوں میں وہ تمام خوبیاں موجود ہیں جو ایک بہترین غزل گو کے ہاں ہونی چاہئیں۔

اردو کے موجودہ شعراء کو تین گروہوں میں تقسیم کیا جا سکتا ہے۔ شعراء کا ایک گروہ تو محض

پرانے اساتذہ کی تقلید میں شعر کہتا ہے اور شاعری برائے شاعری کرتا ہے ۔ دوسرا گروہ وہ ہے جو اگرچہ پرانے اساتذہ کی پیروی میں نظمیں اور غزلیں لکھتا ہے لیکن اُن کی شاعری میں افکار و خیالات نئے ہیں۔ تیسرا گروہ آزاد نظم لکھنے والوں کا ہے ۔ آزاد نظم اگرچہ زیادہ مقبول نہیں، پھر بھی بعض شعراء کی کچھ نظمیں شاہکار کی حیثیت رکھتی ہیں۔ سیاست ، مذہب ، اشتراکیت ، سامراجیت اور سرمایہ داری دوسرے اور تیسرے گروہ کے خاص موضوعات ہیں ۔ ان میں کچھ شعراء مغرب کی شاعری اور اُس کی تہذیب سے متاثر ہیں ۔ اور کچھ اپنی پرانی روایات کو ہی قوم کا سرمایہ اور فخر تصور کرتے ہیں ۔

پاکستان اور ہندوستان میں شاعری کسی خاص طبقے تک محدود نہیں ہے ۔ یہاں کسان ، سرکاری ملازم ، اعلیٰ عہدے دار ، امیر و غریب ، پروفیسر ، ڈاکٹر۔ غرض کہ ہر شخص شعر و شاعری سے دلچسپی رکھتا ہے ۔ اور بہت سے لوگ خود بھی شعر کہتے ہیں ۔ موجودہ شعراء کی فہرست بہت طویل ہے ۔ اسی لئے یہاں درج نہیں کی گئی ۔

مختصر یہ کہ اُردو شاعری کا مستقبل تاریک نہیں ۔ شعراء نئے نئے تجربے کر رہے ہیں، اور اس طرح نئے نئے افکار و خیالات سے اُردو ادب کے خزانے میں برابر اضافہ ہو رہا ہے ۔

آریائی	aryai A1	Aryan
طویل	təvil A1	long, lengthy, extended
محققین	*mwhəqqyqin Mpl [pl. /mwhəqqyq/]	researchers, investigators
غزنوی	γəznəvi M1 A1	Ghaznavi, the dynasty to which Mahmud of Ghazna belonged (invaded India c. 1000 A.D.)
ہندی	hyndi F2 [np] M1 A1	Hindi (language); Indian (adj. and occasionally noun)
میرٹھ	merəTh M1 [np]	Meerut, a city in North India
شور سینی پراکرت	šəwrəseni prakryt F1	Shawraseni Prakrit, one of the Prakrit dialects which developed from -- or existed side by side with -- Sanskrit
قواعد	*qəvayd Mpl [pl. /qayda/]; F1	rules, regulations, regular practice; grammar
کثرت	kəsrət F1 [np]	abundance, plenty
متأثر	mwtəəssyr PA1	affected, influenced, impressed
تُرک	twrk M1 A1	Turk, Turkish
غالباً	γalybən Adv	most probably, in all likelihood, perhaps
تُرکی	twrki M1 [np] F2 [np] A1	Turkey; Turkish (language); Turkish (adj.)
لشکر	ləškər M1	army, military force
دارالحکومت	darwlhwkumət M1	capital
امیرخسرو	əmir xwsrəw PN	Amir Khusraw, an Indian poet who wrote mostly in Persian; 1254-1324

گجرات	gwjrat M1 [np]	Gujarat, a province on the west-central coast of India
آخر	axyr M1	end, latter portion
حیدرآباد	həydərabad M1 [np]	Haydarabad, a province (nearly synonymous with /dəkən/) and also the name of the capital city of that province; also a city in Sindh
سرپرستی	sərpərəsti F2	patronage
ادبی	ədəbi A1	literary
نثر	nəsr F1	prose
جلنا	jwlna	to meet, mix [used only in the echo compound /mylna jwlna/ "to mix, meet, mingle, intermingle"]
صفحه	səfha M2	page
ابتدائی	ybtydai A1	beginning, introductory, elementary, early
قلی قطب شاه	qwli qwtb šah PN	Muhammad Qutb Quli Shah, king of Golkonda; reigned 1580-1611
نصرتی	nwsrəti PN	Muhammad Nusrat Nusrati; d. 1674
وجهی	vəjhi PN	Mulla Vajhi; d. between 1657 and 1671
غواصی	yəvvasi PN	Ghavvasi; d. before 1650
ولی دکنی	vəli dəkəni PN	Vali Muhammad Vali Dakani; 1668-1707
حقیقتاً	həqiqətən Adv	really, in reality, in fact
قدردان	qədrdan [or /qədrdā/] M/F1 A1	appreciator, connoiseur, one who knows the value of something
کلام	kəlam M1	word, speech, discourse; poetry, works (of a poet); theology

447

مقبول	məqbul PA1	accepted, approved, popular
سادگی	sadgi F2	simplicity, plainness
روانی	rəvani F2	fluency, smoothness
دکنی	dəkəni A1	Deccani, of the Deccan
گلشن	gwlšən PN	Shaykh Sad-ullah Gulshan; d. 1727
آرزو	arzu PN	Siraj-ud-din Ali Khan Arzu; 1689-1756
فقیر	fəqir PN	Mir Shams-ud-din Faqir; dates unknown
شاہ حاتم	šah hatym PN	Zuhur-ud-din Hatim; 1699-1781
مظہر جان جاناں	məzhər jan janā PN	Shams-ud-din Mazhar Jan Janan; 1700-1781
اُستاد	wstad M1	teacher, master, expert
وسط	vəst M1 [np]	middle, centre
میر	mir PN	Mir Muhammad Taqi Mir; 1722-1810
غزل گو	ɣəzəlgo M1 A1	/ɣəzəl/-composer, /ɣəzəl/-composing (see below)
سودا	səwda PN	Mirza Muhammad Rafi Sawda; 1713-1780(-81)
قصیدہ گو	qəsidəgo M1 A1	/qəsida/-composer, /qəsida/-composing (see below)
اساتذہ	*əsatyza Mpl [pl. /wstad/]	teachers, masters, experts
پُر اثر	pwrəsər A1	effective, impressive
خیالات	*xyalat Mpl [pl. /xyal/]	thoughts, ideas

تقصیده	qəsida M2	a type of poem, usually written in praise of someone
بلند	bələnd [or /bwlənd/] A1	high, exalted, great
بخشنا	bəxšna [Ic: /ə/]	to give, bestow, grant; forgive
درد	dərd PN	Khvaja Mir Dard; 1719-1785
سوز	soz PN	Muhammad Mir Soz; 1730-1798
قائم	qaym PN	Shaykh Muhammad Qayam-ud-din Qaym; 1730-1792(-93)
غزل	γəzəl F1	"γəzəl," a type of poem roughly corresponding to the sonnet or ode
عروج	wruj M1 [np]	height, climax, zenith
میرحسن	mir həsən PN	Mir Ghulam Hasan; 1727-1786
مثنوی	məsnəvi F2	a type of epic or narrative poem
سحرالبیان	syhrwlbəyan	the name of Mir Hasan's /məsnəvi/; 1785
شاہکار	šahkar [or /šəhkar/] M1	masterpiece
افکار	*əfkar Mpl [pl. /fykr/]	thoughts, ideas
تذکرہ	təzkyra M2	mention; biographical notice, book of brief biographies of poets, etc.
زوال	zəval M1 [np]	decline, decadence, wane, fall
لکھنؤ	ləkhnəu M1 [np]	Lucknow, a city in north-central India
ہجو	həjv F1	ridicule, a poem written to ridicule someone
رباعی	rwbai F2	quatrain, a four line poem

449

صنف	synf F1	kind, sort, species, category, genre
سخن	swxən M1 [np]	speech, eloquence
شاعرانہ	šayrana A1	poetic
صلاحیت	səlahiət F1	capability, ability, capacity, talent
انشا	ynša PN	Insha Allah Khan Insha; 1756(-58)-1817
مصحفی	mwshəfi PN	Shaykh Ghulam Hamdani Mushafi; 1750-1824
نذاق	məzaq M1	joke; (literary) taste
جرأت	jwrət PN	Shaykh Qalandar Bakhsh Jurat; 1743-1810
رنگین	rə̄gin PN	Saadat Yar Khan Rangin; 1756-1834
معشوق	mašuq M1	beloved, sweetheart
حسن	hwsn M1 [np]	beauty, handsomeness
انداز	əndaz M1	way, manner, mode, style
اوقات	*əwqat Mpl [pl. /vəqt/]	times
عریانی	wryani F2	nudity, lewdness, nakedness
اصناف	*əsnaf Fpl [pl. /synf/]	kinds, sorts, species, genres
نظیر اکبر آبادی	nəzir əkbərabadi PN	Vali Muhammad Nazir Akbarabadi; 1740-1830
حلقہ	həlqa M2	circle, group; link (in a chain); ward (of a city)
جاہل	jahyl A1	ignorant, illiterate
گھومنا	ghumna [IIc: /w/]	to turn, revolve, circle, wander

450

پھرنا	phyrna [I: /pherna/: Ie]	to turn, turn back, turn away, wander, rove
موضوعات	*mawzuat Mpl [pl. /mawzu/]	subjects, topics
خالص	xalys A1	pure, genuine, unadulterated
ہندوستانی	hyndostani F2 [np] M1 A1	Hindustani (language); Indian (adj. and occasionally noun)
میلہ	mela M2	fair, large concourse of people
تہوار	tyhvar [or /teohar/] M1	celebration, festival (usually religious)
عید	id F1	"Id, " the name of two great yearly Muslim religious celebrations
نصیحت	nasihat F1	(moral) advice, counsel; lesson, warning
مناظر	*manazyr Mpl [pl. /manzər/]	scenes, sights
قدرت	qwdrat F1	nature; power, ability
کھچنا	khỹcna [or /khycna/] [I: /khẽcna/: Ie]	to be pulled, drawn, attracted
ناسخ	nasyx PN	Shaykh Imam Bakhsh Nasikh; 1774-1838
محاورہ	mwhavra [literary: /mwhavəra/] M2	idiom, expression
اصطلاحات	*ystylahat Fpl [pl. /ystylah/]	(technical) terms
پیچیدہ	pecida A1	complicated, complex, difficult, twisted, involved
شک	šak M1	doubt, uncertainty, suspicion

451

اتش	atyš PN	Khvaja Haydar Ali Atish; 1767-1846
محاورات	*mwhavrat [literary: /mwhavərat/] Mpl [pl. /mwhavra/]	idioms, expressions
روزمرّہ	rozmərra M1 [np] A1 Adv	daily usage, ordinary conversation, daily allowance, daily wages; daily
خوبصورتی	xubsurti F2	beauty, prettiness
نسیم	nəsim PN	Pandit Daya Shankar Kawl Nasim; 1811-1843
گلزارِ نسیم	gwlzare nəsim	the name of Nasim's /məsnəvi/; 1838
تصوّف	təsəvvwf M1 [np]	Sufism, mysticism
غالب	yalyb PN	Mirza Asad-ullah Khan Ghalib; 1797-1869
انوکھا	ənokha A2	novel, unique
سخنور	swxənvər M/F1 A1	eloquent person, eloquent
مہارت	məharət F1 [np]	skill, mastery
دیوان	divan M1	divan, collection of poetry
مرثیہ	mərsia M2	elegy
فلسفیانہ	fəlsəfyana A1	philosophical
حیرت	həyrət F1 [np]	wonder, amazement, astonishment
مقبولیت	məqbuliət F1 [np]	acceptance, popularity
اشعار	*əšar Mpl [pl. /šer/]	verses, couplets
ذوق	zəwq PN	Shaykh Muhammad Ibrahim Zawq; 1789-1854

452

مومن	momyn PN	Hakim Muhammad Momin Khan Momin; 1800-1851
ثناه نصیر	šah nəsir PN	Shah Nasir-ud-din Nasir; 1765-1840
ظفر	zəfər PN	Siraj-ud-din Muhammad Bahadur Shah Zafar, the last Mughal ruler of Delhi; 1775-1862
موسیقی	məwsiqi F2 [np]	music
عشق	yšq M1 [np]	love, romantıc affection
مرثیہ گر	mərsiəgo M1 A1	elegy-composer, elegy-composing
بگڑنا	bygəRna [I: /bygaRna/: If]	to become bad, be spoiled, bungled, ruined; become angry
انیس	ənis PN	Mir Babar Ali Anis; 1802-1874
دبیر	dəbir PN	Mirza Salamat Ali Dabir; 1803-1875
نہایت	nyhayət Adv	extremely, exceedingly
معیار	meyar [or /mear/] M1	standard, level, calibre
کردار	kyrdar M1	character, nature; character (in a story, play, etc.)
مصور	mwsəvvyr M1	artist, painter
قلم	qələm M1 [or F1]	pen
مرثیہ گوئی	mərsiəgoi F2 [np]	composition of elegies
قید	qəyd F1 [np]	imprisonment, bonds, restraint, restriction
رامپور	rampur M1 [np]	Rampur, a princely state in north-central India
داغ دہلوی	daγ dyhləvi PN	Navab Mirza Khan Dagh Dihlavi; 1831-1905

امیر مینائی	əmir minai PN	Amir Ahmad Amir Minai; 1828-1900
جلال لکھنوی	jəlal ləkhnəvi PN	Sayyid Zamin Ali Jalal Lakhnavi; 1834-1909
تشبیہات	*təšbihat Fpl [pl. /təšbih/]	similes
امیراللغات	əmirwllwyat	the name of Amir Minai's great Urdu dictionary; only one volume was published; 1891
گُل	gwl M1	rose, flower
بلبل	bwlbwl F1	nightingale
افسانہ	əfsana [or /fəsana/] M2	tale, story, romance, short story, fiction
رجحان	rwjhan M1	inclination, trend, desire
آزاد	azad PN	Muhammad Husayn Azad; 1830-1910
حالی	hali PN	Altaf Husayn Hali; 1837-1914
روح	ruh F1	spirit, life, soul
پھونکنا	phūkna [If: /w/]	to blow
اسماعیل میرٹھی	ysmail merThi PN	Muhammad Ismail Merathi; 1844-1917
اکبر الہ آبادی	əkbər ylahabadi PN	Sayyid Akbar Husayn Rizvi Akbar Ilahabadi; 1846-1921
طنز	tənz M1 [np]	satire
مزاح	məzah M1 [np]	humour, wit, fun
اقبال	yqbal PN	Dr. Muhammad Iqbal; 1873-1938
چکبست	cəkbəst PN	Pandit Brij Narayn Chakbast; 1882-1926

نلسفی	fəlsəfi M/F1	philosopher
حسرت موہانی	həsrət mohani PN	Fazl-ul-Hasan Hasrat Mohani; 1878-1951
فانی بدایونی	fani bədayuni PN	Shawkat Ali Khan Fani Badayuni; 1879-1941
ریاض خیرآبادی	ryaz xəyrabadi PN	Sayyid Riaz Ahmad Riaz Khayrabadi; 1853-1935
اصغر گزندوی	əsɣər gõDvi PN	Asghar Husayn Asghar Gondvi; 1884-1936
جگر مراد آبادی	jygər moradabadi PN	Ali Sikandar Jigar Moradabadi; 1890-1960
جوش ملیح آبادی	još məlihabadi PN	Shabbir Hasan Khan Josh Malihabadi; 1894-
فراق گورکھپوری	fyraq gorəkhpuri PN	Raghupati Sahai Firaq Gorakhpuri; 1896-
بے شمار	bešwmar A1	countless, innumerable
گروہ	gyroh [or /gwroh/] M1	group, class
تقلید	təqlid F1	imitating, copying, following
برائے	bərae Prep	for
پیروی	pəyrəvi F2	following, adherence, observance (of laws, rules, etc.), pursuit
اشتراکیت	yštyrakiət F1 [np]	communism
سامراجیت	samrajiət F1 [np]	imperialism
سرمایہ داری	sərmayədari F2 [np]	capitalism
روایات	*rəvayat Fpl [pl. /rəvayət/]	narrations, sayings; traditions

سرمایه	sərmaya M2	capital, asset[s]
فخر	fəxr M1	pride
فهرست	fyhryst F1	list
درج	dərj PA1	entered, recorded, listed, registered, included
تاریک	tarik A1	dark

24. 200. WORD STUDY

24.201. /aryai/ A1 "Aryan" is used here in the sense of "Indo-Iranian, " the sub-
group of the Indo-European language stock to which Urdu belongs. Languages of this group
in India-Pakistan include Assamese, Bengali, Gujarati, Kashmiri, Marathi, Nepali, Oriya,
Panjabi, Rajasthani, Sindhi, etc. All of these are modern developments from various
Middle Indic dialects, which in turn go back through one or another Prakrit dialect to some
form of Sanskrit. These Indic languages are related to those of the Iranian group: Persian,
Kurdish, Pashto, Baluchi, etc. (the latter two being found in Pakistan, as well as in Iran
and Afghanistan), and the Indo-Iranian sub-group as a whole is generically related to the
other Indo-European groups: e. g. Latin (and hence to the Romance languages, such as
Spanish, French, etc.), Greek, the Germanic languages (of which English is a member),
the Slavic group, etc.

Quite apart from these Indo-Iranian languages, there are three other major linguistic
stocks in the Subcontinent: (1) the Dravidian stock, which includes the languages of South
India: Tamil, Telegu, Kannada, Malayalam, plus many tribal languages in Central India
and the isolated Brahui language found in Baluchistan; (2) the Munda stock, which includes
many tribal languages in Central and Eastern India; and (3) the Tibeto-Burman group, of
which there are various representatives along India's Himalayan and Eastern frontiers.
There are also several languages presently unrelatable to any of these major stocks: e. g.
Burushaski in Hunza State, West Pakistan.

Scholars are not yet entirely satisfied with the identification of the exact dialect of
Middle Indic from which Urdu originates, but it is generally agreed that this must have been
derived from some form of Shawraseni Prakrit, probably that dialect spoken around Delhi
and Meerut (/merəTh/). Many scholars believe that this dialect was exported to the Deccan
during the campaigns of the Khiljis and the Tughluqs, and this provided the foundation for
Deccani Urdu. In the north, the strong preference for Persian at the court of Delhi hampered
the development of Urdu as a literary language. The Deccan was more provincial, however,
and farther removed from the sources of Persian. It was also more imperative to deal
with the vast Hindu majority in some common language, and Sufis and Muslim missionaries
thus wrote and preached in Deccani Urdu. The kings of Bijapur and Golkonda also patronised
the language and themselves wrote copious divans in Urdu.

Although it is true that Persian held almost universal sway in the north until the coming
of Vali Dakani in 1700 A.D., occasional fragments of Urdu (or some form thereof) are
indeed met with in North Indian Muslim writings dating almost from the beginning of the
Muslim conquest. It is probable that some form of Urdu was used as a lingua franca all
during the Middle Ages, but this was not accepted as a vehicle for literature until after
Vali's poetry set the example for his northern contemporaries. The situation is somewhat
analogous to the use of Norman French at the English court after the Conquest.

In its earliest forms, Urdu was termed simply /hyndvi/ or /hyndi/ "the Indian [language]. "
It was also called /rexta/ M2 which literally means "scattered, dispersed" (probably
referring to the "scattering" of Persian, Arabic, etc. words throughout the Hindi text). The
term /wrdu/ F1 really denotes "army encampment, " indicating that this form was originally

457

the lingua franca employed in the /wrdue mwəlla/ "the Great Camp [of the Mughal Emperor], "
where speakers of Persian, Turkish, etc. mingled with Indians of diverse linguistic origins.
These terms -- /hyndvi/, /hyndi/, /rexta/, and /wrdu/ -- did not denote separate dialects
but were all names for a single amorphous linguistic entity, whose particular form depended
upon the speaker's own background, his knowledge of Hindi, Persian, etc. , and to some
extent upon his own predilections.

In modern India and Pakistan, however, three separate entities can be distinguished:
(1) Urdu, the Perso-Arabicised form of the language; (2) Hindi, the Sanskritised form;
(3) Hindustani, the simple lingua franca of much of North and Central India. All three rest
on the same foundation: they have the same sound system, the same basic grammar (with
but minor differences), and the same basic vocabulary. Urdu, however, depends upon
Persian and Arabic for its more literary vocabulary and for various grammatical constructions, while Hindi borrows or coins its literary terms from Sanskrit. The matter is made
more difficult by the fact that Urdu is written in the Arabic script, while Hindi is written in
the /deva nagəri/ script, a slightly modified form of the alphabet employed for Sanskrit.
After the partition of the Sub-Continent in 1947, Urdu and Hindi have drifted even farther
apart, with Urdu speakers in Pakistan borrowing and coining more and more items from
Perso-Arabic sources, while speakers of Hindi have been similarly busy "purifying" their
literary language from Perso-Arabic elements and substituting Sanskrit-derived forms in
their stead. Now, even if one knows the script, it has become difficult for a member of one
community to read the literature of the other. There are even some differences between
the Urdu used in Pakistan and that employed in India: e. g. Urdu newspapers printed in
India contain a somewhat higher percentage of Sanskrit-derived words than do their Pakistani
counterparts. Although the majority of Hindi-Urdu films produced in India still employ a
fairly Perso-Arabicised vocabulary, there is an increasing tendency to produce films having
a higher percentage of Hindi words in the dialogue. Urdu has had, of course, a longer
currency among the intellectuals of North India, both Hindu and Muslim, and highly
Sanskritised Hindi is still somewhat unfamiliar; nevertheless, the trend appears to be
toward greater and greater linguistic diversity.

Shorn of all these elaborate literary trimmings, the language of the common man of
North Central India may be termed "Hindustani. " It is intelligible to Hindu and Muslim,
Indian and Pakistani, alike, and it is the lingua franca for many millions more whose first
language is neither Hindi nor Urdu.

24. 202. /təvil/ A1 "long, lengthy, extended" is more literary than /ləmba/ A2 "long,
tall. " /təvil/ is also more or less restricted to abstracts: e. g. time, a story, a discussion,
etc. /təvil/ never has the sense of "tall (as a person). " E. g.

> /vw bəhwt ləmba admi həy. /   He's very tall man. [Never /təvil/ in this
> meaning.]
>
> /yy mez bəhwt ləmbi həy. /   This table is very long. [Again, /təvil/
> cannot be substituted.]
>
> /yy xət bəhwt təvil həy. /   This letter is very long. [/ləmba/ can be
> substituted here.]

/ws ne bəhwt təvil wmr pai. / He had [lit. got] a very long life. [/ləmbi/ can be substituted here, but, since the sentence is a trifle literary in style, /təvil/ somehow seems more appropriate.]

23.203. /qəvayd/ has two meanings: (1) the plural of /qayda/ M2 "rule, regulation, order" and (2) "grammar. " In the former sense /qəvayd/ is masculine plural, but in the latter meaning it is feminine singular. E. g.

/ap ko kalyj ke qəvayd ki pabəndi kərni cahie. / You ought to obey the rules of the college. [Here /ke/ shows that /qəvayd/ is Mpl.]

/farsi zəban ki qəvayd bəhwt asan həy. / The grammar of Persian is very easy. [/ki/ and /həy/ show that /qəvayd/ is F1 here.]

23.204. /mwtəəssyr/ PA1 "affected, influenced" and /mwəssyr/ A1 "effective" are both from the same Arabic root as /əsər/ M1 "effect, influence. " /mwəssyr/ is the active participle of Form II of ʔ-θ-r "to imprint, impress, leave a mark upon, " while /mwtəəssyr/ is the active participle of Form V of this root. Note also the compound /pwrəsər/ A1 "effective, impressive" (lit. "full-[of]-influence"); this compound is almost entirely synonymous with /mwəssyr/. E. g.

/məy məwlvi sahəb ke ylm se bəhwt mwtəəssyr hwa. / I was very much impressed with Məwlvi Sahəb's learning.

/həmare masTər sahəb ne bəhwt pwrəsər təqrir ki. / Our teacher gave a very impressive speech. [/mwəssyr/ is substitutable here.]

/hwkumət ka yy yqdam mwəssyr sabyt hwa. / This step of the Government's was proven to be effective. [/pwrəsər/ is substitutable here.]

24.205. /twrk/ M1 A1 "Turk" denotes a person of Turkish ethnic origin (i. e. including not only persons of Turkish ethnic origin but also members of Turkish tribes in the Soviet Union, etc.). /twrki/ M1 [np] F2 [np] A1 has three uses: (1) as a masculine noun denoting "Turkey, " the country (names of countries are treated as masculine in standard Urdu); (2) as a feminine noun denoting the Turkish language; and (3) as an adjective denoting "Turkish, of Turkish nationality. " In common usage, however, when /twrk/ is used as an adjective, it is usually found with nouns denoting persons; /twrki/, on the other hand, is used with inanimate objects, etc. See also Sec. 22.302. E. g.

/ek twrk aya. / A Turk (man) came. [/twrki/ is also possible but less common.]

/ek twrk əwrət ai. / A Turk[ish] woman came. [Again, /twrki əwrət/ is not wrong and specifically denotes a woman of Turkish nationality.]

/twrk nəwjəvanõ ne qəle pər həmla kia. / The Turkish youths attacked the fort.

/twrki bəhwt əccha həy. / Turkey is very good. [Some speakers may say /twrki əcchi həy/, treating nouns ending in /i/ as feminine, but in standard Urdu all countries are masculine.]

/twrki hwkumət ki tərəf se, ek elan jari hwa həy, ky vw əpne vade ko pura kəregi. / An announcement has been issued from [lit. from the direction of] the Turkish Government, that it will fulfill its promise.

24.206. /ləškər/ M1 "army, military force" has much the same meaning as /fəwj/ F1 "army. " /ləškər/, however, is generally used in the sense of a specific body of troops, while /fəwj/ denotes "army" in general. Originally /ləškər/ also meant "military encampment" (as did /wrdu/). E. g.

> /donõ ləškər age bəRhe, əwr ləRai šwru ho gəi. / Both armies advanced, and the battle began. [/fəwjẽ ... bəRhĩ/ can be substituted here since two bodies of troops are meant.]

> /mera ləRka fəwj mẽ həy. / My son is in the army. [/ləškər/ cannot be substituted here since "military service" is meant rather than a specific military force.]

24. 207. At this point a note on Indo-Pakistani proper names (and specifically the names of Urdu poets) seems in order. At birth a child receives a personal name chosen by some elderly male family member. During childhood, the child's close family also usually gives a "pet name" or nickname: e. g. /səyfwddin/ may be called /səyfi/, /zəfər/ may be /zəfru/, etc. Often this nickname has no connection with the child's personal name: e. g. /šəfiqwrrəhman/ may be called /əcchən miā/. This nickname may be employed by the child's parents and close relatives even after the child reaches maturity.

Various family titles are also commonly adopted: e. g. /səyyəd/ denotes that the person traces his descent back to the Prophet Muhammad; /mir/ is another title adopted by /səyyəd/ families; /mirza/ or /myrza/ is an abbreviated form of /əmirzada/ "born of a prince" and is generally a title employed by families of Mughal descent; /xan/ or /xā/ (in English, "Khan") originally meant "king"; /xaja/ meant "learned man, " etc. etc. In some parts of the Subcontinent these titles have taken on some of the characteristics of the Hindu caste system: e. g. a /səyyəd/ will prefer to marry another /səyyəd/; a /šəyx/ will marry a /šəyx/, rather than a member of some other lineage, etc. Originally these titles were placed before the personal name (as in English: e. g. "Lord Ashton"), but in recent times many people have taken to placing them last so that they may serve as a "last name": e. g. /yftyxar əli šəyx/ "Iftikhar Ali Shaykh" instead of /šəyx yftyxar əli/.

As soon as one begins to write poetry, the adoption of a /təxəllws/ M1 "pen-name, pseudonym" becomes necessary. The /təxəllws/ may be some abbreviated form of one's personal name, but it is more often a word of high literary content: e. g. /mir/ "Mir, " actually the title of /mir mwhəmməd təqi/; /azad/ meaning "free, " /momyn/ "believer, " /yalyb/ "surpassing, " /zəwq/ "taste, " /fəqir/ "mendicant, " /atyš/ "fire, " etc. This pen-name is usually retained throughout one's life, but there are many cases of a pen-name being changed for one or another reason: e. g. /myrza əsədwllah xan yalyb/ at one time used /əsəd/ "lion, " but changed to /yalyb/. Some poets have one /təxəllws/ for their Persian verses and another for their Urdu poetry. This pen-name almost always occurs in the last verse of each /yəzəl/ (see Sec. 24. 212) and in various places in other forms of poetry as well.

As a means of further clarification, a person may also add a name denoting his place of origin. These are all adjectival forms ending in /i/ (or, if the place name ends in a vowel, in /vi/ or /əvi/): hence, /dyhləvi/ "of Delhi, " /dəkəni/ "of the Deccan, " /gõDvi/ "of Gonda, " /əkbərabadi/ "of Akbarabad (i. e. Agra), " /əzimabadi/ "of Azimabad (i. e. Patna), " etc. Often the place name is added to a poet's /təxəllws/ to distinguish him from others having the same pen-name: e. g. /həsrət mohani/ "Hasrat of Mohan (a place near

Lucknow)" and /həsrət dyhləvi/ "Hasrat of Delhi. " In speaking of poets, thus, one rarely encounters the poet's full name (i. e. his title, his personal name, his /təxəllws/, and his place name); instead, one employs just the /təxəllws/ or perhaps the /təxəllws/ and the place name: e. g. /myrza əsədwllah xan γalyb dyhləvi/ "Mirza Asad-ullah Khan Ghalib Dihlavi" is simply known as "Ghalib"; /səyyəd əkbər hwsəyn ryzvi əkbər ylahabadi/ "Sayyid Akbar Husayn Rizvi Akbar Ilahabadi" is called "Akbar Ilahabadi" (/ylahabad/ -- English "Allahabad" -- is a city south of Lucknow in North Central India), etc.

24.208. /kəlam/ M1 is only occasionally heard in its original meaning of "word, speech, discourse. " Its commonest meaning is "poetry, verse, works (of a poet). " It also denotes "theology": /ylmwlkəlam/ "the science of theological dialectic. " Followed by an adjective like /məjid/ A1 "glorious, great, " it denotes "the Holy Qwran"; /kəlam məjid/ "the Glorious Qwran" (grammatically /kəlame məjid/, with the Persian /yzafət/). Here one should also note /swxən/ M1 "word, speech, eloquence. " This word shares almost no common environments with /kəlam/, since it rarely occurs alone in modern Urdu, and it is really only common in highly literary compounds or "frozen phrases" having to do with poetry and eloquence. E. g.

/mwjh se kəlam mət kəro! / Don't talk to me! [Commonly /mwjh se bat mət kəro! /.]

/yy myrza γalyb ka kəlam həy. / This is the poetry of Mirza Ghalib.

/synfe swxən/ "literary form, genre. " [/kəlam/ cannot be substituted here.]

24.209. /dərd/ M1 has been introduced in the meaning of "pain. " It also means "sympathy" and "pathos. " E. g.

/ws ki šayri mẽ bəhwt dərd həy. / There is much pathos in his poetry.

/wn ke dyl mẽ qəwm ka dərd tha. / He had sympathy [i. e. deep feeling] for the nation in his heart.

24.210. /xyalat/ Mpl and /əfkar/ Mpl both mean "thoughts, ideas. " The former is common and general, however, while the latter is somewhat literary and tends to connote "thinking, reflections, philosophical ideas. " Note that /əfkar/ is Mpl, while the singular /fykr/ is usually F1 in modern Urdu. /fykr/ also is commonly found meaning "worry" rather than "thinking, idea. " E. g.

/wn ke xyalat bəhwt bələnd hẽy. / His ideas are very exalted.

/wn ke əfkar mẽ gəhrai həy. / There is depth in his thinking. [/gəhrai/ F2 "depth. "]

24.211. Like /əta kərna/ and /ynayət kərna/ (Sec. 17.107), /bəxšna/ Ic "to give, bestow, grant" usually carries honorific connotations. It is used for honours (e. g. a /jagir/ F1 "estate, " /xylət/ F1 "robe of honour") and for abstractions having honorific connotations (e. g. /yzzət/ F1 "honour, " /mwqam/ M1 "rank, position"). /bəxšna/ is not generally employed for "to give" when the thing given is money. The completive form, /bəxš dena/, however, is used for all sorts of things and means "to give (something) away forever. "

/bəxšna/ and /bəxš dena/ also have another quite different meaning: "to forgive (an error, sin). " E. g.

/badšah ne wse ek jagir bəxši. / The king gave him an estate.

/xwda ne wse yzzət bəxši. / God gave him honour. [I. e. He was raised to an honourable position by God's Will.]

/ws ke ysi šahkar ne wse šayri mē bələnd mwqam bəxša. / This master-piece of his bestowed an exalted rank upon him in [the field of] poetry.

/wnhō ne wse yy kytab bəxš di. / He gave away this book to him [forever].

/myhrbani fərma kər, meri xəta bəxš dē! / Please forgive my fault! [/xəta/ F1 "fault, error, transgression. "]

/wnhō ne mwjhe dəs həzar rupəe die. / They gave me ten thousand rupees. [/əta kie/, /əta fərmae/, /ynayət fərmae/, etc. , can be substituted here, but /bəxše/ is less idiomatic.]

24. 212. Since the various forms of Urdu poetry are mentioned passim throughout this Unit, it will be useful to discuss the structure of Urdu poetry and contrast the more important types of poetic composition. It must be understood, of course, that this discussion is only superficial, and the student who wishes to investigate Urdu prosody in detail must seek further elsewhere.

Urdu prosody is based upon a metrical system invented by the Arabs and transmitted through Persia to Muslim India soon after the establishment of the Delhi Sultanate. According to this system, each letter of the alphabet (i. e. including /əlyf/, /vao/ and /ye/ but excluding the short vowel diacritics) is a consonant. Each consonant may be vowelled or unvowelled. All types of syllables are thus reduced to two basic forms: CV (i. e. a consonant + a short vowel diacritic) or CVC (i. e. a consonant + a short vowel diacritic + a consonant). A consonant + a short vowel diacritic + /əlyf/, /vao/, or /ye/ = CVC. There are a great many minor rules for dealing with syllable types which do not fit this basic pattern, and there is also a certain amount of poetic license.

There are eight "perfect metrical feet" (made by employing the two basic syllables in various combinations: CV-CVC-CVC, CVC-CV-CVC-CVC, etc.). When these metrical feet are repeated in various set orders and combinations, nineteen "standard metres" are produced. There are also rules for the addition or subtraction of syllables from one or more of the metrical feet, and by this means a great variety of "imperfect metrical feet" and "non-standard metres" are created. This process is termed "catalexis" in English.

"Rhyme" differs somewhat from that commonly found in Western poetry. In Urdu, words which are completely identical at the end of both lines of a couplet (or at the end of the second hemistich of each verse; see below) are termed /rədif/ F1. Any word or words preceding the /rədif/ which are identical in general pattern but which have different initial or medial consonants are termed /qafia/ M2. For Example:

/əsər bhi hota ... səfər bhi hota ... qəmər bhi hota ... / [Here /əsər/, /səfər/, and /qəmər/ are /qafia/ since they are all of the same pattern: CəCər; /bhi hota/ is identical in each line and is the /rədif/.]

The /qafia/ and /rədif/ need not necessarily occur at the end of each /mysra/ M2 "hemistich, line of a couplet. " As will be seen below, each type of poetic composition has its own rhyme scheme.

Types of poetic composition include:

(1) The commonest form is that of the /ɣəzəl/ F1, which roughly corresponds to the sonnet or ode. The Arabic root of the word /ɣəzəl/ means "to flirt, talk amorously with women, " and the theme of this type of poetry is properly erotic. The love portrayed in the /ɣəzəl/, however, is not usually sexually descriptive, nor is it the attainment of a love-object -- the joy of two young people in love. Instead, the /ɣəzəl/ treats of the haughtiness and cold indifference of the beloved, the suffering and disappointment of the lover, his yearning and inability even to confess his devotion, his madness and the destruction which love has brought him. Other common themes include the mystic doctrines of Sufism, the harshness of this material world, the ephemeral nature of happiness, etc. Sufistic concepts are all-pervasive: almost every verse is open to a mystical interpretation, and indeed this is usually the real meaning intended by the poet. For example, even when the poet praises the beauties of the beloved and laments the fact that he has been ejected from the beloved's assembly of admirers, he may really be saying that the beauties and majesty of God alone are worthy of devotion, and the poet is separated from union with God (perhaps likening himself to Adam, who was turned out of Paradise and thus deprived of his proximity to God). The language and imagery of the /ɣəzəl/ is rather stereotyped, and it is thus possible to employ these as a vehicle (and sometimes a disguise) for all sorts of deeper messages: philosophical, religious, political, and ideological doctrines are commonly found in modern Urdu /ɣəzəl/ writing.

One very important features of the structure of the /ɣəzəl/ is still to be mentioned: each verse of this form of poetry usually expresses a complete idea, and there is no conceptual connection between the verses of a given /ɣəzəl/. The first verse may speak of the joys of wine (perhaps Sufistically denoting the love of God); the second may praise the beauties of the beloved; the third may express some philosophical concept; the fourth lament the lover's madness, etc. Some poets have indeed written /ɣəzlē/ containing connected verses, but these are uncommon. In a /mwšayra/ M2 "poetry-reading" (a common feature of Indo-Pakistani cultural life), each verse of a /ɣəzəl/ is read aloud, the audience is given time to applaud, and if the verse is good, it may be read again; only after the poet has indicated his thanks to the audience for their appreciation will he go on to the next verse. Each verse, thus, must be complete, a poem in two lines.

The minimum number of verses for a /ɣəzəl/ is properly five, and the maximum is seventeen (though some say twenty-five). Poets of the Lucknow school have also written /ɣəzlē/ of much greater length. In any case, the number of verses must be odd and not even.

The first verse of the /ɣəzəl/ is called the /mətla/ M2, and its two hemistiches end in the same /qafia/-/rədif/. The remaining verses have the /qafia/-/rədif/ of the /ɣəzəl/ at the end of the second hemistich only; the first hemistich may end in anything. The rhyme scheme may thus be symbolised as A A, B A, C A, etc. The last verse of the /ɣəzəl/ is called the /məqta/ M2, and it usually contains the poet's /təxəllws/.

(2) The /qəsida/ M2 (pl. /qəsayd/ Mpl) is usually a poem in praise of someone, generally the poet's patron. It may treat of other themes as well, however: mysticism, philosophy, satire, etc. The /qəsida/ commonly begins with an introduction, followed by an

address to the person to whom it is dedicated, then a prayer for the person's health and prosperity, praises of his noble qualities, etc. The last verse often includes the poet's /təxəllws/. The rhyme scheme of the /qəsida/ is identical with that of the /ɣəzəl/: i.e. A A, B A, C A, etc., but the /qəsida/ is much longer, ranging (according to the authorities) from twenty to one hundred and seventy lines.

(3) The /məsnəvi/ F2 (pl. /məsnəviat/ Fpl) is a narrative poem. Usually it relates a story or perhaps a number of short anecdotes or fables. The greatest Urdu examples of this type of poetry are long tales, whose plots, characters, and background are reminiscent of the Arabian Nights. The /məsnəvi/ may, however, also deal with religious topics, philosophy, grammar, and even scientific subjects, although these are less common. The rhyme scheme of the /məsnəvi/ is quite different from that of the /ɣəzəl/: all of the verses have the same metre, but each verse has its own /qafia/-/rədif/. The pattern is thus: A A, B B, C C, D D, etc. There are no restrictions upon the number of lines. The /məsnəvi/ is usually written in only four of the standard metres, although examples in other metres are also occasionally encountered.

(4) The /rwbai/ F2 (pl. /rwbaiat/ Fpl) "quatrain" is a four line poem having the rhyme scheme A A, B A. There are a great many special and difficult metres for the /rwbai/ (modifications of one of the standard metres, /bəhre həzəj/). The subject matter of the /rwbai/ may be almost anything.

(5) The /qyta/ M2 (pl. /qytaat/ Mpl) "fragment" is like the /ɣəzəl/ and the /qəsida/, except that there is no /mətla/ (i.e. the first verse does not have the rhyme scheme A A). The rhyme scheme is thus A B, C B, D B, etc. The /qyta/ may range in length from two verses to any length. It has no special theme and may be written in any of the nineteen metres. The subject matter of the various verses of the /qyta/ is connected, unlike the /ɣəzəl/.

(6) The /mərsia/ M2 (pl. /mərasi/ Mpl) "elegy" is a lament for some deceased person. It recounts his life and good deeds and mourns his passing. In India and Pakistan this form has been highly developed as a vehicle for the retelling of the tragic death of the maternal grandson of the Prophet Muhammad, Imam Husayn, at Karbala in A.H. 61 (680 A.D.). This type of /mərsia/ has thus ceased to be simply an elegy for the dead but instead has become an epic poem dealing with the woeful events of Karbala. Such /mərasi/ are usually written in units of six lines each (called a /mwsəddəs/ F1), the rhyme scheme of which is A A, A A, B B. A /mərsia/ written about some other person may be in any metre or poetic form.

(7) /həjv/ F1 "ridicule" is a poem which pokes fun at some person. It may be written in the form of a /məsnəvi/, a /qəsida/, etc.

There are various other poetic forms: e.g. the /mwsəddəs/ F1, just mentioned above; the /mwxəmməs/ F1, a five-line poem; the /tərkibbənd/ M1 and the /tərjibənd/ M1, which have stanzas separated by a refrain verse; the /mwfrəd/ M1 (pl. mwfrədat/ Mpl) "individual couplet"; etc. Various other forms have been developed under Western influence: e.g. the /nəzm/ F1 (discussed in Sec. 22.218) and the /azad nəzm/ F1 "free [i.e. blank] verse." Of all these types, however, only the /ɣəzəl/ the /rwbai/, the /nəzm/, and lately the /azad nəzm/ are really common in modern Urdu, although occasional practitioners of the other types are found as well.

A collection of a poet's /γəzlẽ/, /qəsayd/, /rwbaiat/, etc. is called a /divan/ Ml "divan. " In this, the /γəzlẽ/ usually are placed first and are alphabetised according to the last letter of the /rədif/. The complete works of a poet are termed his /kwlliat/ Ml "collected works. "

24. 213. /təzkyra/ M2 basically means "mention, " and it is synonymous in this sense with /zykr/ Ml "mention, " which also comes from the same Arabic root. E. g.

/ws ne ap ka təzkyra kia. / He mentioned you. [Or: / ... ka zykr kia/.]

/təzkyra/, however, is more commonly employed for a biographical notice of some person or persons. It is most often applied to a collection of brief biographies of poets (although a /təzkyra/ may deal with great religious leaders, rulers, etc. as well). A /təzkyra/ of poets is usually arranged in alphabetical order according to the /təxəllws/ of each poet. After a brief biography, a selection of each person's verses is given.

24. 214. /məzaq/ Ml denotes "joke" and also "(literary) taste. " It is thus synonymous in some senses with /zəwq/ Ml "taste, " which comes from the same Arabic root. /tənz/ Ml [np] "satire" and /məzah/ Ml [np] "humour, wit, fun" contrast with /məzaq/ just as "satire, " "humour, " and "joke" contrast in English. It may be noted that /həjv/ Fl "ridicule" is in no sense synonymous with /tənz/: the former denotes a particular literary form (usually poetry) in which personal criticism may be carried to great limits; the latter term denotes "satire" in general and is much milder. E. g.

/ws ne mwjh se məzaq kia. / He played a joke on me.

/vw šayri ka əccha məzaq rəkhta həy. / He has good taste in poetry. [/zəwq/ can be substituted here.]

/kytabõ ke yntyxab ke bare mẽ, ws ka zəwq bəhwt əccha həy. / With regard to the selection of books, his taste is very good. [/məzaq/ cannot occur here, since literary taste -- the ability to distinguish good literature from bad -- is not specifically meant.]

/ws ne yy bat məzaq ke təwr pər kəhi. / He said this thing as a joke.

/vw əksər mwjh pər tənz kərta həy. / He generally satirises me. [I. e. teases me.]

/wn ki təbiət mẽ bəhwt məzah həy. / There is much humour in his disposition.

24. 215. In Persian poetry, the model upon which Urdu poetic forms and imagery are based, the "beloved" is conventionally a young man rather than a maiden, and /mašuq/ Ml "beloved" is thus treated as masculine. Explanations for this phenomenon vary: some scholars state that it was common for mystics and poets in early medieval Persian society to gather at the monasteries of Zoroasterian monks (where wine could be obtained against the strict prohibitions of Islam), and the young acolytes who served the wine became natural love-objects, especially in view of the restricted status of women in the society. Other authors emphasise that the apparent homosexuality of Persian-Urdu poetry is only traditional in the vast majority of cases: the "beloved" really stands for God, the "tavern" represents the world, and the "cup-bearer" symbolises one's mystic preceptor. It would not be

fitting to give to God the sexual connotations inherent in a female "beloved," but at the same time it is necessary to express one's love, admiration, etc.; hence the idea of a male beloved. Still others claim that the position of women in the society precluded the open writing of poetry addressed to a maiden. Various modern poets have attempted to change this tradition, and one now encounters "beloveds" in Urdu poetry who are undoubtedly feminine.

In speech, of course, /mašuq/ (or rather its feminine form, /mašuqa/ F1) are heard referring to a real-life feminine beloved.

24.216. /hwsn/ M1 "beauty" denotes a rather abstract quality. It may be employed for the beauty of a person, of a natural scene, etc. but not for the beauty of some small inanimate physical object. /xubsurti/ F2 "beauty, prettiness" covers all of these senses. /hwsn/ is also somewhat more literary than /xubsurti/. E. g.

> /ws ka hwsn dwnya bhər mẽ məšhur tha. / Her beauty [or: his handsomeness] was famous throughout the whole world. [/xubsurti/ can be substituted here.]

> /mə̃y ws ləRki ke hwsn se bəhwt mwtəəssyr tha. / I was much affected by the beauty of that girl. [Again, /xubsurti/ can be substituted.]

> /yy kytab bəRi xubsurti se lykhi gəi həy. / This book is written [i. e. copied by a calligrapher] beautifully [lit. with great beauty]. [/hwsn/ cannot occur here.]

24.217. /əndaz/ M1 "way, style, mode" must be distinguished from /əndaza/ M2 "estimate, guess." Both words are originally from the same Persian root, and in some dialects /əndaz/ also means "estimate, guess."

/əndaz/ must be carefully compared with several other words denoting "way, manner." /təriqa/, /təra/, /təwr/, and /zəria/ were discussed in Sec. 13.104. /tərz/ was discussed in Sec. 20.107. In many contexts these words overlap, and the student must thus explore the possibilities of usage for himself.

24.218. /ghumna/ IIc "to turn, revolve, circle, wander" differs only slightly from /phyrna/ "to turn, turn back, turn away, wander, rove," the intransitive form of /pherna/ Ie "to turn away from, reject, stroke." In the sense of "to wander, rove," /ghumna/ means "to wander with some specified object," while /phyrna/ means "to wander aimlessly." /phyrna/ means "to turn away from, turn back upon," while /ghumna/ does not share this meaning. /ghumna/, on the other hand, means "to whirl, revolve," a meaning which /phyrna/ lacks. E. g.

> /həm dərya ke kynare ghum rəhe the. / We were wandering [i. e. strolling] by the river.

> /vw kafi der tək baγ mẽ phyrta rəha. / He kept wandering [aimlessly or helplessly] in the garden for a long time.

> /vw əpne vade se phyr gəya. / He went back on his promise.

> /ws ka sər phyr gəya. / He went crazy. [Lit. his head turned. An idiom.]

> /zəmin surəj ke gyrd ghumti həy. / The earth revolves around the sun. [/[ke] gyrd/ Comp Post "around, in a circle about. "]

466

24.219. /hyndostani/ M1 A1 is the common word for "Indian, " both as a masculine noun and as an adjective. /hyndi/ M1 A1 F2 may also be used in these senses, but this usage is obsolete. /hyndi/ is now employed only as a F2 noun denoting "the Hindi language. " See Sec. 24.201.

24.220. /id/ F1 "Id" (usually spelled "Eid, " "Eed, " "Ied, " etc. in English works) is the abbreviated name of two major Muslim religious celebrations. The first, /idwlfytr/ "the festival of breaking the fast, " occurs at the end of the month of fasting (/rəmzan/ M1). On this day Muslims break their fast, go to the mosque for prayers, and spend the day visiting friends and feasting. Alms are collected and distributed to the poor, and there is general rejoicing. The second /id/, called variously /idwzzwha/, /idwləzha/, /ide qwrban/, or /bəqrəid/ "the festival of sacrifice, " commemorates the willingness of the Prophet Abraham to sacrifice his son. This /id/ is celebrated on the day following the day of the great yearly pilgrimage (the /həj/ M1) -- i. e. on the 10th of /zwlhyj/ -- and on this occasion every male Muslim who can afford it slaughters a goat, sheep, cow, or camel and distributes a portion of the meat to the poor, a portion to his friends and relatives, and keeps a portion for his own family. Since the Islamic calendar is based on the lunar year (354 days, eight hours, and forty-five minutes in length), these two festivals cannot be correlated with any fixed date in the solar calendar: each year the two /id/ festivals each occur roughly ten days earlier than they did the year before.

24.221. /nəsihət/ F1 always denotes moral or religious advice; /məšvəra/ M2 denotes advice of a more pragmatic nature. /nəsihət/ also means "a lesson (of experience), a warning. " E. g.

/buRhe bap ne əpne beTe ko nəsihət ki, ky həmeša səc bolo! / The old father gave his son the advice, that [he] should always speak the truth. [Note that /nəsihət kərna/ is a Type C complex verbal formation, and /ki/ thus agrees with the number-gender of /nəsihət/. See Secs. 7.123 and 11.306.]

/mwjhe ys vaqəe se nəsihət ho gəi. / I got a lesson from this incident.

/mɛ̃y ne wse məšvəra dia, ky vw lahəwr nə jae. / I advised him not to go to Lahore.

/mɛ̃y ne əpne bhai se ys mwamle mɛ̃ məšvəra kia. / I consulted my brother in this matter.

24.222. /gwlzare nəsim/, the name of Pandit Daya Shankar Kawl Nasim's /məsnəvi/, makes use of the poet's /təxəllws/ (see Sec. 24.207) as part of the title: /gwlzar/ M1 "rosegarden"; /nəsim/ F1 "zephyr. " The title thus means both "The Rosegarden of Nasim" and "The Rosegarden of the Zephyr. "

24.223. The word order in an Urdu verse is often quite different from normal prose order. This is done in order to fit the words into the rigid metrical scheme. Until the student gains experience, he must first rearrange the words of each verse in their usual prose order before trying to understand the meaning. Thus:

/hə̃y əwr bhi dwnya mẽ swxənvər bəhwt əcche -- kəhte hə̃y, ky γalyb ka
  həy əndaze bəyan əwr. /

Becomes:

/dwnya mẽ əwr bhi bəhwt əcche swxənvər hə̃y -- kəhte hə̃y, ky γalyb ka
  əndaze bəyan əwr həy. /   In the world there are other very good poets
  [lit. eloquent ones], [but people] say that Ghalib's style is [still
  something] else. [I. e. that Ghalib's style is unique.]

24. 224. /həyrət/ F1 "wonder, amazement, astonishment" and /təəjjwb/ M1 "wonder,
amazement" are, for all practical purposes, synonyms.

24. 225. /yšq/ M1 "love" is used to refer to romantic affection or to the mystic love
of God. /mwhəbbət/ F1 may also have these meanings but denotes love in other senses as
well; e. g. love of one's parents, love for one's country, etc. /yšq/ also tends to denote
a stronger variety of love. E. g.

/mwjhe ws ləRki se mwhəbbət həy. /   I love that girl. [Lit. to me with
  that girl love is. /yšq/ can be substituted here.]

/mwjhe əpne valydəyn se mwhəbbət həy. /   I love my parents. [/yšq/
  would not ordinarily occur here.]

/mwjhe əpne vətən se bəhwt mwhəbbət həy. /   I love my native land very
  much. [Again, /yšq/ would not ordinarily be substitutable.]

24. 226. /kyrdar/ M1 denotes "character" both in the sense of "temperament, natural
disposition" and also "rôle, part in a play. " E. g.

/ws ka kyrdar əccha nəhĩ. /   He does not have a good character.

/ys Dyrame mẽ, ws ne buRhe ka kyrdar bəhwt xubsurti se əda kia. /   In
  this play he played [lit. performed] the character of the old [man]
  beautifully.

24. 227. /əmirwllwγyat/, the name of Amir Ahmad Amir Minai's dictionary, contains
the pen-name of its author as part of its title (see Sec. 24. 222); /əmir/ M1 A1 "rich,
wealthy" originally meant "prince, 'emir'"; /lwγyat/ Fpl [or Mpl] "dictionaries" is the
plural of /lwγət/ F1 [or M1] "dictionary, vocabulary, stock of words. " The title thus
means "The Prince of Dictionaries. " (Note that since this word ends in /ət/, many modern
speakers treat /lwγət/ as F1, but the great classical dictionaries unanimously list it as M1.
/lwγyat/ "dictionaries" is similarly Fpl in common usage but Mpl in the dictionaries.)

24. 228. /əfsana/ (or /fəsana/) M2 "story, tale" always denotes a fictional narrative,
unlike /kəhani/ F2 and /qyssa/ M2 which denote "story, tale" and also "event, occurrence,
happening" (see Sec. 15. 118). /əfsana/ is now generally employed for "short story. "

24. 229. Note the following idiom:

/azad əwr hali ne əpni šayri se qəwm mẽ ek nəi ruh phũk di. /   Azad and
  Hali by means of [lit. with] their poetry infused [lit. blew] a new
  spirit into the nation.

Another example:

/ws ki təqrir ne mwrda qəwm mẽ ek nəi ruh phūk di. /   His speech
infused a new spirit into the lifeless nation.

For /ruh/ F1 "soul, spirit, life, " see Sec. 23. 201.

24. 230. /təqlid/ F1 "imitating, copying, following" denotes "following the example of
(as a person, a doctrine, etc.)"; /pəyrəvi/ F2 "following, adherence, observance" is
usually employed for adherence to some law, rule, or principle; /pəyrəvi/ also means
"pursuit (of a case in court), " and /ki pəyrəvi mẽ/ is used as a compound postposition to
denote "on the example of, in imitation of"; /nəql/ F1 means "copy (of a document, letter,
etc.)" and is also employed for "copying, apeing" in a bad sense. E. g.

/yn šwəra ne pwrane əsatyza ki təqlid mẽ šer kəhe. /   These poets wrote
[lit. said] verses on the same pattern [lit. in imitation of] the old
masters.

/həm košyš kərte hɔ̃y, ky zyndəgi ke hər šobe mẽ əpne nəbi ki təqlid kərẽ. /
We try to follow [copy, imitate] our Prophet in every sphere of life.

/wnhõ ne yy qədəm yštyrakiət ki təqlid mẽ wThaya. /   They took this step
following [lit. in] the example of Communism.

/vw yn wsulõ ki pəyrəvi kərta həy. /   He adheres to these principles.
[/təqlid/ cannot occur here.]

/vəkil sahəb ys mwqədme ki pəyrəvi kərẽge. /   The lawyer will pursue
this case.

/ys xət ki tin nəqlẽ cahiẽ. /   Three copies of this letter are needed.

/mere lie yy səfha nəql kər do! /   Copy this page for me! [Neither
/təqlid/ nor /pəyrəvi/ can occur in this sense of "copy. "]

/vw xwd kwch nəhĩ janta. həmeša dusrõ ki nəql kərta həy. /   He himself
knows nothing. [He] always copies others. [Here in the sense of
"to ape" /nəql/ alone can occur.]

/vw kəmyunysTõ ki nəql kərta həy. /   He behaves like [lit. copies] the
Communists.

24. 231. /bərae/ Prep "for" is a preposition borrowed from Persian (probably /bə
rah e/ "by way of"). Its use is limited to a few "set phrases" and to occasional rather
literary occurrences where one would otherwise expect /ke lie/ or /ke vaste/ (the latter
being a synonym for /ke lie/). E. g.

/vw bərae nam mwsəlman hɔ̃y. /   They are Muslims only nominally [lit.
for the name].

/bərae myhrbani, mera yy kam kər dijie! /   Please do this work of mine!
[/myhrbani kər ke/ is also possible.]

/yy mal bərae fəroxt həy. /   These goods are for sale. [/ke lie/ is
substitutable.]

/mɔ̃y bərae mwlazmət lahəwr ja rəha hū. /   I'm going to Lahore [to look]
for a job. [/ke lie/ is much commoner in sentences such as this.]

24. 232. /yštyrakiət/ F1 (np) "Communism" is an abstract noun made from the Form
VIII verbal noun of š-r-k "to take part, participate. " It is entirely synonymous with the
English loanword /kəmyunyzm/ F1. The adjectival form, /yštyraki/ M1 A1, is similarly
synonymous with /kəmyunysT/ M1 A1 "Communist. "

24.233. /rəvayət/ F1 (pl. /rəvayat/ Fpl) "narration, saying, tradition" is usually employed for the saying of some great person (often a religious figure). It also denotes "tradition, " overlapping slightly with /rəsm/ F1 "custom" and /rəvaj/ M1 "custom, tradition" (Sec. 19.102). /rəsm/, however, denotes some particular custom or observance; /rəvaj/ refers to something which has become prevalent or popular; /rəvayət/ refers to something which has become an established practice. E. g.

/ek rəvayət həy, ky ek əysa vəqt aega, ky dwnya mē bwraiā bəhwt bəRh jaēgi. / There is a saying [of some authority] that a time will come when evils will greatly increase.

/yy rəvayət həmare bwzwrgō ne qaym ki həy. / Our great men established this tradition [i. e. practice].

/yy ys ydare ki rəvayət həy, ky səb log šam ko car bəje ys kəmre mē ykhəTTe cae piē. / This is a tradition of this institution that everyone drinks tea together in this room at four o'clock in the afternoon.

24.234. Some Complex Verbal Formations.

A:

/bələnd/

/bələnd hona/ to be, become great, high

/[X ko] bələnd kərna/ to make [X] great, high

/dərj/

/[Y mē] dərj hona/ to be entered [in Y]

/[X ko Y mē] dərj kərnā/ to enter [X in Y]

/məqbul/

/məqbul hona/ to be, become popular

/mwtəəssyr/

/[Y se] mwtəəssyr hona/ to be affected, influenced [by Y]

/[X ko] mwtəəssyr kərna/ to influence, affect [X]

/pecida/

/pecida hona/ to be, become complicated

/[X ko] pecida kərna/ to complicate [X]

/qəyd/

/qəyd hona/ to be, become imprisoned

/[X ko] qəyd kərna/ to imprison [X]

/tarik/

/tarik hona/ to be, become dark

/[X ko] tarik kərna/ to darken [X]

B:

/pəyrəvi/

/[X ki] pəyrəvi hona/ [X] to be adhered to, followed, observed

/[X ki] pəyrəvi kərna/ to follow, adhere to, observe [X]

/sərpərəsti/

/[X ki] sərpərəsti kərna/ to patronise [X]

/təqlid/

/[X ki] təqlid kərna/ to copy, imitate, follow the example [of X]

/təzkyra/

/[X ka] təzkyra hona/ [X] to be mentioned

/[X ka] təzkyra kərna/ to mention [X]

C:

/nəsihət/. [See also D.]

/[X ko Y se] nəsihət hona/ [X] to be advised [by Y], [X] to get a lesson [from Y]

/[X ko] nəsihət kərna/ to advise [X]

D:

/nəsihət/. [See also C.]

/[X ko] nəsihət dena/ to give advice [to X]

/[X ko Y se] nəsihət mylna/ [X] to receive advice [from Y]

/təšbih/

/[X ko Y se] təšbih dena/ to liken [X to Y]

/wruj̄/

/[X ko] wruj̄ hona/ [X] to be raised, exalted, brought to a high level

/[X se Y ko] wruj̄ mylna/ [Y] to be exalted, raised, brought to a high level [because of X]

F:

/fəxr/

/[X ko Y pər] fəxr hona/ [X] to be proud [of Y]

/[X pər] fəxr kərna/ to take pride [in X]

/γəzəl/

/γəzəl kəhna/ to compose a /γəzəl/

/həyrət/

/[X ko Y pər] həyrət hona/ [X] to be surprised [at Y]

/[X pər] həyrət kərna/ to be surprised [by, at, X]

/id/

/id hona/ to be the /id/ festival

/id mənana/ to celebrate the /id/ festival

/məzaq/

/[X ka] məzaq wRana/ to make fun of [X]. [/wRana/ "to cause to fly "]

/[X se] məzaq kərna/ to joke [with X], play a joke [upon X]

/mela/

/mela hona/ to be a festival, fair

/mela ləgana/ to hold a fair

/rwjhan/

/[X ka Y ki tərəf] rwjhan hona/ [X] to be inclined [toward Y]

/sərmaya/

/[X mẽ] sərmaya ləgana/ to invest capital [in X]

471

/šək/

    /[X ko Y pər] šək hona/ [X] to be suspicious [of Y]

    /[X pər] šək kərna/ to suspect, be doubtful [of X]

/tənz/

    /[X pər] tənz kərna/ to satirise [X]

/tyhvar/

    /tyhvar mənana/ to celebrate a festival

/yšq/

    /[X ko Y se] yšq hona/ [X] to fall in love [with Y]

    /[X se] yšq kərna/ to love, make love [to X]

/zəval/

    /[X ko] zəval ana, hona/ [X] to decline, degenerate, fall

24.301. Substantive Composition.

The analysis of the various compounds introduced in this Unit is as follows:

/bərae/ Prep "for": See Sec. 24.231.

/darwlhwkumət/ M1 "capital": Arabic /dar/ "house, place of"; /wl/ the Arabic definite article; /hwkumət/ "government."

/γəzəlgo/ M/F1 A1 "/γəzəl/-composer, /γəzəl/-composing": Arabic /γəzəl/ "/γəzəl/, a type of poetry" (see Sec. 24.212); Persian /go/ the present stem of /gwf/ "say, speak."

/mərsiəgo/ M/F1 A1 "elegy-composer, elegy-composing": Arabic /mərsia/ "elegy"; /go/ as above.

/mərsiəgoi/ F2 [np] "composition of elegies": /mərsiəgo/ as above; /i/ the abstract noun formant suffix. /i/ may also be added to /γəzəlgo/, /qəsidəgo/, etc. to form abstract nouns.

/mylna jwlna/ "to mix, meet, mingle together": A Hindi echo compound (see Sec. 19.305) consisting of /mylna/ IIc "to meet, get, mix" + /jwlna/ "to meet." The latter occurs only in this compound. See also Sec. 17.310.

/pəyrəvi/ F2 "following, adherence, pursuit": /pəyrəw/ M/F1 "follower, devotee" was analysed in Sec. 21.301; /i/ the abstract noun formant suffix.

/pwrəsər/ A1 "effective, impressive": Persian /pwr/ "full"; Arabic /əsər/ "effect, trace, indication."

/qədrdan/ [or /qədrdā/] M/F1 A1 "appreciator, connoiseur": Arabic /qədr/ "amount, value, appreciation"; Persian /dan/ present stem of /danys/ "know."

/qəsidəgo/ M/F1 A1 "/qəsida/-composer, /qəsida/-composing": Arabic /qəsida/ "/qəsida/, a type of poetry" (see Sec. 24.212); /go/ as in /γəzəlgo/ above.

/rozmərra/ M1 [np] A1 Adv "daily usage, daily conversation, daily allowance, daily wages; daily": Persian /roz/ "day"; Arabic /mərra/ "one time, once, a turn."

/samrajiət/ F1 [np] "imperialism": Hindi /sam/ "conciliatory means used in politics" (?); /raj/ "government"; /i/ + /ət/ the Arabic abstract noun affixes (see Sec. 17.305 (9)).

/sərmaya/ M2 "capital, assets": Persian /sər/ "head"; /maya/ "wealth."

/sərmayədari/ F2 [np] "capitalism": /sərmaya/ as above; /dar/ present stem of /daš/ "have"; /i/ the abstract noun formant suffix.

/sərpərəsti/ F2 "patronage": Persian /sər/ "head"; /pərəst/ past stem of /pərəst/ "to worship, adore, be devoted to"; /i/ the abstract noun formant suffix.

/šahkar/ M1 "masterpiece": Persian /šah/ "king"; /kar/ "work, deed."

24.302. The <A^1 + /se/ + A^1> Construction: "Even the ... est."

To express "even the ... est, " one employs an adjective + /se/ + the same adjective:
e. g. /mwškyl se mwškyl kam/ "even the most difficult work, " /bəRe se bəRa ləRka/
"even the largest boy, " /choTi se choTi jəga/ "even the smallest place," etc. To emphasise
the "even, " /bhi/ may be added after the noun: /asan se asan bat bhi/ "even the easiest
matter. " This formation is similar in pattern to that of /zyada se zyada/ "as much as
possible" and /kəm se kəm/ "at least, as little as possible" discussed in Sec. 18. 115. E. g.

/vw mwškyl se mwškyl kam kər lega. / He will do even the most difficult
work.

/vw asan se asan səval bhi həl nəhĭ kər səkta. / He cannot solve even
the easiest questions.

/vw bəRe se bəRe admi ki bhi pərva nəhĭ kərte. / He doesn't care even
for the greatest [i. e. most influential, powerful] man.

/vw ūce se ūce dərəxt pər mynTõ mē cəRh jata həy. / He climbs even
the tallest tree in minutes.

/ap ke šəhr ki bəRi se bəRi ymarət bhi syrf aTh mənzyl ki həy. / Even
the biggest building of your city is only eight storeys [high].

/mɛ̃y bədtərin se bədtərin admi ke sath bhi rəh səkta hū̃. / I can get on
[lit. stay] with even the worst person. [This formation is possible
even with the Persian superlative adjective /bədtərin/ Al "worst,
most evil"; see Sec. 15. 302.]

24. 303. The < ... /se le kər/ ... /tək/> Construction: "From ... to ... "

The usual method of expressing "from ... to ... " is / ... se ... tək/: e. g. /kəraci
se lahəwr tək/ "from Karachi to Lahore. " When two poles are expressed, however,
between which some action or state extends unbroken, then the conjunctive participle of
/lena/ "to take" is inserted after /se/: thus, / ... se le kər ... tək/ denotes "[stretching]
from ... to ... " E. g.

/məšryq se le kər məɣryb tək, hər jəga yyhi rəsm pai jati həy. / From
east to west, every place this same custom is found.

/mɛ̃y swba se le kər šam tək kam kərta hū̃. / I work [continuously] from
morning to evening. [This carries a connotation of unbroken continuity;
/swba se šam tək/ simply states the two extremes.]

/ys dwkan pər, ek rupəe se le kər həzar rupəe tək ka mal mylta həy. /
In [lit. on] this shop goods [worth] from one rupee to a thousand rupees
are available. [The implication is that the two extremes are connected
by an unbroken continuity of variously priced items: "all the way from
... to ... "]

/bəccõ se le kər buRhõ tək -- ajkəl səb hi bimar hɛ̃y. / From the
children to the old [people] -- these days everyone is sick.

/yn pəhaRõ ka sylsyla šymal se le kər jwnub tək phəyla hwa həy. / This
mountain chain [lit. the chain of these mountains] extends from north
to south.

24. 304. /šayəd hi/ "Perhaps Not. "

The following examples are from Sec. 24. 000.

/wn ke pas əlfaz ka zəxira ytna tha, ky šayəd hi kysi dusre šayr ke pas
ho. / He had such a store of words as [lit. that] perhaps [no] other
poet had [lit. may have].

474

/wn ke xyalat ytne bələnd, əwr məzamin ys qədr hɔ̃y, ky šayəd hi kysi
dusre šayr ke hã̄ myl səkẽ. / His ideas are so exalted, and [his]
subjects so many, as [lit. that] perhaps can [not] be found in the
poetry [lit. at, with] any other poet.

Note that there is no word for "not" in the clauses introduced by /šayəd hi/ in the above
sentences. Clauses containing /šayəd hi/ imply a negative comparison. They may be
translated with a negative in English (e.g. " ... as perhaps no other poet has") or with a
comparative (e.g. " ... than any other poet perhaps has"). E.g.

/wn ke pas ytni dəwlət həy, ky šayəd hi kysi dusre ke pas ho. / He has
so much wealth, as [lit. that] perhaps [no] other has. [Or: " ...
more wealth than perhaps any other has. "]

/ws ne yy məzmun ys xubsurti se peš kia həy, ky šayəd hi kysi dusre
šayr ne peš kia ho. / He has presented this subject so beautifully
[lit. with this beauty], as [lit. that] perhaps [no] other poet has
[ever] expressed [it].

/mere xyal mẽ, ys vəqt ysmyth sahəb šayəd hi ghər pər hõ. / In my
opinion, at this time perhaps Mr. Smith will [not] be at home.

/mɔ̃y šayəd hi lahəwr jaū̃. / Perhaps I will [not] go to Lahore. [Note
that in all of these examples conditional forms of the verb are employed.]

It is possible to omit /hi/ in the above sentences, but then the expected negative /nə/
or /nəhī̃/ must be inserted. Semantically, clauses containing /šayəd hi/ carry greater
negative force than do the same clauses with /šayəd ... nəhī̃/. When /šayəd hi/ is used,
there is little or no chance of the action or condition taking place, whereas with /šayəd ...
nəhī̃/ there is still some possibility. E.g.

/ws ke pas ytni dəwlət həy, ky šayəd kysi dusre ke pas nə ho. / He has
so much wealth as [lit. that] perhaps no other has. [The possibility
of someone else having an equal amount of wealth still exists, however.]

/mere xyal mẽ, ys vəqt ysmyth sahəb šayəd ghər pər nə hõ. / In my
opinion, perhaps Mr. Smith will not be at home at this time.

/mɔ̃y šayəd lahəwr nə jaū̃. / Perhaps I will not go to Lahore.

24. 305. The Verb: The Participles + /ana/, /cəla ana/, and /cəla jana/.

Continuity over an extended period of time is expressed by a participle + an inflected
form of /ana/ "to come, " or, with a greater sense of unbroken continuity, by a participle
+ /cəla ana/. This construction denotes a continuous action or state extending from some
point in the past up to the present. The verb forms employed are almost always continuative
(e.g. /kərta a rəha həy/, /kərta cəla a rəha həy/, /kərta cəla a rəha tha/, etc.) or present
perfect (e.g. /kərta aya həy/, /kərta cəla aya həy/, etc.). Both present and past participles
are found in this construction, but the latter are rather rare and are restricted idiomatically
to a few intransitive verbs only. In fact, except for a few very common occurrences, this
construction is rather uncommon, other continuative formations (e.g. <S + /rəha həy/>,
<PreP + /rəhna/>, <OPasP + /jana/>) being used instead. E.g.

/həm ərse se yyhi qyssa swnte cəle a rəhe hɔ̃y. / We have been
[continuously] hearing this story for a long time. [/swnte a rəhe hɔ̃y/
or /swn rəhe hɔ̃y/ may be substituted. /swnte cəle a rəhe hɔ̃y/ is
one of the common uses of this construction.]

/həm ərse se yyhi qysse swnte cəle ae hə̄y. / We have been hearing this story for a long time. [/swnte ae hə̄y/ is substitutable. The use of the present perfect denotes that the "hearing" was continuous in the past and has effects upon the present context.]

/həm do məhine se cavəl khate cəle a rəhe hə̄y. / We have been [continuously] eating rice for the [last] two months. [/khate a rəhe hə̄y/ is substitutable.]

/həmara yskul car sal se harta cəla a rəha həy. / Our school has been [continuously] losing [at some sport] for four years. [/har rəha həy/ and /harta a rəha həy/ are substitutable.]

/do sal se həm yyhi sylsyla dekhte cəle a rəhe hə̄y. / For two years we have been [continuously] seeing this sequence [of events].

/pā̃c sal se mə̄y yyhi saRi pəhnti cəli a rəhi hū̃. / I have been wearing this sari for five years. [I. e. I have no other and must wear this.]

/vw bərsō se kəpRe ki tyjarət kərta cəla a rəha tha. / He had been dealing in cloth for years. [Or: /kərta a rəha tha/.]

/sədiō se yyhi hota cəla aya həy. / This has been going on for centuries. [Or: /hota aya həy/.]

/vw dəs sal se yyhi bat kəhte cəle ae hə̄y. / They have been [continuously] saying this for ten years. [Or: /kəhte ae hə̄y/.]

/həm bwzwrgō se yyhi swnte cəle ae hə̄y. / We have been hearing this [continuously] from [our] elders. [Or: /swnte ae hə̄y/.]

Examples of <PasP + /cəla ana/ or /ana/>:

/ap əpna kəlam swnaie! səb log khȳce cəle aẽge. / Please recite your poetry. Everyone will be attracted. [Lit. will continuously be drawn.]

/həm sədiō se yn hi rwsumat mē bədhe cəle a rəhe hə̄y. / We have been chained to [lit. bound in] these same customs for centuries.

The <PreP + /jana/> construction was discussed in Sec. 15.310. It denotes "to gradually go on ... ing" and "to keep on ... ing (perhaps in spite of some obstacle)." The <PreP + /cəla jana/> formation has almost the same meaning but is somewhat more emphatic. It may also denote a longer period of continuity. It is uncommon, and other continuative formations (e.g. <S + /rəha həy/>, <PreP + /rəhna/>, <OPasP + /jana/>) are more often employed instead. See also Sec. 21.304. E.g.

/jəyse ap bətaẽge, həm vəyse hi kərte cəle jaẽge. / Just as you say [lit. will tell], just thus will we go on doing. [Here /kərte rəhẽge/, /kərte jaẽge/, and /kie jaẽge/ may be substituted.]

/həm mwsibtō ka samna kərte ae hə̄y, əwr kərte cəle jaẽge. / We have been [continuously] facing calamities, and we will go on [facing them]. /kərte rəhẽge/ and /kie jaẽge/ are substitutable.]

/ws ke peT ka dərd bəRhta cəla gəya. / The pain in [lit. of] his stomach kept on increasing. [Here /bəRhta rəha/ and /bəRhta gəya/ are also possible.]

/yn halat ki vəja se, mwyəl səltənət kəmzor hoti gəi. / Because of these conditions, the Mughal Empire kept on getting weaker. [Here /hoti cəli gəi/ can be substituted.]

/ləRka kəi mil tək dərya mē bəhta cəla gəya. / The boy floated for several miles down [lit. in] the river.

24.400. SUPPLEMENTARY VOCABULARY

24.401. Supplementary Vocabulary.

*lwγat Fpl [or Mpl]	dictionaries, vocabularies, words
lwγət Ml [or Fl]	dictionary, vocabulary, stock of words
mwhəqqyq Ml	researcher, investigator
qayda M2	rule, regulation, regular practice
rəvayət Fl	narration, saying; tradition
təšbih Fl	simile
wryā Al	nude, naked, lewd
ystylah Fl	(technical) term

24.402. Supplementary Exercise I: Substitution.

1. ys kytab   mẽ   yy qyssa   məwjud həy.

    this dictionary   this term

    this investigator's book   this tradition

    that təzkyra   that poet's verse

    these dictionaries   this idiom

    this list   the name of this prince

2. ys təzkyre mẽ,   do səw pəcəttər   šwəra šamyl kie gəe hə̃y.

    seven hundred and twenty-six

    eleven hundred and thirty-five

    nine hundred and seventy-four

    eight hundred and ninety-nine

    six hundred and fifty-two

24.403. Supplementary Exercise II: Translation.

1. Translate the following sentences into Urdu.

    a. In this dictionary most terms ρf poetry will be found.

    b. The poet likened [lit. gave the simile of] this world to a prison.

    c. This tradition is found [lit. present] in the books of the Jews.

    d. In order to please [/xwš kərna/] the king, he wrote lewd verses.

    e. The Government has issued a new regulation dealing with [lit. for] the export of cotton wool.

24.501. Substitution.

1. <u>səb log</u>   <u>məwlvi sahəb ki təqrir</u>   se bəhwt mwtəəssyr hwe. [1]

the poets   this γəzəl

the president   the criticism of the opposition party
of the state

I   her song

our industrial   these recommendations
projects

our culture   Western ideas

      [1]Change /hwe/ to agree with the number-gender of the subject in each
      sentence.

2. <u>õgrezõ</u>   ne   <u>bəhadwr šah zəfər</u>   ko qəyd kər lia.

the soldiers   five Turks

our government   all communist leaders

the army   the Caliph

the Raja   that Iranian poet

the French   our ambassador

3. <u>mwyəl badšahõ</u>   ne   <u>farsi ədəb</u>   ki sərpərəsti ki.

the Navabs of   countless Urdu poets
Rampur

the Deccani kings   the Urdu language

the British   Urdu prose

the prince   this artist

the notables of the   the composition of
court   elegies

4. šayr ne   <u>ws ke balõ</u>   ko   <u>rat</u>   se təšbih di.

      the beloved's   the voice of the
      voice   nightingale

      her beauty   the sun

      her face   a flower

      his love   fire

      the bride   the moon

5. ws ki   <u>məsnəvi</u>   bəhwt pwrəsər thi.

      quatrain

      prose

      lecture

      poem

      γəzəl

6. wnhõ ne <u>šayri</u>   ke meyar ko gyrne nə dia.

      elegies

      examination

      qəsida

478

　　　　　　　satire

　　　　　　　short story

7.　ws ne　　ys ləfz　　　ko nyhayət xubsurti se ystemal kia həy.

　　　　　　　these words

　　　　　　　this example

　　　　　　　these terms

　　　　　　　this idiom

　　　　　　　these idioms

8.　sərkari əfsər　　ne　　mera nam　　ys fyhryst　　mē dərj kia həy. [1]

　　the village-elder　　　　the numbers of　　the register
　　　　　　　　　　　　　　the houses

　　the landowner　　　　　the number of　　　the copybook
　　　　　　　　　　　　　　labourers

　　the historian　　　　　　the names of　　　his history
　　　　　　　　　　　　　　the ministers
　　　　　　　　　　　　　　of this period

　　the owner of the　　　　my address　　　　the register
　　hotel

　　the Iranian ambassador　these details　　　his book

　　　　[1]Change /kia həy/ to agree with the number-gender of the object in these
　　　　sentences.

9.　həmē　　ys mwamle　　mē yn mwfəssyrin　　ki təqlid kərni cahie.

　　　　　every sphere of　　　our Prophet
　　　　　life

　　　　　this policy　　　　　America

　　　　　these matters　　　　our great [one]s

　　　　　national life　　　　these principles

　　　　　the γəzəl　　　　　　the old masters

10.　ys dəwr ke wdəba　　mwškyl zəban əwr mwhavərat　　pər fəxr kərte the.

　　the old masters　　　complicated terms

　　the tribes of Turkey　　their traditions

　　the early poets of Urdu　their Persian poetry

　　the people of that time　this masterpiece
　　also

　　Mirza Ghalib　　　　　his novel style of expression

11.　sətrəvī sədi　　　mē　　wrdu šayri　　　ko wruj myla.

　　the last period of　　　　Urdu literature
　　the Mughal Empire

　　the middle of the　　　　Deccani Hindi
　　nineteenth century

　　the end of the eighteenth　the Urdu məsnəvi
　　century

　　the beginning of the　　　the composition of elegies
　　nineteenth century

　　the period of this poet　　satire and wit

12.　wn ki šayri mē　wryani　　həy.

　　　　　　　　　　fluency

479

simplicity
mysticism
pathos
philosophy

13. <u>ys šayr</u>   ne <u>ɣəzəl</u>   me ek nəi ruh phūk di.

    his lecture   the nation

    his reforms   the Turks

    his satire and   literature
    humour

    his style of   Arabic poetry
    expression

    this step   the people

14. <u>wn ka divan</u> <u>do səw ɣəzlõ</u>   pər mwštəmyl həy.

    this ɣəzəl   nine verses

    this short story   forty pages

    this təzkyra   only ɣəzəl-composing
                     poets

    this dictionary   twenty-two thousand
                     words

    this book   eighteen chapters

15. ws ne Dyrame mẽ <u>buRhe</u>   ka kyrdar bəRi xubsurti se əda kia.

    the Pakistani
    officer

    the ambassador

    the student

    the husband

    the gardener

24. 502. Transformation.

1.   Change the underlined verb forms in the following sentences to (a) the <PreP + /a rəha həy/> formation, and (b) the <PreP + /cəla a rəha həy/> formation. E. g. /kər rəha hə̃y/ to (a) /kərte a rəhe hə̃y/ and (b) /kərte cəle a rəhe hə̃y/.

    a.   həm ərse se yyhi <u>swn rəhe hə̃y</u>.

    b.   həm pãc sal se wn ka xərc <u>de rəhe hə̃y</u>.

    c.   həm sal bhər se yyhi <u>kəh rəhe hə̃y</u>.

    d.   dhobi salõ se dərya ke kynare ysi təra kəpRe <u>dho rəhe hə̃y</u>.

    e.   mə̃y bəcpən se yyhi dəvai <u>pi rəhi hū̃</u>.

    f.   vw do sal se yyhi qəmis <u>pəhn rəha həy</u>.

    g.   həm ys yskul mẽ tisri jəmat se <u>pəRh rəhe hə̃y</u>.

    h.   mə̃y ərse se pwrani kytabẽ <u>xərid rəha hū̃</u>.

    i.   šwəra sədiõ se ys məwzu pər nəzmẽ <u>lykh rəhe hə̃y</u>.

    j.   vw xwda se yyhi doa <u>mã̄g rəhi hə̃y</u>.

24. 503. Fill the Blanks.

1. Fill the blanks in the following sentences with the most appropriate word or phrase from among those given at the end of the exercise. Drill each sentence for fluency.

۱۔ معنی کے لحاظ سے ـــــــ کے اشعار آپس میں کوئی تعلّق نہیں رکھتے ۔

۲۔ اُردو کی سب سے مشہور ـــــــ میر حسن دہلوی کی ہے ۔

۳۔ اُردو کے شعراء نے فارسی کی سب ـــــــ اپنائی ہیں ۔

۴۔ تصوّف کی اصطلاح میں ـــــــ خدا کو کہتے ہیں ۔

۵۔ ـــــــ میں صرف دو شعر ہوتے ہیں ۔

۶۔ ذوق نے مختلف امراء کی تعریف میں ـــــــ لکھے ہیں ۔

۷۔ میر انیس کے ـــــــ سن کر لوگ رو دیتے ہیں ۔

۸۔ ایک روایت ہے کہ ذوق کا ـــــــ غدر میں ضائع ہو گیا ۔

۹۔ میر تقی میر نے اُردو شعراء کا سب سے پہلا ـــــــ بھی لکھا ہے ۔

۱۰۔ اکبر الہ آبادی نے اِس شعر میں معاشرے پر ـــــــ کیا ہے ۔

۱۱۔ امیر اللّغات املی درجے کے ـــــــ میں سے ایک ہے ۔

۱۲۔ آجکل پاکستان میں ـــــــ کا بہت رواج ہے ۔

۱۳۔ مصنّف اور انتقاد نے ایک دوسرے کی خوب ـــــــ لکھیں ۔

۱۴۔ غالبؔ کے ـــــــ میں بلند خیالات و انکار پائے جاتے ہیں ۔

۱۵۔ موجودہ دور میں امریکہ میں ـــــــ کا رواج زیادہ ہے اور شاعری کم ۔

۱۶۔ آجکل اُردو شاعری میں گل و بلبل کے ـــــــ کے علاوہ اور بھی بہت سے مضامین ہتے ہیں ۔

۱۷۔ میر تقی میر ایک ـــــــ شاعر کی حیثیت سے یاد کئے جاتے ہیں ۔

481

۱۸۔ دکنی بادشاہوں کی سرپرستی کی وجہ سے اردو ۔۔۔۔۔۔۔کو عروج ملا ۔

۱۹۔ ناسخؔ کے کلام میں بہت پیچیدہ ۔۔۔۔۔۔۔ ملتی ہیں ۔

۲۰۔ اکثر مثنویوں میں ۔۔۔۔۔۔ کی کہانی بیان کی جاتی ہے ۔

مثنوی   اصنافِ سخن   لغات   شاعری   غزل   غزلگو   طنز   معشوق

ہجویں   حسن وعشق   نثر   تذکرہ   رباعی   محاورات و اصطلاحات   آزاد نظم

دیوان   قصیدے   کلام   افسانوں   مرثیے

24. 504. Variation.

۱۔ اُن کی تقریر نے ہجوم کو بہت متأثّر کیا ۔

اُس کی اِس غزل نے سننے والوں کو بہت متأثّر کیا ۔

صدر کی سادہ زندگی اور کردار نے غیر ممالک کے سفیروں کو بہت متأثّر کیا ۔

ذوقؔ کے اِس قصیدے نے بادشاہ کو بہت متأثّر کیا ۔

اُس فرانسیسی محقّق کی اردو نے سب لوگوں کو بہت متأثّر کیا ۔

میرانیسؔ کے مرثیوں نے لوگوں کو جتنا متأثّر کیا ہے، شاید ہی کسی دوسرے شاعر کے
مرثیوں نے کیا ہو ۔

۲۔ آج کل ہمارے شعرا کا رجحان آزاد نظموں کی طرف ہے ۔

اِس دَور کے شعرا کا رجحان روزمرّہ اور آسان زبان کی طرف ہے ۔

آج کل ہندوستانی موسیقاروں کا رجحان مغربی موسیقی کی طرف ہے ۔

اُنیسویں صدی کے آغاز سے ہی لکھنؤ کے شعرا کا رجحان طویل غزلوں کی طرف ہے ۔

482

اُنیسویں صدی کے وسط میں اردو کے شعراء کا رجحان مشکل اور پیچیدہ محاورات کی طرف تھا۔

قید ہونے کے بعد اُس کی شاعری کا رجحان اِشتراکیت کی طرف ہو گیا۔

۳- اِس گروہ کی رائے کے مطابق اِشتراکیت دنیا کے لئے سب سے مفید نظام ہے۔

اُس کی رائے کے مطابق سرمایہ داری کے کچھ اچھے پہلو بھی ہیں۔

کمیونسٹوں کے مطابق سرمایہ داری دنیا کو نقصان پہنچا رہی ہے۔

امریکہ کے مطابق دنیا صرف جمہوری نظام کے تحت ترقّی کر سکتی ہے۔

میرے خیال کے مطابق ہر بڑے ملک کی تاریخ میں سامراجیت کسی نہ کسی شکل میں ضرور ملے گی۔

اِس محقق کے نظریہ کے مطابق سرمایہ داری اور اِشتراکیت دونوں ختم ہو جائیں گی اور اِن کی جگہ ایک نیا سیاسی نظام وجود میں آئے گا۔

۴- ہر مسلمان کو اِن عقائد کی پیَروی کرنی چاہئے۔

آپ کو اِن قواعد کی پیَروی کرنی پڑے گی۔

اُس نے قدیم اساتذہ کی پیَروی میں ایک طویل مثنوی لکھی ہے۔

اگر ہم اِن اصولوں کی پیَروی کریں تو ہمارے تمدن کو کبھی زوال نہیں آئے گا۔

اگر ہم اسلامی قوانین کی پیَروی کریں تو زندگی بہتر بن سکتی ہے۔

ہمارے وکیل صاحب اِس مقدمے کی پیَروی کریں گے۔

۵- اُنہوں نے ایسی غزلیں کہی ہیں کہ شاید ہی کسی دوسرے غزل گو نے کہی ہوں۔

اُس نے غریبوں پر جو ظلم کیا ہے وہ شاید ہی کسی اور بادشاہ نے کیا ہو۔

اُس نے اپنے اِنشائوں میں مناظرِقدرت اِس خوبصورتی سے پیش کئے ہیں کہ شاید ہی کسی دوسرے نے پیش کئے ہوں۔

483

اُن کے کلام میں نئی نئی اصطلاحات اور محاورات اِس کثرت سے ہیں کہ شاید ہی کسی اور شاعر کے کلام میں ہوں۔

اُس زمانے میں غزل کو اتنا عروج بلا کہ شاید ہی کسی اور زمانے میں ملا ہو۔

جو مقبولیت غالبؔ کو حاصل ہوئی ہے وہ شاید ہی کسی دوسرے کو حاصل ہوئی ہو۔

۶۔ جاہل سے جاہل آدمی بھی اِس بات کو سمجھ سکتا ہے۔

امیر سے امیر آدمی بھی اِس کا خرچ برداشت نہیں کر سکتا۔

غریب سے غریب آدمی بھی اللہ کے راستے میں پانچ روپے دے سکتا ہے۔

وہ پیچیدہ سے پیچیدہ مضامین کو آسان لفظوں میں پیش کرتا ہے۔

وہ آسان سے آسان سوال بھی حل نہیں کر سکتا۔

اُسے اچھے سے اچھا کپڑا بھی پسند نہیں آتا۔

۷۔ صرف اِس تذکرے میں اِس شاعر کا ذکر ملتا ہے۔

آپ کو تقریباً ہر تذکرے میں اِن اساتذہ کا ذکر ملے گا۔

آپ کو ہر تاریخ میں اِس بادشاہ کے ظلم کا ذکر ملے گا۔

آپ کو اِس تاریخ میں اِس جنگ کا ذکر نہیں ملے گا۔

پرانے تذکروں میں شعراء کے اِس گروہ کا ذکر نہیں ملے گا۔

اُس کے ہر قصیدے میں اِس وزیر کا ذکر ملتا ہے۔

۸۔ آریائی زبانوں میں اُردو بھی شامل ہے۔

اِس تاریخ میں بعض ایرانی سیاست دانوں کے حالات بھی شامل ہیں۔

اِس گروہ میں بہت سے غیر ملکی محققین بھی شامل تھے۔

غالبؔ کے دیوان میں غزلوں کے علاوہ کچھ قصیدے بھی شامل ہیں۔

انتخاؔب کے دیوان میں ترکی ، عربی اور فارسی کے اشعار بھی شامل ہیں۔

انھوں نے اپنی کتاب میں بعض ایسی روایات بھی شامل کر دی ہیں جو مستند نہیں۔

۹۔   بادشاہ کو سفیر کی باتوں پر شک تھا۔

مجھے اُس آدمی پر شک تھا کہ وہ چور ہے۔

ابتدا ہی سے مجھے اُس پر شک تھا۔ اسی لئے میں نے اُسے وہاں جانے کی اجازت نہیں دی۔

مجھے اِس محاورے کے صحیح ہونے پر شک ہے۔

اگرچہ پولیس کو اُس پر شک تھا۔ مگر اُس نے اُسے گرفتار نہیں کیا۔

اُس کی یہ حرکت دیکھ کر مجھے شک ہوا کہ وہ اچھا آدمی نہیں ہے۔

۱۰۔   وہ سمندر کے کنارے گھوم رہے تھے۔

وہ چار گھنٹے تک سمندر کے کنارے گھومتے رہے۔

وہ ہر روز شام کو سمندر کے کنارے گھومنے جاتے ہیں۔

اُس زمانے میں ہم ہر روز شام کو سمندر کے کنارے گھوما کرتے تھے۔

زبان سیکھنے کے لئے وہ شہر کی گلیوں اور بازاروں میں گھومتا پھرتا تھا۔

جب ہم گاڑی میں سفر کرتے ہیں تو ایسا محسوس ہوتا ہے کہ زمین گھوم رہی ہے۔

۱۱۔   پریشانی کی وجہ سے وہ تمام رات سڑکوں پر پھرتا رہا۔

میں ہوائی ڈاک کے لفافے کی تلاش میں ایک گھنٹے تک پھرتی رہی۔

دولت کے لئے وہ اپنے مذہب سے پھر گیا۔

اُس نے اپنے خاندان کی عزت کا بھی خیال نہ کیا اور اپنے وعدے سے پھر گیا۔

دہ اپنی منزل سے ناکام پھرا۔

اُس کی باتوں کی پروا   نہ کریں ۔ اُس کا تو سر پھر گیا ہے ۔

۱۲۔ غریب سے لے کر امیر تک ہر قسم کے لوگ اُس کے حلقے میں شامل تھے۔

بچے سے لے کر بوڑھے تک سب ہی اُس کا گانا سننے کے لئے آتے تھے۔

غلام سے لے کر بادشاہ تک سب ہی اُس بزرگ کے مزار پر آتے ہیں۔

اُس کی شاعری مغرب سے لے کر مشرق تک مشہور ہے ۔

یہ سڑک کلکتے سے لے کر پشاور تک جاتی ہے۔

ڈاکٹر صاحب سات بجے سے لے کر آٹھ بجے شام تک دفتر میں رہتے ہیں۔

۱۳۔ شعراء عرصے سے اِس موضوع پر لکھتے چلے آ رہے ہیں۔

عرب لیڈر عرصے سے اِسی سوال کو دوہراتے چلے آ رہے ہیں۔

مسلمان صدیوں سے اِس تہوار کو مناتے چلے آ رہے ہیں ۔

ہم لوگ اِن ہی اصولوں پر عمل کرتے چلے آئے ہیں۔

ہم لوگ اِن ہی اصولوں پر عمل کرتے آئے ہیں۔

ہم لوگ اِن ہی اصولوں پر عمل کرتے آئے ہیں اور کرتے رہیں گے۔

۱۴۔ اُس کی اِس حرکت سے سارا کام بگڑ گیا۔

بادشاہ کی کمزوری کی وجہ سے سلطنت کا نظام بگڑ گیا۔

کمزوری کی وجہ سے اُس کی حالت اور بھی بگڑ گئی ۔

انگریزی الفاظ کی کثرت کی وجہ سے ہماری زبان بگڑتی جا رہی ہے۔

یہ بات سن کر وہ ایک دم بگڑ گئے۔

سپاہی کی یہ بات سن کر وہ بگڑنے لگے۔

۵۱۔ اِس عمارت کی تعمیر نے ہمارے دارالحکومت کو ایک نیا حسن بخشا ہے۔

بادشاہ نے انعام کے طور پر سفیر کو ایک جاگیر بخشی۔

بادشاہ نے فوجی افسران کو انعام کے طور پر ایک ایک ہزار روپے عطا کئے۔

بادشاہ نے سپہ سالار کو ایک بڑی جاگیر عنایت فرمائی۔

اِس بیماری کے بعد اللہ نے اُسے ایک نئی زندگی بخشی۔

ہمیں امید ہے کہ اللہ ہمارے گناہوں کو بخش دے گا۔

24. 505. Translation.

1. Translate the following sentences from Urdu to English:

۱۔ اُس زمانے کی دکنی اُردو اور دہلی کی اُردو میں زیادہ فرق نہیں ہے۔ دکنی لغات میں مقامی
ہندی کے الفاظ زیادہ ہیں۔ مگر قواعد تقریباً ایک ہی ہے۔

۲۔ اُردو کی بنیاد ہندی ہے۔ یہ ایک آریائی زبان ہے۔ اگرچہ اُردو میں عربی سے بھی بہت سے
الفاظ لئے گئے ہیں۔ مگر بنیادی طور پر اُردو اور عربی الگ الگ خاندانوں سے ہیں۔

۳۔ اگرچہ غزل کے عام اور مقبول مضامین حسن و عشق ہیں۔ لیکن اِس صنفِ سخن میں تقریباً ہر
موضوع ملتا ہے۔ مثلاً تصوّف، فلسفہ، مذہب وغیرہ۔ آجکل کی غزلوں میں ایسے موضوعات
جیسے اشتراکیت، جمہوریت، سامراجیت وغیرہ بھی ملتے ہیں۔

۴۔ انشاء اللہ خاں انشاؔ سب سے پہلے ہندوستانی میں جنہوں نے اُردو زبان کی قواعد پر کتاب لکھی
اِس میں دہلی کے روزمرّہ سے لے کر پیچیدہ ادبی زبان تک ہر قسم کی اُردو پر بحث کی گئی ہے۔
اِس کتاب میں بعض ایسی باتیں بھی ہیں جن پر اب تک تحقیق کی نظر نہیں ڈالی گئی۔ یہ

487

کتاب ششماہ میں لکھی گئی تھی اور اب تک کئی دفعہ شائع ہو چکی ہے۔

۵۔ بابر کی اصل زبان ترکی تھی۔ چونکہ اُس وقت ترکوں میں بھی فارسی بولنے اور لکھنے کا رواج تھا، چنانچہ بابر کے دربار کی زبان بھی فارسی ہی تھی۔ لیکن بابر نے اپنے حالات ترکی زبان میں لکھے ہیں جو نہایت دلچسپ ہیں۔

۶۔ مرزا غالب کی سب سے بڑی خوبی اُن کا طرزِ بیان ہے۔ وہ پرانے مضامین کو ایک نئے انداز میں پیش کرتے ہیں۔ اُن کی شاعری سے اندازہ ہوتا ہے کہ اُنہوں نے زندگی کا گہرا مطالعہ کیا ہے۔ یہی وجہ ہے کہ اُن کا کلام بہت پُر اثر ہے۔

۷۔ اردو کے بہت کم ایسے شعراء ہیں جنہوں نے خالص ہندوستانی موضوعات پر شعر کہے ہیں۔ اکثر شعراء نے فارسی سے نہ صرف زبان، اندازِ بیان، محاورات و اصطلاحات لی ہیں بلکہ اُن کے خیالات بھی اپنائے ہیں۔ اصنافِ سخن تو سب کی سب فارسی ہیں۔ اردو میں غزل اور رباعی وغیرہ کے مضامین بھی اکثر فارسی سے لیے گئے ہیں۔ البتہ بعض مثنویاں ہندوستانی قصوں پر لکھی گئی ہیں جن میں خالص ہندوستانی ماحول پیش کیا گیا ہے۔

۸۔ جب افغانوں کا لشکر پہاڑ کے پاس پہنچا تو اُس کے سردار نے دیکھا کہ مغلوں کی فوج دریا کے کنارے کھڑی ہے۔ نزدیک جا کر اُس نے یہ بھی دیکھا کہ دشمن کی فوج بہت کم ہے چنانچہ اُس نے فوراً اپنے افسروں کو بلایا اور حملہ کرنے کا حکم دے دیا۔ حملے کا حکم ملتے ہی افغان لشکر آگے بڑھا اور لڑائی شروع ہو گئی۔ اتنے میں مغل سپہ سالار کے اشارے پر اُس پہاڑ کے پیچھے سے اور فوج نکل آئی جس نے افغانوں کے لشکر پر پیچھے سے حملہ کر دیا۔ جب لشکر کے سردار نے دیکھا کہ اُس کی فوج دونوں فوجوں کے بیچ میں آ گئی ہے تو اُس نے واپس ہونے کا حکم دے دیا۔

۹- مرثیے کو جتنا عروج اردو ادب میں حاصل ہوا ہے اتنا اس صنفِ سخن کو شاید کسی اور ادب
میں حاصل نہیں ہوا۔ انیس اور دبیر کے مرثیے اس صنفِ سخن میں ان کی مہارت کا ثبوت
ہیں۔ لوگ ان کے مرثیے آج بھی نہایت شوق سے پڑھتے اور سنتے ہیں۔

۱۰- اردو شاعری کے دکن میں جلد مقبول ہونے کی وجہ یہ تھی کہ وہاں کی حکومتوں اور ریاستوں میں
ہندی بولنے والوں کی اکثریت تھی۔ مقامی بادشاہوں کے درباروں میں بڑے بڑے ہندو
عہدے دار بھی تھے اور حکومت کا اکثر کام ان ہی کی زبان میں ہوتا تھا۔ یہی وہ لوگ
تھے جو شاعروں کی سرپرستی کرتے تھے۔ اسی لئے دکنی اردو پر فارسی یا عربی کی بجائے
ہندی کا اثر زیادہ ہے۔

۱۱- دہلی کے اکثر امراء اور شاہزادوں کو شعرو شاعری کا ذوق تھا۔ وہ شعراء کے قدر دان تھے۔
چنانچہ یہ ان ہی کی سرپرستی کا نتیجہ ہے کہ اردو شاعری نے اتنی ترقی کی۔

۱۲- اردو کے قدیم شعراء کے کلام میں اکثر تصوف کے خیالات و افکار پائے جاتے ہیں۔ تصوّف
کی زبان میں معشوق کا اشارہ اللہ کی طرف ہوتا ہے اور اسی طرح عشق کا مطلب اللہ
سے محبت کرنا ہے۔

۱۳- اردو شاعری میں مصنّف کا مقام بہت بلند ہے۔ وہ نہ صرف خود اچھے شاعر تھے بلکہ وہ
بہت سے مشہور شعراء کے استاد بھی تھے۔

۱۴- پرانے زمانے میں کتابیں ہاتھ سے لکھی جاتی تھیں۔ اور اسے ایک باقاعدہ فن کی حیثیت
حاصل تھی۔ جو کتابیں بادشاہوں کے لئے لکھی جاتی تھیں وہ نہایت خوبصورت ہوتی تھیں۔
ان کتابوں میں دربار کے مصوّر تصویریں بھی بناتے تھے۔ جن میں مختلف قسم کے رنگ
بھرتے تھے۔ بادشاہ ایسی کتابوں پر شاعروں اور مصوّروں کو بھاری انعام دیا کرتے تھے۔

489

۵۱- اردو میں محاورات کا سرمایہ بہت وسیع ہے ۔ اگرچہ محاورات کے کئی لغات شائع ہو چکے ہیں، پھر بھی محققین کا کام جاری ہے ۔ اس سلسلے میں سب سے بڑی مشکل یہ ہے کہ ہر علاقے کے محاورے مختلف ہیں جن کا ایک جگہ جمع کرنا اور اُن کے معنی بیان کرنا کوئی آسان کام نہیں ہے ۔

۱۶- بادشاہوں کے درباروں میں شعراء کی سرپرستی کا ایک نتیجہ یہ بھی ہوا کہ خود شعراء ایک دوسرے کی ہجو لکھنے لگے ۔ اس کی اصل وجہ یہ تھی کہ بادشاہ جس شاعر سے خوش ہوتا تھا-اُس کو انعام دیتا تھا اور اُس کی قدر کرتا تھا۔ چنانچہ شعراء کا آپس میں مقابلہ ہونے لگا اور ہجویں لکھی جانے لگیں ۔

۱۷- قدیم دکنی ادب کے بارے میں اب تک بہت کم معلومات حاصل تھیں ۔ لیکن بعض محققین کی زبردست کوششوں سے آہستہ آہستہ دکنی شعراء کے دیوان اور مثنویاں وغیرہ سامنے آنے لگی ہیں ۔ جس سے اردو کے ابتدائی دَور پر روشنی پڑتی ہے ۔ اِن معلومات کی روشنی میں دکنی ادب کی ایک مستند تاریخ بھی لکھی گئی ہے-اِس کے علاوہ ابھی پچھلے دِنوں دکنی ادب کے بعض شاہکار بھی شائع ہوئے ہیں ۔

۱۸- آج کل قصیدے لکھنے کا رواج نہیں کیونکہ اب وہ ماحول نہیں رہا-جب شعراء درباروں میں بادشاہوں کی تعریف میں قصیدے پڑھا کرتے تھے ۔ اُس زمانے میں تقریباً ہر دربار میں شعراء ہوتے تھے جن کا کام ہی یہ تھا کہ اپنے بادشاہ یا نواب کی تعریف میں قصیدے لکھیں اور اُنہیں خوش کریں ۔ دربار کے اِن خاص شعراء کو تنخواہوں کے علاوہ انعام بھی دیے جاتے تھے ۔

۱۹- ہمارے گاؤں میں ہر سال ایک میلہ لگتا تھا ۔ جس میں چاروں طرف کے گاؤں سے

490

لوگ آتے تھے۔ جو دو تین دن تک رہتے تھے۔ رات کو چراغوں کی روشنی کی جاتی تھی۔

اور ڈرامے ہوتے تھے۔ لوگ دن رات خوب ناچتے اور گاتے تھے۔ میلے میں ہر طرف چھوٹی

چھوٹی دکانیں بھی ہوتی تھیں جہاں سے ہر قسم کے پھل، مٹھائی اور دوسرا سامان خریدا

جا سکتا تھا۔ معلوم نہیں یہ میلہ اب بھی ہوتا ہے یا نہیں۔

۲۔ ابتدائی اردو شاعری میں آسان زبان، مقامی محاورات اور سادہ خیالات ملتے ہیں مگر بعد

میں فارسی زبان کے اثر کے تحت اس میں شکل اصطلاحات، پیچیدہ خیالات اور انوکھی

تشبیہات آ گئیں۔

2. Translate the following sentences into Urdu and write them out in the Urdu script.

a. After the decline of Delhi, many poets went to [lit. in] Lucknow, Rampur, and many other states, where the kings and navabs patronised them.

b. Sometimes his poetry reaches the limit [lit. up to the limit] of lewdness.

c. He presents scenes of nature in his məsnəvis more beautifully [lit. with this beauty] than [lit. that] perhaps any artist can do [lit. may be able to present] with the pen.

d. In modern poetry one group [lit. one group is such which] composes [lit. says] poetry in imitation of the old masters, and the other group writes poems on imperialism, communism, capitalism, and other subjects.

e. During the time of the Navabs of Lucknow, the elegy reached its zenith. The elegies of Mir Anis and Mirza Dabir are the monuments of that period.

f. [It] is the opinion of most researchers, that Insha wasted his poetic talents in joking [lit. in joke].

g. Communism has spread much in Africa and Asia because its leaders have promised that every person will get an ox, waterbuffalo, cow, land, house, etc., and the difference between [lit. of] rich and poor will not remain.

h. In this country revolutions constantly [/əksər/] keep taking place [lit. keep becoming]. Therefore foreign people do not want to invest capital in its industry.

i. He speaks Urdu with great fluency, but [he] does not know the true use of the idioms.

j. Because of his sudden death, our nation suffered a great loss [lit. to our nation a great loss arrived].

k. So long as [/jəb tək/] a Mughal Government was in [lit. on] Delhi, great [lit. big big] poets and writers remained [lit. were present] there, but after the decline of Delhi, everyone began to flee to [lit. in] the nearby [lit. near's] states.

l. From this incident I got a lesson [lit. counsel], that [one] should not become [/bənna/] a member of such a group, but [/bəlke/] [one] should remain far from such people.

m. You will find the word "imperialism" [lit. the word of imperialism] on page number [/nəmbər/] five hundred and thirty of this dictionary.

n. In his temperament are satire and humour. Therefore his poetry has received such popularity [lit. to his poetry so much popularity has become acquired].

o. Up to the middle of the Nineteenth Century, the language of the court of Delhi was Persian, and most of [/əksər/] the poets used to compose [lit. say] poetry in Persian. But after the coming of Vali Dakani, Urdu poetry began to be popular, and the great [lit. big big] poets [lit. eloquent ones] of Delhi began to compose [lit. say] poetry in Urdu.

p. He used to wander about in the markets [and] lanes of Lucknow every day. [He] used to meet the people. [He] used to take part [lit. sit] in various circles. This [/yyhi/] is the reason that he learned Urdu so quickly [/ytni jəld/].

q. Tomorrow is Id. My father has bought a goat. After coming back from the Id prayers [lit. the prayer of Id], he will slaughter [lit. will cut] it. Of [lit. from in] its meat, one portion will be given to the poor, one portion to friends and relatives, and one portion we ourselves will keep [/rəkhna/].

r. In this təzkyra are only Deccani poets. Therefore [it] will not be useful [lit. will not come [into] work] in my research.

s. Probably he was the last poet who wrote a məsnəvi in this style.

t. The poetry of Insha and Rangin throws light upon the society of that time.

24.506. Script.

1. Write out the following words in the Urdu script and place them in Urdu alphabetical order.

a.	cwnãce	k.	bezar
b.	səfha	l.	yttyfaqən
c.	sədarət	m.	xamoš
d.	behoš	n.	tənz
e.	chwpna	o.	fəxr
f.	səlahiət	p.	təavwn
g.	yəzəlgo	q.	yšq
h.	mwhəzzəb	r.	nali
i.	sabyt	s.	tərbiət
j.	gwmrah	t.	bheR

2. Look up the following words in an Urdu-English dictionary. Write out each entry. Note whether the dictionary gives such information as gender, possible plurals, complex verbal formations, idioms, etc.

492

a.	مفت	f.	روشن
b.	درخواست	g.	بے وفا
c.	جیتنا	h.	ناممکن
d.	مخلص	i.	لعنت
e.	بالوس	j.	قرضہ

3. Look up the following words in an English-Urdu dictionary. Write out each entry.
Note the presence or absence of the information listed under (2) above.

a.	rib	f.	recognise
b.	snake	g.	face [noun]
c.	birth	h.	tour
d.	adorable	i.	bird
e.	purify	j.	danger

24. 507. Response.

1. Answer the following questions verbally:

١۔ کیا، آپ کے ملک میں شاعری مقبول ہے ؟

٢۔ آپ کے شعراء کے ہاں معشوق کا کیا تصوّر ہے ؟

٣۔ آپ کی نظر میں انگریزی شاعری کا سب سے بڑا شاہکار کونسا ہے ؟

٤۔ اُردو کے مقابلے میں انگریزی کی قواعد آسان ہے یا پیچیدہ ؟

٥۔ کیا آپ نے کبھی شعر کہے ہیں ؟

٦۔ آپ کے ملک میں شاعری کا مستقبل تاریک ہے یا روشن ؟

٧۔ کیا آپ ہندی کے رسم الخط سے بھی واقف ہیں ؟

٨۔ کیا آپ ہندوستانی موسیقی سے لطف اٹھاتے ہیں ؟

۹۔ کیا آپ شعر کہنے کی صلاحیت رکھتے ہیں ؟

۱۰۔ آپ کے ہاں پہلے نثر مقبول ہوئی یا نظم ؟

۱۱۔ کیا آپ کے ہاں کبھی طویل کہانیاں نظم کی شکل میں لکھنے کا رواج تھا ؟

۱۲۔ آپ انگریزی کے کس شاعر سے متاثر ہیں ؟

۱۳۔ آپ کو کس کے افسانے پسند ہیں ۔ اور کیوں ؟

۱۴۔ کیا آپ کے ملک کے شعرا، اب تک پرانے اساتذہ کی تقلید کر رہے ہیں یا انہوں نے کوئی نیا انداز اختیار کیا ہے ؟

۱۵۔ مغربی ممالک میں فارسی کا ایک شاعر اپنی رباعیوں کی وجہ سے بہت مشہور ہے ۔ اس شاعر کے متعلق آپ کیا جانتے ہیں ؟

2.   Write out the answers to the following questions in Urdu.   Answers to these may be found in Sec. 24. 000 or in the Word Study Section.

۱۔ اردو زبان کس خاندان سے تعلق رکھتی ہے ؟

۲۔ کیا دلّی دکنی کا کلام دیگر شعرا کے مقابلے میں فارسی اور عربی سے زیادہ متاثر ہے ؟

۳۔ نظیر اکبر آبادی کس دربار سے تعلق رکھتے تھے ؟

۴۔ نظیر اکبر آبادی نے کن موضوعات پر نظمیں لکھیں ؟

۵۔ کیا اردو اور انگریزی ایک ہی خاندان سے تعلق رکھتی ہیں ؟

۶۔ غزل میں کم سے کم کتنے اشعار ہونے چاہییں ؟

۷۔ آتش اور ناسخ میں سے کس کا کلام زیادہ پیچیدہ ہے ؟

۸۔ امیر مینائی اور داغؔ کی شاعری کا مقابلہ کیجیے ۔

494

۹۔ کیا اقبال کی شاعری میں صرف حُسن و عشق کی باتیں پائی جاتی ہیں؟

۱۰۔ موجودہ شعراء کو آپ کتنے گروہوں میں تقسیم کر سکتے ہیں؟

۱۱۔ حالی اپنی شاعری میں کیا پیغام دیتے ہیں؟

۱۲۔ کیا یہ صحیح ہے کہ مرزا دبیر اُردو کے پہلے مرثیہ گو شاعر ہیں؟

۱۳۔ اُردو کی وہ کون کون سی اصنافِ سخن ہیں جن کا ذکر اِس سبق میں آیا ہے؟

۱۴۔ میرانیؔس کی شاعری کی خوبیاں بیان کیجئے ۔

۱۵۔ غالب کے کلام کی سب سے بڑی خوبی کیا ہے؟

24. 508. Conversation Practice.

Mr. Smith is discussing the essay given in Sec. 24. 000 with Dr. Rəhim.

اسمتھ۔ آپ کے ہاں نثر کے مقابلے میں شاعری زیادہ مقبول ہے ۔ لیکن ہمارے ملک میں لوگ
نثر سے زیادہ لطف اٹھاتے ہیں ۔

رحیم۔ دراصل اُردو ادب کی ابتدا ہی شاعری سے ہوتی ہے ۔ چنانچہ شروع سے ہی لوگوں کو شعر
کہنے اور شعر سننے کا بہت شوق ہے ۔

اسمتھ۔ ہمارے ملک میں بھی پرانے زمانے میں شاعری بہت پسند کی جاتی تھی ۔ لیکن آج کل
زیادہ مقبول نہیں۔

رحیم۔ آپ کے ہاں ڈرامے اور افسانے وغیرہ نے اتنی ترقی کی ہے کہ لوگ اُن سے زیادہ
لطف اٹھاتے ہیں اور شاعری میں زیادہ دلچسپی نہیں لیتے ۔ ہمارے ملک میں بھی آج سے
کچھ عرصہ پہلے افسانہ یا ڈرامہ مقبول نہیں تھا۔ لیکن اب رفتہ رفتہ اِن کی مقبولیت بڑھتی

جا رہی ہے ۔

اسمتہ۔ میرے خیال میں خواہ وہ نثر ہو یا نظم اِن کی مقبولیت اپنے اپنے ماحول اور معاشرے سے تعلق رکھتی ہے ۔ ہوسکتا ہے کہ بعض چیزیں جو آپ کے معاشرے میں پسند کی جاتی ہیں وہ ہمارے ہاں پسند نہ کی جائیں ۔

رحیم۔ جی ہاں! آپ نے بالکل صحیح فرمایا ۔ مثال کے طور پر ہمارے ہاں اکثر شعرا۔ ایک جگہ جمع ہوتے ہیں اور اپنا اپنا کلام سناتے ہیں۔ اور لوگ ہزاروں کی تعداد میں دُور دُور سے اُن کا کلام سننے کے لئے آتے ہیں اور گھنٹوں بیٹھ کر بڑی دلچسپی سے سنتے ہیں ۔ مگر آپ کے ہاں ایسا نہیں ہوتا ۔ شاید آپ لوگ اِسے وقت ضائع کرنے کا ایک ذریعہ سمجھیں ۔ اِس کے مقابلے میں آپ لوگ ڈراموں اور افسانوں وغیرہ سے لطف اٹھاتے ہیں ۔

اسمتہ۔ آپ کسی حدتک صحیح فرماتے ہیں .... کیا موجودہ دَور کے شعرا۔ بھی قصیدے لکھتے ہیں؟

رحیم۔ قصیدوں کا تعلق درباروں سے ہوتا تھا ۔ بادشاہ ، نواب اور امرا۔ کے درباروں میں شعرا۔ ہوتے تھے جن کا کام ہی یہ تھا کہ وہ اُن کی تعریف میں قصیدے لکھیں ۔ اِن شاعروں کو باقاعدہ تنخواہیں ملتی تھیں ۔ اور اِس کے علاوہ مختلف موقعوں پر انعام وغیرہ بھی دیے جاتے تھے ۔ لیکن آج کل ماحول بدل چکا ہے ۔ اب نہ تو دربار ہیں اور نہ ہی قصیدہ گو شعرا۔ ۔ قصیدے کی طرح موجودہ شعرا۔ مثنوی بھی نہیں لکھتے ۔ اِن کی جگہ افسانوں اور ڈراموں نے لے لی ہے ۔

اسمتہ۔ مثنوی اور نظم میں کیا فرق ہے ؟

رحیم۔ نظم میں عام طور پر کوئی قصّہ یا کہانی نہیں بیان کی جاتی ۔ اور اگر کوئی شاعر نظم میں

کہانی بیان کرتا بھی ہے تو وہ اِتنی طویل نہیں ہوتی ۔ نظم عام موضوعات پر لکھی جاتی ہے؛ جیسے مناظرِ قدرت وغیرہ ۔ مثنوی ایک ایسی طویل نظم کا نام ہے جس میں کوئی قصّہ یا کہانی بیان کی جاتی ہے ۔ یا ایک ہی موضوع کے تحت مختلف کہانیاں لکھی جاتی ہیں۔ اُردو زبان کی اکثر مثنویاں حُسن و عشق کی کہانیوں پر مشتمل ہیں۔

اسمتھ۔ میں نے یہ محسوس کیا ہے کہ آپ لوگوں کو ایسی شاعری پسند ہے جس میں درد وغم ہو اِس کی کیا وجہ ہے؟

رحیم۔ ہر انسان کی زندگی میں کچھ مشکلیں اور پریشانیاں ہوتی ہیں ۔ لوگ ایسی شاعری کو اِس لئے پسند کرتے ہیں کہ اُنہیں اِس میں اپنی زندگی نظر آتی ہے ۔ غالباً یہی وجہ ہے کہ انگلستان کے ایک مشہور شاعر نے کہا ہے کہ درد بھری شاعری ہی سب سے اچّھی شاعری ہے۔

اسمتھ۔ کیا سودؔا نے بھی غزلیں لکھی ہیں؟

رحیم۔ جی ہاں! اُن کی غزلوں کا پورا دیوان موجود ہے ۔ لیکن اُن کی غزلوں کو وہ مقام حاصل نہیں جو اُن کے قصیدوں کو ہے ۔ اُردو ادب میں وہ اپنے قصیدوں اور ہجو کی وجہ سے زیادہ مشہور ہیں۔

اسمتھ۔ مصطفٰی اور انشاؔ جیسے بڑے اساتذہ نے اپنی شاعرانہ صلاحیتوں کو غلط طریقے سے کیوں استعمال کیا؟

رحیم۔ دراصل اُس زمانے کا ماحول ہی کچھ ایسا تھا۔ اچّھے اور قابل بادشاہوں اور نوابوں کی کمی تھی۔ یہ لوگ عیش و آرام کی زندگی بسر کرتے تھے اور حکومت کے کاموں میں دلچسپی نہ لیتے تھے۔ اُن کی زندگی میں اِس قسم کی عریاں اور مذاق سے بھری ہوئی شاعری بڑی

اہمیت رکھتی تھی۔ کیونکہ وہ اپنا سارا وقت اِسی قسم کی باتوں میں گذارتے تھے ۔ چنانچہ اِس دَور کے اکثر شعرا نے اُن کو خوش کرنے کے لئے ایسی شاعری شروع کی جس میں سوائے عریانی اور مذاق کے کچھ نہ ہوتا تھا۔

اسمتھ۔ تیر کی شاعری میں درد وغم اورعشق کے مضامین بہت ملتے ہیں ۔ اکثر ایسا محسوس ہوتا ہے کہ وہ اپنے حالات لکھ رہے ہیں ۔

رحیم۔ جی ہاں ، اگر آپ اُن کی زندگی کے حالات پڑھیں تو پتہ چلتا ہے کہ تیر کو بچپن ہی سے مصیبتوں کا سامنا کرنا پڑا۔ دس سال کی عُمر میں باپ کا انتقال ہوگیا ۔ اِس عمر میں نوکری کی تلاش شروع کی ۔ بڑے بھائی نے بھی مدد نہ کی ۔ اُنہوں نے دہلی کو برباد ہوتے اور اپنے دوستوں ، عزیزوں اور خاندان والوں کو تباہ ہوتے دیکھا۔ بعض لوگوں کا خیال ہے کہ وہ کسی سے عشق بھی کرتے تھے ۔ جسے وہ حاصل نہ کر سکے ۔ اور عُمر بھر عشق کی آگ میں جلتے رہے ۔ یہی وجہ ہے کہ اُن کی شاعری میں درد وغم اور عشق کے مضامین کثرت سے پائے جاتے ہیں ۔

اسمتھ۔ آپ کا دیوانِ غالب میرے پاس ہے ۔ آج کل میں اُس کا مطالعہ کر رہا ہوں ۔ انشاءاللہ اگلے ہفتے واپس کر دوں گا ۔

رحیم۔ کوئی بات نہیں ، جب آپ کی مرضی ہو واپس کر دیجئے گا ۔

اسمتھ۔ آپ کی بہت مہربانی ۔ خدا حافظ ۔

رحیم۔ خدا حافظ ۔

24.509. Conversation Stimulus.

Topics may include:
1.   The status of poetry in one's own country.
2.   One's own view of poetry.
3.   Poetry versus prose.
4.   Poetry and politics.
5.   The place of literature in language learning.

aryai A1	Aryan
axyr M1	end, latter portion
ədəbi A1	literary
*əfkar Mpl	pl. /fykr/
əfsana [or /fəsana/] M2	tale, story, romance, short story, fiction
əndaz M1	way, manner, mode, style
ənokha A2	novel, unique
*əsatyza Mpl	pl. /wstad/
*əsnaf Fpl	pl. /synf/
*əšar Mpl	pl. /šer/
*əwqat Mpl	pl. /vəqt/
bələnd [or /bwlənd/] A1	high, exalted, great
bərae Prep	for
bəxšna [Ic: /ə/]	to give, bestow, grant; forgive
bešwmar A1	countless, innumerable
bwlbwl F1	nightingale
bygəRna [I: /bygaRna/: If]	to become bad, be spoiled, bungled, ruined, become angry
darwlhwkumət M1	capital (city)
dəkəni A1	Deccani, of the Deccan
dərj PA1	entered, recorded, listed, registered, included
divan M1	divan, a collection of a poet's verses
fəlsəfi M/F1	philosopher
fəlsəfyana A1	philosophical
fəxr M1	pride
fyhryst F1	list
ghumna [IIc: /w/]	to turn, revolve, circle, wander
gwjrat M1 [np]	Gujarat, a province on the west-central coast of India
gwl M1	rose, flower
gyroh [or /gwroh/] M1	group, class
γalybən Adv	most probably, in all likelihood, perhaps
γəzəl F1	"γəzəl," a type of poem roughly corresponding to the sonnet or ode
γəzəlgo M/F1 A1	/γəzəl/-composing
həjv F1	ridicule, a poem (or other composition) ridiculing someone
həlqa M2	circle, group; link (in a chain); ward (of a city)
həqiqətən Adv	really, in reality, in fact
həydərabad M1 [np]	Haydarabad, both a province (nearly synonymous with /dəkən/) and the capital city of that province

həyrət F1 [np]	wonder, amazement, astonishment
hwsn M1 [np]	beauty, handsomeness
hyndi F2 [np] M1 A1	Hindi (language); Indian (nearly obsolete usage)
hyndostani F2 [np] M1 A1	Hindustani (language); Indian
id F1	"Id, " the name of two major yearly Muslim religious celebrations
jahyl A1	ignorant, illiterate
jwlna	to meet, mix [used only in the echo compound /mylna jwlna/ "to mix, meet, mingle together"]
kəlam M1	word, speech, discourse; poetry, works (of a poet); theology
kəsrət F1 [np]	abundance, plenty
khȳcna [or /khycna/] [I; /khɛ̄cna/; Ie]	to be pulled, drawn, attracted
kyrdar M1	character, nature; character (in a story, etc.)
ləkhnəu M1 [np]	Lucknow, a city in north-central India
ləškər M1	army, military force
*lwɣat Fpl [or Mpl]	pl. /lwɣət/
lwɣət F1 [or M1]	dictionary, vocabulary, stock of words
mašuq M1	beloved, sweetheart
məharət F1 [np]	skill, mastery
*mənazyr Mpl	pl. /mənzər/
məqbul PA1	accepted, approved, popular
məqbuliət F1 [np]	acceptance, popularity
mərsia M2	elegy, "mərsia"
mərsiəgo M/F1 A1	elegy-composing
mərsiəgoi F2 [np]	composition of elegies
məsnəvi F2	"məsnəvi, " a type of epic or narrative poem
məwsiqi F2 [np]	music
*məwzuat Mpl	pl. /məwzu/
məzah M1 [np]	humour, wit, fun
məzaq M1	joke; (literary) taste
mela M2	fair, large concourse of people
merəTh M1 [np]	Meerut, a city in north India
meyar [or /mear/] M1	standard, level, calibre
mwhavra [literary: /mwhavəra/] M2	idiom, expression
*mwhavrat [literary: /mwhavərat/] Mpl	pl. /mwhavra/
mwhəqqyq M1	researcher, investigator
*mwhəqqyqin Mpl	pl. /mwhəqqyq/
mwsəvvyr M1	artist, painter
mwtəəssyr PA1	affected, influenced, impressed
nəsihət F1	(moral) advice, counsel; lesson, warning
nəsr F1	prose
nyhayət Adv	extremely, exceedingly
pəyrəvi F2	following, adherence, observance (of laws, etc.); pursuit

pecida A1	complicated, complex, difficult, twisted, involved
phūkna [If: /w/]	to blow
phyrna [I: /pherna/: le]	to turn, turn back, turn away, wander, rove
pwrəsər A1	effective, impressive
qayda M2	rule, regulation, regular practice
qədrdan [or /qədrdā/] M/F1 A1	appreciator, connoiseur, one who knows the value of something
qələm M1 [or F1]	pen
qəsida M2	"qəsida," a type of poem usually containing praise of someone
qəsidəgo M/F1 A1	/qəsida/-composing
*qəvayd Mpl F1	pl. /qayda/; grammar
qəyd F1 [np]	imprisonment, bonds, restraint, restriction
qwdrət F1	nature; power, ability
rampur M1 [np]	Rampur, a princely state in north-central India
rəvani F2	fluency, smoothness
*rəvayat Fpl	pl. /rəvayət/
rəvayət F1	narration, saying; tradition
rozmərra M1 [np] A1 Adv	daily usage, ordinary conversation, daily allowance, daily wages; daily
ruh F1	spirit, life, soul
rwbai F2	quatrain, a four line poem
rwjhan M1	inclination, trend, desire
sadgi F2	simplicity, plainness
samrajiət F1 [np]	imperialism
səfha M2	page
səlahiət F1	capability, ability, capacity, talent
sərmaya M2	capital, asset[s]
sərmayədari F2 [np]	capitalism
sərpərəsti F2	patronage
swxən M1 [np]	speech, eloquence
swxənvər M/F1 A1	eloquent person, eloquent
synf F1	kind, sort, species, category, genre
šahkar [or /šəhkar/] M1	masterpiece
šayrana A1	poetic
šək M1	doubt, uncertainty, suspicion
tarik A1	dark
tənz M1 [np]	satire
təqlid F1	imitating, copying, following
təsəvvwf M1 [np]	Sufism, mysticism
təšbih F1	simile
*təšbihat Fpl	pl. /təšbih/
təvil A1	long, lengthy, extended

təzkyra M2	mention; biographical notice, book of brief biographies of poets, etc.
twrk M1 A1	Turk; Turkish
twrki M1 [np] F2 [np] A1	Turkey; Turkish (language); Turkish
tyhvar [or /teohar/] M1	celebration, festival (usually religious)
vəst M1 [np]	middle, centre
wruj M1 [np]	height, climax, zenith
wryani F2	nudity, nakedness, lewdness
wryã A1	nude, naked, lewd
wstad M1	teacher, master, expert
xalys A1	pure, genuine, unadulterated
xubsurti F2	beauty, prettiness
*xyalat Mpl	pl. /xyal/
ybtydai A1	beginning, introductory, elementary, early
ystylah F1	(technical) term
*ystylahat Fpl	pl. /ystylah/
yšq M1 [np]	love, romantic affection
yštyrakiət F1 [np]	communism
zəval M1 [np]	decline, decadence, wane, fall

Mirza Asad-ullah Khan Ghalib, one of the greatest poets
of Urdu.

اردو ادب کی مختصر تاریخ

(دوسرا حصّہ)

پچھلے سبق کے پڑھنے سے ہمیں یہ پتہ چلتا ہے کہ اردو کی پیدائش دہلی اور اس کے ارد گرد کے
علاقوں میں ہوئی اور یہ زبان جلد ہی سارے شمالی ہندوستان میں پھیل گئی ۔ اردو شاعری نے دہلی اور
دکن کے علاقوں میں خاص طور پر بہت ترقّی کی ۔ لیکن اردو نثر کی ترقّی دکن سے شروع ہوئی۔ایسا کیوں
ہوا کہ شاعری نے تو اِن علاقوں میں اتنی ترقّی کی اور نثر گمنامی میں پڑی رہی ۔ غالباً اِس کی وجہ یہ
تھی کہ شمالی ہندوستان میں فارسی کا عام رواج تھا۔ فارسی درباری زبان تھی ۔ ہر قسم کی تحریریں فارسی
ہی میں لکھی جاتی تھیں ۔ جو لوگ نثر لکھتے تھے وہ بہت مشکل ہوتی تھی ۔ موٹے موٹے فارسی اور
عربی الفاظ استعمال کئے جاتے تھے ۔معمولی سے معمولی اور آسان سے آسان بات بھی نہایت رنگین اور
پُرتکلف انداز میں بیان کی جاتی تھی ۔ دوسرے، شاعری اُس زمانے میں باعثِ امتیاز سمجھی جاتی تھی۔
اور لوگ نثر کو اہمیت نہ دیتے تھے۔اِن وجوہات کی بنا، پر نثر کی ترقّی نہ ہو سکی ۔

موجودہ محقّقین کے مطابق دکن کے شیخ عین الدّین گنج العلم کے چند رسالے اردو نثر کے
سب سے قدیم رسالے ہیں ۔ اگرچہ یہ رسالے آج کل نہیں ملتے ۔ اس سے اتنا اندازہ ضرور لگایا
جا سکتا ہے کہ آٹھویں صدی ہجری میں اردو نثر موجود تھی ۔ یہ رسالے مذہبی مسائل اور بزرگانِ
دین کے اقوال وغیرہ پر مشتمل ہیں ۔ خواجہ گیسو دراز کی "معراج العاشقین" غالباً اردو نثر کی سب سے قدیم
کتاب ہے جو شائع ہو چکی ہے ۔ اس کتاب کا موضوع بھی مذہب ہے ۔ اگر ہم قدیم دکنی ادب

505

کا جائزہ لیں تو نثر کی بہت سی اور بھی کتابیں ملتی ہیں۔ جن میں وجہی کی "سب رس" اور شاہ میران کی "جبلتنگ" مشہور ہیں۔

جب اردو نثر دکن سے شمالی ہندوستان میں آئی تو بہت سی فارسی اور عربی کتابوں کا ترجمہ اردو میں ہو چکا تھا۔ ان میں سب سے مشہور فنّی کی "دہ مجلس" ہے۔ جو ایرانی مصنف حسین واعظ کاشفی کی "روضۃ الشہداء" کا ترجمہ ہے۔ اس کی عبارت پیچیدہ اور مشکل ہے۔ اسی طرح نثر کا ایک مختصر نمونہ "کلیاتِ سودا" کے دیباچے میں ملتا ہے۔ جس سے اُس زمانے کی نثر کا اندازہ ہوتا ہے۔

انشا کی مشہور قواعد کی کتاب "دریائے لطافت" اگرچہ فارسی میں ہے لیکن اس میں مختلف اہلِ پیشہ کی بولیاں اور دہلی اور لکھنؤ کی زبان و محاورے کا فرق بتایا گیا ہے۔ یہ کتاب اُس زمانے کی نثر کا نمونہ ہے۔ اس عہد کی ایک اور کتاب "نو طرزِ مرصّع" ہے جس کے مصنف میر محمد حسین تحسین ہیں۔ یہ کتاب امیر خسرو کے "قصۂ چہار درویش" کا اردو ترجمہ ہے۔ کتاب کی عبارت بہت رنگین اور پیچیدہ ہے۔ ان کتابوں کے علاوہ اس دَور میں قرآن شریف کے ترجمے بھی ملتے ہیں۔ جن کے مترجم شاہ رفیع الدین اور شاہ عبد القادر ہیں۔

مندرجہ بالا کتابوں سے پتہ چلتا ہے کہ اکثر کتابیں یا تو عربی اور فارسی کتب کا ترجمہ ہیں یا مذہبی موضوعات اور مسائل پر لکھی گئی ہیں۔

سبق نمبر ۲۲ میں اس بات کی طرف اشارہ کیا گیا تھا کہ سترہویں صدی عیسوی کے وسط میں انگریز ہندوستان میں تجارت کی غرض سے آئے۔ اُس وقت یہاں انگریزوں کے علاوہ پرتگالی اور فرانسیسی بھی موجود تھے۔ ان غیر ملکیوں کا اصل مقصد تو تجارت تھا لیکن مقامی بادشاہوں کی کمزوری سے فائدہ اٹھا کر اُنہوں نے ملک کے سیاسی معاملات میں بھی دخل دینا شروع کر دیا۔

جب انگریزوں کی تجارت اور اُن کا اثر ملک میں بڑھنے لگا تو اُنہوں نے مقامی زبانیں سیکھنا
ضروری سمجھا۔ چنانچہ سنہ۱۸۰۰ میں کلکتّہ میں فورٹ ولیم کالج کے نام سے ایک ادارے کی
بنیاد رکھی گئی۔ جس میں انگریز افسر مقامی زبانیں سیکھتے تھے۔ ڈاکٹر گِل کرسٹ جو اِس کالج کے پہلے
منتظمِ اعلیٰ تھے، اردو زبان کے بہت بڑے سرپرست تھے۔ اُنہوں نے اُس وقت کے بڑے بڑے
اہلِ قلم کو اپنے کالج میں پڑھانے اور اردو زبان پر کام کرنے کی دعوت دی۔ اِن میں میر امّن،
شیر علی افسوس، کاظم علی جوان، نہال چند لاہوری، مرزا علی لطف اور سیّد حیدربخش حیدری
قابلِ ذکر ہیں۔

میر امّن اِس دَور کے ممتاز نثر نگار ہیں۔ اُنہوں نے امیرخسرو کے "قصّۂ چہار درویش" کا "باغ و بہار"
کے نام سے آسان اردو میں ترجمہ کیا۔ یہ کتاب آج بھی بہت مقبول ہے۔ "باغ و بہار"
صرف ایک دلچسپ قصّہ ہی نہیں بلکہ اُس زمانے کے رسم و رواج اور طرزِ زندگی کی ایک
اچّھی تصویر ہے۔

شیر علی افسوس نے "گلستانِ سعدی" اور نہال چند لاہوری نے "قصّۂ گل بکاؤلی" کا اردو
میں ترجمہ کیا۔ حیدری کی "آرائشِ محفل" اور مرزا علی لطف کا"تذکرہ گلشنِ ہند" بھی اِس دَور
کی یادگار ہیں۔

فورٹ ولیم کالج کی وجہ سے غیر ملکیوں میں اردو سیکھنے اور اردو زبان پر کام کرنے کا شوق پیدا
ہوا۔ یہی وجہ تھی کہ آگے چل کر بہت سے غیر ملکی مصنفین نے اردو زبان، قواعد اور لسانیات پر
بیسیوں کتابیں لکھیں۔ اِن میں جان شیکسپیئر، ڈاکٹر گریرسن، جان پلیٹس، مسٹر فینن، مسٹر فوربز
اور گارساں دتاسی وغیرہ بہت مشہور ہیں۔

مختصر یہ کہ فورٹ ولیم کالج نے اردو نثر کی شاندار خدمات سرانجام دیں۔ اردو ٹائپ کا

سب سے پہلا چھاپہ خانہ اسی کالج کے تحت قائم ہوا۔ اس کالج کی خدمات کم و بیش بیس برس جاری
رہیں۔ اس عرصے میں اٹھارہ مصنفین نے ۵۰ کتابیں اردو میں تصنیف، تالیف اور ترجمہ کیں۔ کالج
کی تالیفات مختلف موضوعات پر مشتمل ہیں۔ جیسے افسانہ، تذکرہ، قواعد، تاریخ، اخلاق، قرآن شریف
و انجیل کے ترجمہ وغیرہ۔ کالج کی سب سے بڑی خدمت یہ ہے کہ اس نے اردو نثر کو آسان اور
سلیس راہ پر ڈالا۔

اردو نثر کی یہ ترقی صرف فورٹ ولیم کالج تک ہی محدود نہیں رہی بلکہ دہلی اور لکھنؤ میں بھی اہل
قلم حضرات نے اس میدان میں قدم بڑھایا۔ لکھنؤ میں فقیر محمد گویا نے حسین واعظ کاشفی کی کتاب
"انوارِ سہیلی" کا "بستانِ حکمت" کے نام سے اردو میں ترجمہ کیا۔ بستانِ حکمت کی زبان بہت مشکل
ہے۔ اور عربی اور فارسی الفاظ سے بھری ہوئی ہے۔ اسی طرح مرزا رجب علی بیگ سرور کا "فسانۂ
عجائب" غالباً اس دور کی سب سے مشہور کتاب ہے۔ یہ کتاب حسن و عشق کا ایک فرضی قصہ
ہے۔ اس کی عبارت بہت رنگین اور پُرتکلف ہے۔ لیکن چونکہ اس قسم کی نثر اُس زمانے میں
بہت پسند کی جاتی تھی۔ اس لئے بہت مقبول ہوئی۔ سرور رنگین اور پُرتکلف طرز تحریر کے ماہر ہیں۔
اُن کی نثر اُس زمانے میں اتنی مقبول ہوئی کہ لوگ اُن کے دیگر پہلو جیسے خوش نویسی، موسیقی اور
شاعری کو بھول گئے۔ اس کتاب کے علاوہ اُن کی اور بھی بہت سی تصانیف ہیں۔

مرزا غالب جو اردو ادب میں عام طور پر ایک شاعر کی حیثیت سے مشہور ہیں فارسی اور اردو
کے ممتاز نثر نگار بھی تھے۔ اُن کی اردو نثر زیادہ تر اُن کے خطوط، چند دیباچوں اور چند
رسالوں پر مشتمل ہے۔ اُنہوں نے اپنے دوستوں۔ عزیزوں اور رشتہ داروں کو کئی سو خطوط
لکھے جو اُس زمانے کے سیاسی، معاشی اور تاریخی حالات پر روشنی ڈالتے ہیں۔ خطوط کی زبان
نہایت سادہ اور شیریں ہے اور تکلف اور بناوٹ سے خالی ہے۔ انداز تحریر ایسا ہے کہ

محسوس ہوتا ہے جیسے دو آدمی آمنے سامنے بیٹھے باتیں کر رہے ہیں یا کوئی مکالمہ ہو رہا ہے ۔ اُن کی
تحریر میں ظرافت اور شوخی کے اعلیٰ نمونے ملتے ہیں ۔

انیسویں صدی کے وسط سے اردو نثر کا ایک نیا دَور شروع ہوتا ہے ۔ اس دَور میں اردو اپنے
عروج پر پہنچی ۔ سرسید احمد خان اس دَور کی عظیم شخصیتوں میں سے ایک ہیں ۔ سرسید کا احسان
اردو ادب اور ہندوستانی مسلمان کبھی نہیں بھول سکتے ۔ سرسید کی ادبی خدمات اُن کے رسالے
تہذیب الاخلاق سے شروع ہوتی ہیں ۔ اُنہوں نے یہ رسالہ سنۃ ۱۸۷۰ء میں جاری کیا ۔ اس میں
اُس وقت کے نامور اہلِ قلم مختلف موضوعات پر مضامین لکھتے تھے ۔ اس رسالے نے اردو نثر
میں ایک انقلاب پیدا کر دیا ۔ سرسید خود بھی اس میں مضامین لکھتے تھے ۔ سرسید کی نثر بہت سادہ اور پُراثر
ہے ۔ وہ قواعد کی زیادہ پابندی نہیں کرتے بلکہ بے تکلف عبارت لکھتے ہیں ۔ وہ اپنے مضامین کو رنگینی اور
پیچیدگی کا لباس نہیں پہناتے بلکہ زبان کی سادگی اور بے تکلفی ہی اُن کی تحریر کا حسن اور زیور ہے ۔ سرسید
اپنے طرزِ تحریک کے خود موجد ہیں ۔ اُن کا طرزِ تحریر اتنا مقبول ہوا کہ اُس عہد کے اکثر اہلِ قلم نے اُسے اپنایا
سرسید نے اُس عہد کے بڑے بڑے ادبا کو اپنے حلقے میں لیا جنہوں نے اردو نثر کی ترقی میں نمایاں حصہ لیا ۔

سرسید کے ساتھیوں اور اس عہد کے دیگر اہلِ قلم حضرات میں محسن الملک ، وحید الدین سلیم
سید علی بلگرامی ، نذیر احمد ، شبلی ، ذکاءاللہ ، مولوی چراغ علی ، مولانا حالی اور آزاد قابلِ ذکر ہیں ۔

نذیر احمد نے بہت سے اصلاحی ناول لکھے اور بہت سی مذہبی اور قانونی کتابوں کا اردو میں
ترجمہ کیا ۔ وہ اردو کے پہلے ناول نویس ہیں ۔ اُن کی زبان سادہ اور آسان ہے ۔ اُن کے ناول
اتنے مقبول ہوئے کہ شاید ہی کوئی ایسا گھر ہوگا جہاں اُن کا ناول " مرآۃ العروس " نہ ہو ۔
" توبۃ النصوح " " ابن الوقت " اور " بنات النعش " اُن کے دوسرے مشہور ناول ہیں ۔

شبلی ایک عالم ، موزخ ، ادیب ، محقق ، نقّاد اور شاعر تھے ۔ اُنہوں نے تاریخ اور

۵۰۹

تنقید میں بہت سی نئی راہیں دکھائیں۔ "سیرۃ النبی" ، "الفاروق" اور "شعرالعجم" اُن کی مشہور تصانیف ہیں۔

مولانا ذکاءاللہ نے ریاضی ، تاریخ ، جغرافیہ اور سائنس پر بہت سی کتابیں اور مضامین لکھے لیکن وہ مورخ کی حیثیت سے زیادہ مشہور ہیں۔ "تاریخِ ہندوستان" کی دس جلدیں اُن کی یادگار ہیں۔

مولوی چراغ علی نے مختلف موضوعات پر بیسیوں مضامین اور کتابیں لکھیں۔ لیکن اُن کے مذہبی مضامین خاص انفرادیت رکھتے ہیں۔

مولانا حالی نے "مقدمۂ شعر و شاعری" لکھ کر ادبی تنقید کا آغاز کیا۔ اِسی طرح "حیاتِ سعدی" اور "حیاتِ جاوید" لکھ کر اردو میں سوانح نگاری کی ابتدا کی۔

محمد حسین آزاد اردو نثر کی ایک ممتاز شخصیت ہیں۔ اُن کا دلکش اندازِ تحریر اردو نثر کی جان ہے۔ اُن کی نثر میں موسیقی ہے۔ حقیقت تو یہ ہے کہ وہ نثر میں شعر کہتے ہیں۔ موضوع کتنا ہی خشک کیوں نہ ہو، اُس میں دلچسپی پیدا کرنا آزاد کے اندازِ بیان کا کمال ہے۔ "آبِ حیات"، "دربارِ اکبری" اور "نیرنگِ خیال" اُن کے شاہکار ہیں۔

مندرجۂ بالا حضرات جدید نثر کے بانی ہیں۔ اِن ہی کی وجہ سے اردو نثر نے پچاس برس میں اِتنی ترقی کی۔ اِن کی وجہ سے زبان ، موضوعات اور مضامین کو بہت وسعت ملی۔ تاریخ ، تنقید، مذہب ، سیاست ، سائنس۔غرض کہ ہر موضوع اردو نثر میں آگیا۔ ملک میں اخبار اور رسالے عام ہو گئے اور دوسرے لوگوں نے بھی مضامین اور کتابیں لکھنی شروع کیں۔ اخباروں اور رسالوں نے نثر کو عوام میں بھی بہت مقبول بنا دیا۔ اخباروں میں منشی نول کشور کا "اودھ اخبار"، منشی محبوب عالم کا "پیسہ اخبار"، ظفر علی خان کا "زمیندار"، محمد علی جوہر کا "ہمدرد" اور

510

ابوالکلام آزاد کا " الہلال " صحافت میں بلند مقام رکھتے ہیں ۔ اور رسالوں میں منشی سجاد حسین کے
"اودھ پنچ"، سر عبدالقادر کے " مخزن " میر ناصر علی کے "مطلائے عام " اور نیاز فتح پوری کے "نگار "نے
اردو ادب کی ترقی میں نمایاں حصہ لیا ۔

اخباروں اور رسالوں کے علاوہ ہندوستان میں اردو ادب کی ترقی کے لئے کئی انجمنیں وجود
میں آئیں ۔ جن میں "انجمن ترقی اردو ہند" خاص طور پر قابل ذکر ہے ۔ مولوی عبدالحق کے
زیر سرپرستی اس انجمن نے اردو ادب کی وہ خدمات سرانجام دیں کہ اس صدی میں شاید ہی کسی
دوسری انجمن نے دی ہوں ۔ مولوی عبدالحق بیسویں صدی کے اردو زبان کے سب سے بڑے
محقق اور نقاد ہیں ۔ انہوں نے اپنی ساری زندگی اردو کے لئے وقف کردی ۔ ان کی سرپرستی
میں ہزاروں کتابیں تالیف ، ترجمہ اور تصنیف ہوئیں ، سینکڑوں پرانی اور نایاب کتابیں ان کی
نگرانی میں شائع ہوئیں ۔ یہ ان ہی کی کوششوں کا نتیجہ تھا کہ کراچی میں اردو یونیورسٹی قائم ہوئی ۔
ان کی ان خدمات کی وجہ سے آج بھی قوم انہیں "بابائے اردو " کے نام سے یاد کرتی ہے ۔

اب ہم مختصر طور پر اردو میں ناول نویسی ، ڈرامے اور افسانہ نویسی کا ذکر کریں گے ۔

اردو ناول کی بنیاد نذیر احمد نے رکھی ۔ ان کے ناول بہت مقبول ہوئے ۔ ان کے بعد
بہت سے لوگوں نے ناول لکھے ۔ لیکن سرشار ، عبدالحلیم شرر ، مرزا رسوا اور راشد الخیری قابل
ذکر ہیں ۔ سرشار نے اپنی افسانہ نویسی اور ناول نویسی کی وجہ سے اردو ادب میں ایک خاص
مقام پیدا کیا ۔ ان کی نثر میں ظرافت اور شوخی ہے ۔ ہر قسم کے موضوع میں دلچسپی پیدا کرتے
ہیں ۔ ان کی زبان خاص لکھنؤ کی زبان ہے اور ان کے افسانوں اور ناولوں میں لکھنؤ کی
تہذیب ملتی ہے ۔ " فسانہ آزاد " "بپی کہاں "اور "سیر کہسار" ان کے مشہور ناول ہیں ۔
شرر نے اسلامی اور تاریخی ناولوں کی طرف توجہ دی اور بڑا نام پیدا کیا ۔ ان کی زبان بہت

511

سلیس اور با محاورہ ہے ۔مسلمانوں کی عظمتِ گذشتہ کے واقعات خوب بیان کرتے ہیں ۔ مرزا رسوا
نے لوگوں کو ناول نویسی کے فن سے آگاہ کرایا۔وہ اپنے ناولوں کے اکثر پلاٹ روز مرّہ کی زندگی
سے لیتے ہیں ۔ اس لئے اُن کے ناول حقیقت معلوم ہوتے ہیں ۔"امراؤ جان آدا" اُن کا
مقبول ترین ناول ہے ۔

راشد الخیری کا اپنا ایک خاص میدان ہے ۔ اُنہوں نے عورتوں کی تعلیم و تربیت کے موضوع
پر ناول لکھے ۔اُن کا ہر افسانہ اور ہر ناول یاس و ناامیدی اور درد وغم سے بھرا ہوا ہے ۔ وہ
بیماری ، موت اور تکالیف کے مناظر اس طرح کھینچتے ہیں کہ پڑھنے والے کی آنکھوں میں آنسو
آجاتے ہیں ۔ اِسی وجہ سے وہ مصوّرِ غم کے نام سے مشہور ہیں۔

اردو میں ناول کی مقبولیت بڑھتی رہی اور کانی لوگوں نے ناول لکھے لیکن ان میں پریم چند اور
کرشن چندر کے ناول بہت مقبول ہوئے ۔ اب بھی بہت سے لوگ ناول لکھتے ہیں ۔لیکن صحیح معنوں
میں اچھے ناول نویسوں کی تعداد بہت کم ہے ۔ موجودہ دَور میں عصمت چغتائی ، عزیز احمد ،
رشید اختر ندوی ، اے۔آر۔خاتون اور قیسی رام پوری بہت مشہور ہیں ۔

اردو ڈرامے کی تاریخ بہت ہی مختصر ہے ۔ ۱۸۵۳ء میں امانت لکھنوی نے "اندر سبھا" کے
نام سے سب سے پہلا ڈرامہ لکھا۔ "اندر سبھا" سے پہلے ہندوستان میں ڈرامہ اس شکل میں موجود
تھا کہ ہندو تہواروں اور میلوں پر مذہبی نقطۂ ڈرامے کی صورت میں پیش کئے جاتے تھے ۔ جیسے "رامائن"
اور"مہا بھارت" وغیرہ ۔ "اندر سبھا" اپنے دَور میں بہت پسند کیا گیا۔ اس کی مقبولیت کا
اندازہ اس بات سے لگایا جا سکتا ہے کہ بہت سی مقامی زبانوں میں اس کا ترجمہ ہوا۔ اور یہ
جگہ جگہ دکھایا گیا ۔ بعد میں لوگوں نے بہت سی تھیئٹر کمپنیاں قائم کیں جو مختلف قسم کے ڈرامے
دکھاتی تھیں ۔ چنانچہ لوگوں نے ڈرامے لکھنے شروع کئے ۔ انگریزی ڈراموں کا بھی اردو میں ترجمہ

512

ہونے لگا اور اسٹیج کٹے جانے لگے ۔ اس طرح تھیٹر اور ڈرامہ خاصا مقبول ہو گیا ۔ لیکن فن کے

اعتبار سے ڈرامے نے کوئی ترقی نہ کی ۔ اس کی پہلی وجہ تو یہ ہے کہ ہندوستان پر مسلمانوں کی حکومت

تھی ۔ اسلام میں اداکاری ، بت تراشی ، موسیقی اور ناچ وغیرہ منع ہیں ۔ اس لئے لوگ اس قسم کی

چیزیں لکھنے اور اسٹیج پر پیش کرنے سے پرہیز کرتے تھے ۔ دوسرے کوئی شریف خاندان کی لڑکی یا

لڑکا ڈراموں میں حصہ نہ لیتا تھا ۔ اس لئے لوگ ڈرامے اور تھیٹر کو اپنے معاشرے میں اجنبی سمجھتے

تھے ۔ اور سب سے بڑی وجہ یہ ہے کہ فلم کی ایجاد نے اسٹیج کی تھوڑی بہت مقبولیت کو بھی

ختم کر دیا ۔ فلمی صنعت نے ہندوستان اور پاکستان میں بہت ترقی کی ۔ خاص طور پر ہندوستان نے

بہت سی معیاری فلمیں پیش کیں جو دنیا بھر میں پسند کی گئیں ۔

تاہم جن لوگوں نے اچھے ڈرامے لکھے ان میں آغا حشر ، طالب بنارسی ، احمد شجاع اور

امتیاز علی تاج مشہور ہیں ۔

موجودہ دور میں افسانہ نویسی اردو نثر کی سب سے مقبول صنف ہے ۔ افسانہ نویسی کی بنیاد سرشار

نے رکھی ۔ ان کے بعد لوگ افسانے لکھتے رہے لیکن منشی پریم چند نے افسانے کو عروج پر پہنچایا ۔ افسانہ

نویسی میں پریم چند کی وہی حیثیت ہے جو میر تقی میر کی غزل میں ۔ پریم چند سے پہلے افسانے صرف

محبت ، جرم و سزا اور اسی قسم کے دوسرے موضوعات پر لکھے جاتے تھے ۔ لیکن پریم چند نے اپنی

نگارانہ صلاحیت سے افسانے میں ایک نئی روح پھونکی ۔ ان کے افسانے انسانی کردار کا آئینہ

ہیں ۔ وہ معاشرے کی خرابیوں ، قدیم رسومات اور پرانے عقائد پر اکثر تنقید کرتے ہیں ۔ پریم چند

کی زبان کی سادگی اور کردار نگاری ان کے انسانوں اور ناولوں میں جادو کا سا اثر رکھتی ہے ۔

انہوں نے بہت سے افسانے اور ناول لکھے ہیں ۔ ان کے ناولوں میں "گؤدان" اور افسانوں میں

"کفن" شاہکار سمجھے جاتے ہیں ۔ دورِ جدید کے افسانہ نگار مختلف موضوعات پر افسانے لکھتے ہیں

کچھ لوگوں نے دوسری زبانوں کے افسانوں کا اردو میں ترجمہ کیا ہے ۔ کچھ مغربی افسانہ نگاروں
سے متاثر ہیں ۔ بعض کا موضوع جنسیات ہے جیسے سعادت حسن منٹو اور عصمت چغتائی۔ اور
بعض مزاحیہ افسانے لکھنے میں مہارت رکھتے ہیں ۔ جیسے پطرس ، شوکت تھانوی اور کنہیا لال کپور
وغیرہ ۔ گھریلو مسائل ، غربت ،ظلم ، گاؤں کی پسماندہ زندگی ،اشتراکیت ، سرمایہ داری اور محبت موجودہ
افسانہ نگاروں کے خاص موضوع ہیں۔

پیدائش	pəydayš F1	birth, creation
[کے] ارد گرد	[ke] yrd gyrd Adv Comp Post	surrounding, in the environs of, around
گمنامی	gwmnami F2	anonymity, namelessness, obscurity
درباری	dərbari M1 A1	courtier; court (adj.), courtly
موٹا	moTa A2	fat, thick, bulky
رنگین	rəgin A1	colourful, ornamented, flowery, ornate
پُرتکلّف	pwrtəkəllwf A1	ceremonious, full of elaborate courtesy
باعث	bays M1 [np]	cause, reason
امتیاز	ymtiaz M1	distinction, discernment, preeminence
شیخ عین الدین گنج العلم	šəyx əynwddin gənjwlylm PN	Shaykh Ayn-ud-din Ganj-ul-Ilm; 1306-1393
ہجری	hyjri A1	After the Hijra, the starting point of the Islamic calendar, dating from the departure of the Prophet Muhammad from Mecca for Medina in 622 A.D.
اقوال	*əqval Mpl [pl. /qəwl/]	sayings, words
خواجہ گیسو دراز	xaja gesu dəraz PN	Khvaja Gesu Daraz; 1330-1431
معراج العاشقین	myrajwlašyqin	a tract on Sufism by Khvaja Gesu Daraz; 1422
وجہی	vəjhi PN	Mulla Vajhi; d. between 1657-71
سب رس	səb rəs	a tale by Vajhi; 1635
شاہ میران	šah miran PN	Shah Miran (also called Miran Shah); d. 1496
جل ترنگ	jəl tərəg	a book by Shah Miran

515

ترجمہ	tərjəma [common /tərjwma/] M2	translation
فضلی	fəzli PN	Shah Fazl Ali Fazli; d. 1770
دہ مجلس	dəh məjlys	a religious work by Fazli; 1731
مصنف	mwsənnyf M/F1	author, writer
حسین واعظ کاشفی	hwsəyn vayz kašyfi PN	Husayn Ibn Ali Vaiz Kashifi; d. 1504
روضۃ الشہدار	rəwzətwššwhəda	a religious treatise in Persian by Husayn Vaiz Kashifi
عبارت	ybarət F1	writing, composition, text, passage
نمونہ	nəmuna M2	sample, specimen, example
کلیات	kwlliat M1 [or F1]	collected works (of a poet)
سودا	səwda PN	Mirza Muhammad Rafi Sawda; 1713-1780(-81)
دیباچہ	dibaca M2	introduction (to a book), preface
انشاء	´ynša PN	Insha Allah Khan Insha; 1756(-58)-1817
دریاۓ لطافت	dəryae lətafət	Insha's treatise on Urdu grammar (written in Persian); 1802
اہل	əhl Mpl	people [in compounds with the /yzafət/ only: e.g. /əhle qələm/ Mpl "literary people, writers"]
بولی	boli F2	language, speech, dialect
نوطرزہ مرصع	nəw tərze mwrəssa	a book of tales by Mir Muhammad Husayn Tahsin; written between 1768 and 1775
میر محمد حسین تحسین	mir mwhəmməd hwsəyn təhsin PN	Mir Muhammad Husayn Ata Khan Tahsin; d. between 1779 and 1781

امیر خسرو	əmir xwsrəw PN	Amir Khusraw; 1254-1324
قصهٔ چهار درویش	qyssəe cəhar dərveš	the name of Amir Khusraw's book of tales
مترجم	mwtərjym M/F1	translator
شاه رفیع الدّین	šah rəfiwddin PN	Shah Rafi-ud-din; 1749-1818
شاه عبدالقادر	šah əbdwlqadyr PN	Shah Abd-ul-Qadir; 1753-1814
مندرجهٔ بالا	mwndərjəe bala A1	above-mentioned
کتب	*kwtwb Fpl [pl. /kytab/]	books
فورٹ ولیم کالج	forT vylyəm kalyj M1 [np]	Fort William College; 1800-1820
ڈاکٹر گل کرسٹ	DakTər gylkərysT PN	Doctor John Gilchrist; 1759-1841
سرپرست	sərpərəst M/F1 A1	patron
میر امّن	mir əmmən PN	Mir Amman Dihlavi; 1733-1803
شیر علی افسوس	šer əli əfsos PN	Sher Ali Afsos; 1735(-47)-1809
کاظم علی جوان	kazym əli jəvan PN	Kazim Ali Javan; d. after 1815
نہال چند لاہوری	nyhal cənd lahəwri PN	Nihal Chand Lahori; dates unknown
مرزا علی لطف	myrza əli lwtf PN	Mirza Ali Lutf; d. 1822
سیّد حیدر بخش حیدری	səyyəd həydər bəxš həydəri PN	Sayyid Haydar Bakhsh Haydari; d. 1833
ممتاز	mwmtaz A1	distinguished
نثر نگار	nəsrnygar M/F1	prose writer
باغ و بہار	baɣ o bəhar	the name of Mir Amman's book; 1801

517

گلستانِ سعدی	gwlystane sadi	a book by the famous Persian poet Sadi of Shiraz; 1175-1291(-92)
قصۂ گل بکاؤلی	qyssəe gwl bəkaoli	a traditional romance; Nihal Chand's version entitled /məzhəbe yšq/ was published in 1803(-04)
آرائشِ محفل	arayše məhfyl	Haydari's version of the story of Hatim Tai; 1802
تذکرۂ گلشنِ ہند	təzkyrəe gwlšəne hynd	Mirza Ali Lutf's təzkyra of Urdu poets; 1801
مصنّفین	*mwsənnyfin Mpl [pl. /mwsənnyf/]	authors
لسانیات	lysaniat F1 [np]	linguistics
جان شیکسپیئر	jan šəykspir PN	John Shakespear; 1774-1858
ڈاکٹر گریرسن	DakTər gərirsən PN	Dr. George A. Grierson; 1851-1941
جان پلیٹس	jan pyləyTs PN	John Platts; 1830-1904
مسٹر فیلن	mysTər fəylən PN	S. W. Fallon; 1817-1880
مسٹر فوربز	mysTər forbz PN	Duncan Forbes; 1798-1868
گرساں دتاسی	gərsā dətasi PN	M. Garcin de Tassy; 1794-1878
ٹائپ	Tayp M1	type (type font)
چھاپہ خانہ	chapəxana M2	press, publishing house
کم و بیش	kəmobeš Adv	more or less
تصنیف	təsnif F1	writing, authoring, literary composition
تالیف	talif F1	compilation, editing
تالیفات	*talifat Fpl [pl. /talif/]	compilations, edited works

سلیس	səlis Al	smooth, simple, fluent, easy (of language only)
راه	rah Fl	road, way
حضرات	*həzrat Mpl [pl. /həzrət/]	gentlemen, (honoured) persons
فقیر محمد گویا	fəqir mwhəmməd goya PN	Navab Faqir Muhammad Khan Goya; d. 1850
انوارِ سہیلی	ənvare swhəyli	a book of tales by Husayn Vaiz Kashifi
بستانِ حکمت	bwstane hykmət	the name of Goya's translation of the foregoing; 1835
مرزا رجب علی بیگ سرور	myrza rəjəb əli beg swrur PN	Mirza Rajab Ali Beg Surur; 1787-1867
فسانۂ عجائب	fəsanəe əjayb	Surur's romantic novel; 1824
فرضی	fərzi Al	imaginary, fictitious, hypothetical; incumbent, obligatory
نثر نگاری	nəsrnygari F2 [np]	prose writing
خوش نویسی	xwšnəvisi F2 [np]	calligraphy
تصانیف	*təsanif Fpl [pl. /təsnif/]	writings, works
مرزا غالب	myrza yalyb PN	Mirza Asad-ullah Khan Ghalib; 1797-1869
خطوط	*xwtut Mpl [pl. /xət/]	letters, correspondence
شیریں	širī Al	sweet
تکلف	təkəllwf Ml	ceremony, formality, elaborate courtesy
آمنے سامنے	amne samne Adv	face to face, opposite one another

مکالمہ	mwkaləma M2	dialogue
ظرافت	zərafət F1 [np]	joviality, humour, fun
شوخی	šoxi F2	liveliness, pertness, sauciness
سرسید احمد خان	sər səyyəd əhməd xan [or /xā/] PN	Sir Sayyid Ahmad Khan; 1817-1898
عظیم	əzim A1	great, high, exalted
شخصیت	šəxsiət F1	personality, great person, important figure
احسان	yhsan M1	kindness, benevolence, goodness, favour
تہذیب الاخلاق	təhzibwləxlaq	Sir Sayyid Ahmad Khan's journal; published with interruptions between 1870 and 1897
نامور	namvər A1	famous
بے تکلف	betəkəllwf A1	informal, without elaborate courtesy, free, frank
رنگینی	rəgini F2	colourfulness, ornateness, floweriness
پیچیدگی	pecidgi F2	complication, complexity
لباس	lybas M1	costume, dress
پہنانا	pəhnana [C: /pəhnna/: Ic]	to cause to wear, put (a garment) on (someone), dress (someone)
بے تکلفی	betəkəllwfi F2	informality, lack of elaborate courtesies
موجد	mujyd M/F1	inventor
نمایاں	nwmayā A1	prominent, evident, clear
محسن الملک	mwhsynwlmwlk PN	Navab Sayyid Mahdi Ali Khan Muhsin-ul-Mulk; 1837-1907

وحید الدین سلیم	vəhidwddin səlim PN	Vahid-ud-din Salim; 1869-1928
سید علی بلگرامی	səyyəd əli bylgrami PN	Sayyid Ali Bilgrami; 1851-1911
نذیر احمد	nəzir əhməd PN	Nazir Ahmad; 1836-1912
شبلی	šybli PN	Mawlana Shibli Nawmani; 1857-1914
ذکاء الله	zəkawllah PN	Mawlvi Zaka-ullah; 1832-1910
مولوی چراغ علی	məwlvi cyraɣ əli PN	Mawlvi Chiragh Ali; 1844-1895
مولانا حالی	məwlana hali PN	Mawlana Altaf Husayn Hali; 1837-1914
آزاد	azad PN	Mawlana Muhammad Husayn Azad; 1830-1910
اصلاحی	yslahi Al	reform (adj.), reformative, for purposes of reform
ناول	navəl Ml	novel
قانونی	qanuni Al	legal
ناول نویس	navəlnəvis M/Fl	novelist, novel writer
مرآة العروس	myratwlwrus	a novel by Nazir Ahmad; 1869
توبة النصوح	təwbətwnnwsuh	another of Nazir Ahmad's novels; 1877
ابن الوقت	ybnwlvəqt	another of Nazir Ahmad's novels; 1888
بنات النعش	bənatwnnaš	another of Nazir Ahmad's novels; 1873
نقاد	nəqqad M/Fl	critic
سیرة النبی	sirətwnnəbi	Shibli's great work on the life of the Prophet Muhammad; completed posthumously by Mawlvi Sulayman Nadvi

521

الفاروق	əlfaruq	Shibli's biography of the 2nd Caliph Umar; 1899
شعرالعجم	šerwləjəm	Shibli's great history of Persian poetry; 4 vols. published in 1908, 1909, 1910, and 1912, with a posthumous 5th vol. published in 1918
ریاضی	ryazi F2 [np]	mathematics
جغرافیہ	jwɣrafia M2 [np]	geography
سائنس	sayns F1	science
تاریخ ہندوستان	tarixe hyndostan	Mawlvi Zaka-ullah's 10 vol. history of India
جلد	jyld F1	volume (of a book); binding (of a book); skin
الفرادیت	ynfyradiət F1 [np]	individuality
مقدمۂ شعر و شاعری	mwqəddəməe šer o šayri	Mawlana Hali's book on literary criticism; 1893
حیاتِ سعدی	həyate sadi	Hali's biography of the great Persian poet Sadi; 1893
حیاتِ جاوید	həyate javed	Hali's biography of Sir Sayyid Ahmad Khan; 1901
سوانح نگاری	səvanenygari [literary: /səvanyhnygari/] F2 [np]	biography writing
خشک	xwšk A1	dry, dessicated
کمال	kəmal M1	perfection, excellence, superior quality
آبِ حیات	abe həyat	Azad's history of Urdu literature; 1881
دربارِ اکبری	dərbare əkbəri	Azad's history of the times of the Emperor Akbar; 1898

نیرنگِ خیال	nəyrãge xyal	Azad's book of allegorical essays; 1880
وسعت	vwsət Fl	breadth, expansion, spaciousness, capacity
منشی نِول کشور	mwnši nyvəl kyšor PN	Munshi Nival Kishor; 1836-1895
اودھ اخبار	əvədh əxbar	the name of Munshi Nival Kishor's newspaper; begun iň 1858
منشی محبوب عالم	mwnši məhbub aləm PN	Munshi Mahbub Alam; 1865-1933
پیسہ اخبار	pəysa əxbar	Munshi Mahbub Alam's newspaper; begun in 1887
ظفر علی خان	zəfər əli xã [or /xan/] PN	Zafar Ali Khan; 1870-1956
زمیندار	zəmindar	Zafar Ali Khan's newspaper; begun in 1903
محمد علی جوہر	mwhəmməd əli jəwhər PN	Muhammad Ali Jawhar; 1878-1931
ہمدرد	həmdərd	Muhammad Ali Jawhar's newspaper; begun in 1913
ابو الکلام آزاد	əbwlkəlam azad PN	Abu-1-Kalam Azad; 1889-1958
الہلال	əlhylal	Abu-1-Kalam Azad's newspaper; begun in 1912
صحافت	səhafət Fl [np]	journalism
منشی سجّاد حسین	mwnši səjjad hwsəyn PN	Munshi Sajjad Husayn; 1856-1915
اودھ پنچ	əvədh pãc	Avadh Punch, the name of Munshi Sajjad Husayn's journal; 1887-1912
سر عبدالقادر	sər əbdwlqadyr PN	Sir Abd-ul-Qadir; 1878-1950

مخزن	məxzən	Sir Abd-ul-Qadir's journal; begun in 1901
میرناصرعلی	mir nasyr əli PN	Mir Nasir Ali; 1847-1933
صلائے عام	səlae am	the name of Mir Nasir Ali's journal; begun in 1888 (?)
نیاز فتح پوری	niaz fətepuri PN	Niaz Fatahpuri; 1887-1966
نگار	nygar	Niaz Fatahpuri's journal; begun in 1921
مولوی عبدالحق	məwlvi əbdwlhəq PN	Mawlvi Abd-ul-Haqq; 1870-1961
[کے] زیر سرپرستی	[ke] zere sərpəresti Comp Post Adv	under the patronage of [/zer/ M1 "under, below; the symbol for the vowel /y/" occurs often as a compound postposition or adverb; /zer/ + the /yzafət/ + a following noun = "under the . . . of. "]
وقف	vəqf M1	devotion; a bequest, trust, or endowment made for pious purposes
نایاب	nayab A1	unavailable, rare
نگرانی	nygrani F2	supervision, care, looking after
بابائے اردو	babae wrdu PN	"The Father of Urdu, " a title given to Mawlvi Abd-ul-Haqq. [/baba/ M1 "father. "]
ناول نویسی	navəlnəvisi F2 [np]	novel writing
افسانہ نویسی	əfsanənəvisi F2 [np]	short story writing
سرشار	səršar PN	Pandit Ratan Nath Sarshar; 1845-1903
عبدالحلیم شرر	əbdwlhəlim šərər PN	Abd-ul-Halim Sharar; 1860-1926

مرزا رسوا	myrza rwsva PN	Mirza Muhammad Hadi Rusva; 1858-1931
راشدالخیری	raʃydwlxəyri PN	Rashid-ul-Khayri; 1868-1936
فسانۂ آزاد	fəsanəe azad	a long novel by Sarshar; first published in installments between 1878 and 1879
پی کہاں	pi kəhā̃	another of Sarshar's novels
سیرِ کوہسار	səyre kohsar	another of Sarshar's novels
توجہ	təvəjjo [literary: /təvəjjwh/] F1	attention, consideration
با محاورہ	bamwhavra [or /bamwhavəra/] A1	idiomatic, full of idioms
آگاہ	agah PA1	aware, informed, acquainted
پلاٹ	pylaT M1	plot (of a story, etc.)
امراؤ جان ادا	wmrao jan əda	one of Mirza Rusva's novels; 1899
مقبول ترین	məqbultərin A1	most popular
یاس	yas F1 [np]	despair, desperation, hopelessness
نا امیدی	nawmmidi [or /nawmidi/] F2 [np]	hopelessness, disappointment
موت	məwt F1	death
پریم چند	prem cənd PN	Dhanpat Rai Prem Chand; 1880-1936
کرشن چندر	kryʃən cəndər PN	Krishna Chandra; 1914-
عصمت چغتائی	əsmət cwɣtai PN	Asmat Chughtai; living
عزیز احمد	əziz əhməd PN	Aziz Ahmad; 1914-
رشید اختر ندوی	rəʃid əxtər nədvi PN	Rashid Akhtar Nadvi; 1915-

اسے آر خاتون	e ar xatun PN	A. R. Khatun; 1900-1965
قیسی رام پوری	qəysi rampuri PN	Qaysi Rampuri; living
امانت لکھنوی	əmanət ləkhnəvi PN	Sayyid Agha Hasan Amanat Lakhnavi; 1816-1858
اندر سبھا	yndər səbha	a drama by Amanat; 1853
رامائن	ramayən M1 [np]	the Ramayana, the 2nd great Hindu religious epic (the 1st being the Mahabharata). In modern India people speaking of this book usually mean the Eastern Hindi version by Tulsi Das (1532-1624) rather than the Sanskrit version ascribed to Valmiki.
مہا بھارت	məhabharət M1 [np]	the Mahabharata, the great Hindu religious epic, parts of which may date back to the Tenth Century B.C. [This work is traditionally ascribed to Vyasa.]
تھیٹر	theTər M1	theatre
اسٹیج	ysTej M1	stage
خاصا	xasa A2	quite a few, rather, quite, pretty
اعتبار	etybar M1 [np]	confidence, trust, reliance [/[ke] etybar se/ Comp Post "from the point of view of, in respect to. "]
ادا کاری	ədakari F2 [np]	acting (on the stage, etc.)
بت تراشی	bwttəraši F2 [np]	idol-making, sculpture
پرہیز	pərhez M1 [np]	abstention, keeping away from, forbearance, restraint
اجنبی	əjnəbi M/F1 A1	stranger, foreigner; strange, foreign
فلم	fylm F1	film
ایجاد	ijad F1	invention
فلمی	fylmi A1	film (adj.), cinematic

معیاری	meyari A1	standard, of high calibre
تاہم	tahəm Conj	however, nevertheless
آغا حشر	aɣa həšər PN	Agha Muhammad Shah Hashar; 1879-1934
طالب بنارسی	talyb bənarsi PN	Munshi Banayak Prashad Talib Banarsi; d. 1914
احمد شجاع	əhməd šwja PN	Hakim Ahmad Shuja; 1893-
امتیاز علی تاج	ymtiaz əli taj PN	Sayyid Imtiaz Ali Taj; 1900-
جرم	jwrm M1	crime, offense
فنکارانہ	fənkarana A1	artistic
انسانی	ynsani A1	human (adj.)
آئینہ	aina M2	mirror
کردار نگاری	kyrdarnygari F2 [np]	delineation of character[s], characterisation
جادو	jadu M1	magic, enchantment
گؤدان	gəudan	a novel by Prem Chand; 1936
کفن	kəfən	a short story by Prem Chand
افسانہ نگار	əfsanənygar M/F1	short story writer
جنسیات	jynsiat F1 [np]	sex
سعادت حسن منٹو	səadət həsən mənTo PN	Saadat Hasan Manto; 1912-1955
مزاحیہ	məzahia A1	humorous
پطرس	pətrəs PN	Ahmad Ali Shah Bukhari Patras; 1898-1958

شوکت تھانوی	šəwkət thanvi PN	Muhammad Umar Shawkat Thanvi; 1909-1963
کنہیّا لال کپور	kənhəyya lal kəpur PN	Kanhayya Lal Kapur; 1910-
گھریلو	ghərelu A1	domestic, homey
غربت	γwrbət F1	poverty
پسماندہ	pəsmanda A1	backward, undeveloped

25. 201. /[ke] yrd gyrd/ Comp Post Adv and /[ke] aspas/ Comp Post Adv both mean "around, in the environs of. " If there is any semantic difference at all, it may be that the former has a connotation of "surrounding (a central object), " while the latter simply means "around, in the vicinity of. "

/[ke] gyrd/ also occurs as a compound postposition meaning "surrounding, revolving around. " E. g.

/zəmin surəj ke gyrd ghumti həy. / The earth revolves around the sun. [Neither /[ke] yrd gyrd/ nor /[ke] aspas/ can be substituted here.]

25. 202. /təkəllwf/ M1 denotes the complex of polite ceremony and formality which once pervaded much of North Indian Muslim (and to some extent Hindu also) urban society. In the court circles of Delhi and Lucknow this elaborate code of etiquette affected every facet of social intercourse, and it was often carried to excessive lengths. Under the impact of industrialisation and Westernisation, however, many of these polite forms have become obsolete, at least in so-called "modernised" circles. /təkəllwf/ is still found, nevertheless, among the Old Culture aristocratic circles of Lucknow, Delhi, and other urban centres. Some examples of usage:

/təkəllwf nə kijie! / Please don't stand on ceremony! [I. e. relax, make yourself at home!]

/ap ne təkəllwf se kam lia, vərna əgər ap yy ciz mãgte, to vw zərur de dete. / You were too formal; otherwise if you had asked for this thing he would certainly have given it. [I. e. you were too polite to make a frank request.]

/əy zəwq, təkəllwf mẽ həy təklif sərasər -- aram se hə̃y, vw jo təkəllwf nəhĩ kərte. / Oh Zawq, in [standing on] ceremony there is solely hardship. -- Those who do not stand on [lit. do] ceremony are comfortable. [A verse from the poet Zawq (1789-1854). /sərasər/ Adv "totally, wholly, solely. "]

The s' dent should also note the formations /pwrtəkəllwf/ A1 "ceremonious, full of elaborate courtesy, " /betəkəllwf/ A1 "informal, without elaborate courtesy, free, frank, " and /betəkəllwfi/ F2 "informality, frankness. " E. g.

/wnhõ ne bəhwt pwrtəkəllwf davət di. / He gave a very formal [i. e. fancy, splendid] party.

/vw mera betəkəllwf dost həy. / He is my very close [i. e. frank] friend.

/həm log apəs mẽ betəkəllwf hə̃y. / We are informal among ourselves.

/wn ki təhrir mẽ betəkəllwfi həy. / In his writing there is informality [i. e. free, loose, informal style].

25. 203. /bays/ M1 [np] "cause, reason" is rather literary but has the same meaning as /vəja/ F1 or /səbəb/ M1. See Sec. 23. 220. E. g.

/baryš ke bays, fəslõ ko bəhwt nwqsan pəhw̄ca. / Because of the rain, the crops were much damaged. [/ke səbəb/ or /ki vəja se/ are substitutable here.]

/meri pərešani ka bays yy tha. / This was the cause of my anxiety.
[/səbəb ... tha/ or /vəja ... thi/ are substitutable.]

25. 204. /təmiz/ F1 "discrimination, distinction, discernment" was introduced in Unit
XVII. /ymtiaz/ M1 "distinction, discernment, pre-eminence" is from the same Arabic
root (m-y-z "to separate, keep apart, distinguish"), /təmiz/ being a verbal noun of Form
II and /ymtiaz/ a verbal noun of Form VIII (see Sec. 17. 301). Both of these words are
employed in the sense of "discrimination (between two things), " but /ymtiaz/ is less common
in this meaning. /ymtiaz/ is more often found meaning "distinction, pre-eminence,
superiority, " while /təmiz/ cannot occur in this sense.

Note also /mwmtaz/ A1 "distinguished, " the participle (either active or passive) of
Form VIII of m-y-z. See Sec. 17. 301. E. g.

/vw əcche əwr bwre mẽ ymtiaz nəhĩ kər səkta. / He cannot distinguish
between good and evil. [/təmiz/ is substitutable here.]

/wse əcche əwr bwre ki təmiz nəhĩ. / He does not have [the power of]
discrimination between [lit. of] good and evil. [/ymtiaz/ usually
does not occur here.]

/wse koi təmiz nəhĩ. / He lacks manners.

/ws ne tarix ke ymtyhan mẽ ymtiaz hasyl kia. / He attained distinction
[i. e. passed with honour] in the history examination.

/yy whda wn ke xandan ke lie bayse ymtiaz tha. / This post was an
occasion for distinction for their family. [/bayse ymtiaz/ "reason
for distinction. " /təmiz/ never occurs here.]

/wrdu ke baz mwmtaz nəsrnygar bhi jəlse mẽ šərik the. / Some
distinguished prose writers of Urdu were also in the meeting.

25. 205. /rysala/ M2 was introduced in Unit XXII in the meaning of "magazine,
journal. " It also means "tract, booklet, treatise (usually on some scholarly subject). "
/rysala/ also denotes "squadron of cavalry. "

25. 206. /qəwl/ M1 "word, saying" is usually employed for the saying of some
respected person. Its Arabic plural is /əqval/ Mpl. E. g.

/mere valyd sahəb ka qəwl həy, ky mwsibət mẽ həmeša əllah se mədəd
mãgo. / It is my father's saying that [you] should always ask help
from God [when] in trouble.

25. 207. /ybarət/ F1 denotes "writing, text, passage (in the sense of a specific
passage). " /təhrir/ F1 means "writing" in general. These two words occasionally overlap in the sense of "style. " E. g.

/mãy ne wn ki təhrir pəRhi həy. / I have read his writing.

/mãy ne yy ybarət pəRhi həy. / I have read this passage. [I. e. this
piece of writing.]

/wn ki təhrir mẽ šoxi əwr zərafət ke ala nəmune mylte hãy. / In his
writing the best [lit. highest] specimens of liveliness and humour
are found. [Here /təhrir/ is synonymous with /tərze təhrir/ "style
of writing. " /ybarət/ can also be substituted here.]

/mãy ne xət ki ybarət dekhi thi, lekyn ws mẽ ys bat ka koi zykr nə tha. /
I looked at the text of the letter, but there was no mention of this
matter in it. [/təhrir/ cannot occur here since a specific passage

is meant.]

/sər səyyəd ki ybarət sada əwr təkəllwf se xali həy. / The writing[s] of
Sir Sayyid are simple and free of formality. [/təhrir/ can be
substituted here.]

25.208. Wherever /nəmuna/ M2 "sample, specimen, example" denotes "example, "
/mysal/ F1 "example" may be substituted. Otherwise these two words do not overlap. E.g.

/myrza γalyb ka yy xət šoxi əwr zərafət ka əccha nəmuna həy. / This
letter of Mirza Ghalib's is a good example of liveliness and humour.
[/... ki əcchi mysal/ is also correct here.]

/wnhõ ne yy kəpRa nəmune ke təwr pər bheja. / They sent this cloth as
a sample. [/mysal/ cannot occur here.]

25.209. As a noun, /əhl/ Mpl "people" occurs only in compounds with the /yzafət/.
E.g.

/əhle peša/ people of different professions, professional people. [/peša/
M2 "occupation, profession. "]

/əhle qələm/ literary people, writers. [/qələm/ M1 "pen. "]

/əhle šəhr/ people of the city. [/šəhr/ M1 "city. "]

/əhle zəban/ native speakers, speakers of the most prestigeful form of
a language. [/zəban/ F1 "language. "]

/əhle zəwq/ people of taste, connoiseurs. [/zəwq/ M1 "taste. "]

/əhle məγryb/ Westerners, Europeans. [/məγryb/ M1 "west. "]

/əhle pakystan/ people of Pakistan. [/pakystan/ M1 [np] "Pakistən. "]

/əhle kytab/ people of the Book. [A technical religious term for those
three religions which, according to Islam, have received a revealed
Book of Revelation: i.e. Jews, Christians, and Muslims. /kytab/
F1 "book. "]

/əhle dyl/ sensitive people, sentimental people, romantics. [/dyl/ M1
"heart. "]

/əhl/ is also found as a sort of predicate adjective meaning "worthy, fitting, suitable,
capable. " In this usage it follows the Type B pattern but occurs only with forms of /hona/
"to be" and also in a few idiomatic environments. E.g.

/mere xyal mẽ, vw ys ka əhl nəhĩ. / In my opinion, he is not suitable for
[lit. of] this. [Or: "... worthy of this. "]

/vw ys whde ki əhl nə thi. / She was not suitable for [lit. of] this post.
[Note that /ki/ agrees with the gender of the subject.]

/mãy ys ynam ka əhl nəhĩ hũ. / I am not worthy of this reward. [Here
again /ka/ agrees with the contextual gender of /mãy/.]

/mãy wse ys mənsube pər kam kərne ka əhl nəhĩ səməjhta. / I don't
consider him suitable to [lit. of] work on this project.

25.210. /boli/ F2 "dialect, language, speech" denotes "language" on a more
colloquial, spoken level than /zəban/ F1 "language. " E.g.

/ys zyle ki boli wrdu se mylti jwlti həy. / The dialect [i.e. spoken
form] of this district is somewhat related to [lit. mingles with]
Urdu.

/ws šəhr ki boli bəhwt xərab həy. / The dialect of that city is very bad.
[I.e. non-standard.]

/vw wrdu zəban janta həy. / He knows the Urdu language. [/boli/ cannot be substituted here since the totality of the language is meant, including its standard literary forms.]

25.211. /mwndərjəe bala/ Al "above-mentioned" is a compound of /mwndərəja/ "entered, inserted, included" (the feminine passive participle of Form VIII of the Arabic root d-r-j "to approach gradually, " which also has derived forms meaning "to insert, include"; see Sec. 17.301) + /bala/ PAl "above, up, over" (from Persian). "Below-mentioned" is similarly /mwndərjəe zəyl/ Al; /zəyl/ Ml "lower-part, beneath, below." Both /zəyl/ and /bala/ are found as independent words in Urdu, although they are rather literary. E.g.

> /mwndərjəe bala kytabē fəroxt ki jaēgi. / The above-mentioned books will be sold.

> /mwndərjəe zəyl həzrat jəlse mē məwjud the. / The below-mentioned gentlemen were present in the meeting.

> /wn ki šəxsiət yn cizõ se bala həy. / His personality is above all these [petty] things.

> /ws ka mwqam ys se kəhī bala həy. / His rank is far [lit. somewhere] above this.

> /yy təmam šərayt zəyl mē dərj ki jati hõy. / All these conditions are listed [lit. included, entered] below [lit. in the lower part]. [/dərj/ PAl "entered, included" is also from the same root as /mwndərja/.]

25.212. The Persian present stems /nəvis/ (from /nəvyš/ "write") and /nygar/ (from /nygaš/ or /nygar/ "paint, draw, embellish, write") are almost completely substitutable in such compounds as /navəlnəvis/ or /navəlnygar/ M/Fl "novelist, " /əfsanənəvis/ or /əfsanənygar/ M/Fl "short story writer, " /nəsrnəvis/ or /nəsrnygar/ M/Fl "prose, writer, " etc. Various items have become standardised with one or the other of these stems, however: e.g. /əxbarnəvis/ M/Fl "newspaper writer, reporter, correspondent" (and almost never **/əxbarnygar/).

Abstract nouns for these forms are made by the addition of the suffix /i/: e.g. /navəlnəvisi/ or /navəlnygari/ F2 [np] "novel writing, " /əfsanənəvisi/ or /əfsanənygari/ F2 [np] "short story writing, " etc.

It should be remembered that many forms of poetry are not "written" but "said, " and one thus finds /γəzəlgo/ M/Fl "/γəzəl/-composer" and /γəzəlgoi/ F2 [np] "/γəzəl/-composing, " etc. instead of **/γəzəlnəvis/ and **/γəzəlnəvisi/, etc.

25.213. Note the following idiom:

> /yyhi vəja thi, ky age cəl kər, bəhwt se γəyrmwlki mwsənnyfin ne wrdu zəban, qəvayd, əwr lysaniat pər bisiõ kytabē lykhī. / This is the reason that, later on, many foreign authors wrote scores of books on the Urdu language, grammar, and linguistics. [/age cəl kər/ here means "later on, further."]

Another example:

> /wnhõ ne age cəl kər kəha, ky həm dwšmənõ ka mwqabla bəhadri se kərēge. / He further said that we will face the enemy with courage [lit. with heroism]. [This usage of /age cəl kər/ is quite common in newspaper prose.]

25.214. /səlis/ Al "smooth, simple, fluent, easy" is used only in reference to a person's language or style of writing: i.e. /səlis zəban/ is that language which is both expressive and yet simple and clear. /səlis/ thus is not a true synonym for /asan/ Al "easy," even when referring to language or writing style. E.g.

/vw səlis zəban lykhta həy./ He writes clear language. [I.e. his style of writing is both simple and expressive.]

25.215. /rah/ Fl "road, way" overlaps somewhat with /rasta/ M2 "road, way, path." Both are used in the sense of a non-physical "way," but only the latter can mean "road" in the physical sense. E.g.

/ws ne wse sidhi rah dykhai./ He showed him the correct [lit. straight] path. [/... sidha rasta dykhaya/ is also substitutable.]

/mɐ̃y ne wse lahəwr ka rasta bətaya./ I told him the way to Lahore. [/rasta/ here denotes a physical "road," and thus /rah/ cannot be substituted.]

25.216. /fərzi/ Al is mostly employed in the meaning of "hypothetical, suppositional, imaginary, fictitious," but it also means "incumbent, obligatory" (as one might expect) in some limited contexts. E.g.

/yy syrf ek fərzi qyssa həy./ This is only an imaginary story.

/yy roze fərzi hɐ̃y./ These fast[day]s are obligatory.

/fərz/ Ml has already been introduced in the meaning of "duty, obligation"; it, too, may mean "supposition" in certain contexts. E.g.

/fərz kijie, ky mɐ̃y yəhã məwjud nəhĩ./ Suppose that I am not here. [/fərz kərna/ is common in the meaning of "to imagine, suppose." It also means "to make obligatory," and the context must determine which meaning is meant. Contrast:]

/əllah ne mwsəlmanõ pər tis roze fərz kie./ God made thirty fast[day]s obligatory upon the Muslims.

25.217. /širĩ/ Al "sweet" is from Persian. It is synonymous with the Hindi-derived word /miTha/ A2 "sweet" but is more literary. E.g.

/yy phəl bəhwt širĩ həy./ This fruit is very sweet. [/miTha/ is more common here.]

25.218. /bənavəT/ Fl was introduced as "structure, make-up" in Unit XIX. It also means "affectation, artificiality, exaggeration." E.g.

/ws ke bəyan mẽ həqiqət kəm əwr bənavəT zyada həy./ In his statement there is less truth and more exaggeration. [I.e. "affectation, putting on airs."]

25.219. /zərafət/ Fl [np] "joviality, humour, fun" is used for humour which arouses real laughter; /məzah/ Ml [np] "humour, wit, fun" is used more in the sense of clever wit.

25.220. /šəxsiət/ Fl "personality" is more often found in the sense of "great person, important figure" (e.g. "He was one of the great personalities of his age.") than in the

meaning of "character, temperament" (e.g. "In his personality there are many defects. ").
In the latter sense /kyrdar/ M1 "character" is common.

25.221. /yhsan/ M1 "kindness, benevolence, goodness, favour" connotes a larger
and more important act of kindness than does /myhrbani/ F2 "kindness." E.g.

> /əgər ap ys mwškyl mē meri mədəd kərēge, to yy ap ka bəhwt bəRa yhsan
> hoga. / If you will help me in this difficulty, it will be a great favour
> [lit. this will be your very great kindness]. [/ ... ap ki bəRi
> myhrbani hogi/ is substitutable here but connotes a somewhat more
> minor act of kindness.]

> /māy ap ka yhsan kəbhi nəhī bhul səkta. / I can never forget this kindness
> of yours. [/yhsan/ here implies a rather large favour.]

25.222. /namvər/ A1 "famous" is synonymous with /məšhur/ A1 "famous." The
latter, however, occurs in various complex verbal formations (e.g. /məšhur kərna/ "to
make famous"), while /namvər/ is employed only as an adjective.

25.223. /zer/ M1 "lower, beneath, inferior, lower part" is found as an independent
word in Urdu (a) as the name of the symbol denoting the short vowel /y/ (i.e. the little
diagonal line written under a consonantal letter to denote /y/; see Sec. 6.101), and (b) in
various complex verbal formations with /kərna/ "to do" and /hona/ "to be, become. " In
literary Urdu, /zer/ is also extremely common in compounds made with the Persian
/yzafət/. These are used as adverbs or (preceded by /ke/) as compound postpositions.
E.g.

> /həmari fəwj ne ek hi dyn mē dwšmənō ko zer kər lia. / Our army
> overthrew the enemies in only one day. [/zer kərna/ "to overpower,
> overthrow, conquer"; lit. "to make lower."]

> /yy təjviz bhi ajkəl kabina ke zere γəwr həy. / This proposal also is
> under the consideration of the cabinet these days. [/[ke] zere γəwr/
> "under investigation, consideration.]

> /zere nəzər məsyla yy həy, ky əqvame mwttəhyda ys sylsyle mē kya qədəm
> wThaegi. / The question under consideration is this, that what step
> will the United Nations take in this connection. [/zere nəzər/ is
> here employed as an adjective, a rather less common usage.]

> /bərsō wrdu ədəb farsi ke zere əsər rəha. / For years Urdu literature
> lay [lit. stayed] under the influence of Persian. [/[ke] zere əsər/
> "under the effect of, under the influence of. "]

> /yy ydara həmari ənjwmən ke zere nygrani kam kərega. / This institution
> will work under the supervision of our organisation. [/[ke] zere
> nygrani/ "under the supervision of. "]

> /yy jəlsa vəzire azəm ke zere sədarət hoga. / This meeting will be
> presided over by the prime minister. [/[ke] zere sədarət/ "under
> the presidency of, presided over by. " Or:]

> /yy jəlsa zere sədarət mysTər ysmyth hoga. / This meeting will be
> presided over by Mr. Smith. [/zere sədarət/ here is used as a sort
> of preposition. The Persian /yzafət/ might have been expected here
> -- i.e. /zere sədarəte mysTər ysmyth/ -- but this is not idiomatic.]

> /mere tinō bəcce zere talim hāy. / All three of my children are being
> educated. [/zere talim/ is used here as a sort of predicate adjective;
> lit. "under education. "]

25.224. /baba/ Ml "father" is used by many people as a familiar form of address for one's father (and often by extension to other elderly male relatives as well). It is thus rather similar to /bap/ Ml "father." Both of these terms lack the honorific connotations of /valyd/ Ml "father," however.

In colloquial and familiar usage, /baba/ is also often employed to address any elderly male: e. g. an old servant, an elderly bearded villager, an elderly stranger of the middle or lower classes, etc. It is important to use this term properly, and the student is perhaps better advised to avoid it rather than risk giving offense.

25.225. /xasa/ A2 is used as an adjective in the sense of "quite a few, quite a good number." It is also found before adjectives meaning "rather, quite, pretty." E.g.

/jəlse mẽ xase log the./ There were quite a number of people in the meeting.

/vw xasa əccha əfsanənygar həy./ He is quite a good short story writer. [The connotation is that he is good but not really superlative.]

/ys məwzu pər, yy xasi əcchi kytab həy./ On this subject this is quite a good book.

/ap ka məkan xasa bəRa həy./ Your house is quite large.

/yy xasa mwškyl kam həy./ This is rather difficult work.

25.226. /etybar/ Ml "reliance, trust, confidence" occurs in a compound postpositional formation having a rather unlooked for meaning: /[ke] etybar se/ "with respect to, regarding, from the point of view of." In this usage, /[ke] etybar se/ overlaps /[ke] lyhaz se/ "with respect to, from the point of view of" and also /[ke] nwqtəe nəzər se/ "from the point of view of," although the latter is only employed in contexts where there is a real opinion involved. See Sec. 18.122. E. g.

/abadi ke etybar se, məšryqi pakystan məɣrybi pakystan se bəRa həy./ With respect to population, East Pakistan is larger than West Pakistan. [/[ke] lyhaz se/ can be substituted here but not /[ke] nwqtəe nəzər se/ since there is really no "point of view" involved.]

/fəne tamir ke etybar se, yy ymarət bəhwt xubsurət həy./ With respect to art, this building is very beautiful. [/[ke] lyhaz se/ can be substituted here also. One can also employ the adjective /fənni/ "artistic" and say /fənni etybar se/ "from the artistic point of view."]

/yslami nwqtəe nəzər se, yy ciz məna həy./ From the Islamic point of view, this thing is forbidden. [Here where there is a real "point of view" involved, /[ke] etybar se/ and /[ke] lyhaz se/ -- strictly speaking -- cannot occur.]

25.227. /pərhez/ Ml [np] "abstention, keeping away from, forbearance, restraint" is often used in somewhat the same sense as the English word "diet." /pərhez/ is more inclusive, however: it includes abstention from all sorts of activities which might be unhealthy or injurious. E. g.

/vw gošt khane se pərhez kərta həy./ He refrains from eating meat. [I. e. as a dietary rule for his health's sake, for religious reasons, etc.]

/ylaj ke sath sath, pərhez bhi zəruri həy./ Along with the [medical] treatment, diet [etc.] is also necessary.

/bwre logõ se pərhez kərna cahie. / [One] should keep away from evil
people.

25.228. /thoRa bəhwt/ Al denotes "just a little, a very little. " E. g.

/thoRi bəhwt rəqəm jo mere pas thi, mãy ne wse de di. / The small
amount [of money] that I had I gave to him. [The sense is "whatever
small amount. "]

/məriz ko thoRa bəhwt zərur khana cahie. / The patient should certainly
eat a little something.

/khyRki khol do, take thoRi bəhwt həva ati rəhe. / Open the window in
order that a little air may come in [lit. may keep coming].

/ws ki ys hərəkət se, ws ki thoRi bəhwt yzzət bhi xətm ho gəi. / Due to
[lit. from] this action of his, whatever little honour [he had left]
also is gone [lit. has finished].

25.229. Some Complex Verbal Formations.

A:

/agah/

/[X se] agah hona/ to be, become acquainted with, aware [of X]

/[X ko Y se] agah kərna/ to acquaint, inform [X of Y]

/ijad/

/ijad hona/ to be invented

/[X ko] ijad kərna/ to invent [X]

/nwmayã/

/nwmayã hona/ to become clear, evident, prominent

/[X ko] nwmayã kərna/ to make [X] clear, evident, prominent

/talif/

/talif hona/ to be compiled, edited

/[X ko] talif kərna/ to compile, edit [X]

/Tayp/

/Tayp hona/ to be typed

/[X ko] Tayp kərna/ to type [X]

/vəqf/

/vəqf hona/ to be dedicated, made into a bequest

/[X ko Y ke lie] vəqf kərna/ to dedicate [X to Y], make a bequest [of X for Y]

/xwšk/

/xwšk hona/ to become dry, dessicated

/[X ko] xwšk kərna/ to dry, dessicate [X]

/ysTej/

/ysTej hona/ to be staged, performed (drama)

/[X ko] ysTej kərna/ to stage, perform [X]

B:

/nygrani/

/[X ki] nygrani hona/ [X] to be supervised

/[X ki] nygrani kərna/ to supervise [X]
/tərjəma/
    /[X ka Y mẽ] tərjəma hona/ [X] to be translated [into Y (a language)]
    /[X ka Y mẽ] tərjəma kərna/ to translate [X into Y (a language)]
/təsnif/
    /[X ki] təsnif hona/ [X] to be written
    /[X ki] təsnif kərna/ to write [X]

D:

/vwsət/
    /[X ko] vwsət dena/ to expand, broaden, give scope [to X]
    /[X ko] vwsət mylna/ [X] to be expanded, broadened, given greater scope

F:

/ədakari/
    /[X mẽ] ədakari kərna/ to act [in X (a drama)]
/bays/
    /[X ka] bays bənna, hona/ to be, become the cause [of X]
/etybar/
    /[X ko Y pər] etybar hona/ [X] to have confidence [in Y]
    /[X pər] etybar kərna/ to rely [upon X], have confidence [in X]
/jadu/
    /[X pər Y ka] jadu cəlna/ [X] to be enchanted [by Y]
    /[X pər] jadu hona/ [X] to be laid under a spell, enchanted
    /[X pər] jadu kərna/ to perform magic, enchant, lay a spell [upon X]
/jwrm/
    /jwrm hona/ to be committed (a crime)
    /jwrm kərna/ to commit a crime
/jyld/
    /jyld bã̄dhna/ to bind a book
/kəmal/
    /[X mẽ] kəmal dykhana/ to show [one's] prowess, skill, greatness [in X]
    /kəmal kərna/ to do something marvellous, amazing
/məwt/
    /[X ki] məwt hona/ [X] to die
/nawmmidi/
    /[X ko Y mẽ] nawmmidi hona/ [X] to be disappointed [in Y]
/pərhez/
    /[X se] pərhez kərna/ to refrain, abstain, keep away [from X]
/pəydayš/
    /[X ki] pəydayš hona/ [X] to be born
/rah/
    /[X ko] rah dykhana/ to show the way, method [to X]
    /rah nykalna/ to find a way, lead the way

/təkəllwf/

    /təkəllwf hona/ to be elaborately courteous, (formality) to be practiced

    /təkəllwf kərna/ to practice elaborate formality

/təvəjjo/

    /[X pər] təvəjjo dena/ to pay attention [to X]

    /[X pər Y ki] təvəjjo hona/ [Y] to be attentive, pay attention [to X]

    /[X pər] təvəjjo kərna/ to pay attention [to X]

    /[X ki tərəf] təvəjjo kərna/ to turn [one's] attention [to X]

/yhsan/

    /[X pər] yhsan hona/ [X] to receive a favour, act of kindness, benevolence

    /[X pər] yhsan kərna/ to do a favour [for X], perform an act of kindness
      [for X]

/ymtiaz/

    /[X əwr Y mē] ymtiaz kərna/ to distinguish [between X and Y]

25.301. Substantive Composition.

The analysis of various compounds introduced in this Unit is as follows:

/amne samne/ Adv "face to face, opposite one another": Hindi echo compound in which the first element is meaningless (see Sec. 19.305); Hindi /samna/ M2 "confrontation, encounter." /amne samne/ is used only as an adverb in modern Urdu.

/ədakari/ F2 [np] "acting": Persian /əda/ F1 "grace, blandishment, act of coquetry"; /kar/ "work, deed, act" (only in compounds in Urdu); /i/ the abstract noun formant suffix.

/əfsanənəvisi/ F2 [np] "short story writing": Persian /əfsana/ M2 "short story, tale"; /nəvis/ present stem of /nəvyš/ "write"; /i/ abstract noun formant suffix.

/əfsanənygar/ M/F1 "short story writer": /əfsana/ see above; /nygar/ present stem of /nygaš/ or /nygar/ "paint, draw, decorate, embellish, write."

/bwttəraši/ F2 [np] "idol-making, sculpture": Persian /bwt/ M1 "idol, image"; /təraš/ present stem of /təraš/ "cut, pare, scrape, engrave"; /i/ abstract noun formant suffix.

/chapəxana/ M2 "press, publishing house": Hindi /chapa/ M2 "seal, stamp, impression, printing"; Persian /xana/ M2 "house, room for, building for."

/fənkarana/ A1 "artistic": Arabic /fən/ (/fənn/) M1 "art, skill"; Persian /kar/ "work, deed, act"; /ana/ adjective formant suffix (see Sec. 18.305).

/gwmnami/ F2 "anonymity, namelessness, obscurity": Persian /gwm/ PA1 "lost"; /nam/ M1 "name"; /i/ abstract noun formant suffix.

/kəmobeš/ Adv "more or less": Persian /kəm/ A1 Adv "little, less"; /o/ "and"; /beš/ "more" (rarely alone in Urdu).

/kyrdarnygari/ F2 [np] "delineation of character[s], characterisation": /kyrdar/ M1 "character, nature"; /nygar/ see /əfsanənygar/ above; /i/ abstract noun formant suffix.

/mwndərjəe bala/ A1 "above-mentioned": see Sec. 25.211.

/mwndərjəe zəyl/ A1 "following, below-mentioned": see Sec. 25.211.

/navəlnəvis/ M/F1 "novelist": English /navəl/ M1 "novel"; /nəvis/ see /əfsanənəvisi/ above.

/navəlnəvisi/ F2 [np] "novel writing": see /navəlnəvis/ above; /i/ abstract noun formant suffix.

/nəsrnygar/ M/F1 "prose writer": Arabic /nəsr/ F1 "prose"; /nygar/ see /əfsanənygar/ above.

/nəsrnygari/ F2 [np] "prose writing": see /nəsrnygar/ above; /i/ abstract noun formant suffix.

/pəsmanda/ A1 "backward, undeveloped": Persian /pəs/ "after, back"; /manda/

past participle of /man/ "remain, stay."

/pwrtəkəllwf/ A1 "ceremonious, full of elaborate courtesy": Persian /pwr/
"full"; Arabic /təkəllwf/ M1 "ceremony, formality, elaborate courtesy."

/sərpərəst/ M/F1 A1 "patron": Persian /sər/ "head, end, chief"; /pərəst/
present stem of /pərəst/ "worship."

/səvanenygari/ F2 [np] "biography writing": Arabic broken plural /səvanyh/
"accidents, events, occurrences" (the singular, /sanyh/, is not used in Urdu);
Persian /nygar/ see /əfsanənygar/ above; /i/ abstract noun formant suffix.

/səvanewmri/ F2 "biography": /səvanyh/ as above; Arabic /wmr/ F1 "life";
/i/ abstract noun formant suffix.

/xwšnəvisi/ F2 [np] "calligraphy": Persian /xwš/ PA1 "happy, glad, good";
/nəvis/ see /əfsanənəvisi/ above; /i/ abstract noun formant suffix.

/[ke] yrd gyrd/ Adv Comp Post "surrounding, in the environs of, around": Hindi
echo compound in which the first element is meaningless (see Sec. 19. 305);
Persian /gyrd/ "surrounding, revolving around."

25. 302. Other Formations.

Most of the grammatical apparatus of modern Urdu has now been introduced. There
are still various constructions, however, which have not been included in this Course.
These were felt to be either archaic in present-day Urdu or else so infrequent as to be of
little use to the student at this stage of his studies.

As an example of a substantive which is now uncommon in the modern language, one
may cite the pronoun /tu/ "thou." This form is now employed only in addresses to the Deity,
occasionally to small children (although many modern Pakistani parents now employ /twm/
"you [nonhonorific]" or even /ap/ "you [honorific]" in preference to /tu/), and sometimes
to young servant boys or girls. In poetry, however, /tu/ and its forms are very common,
and at that stage the student must include it in his active vocabulary. E. g.

> /tu a!/ Come thou! [The imperative form of the verb used with /tu/
> consists of the verb stem alone.]

> /əy əllah, tu həmare gwnahõ ko maf kərnevala həy./ O God, Thou art
> the forgiver of our sins! [/tu/ is always treated as singular; the
> verbal paradigm employed with it is thus identical with that used with
> the singular forms of /yy/ "this, he, she, it" and /vw/ "that, he,
> she, it." Adjectives, etc. are similarly MS or FS.]

> /beTi, tu kyõ ro rəhi həy. məy twjh se naraz nəhĩ hū./ Daughter, why
> art thou weeping? I am not angry with thee. [The oblique form of
> /tu/ is /twjh/; the special object form is similarly /twjhe/.]

> /kya, teri kytab kho gəi həy?/ Has thy book been lost? [/tera/ A2
> "thy. "]

There are also various infrequent or obsolete verbal formations which have not been
introduced in this Course. E. g.

(1) <PasP + /jana/> "to be on the verge of, on the point of ... " The past participle of
an intransitive verb (agreeing in number-gender with its subject) is followed by an inflected
form of /jana/ "to go" (usually the simple present or the present or past continuous). This
formation is employed for action which has not yet begun but which is impending. Its usage

is quite restricted. E. g.

/divar gyri jati həy./　The wall is on the verge of falling down. [The action of falling has not yet begun, but it appears that any moment the wall may collapse.]

/jəhaz Duba ja rəha həy./　The ship is on the point of sinking. [The continuous form implies that some part of the action has indeed begun, but it has not yet been completed; this sentence might thus indicate that some sections of the ship were actually awash, but the major portion was still above water in the process of sinking.]

/ap ka dəm kyõ nykla ja rəha həy./　Why are you so upset? [Lit. "Why is your breath going out?" -- i. e. "Why are you on the verge of dying?" /dəm nykəlna/ is an idiom denoting "to expire, die. "]

(2)　<PasP + /cahna/>　"to be about to ... " The past participle of certain verbs (transitive or intransitive) is followed by a present general or imperfect form of /cahna/ "to wish, want, desire. " The past participle is always MS in form; cf. the "habitual" formation discussed in Sec. 14. 306. Like the habitual formation, too, the <PasP + /cahna/> construction is treated as intransitive: the subject is nominative, no /ne/ occurs, and the occurring form of /cahna/ agrees with its subject in number-gender. This formation is semantically almost the same as the <OI + /vala/> construction seen in Sec. 15. 312. The <PasP + /cahna/> formation has mostly become obsolete in modern Urdu, being replaced by the <OI + /vala/> form. E. g.

/gaRi aya cahti həy./　The train is about to come. [I. e. Its arrival is expected any moment. /ane vali həy/ is substitutable. Note that /aya/ is MS, although /gaRi/ "train, car, cart" is F2.]

/swba hwa cahti həy./　Morning is about to dawn [lit. become]. [/hone vali həy/ is substitutable.]

/vw sərdar pər həmla kia cahta tha, ky mɛ̃y ne wse piche se pəkəR lia./ He was about to make an attack on the chief when [lit. that] I seized him from behind. [The subject /vw/ is nominative and agrees in number-gender with /cahta tha/ in spite of the presence of /kia/. Here, /kərne hi vala tha/ is substitutable.]

　　Still other formations exist which have not been presented in this book. Some of these may be introduced in the newspaper reader and poetry reader which are to follow this Course. For obsolete constructions (such as are found in classical Urdu works like the /baɣ o bəhar/ and /fəsanəe əjayb/), however, the student will find that there is something to be gleaned from a perusal of such older work as Platts' "A Grammar of the Hindustani or Urdu Language, " Phillott's "Hindustani Manual" and "Hindustani Stumbling Blocks, " Forbes' "Hindustani Grammar" and "Hindustani Manual, " Kempson's "The Syntax and Idioms of Hindustani, " etc. The student must remember, of course, that linguistic changes have occurred in Urdu -- as in all languages -- and that thus portions of what these earlier writers say may no longer be applicable to modern Urdu. This is even true to some extent of Platts' monumental Urdu-English dictionary ("A Dictionary of Urdu, Classical Hindi, and English"). This is not to denigrate the work of these earlier authors by any means, but the student of modern Urdu must still check such matters as pronunciation, gender, meaning, complex verbal formations, etc. with an Urdu speaker in order to be certain of present-day usage.

25.401. Supplementary Vocabulary.

baba M1	father [familiar]
[ke] gyrd Comp Post	surrounding, revolving around
mwndərjəe zəyl A1	following, below-mentioned
qəwl M1	saying, word
səvanewmri [literary: /səvanyhwmri/] F2	biography

25.402. Supplementary Exercise I: Substitution.

1. wn ki pəydayš   <u>sətra səw əTThara</u>   mē hwi.

    nine hundred and eighty-four

    eighteen hundred and sixty-eight

    nineteen hundred and forty-six

    two hundred and six B.C.

    eight hundred and seventy-two Hijri

25.403. Fill the Blanks.

1. Fill the blanks in the following sentences with the most appropriate word from those given in Sec. 25.401.

    a. ___, zəra meri bat swnie!

    b. ys kytab mē, bəhwt se šwəra ki ___ myl jaegi.

    c. həmare dusre xəlifa ki səb se əcchi ____ šybli ne lykkhi həy.

    d. mwhəmməd əli jynah ko ____e qəwm ke nam se yad kia jata həy.

    e. bwzwrgō ka ____ həy, ky dwšmənō ke sath bhi əccha swluk kəro!

25.404. Translation.

1. Translate the following sentences into Urdu.

    a. Around the school is a beautiful garden.

    b. [It] is [a] saying of our Prophet, that the best man is he who is the best husband.

    c. The reasons for [lit. of] the decline of the Mughals are listed below [lit. are below-mentioned].

    d. Around the palace a canal flows.

    e. The conditions of this treaty are as follows [lit. are below-mentioned].

25.501. Substitution.

1. | hwkumət | ne | əmrika ke səfir | ko | əpne fəysle | se... |

the newspapers   the public   this event

the village elder   the villagers   this new law

the police   the citizens   these restrictions

the Commander-in-Chief   the army   the new command

the labourers   the owner of the factory   their demand

... agah kər dia.

2. ws zəmane mē   šayri   bayse ymtiaz səmjhi jati thi.

calligraphy

biography writing

elegy composition

short story writing

novel writing

3. ws ki təhrir mē   šoxi əwr zərafət   pai jati həy. [1]

sarcasm and humour

hopelessness and despair

ornateness

simplicity

a special individuality

[1]Change /pai jati həy/ to agree with the number-gender of the subject in each sentence.

4. əhle qələm   ki təjviz yy həy, ky   mwsənnyfin   ke lie ek xas...

language   the teaching of the language

city   the cleanliness of the city

Pakistan   technical training

literature   the writing of books

West   the progress of backward countries

... ydara qaym kia jae.

5. wn ke zere sərpərəsti,   bəhwt si kytabē   təsnif   hwī. [1]

many rare tracts   published

this research   complete

the collected works of Sawda   edited

this project   successful

this organisation   established

¹Change /hwĩ/ to agree with the number-gender of the subject in each of these sentences.

6. ys məzmun ki ybarət bəhwt   <u>pwrtəkəllwf</u>   həy.
                                      smooth
                                      dry
                                      colourful
                                      idiomatic
                                      complicated

7. sədiõ tək yy <u>navəl</u>   gwmnami mẽ pəRe rəhe.
                   short stories
                   dramas
                   letters
                   translations
                   articles

8. <u>məwlvi sahəb</u>   ne əpni sari zyndəgi   <u>yslam</u>   ke lie vəqf kər di həy.
    that scholar   mathmatics
                                   and science
    those poets   qəsidas
    this critic   the progress of
                                   the language
    many Englishmen   Urdu
    that girl   acting

9. ap ko   <u>gošt</u>   se pərhez kərna cahie.
              evil people's
              friendship
              quarreling [lit.
              fight-quarrel]
              spices
              mangoes
              wine

10. γalybən <u>fəransisiõ</u>   ne   <u>chapəxana</u>   ijad kia.
      the Americans   the airplane
      the Englishmen   the cinema
      the Greeks   the theatre
      the Dravidians   this script
      the Aryans   the chariot

11. ys ke bad, wnhõ ne   <u>tənqid</u>   ki tərəf təvəjjo ki.
                      journalism
                      linguistics
                      domestic matters
                      short story writing
                      prose writing

12. wnhõ ne   <u>ys qysse</u>   ka <u>farsi</u>   me tərjəma kia həy.

	this short story	Urdu
	that novel	Turkish
	his biography	English
	this passage	Portuguese
	my preface	Hindi

13. wnhõ ne <u>syasiat</u>   pər ek məzmun lykha.

Pakistani journalism

sex

linguistics

sculpture

technical education

14. <u>mwndərjəe bala həzrat</u>   ne   <u>wrdu</u>   ki tərəqqi mẽ nwmayā kyrdar əda kia.

the below-mentioned authors   prose

these prose writers   biography writing

these five short story writers   the short story

those novelists   the novel

these poets   free verse

15. yy <u>bwt</u>   <u>bwttəraši</u>   ka əccha nəmuna həy.

passage	his writing
yəzəl	Urdu poetry
short story	ornate prose
novel	characterisation
article	liveliness and humour

25.502. Fill the Blanks.

1. Fill the blanks in the following sentences with the most appropriate word or phrase from among those given at the end of the exercise. Drill each sentence for fluency.

١۔ نذیر احمد کو اردو کا سب سے پہلا ـــــــ ہونے کا امتیاز حاصل ہے۔

۲۔ مولوی عبدالحق کے زیرِسرپرستی بہت سی قدیم کتابیں ـــــــ ہوئیں۔

۳۔ اس افسانے کا ـــــــ ایک مغربی مصنف کے افسانے سے لیا گیا ہے۔

۴۔ مغل سلطنت کے زمانے میں فارسی ـــــــ زبان تھی۔

۵۔ ڈاکٹر گل کرسٹ کے زیرِ سرپرستی اردو کا سب سے پہلا ـــــــ قائم ہوا۔

۶- راشدالخیری کے ناول ــــــ سے بھرے ہوئے ہیں ۔

۷- شاہ رفیع الدّینؒ نے قرآن شریف کا اردو میں ــــــ کیا جو اب تک بہت مقبول ہے ۔

۸- ایک امریکن نے ٹیلی فون ــــــ کیا ۔

۹- بارہویں صدی ــــــ میں اردو نثر نگاری کو بہت وسعت ملی ۔

۱۰- مولوی عبدالحق نے اردو کی ترقی کے لئے اپنی زندگی ــــــ کر دی تھی ۔

۱۱- دہلی کے ارد گرد کے علاقوں میں مختلف ــــــ بولی جاتی ہیں ۔

۱۲- دکنی نثر کے یہ شاہکار کم وبیش چار سو سال تک ــــــ میں پڑے رہے ۔

۱۳- اٹھارہویں صدی کی نثر پیچیدہ اور ــــــ ہے ۔

۱۴- عیسائی ، یہودی اور مسلمان تینوں ــــــ کہلاتے ہیں ۔

۱۵- مرزا غالب کی تحریر میں ــــــ پائی جاتی ہے ۔

۱۶- مولانا آزاد کی زبان نہایت سلیس و ــــــ ہے ۔

۱۷- اکثر کتابیں ــــــ سے شروع ہوتی ہیں ۔

۱۸- شوکت تھانوی کے ــــــ افسانے بہت مقبول ہیں ۔

۱۹- قدیم دکنی مذہبی رسالوں میں اکثر بزرگانِ دین کے ــــــ پیش کئے گئے ہیں ۔

۲۰- فورٹ ولیم کالج کی خدمات ــــــ بیس برس تک جاری رہیں ۔

پلاٹ	درباری	تائید	یاس و نا امیدی	ناول نویس
چھاپہ خانہ	ایجاد	ترجمہ	بولیاں	وقف
ہجری	اہلِ کتاب	گمنامی	شوخی و ظرافت	پُر تکلّف
ویبلاچے	با محاورہ	کم وبیش	مزاحیہ	اقوال

546

25. 503. Variation.

۱۔ میرا اور اُن کا مکان آمنے سامنے ہے ۔

دونوں عمارتیں آمنے سامنے واقع ہیں ۔

دونوں گاڑیاں ایک دم آمنے سامنے آگئیں ۔

اِن کرسیوں کو آمنے سامنے رکھ دو !

وہ آمنے سامنے بیٹھے باتیں کر رہے ہیں ۔

مالک اور مزدور آمنے سامنے بیٹھے بحث کر رہے ہیں ۔

۲۔ آج کا جلسہ مولوی صاحب کے زیرِ صدارت ہوگا ۔

یہ لغت ہمارے ادارے کے زیرِ سرپرستی شائع ہوگا ۔

یہ چھاپہ خانہ ہماری انجمن کے زیرِ نگرانی کام کرے گا ۔

ہمارے شہر کے پندرہ نئی صدی لڑکے زیرِ تعلیم ہیں ۔

زیرِ بحث مسئلہ یہ ہے کہ اسلام میں عورت کا کیا مقام ہے ۔

زیرِ نظر کتاب جنسیات کے موضوع پر بہترین کتاب ہے ۔

۳۔ مندرجہ بالا کتابیں اسکولوں کے لئے منظور کی گئی ہیں ۔

مندرجہ ذیل حضرات کو ایک ہزار روپے انعام دیئے گئے ہیں ۔

مندرجہ بالا لڑکوں نے جغرافیہ کے امتحان میں امتیاز حاصل کیا ہے ۔

مندرجہ ذیل غیر ملکی مصنفین نے اردو کی ترقی میں نمایاں حصہ لیا ہے ۔

مندرجہ ذیل کتب دو سو سال پہلے تصنیف ہوئی تھیں ۔

مندرجہ بالا کتابوں کے ترجمے آج سے پچاس سال پہلے شائع ہوئے تھے ۔

547

۴۔ اگرچہ اِن اِنسانوں کے پلاٹ مغربی ہیں مگر کردار خاص ہندوستانی ہیں۔

اگرچہ اُن کے مضمون کا موضوع فلسفہ ہے مگر عبارت بہت سلیس ہے۔

اگرچہ خیالات پرانے ہیں مگر غالبؔ نے اُنہیں نئے انداز سے پیش کیا ہے۔

اگرچہ اُن کی ساری زندگی عیش و آرام میں گزری مگر اُن کی شاعری میں یاس و نا امیدی پائی جاتی ہے۔

اگرچہ یہ ڈرامہ بہت اچھا ہے مگر اِس کا اسٹیج کرنا خاصا مشکل ہے۔

اگرچہ اُن کا طرزِ تحریر پُرتکلف ہے مگر کہیں کہیں سادگی بھی پائی جاتی ہے۔

۵۔ اب تک کسی ناول نویس نے اِس پہلو پر توجہ نہیں دی۔

اب تک ہمارے ماہرینِ لسانیات نے اِن مسئلوں پر توجہ نہیں دی۔

اب تک کسی مترجم نے اُن کے اِس ناول کی طرف توجہ نہیں کی۔

اب تک اردو کے نقادوں نے اُس کی شاعری کی طرف توجہ نہیں کی۔

اب تک کسی افسانہ نگار نے اِس موضوع کو قابلِ توجہ نہیں سمجھا۔

۶۔ میں اُن کی باتوں پر اعتبار نہیں کر سکتا۔

مجھے اُن کے وعدے پر اعتبار ہے۔

کیا آپ اُن کا یہ خط دیکھنے کے بعد بھی اُن پر اعتبار کریں گے؟

اُن کا سلوک بہت اچھا ہے۔ امیر اور غریب سب ہی اُن پر اعتبار کرتے ہیں۔

اُس کی اِس حرکت کے بعد مجھے اُس پر اعتبار نہیں رہا۔

اگرچہ وہ غریب ہے مگر وہ قابلِ اعتبار آدمی ہے۔

۷۔ کالج کے اِردگرد بعض بہت اچھے چھاپہ خانے ہیں۔

ہمارے مکان کے اِردگرد بہت سے غریب لوگ رہتے ہیں۔

آج کل بہت سے خانہ بدوش شہر کے اردگرد بیرے ہوتے ہیں ۔

ہمارے شہر کے اردگرد دراوڑ تہذیب کے آثار پائے جاتے ہیں ۔

دشمن نے ہمارے قلعے کے گرد فوج ڈال دی ۔

دشمنوں نے شہر کے گرد ایک دیوار بنائی تاکہ کوئی باہر نہ نکل سکے ۔

۸۔ اُس زمانے میں شعرو شاعری کے خاصے قدردان موجود تھے ۔

اُس زمانے میں فارسی کی خاصی کتابوں کا اردو میں ترجمہ ہوا ۔

اُس دَور میں رنگین اور پُرتکلف نثر خاصی مقبول تھی ۔

آج کل ایسی قدیم کتابیں خاصی نایاب ہیں ۔

اس دوران میں وہ خاصا موٹا ہوگیا ۔

چند سال پہلے اصلاحی ناول خاصے عام تھے مگر اب بہت کم لکھے جاتے ہیں ۔

۹۔ پلاٹ کے اعتبار سے اُن کے ڈرامے پیچیدہ ہیں ۔

زبان کے اعتبار سے اُس زمانے کی نثر خاصی پیچیدہ اور پُرتکلف تھی ۔

اسلامی عقائد کے اعتبار سے بت تراشی سے پرہیز کرنا چاہئے ۔

قانونی اعتبار سے حکومت کا یہ فیصلہ بالکل غلط تھا ۔

مقبولیت کے اعتبار سے اِس ناول کی خاصی اہمیت ہے مگر حقیقتہً بنیات کے سوا اِس میں کچھ نہیں ۔

انداز تحریر کے لحاظ سے مولوی صاحب کی تصانیف خاص انفرادیت رکھتی ہیں ۔

مہاجرین کے نقطۂ نظر سے حکومت کے یہ اقدامات بہت ضروری تھے ۔

۱۰۔ اُن کی کامیابی سب کے لئے باعثِ خوشی ہے ۔

اِس مسجد کی خوبصورتی سارے شہر کے لئے باعثِ فخر ہے ۔

آپ کی یہ حرکات آپ کے والدین کے لئے باعثِ تکلیف ہوں گی ۔

اُن کی فوجی خدمات خاندان بھر کے لئے باعثِ امتیاز ہیں ۔

آپ لوگوں کی دشمنی میرے لئے باعثِ مصیبت بن گئی ہے ۔

اِس غلطی کی وجہ سے وہ گاؤں والوں کے لئے باعثِ مذاق بن گیا ہے ۔

۱۱۔ ہماری انجمن ترجمے کے کام کی نگرانی کر رہی ہے ۔

فوجی افسران نے بند کی تعمیر کی نگرانی کی ۔

اُن کا کلیات ایک نامور عالم کی نگرانی میں تالیف ہوا تھا ۔

اردو کتب کی یہ فہرست میری نگرانی میں تیّار کی گئی ۔

یہ لغت موجودہ دَور کے نامور اہلِ قلم حضرات کی نگرانی میں تیّار ہوا ہے ۔

یہ فلم انگلستان کی ایک فلم کمپنی کی نگرانی میں بنی تھی ۔

۱۲۔ اُس کے دورِ حکومت میں مغل سلطنت کو خاصی وسعت ملی ۔

اِن مشکلات کے باوجود اردو افسانہ نگاری کو اُنّیسویں صدی میں کافی وسعت ملی ۔

مغربی کتب کے ترجموں سے اردو ادب کو خاصی وسعت ملی ۔

اِن پابندیوں کو ختم کر دینے سے ہماری فلمی صنعت کو کافی وسعت ملی ۔

اُس بادشاہ نے اپنی فتوحات سے سلطنت کو وسعت دی ۔

اُنہوں نے نئی نئی تشبیہات اور محاوروں سے زبان کو وسعت دی ۔

۱۳۔ اُنّیسویں صدی میں فلم کی ایجاد ہوئی جس سے ہمارے معاشرے پر خاصا اثر پڑا ۔

پندرہویں صدی میں امریکہ دریافت ہوا ۔ جس سے مغربی ممالک کے اقتصادی نظام پر بہت اثر پڑا ۔

بارھویں صدی عیسوی میں بندوق کی ایجاد چین میں ہوئی جس سے دنیا کی تاریخ میں انقلاب آ گیا ۔

اٹھارہویں صدی میں ایک انگریز نے بجلی ایجاد کی جس سے دنیا کی حالت بدل گئی۔

بیسویں صدی کے آغاز میں امریکنوں نے ہوائی جہاز ایجاد کیا جس کی وجہ سے اب کوئی جگہ دُور نہیں رہی۔

چار ہزار سال قبل از مسیح مصر میں رسم الخط کی ایجاد ہوئی جس کے سبب وہاں کی تہذیب نے بہت جلد ترقی کی۔

۱۴۔ اُنہوں نے ایک سونے کی انگوٹھی نمونے کے طور پر بھیجی ہے۔

اُس دکاندار نے دو سیر چاول نمونے کے طور پر بھیجے ہیں۔

شاعر نے ایک قصیدہ نمونے کے طور پر لکھا۔

اُس کے پاس خوش نویسی کے چند بہت اچھے نمونے موجود ہیں۔

یہ عبارت اُن کی تحریر کا ایک اچھا نمونہ ہے۔

اُنہوں نے نئے ٹائپ کے چند نمونے میرے پاس بھیجے تھے۔

۱۵۔ اگرچہ اُن کے کردار میں بہت سی خرابیاں ہیں تاہم لوگ اُنہیں پسند کرتے ہیں۔

اگرچہ یہ دوائی آج کل نہیں ملتی تاہم نایاب نہیں۔

اگرچہ وہ اجنبی تھا تاہم اُس نے ہمارے معاشرے پر ایک اچھی کتاب لکھی ہے۔

اگرچہ میں موقع پر موجود نہ تھا تاہم مجھے یقین ہے کہ اُنہوں نے یہ جرم نہیں کیا۔

اگرچہ یہ وہ کتاب نہیں جس کی ہمیں ضرورت ہے تاہم ہمارے کام آسکتی ہے۔

اگرچہ آج کل وہ بہت مصروف ہیں تاہم آپ سے ملنے ضرور آئیں گے۔

25. 504. Translation.

1. Translate the following sentences into English.

۱۔ اُنیسویں صدی کے وسط میں اُردو ناول نویسی کو عروج ملا۔ اِن دور میں اردو کے بڑے بڑے ناول نویس

پیدا ہوئے ۔ جنہوں نے مغربی ناول نویسی کے اصولوں کو اپنایا اور اِس طرح اپنی تصانیف سے اردو ادب کے خزانے میں قیمتی اضافہ کیا ۔

۲۔ اِس مصنف کو اُس دَور میں بڑی مقبولیت حاصل ہوئی کیونکہ اُس زمانے میں رنگین اور مترنکلف نثر لکھنے کا رواج تھا ۔ پیچیدہ بیان اور مشکل اصطلاحات عام تھیں اور اِس مصنف کی تحریر میں یہ تمام چیزیں موجود تھیں ۔ مگر آج کل ہمارے ادیب آسان اور سلیس زبان لکھتے ہیں ۔ البتّہ فلسفہ اور مذہب وغیرہ سے متعلق مضامین میں آج بھی فارسی اور عربی الفاظ اور اصطلاحات کثرت سے ملتی ہیں ۔

۳۔ آج کل پاکستان میں ایسی معیاری فلمیں بنتی ہیں جو دنیا کے دیگر ممالک کی فلموں سے مقابلہ کرسکتی ہیں ۔ ابھی ردم کے فلمی میلے میں ہماری ایک فلم کو انعام ملا ہے ۔ تاہم اکثر فلمیں اعلیٰ معیار کی نہیں ہوتیں ۔ ہماری بعض فلمیں تو ایسی ہیں جن میں نہ کوئی پلاٹ ہے اور نہ کردار نگاری ۔

۴۔ اُن کے افسانوں میں یاس و ناامیدی پائی جاتی ہے ۔ اُن کے نزدیک زندگی صرف ایک سزا ہے ۔ اور دنیا میں خوشی کا حاصل ہونا ممکن نہیں ۔ اُنہوں نے اپنی ایک کتاب کے دیباچے میں لکھا ہے کہ یہ زندگی ایک طویل سفر ہے جس میں سوائے تکالیف کے، اور کچھ نہیں ۔ آرام اور خوشی صرف اُس زندگی میں حاصل ہوں گے جو مرنے کے بعد ملے گی ۔

۵۔ اُس زمانے کے معاشرے میں عورتوں کو کوئی خاص مقام حاصل نہ تھا ۔ چنانچہ اُنہوں نے اپنے ناولوں میں عورتوں کے حقوق، تعلیم اور بچوں کی تربیت وغیرہ پر زور دیا ۔ اِس کے ساتھ ہی اُنہوں نے اُن قدیم رسومات پر بھی سخت تنقید کی جو معاشرے میں برائیاں پھیلانے کی ذمّہ دار تھیں ۔

۶۔ لکھنؤ کا تکلف مشہور ہے ۔ اِس سلسلے میں ہم آپ کو ایک دلچسپ قصّہ سناتے ہیں ۔ ایک دفعہ دو بزرگ آدمی سفر کی غرض سے اسٹیشن پہنچے ۔ جب گاڑی آئی تو دونوں ایک ہی ڈبّے میں جانے

کے لئے آگے بڑھے مگر ڈبّے کے دروازے پر پہنچ کر دونوں رک گئے۔ اُن میں سے ایک نے دوسرے سے کہا "جناب! پہلے آپ"۔ دوسرے نے کہا "نہیں نہیں۔ پہلے آپ"۔ پہلے نے کہا "نہیں جناب! پہلے آپ"۔ اِس دوران گاڑی اپنے سفر پر دوبارہ روانہ ہوگئی۔ اور وہ دونوں بزرگ "پہلے آپ، پہلے آپ" کہتے اسٹیشن ہی پر رہ گئے۔

۷۔ ہندو مذہب کے مطابق بعض ذِنّے گوشت کھا سکتے ہیں اور بعض نہیں کھا سکتے۔ بعض مچھلی اور انڈے سے بھی پرہیز کرتے ہیں۔

۸۔ اُس کی جو کتاب حال ہی میں شائع ہوئی ہے، اُس میں قدیم اردو نثر کے چند نمونے دیئے گئے ہیں۔ یہ اردو موجودہ اردو سے بہت مختلف ہے۔ پچھلے بیس برس میں دکنی زبان سے متعلق جو قدیم کتب ملی ہیں، اِس کتاب میں اُن تمام کتب کی مختصر تاریخ۔ یعنی مصنف کا نام، اُس کے حالاتِ زندگی اور تصنیف کی تاریخ وغیرہ بھی دی گئی ہے۔

۹۔ وہ اچھے اور بُرے میں امتیاز کرنے کی صلاحیت نہیں رکھتا۔ یہی وجہ ہے کہ اُسے زندگی میں بڑی تکالیف کا سامنا کرنا پڑا۔

۱۰۔ یہ ڈرامہ لکھ کر اِنہوں نے اپنی فنکارانہ صلاحیت کا ثبوت دیا ہے۔ پلاٹ، کردار اور مکالمے۔ غرض کہ ہر اعتبار سے اِسے ایک معیاری ڈرامہ کہا جا سکتا ہے۔

۱۱۔ اِس معاملے میں مجھے صحیح راہ دکھانے والا کوئی نہیں تھا۔ یہ آپ کا احسان ہے کہ آپ نے مجھے صحیح مشورہ دے کر پریشانیوں سے بچا لیا۔

۱۲۔ مندرجہ بالا مصنفین کی مندرجہ ذیل تصانیف اِس موضوع پر مستند کتابیں سمجھی جاتی ہیں۔

۱۳۔ میرا خیال تھا کہ اُن کی پیدائش ۱۸۵۵ء میں ہوئی۔ مگر ایک تذکرے میں اُن کے متعلق یہ عبارت نظر آئی "وہ غدر کے دو سال بعد دلی میں پیدا ہوئے۔ بچپن ہی میں دلی سے اگرے چلے گئے۔ جہاں

553.

شعر و شاعری عروج پر تھی ۔اُن کے گھر پر اکثر اُن کے والد کے زیرِ صدارت ادبی جلسے ہوا
کرتے تھے جس سے اُنہیں بھی شعر و شاعری کا شوق پیدا ہوا۔"

۱۳۔ مولانا حالی نے سرسید احمد خان کی سوانح عمری لکھ کر اردو میں سوانح نگاری کی ابتدا کی ۔اِس سے
پہلے ہندوستان میں اِس طرز کی سوانح عمری کبھی نہیں لکھی گئی تھی ۔

۱۵۔ آج کل اُن کی تصانیف نایاب ہیں ۔ اگر کبھی بازار میں کہیں سے اُن کی ایک دو کتابیں آجاتی ہیں
تو فوراً ہی فروخت ہو جاتی ہیں ۔

۱۶۔ پاکستان میں اردو ٹائپ کے کئی چھاپہ خانے ہیں ۔ جو خاصی خوبصورت کتابیں شائع کرتے ہیں ۔

۱۷۔ کل ہماری انجمن کا جلسہ مولوی صاحب کے زیرِ صدارت ہوا ۔ شروع میں لوگ خاصے کم تھے مگر
تھوڑی ہی دیر میں کمرہ لوگوں سے بھر گیا اور کھڑے ہونے کی بھی جگہ نہیں رہی ۔ جلسے میں مولوی
صاحب نے ایک فلسفیانہ تقریر کی ۔ اُن کے بعد دو ممتاز غیر ملکی مصنفین نے اپنے مضامین
پڑھے ۔ جن پر چار بجے تک بحث جاری رہی ۔ جلسہ ختم ہونے پر تمام لوگوں کو چائے پیش کی گئی ۔

۱۸۔ شہروں کے مقابلے میں گاؤں کی زندگی پسماندہ کہی جا سکتی ہے ۔ مگر شہر اور گاؤں کی زندگی کا
مقابلہ کرنا بنیادی طور پر ایک غلط بات ہے ۔کیونکہ گاؤں کی زندگی اپنی جگہ پر ایک دلکش
زندگی ہے اور شہر کی زندگی اپنی جگہ پر ۔ مگر مجھے شہر کے مقابلے میں گاؤں کی سادہ زندگی
زیادہ پسند ہے ۔

۱۹۔ دشمن نے قلعے کے اِردگرد کے تمام گاؤں کو جلا دیا ۔ ہم لوگ رات بھر قلعے کی دیواروں پر
سے اُنہیں جلتا ہوا دیکھتے رہے ۔ جب صبح ہوئی تو دشمن کے لشکر نے ہمارے قلعے پر بھی حملہ
کیا۔ یہ قلعہ اگرچہ اِس سلطنت میں سب سے قدیم ہے مگر دوسرے تمام قلعوں سے مضبوط ہے ۔
دشمن کے سپاہیوں نے قلعے کے اندر گھسنے کی بہت کوشش کی مگر اُنہیں کامیابی نہ ہوئی۔

ہمارے پاس قلعے میں کئی مہینے کا کھانے پینے کا سامان موجود تھا۔ اس لئے دشمن کو آخر کار ہار کر واپس

جانا پڑا۔ اور آخر میں فتح ہماری ہوئی۔

۲۰۔ لڑکی کو شہزادے پر بڑا غصہ آیا۔ اُس نے شہزادے پر جادو کر کے اُسے کُتّا بنا دیا۔ شہزادہ کُتّا بنتے

ہی بھینچنے لگا ۔ اور دو دو کر لڑکی سے معافی مانگنے لگا۔ لیکن لڑکی نے اُس کے رونے کی کوئی پروا

نہیں کی اور ہنس کر وہاں سے چلی گئی ۔ شہزادہ کُتّا بن جانے سے بہت اداس ہوا۔ آخر کار وہ آہستہ

آہستہ اپنے محل کی طرف چلا ۔ وہاں جب شہزادے کے نوکروں نے ایک کُتّے کو محل میں داخل

ہوتے دیکھا تو شور مچا دیا اور اُسے مار کر محل سے نکال دیا۔ شہزادہ اپنے نوکروں کے اس سلوک

سے بہت پریشان ہوا۔ مگر وہ اس حالت میں کیا کر سکتا تھا۔ شہزادہ پھر کُتّے کی شکل میں گلیوں

اور بازاروں میں گھومنے لگا ۔ آخر کار اُس پر ایک بوڑھی عورت کی نظر پڑی ۔ اُسے اپنے جادو

سے فوراً ہی معلوم ہو گیا کہ یہ کُتّا نہیں ، بلکہ اس ملک کا شہزادہ ہے ۔ چنانچہ اُس نے اُس کُتّے

کو اپنے جادو سے پھر انسان میں تبدیل کر دیا ۔ شہزادہ اپنی اصلی حالت میں آ کر بہت خوش ہوا۔

اور محل واپس پہنچ کر اُس بوڑھی عورت کو بہت سا انعام دیا۔

2. Translate the following sentences into Urdu and write them out in the Urdu script.

a. His novels have [lit. keep] a special individuality.

b. He is one of [lit. from in] those great personalities of the Twentieth Century of India whose services the nation cannot ever forget.

c. Məwlvi sahəb took [lit. had taken] a prominent part in the Freedom Movement [lit. in the movement of freedom].

d. He devoted [lit. had devoted] his life to [lit. for] Urdu literature. It [lit. this] is the result of his [/wn hi ki/] efforts that many old and rare books have been published [/šae hwī/] again.

e. This play has been staged [/ysTej ho cwka həy/] before, but [at] that time I did not get [lit. had not got] an opportunity of seeing [it].

f. I acquainted them with the whole situation [/təmam halat se/] on the telephone. After that [I] wrote a letter also, in which [I] explained everything [lit. every matter] in [lit. with] detail.

g. Because of the patronage of the Navabs and other notables, Urdu poetry was

555

greatly augmented [lit. received much expansion].

h. Prem Chand [lit. poured] Urdu short story writing on a new path. Nowadays most short story writers follow him only [/wn hi ki təqlid kərte hɛ̄y/].

i. In my district three different dialects are spoken: one in [lit. on] the mountains, another in the village[s], and the third in the city, which is similar to [lit. mixes with] Urdu.

j. In the last twenty years Indian films have made such [lit. this much] progress as [lit. that] [they] never made [lit. had made] before this.

k. His real objective is the reform of the society. Therefore most of his novels are connected with [/... se mwtəəllyq/] domestic life, in which the evils of the society have been presented.

l. His style of writing is so [lit. this much] dry, that I could not ever [/kəbhi/] read even [/bhi/] one of his short stories completely [/pura/].

m. We are not formal [lit. do etiquette] at all [/bylkwl/]. When any person comes [to] our house, we give [lit. do with] him the same [/vwhi/] treatment which we give [lit. do with] our friends and relatives.

n. Under the supervision of our college two important books are being edited: one will be published this [/ysi/] month, and the other will probably be ready next year.

o. By means of [lit. with] his artistic talents, Prem Chand brought the short story to [its] zenith. His short stories and novels are very popular even [/bhi/] today.

p. The doctors gave him the advice that he should abstain from meat and eggs.

q. This was his very first [/səb se pəhla/] short story. On its being published [/šae hote hi/] he became famous throughout the country, and in a very short time [/thoRe hi dynõ mẽ/] he became [/bən gəya/] our most popular short story writer.

r. He is the translator of the Holy [lit. noble] Qwran. Aside from this, he has also edited an old book which throws [lit. pours] quite a bit of [lit. enough] light on Deccani history.

s. I typed [lit. having typed] this article [and] at once sent it to a journal.

t. Although the court language was Persian, nevertheless he wrote two religious tracts in Urdu for the king.

25.505. Script.

1. Write out the following words in the Urdu script and place them in Urdu alphabetical order.

a.	dibaca	f.	yhsan
b.	əzim	g.	vwsət
c.	azəm	h.	meyari
d.	etybar	i.	zərafət
e.	əhl	j.	səhafət

k.	bays	p.	nəzm
l.	Tayp	q.	həmləavər
m.	ərz	r.	əsl
n.	həysiət	s.	lwtf
o.	nəsr	t.	yas

2. Look up the following words in an Urdu-Urdu dictionary (if one is available; otherwise this exercise may be done with an Urdu-English dictionary). Note whether the dictionary gives such information as gender, possible plurals, complex verbal formations, idioms, and how it indicates pronunciation.

a.	مبنی	f.	تخیّل
b.	ضمانت	g.	تخصیص
c.	لطیفہ	h.	دھمکی
d.	نصاب	i.	رابطہ
e.	ناٹک	j.	بوئی

3. Look up the following words in an English-Urdu dictionary. Write out each entry and note the presence or absence of the information listed under (2) above.

a.	shame	f.	trap [noun]
b.	lock	g.	finger
c.	caste	h.	beard
d.	lips	i.	wheel
e.	supply	j.	ivory

25. 506. Response.

1. Answer the following questions verbally.

۱۔ کیا آپ کو ناول پڑھنے کا شوق ہے ؟ اگر ہے تو آپ کو کونسا ناول نویس پسند ہے ؟

۲۔ کیا آپ موت سے ڈرتے ہیں ؟

۳۔ کیا آپ اقوامِ متحدہ میں مترجم بننے کی خواہش رکھتے ہیں ؟

۴۔ آج کل آپ کے ملک میں رنگین اور پُرتکلف نثر لکھنے کا رواج ہے یا نہیں ؟

۵۔ کیا آپ نے کبھی کسی ڈرامے میں کوئی کردار ادا کیا ہے ؟

۶۔ کیا آپ نے پاکستانی فلمیں دیکھی ہیں ؟

۷۔ ریڈیو کے موجد کا کیا نام ہے ؟

۸۔ کیا آپ اپنی زندگی سائنس کی ترقی کے لئے وقف کرنے کو تیّار ہیں ؟

۹۔ آپ کو مزاحیہ نقطے زیادہ پسند ہیں یا یاس و ناامیدی سے بھری ہوئی کہانیاں ؟

۱۰۔ کیا آپ مذہبی وجوہات کی بنا پر کسی چیز سے پرہیز کرتے ہیں ؟

۱۱۔ ہوائی جہاز کس نے ایجاد کیا ؟

۱۲۔ آپ اپنے دوستوں اور رشتہ داروں کو جو خطوط لکھتے ہیں کیا آپ اُن کی نقلیں بھی رکھتے ہیں ؟

۱۳۔ کیا آپ نے کبھی افسانہ نگاری کی طرف توجّہ دی ہے ؟

۱۴۔ کیا آپ کی رائے میں تکلّف تہذیب کے لئے ضروری ہے ؟

۱۵۔ کیا آپ فلمی نقّادوں کی رائے پڑھنے کے بعد سنیما دیکھتے ہیں ؟

۱۶۔ آپ کی پیدائش کہاں ہوئی ؟

۱۷۔ کیا آپ کو ریاضی سے دلچسپی ہے ؟

۱۸۔ کیا آپ بھی اداکاری کو بُرا سمجھتے ہیں ؟

۱۹۔ ایک سال میں آپ کتنی دفعہ تھیئٹر جاتے ہیں ؟

۲۰۔ کیا آپ کی کچھ تصانیف بھی ہیں ؟

2. Write out the answers to the following questions in Urdu. Answers to these may
be found in Sec. 25, 000.

۱۔ اُردو کا سب سے پہلا ناول نویس کون تھا ؟

۲۔ کیا امانت لکھنوی کے ڈرامے "اندر سبھا" سے پہلے بھی ہندوستان میں ڈرامے موجود تھے ؟

۳۔ کیا یہ صحیح ہے کہ مولانا ذکاءاللہ نے اردو کا سب سے قدیم تذکرہ تصنیف کیا؟

۴۔ "باغ و بہار" کس کتاب کا ترجمہ ہے؟

۵۔ "فسانۂ آزاد" کا مصنف کون ہے؟

۶۔ ہندوستان میں ڈرامے کے مقبول نہ ہونے کی کیا وجوہات ہیں؟

۷۔ اردو ٹائپ کا سب سے پہلا چھاپہ خانہ کہاں قائم ہوا؟

۸۔ جدید افسانہ نگاروں کے خاص موضوعات کیا ہیں؟

۹۔ کیا یہ صحیح ہے کہ مولانا حالی صرف شاعر کی حیثیت سے مشہور ہیں؟

۱۰۔ ڈاکٹر گلکرسٹ کس کالج میں ملازم تھے؟

۱۱۔ اردو ادب میں پریم چند کی کیا حیثیت ہے؟

۱۲۔ کیا اسلامی عقائد کے اعتبار سے بت تراشی منع ہے؟

۱۳۔ سرور ناول نویسی کے علاوہ اور کن چیزوں سے دلچسپی رکھتے تھے؟

۱۴۔ اردو کی پیدائش کن علاقوں میں ہوئی؟

۱۵۔ اردو کے کس ادیب کو "مصورِ غم" کا نام دیا گیا ہے؟

۱۶۔ کیا یہ غلط ہے کہ غالب کے اکثر خطوط انگریزوں کے نام ہیں؟

۱۷۔ ڈاکٹر گلکرسٹ نے جن اہل قلم حضرات کو اردو زبان پر کام کرنے کی دعوت دی تھی اُن میں سے قابلِ ذکر مصنفین کے نام بتائیے۔

۱۸۔ کیا سرسید احمد خان کے اندازِ تحریر میں بے تکلفی پائی جاتی ہے؟

۱۹۔ سرسید کے کس ساتھی نے ریاضی، جغرافیہ، سائنس اور تاریخ وغیرہ پر کتابیں تصنیف کیں؟

۲۰۔ مولوی عبدالحق نے اردو کی ترقی کے لئے کیا خدمات انجام دیں؟

25. 507. Conversation Practice.

Mr. Smith is discussing the essay given in Sec. 25. 000 with Dr. Rəhim.

اسمتھ۔   اگرچہ یہ حقیقت ہے کہ آج کل جدید ادب بہت مقبول ہے ۔ لیکن کیا لوگ اب بھی
مثنویوں کہانیوں اور قصوں سے لطف اٹھاتے ہیں یا محض ادب کی تاریخ پڑھنے کے لئے
اُن کا مطالعہ کرتے ہیں ؟

رحیم۔   قدیم دَور کے بعض ادبا۔ اور شعرا۔ آج بھی بہت مقبول ہیں ۔ مثلاً میر ، غالب ، اور انیس
جیسے عظیم شعرا۔ کا کلام لوگ نہ صرف پڑھتے ہیں بلکہ بہت سے لوگوں کو اُن کے سینکڑوں
اشعار بھی یاد ہیں ۔ اسی طرح بعض مثنویاں جیسے "سحرالبیان" "گلزارِ نسیم" وغیرہ بھی بڑی
دلچسپی سے پڑھی جاتی ہیں ۔ قصوں میں "باغ و بہار"۔ "آرائشِ محفل" اور "فسانۂ عجائب"
وغیرہ بھی کافی مقبول ہیں ۔ یہ کتابیں کالجوں اور یونیورسٹیوں میں بھی پڑھائی جاتی ہیں،
مگر اُردو پڑھنے والوں کی اکثریت کا رجحان جدید ادب کی طرف ہے ۔ چنانچہ اُن میں افسانے،
ناول اور جدید شعرا۔ کا کلام زیادہ مقبول ہے ۔

اسمتھ۔   قدیم اُردو ادب میں ناول اور افسانے موجود نہ تھے لیکن موجودہ دَور میں یہ اِتنے کیوں
پسند کئے جاتے ہیں۔

رحیم۔   میرے خیال میں اِس کی وجہ یہ ہے کہ قدیم ادب کے قصے، کہانیوں اور مثنویوں میں عام
طور پر بادشاہوں ، شہزادوں اور محبوبوں کا ذکر ہوتا تھا اور اگر کبھی کسی عام آدمی کا کردار
ہوتا بھی تھا تو وہ انسانی جذبات اور زندگی کی صحیح تصویر نہیں پیش کرتا تھا ۔ بلکہ پلاٹ میں
اُس کی حیثیت محض ایک کھلونے کی ہوتی تھی۔ اِس کے برعکس جدید افسانوں اور ناولوں کے
پلاٹ ہماری روز مرّہ کی زندگی سے لئے جاتے ہیں ۔ اِن کے کردار ہماری ہی طرح کے انسان

560

موتے ہیں اور اُنہیں ہماری ہی طرح کے مسائل کا سامنا کرنا پڑتا ہے جو پڑھنے والوں کے لئے کافی دلچسپی رکھتے ہیں۔

استفہ۔ میں نے غیر ملکی مصنفین کے لکھے ہوئے اُردو لغات کے علاوہ قدیم مقامی علماء کے بعض لغات بھی دیکھے ہیں لیکن کیا اُردو کے موجودہ ادباء بھی اِس طرف توجّہ دے رہے ہیں ؟

رحیم۔ جی ہاں ، ہمارے ادباء نے ہمیشہ اِس کی اہمیت کو سمجھا ہے ۔ آپ نے اُنیسویں صدی کے لغات دیکھے ہیں ۔ بیسویں صدی میں مولوی عبدالحق اور دوسرے ادیبوں کے لغات بہت اچھے ہیں۔اُنہیں ضرور دیکھّے ۔ اُن میں تفصیل سے ایک ایک لفظ کی بناوٹ ، اُن کے معنی اور اُن کے استعمال کا ذکر کیا گیا ہے ۔ اِس وقت بھی حکومتِ پاکستان کی نگرانی میں اُردو کا ایک لغت تیّار کیا جا رہا ہے ۔ اِس کام میں ملک کے مشہور ادباء مدد دے رہے ہیں۔ اُمید ہے یہ لغت موجودہ اُردو کا بہترین لغت ہوگا۔ مغربی علماء کا کام اِس اعتبار سے نہایت قابلِ تعریف ہے کہ اُنہوں نے اُردو کے لغات اُس وقت لکھے جب کہ اُردو کا کوئی لغت موجود نہ تھا۔

استفہ۔ آج کل اُردو ادب سب سے زیادہ کس ادب سے متأثر ہے ؟

رحیم۔ اُردو ادب اب تک فارسی کے زیرِ اثر رہا ہے ۔ مگر موجودہ دَور کے مصنفین نے غیر ملکی ادب۔خاص طور پر انگریزی ادب۔کا گہرا مطالعہ کیا ہے ۔ جس کی وجہ سے اُردو کے جدید ادب پر انگریزی اور فرانسیسی کا خاصا اثر ہے ۔ یہی وجہ ہے کہ ہمارے قدیم ادب میں افسانے ، ناول اور ڈرامے وغیرہ نہیں ملتے ۔ لیکن جدید ادب میں یہ تمام اصناف موجود ہیں۔

استفہ۔ کل میں نے اخبار میں پڑھا تھا کہ لاہور کا کوئی ادارہ اتوار کو ایک ڈرامہ پیش کر رہا ہے ۔ کیا آپ نے اِس کے بارے میں کچھ سنا ہے؟

رحیم۔ جی ہاں، دراصل ہمارے نوجوانوں کے ایک گروہ نے پچھلے چند سالوں سے ڈراموں میں دلچسپی لینی شروع کی ہے۔ ان میں سے اکثر نے نہ صرف غیر ممالک میں تعلیم حاصل کی ہے۔ بلکہ وہاں انہوں نے ڈرامے اور اسٹیج کی تربیت بھی لی ہے۔ یہ شوق انہیں غیر ممالک میں تعلیم کے دوران پیدا ہوا۔ اور جب وہ وطن واپس آئے تو یہاں بھی انہیں ایسے نوجوان مل گئے جنہوں نے انگریزی، فرانسیسی اور دیگر غیر ممالک کے ادب کا مطالعہ کیا تھا اور جو مغرب میں اسٹیج کی اہمیت سے بھی واقف تھے۔ چنانچہ انہوں نے یہاں بھی ڈراموں کو مقبول بنانے کے لئے ادارے قائم کئے۔ آج کل لاہور اور کراچی میں ایسے کئی ادارے موجود ہیں۔ میں یہ ڈرامہ دیکھنے جاؤں گا۔ اگر آپ بھی دیکھنا چاہتے ہوں تو ہم لوگ ساتھ ہی چلیں۔

اسمتھ۔ جی ہاں، میں بھی جانا چاہتا ہوں۔ کیونکہ مجھے بھی ڈراموں سے خاصی دلچسپی ہے۔ لیکن ذرا یہ بتائیے کہ ان اداروں کے پیش کئے ہوئے ڈرامے مقبول بھی ہوئے ہیں یا نہیں۔ میں نے اب تک صرف ایک یا دو ڈرامے دیکھے ہیں جن سے میں کوئی اندازہ نہیں لگا سکا۔

رحیم۔ یہ ڈرامے ایک محدود حلقے میں تو ضرور پسند کئے گئے مگر انہیں عوام کی مقبولیت حاصل نہیں ہوئی۔ کیونکہ ہمارے عوام کا مذاق مختلف ہے۔ وہ ڈراموں کے مقابلے میں فلمیں دیکھنا زیادہ پسند کرتے ہیں۔ اس کے علاوہ جیسا کہ آپ جانتے ہیں کہ ابھی ہمارا اسٹیج فنی اعتبار سے بالکل ابتدائی منزل پر ہے۔ اس لئے فوراً عوام کی دلچسپی کا مرکز نہیں بن سکتا۔ اس کے لئے کافی وقت چاہئے۔

اسمتھ۔ مغربی فلمی صنعت نے ہندوستان اور پاکستان کی فلموں پر کہاں تک اثر ڈالا ہے؟

رحیم۔ ہماری فلمی صنعت خاص طور پر فنی میدان میں مغربی فلمی صنعت سے بہت متاثر ہوئی

562

ہے ۔ کیونکہ اِس صنعت میں کام کرنے والوں میں سے بہت سے لوگوں نے امریکہ اور انگلستان
کے فلمی اداروں سے تربیت حاصل کی ۔ اُنہوں نے وہاں فلمیں بنانے کے جو نئے طریقے
سیکھے اُن سے ہماری فلمی صنعت کو ترقی کرنے میں بڑی مدد ملی ۔ ہماری فلمی موسیقی پر
بھی مغربی موسیقی کا اثر پڑا ہے ۔ اگرچہ ہندوستانی اور پاکستانی فلموں کی موسیقی بنیادی
طور پر مقامی ہے ۔ مگر ہمارے اکثر موسیقار فلموں کے لئے مقامی اور مغربی موسیقی کو
ملا کر ایک نئے طرز کی موسیقی پیش کرتے ہیں ۔ اِس طرح عام طور پر فلموں میں خالص مقامی
موسیقی نہیں ہوتی بلکہ اُس کی بدلی ہوئی شکل ملتی ہے ۔ موضوع کے اعتبار سے ہماری فلموں
پر مغربی فلموں کا بہت کم اثر ہوا ہے ۔ عام طور پر ہماری فلمیں مقامی تاریخی واقعات،
مختلف فرقوں کی سماجی اور معاشی زندگی اور ایسے رسم و رواج پر بنائی جاتی ہیں جو ہماری
روز مرّہ کی زندگی سے تعلق رکھتے ہیں ۔ چنانچہ مشہور ناول نویسوں مثلاً پریم چند اور مرزا
رسوا وغیرہ کے ناولوں کو فلم کی شکل میں پیش کیا جا چکا ہے ۔ اگر کبھی کسی مغربی فلم یا
مغربی ناول کی کہانی پر کوئی فلم بنائی جاتی ہے ۔ تو اُسے بھی خالص مقامی کرداروں کے
ذریعہ پیش کیا جاتا ہے ۔ ہندوستان اور پاکستان نے ایسی بہت سی فلمیں بنائی ہیں
جو اداکاری ، کہانی اور فنی اعتبار سے غیر ممالک کی بہترین فلموں کے مقابلے میں
پیش کی جا سکتی ہیں۔

استفہ۔ کیا آج کل کے مشہور ادیب فلموں کے لئے کہانیاں، گانے اور مکالمے وغیرہ لکھتے ہیں ؟

رحیم۔ عام طور پر ہمارے مشہور ادیب فلموں کے لئے نہیں لکھتے لیکن اگر کوئی فلم کمپنی اِن کے
کسی ناول کو فلم کی شکل میں پیش کرنا چاہتی ہے تو وہ فلم کی ضرورت کے مطابق اپنی
کہانی وغیرہ کے تبدیل کرنے میں مدد دیتے ہیں ۔ اِس طرح بعض ادیب فلموں کے مکالمے

563

اور گانے بھی لکھتے ہیں ۔ عام طور پر فلمی ادیب الگ ہوتے ہیں جو صرف فلموں کے لئے ہی لکھتے ہیں ۔

اسمتہ۔   آپ کے یہاں ادیبوں کی جو انجمنیں ہیں کیا وہ اُن کے حقوق کی بھی حفاظت کرتی ہیں؟

رحیم۔   جی نہیں ۔ اگرچہ ہندوستان اور پاکستان دونوں ملکوں میں ادبا کی باقاعدہ انجمنیں موجود ہیں مگر یہ انجمنیں پیشے کی بنیاد پر نہیں ہیں بلکہ خاص ادبی بنیادوں پر قائم کی گئی ہیں ۔البتہ حال ہی میں پاکستان میں ادیبوں کے حقوق کی حفاظت کے لئے ایک قانون نافذ کیا گیا ہے ۔ ادیبوں کی انجمنیں صرف ادبی باتوں سے تعلق رکھتی ہیں ۔ اُن کا ہفتے یا مہینے میں ایک بار جلسہ ہوتا ہے جس میں یہ ادیب اپنے افسانے نظمیں اور مضامین پڑھتے ہیں ۔ پھر مجلسے میں موجودہ ادبا اُن پر تنقید اور بحث کرتے ہیں ۔

اسمتہ۔   اچھا رحیم صاحب ، میں نے آپ کا کافی وقت لیا۔ اب میں اجازت چاہوں گا۔ اور ہاں یہ تو بتایئے کہ اتوار کو ڈرامے میں جانے کے لئے ہم لوگ کہاں ملیں؟ میرے خیال میں آپ میرے گھر آجائیں۔ وہاں سے وہ جگہ نزدیک ہوگی۔

رحیم۔   بہت اچھا۔ میں اور میری بیگم انشاءاللہ آٹھ بجے آپ کے گھر آجائیں گے۔

اسمتہ۔   بہت خوب ۔ میں آپ کا انتظار کروں گا ۔ اچھا۔ خدا حافظ ۔

رحیم   خدا حافظ ۔

25. 508. Conversation Stimulus.

Topics may include:
1. An essay on an Urdu poet or novelist (based on outside reading).
2. A favourite novel.
3. The development of the theatre in Europe and America.
4. Literature and nationalism.
5. A brief short story.

agah PA1	aware, informed, acquainted
aina M2	mirror
amne samne Adv	face to face, opposite one another
ədakari F2 [np]	acting
əfsanənəvisi F2 [np]	short story writing
əfsanənygar M/F1	short story writer
əhl Mpl	people [in compounds with the /yzafət/ only: e.g. /əhle qələm/ Mpl "literary people, writers"]
əjnəbi M/F1 A1	stranger, foreigner; strange, foreign
*əqval Mpl	pl. /qəwl/
əzim A1	great, high, exalted
baba M1	father [familiar]
bamwhavra [or /bamwhavəra/] A1	idiomatic
bays M1	cause, reason
betəkəllwf A1	informal, without elaborate courtesy, free, frank
betəkəllwfi F2	informality, lack of elaborate courtesies
boli F2	language, dialect, speech
bwttəraši F2 [np]	idol-making, sculpture
chapəxana M2	press, publishing house
dərbari M1 A1	courtier; court (adj.), courtly
dibaca M2	introduction (to a book), preface
etybar M1 [np]	confidence, trust, reliance [/[ke] etybar se/ Comp Post "from the point of view of, in respect to"]
fənkarana A1	artistic
fərzi A1	imaginary, fictitious, hypothetical; incumbent, obligatory
fylm F1	film
fylmi A1	film (adj.), cinematic
ghərelu A1	domestic, homey
gwmnami F2	anonymity, namelessness, obscurity
[ke] gyrd Comp Post	surrounding, revolving around
ɣwrbət F1 [np]	poverty
*həzrat Mpl	pl. /həzrət/
hyjri A1	After the Hijra, the starting point of the Muslim era, dating from the departure of the Prophet Muhammad from Mecca to Medina in 622 A.D.
ijad F1	invention
jadu M1	magic, enchantment
jwɣrafia M2 [np]	geography
jwrm M1	crime, offense

jyld F1	volume (of a book); binding (of a book); skin
jynsiat F1 [np]	sex
kəmal M1	perfection, excellence, superior quality
kəmobeš Adv	more or less
kwlliat M1 [or F1]	collected works (of a poet)
*kwtwb Fpl	pl. /kytab/
kyrdarnygəri F2 [np]	delineation of character[s], characterisation
lybas M1	costume, dress
lysaniat F1 [np]	linguistics
məqbultərin A1	most populaɪ
məwt F1	death
məzahia A1	humourous
meyari A1	standard, of high calibre
moTa A2	fat, thick, bulky
mujyd M/F1	inventor
mwkaləma M2	dialogue
mwmtaz A1	distinguished
mwndərjəe bala A1	above-mentioned
mwndərjəe zəyl A1	following, below-mentioned
mwsənnyf M/F1	author, writer
*mwsənnyfin Mpl	pl. /mwsənnyf/
mwtərjym M/F1	translator
namvər A1	famous
navəl M1	novel
navəlnəvis M/F1	novelist
navəlnəvisi F2 [np]	novel writing
nawmmidi [or /nawmidi/] F2 [np]	hopelessness, disappointment
nayab A1	unavailable, rare
nəmuna M2	sample, specimen, example
nəqqad M/F1	critic
nəsrnygar M/F1	prose writer
nəsrnygari F2 [np]	prose writing
nwmayã A1	prominent, evident, clear
nygrani F2	supervision, care, looking after
pəhnana [C: /pəhnna/: Ic]	to cause to wear, put (a garment) on (someone), dress (someone)
pərhez M1 [np]	abstention, keeping away from, forbearance, restraint
pəsmanda A1	backward, undeveloped
pəydayš F1	birth, creation
pecidgi F2	complication, complexity
pwrtəkəllwf A1	ceremonious, full of elaborate courtesy
pylaT M1	plot
qanuni A1	legal

qəwl M1	saying, word
rah F1	road, way
rǝ̄gin A1	colourful, ornamented, flowery, ornate
rǝ̄gini F2	colourfulness, ornateness, floweriness
ryazi F2 [np]	mathematics
sayns F1	science
səhafət F1	journalism
səlis A1	smooth, simple, fluent, easy (of language only)
sərpərəst M/F1 A1	patron
səvanenygari [literary: /səvanyhnygari/] F2 [np]	biography writing
səvanewmri [literary: səvanyhwmri/] F2	biography
šəxsiət F1	personality, great person, important figure
širī A1	sweet
šoxi F2	liveliness, pertness, sauciness
tahəm Conj	however, nevertheless
talif F1	compilation, editing
*talifat Fpl	pl. /talif/
təkəllwf M1	ceremony, formality, elaborate courtesy
tərjəma [common: /tərjwma/] M2	translation
*təsanif Fpl	pl. /təsnif/
təsnif F1	writing, authoring, literary composition
təvəjjo [literary: /təvəjjwh/] F1	attention, consideration
theTər M1	theatre
Tayp M1	type (type font)
vəqf M1	devotion, dedication, a bequest or endowment or trust made for pious purposes
vwsət F1	breadth, expansion, spaciousness, capacity, scope
xasa A2	quite a few, rather, quite, pretty
xwšk A1	dry, dessicated
xwšnəvisi F2 [np]	calligraphy
*xwtut Mpl	pl. /xət/
yas F1 [np]	despair, desperation, hopelessness
ybarət F1	writing, composition, text, passage
yhsan M1	kindness, benevolence, goodness, favour
ymtiaz M1	distinction, discernment, preeminence
ynfyradiət F1 [np]	individuality
ynsani A1	human (adj.)
[ke] yrd gyrd Adv Comp Post	surrounding, in the environs of, around
yslahi A1	reform (adj.), for purposes of reform
ysTej M1	stage (dramatic)
zərafət F1 [np]	joviality, humour, fun

568

[ke] zere ... Comp Post Adv   under ... [/zer/ Ml "the symbol for the vowel /y/; under, below." As an adverb or compound postposition, /zer/ + the /yzafət/ is always followed by some other word: e.g. /[ke] zere sərpərəsti/ "under the patronage of," /[ke] zere sədarət/ "under the presidency of, presided over by," etc.]